AN INQUIRY INTO THE EXISTENCE OF GLOBAL VALUES

The world appears to be globalising economically, technologically and even, to a halting extent, politically. This process of globalisation raises the possibility of an international legal framework, a possibility which has gained pressing relevance in the wake of the recent global economic crisis. But for any international legal framework to exist, normative agreement between countries, with very different political, economic, cultural and legal traditions, becomes necessary.

This work explores the possibility of such a normative agreement through the prism of national constitutional norms. Since 1945, more than a hundred countries have adopted constitutional texts which incorporate, at least in part, a Bill of Rights. These texts reveal significant similarities; the Canadian Charter of Rights and Freedoms, for instance, had a marked influence on the drafting of the Bill of Rights for South Africa, New Zealand and Hong Kong as well as the Basic Law of Israel. Similarly, the drafts of Eastern European constitutions reflect significant borrowing from older texts.

The essays in this book examine the depth of these similarities; in particular the extent to which textual borrowings point to the development of foundational values in these different national legal systems and the extent of the similarities or differences between these values and the priorities accorded to them. From these national studies the work analyses the rise of constitutionalism since the Second World War, and charts the possibility of a consensus on values which might plausibly underpin an effective and legitimate international legal order.

Volume 7 in the series Hart Studies in Comparative Public Law

Hart Studies in Comparative Public Law

Recent titles in this series:

The Use of Foreign Precedents by Constitutional Judges
Edited by Tania Groppi and Marie-Claire Ponthoreau

Israeli Constitutional Law in the Making
Edited by Gideon Sapir, Daphne Barak-Erez and Aharon Barak

Judicial Decision-Making in a Globalised World
A Comparative Analysis of the Changing Practices of Western Highest Courts
Elaine Mak

Constitutionalising Secession
David Haljan

Parliaments and Human Rights
Redressing the Democratic Deficit
Edited by Murray Hunt, Hayley Hooper and Paul Yowell

The Right to Freedom of Assembly
A Comparative Study
Orsolya Salát

An Inquiry into the Existence of Global Values

Through the Lens of Comparative Constitutional Law

Edited by
Dennis Davis
Alan Richter
and
Cheryl Saunders

·HART·
PUBLISHING
OXFORD AND PORTLAND, OREGON
2017

Hart Publishing
An imprint of Bloomsbury Publishing Plc

Hart Publishing Ltd
Kemp House
Chawley Park
Cumnor Hill
Oxford OX2 9PH
UK

Bloomsbury Publishing Plc
50 Bedford Square
London
WC1B 3DP
UK

www.hartpub.co.uk
www.bloomsbury.com

Published in North America (US and Canada) by
Hart Publishing
c/o International Specialized Book Services
920 NE 58th Avenue, Suite 300
Portland, OR 97213-3786
USA

www.isbs.com

First published in hardback, 2015
Paperback edition, 2017

British Library Cataloguing-in-Publication Data
A catalogue record for this book is available from the British Library.

ISBN: PB: 978-1-50991-770-9
HB: 978-1-84113-855-8

Typeset by Compuscript Ltd, Shannon
Printed and bound in Great Britain by
Lightning Source UK Ltd

Contents

List of Contributors

Catherine Albertyn Professor of Law, School of Law, University of the Witwatersrand

Allan R Brewer-Carías Professor, Central University of Venezuela; Adjunct Professor of Law, Columbia Law School, New York (2006–2007)

Fábio Carvalho Leite Assistant Professor, Department of Law, Pontifícia Universidade Católica do Rio de Janeiro (PUC-Rio)

Albert HY Chen Chan Professor in Constitutional Law, Faculty of Law, University of Hong Kong

Dennis Davis Judge of High Court, South Africa, and Professor of Law, University of Cape Town

Megan Donaldson Doctoral candidate, New York University School of Law

Nazila Ghanea University Lecturer in International Human Rights Law, University of Oxford

Dieter Grimm Professor of Law, Humboldt University Berlin, Former Justice, Federal Constitutional Court of Germany

Aeyal M Gross Professor of Law, Tel-Aviv University

Menaka Guruswamy Advocate at the Supreme Court of India

Yasuo Hasebe Professor of Law at Waseda University, Tokyo

Florian F Hoffmann Lecturer, Department of Law, London School of Economics and Political Science (LSE)

Jeffrey Jowell QC Director, Bingham Centre, British Institute of International and Comparative Law

Colm O'Cinneide Reader in Law, University College, London

Martta October General Secretary, Social Democratic Group in the Parliament of Finland

Alan Richter President, QED Consulting

Riikka Salonen Manager, Workforce Equity and Inclusion, Oregon Health & Science University

Cheryl Saunders Laureate Professor Emeritus, University of Melbourne

Ruti Teitel Ernst C Stiefel Professor of Comparative Law, New York Law School; Visiting Fellow, London School of Economics and Political Science (LSE)

Michel Troper Professor Emeritus at the University of Paris Ouest—Nanterre—La Défense

Lorraine E Weinrib Professor of Law, Faculty of Law, University of Toronto

1

Introduction

DENNIS DAVIS, ALAN RICHTER AND CHERYL SAUNDERS

I. OUTLINE OF PROJECT

THE PAST 25 years have seen a new rights revolution.[1] With the fall of the Berlin Wall, the collapse of the Soviet Empire and the dismantling of apartheid in the South, a significant number of the national states that emerged from these tectonic developments embraced a constitutional system with a Bill of Rights as a central component of their chosen constitutional text.

Simultaneously a new system of the free movement of goods, services and capital emerged across national boundaries. In many instances, limitations on government action through legally enforceable contractual mechanisms were viewed as a preferable means of safeguarding gains made towards global free markets in the post-Cold War era.[2] These two developments, constitutionalism and the erosion of national economic sovereignty, have been the key characteristics of global governance over recent decades. One question that arises from this duality is whether the form of economic globalisation which developed during the 1990s, and which provided almost unfettered scope to multinationals and finance capital, could be regulated, to any degree, by a universal human rights jurisprudence.

Heinz Klug[3] has noted that of the 197 national constitutions which were in effect in 1991, only 20 pre-dated 1950. John and Jean Comaroff have commented on this increase in national constitutions, that it is striking that there is 'the almost salvific belief in the capacity to conjure up equitable, just ethically founded pacific polities; this in the midst of the law that has accompanied laissez faire in so many places'.[4] According to the

[1] M Ignatieff, *The Rights Revolution* (Toronto, Anansi, 2000).

[2] See David Schneiderman, *Constitutionalising Economic Globalisation: Investment Rules and Democracies Promise* (Cambridge, Cambridge University Press, 2008).

[3] Heinz Klug, *Constituting Democracy: Law Globalism and South Africa's Political Reconstruction* (Cambridge, Cambridge University Press, 2000).

[4] John L Comaroff and Jean Comaroff, *Law and Disorder in the Postcolony* (Chicago, University of Chicago Press, 2006) 22.

Comaroffs, this move to law has resulted in the judicialisation of politics. Thus

> conflicts once joined in parliaments by means of street protests, mass demonstrations and media campaigns through labour strikes, boycotts, blockades and other instruments of assertion, tend more and more—if not only, or in just the same way everywhere—to find their way to the judiciary. Class struggles seem to have metamorphosed into class actions … people drawn together by social or material predicament, culture, race, sexual preference, residential proximity, faith and habits of consumption become legal persons as their common plaints turns them into plaintiffs with common law identities—against antagonists, who allegedly, have acted illegally against them.[5]

A nascent global human rights regime which has risen within the context of economic globalisation, with a concomitant judicialisation of politics points to the significance of the rights framework as an important area of enquiry if we are to understand the broader possible correspondence between human rights discourse and the core of the rules governing the process and key institutions which appear to underpin economic globalisation.

This project thus concentrates on a key question, the answer to which can promote further inquiry into the creation of a more coherent body of international human rights law. Most of the texts which have emerged over recent decades have ultimately been sourced in earlier constitutional documents, whether from the United States of America, Germany, the European Convention of Human Rights, United Nations Human Rights instruments or, more recently, the Canadian Charter. The extent to which their forms show similarity is easy to ascertain. Far more important is the determination of whether these instruments, as practised, share a common ethical foundation. Expressed differently, in an era of economic globalisation, is there a parallel development of human rights globalisation where the content of such human rights is shared across boundaries? The existence of shared values across constitutional systems could then provide the potential basis for more meaningful form of international human rights law.

Contributors from a range of countries were asked to assess whether and how their national constitutional orders reflected certain values, whether their constitutional order prioritised particular values and whether the values reflected in their constitutional order, understood to include both text and any associated jurisprudence, were congruent with values which were respected in the society of which the constitution was a part. Take for example the value of freedom. In the United States, freedom is essentially defined as an absence of state control. Following the French conception, in some continental systems, of which Germany is an example, liberty is secured through the state, which thus has positive obligations, through the

[5] ibid, 26–27.

equal subjection of all citizens to law.[6] Both the Indian and Canadian texts expressly provide for four 'freedoms'; thought and expression, association, assembly, and conscience and religion in the case of Canada and speech/expression, assembly, association (including the forming of unions) and movement in India. In Israel the concept of freedom has played a central role in all forms of due process law. In South Africa, freedom has to be given a content which does not place it at odds with the other key values of dignity and equality. Thus in relation to say Israel and the United States, it may be that there is a degree of convergence in constitutional jurisprudence with regard to the concept of freedom. By contrast, French and American jurisprudence differ significantly from each other in their conception of freedom in the context of the role of the state. South Africa also is inclined to the continental approach.

The project gives rise to a range of epistemological and methodological challenges, including:

- Which constitutional orders to compare.
- How to conceptualise 'values'; how to distinguish them from rights; and whether values are susceptible to objective definition.
- How to select a set of values upon which to base the comparison.
- How to establish a connection between a particular feature of the constitutional order and the value(s) that could be said to underlie it.

II. COMPARATIVE LAW AND CONSTITUTIONALISM

The literature in the field of comparative law offers no pre-existing frameworks for this study. Indeed, even as comparative law becomes more prevalent and significant, much contemporary comparative law scholarship acknowledges the absence of a coherent explanation of its purpose or its methods.[7] Comparative law also carries with it certain epistemological biases: until relatively recently, comparative law has tended to privilege similarity over difference, and to assume, more or less explicitly, the desirability of bringing legal systems more closely into alignment with a model of perceived best practice.[8]

In the field of comparative constitutional law, four different approaches have dominated the scholarship. The most common form is the single-country

[6] Dieter Grimm, 'The protective function of the State' in Georg Nolte (ed), *European and US Constitutionalism* (Cambridge, Cambridge University Press, 2005) 137, 146.

[7] Esin Örücü, '*Unde Venit, Quo Tendit* Comparative Law' in Andrew Harding and Esin Örücü (eds), *Comparative Law in the 21st Century* (London, Kluwer, 2002) 1; Ran Hirschl, 'On the Blurred Methodological Matrix of Comparative Constitutional Law' in Sujit Choudhry (ed), *The Migration of Constitutional Ideas* (New York, Cambridge University Press, 2006) 39.

[8] Roger Cotterrell, 'Seeking Similarity, Appreciating Difference: Comparative Law and Communities' in Andrew Harding and Esin Örücü (eds), *Comparative Law in the 21st Century* (London, Kluwer, 2002) 36, 44; Angus McDonald, 'Hundred Headless Europe: Comparison, Constitution and Culture' in Harding and Örücü (eds), *Comparative Law*, 194.

study which generally concerns a country other than that in which the author resides. The particular jurisdiction is then examined through the prism of the author's own constitutional system.[9] A second more expansive form of comparative constitutional law concerns a search for a better answer in a designated domestic jurisdiction by way of examination with a view to emulation of constitutional solutions developed elsewhere. These studies often concentrate on the constitutional jurisprudence of established constitutional regimes: the United States, Germany, Canada, and the European Union.[10]

A third approach which, in essence, is a variation of the second, seeks to explore the similarity of national constitutional jurisprudence and thereby claims to have found some form of universalist constitutional discourse. This approach derives some support from judicial borrowings of constitutional ideas across jurisdictional boundaries, suggesting at least a developing international constitutional discourse, if not constitutional convergence.[11]

In a useful critique of the discipline, Ran Hirschl[12] suggests a possible fourth approach to comparative constitutional law 'based on a notion that a good theory requires clarifying concepts as well as offering causal explanations for observed phenomena employing social science techniques'. Here, theory-building through causal inference seeks to explain particular constitutional choices which had been made by different countries. For example, Salzberger and Voigt[13] examine a number of countries in Eastern and Central Europe which undertook a peaceful transition to democracy after half a century of communist rule. and compare these developments to Israel where a constitutional process has been underway for some 50 years, albeit in the absence of a complete constitutional document. The authors seek to determine possible sources of institutional similarities and differences amongst these governmental regimes and to provide sociological explanations for these phenomena and the possible effect of differences on collective decision-making processes.

This project can probably best be explained by reference to the third form of comparative scholarship. It adopted as its initial hypothesis a measure of convergence between the various constitutional texts, at least at the level of fundamental values. However, the project was deliberately designed to examine the nuances and differences between the various constitutional orders, both in the manner in which the jurisprudence develops through

[9] See D Kommers, *The Constitutional Jurisprudence of the Federal Republic of Germany* (Durham NC, Duke University Press 1997).

[10] See AM Slaughter, *A New World Order* (Princeton NJ, Princeton University Press, 2004).

[11] See V Jackson and M Tushnet, *Comparative Constitutional Law* (Chicago, Foundation Press, 1999); DB Beatty, *The Ultimate Rule of Law* (Oxford, Oxford University Press, 2004).

[12] Ran Hirschl, 'On the Blurred Methodological Matrix of Comparative Constitutional Law' in S Choudhry (ed), *The Migration of Constitutional Ideas* ch 2.

[13] 'On constitutional processors and the delegation of power, a special emphasis on Israel and Central and Eastern Europe' 2002 (3) *Theoretical Enquiries in Law* 207. This entire volume of *Theoretical Enquiries in Law* was devoted to a symposium on economic analyses of constitutional law which is reflective of this particular form of comparative study.

the courts and in the form in which constitutions operate in practice in the countries under review.

The project demonstrates, at the very least, that convergence cannot conclusively be established, in part because values, as defined, are not susceptible to objective definition. The project nevertheless has yielded interesting results. Whatever it may say about the similarity in underlying values across systems, the project demonstrates the many different ways in which constitutional systems manifest a single value, and the many different ways in which a single value can be understood. This suggests that, despite textual or conceptual similarities between constitutions, there is significant diversity between them, sometimes revealed by a jurisprudence of considerable complexity. In itself, this drives the project towards an enquiry into the political and ethical bases which inform the development of the constitutional foundations of the countries under review.

III. CONSTITUTIONAL SYSTEMS—CONVERGENCE AND PARTICULARISM

The project took shape against a backdrop of growing similarities between national constitutional orders. In 1989 Fukuyama claimed that the fall of the Berlin Wall and the collapse of Soviet Russia marked the 'end point of mankind's ideological evolution', being 'the universalization of Western liberal democracy as the final form of human government'.[14] Less hyperbolically, there is currently a sense in the disciplines of political philosophy and constitutional law, crystallised particularly in discussions of human rights, that national constitutional orders are increasingly exhibiting certain shared features.

Several distinct phenomena contribute to this impression. First, it is true that a number of post-WWII constitutions drew heavily on existing constitutional texts, leading inevitably to certain similarities in their constitutional structures. Some existing constitutions have also been amended to incorporate more explicit human rights protection. Secondly, it is true that there is an increasing level of 'transnational judicial dialogue' about constitutional questions, particularly questions of human rights.[15] The extent to which growing (but limited and patchy) attention to foreign and international

[14] Francis Fukuyama, 'The End of History' (Summer 1989) *The National Interest* 3–18.

[15] See, eg, Justice Michael Kirby, 'To Judge is to Learn', paper delivered at a conference in December 2006 on *Transnational Judicial Dialogue: Strengthening Networks and Mechanisms for Judicial Consultation and Cooperation*, sponsored by the American Society of International Law, available from www.asil.org/judicial/transnational/papers.html. Dialogue, in the form of meetings and discussions or merely of cross-citation, is itself one part of a broader phenomenon. Anne-Marie Slaughter has identified five aspects of 'judicial globalisation': relations between national courts in EU countries and the European Court of Justice; relations between EU national courts and the European Court of Justice; judicial comity in transnational litigation; 'constitutional cross-fertilisation'; and face-to-face meetings between judges: 'Judicial Globalization' (2000) 40 *Virginia Journal of International Law* 1103, 1104.

materials by national constitutional courts actually does result in cross-fertilisation between different systems is, however, still open to debate.

Both of these developments have been fuelled by changes at the regional and international level, including the proliferation of treaties and rights instruments, and the production of jurisprudence by supranational courts and tribunals dealing with rights matters.

However, any impression that national constitutional orders are converging needs to be qualified. While there are similarities between long-standing liberal democratic constitutional arrangements, and while there have been a great number of 'transplants' or 'borrowings' from these older texts in the drafting of newer constitutions, even very similar constitutional provisions may be interpreted differently, in light of matters particular to national history or legal tradition. Moreover, the purported universality of the rights which are typically part and parcel of the liberal constitutional paradigm remains contested. There is a substantial literature contending that these putatively universal rights are merely Western constructs imposed upon other states whose indigenous traditions and value systems may be very different.[16]

The history of the Universal Declaration of Human Rights reflects the complexities of cross-cultural dialogue about fundamental values, as they inform rights. Mary-Ann Glendon's account of the drafting of this instrument describes two separate comparative exercises associated with the drafting of the document that would come to be the Declaration. First, John Humphrey, at the UN Secretariat, had asked staff to study all existing constitutions and rights instruments, as well as various proposals submitted by states, NGOs and individuals. Extant instruments included a draft Pan-American declaration, influenced by both continental European and Anglo-American traditions, and a 1944 'Statement of Essential Human Rights' produced on the basis of a study by the American Law Institute, involving consultation with experts from Arabic, British, Canadian, Chinese, French, German, Italian, Indian, Latin American, Polish, Soviet Russian and Spanish cultures.[17] Following a review of this material, Humphrey and an aide produced 48 articles that reflected the systems surveyed. There appears to have been little analysis done at this stage; the intention was to capture the breadth of rights protected. It covered what are now considered the key civil and political rights, and a broad array of economic and social rights. Secondly, UNESCO, of its own initiative, recruited leading thinkers for a 'Committee on the Theoretical Bases of Human Rights'.[18] The Committee

[16] See, eg, Makau Wa Mutua, 'The Ideology of Human Rights' (1996) 36 *Virginia Journal of International Law* 589; Josiah AM Cobbah, 'African Values and the Human Rights Debate' (1987) 9 *Human Rights Quarterly* 309; Bilahari Kausikan, 'Asia's Different Standard' (1993) 92 *Foreign Policy* 24.

[17] Mary-Ann Glendon, *The World Made New: Eleanor Roosevelt and the Universal Declaration of Human Rights* (New York, Random House, 2001) 56–57.

[18] The work of the Committee is discussed briefly in Glendon, *A World Made New* 73–78 and more fully in UNESCO (ed), *Human Rights: Comments and Interpretations* (New York, Columbia University Press, 1949).

prepared a memorandum/questionnaire and sent it to various thinkers in member states of UNESCO, outlining the history of declarations of rights and inviting responses. 'Lines of enquiry' identified in the memorandum included complex questions such as 'What are the relations between the political, the social and the economic rights of individuals (of different sexes and ages) and of groups, in societies of different types and in different historical circumstances' and 'What … are the theoretical grounds, the practical extent, and the efficient guarantees of specific rights and freedoms such as [there followed 24 enumerated rights/freedoms]'.[19] There were efforts to disseminate this questionnaire to experts on Hindu, Islamic and Chinese traditions, as well as experts on 'primitive peoples'. However, this was a highly academic consultation, rather than an exercise aimed at eliciting the views of non-specialists. Mahatma Gandhi, for example, wrote briefly that he was 'a poor reader of literature past or present … I had no leisure to do the necessary reading' and thus 'can't give you anything approaching your minimum'.[20]

The Committee took the many and varied communications it received and prepared a report identifying 15 'fundamental rights on which, the [Committee] is convinced, all men are agreed'. They included life, health, work, 'maintenance' (minimal welfare support), property, education, information, thought and free inquiry, self-expression, justice, political action, freedom of speech, assembly, association, worship and the press, citizenship (a right to abandon existing citizenship and take up citizenship of any other nation that is willing to extend it), rights of rebellion and revolution, and a right to share in progress.[21] Perhaps sadly, the UNESCO report received 'little attention from the [Human Rights] Commission'. Glendon suggests that the Commission 'probably regarded it as confirming the results of Humphrey's study of the world's rights instruments, even though UNESCO had solicited advice from parts of the world where such documents did not yet exist'.[22]

It is clear that, even without entertaining the complexities involved in the UNESCO report, the drafters of the Declaration accepted that there was no consensus on either the justification for rights, or how they should be implemented. Jacques Maritain (on the UNESCO Committee) wrote that, although 'a Christian and a rationalist' might both support a democratic charter, their reasons for doing so would be mutually incompatible.[23] This is borne out by Glendon's account of the painful drafting of article 1, which serves as a kind of philosophical framing of the human rights that follow. It caused lengthy arguments within the drafting committee and was then debated for six days when the draft went to the Third Committee of the

[19] The entire memorandum/questionnaire is reproduced as Appendix I, UNESCO (ed), *Human Rights* 251.
[20] Letter from Gandhi to Committee, reproduced at UNESCO (ed), *Human Rights* 18.
[21] UNESCO (ed), *Human Rights* 268–71.
[22] Glendon, *A World Made New* 83–84.
[23] Maritain, in UNESCO (ed), *Human Rights* 10–11.

General Assembly.[24] It is also reflected in the ongoing tensions as to whether the rights-holding individual should be conceptualised as an individual full stop, or as an individual inextricably connected to his society: these competing visions rested on very different understandings of the foundation of rights. Doubts attended not only the basis of rights, but their implications. Glendon notes that Roosevelt and the other drafters were conscious of the need to avoid being too prescriptive about how rights were to be protected, to allow countries to implement rights in their own way.[25] This was particularly the case with economic and social rights. There was obviously an element of pragmatism at play, but this also points to the fact that countries probably had very different understandings of what specific rights meant.

The ambiguity surrounding the foundations and implications of supposedly 'universal' rights highlights the importance for this project of comparison that is attentive to the differences that might divide constitutional regimes which are, on their face, very similar.

This debate provides a basis for understanding the genesis of this project. In 2001 Alan Richter, as a member of the Diversity Collegium, collaborated with the American Institute for Managing Diversity to organise a symposium for select diversity practitioners to explore the myriad approaches to their work and to attempt to come to some common framework for understanding. One outcome of this symposium was a challenge as to whether the set of global values that were proposed to help understand the various approaches to diversity work were in fact global. In subsequent meetings, after the sobering events of September 11 2001, the Collegium resolved to explore the issue further, but soon came to the realisation that this really was a major research question with profound community, social, political and leadership implications. The Collegium did not follow through on its own but in 2004 Alan Richter, in conversation with Dennis Davis and Cheryl Saunders, decided to undertake this research through the lens of the jurisprudence of national constitutional systems.

IV. IDENTIFYING CONSTITUTIONAL SYSTEMS FOR COMPARISON

Before World War I, constitutional review was to be found in the United States Constitution after the doctrine of review was established in *Marbury v Madison*. In 1872, in a development of an entirely different kind, the French Conseil d'Etat was authorised to resolve complaints against administrative officials and agencies, and even to impose damages on behalf of injured complainants. After World War I the Austrians developed a constitution in which a court was given the power of reviewing the work of elected and

24 Glendon, *A World Made New* 144.
25 ibid, 230–31.

other public officials. After World War II the defeated powers as well as India and the members of the Council of Europe all embraced this form of constitutionalism. With the fall of the Berlin wall, judicial review spread into Central and Eastern Europe and more broadly throughout Africa, Asia and the Middle East.[26]

Notwithstanding the often aggressively national character of written constitutions, it is apparent that most of these systems are or were derivative in part, with the possible exceptions of the earliest systems of the United Kingdom, the United States and France.[27]

More recent developments have given rise to confident claims about the nature of universal constitutionalism. Thus David Beatty[28] writes: 'By the end of the twentieth century, constitutional democracies had taken root on every continent, giving credence to the claim of one leading theorist that the idea of judicial review and enforcement of basic human rights is the single most important contribution the United States has made to political theory.'

Klug is somewhat more cautious but tends to articulate a similar view:

> While there are clearly counter-hegemonic examples and trends—particularly in the adoption of explicitly Islamic constitutions in a number of states—local or national events still determine the particular nature and even timing of political reconstruction in different states in this latest wave. Yet, it is the existence of a particular hegemonic form of international political culture, itself the product of struggles for human rights and democracy, as well as the triumph of the market in the economic realm, that provides the broad framework under which local political forces confront and accommodated their own histories and divisions.[29]

This passage reflects the purpose of the present inquiry. The textual commonality of pedigree notwithstanding, the question remains as to whether the explosion of national constitutionalism represents a triumph of a universal struggle for human rights and democracy or whether the manner in which these constitutions operate in their respective countries is rather a product of indigenous history and culture, albeit within an interdependent world. If so, upon closer examination, no commonality of enterprise actually exists across national boundaries.

The rationale for the selection of the various cases in this study must be understood in this light. The states representing the earliest manifestations of the constitutional rights enterprise were chosen for that reason alone: the United States, France and the United Kingdom, each with its different

[26] For a review of the globalisation of constitutionalism, see Ran Herschl, 'The political origins of judicial empowerment through constitutionalization' (2000) 25 *Law and Society Enquiry* 91.

[27] Cheryl Saunders, 'A constitutional culture in tradition' in M Wyrzykowski (ed), *Constitutional Cultures* (Warsaw, Institute of Public Affairs, 2000).

[28] Beatty, *The Ultimate Rule of Law* 42.

[29] Klug, *Constituting Democracy* 11.

form of constitutionally democratic system. Germany, Canada and South Africa were included as more recent constitutional models that have had a significant influence of the form and structure of constitutional democracies over recent decades. The remainder comprise countries in which there is an active constitutional rights discourse but which otherwise are diverse in a multiplicity of ways, in terms of geography, demography, culture, political system, economic circumstances, legal tradition and religious influence. These are Australia, Brazil, China, Finland, India, Iran, Israel, Japan, and Venezuela. No doubt it is possible to identify a combination of other countries that would offer an equally diverse mix. This selection, however, is more than adequate for the exploration of the extent of commonality of constitutional values. The editors are grateful to the authors of country chapters who have participated so willingly in the task.

V. DEFINING VALUES

In order to narrow the focus of the project and to provide a framework within which an inquiry into common values could be pursued, the authors were provided with a list of familiar common values and asked to endeavour to address them all: fairness/justice; freedom/independence; community/family; responsibility/accountability; integrity/honesty; compassion/caring; respect/tolerance; reverence for life; spirituality; and learning/education. Because the language of values is not universally a part of jurisprudence, the project design turned to other fields of knowledge to guide the choice of values, while retaining jurisprudence as the lens through which values were examined, because of the availability of data. It drew in particular on work undertaken by Rushworth Kidder and the Institute for Global Ethics, in seeking to identify a global code of ethics that transcends cultural difference. This study involved interviews with 24 individuals from different national, cultural and political backgrounds, each of whom had been recognised by peers as a moral leader. Each interviewee was asked what values they would bring from their own experience to be included in a hypothetical list of global values. Following the interviews, the responses were compared and a list of eight of the most commonly identified values was distilled.[30] The preparation of the list required a certain approximation between values identified—for example, references to individual conscience and the right to differ from authority were assimilated into 'liberty', rather than being listed separately.[31] The list arising

[30] Rushworth Kidder, *Shared Values for a Troubled World: Conversations with Men and Women of Conscience* (San Francisco CA, Jossey-Bass, 1994) 16–17, 311–13.
[31] ibid 312.

from this study was adapted for the current project: love; truthfulness; fairness/justice; freedom/liberty/independence; unity/fraternity/solidarity; tolerance; responsibility; and respect for life.

Thanks to a grant from the Rockefeller Foundation we were able to meet with some of the authors in 2008, and after much discussion at Bellagio further values were included in the study such as security, dignity, diversity, participation/inclusion, environment, privacy and property. As with the choice of countries, however, the precise selection is less important, as long as it enables an examination of values that are reasonably representative of what societies might hold in common.

Kidder argued that the values included on his list were values that are of 'intrinsic worth', as distinguished from, for example, concerns about racial inequality, ensuring respect for women's rights, and protecting the environment, which are of worth *because* they manifest or advance one or more of the listed values. They have been embellished for this project,

The values deliberately were cast in terms that were broad and capable, in many cases, of encompassing both the individual and group meanings of the term. In dealing with each value, authors necessarily examine both its relevance and its nuances from their national perspective. Authors were also encouraged to include other values that are manifest in their country's jurisprudence, which were not included on the original list. Many of the chapters do so, although in some cases there is a question whether the differences are semantic rather than matters of substance. In the course of this part of the exercise, it also became evident that it is not always possible to attribute particular rights to a single value, particularly where values are understood at a level of significant abstraction.

It is difficult to articulate a clear definition of 'values'. Some constitutional systems, such as that of South Africa, explicitly identify a number of 'values' that underlie the constitution itself. In other systems, such as France, the term 'value' has no real resonance; the terms 'principle' or 'norm' are more commonly used, and may mean something different to what an Anglo-American scholar would understand by 'value'. As a working definition for the purposes of this project, a value can best be understood as an ethical imperative expressed at a high degree of abstraction, and possessing the quality of an ultimate goal. Values, in this sense, are distinct from rights, which exist to serve and advance particular values, although it may be true that any discussion of values in a legal system is most likely to occur in the context of rights.

Joseph Raz has developed a typology of values that also distinguishes between 'ultimate' and other values. In Raz's analysis, things of instrumental value derive their value from the value of their consequences, the consequences that they are likely to have, or the consequences they can be used to produce. Things of intrinsic value are things which are of value other than because their consequences are of value. Things of ultimate value are a subset of things of intrinsic value:

> The aspects of a good in itself which are of ultimate value are those which explain and justify the judgment that it is good in itself, and which are such that their own value need not be explained or be justified by reference to (their contribution to) other values. The relation of ultimate values to intrinsic values which are not ultimate is an explanatory or justificatory one. Ultimate values are referred to in explaining the value of non-ultimate goods.[32]

Raz does not establish a finite list of goods of intrinsic value or ultimate value.

The distinction made by Kidder between intrinsic values, whose worth is self-evident or incapable of explanation with reference to other values, and 'goals' such as racial harmony, whose worth is explicable by reference to intrinsic values, may be difficult to maintain. The example used by Kidder, that the question 'Why does truthfulness matter?' will elicit either 'a slack-jawed stare of amazement that anyone would have to ask' or 'an extended and complex metaphysical discussion touching on God, man, and the nature of good and evil', illustrates the problem. First, stares of amazement are not the only alternative to a metaphysical account. It might be possible to generate an instrumental justification for truthfulness, along the lines that it protects trust, facilitates social interaction and the sharing of labour, without referring to the moral worth of truthfulness. Secondly, even a metaphysical response would refer to some higher value. For example, if we believe that truthfulness is desirable because our religion so prescribes, and act on this belief, then our actions are referable to an antecedent belief in the value of our religion.

It may be that the better distinction between 'values' and 'goals', in Kidder's terms, or 'ultimate values' and other values, in Raz's terms, is one of the degree of abstraction with which they are expressed. This makes sense of the distinction between values and rights. Raz notes:

> Assertions of rights are typically *intermediate conclusions in arguments from ultimate values to duties* ... Such intermediate conclusions are used and referred to as if they were themselves complete reasons. The fact that practical arguments proceed through the mediation of intermediate stages so that not every time a practical question arises does one refer to ultimate values for an answer is ... of crucial importance in making social life possible, not only because it saves time and tediousness, but primarily because it enables a common culture to be formed round shared intermediate conclusions, in spite of a great degree of haziness and disagreement concerning ultimate values.[33]

In other words, we refer to rights as though their importance and justification are self-evident, because this facilitates dialogue and allows us to form a limited consensus, whereas referring always to the ultimate values upon which rights are truly founded might open a sphere of uncertainty or disagreement.

[32] Joseph Raz, *The Morality of Freedom* (Oxford, Clarendon Press, 1986) 200.
[33] ibid, 181 (emphasis added).

Two further problems emerge. The first is the question of whether values of the kind identified for the project have some objective meaning. The second, and related, question is whether it is possible to draw a connection between a value, expressed at a high level of abstraction, and various rights or other concrete features of a legal system.

On one view, values of the kind drawn on for the project do possess some core of objective meaning. This is the view which informed Isaiah Berlin's argument that there is a fundamental conflict between liberal values:

> Both liberty and equality are among the primary goals pursued by human beings through many centuries; but total liberty for wolves is death to the lambs, total liberty of the powerful, the gifted, is not compatible with the rights to a decent existence of the weak and the less gifted.[34]

When Berlin suggests, for example, that there is an irreconcilable tension between liberty and equality, such that it is not possible for a society to realise both values simultaneously, he assumes that these values have an objective definition.

Others have emphasised the contingency and fluidity of definitions of values. Dworkin, for example, contends that there are competing conceptions of liberty, some of which are compatible with equality: if liberty is understood as the freedom to do whatever one wishes provided that one respects the moral rights of others, it is possible to understand how liberty and equality could be reconciled.[35] If democracy is understood as a complex system incorporating certain rights for all citizens, rather than as simple majoritarianism, much of the controversy about the compatibility of democracy and judicial review slips into irrelevance.[36] However, the main implication of fluidity in the definition of values is not that all conflict can be defined away, but that all values are always open for political contestation.

> [Political concepts] serve as abstract plateaus of agreement. Almost everyone agrees that the values in question are of at least some importance, and perhaps very great importance, but that agreement leaves open crucial substantive issues about what more precisely these values are or mean. We see this most dramatically in the case of the most abstract political conception of all: justice. People do not much dispute the importance of justice ... Disputes about justice almost always take the form of argument, not about how important justice is or when it should be sacrificed to other values, but what it is.[37]

[34] Isaiah Berlin, 'On the Pursuit of the Ideal' in Henry Hardy (ed), *The Crooked Timber of Humanity: Chapters in the History of Ideas* (London, John Murray, 1990).

[35] See Ronald Dworkin, 'Moral Pluralism' in *Justice in Robes* (Cambridge MA, Harvard University Press, 2006) 105, 112. Another aspect of the argument, not relevant for our purposes, is whether it is actually desirable to be able to reconcile fundamental values into one coherent system. Berlin would suggest that this monist tendency is dangerous.

[36] Ronald Dworkin, 'Hart's Postscript and the Point of Political Philosophy' in *Justice in Robes* 140, 147–48.

[37] ibid, 148.

This poses a serious problem for a comparative enterprise based on identification of whether particular values are manifested in national constitutional systems. Contributors may have competing understandings of particular values. One obvious example is equality: the Anglo-American tradition has a very narrow and procedural understanding of equality, as equality to participate in political processes and equality before the law, whereas regimes with a strong social democratic tradition might conceive equality in broader terms, as requiring some measure of redistributive or transformative action by the state to remedy gross inequalities in wealth and opportunity. Liberty poses similar problems. In the American tradition, liberty tends to be understood as freedom from constraints imposed by the state. In some European systems, liberty is precisely a product of citizens' equal subjection to the law. Rights are held through the state, rather than against it.[38] These differences in the understanding of values, along with institutional differences, are an important aspect of what might be described as 'constitutional culture'.

Short of providing our own, fixed definitions of the values nominated for comparison—an exercise which would itself be fraught with difficulty, and would still leave aspects of the definition open to interpretation—the only way of proceeding seems to be to ask contributors to reflect not only on whether their national constitutional system reflects particular values, but what conception of those values appears to predominate. Contributors have also been asked to comment on which values are prioritised over others in their national systems, but it may be that much of the national particularity around values arises in the understanding of values themselves.

There are further difficulties that arise in ascertaining whether particular constitutional systems reflect certain values. Various features of a constitutional regime may well be attributable to more than one value. Unless the constitutional text or the jurisprudence explicitly connects particular features of the constitutional order to underlying values, establishing these connections is essentially an interpretive exercise.

Now, by way of introducing the succeeding chapters, each author was asked to research three things:

1. Review their country's bill of rights, constitution, and/or its key legal cases, and determine if each value on the list of values under study are (or are not) clearly articulated.
2. Comment on the prioritisation of values.
3. Comment on 'congruence', that is, the extent to which the aspirant values are or are not 'lived' in that country. That is, contributors will provide their opinion on whether particular values manifested in the legal system do, or do not, reflect societal values.

[38] Dieter Grimm, 'The Protective Function of the State' in Georg Nolte (ed), *European and US Constitutionalism* (Cambridge, Cambridge University Press, 2005) 137.

2

Values in Australian Constitutionalism

CHERYL SAUNDERS AND MEGAN DONALDSON

I. THE AUSTRALIAN DILEMMA

AUSTRALIA IS A liberal democracy in the common law tradition. Most of the rights that are recognised and protected in comparable countries elsewhere are broadly respected in Australia. Australia typically ranks well on world indices of democracy and civil liberties, although neither its past nor its present record suggests that there are any grounds for complacency.[1]

An Australian contribution to a project of this kind is complicated, however, by certain features of the Australian constitutional and political system. One is the absence of a national statement of rights in any form. Two regions of the country have their own legislative bills of rights, covering largely civil and political rights,[2] but there is no specific legal or even declaratory

[1] Australia appears in the first rank of 'free countries' in the Freedom House annual 'Freedom in the World' survey (available at www.freedomhouse.org/report-types/freedom-world); was ranked 25th in 2015 in the worldwide press freedom rankings by Reporters without Borders (available at http://index.rsf.org/#!/); and was ranked 9th in the Economist Intelligence Unit Democracy Index in 2014 (Economist Intelligence Unit, *Democracy Index 2014: Democracy and Its Discontents* (London, EIU, 2015)).

[2] Human Rights Act 2004 (ACT); Charter of Human Rights and Responsibilities Act 2006 (Vic). Neither allows for the invalidation of statutes inconsistent with rights. In both instruments, rights may be subject to 'reasonable limits' that can be 'demonstrably justified in a free and democratic society': Human Rights Act s 28(1); Charter s 7(2). The Human Rights Act was amended in 2012 to include immediately realisable aspects of the right to education (although public authorities were not required to act consistently with this right), and to require the Attorney-General to report by January 2015 to the Legislative Assembly on, inter alia, the inclusion of further economic, social and cultural rights ('ESC rights') in the Act. This report recommended that the Act be amended to require public authorities to act consistently with immediately realisable aspects of the right to education, but recommended against the inclusion of various other ESC rights: ACT Justice and Community Safety Directorate, *Economic, Social and Cultural Rights in the Human Rights Act 2004—Section 43 Review* (November 2014). There have been proposals for the introduction of statutory bills of rights similar to those in the ACT and Victoria in some other states, but as of February 2015 there are no active

protection for rights that applies nationwide (and one of the state bills of rights may in future be further reduced in its effects).[3] A national consultation, established in 2008 to elicit views from the community as to which human rights should be protected and promoted, whether these rights are currently adequately protected and promoted, and how Australia could better protect and promote rights, recommended adoption of a legislative bill of rights on the 'dialogue' model,[4] but the federal Government rejected this recommendation on the basis that 'many Australians remain concerned about the possible consequences of such an Act [and] [t]he Government believes that the enhancement of human rights should be done in a way that as far as possible unites, rather than divides, our community'.[5] The Government's 'National Human Rights Framework' instead committed, in particular, to greater human rights education for public servants and the public at large, and reforms to parliamentary scrutiny of legislation, and policy-making and implementation within the federal bureaucracy.[6] However, some of these initiatives have been abandoned, and a review of the Framework scheduled for 2014 has not been carried out.[7]

Insofar as a rights instrument codifies or reflects values, the chapter is, at least for now, deprived of its obvious starting point. More significantly still, it is deprived of a readily identifiable context in which relevant values might be articulated and through which they might have been tested,

initiatives. In Tasmania, a 2007 report of the Law Reform Institute recommended adoption of a statutory charter of rights, and further consultations as to the form of a charter were conducted by the Department of Justice in 2010–11, but in 2012 the Government put further work on hold, citing budgetary constraints. In Western Australia, a Consultation Committee for a Proposed WA Human Rights Act similarly recommended adoption of a statutory bill of rights in 2007, but no action was taken to implement such a bill. Previous inquiries by parliamentary committees in New South Wales and Queensland have rejected adoption of a human rights act or like instrument.

[3] A four-year review of the Victorian Charter by the Scrutiny of Acts and Regulations Committee found it had brought some benefits (including improving statutory drafting and promoting informed discussion of rights implications of bills), but incurred significant costs. In light of the legal uncertainties surrounding key provisions of the Charter (see below n 19, text accompanying n 47) a divided Committee provided three options for reform: complete abolition of the Charter, reduction of the Charter to arrangements for scrutiny of legislation only (possibly against a broader range of rights than currently provided); and the status quo with some more minor amendments: Scrutiny of Acts and Regulations Committee, Parliament of Victoria, *Review of the Charter of Human Rights and Responsibilities Act 2006* (September 2011). No major changes have yet been made but a further review is due in October 2015.

[4] National Human Rights Consultation Commission, *National Human Rights Consultation Report* (September 2009) Recommendations 18–19, xxxiv (hereafter 'Consultation Report').

[5] Attorney-General's Department, 'Australia's Human Rights Framework' (April 2010) 1 (hereafter 'Human Rights Framework').

[6] ibid 1.

[7] Australian Human Rights Commission, *Australia's Universal Periodic Review: Progress Report Prepared by the Australian Human Rights Commission on behalf of the Australian Council of Human Rights Authorities* (December 2014) ('*AHRC UPR Progress Report (December 2014)*').

causing priorities to emerge. The National Human Rights Consultation Committee envisaged that, if a federal bill of rights was not adopted, there should nevertheless be some process of listing core rights that the Government was particularly committed to protecting and promoting, and the Consultation Committee recommended that the Government operate on the assumption that all rights under seven major human rights conventions be on that list (unless Australia had entered a reservation to the contrary).[8] The decision to have regard, in new processes of scrutiny of primary and secondary legislation, to all rights under these conventions no doubt accorded best with Australia's international obligations, but it also circumvented the task of identifying rights of particular importance in or to Australia, and differentiating between rights deemed more or less important.[9]

As the Constitution itself contains few rights provisions and no explicit statement of values, the task of examining Australian values through the lens of national constitutional jurisprudence requires attention to a range of sources that potentially is very wide. It encompasses not only the Constitution, including the cases interpreting its few rights provisions, but also the institutional provisions of the Constitution that indirectly offer rights protection by distributing power. In addition, there is a case for including a much larger body of case law arising in fields of private law, as well as legislation, international instruments to which Australia is a party, and various statements of executive policy. This possibility presents a question as to where this chapter should draw the boundary between the constitutional order and the rest of the body of Australian law.

This chapter is structured as follows. Section II provides an overview of the Australian constitutional order and Australia's current approach to rights protection, as a guide to the sources in which values may be reflected. Section III explores the extent to which the values specifically identified for this project are manifested in the Australian constitutional order, the form these values take in Australia, and the relative priorities these values hold. Section IV considers the issue of congruence.

[8] Consultation Report (n 4) Recommendation 17, xxxiv.

[9] This decision also meant that no formal distinction was made between civil and political rights, on the one hand, and ESC rights, on the other. The two sub-national bills of rights largely only cover civil and political rights (see above n 2), and the Consultation Report had recommended that a federal bill of rights do the same or that, if it provided for ESC rights, these be non-justiciable: ibid, Recommendation 22, xxxv. However, the National Human Rights Consultation Committee noted that some of the ESC rights, particularly to an adequate standard of living, to food, health and education, were precisely the rights thought to be of most immediate and practical importance both to vulnerable groups, and to Australians surveyed by a social research firm in connection with the Consultation: ibid 78–82.

II. THE AUSTRALIAN CONTEXT: MEANING AND SOURCES OF 'VALUES'

As far as protection of rights is concerned, Australia is a country in what was once thought of as the British tradition. In the absence of a national bill of rights, rights protection depends on the 'capacity of a democratic society to preserve for itself its own shared values',[10] institutionalised through the principles and practices of responsible government, supplemented by the common law, developed and applied by independent courts assuming liberty as their starting point. The Australian position thus draws directly on the views of AV Dicey, as articulated at the turn of the twentieth century, when the Australian Constitution was being framed, claiming the centrality of parliamentary sovereignty, repudiating reliance on rights instruments, and relying on the common law as a bridge between the omnipotence of Parliament and the rule of law. This position has been defended by successive political leaders against proposals for specific rights protection.[11] Procedures adopted in the wake of the National Human Rights Consultation, particularly the gradual review of all federal legislation and policy for human rights compliance, a requirement that all bills be accompanied by statements assessing compatibility with seven major UN human rights conventions,[12] and establishment of a Parliamentary Joint Committee on Human Rights with a mandate to review bills and delegated legislative instruments against these same conventions, have given human rights greater prominence, but in a manner which retains the centrality of legislative, rather than judicial, deliberation.[13] This regime of parliamentary

[10] *Australian Capital Television v Commonwealth* (1992) 177 CLR 106, 183 (Dawson J).

[11] For example, in a 2006 Australia Day address, Australia's then Prime Minister repudiated the notion of a bill of rights for Australia, attributing the 'strength and vitality of Australian democracy' instead to 'parliament with its tradition of robust debate; the rule of law upheld by an independent and admirably incorruptible judiciary; and a free and sceptical press': John Howard, 'A sense of balance: the Australian achievement in 2006', Speech delivered at the National Press Club, Canberra, 25 January 2006, available at australianpolitics.com/news/2006/01/06-01-25_howard.shtml. Although the Australian Labor Party has historically been more supportive of a national bill of rights, the Labor Government stipulated in 2008 that options identified by the Consultation Committee for the enhancement of protection and promotion of human rights 'should preserve the sovereignty of the Parliament and not include a constitutionally entrenched bill of rights': Appendix A to the Consultation Report (n 4).

[12] The conventions are: International Convention on Civil and Political Rights ('ICCPR'); International Convention on Economic, Social and Cultural Rights ('ICESCR'); International Convention on the Elimination of All Forms of Racial Discrimination; Convention on the Elimination of All Forms of Discrimination against Women; Convention against Torture and other Cruel, Inhuman and Degrading Treatment or Punishment ('CAT'); Convention on the Rights of the Child; and Convention on the Rights of Persons with Disabilities.

[13] Human Rights (Parliamentary Scrutiny) Act 2011 (Cth). The Government has indicated that it is considering other recommendations made in the Consultation Report, including integrating compliance with human rights into the Australian Public Service Values and Code of Conduct, but appears not to have taken up a recommendation that Australia's international human rights obligations be specifically listed in the Administrative Decisions (Judicial Review) Act 1977 (Cth) as a relevant consideration which must be taken into account by a decision-maker: Human Rights Framework (n 5).

scrutiny currently enjoys bipartisan support but, having its basis in statute only, remains vulnerable to changing political preferences.

Australia departs from the British tradition of constitutionalism in having a national Constitution that is fundamental law. The initial purpose of the Constitution was to provide a secure framework for federalism. Necessarily, however, it also entrenched the institutions of national government in a form that has ultimately been interpreted as requiring a separation of powers. This separation is incomplete as between the legislature and the executive, but very strict as regards the judiciary.

Similarly, some institutional provisions of the Constitution either establish a framework within which certain rights are, as a practical matter, protected, or have been interpreted as giving rise to certain rights and freedoms 'implied' from the text of the Constitution. For example, various provisions providing for a bicameral Parliament, elected directly by the people, have been held to enshrine a system of representative government. This in turn gives rise to a limited 'freedom of political communication': the High Court has held that, as sections 7 and 24 of the Constitution respectively require the members of the Senate and of the House of Representatives to be 'directly chosen by the people', these sections 'necessarily protect that freedom of communication between the people concerning political or governmental matters which enables the people to exercise a free and informed choice as electors'.[14] Within the framework established by the Constitution, there are certain conventions of government imported from the Westminster system, such as ministerial responsibility and a recognised Opposition party, that contribute to the effective operation of democracy and in turn the protection of rights. The Constitution also includes a few scattered provisions that in other systems might have evolved into robust rights (such as, to a jury trial, or to freedom of religion). For the most part these have been construed narrowly and have no particular interest for present purposes.

The absence of express protection for rights in the Constitution, and the institutional stance that Australia continues to take on the question of rights protection, itself indicates adherence to particular values; most obviously to the ideal of a particular form of democratic community through which decisions are taken by majority vote and accepted as legitimate by the community as a whole. Further support for this interpretation is suggested by several distinctive features of Australian representative democracy, including the requirements for compulsory voting. This possibility will be examined further in the next part, by reference to the values in question. In addition, however, the justification of the Australian position assumes that a measure

[14] *Lange v Australian Broadcasting Corporation* (1997) 189 CLR 520, 559. This freedom, however, is not a personal right analogous to freedom of speech in the US, but merely prohibits executive or legislative action that would curtail the protected communication, where such action is not both directed to a legitimate end and appropriately adapted to achieve that end.

of rights protection may be derived from the common law and raises the possibility that values may also be identified in this context.

The protection of rights through the common law takes two principal forms. First, the common law itself identifies particular rights on which individuals might in some cases rely. The right to a fair trial is one example. In the absence of legislative intervention, power to ensure the fairness of trials lies entirely with the courts.[15] Common law rights are not necessarily co-extensive with values, but cases giving them effect typically are underpinned by values, whether these are explicitly articulated or are left to be surmised.[16] Secondly, common law principles of statutory interpretation shield a limited set of what are often called 'fundamental' rights against abrogation by statute in cases where the statute is not sufficiently clear.[17] This 'principle of legality' requires the Parliament to manifest an intention to abrogate rights 'by clear and unequivocal language for which Parliament may be accountable to the electorate'.[18] The principle of legality now finds statutory reflection, in application to specified rights, in sub-national bills of rights.[19] A further common law principle (discussed in more detail below), requiring statutes to be interpreted, insofar as their language permits, in accordance with international law, may also play some role in the protection of rights.[20]

Cases providing protection for common law rights are not the only potential source of values in Australian jurisprudence, however. Values also emerge in connection with other areas of law, including contract, tort, property and

[15] See, eg, *Dietrich v R* (1992) 177 CLR 292.

[16] See, eg, *Momcilovic v The Queen* (2011) 245 CLR 1, 47 (French CJ) ('The common law "presumption of innocence" in criminal proceedings is an important incident of the liberty of the subject.')

[17] See, eg, *Al-Kateb v Godwin* (2004) 219 CLR 562, 577 (Gleeson CJ); *Coco v The Queen* (1994) 179 CLR 427, 437 (Mason CJ, Brennan, Gaudron and McHugh JJ); *Re Bolton, ex p Beane* (1987) 162 CLR 514, 523 (Brennan J). The principle of legality is a longstanding feature of statutory interpretation: see *Potter v Minahan* (1908) 7 CLR 277, 304 and old English authority there cited. For a discussion of the rights now protected by the principle, see James Spigelman (then Chief Justice of New South Wales, speaking extracurially), 'The Common Law Bill of Rights' (First 2008 McPherson Lecture, University of Queensland, Brisbane, 10 March 2008); Dan Meagher, 'The Common Law Principle of Legality' (2011) 35 *Melbourne University Law Review* 449.

[18] *Momcilovic v The Queen* (2011) 245 CLR 1, 46 (French CJ).

[19] See Charter of Human Rights and Responsibilities Act 2006 (Vic) s 32(1) ('So far as it is possible to do so consistently with their purpose, all statutory provisions must be interpreted in a way that is compatible with human rights' [as defined in the Act]); Human Rights Act 2004 (ACT) s 30. There had been some question as to whether the Victorian provision required courts to depart from ordinary principles of statutory interpretation. The High Court in *Momcilovic* confirmed that it did not (Heydon J dissenting), but the Court divided on a related question about whether to assess a statute against the bare rights as enumerated in the Charter (French CJ, Crennan and Kiefel JJ), or against the rights coupled with a provision permitting limitations to rights in certain circumstances (Gummow and Hayne JJ, Heydon J, Bell J): *Momcilovic v The Queen* (2011) 245 CLR 1.

[20] On the potential for some future intersection between the principle of legality and the principle of interpretation consistent with international law, see Meagher (n 17) 466–68.

family law. In *Mabo v Queensland [No 2]*, the case in which the High Court accepted that the common law of Australia recognised native title as a form of property, and effectively overturned the assumption that Australia was *terra nullius* at the time of European settlement, the leading judgment of Brennan J drew upon the 'fundamental values' of the common law, and in particular those associated with justice.[21]

Another possible source of guidance as to the values underlying Australia's constitutional order lies in statute. Statutory regimes are inherently amenable to change and are therefore less likely to be a reliable indicator of longstanding values. On the other hand, the Australian approach to rights protection assumes that Parliaments will actively protect rights, and such initiatives are often responsive to perceived underlying values. Statutes of particular interest for present purposes are those that have endured for a considerable period already, were enacted on the basis of Australia's international obligations, or are recognised as having some moral significance. Legislation falling with these categories includes anti-discrimination legislation, which exists at both federal and state levels, and statutes recognising certain rights of the indigenous peoples. Other statutory regimes of obvious interest are sub-national legislative bills of rights. These statutes are often motivated (at least in part) by, and reflect, underlying values. The Preamble to the Charter of Human Rights and Responsibilities Act 2006 (Vic), for example, includes a statement that 'human rights are essential in a democratic and inclusive society that respects the rule of law, human dignity, equality and freedom'.

Australia's international commitments may also reflect national values. Australia is a relatively active participant in international law-making and has been broadly supportive of human rights instruments. However, Australia is a dualist system in which international law has no binding force unless it is implemented in the national legal system. Federal statutes, particularly anti-discrimination legislation, have given force to commitments under major human rights treaties, but much international law, particularly as it concerns human rights, has not been incorporated into national law, and Australian governments have been selective in their engagement with treaty bodies.[22] There has been significant debate about the role of

[21] *Mabo v Queensland [No 2]* (1992) 175 CLR 1, 42, 58.

[22] In 1992, in response to an individual petition to the Human Rights Committee under the Optional Protocol to the ICCPR, the then federal Government conceded that a prohibition of sexual conduct between men in the criminal law of the State of Tasmania violated, inter alia, the right to privacy under the ICCPR, and that the prohibition could not be justified on health or moral grounds (Human Rights Committee, *Toonen v Australia*, 31 March 1994, CCPR/C/50/D/488/1992). Following the Human Rights Committee's adoption of views that the Tasmanian provisions did constitute a violation of the right to privacy, the federal Government passed legislation overriding the Tasmanian provisions. Australia has been much less receptive to the views of the Human Rights Committee in subsequent cases, a number of which concerned aspects of Australia's regime of immigration detention, simply rejecting the Committee's views and declining to take the actions recommended.

international law on both the interpretation of the Australian Constitution and the development of the common law. The position appears to be that international law does not limit the powers granted to the legislature by the Constitution, such that, for example, the federal Government is free to enact statutory provisions that might result in the indefinite detention of a stateless person who was not accepted by any other country for resettlement, despite a body of international law limiting arbitrary, indefinite or non-judicial detention.[23] International law may have some influence on the development of the common law,[24] and may influence statutory interpretation to some degree, under the common law principle that statutes should be interpreted, insofar as is possible, in a manner consistent with international law.[25] On the other hand, a suggestion by the High Court that ratification of a treaty could found a legitimate expectation that, absent statutory or executive indication to the contrary, administrative decision-makers would act in accordance with Australia's treaty commitments,[26] met strong opposition from the executive, and the Court has now moved away from this position.[27]

Perhaps surprisingly, given this backdrop of formal separation between international and national law, the National Human Rights Framework gave international commitments a much higher profile within the national discourse on human rights. The current National Human Rights Action Plan (2012) is closely engaged with international commitments, although many

[23] *Al-Kateb v Godwin* (2004) 219 CLR 562.

[24] See, eg, *Mabo v Queensland [No 2]* (1992) 175 CLR 1, 32 (Brennan J).

[25] See, eg, *Polites v Commonwealth* (1945) 70 CLR 60, 68 (Latham CJ), 74 (Rich J), 77 (Dixon J), 79 (McTiernan J), 80–81 (Williams J); *Kartinyeri v Commonwealth* (1998) 195 CLR 337, 386 (Gummow and Hayne JJ); but see a strong criticism of the principle, given the vast reach and diversity of contemporary international law, in *Al-Kateb v Godwin* (2004) 219 CLR 562, 590–91 (McHugh J). Some judgments in *Maloney v The Queen* [2013] HCA 28 reflect a cautious, indeed arguably overly restrictive, use of international law and legal materials in the interpretation of the Racial Discrimination Act (implementing in Australia the International Convention on the Elimination of All Forms of Racial Discrimination). In other cases, where the international norm in question is fully codified and readily ascertainable, and it is clear on the face of the legislation that Parliament had reference to Australia's international law obligations in enacting the statute, as with the Migration Act 1958 (Cth) and the Convention relating to the Status of Refugees, the approach has been different. Australia's obligations under that Convention were an important element in interpretation of relevant provisions of the Migration Act to preclude 'offshore processing' of asylum-seekers in Malaysia, a state which did not satisfy requirements under the Convention in terms of the protections afforded to refugees: *Plaintiff M70/2011 v Minister for Immigration and Citizenship* (2011) 244 CLR 144, 190–91, 195–97 (Gummow, Hayne, Crennan and Bell JJ). The sub-national bills of rights contain provisions explicitly permitting consideration of international law and the judgments of foreign and international tribunals in interpreting protected human rights or, in the case of Victoria, any statutory provision. However, the view has been expressed that these provisions add nothing to the status quo: *Momcilovic* (2011) 245 CLR 1, 36 (French CJ).

[26] *Minister for Immigration and Ethnic Affairs v Teoh* (1995) 183 CLR 273, 291 (Mason CJ and Deane J).

[27] *Minister for Immigration and Multicultural Affairs, ex p Lam* (2003) 214 CLR 1.

of the items in the Action Plan have not been achieved.[28] New processes of parliamentary scrutiny of legislation are informed by assessments of compliance of draft bills with major human rights conventions (and now with the interpretations of those conventions by treaty bodies).[29] The Committee's challenges to what it perceives as inadequate statements of compatibility, and responses of ministerial departments to these challenges, might indicate a growing attention to the corpus of international human rights law, although there is not yet much evidence of meaningful change at the level of policy formulation.[30]

A final category of potential sources from which to identify underlying values of a constitutional kind comprises various executive policy instruments, such as the statement of 'Our democratic beliefs' in a booklet outlining information on which citizenship applicants will be tested.[31]

The sources in which the values of Australian constitutionalism find reflection must also be understood in the context of the nation's political and judicial culture. Observations on a topic as broad as a national political culture are dangerous but, to risk a generalisation, Australia does not have a strong tradition of connecting political choices and policies to abstract ideals such as 'freedom' or 'dignity'. There is broad agreement on many issues between the two major parties,[32] and the recourse to overarching values in political discourse is probably less frequent than in other liberal

[28] In particular, commitments to review reservations under various rights treaties, and work towards ratifying some new instruments, including the Optional Protocol to CAT. A recent report tracking action against recommendations made in the course of Australia's Universal Periodic Review identifies several recommendations accepted by Australia which have not been subject to any further action by the Government: see *AHRC UPR Progress Report (December 2014)* (n 7).

[29] See Commonwealth of Australia, Parliamentary Joint Committee on Human Rights, Guidance Note 1 (September 2012), available at http://www.aph.gov.au/Parliamentary_Business/Committees/Joint/Human_Rights/Guidance_Notes_and_Resources.

[30] For example, the Committee's report on a suite of legislative arrangements providing for 'offshore processing' of asylum-seekers in Papua New Guinea and Nauru was a substantive one. The Committee was critical of the inadequacy of the statements of compatibility offered for some of the legislative measures, and concluded that 'the measures as currently implemented carry a significant risk of being incompatible with a range of human rights': Parliamentary Joint Committee on Human Rights, *Examination of legislation ... Migration Legislation Amendment (Regional Processing and Other Measures) Act 2012 and related legislation* (June 2013), 51–52, 84.

[31] 'Australian Citizenship: Our Common Bond' (2014), available at http://www.citizenship.gov.au/learn/cit_test/test_resource/_pdf/our-common-bond-2014.pdf. The beliefs listed are 'Parliamentary democracy', 'the rule of law', 'living peacefully', 'respect for all individuals regardless of background' and 'compassion for those in need'. The booklet also lists 'freedoms' of speech and expression, association, religion and secular government, and 'equalities' between genders, and of opportunity.

[32] National and, to a large extent, state politics in Australia are dominated by the Australian Labor Party (formally identified as a social democratic party but supportive of a broadly neoliberal economic programme), and a centre-right coalition of the Liberal and National parties.

democracies featured in this volume, such as the United States or France.[33] This is not to suggest that politics is not informed by values; it is simply to observe that the values underlying particular positions tend not to be articulated at the same level of abstraction that one might find in other systems.

There are some exceptions to this generalisation. References to 'human rights' are much more common in executive policy documents now than they were even 10 years ago (although, as indicated above, the approach currently taken affords little insight into which rights are of most significance to Australia, and thus little insight into particular values). Equality is frequently invoked, although often in more colloquial terms. It appears, for example, in the distinctively Australian expression, a 'fair go', meaning a reasonable opportunity or chance to participate, or a common sense understanding of what fairness or decency requires. An appeal to the idea of the 'fair go' was mentioned by the Prime Minister in his explanation of the need for an apology for the nation's past treatment of indigenous people, given in 2008.[34] However, historic inequalities in the Australian polity, as well as the complexities inherent in the very idea of equality—rarely teased out in political discourse—suggest that even this frequently mentioned value may not have the influence sometimes attributed to it.[35]

Australia's constitutional framework and prevailing political culture is reflected in the typical style of judicial reasoning, which leaves little scope for substantive discussion of values by the judiciary. Most discussion of 'values' by the judiciary has been either at a very abstract level, connected only tenuously to the body of reasoning, or at a much more concrete level, focusing on the detail of what a value means in particular practical circumstances. Nevertheless, there has been some conceptual discussion of the nature of 'values' and their role in the determination of cases. In *Mabo [No 2]* Justice Brennan observed that 'no case can command unquestioning

[33] One (no doubt contestable) explanation for this tendency is the enduring legacy of a 'Benthamist' philosophy—utilitarian, legalist and positivist—that flourished in Australia's nineteenth-century settler society (see Hugh Collins, 'Political Ideology in Australia: The Distinctiveness of a Benthamite Society' in Stephen R Graubard (ed), *Australia: The Daedalus Symposium* (North Ryde, Angus & Robertson, 1985) 147–70). Within the Benthamist world view, politics was a secular and instrumental endeavour, guided by interests rather than ideals: Collins, 'Political Ideology in Australia', 149, 155.

[34] 'There is a further reason for an apology as well: it is that reconciliation is in fact an expression of a core value of our nation—and that value is a fair go for all. There is a deep and abiding belief in the Australian community that, for the Stolen Generations, there was no fair go at all. And there is a pretty basic [Australian] belief that says it is time to put right this most outrageous of wrongs': Parliamentary motion apologising to the Stolen Generations, made by the Prime Minister on 13 February 2008, available at http://www.australia.gov.au/about-australia/our-country/our-people/apology-to-australias-indigenous-peoples.

[35] See Elaine Thompson, *Fair Enough: Egalitarianism in Australia* (Kensington, University of New South Wales Press, 1994); Rodney Smith, *Australian Political Culture* (Frenchs Forest, Pearson, 2001) 96–121. For the prevalence of the 'fair go' framing in discussions of rights, and its limits, see Consultation Report (n 4) 58, 97, 99, 149, 344.

adherence if the rule it expresses seriously offends the values of justice and human rights ... which are aspirations of the contemporary Australian legal system'.[36] His Honour held that the 'unjust and discriminatory doctrine' underpinning a failure to recognise the pre-existing rights and interests of indigenous inhabitants of settled colonies was contrary to 'the fundamental values of our common law', and thus required reconsideration.[37]

In the course of the debate that followed the decision in *Mabo,* and after his retirement from the bench, Sir Gerard Brennan drew a distinction between 'relatively permanent values of the Australian community', which may, in certain circumstances, inform judicial deliberations, and 'transient notions which emerge in reaction to a particular event or which are inspired by a publicity campaign conducted by an interest group', which should not influence judicial decision-making.[38]

The distinction drawn between permanent 'values' and transient 'attitudes', of course, turns not only on the stability of the mind-set in question, but on the degree of abstraction with which it is expressed.[39] 'Values' such as justice and fairness are longstanding and slow to change, but their permanence is probably due at least in part to the fact that they are expressed at such a high level of generality.[40] When they are invoked in a specific instance their meaning crystallises in particular circumstances. While the value itself may endure, this meaning changes over time, shaped by something that is neither inherent in the value itself, nor, perhaps, reducible to the status of a transient 'attitude'. For example, the commitment to fairness in curial process has long been a feature of the common law. This fairness can be understood as a 'value', but the *meaning* of this value has evolved:

> While the law's insistence that there be no conviction without a fair trial according to law has been long established, the practical content of the requirement that a criminal trial be fair may vary with changing social standards and circumstances.[41]

[36] *Mabo v Queensland [No 2]* (1992) 175 CLR 1, 30.

[37] ibid 42.

[38] Sir Gerard Brennan (formerly Chief Justice of the High Court), 'Values' in Tony Blackshield, Michael Coper and George Williams (eds), *Oxford Companion to the High Court of Australia* (Melbourne, Oxford University Press, 2001) 695, 696. One finds a similar distinction in some of the academic literature. John Braithwaite (citing the work of Milton Rokeach) has defined a value as 'a single belief of a specific kind ... a trans-situational guide to attitudes, actions and judgments [that] lifts us above attitudes about specific objects and situations, to more ultimate goals that affect how we should judge a wide sweep of objects and situations': John Braithwaite, 'Symposium on Community Values in Law' (1995) 17 *Sydney Law Review* 351, 354, citing Milton Rokeach, *Beliefs, Attitudes and Values* (1968) and *The Nature of Human Values* (1973).

[39] Jeremy Kirk, 'Rights, Review and Reasons for Restraint' (2001) 23 *Sydney Law Review* 19, 47–49.

[40] Martin Krygier and Arthur Glass, 'Shaky Premises: Values, Attitudes and the Law' (1995) 17 *Sydney Law Review* 385, 389.

[41] *Dietrich v R* (1992) 177 CLR 292, 328 (Deane J).

A 'fair trial' now requires compliance with many safeguards that would not always have been observed in previous decades. It is now accepted, for example, that where an accused is charged with serious offences, legal representation will usually be essential to the conduct of a fair trial.[42]

The range of sources from which values may be drawn in the Australian system presents potential for conflict between different sources, and thus a problem of selection. It also complicates comparison with other jurisdictions, where consideration of values can be confined more strictly to the Constitution. Accordingly, it is necessary to impose some limits on the sources to which reference will be made.

One limit concerns the reliability of sources as indicators of lasting values rather than passing trends. The text of the Constitution has changed little since its passage as an Act of the British Parliament in 1900. Subject to the evolution noted above in the content and practical implications of particular values, jurisprudence also tends to be relatively enduring. Statutes and executive policy, on the other hand, are both inherently subject to change with fluctuations in the balance of party political power. Therefore, only longstanding statutory regimes recognised as significant for their centrality to the political process, or for the interests they protect, and executive policies or statements recognised as being of great historic or symbolic significance, will be relied upon.

A second limit concerns the nature of the source, and specifically whether it may be understood as part of the Australian constitutional order. For the purposes of this chapter, we have adopted a broad, impressionistic definition of the constitutional order as encompassing any matter going to the exercise of public power, or to the involvement of the state in the protection of individuals or groups as members of the polity. On this definition, legislation prohibiting discrimination on the basis of race or gender, and providing recourse for those suffering discrimination, is part of the constitutional order, because it has a public and political dimension, whereas legislation prohibiting, for example, misleading and deceptive conduct in commerce, and providing recourse against these wrongs, falls outside it. Even recognising the impossibility of any principled distinction between public and private, the latter is somewhat further removed from questions of political status. Similarly, while a right to life enshrined in a sub-national rights instrument is part of the constitutional order, considerations on the value of life that have informed tort cases—essentially matters between private individuals as such—are not. In light of Australia's dualist approach to the relationship between municipal and international law, Australia's international commitments will generally be excluded from the analysis, unless

[42] ibid 311 (Mason CJ and McHugh J), 336 (Deane J), 371 (Gaudron J).

they are incorporated by legislation of the kind described above. Further, no reference is made to specific rights relevant in Australia only as a result of being included in the seven major human rights conventions which form a baseline for legislative scrutiny; these are not directly binding and, although these rights no doubt evidence certain values, the sheer range of rights involved and the lack of any formal discrimination between them makes it difficult to discern from them any commitment to *particular* values. Despite these restrictions on the subject matter for analysis, brief reference is sometimes made to relevant developments beyond the constitutional order to place the constitutional position, or lack thereof, in context.

III. WHICH VALUES?

Subject to all that has been said above regarding the methodological difficulties of this project in the case of Australia, section III sets out our survey of the extent to which the Australian constitutional order manifests the values listed for comparison. We have taken an expansive view of some of the listed values in order to accommodate the Australian case while also facilitating comparison with other systems. Thus, for example, the listed value of community is stretched to encompass Australian practices of majoritarian democracy.

Given that some of the listed values are very significant in the Australian constitutional order, while others have virtually no relevance, we have modified the order of the list of values somewhat, such that the most important values are considered first. However, within this general approach, the order of values chosen is not intended to convey any precise hierarchy. In a system of this kind, in which evidence of values is so dispersed and contestable, it is difficult to identify formal priorities of values. Some general comments on the question of priority are set out in section IIIB below.

A. Review of Listed Values

i. Justice/Fairness

Both justice and fairness are very important in Australian constitutionalism, although in the Australian context these values tend to be manifested in formal, institutional and procedural requirements, rather than substantive redistributive policies. Justice and fairness are connected and mutually reinforcing values. However, for the purposes of clarity, this chapter distinguishes between fairness at large, dealt with primarily under 'Equality' below, and fairness in the context of adjudication, which is intimately connected to the value of justice, and is dealt with in the later part of this section.

The importance of justice to the Australian constitutional order—in the sense of a well-functioning and independent judiciary acting within a relatively rigid definition of judicial power—is recognised most obviously in the structure of the Constitution, and the way in which the High Court has historically policed the limits of the judicial function. The structure of the Constitution, which accords 'The Judicature' a chapter of its own, alongside 'The Parliament' and 'The Executive Government', as a distinct branch of government, is one basis on which the High Court has held that the Constitution mandates a strict separation of powers, such that the judicial power of the Commonwealth may only be vested in those courts envisaged by Chapter III and, conversely, these courts may not undertake tasks other than those within the bounds of, or ancillary to, the judicial power.[43] A similar principle precludes individual judges being appointed in their personal capacities to carry out non-judicial functions that are repugnant to or incompatible with the judicial function.[44] The separation of powers at the federal level also prevents state courts and judges, which exercise federal judicial power in some instances, from being vested with a power under state law that is repugnant to or incompatible with the exercise of federal judicial power.[45] This principle has posed a difficulty inter alia for sub-national bills of rights. The High Court has indicated that a provision in the Victorian Charter authorising that state's Supreme Court to make a 'declaration of incompatibility'[46] between statutory provisions and protected rights is constitutional, but by a narrow majority only. For two of the four judges in the majority this conclusion was reached on grounds implying

[43] See, eg, *R v Kirby, ex p Boilermakers' Society of Australia* (1956) 94 CLR 254.

[44] See, eg, *Wilson v Minister for Aboriginal and Torres Strait Islander Affairs* (1996) 189 CLR 1.

[45] *Kable v Director of Public Prosecutions (NSW)* (1995) 189 CLR 51. See also, eg, *South Australia v Totani* (2010) 242 CLR 1, *Kuczborski v Queensland* [2014] HCA 46 (14 November 2014). The principle was extended to individual state judges in *Wainohu v New South Wales* (2011) 243 CLR 181. It has been observed that the notions of repugnancy and incompatibility may not be susceptible of precise ex ante definition. Cases in which state legislation has been held invalid on these grounds have involved provisions: empowering courts to order the detention of an individual for a specified period if satisfied on reasonable grounds that he was more likely than not to commit a serious act of violence, and that it was appropriate for the protection of the individual, or the community generally, that he be held in custody; requiring the making of ex parte orders for the sequestration of property upon suspicion of wrongdoing, for an indeterminate duration, with the only possibility of release from the order depending on proof of a complex negative proposition; requiring courts to make a control order against an individual if satisfied that the person is a member of a declared organisation (this declaration being made by the executive); and empowering the courts to declare organisations as 'criminal organisations' without giving reasons. See discussion in *Assistant Commissioner Michael James Condon v Pompano Pty Ltd* [2013] HCA 7 (14 March 2013) [122]–[135] (Hayne, Crennan, Kiefel and Bell JJ).

[46] Such declarations do not affect the validity of the statutory provision subject to the declaration, although the Minister concerned is required to table in Parliament a response to the declaration.

that an analogous provision could not be validly conferred on a Chapter III federal court in any future national legislative bill of rights.[47]

The Constitution, together with statutory regimes, goes some way to securing the institutional independence of the judiciary, although protections are considerably weaker for state judges and magistrates than for their federal counterparts. Each of the federal courts now has extensive administrative independence, managing its own affairs with funds allocated to it in a single line appropriation in the budget.[48] Judges of both federal and state courts in Australia are appointed by the relevant executive[49] in accordance with minimum qualifications set out in statute.[50] Such a process arguably provides scope for politically motivated appointments. However, appointments to the High Court, while they attract some degree of public comment, are rarely subject to serious criticism or challenge. Federal judges have constitutionally entrenched security of tenure (at least until retirement at a fixed age) and a guarantee that remuneration will not be reduced during a term of office.[51] In state courts, on the other hand, there is significant scope for the appointment of acting judges for fixed terms. Although such arrangements

[47] The case in question could have been disposed of on much narrower grounds, but all justices discussed the constitutional issues it raised. A majority considered that the provision empowering the court to make a declaration of incompatibility was valid, either because, while this power was not judicial or incidental to judicial power, it did not impair the integrity of the Victorian Supreme Court as a repository of federal judicial power (*Momcilovic v The Queen* (2011) 245 CLR 1, 67–68, 241 (French CJ, Bell J)); or because it was incidental to judicial power and, insofar as further scrutiny under *Kable* was required, did not impair the institutional integrity of the state court (224–28 (Crennan and Kiefel JJ)). Gummow and Hayne JJ found the provision incompatible with federal judicial power (97, 123); Heydon J found the Charter as a whole invalid, primarily on other grounds. However, two of the judges in the majority, Crennan and Kiefel JJ, held that there was a discretion not to make the declaration and that no declaration should have been made; making the declaration placed the court below in the position of both upholding the validity of a conviction while acknowledging that the trial had violated the defendant's Charter rights (228–29) (the reasons of Gummow J specifically criticised the role that reading the relevant provision as discretionary played in the reasons of Crennan and Kiefel JJ on the question of validity, and their statements regarding the exercise of the discretion in criminal proceedings: 96).

[48] See, eg, High Court of Australia Act 1979 (Cth) s 17; Federal Court of Australia Act 1976 (Cth) s 18A; Family Law Act 1975 (Cth) s 38A.

[49] While the only formal requirement for consultation of other parties in relation to the appointment of High Court justices is for consultation by the federal Attorney-General with state Attorneys-General (High Court of Australia Act 1979 (Cth) s 6), there is usually, in practice, consultation with the Chief Justice and senior members of the profession: see comments of Sir Harry Gibbs, former Chief Justice, quoted in Enid Campbell and HP Lee, *The Australian Judiciary* (Melbourne, Cambridge University Press, 2001).

[50] See, eg, High Court of Australia Act 1979 (Cth) s 7; Family Law Act 1975 (Cth) s 22.

[51] Section 72 of the Constitution requires the term of office of High Court and other federal justices to continue until they attain the age of 70 (or, for justices other than High Court justices, a lesser age if Parliament so provides), subject to removal only following an address by both Houses of Parliament on the ground of 'proved misbehaviour or incapacity'. Section 72 provides that remuneration will be as the Parliament provides, but may not be reduced during a term of office. In practice remuneration of federal justices is determined by the Remuneration Tribunal, an independent statutory authority.

have been held not to pose a constitutional difficulty per se,[52] their perceived threat to independence has been a matter of concern for some judges and academics.[53] Institutional provision for independence needs to be assessed against a backdrop that includes increasing criticism of the judiciary by politicians and the media,[54] and, of particular relevance for state judges and magistrates, ongoing attacks on what are perceived to be overly lenient sentencing practices.[55]

Australia has a comprehensive body of administrative law allowing individuals to seek review of decisions made by executive agencies. The scope and fora for review of executive action varies for the different decisions in issue. In some cases, a full merits review is available through another executive decision-maker or an external tribunal. Courts are confined to a more limited judicial review, the basis and scope of which varies,[56] but which generally determines whether the decision made was within the power of the decision-maker. The High Court has also enunciated a common law duty to accord procedural fairness in making a decision which affects rights or interests, broadly understood, unless a relevant statute clearly manifests a contrary intention.[57] Legislatures have from time to time enacted 'privative clauses' purporting to limit the scope and availability of judicial review of particular classes of decisions, but such clauses cannot oust the jurisdiction for which the Constitution provides.[58]

[52] An argument that provisions allowing appointment of an acting judge to a state Supreme Court were constitutionally invalid, on the basis that such an appointment was incompatible with the vesting in state Supreme Courts of federal judicial power, failed in *Forge v Australian Securities and Investments Commission* (2006) 228 CLR 45.

[53] HP Lee, 'Appointment, Discipline and Removal of Judges in Australia' in HP Lee (ed), *Judiciaries in Comparative Perspective* (Cambridge, Cambridge University Press, 2011) 27, 32–35.

[54] See then Attorney-General Daryl Williams, 'The Role of the Attorney-General' (2003) 13 *Public Law Review* 252, 258–61.

[55] See Karen Gelb (for the Sentencing Advisory Council of Victoria), *Myths and Misconceptions: Public Opinion versus Public Judgment about Sentencing* (July 2006), available at https://www.sentencingcouncil.vic.gov.au/publications-by-year/2006.

[56] The High Court has held that the Constitution's grant to the Court of jurisdiction in all matters in which a writ of mandamus or prohibition or an injunction is sought against an officer of the Commonwealth gives rise to an 'entrenched minimum provision of judicial review' (*Plaintiff S157/2002 v Commonwealth* (2003) 211 CLR 476, 513 (Gaudron, McHugh, Gummow, Kirby and Hayne JJ)). Other bases for judicial review at the federal level include the Administrative Decisions (Judicial Review) Act 1977 (though migration decisions have been specifically exempted from this regime), and various other statutory regimes for review or appeal: see Administrative Review Council, *Federal Judicial Review in Australia* (September 2012) 45–71. Migration cases have furnished an important impetus for shifts in the conceptualisation of judicial review: see Stephen Gageler SC, 'Impact of Migration Law on the Development of Australian Administrative Law' (2010) 17 *Australian Journal of Administrative Law* 92.

[57] *Kioa v Minister for Immigration and Ethnic Affairs* (1985) 159 CLR 550, 584. However, what will be required in order to ensure that a decision is attended with procedural fairness differs depending on the nature of the decision, and what is at stake for the individual subject to it.

[58] *Plaintiff S157/2002 v Commonwealth* (2003) 211 CLR 476 (and see above n 56). The High Court has held that state Supreme Courts similarly enjoy a core jurisdiction to review for jurisdictional error (*Kirk v Industrial Court (NSW)* (2010) 239 CLR 531). However, in

The judicial process is subject to a number of provisions and doctrines designed to protect its integrity, and further the administration of justice. With some exceptions,[59] courts in Australia operate on an adversarial model, whereby each party seeks to establish the truth of its own version of events before an impartial judge (and sometimes jury). The nature of the adversarial system is such that fairness between contending parties—at least in the procedural sense—is a central element of the workings of the justice system.[60] In this respect the values of fairness and justice are intertwined.

'Fairness' takes on a particular meaning in the context of the criminal law. In light of the disparity of resources between the state and the accused, and the seriousness of the consequences flowing from conviction, it is accepted that it is better for many guilty men to escape justice than it is for one innocent man to suffer unjust punishment.[61] The courts thus act on principles designed to safeguard the rights of the accused.

Section 80 of the Constitution contains a requirement that 'the trial on indictment of any offence against any law of the Commonwealth shall be by jury'. At first glance this appears to guarantee a jury trial for serious criminal offences. However, it is the legislature that decides whether particular offences will be tried summarily or on indictment, and the High Court has held that, if an offence is not triable on indictment, section 80 does not apply.[62] This position has been subject to forceful dissenting judgments, based in part on the way in which juries enhance the transparency and fairness of proceedings.[63] The Court has held that, where section 80 does apply,

the wake of *Federal Commissioner of Taxation v Futuris Corp Ltd* (2008) 237 CLR 146 there remains an open question about the extent to which legislatures may use so-called 'no invalidity' clauses, which provide that an act done or decision made in violation of another statutory provision, or rule of administrative law, is not for that reason invalid, and thus purport to take errors of this kind beyond the class of jurisdictional error.

[59] Such as specialist courts in the state jurisdictions, including Koori Courts (which have jurisdiction in some cases involving indigenous accused) and Drug Courts (which have jurisdiction in some cases involving drug-dependent accused).

[60] It has recently been said that '[Chapter] III of the Constitution mandates the observance of procedural fairness as an immutable characteristics of a Supreme Court and of every other court in Australia': *Assistant Commissioner Michael James Condon v Pompano Pty Ltd* [2013] HCA 7 (14 March 2013) [177] (Gageler J). However, the significance of this constitutional grounding of procedural fairness falls to be considered in accordance with the variable content of what procedural fairness requires, examined further below.

[61] See, eg, *R v Carroll* (2002) 213 CLR 635, 643 (Gleeson CJ and Hayne J).

[62] *R v Federal Court of Bankruptcy, ex p Lowenstein* (1938) 59 CLR 556; *Kingswell v The Queen* (1985) 159 CLR 264.

[63] See, eg, *Kingswell v The Queen* (1985) 159 CLR 264, 301 (Deane J): 'A system of criminal law cannot be attuned to the needs of the people whom it exists to serve unless its administration, proceedings and judgments are comprehensible by both the accused and the general public ... [in a jury trial] the participating lawyers are constrained to present the evidence and issues in a manner that can be understood by laymen.... The presence and function of a jury in a criminal trial and the well-known tendency of jurors to identify and side with a fellow-citizen who is, in their view, being denied a 'fair go' tend to ensure observance of the consideration and respect to which ordinary notions of fair play entitle an accused or a witness.'

it requires a unanimous verdict, rather than merely a majority verdict, in order for an accused to be convicted. The requirement of unanimity invokes the 'fundamental thesis' that an accused should be given the benefit of any reasonable doubt, and minimises the risk of conviction of the innocent.[64]

Beyond this limited constitutional protection for jury trials, the requirement that trials be 'fair' has its origins in the common law.[65] Ensuring the fair conduct of a trial has been recognised as central to the judicial function.[66] Fairness encompasses certain recognised requirements, but is not limited to these, and may continue to evolve.[67] One manifestation of 'fairness' that may find application even before a trial commences is the set of doctrines usually collected under the prohibition on 'double jeopardy'. There is a longstanding common law principle that an individual 'shall not be twice vexed for one and the same cause'.[68] Within this concept there are several distinct doctrines relating to different stages of criminal process, from prosecution to punishment.[69] One is that an individual must not be prosecuted for an offence the elements of which are either the same as, or fall within the elements of, another offence for which the individual has been, or is being, prosecuted.[70]

Courts have a power to permanently stay criminal prosecutions to prevent an abuse of process, or the prosecution of a criminal proceeding that will result in a trial that is unfair.[71] Although abuse of process and unfairness may not be distinct concepts, cases analysed under the rubric of 'abuse of process' include those in which proceedings have been instituted not to prosecute an offence to a conclusion but to achieve some collateral end for which the criminal law is not designed,[72] and those in which new proceedings will

[64] *Cheatle v The Queen* (1993) 177 CLR 541, 553.

[65] The right to a fair trial and to certain protections in criminal process is made explicit in the sub-national rights instruments: Human Rights Act 2004 (ACT) ss 21, 22; Charter of Human Rights and Responsibilities Act 2006 (Vic) ss 21, 22.

[66] *RPS v The Queen* (2000) 199 CLR 620, 637; see also *Hinch v Attorney-General (Victoria)* (1987) 164 CLR 15, 58 (Deane J): 'The right to a fair and unprejudiced trial is an essential safeguard of the liberty of the individual under the law. The ability of a society to provide a fair and unprejudiced trial is an indispensable basis of any acceptable justification of the restraints and penalties of the criminal law. Indeed, it is a touchstone of the existence of the rule of law.'

[67] Common law rights may of course be abrogated by statute, but, to the extent that there have been indications that the federal courts cannot be required to exercise power 'in a manner which is inconsistent with the essential requirements of a court or with the nature of judicial power', there may be a constitutional basis on which core procedural safeguards are maintained even in the face of statutory provisions to the contrary: *Polyukhovich v The Commonwealth of Australia* (1992) 172 CLR 501, 607 (Deane J); see also *Chu Kheng Lim v Minister for Immigration* (1992) 176 CLR 1, 27 (Brennan, Deane and Dawson JJ).

[68] From the Latin maxim 'nemo debet bis vexari pro una et eadem causa'.

[69] See *Pearce v The Queen* (1998) 194 CLR 610, 614 (McHugh, Hayne and Callinan J), 629 (Gummow J).

[70] *Pearce v The Queen* (1998) 194 CLR 610.

[71] See, eg, *Barton v The Queen* (1980) 147 CLR 75; *Moti v The Queen* (2011) 245 CLR 456.

[72] See, eg, *Williams v Spautz* (1992) 174 CLR 509.

involve controverting a prior acquittal.[73] The power to grant a permanent stay to prevent an unfair trial may be exercised where there has been unreasonable delay in prosecution,[74] or where intense media coverage may give rise to bias in jurors,[75] though only in exceptional cases where there would be a fundamental defect in the trial such that no steps taken by the trial judge (such as adjournment or jury directions) could relieve against the unfair consequences for the accused. Further, in most cases in which an accused is charged with a serious criminal offence, representation will be essential to a fair trial, and it has been held that, where such representation cannot be obtained (other than through the accused's own fault), in all but exceptional cases a judge should stay, adjourn or postpone proceedings until representation is available.[76]

A concern with fairness, in the sense of protecting the accused against the greater might of the prosecuting authority, underlies the whole of the procedural law, for example the exclusion of evidence resulting from illegal conduct by police[77] and confessional statements not made voluntarily,[78] and the discretion to exclude evidence that is unfairly prejudicial or is propensity evidence.[79]

Another manifestation of the values of justice and fairness lies in the requirement for an impartial judge. In both criminal and civil proceedings, judges are disqualified from hearing cases not only if they may actually be biased against a party, but if 'a fair-minded lay observer might reasonably apprehend that the judge might not bring an impartial mind to the resolution of the question the judge is required to decide'.[80] The centrality of justice and fairness to the Australian system is such that there is a strong emphasis on conducting proceedings in such a way that their integrity is manifest to both those involved, and the wider public. The doctrine noted above in relation to separation of powers, precluding courts and individual judges being pressed into roles inimical to the judicial function, is closely bound up with perceptions of the judicial system and in particular the need to protect the appearance as well as the fact of independence. Many of the rules governing court process '[give] effect to the requirement that justice should both be done and be seen to be done'.[81] Most obviously, the vast majority of court

[73] *R v Carroll* (2002) 213 CLR 632.

[74] *Jago v District Court of New South Wales* (1989) 168 CLR 23.

[75] *R v Glennon* (1992) 173 CLR 592.

[76] *Dietrich v R* (1992) 177 CLR 292.

[77] *Ridgeway v The Queen* (1995) 184 CLR 19.

[78] See, eg, *R v Thomas* (2006) 14 VR 475, 497–503.

[79] *Pfennig v The Queen* (1995) 182 CLR 461.

[80] *Ebner v Official Trustee in Bankruptcy* (2000) 205 CLR 337, 344; see also *R v Watson, ex p Armstrong* (1976) 136 CLR 248; *Livesey v NSW Bar Association* (1983) 151 CLR 288; *Vakauta v Kelly* (1989) 167 CLR 568.

[81] *Ebner v Official Trustee in Bankruptcy* (2000) 205 CLR 337, 344 (concerning apprehension of bias on the part of a judge).

hearings in Australia are public. The High Court has commented that 'the fact that courts of law are held openly and not in secret is an essential aspect of their character', noting that openness 'has the virtue that the proceedings of every court are fully exposed to public and professional scrutiny and criticism, without which abuses may flourish undetected' and 'the public administration of justice tends to maintain confidence in the integrity and independence of the courts'.[82] Similarly, although there are provisions allowing courts to forbid or restrict publication of evidence, or the names of parties and witnesses, in certain circumstances,[83] these provisions are interpreted in light of a strong principle of 'open justice'.[84]

ii. Equality

Like justice, equality manifests itself primarily in formal and procedural provisions, rather than in guarantees of substantive outcomes. Unlike justice, however, equality has very little grounding in the Constitution. Most protection takes the form of statutory regimes prohibiting particular forms of discrimination and providing systems for complaint.

The High Court has rejected arguments that the Constitution contains a general implication of equality before the law.[85] Indeed, the Constitution

[82] *Russell v Russell* (1976) 134 CLR 495, 520 (Gibbs J); see also *Grollo v Palmer* (1995) 184 CLR 348, 379 (McHugh J): 'Open justice is the hallmark of the common law system of justice and is an essential characteristic of the exercise of federal judicial power'. The general requirement that hearings be public has always been subject to very limited common law exceptions (usually confined to circumstances where justice cannot be done if the proceeding is heard in public). There are also statutory exceptions in force in different Australian jurisdictions, pertaining for example to committal proceedings, and proceedings involving children or sexual offences. The National Security Information (Civil and Criminal Proceedings) Act 2004 (Cth) s 29 requires certain hearings held in the course of federal criminal proceedings, involving information which, if disclosed, may harm national security, to be held in camera (and even, in some cases, in the absence of the defendant and his or her legal representative).

[83] See, eg, Federal Court of Australia Act 1976 (Cth) s 50; Supreme Court Act 1986 (Vic) ss 18, 19.

[84] In relation to s 50 Federal Court of Australia Act, it has been said that the principle of open justice is the 'underlying assumption upon which [s 50] is based'; see also *Herald Weekly Times Ltd v Gregory D Williams (formerly identified as VAI)* (2003) 130 FCR 435: *Applicant Y v Australian Prudential Regulation Authority* [2005] FCAFC 222 (28 October 2005) [15]. For other comments on the importance of open justice, see, eg, *Australian Broadcasting Commission v Parish & Ors* (1980) 43 FLR 129; *Johnston v Cameron* (2002) 124 FCR 160; *Raybos Australia Pty Ltd v Jones* [1985] 2 NSWLR 47.

[85] Expressed by a minority in *Leeth v Commonwealth* (1992) 174 CLR 455, 485–92 (Deane and Toohey JJ), 502–03 (Gaudron J), but rejected by the majority. At issue in *Leeth* was inequality in the sentencing of federal offenders arising out of the (ongoing) reliance on state and territory courts, applying different sentencing regimes, to try a growing list of federal crimes. The problem was discussed in Australian Law Reform Commission, *Same Crime, Same Time: Sentencing of Federal Offenders*, Report No 103 (2006), but the major reforms proposed in that report have not come to pass. The High Court endeavoured to provide guidance to state and territory courts on the importance of consistency, and regard for the approach to sentencing taken by other intermediate appellate courts, in *Hili v The Queen* (2010) 242 CLR 520.

still allocates to the federal Parliament a power to make laws with respect to 'the people of any race ... for whom it is deemed necessary to make special laws', and this power has not been conclusively interpreted as supporting only laws for the benefit of particular races.[86] However, particular aspects of the Constitution's operation may be subject to some requirement to respect equality. There are signs that the Court may ultimately favour some attenuated view that the separation of powers inherent in the Constitution, and the nature of judicial power, prevents the conferral of powers on the courts that, by their nature, must be exercised in a discriminatory way.[87] In relation to the franchise, the High Court has commented that, in today's world, an abandonment of universal adult suffrage as the basis for the franchise would be inconsistent with the requirements in sections 7 and 24 that members of the Senate and the House of Representatives be 'directly chosen by the people'.[88]

Section 24, in providing that the number of members of the federal House of Representatives chosen in the several states shall be in proportion to their numbers (subject to a requirement that at least five members be chosen by each original state, giving the relatively less populous Tasmania a boost), preserves some basic equality in the representation of state populations in the lower house. The High Court has rejected any strong notion that state electoral districts need to be drawn in such a way that individual votes have roughly equal weight,[89] although all states now have legislative regimes aimed at ensuring some parity in the value of a vote for at least the lower house (in some cases with tolerance for variation or special arrangements for particularly sparsely populated or remote seats).

At the most general level, section 117 of the Constitution protects political equality within the federation by providing that states must not impose on a resident of another state any 'disability or discrimination' which would not be applicable to a the state's own residents. However, perhaps because most state discrimination arises in relation to regulatory legislation, section 117 has not played a significant role in rights protection. It is also an inevitable incident of Australia's federal structure, and particularly the fact that many aspects of health and education remain within the purview of state governments, that significant disparities can exist between the benefits and facilities available in one state, and those available in another. Comments

[86] *Kartinyeri v The Commonwealth of Australia* (1998) 195 CLR 337.

[87] See *Kruger v Commonwealth* (1997) 190 CLR 1, 116–18 (Gaudron J).

[88] See, eg, *McGinty v Western Australia* (1996) 186 CLR 140, 170 (Brennan J), 286–87 (Gummow J); *Roach v Electoral Commissioner* (2007) 233 CLR 162, 173 (Gleeson CJ); *Rowe v Electoral Commissioner* (2010) 243 CLR 1, 18 (French CJ).

[89] *McGinty v Western Australia* (1996) 186 CLR 140.

to the National Human Rights Consultation make clear how keenly these disparities are felt in areas close to state borders.[90]

The two sub-national rights instruments include express rights to freedom from discrimination in the enjoyment of human rights, and to equality before the law.[91]

Statutes at both federal and state levels prohibit discrimination on the grounds of personal characteristics such as race and gender. For example, the Racial Discrimination Act 1975 (Cth) prohibits a person from doing any act

> involving a distinction, exclusion, restriction or preference based on race, colour, descent or national or ethnic origin which has the purpose or effect of nullifying or impairing the recognition, enjoyment or exercise, on an equal footing, of any human right or fundamental freedom in the political, economic, social, cultural or any other field of public life.[92]

Without prejudice to the generality of this prohibition, subsequent provisions deal with racial discrimination in relation to specific areas.[93] As well as prohibiting direct discrimination on the grounds of race, the Act prohibits what is often called 'indirect discrimination': requiring a person to comply with a term, requirement or condition that is not reasonable in the circumstances, where the requirement to comply has the purpose or effect of nullifying or impairing recognition, enjoyment or exercise of human rights or fundamental freedoms, on an equal footing, by persons of different race.[94] Other federal statutes prohibiting discrimination include the Sex Discrimination Act 1984 (Cth), the Disability Discrimination Act 1992 (Cth) and the Age Discrimination Act 2004 (Cth). State anti-discrimination statutes cover broadly similar ground to federal statutes.[95]

Generally, prohibitions on discrimination are civil, rather than criminal, provisions. Complaints about breaches of any of the federal Acts may be made to the Australian Human Rights Commission, which undertakes a

[90] See, eg, Consultation Report (n 4) 33, reporting that a round-table participant 'was dismayed at the great difference in mental health service provision in a town a few hundred kilometres away across the border: "Warrnambool has excellent services. Mt Gambier has nothing".'

[91] Human Rights Act 2004 (ACT) ss 8(2), (3); Charter of Human Rights and Responsibilities Act 2006 (Vic) ss 8(2), (3).

[92] Section 9(1). These rights and freedoms are defined by reference to art 5 of the International Convention on the Elimination of all Forms of Racial Discrimination, which refers to 'equality before the law', and then indicates that this encompasses a wide array of rights, some of which are mentioned in a non-exhaustive list.

[93] Such as laws providing for the management of property: s 10(3); access to public places and vehicles: s 11; the purchasing, sale or leasing of real property: s 12; refusal to supply goods or services: s 13; membership of trade unions: s 14; and employment: s 15.

[94] Racial Discrimination Act 1975 (Cth) s 9(1A).

[95] See, eg, Anti-Discrimination Act 1977 (NSW); Equal Opportunity Act 1984 (SA); Equal Opportunity Act 1984 (WA); Discrimination Act 1991 (ACT); Anti-Discrimination Act 1991 (Qld); Anti-Discrimination Act 1992 (NT); Equal Opportunity Act 2010 (Vic); Anti-Discrimination Act 1998 (Tas).

process of conciliation.[96] If the Commission terminates investigation of the complaint, the complainant may pursue it in court, and the court has jurisdiction to grant compensation and a range of other orders.[97] Additionally, the Fair Work Act 2009 (Cth) prohibits discrimination in the employment context on grounds such as race, sex, age, disability, marital status, sexual preference, or religion,[98] and provides for employees affected, unions or inspectors to apply for court orders regarding the contravention, including orders for compensation. State anti-discrimination statutes provide for complaints to be made to state discrimination commissioners or boards.

Although the statutory anti-discrimination framework appears extensive, it is by no means a comprehensive guarantee of equality. For example, although most state anti-discrimination statutes apply also to discrimination on the basis of sexual preference, there remain a number of areas in which the law discriminates between homosexual and heterosexual couples. In particular, homosexual couples cannot be 'married' in a legal sense,[99] and in some states they are restricted in their access to assisted reproductive technology and adoption. A 2007 audit of federal legislation identified many instances in which homosexual couples and their children were disadvantaged as compared to heterosexual couples,[100] although the Government has now moved to address many of these inconsistencies.[101]

[96] Australian Human Rights Commission Act 1986 (Cth) ss 46P, 46PF.

[97] Australian Human Rights Commission Act 1986 (Cth) s 46PO.

[98] Section 351 (subject to qualifications regarding inherent requirements of the position, religious institutions, and to conduct permitted by state anti-discrimination legislation applicable to the relevant workplace).

[99] In 2004 the Liberal Government, motivated by a 'commitment to protect the institution of marriage' (Explanatory Memorandum to the Marriage Legislation Amendment Bill 2004) passed legislation to define marriage in the Marriage Act 1961 (Cth) as 'the union of a man and a woman to the exclusion of all others, voluntarily entered into for life' and to provide that unions between same-sex partners, solemnised in another country, must not be recognised in Australia as marriages: Marriage Legislation Amendment Act 2004 (Cth) Sch 1, items 1 and 3. The federal Marriage Act provisions preclude legislation in the Australian Capital Territory that would recognise marriage or civil unions analogous to marriage for same-sex couples (see, most recently, *Commonwealth v Australian Capital Territory* (2013) 250 CLR 441). However, there have been a number of bills to permit same-sex marriage introduced in the federal Parliament since 2009, and momentum may be building for reform at the federal level.

[100] The audit of legislation focused on financial and workplace entitlements, and found discrimination in such diverse areas as employment law, workers' compensation, tax, social security, veterans' entitlements, health care costs, superannuation, aged care and migration: Human Rights and Equal Opportunity Commission [now Australian Human Rights Commission], *Same-Sex, Same Entitlements: National Inquiry into Discrimination against People in Same-Sex Relationships: Financial and Work-Related Entitlements and Benefits* (2007), available at https://www.humanrights.gov.au/publications/same-sex-same-entitlements.

[101] See, eg, Same-Sex Relationships (Equal Treatment in Commonwealth Laws—General Law Reform) Act 2008 (Cth); Same-Sex Relationships (Equal Treatment in Commonwealth Laws—Superannuation) Act 2008 (Cth). Over the last decade, most states have been working to remove discrimination of this kind from their own statutes: see eg Property (Relationships) Amendment Act 1999 (NSW); Miscellaneous Acts Amendment (Relationships) Act 2002 (NSW); Discrimination Law Amendment Act 2002 (Qld); Statute Law Amendment (Relationships) Act 2001 (Vic); Statute Law Further Amendment (Relationships) Act 2001 (Vic).

Furthermore, statutory regimes are subject to exceptions. The Racial Discrimination Act has been suspended on three occasions, most recently in 2008, when the federal Government, with bipartisan support, undertook a large-scale 'intervention' into indigenous communities in 'prescribed areas' in the Northern Territory, with the aim of addressing, inter alia, child welfare concerns, family violence, and the perceived breakdown of law and order. The statutory provisions underpinning the 'intervention' affected some 500 communities and 45,000 people, and included, for a subset of these communities, an intrusive 'income management' scheme quarantining a portion of welfare payments and permitting them to be spent only on such items as food, clothing, education and child care.[102] The 'intervention' legislation was excluded from the purview of the Racial Discrimination Act as 'special measures' within the meaning of the Act and the International Convention on the Elimination of All Forms of Racial Discrimination.[103] Indigenous communities are perhaps particularly vulnerable to differential measures of this kind, but the suspension of the Racial Discrimination Act also illustrates a larger point that, although statutory regimes intended to secure equality do provide some measure of protection, this protection is sometimes partial and always contingent on the will of the political majority.

iii. Community

Aside from basic protections for the states as distinct political communities, and some degree of acknowledgment of the special position of indigenous Australians, the Australian constitutional order does not recognise the value of community as such, and contains little explicit acknowledgment of, or protection for, particular communities existing within the nation. Aspects of the constitutional order may, however, be read as instantiating a particular notion of the nation itself as a community.

[102] Although some elements of the intervention have been welcomed by indigenous people in some communities, particularly women, the more draconian aspects of the intervention and the way in which the project was framed and imposed had a particular and offensive resonance in light of Australia's past treatment of the indigenous population. A one-year review of the intervention observed: 'There is a strong sense of injustice that Aboriginal people and their culture have been seen as exclusively responsible for problems within their communities that have arisen from decades of cumulative neglect by governments in failing to provide the most basic standards of health, housing, education and ancillary services enjoyed by the wider Australian community': *Report of the Northern Territory Emergency Response Review Board* (October 2008) 9, available at www.nterreview.gov.au/docs/report_nter_review/default.htm.

[103] Northern Territory National Emergency Response Act 2007 (Cth) s 132. In a 2013 case, the High Court ruled that 'special measures' could include criminalisation of conduct (in that case, possession of alcohol within a certain area), and were not required to be subject to prior informed consent or consultation with affected communities (contrary to the position adopted by the ICERD Committee on 'special measures' under the Convention): *Maloney v The Queen* [2013] HCA 28.

The Constitution establishes a federal structure, and is predicated on the continued existence of the Commonwealth and the states as separate polities. The Constitution's provision for the states has been held to give rise to a limitation on the Commonwealth's express legislative powers, precluding statutes which place a special burden on the states, or curtail their capacity to function as separate polities.[104]

The common law recognition of native title—a key element of the relationship between indigenous and non-indigenous Australia—turns on an acknowledgment that indigenous people lived in distinct communities (whether defined as tribes, clans or groups), and that the laws and customs of those communities could found an ongoing title to land.[105] A complex statutory regime now governs claims to the native title recognised at common law, and provides for adjudication of claims and the interrelation of native title and other property rights. In this way Australian law now makes some concession to the distinct culture of indigenous communities (which of course differ also among themselves in culture and in history) within the Australian state.[106] Australia is bound to respect a right of self-determination provided in the ICCPR and ICESCR, and reiterated in the Declaration on the Rights of Indigenous Peoples, although this has always been interpreted in Australia as requiring consultation with indigenous groups—and sometimes not even that—rather than any stronger notion of political independence. In the wake of Australia's 2009 endorsement of the

[104] *Melbourne Corporation v Commonwealth* (1947) 74 CLR 31; *Austin v Commonwealth* (2003) 215 CLR 185. Recent decisions on the scope of Commonwealth powers to appropriate and spend moneys have also had a practical effect on the ability of the Commonwealth to unilaterally implement policies affecting the states, other than pursuant to a specific head of legislative power or within the (still contestable) limits of federal executive power, and have been grounded in part on a strong notion of Australia's federal design, and the power of spending arrangements to undermine it: see, eg, *Williams v Commonwealth of Australia* (2012) 248 CLR 156, 178, 216 (French CJ), 235–36 (Gummow and Bell JJ). In a subsequent case the Court struck down, in its operation with respect to funding at issue in the case, remedial legislation intended to provide legislative authority for the payments previously held to have been invalidly made, and an array of other payments to be made under similar arrangements: *Williams v Commonwealth of Australia* [2014] HCA 23 (19 June 2014).

[105] See, eg, *Mabo v Queensland [No 2]* (1992) 175 CLR 1, 51–52 (Brennan J), 88 (Deane and Gaudron JJ).

[106] This stands in contrast to the initial exclusion of indigenous people from the polity. Prior to a referendum in 1967, the Constitution contained a provision that 'In reckoning the numbers of the people of the Commonwealth, or of a State or other part of the Commonwealth, Aboriginal natives shall not be counted' (intended to prevent Queensland and Western Australia, which initially had small white populations, from obtaining additional seats in the legislature or Commonwealth funding on the strength of their significant indigenous population), and the federal power to make laws with respect to a particular race expressly did not extend to indigenous people. The latter exclusion was deleted in 1967, leaving the somewhat anomalous constitutional provision—to make laws with respect to 'The people of any race, for whom it is deemed necessary to make special laws'—discussed under 'Equality' above.

Declaration[107] there are proposals for some kind of constitutional recognition for indigenous language and culture.

The two sub-national charters of rights recognise the rights of minorities to enjoy their culture, declare and practise their religion, and use their language.[108]

Beyond this limited recognition of sub-national communities, citizenship, the franchise, compulsory voting, and the absence of any comprehensive protection for rights that would curtail majoritarian politics might be said to reflect a particular notion of the nation itself as a community (although some of these aspects could also be said to reflect a distinct value of democracy, rather than any value of community as such). However, there is a surprising fluidity to definitions of the Australian political community. Neither the bounds of citizenship nor the extent of the franchise is fixed. There is no definition of 'citizenship' in the Constitution.[109] At the time of the drafting of the Constitution, there was no notion of Australian citizenship as such: persons in Australia were subjects of the British Crown, or aliens. The first statute prescribing the bounds of Australian citizenship, the Nationality and Citizenship Act 1948 (Cth), granted an entitlement to citizenship to, inter alia, all persons born within Australia,[110] including indigenous people,[111] and provided a means whereby persons born overseas could receive certificates of naturalisation and thereby become Australian citizens.[112] The

[107] The Liberal Government had originally declined to support the Declaration in 2007, citing inter alia concerns about references to self-determination and customary law. In endorsing the Declaration two years later the Labor Government emphasised the aspirational and non-binding quality of its treatment of self-determination: Jenny Macklin MP, 'Statement on the United Nations Declaration on the Rights of Indigenous Peoples', 3 April 2009, available at www.un.org/esa/socdev/unpfii/documents/Australia_official_statement_endorsement_UNDRIP.pdf.

[108] Human Rights Act 2004 (ACT) s 27; Charter of Human Rights and Responsibilities Act 2006 (Vic) s 19(1); see also s 19(2) on specific rights of Aboriginal people.

[109] In fact, citizenship is only ever mentioned in the context of prohibition in s 44 on the election of a person being a 'citizen of a foreign power'. The absence of reference to citizenship has been attributed to a reluctance to use a term particularly associated with republican government: see John Quick and Robert Garran, *The Annotated Constitution of the Australian Commonwealth* (Sydney, Angus & Robertson, 1901) 957.

[110] Except persons whose fathers were accredited diplomatic envoys, and persons born in enemy occupied territory to a father who was an enemy alien: see s 10(2).

[111] Although the extension of citizenship to indigenous people was at that time a formality only: most indigenous people were not able to vote, could not access a number of welfare benefits available to non-indigenous people, and were subject to restrictive regulations and powers that had no application to non-indigenous people: John Chesterman and Brian Galligan, 'Indigenous Rights and Australian Citizenship' in Kim Rubenstein (ed), *Individual, Community, Nation: Fifty Years of Australian Citizenship* (Melbourne, Australian Scholarly Publishing, 2000) 64–72.

[112] See ss 14 and 15. Naturalisation was subject to satisfaction of requirements including that the applicant be of good character, and have an adequate knowledge of the English language and the responsibilities and privileges of Australian citizenship: s 15(1)(a). Separate provisions applied to persons born overseas to fathers who were Australian citizens and eligible to be citizens by descent (s 11), and to persons who were already, under legislation applicable in other specified Commonwealth countries, citizens of those countries (s 12).

current iteration of this legislation, the Australian Citizenship Act 2007 (Cth), contains a preamble articulating the connection between citizenship and the national community:

> The Parliament recognises that Australian citizenship represents full and formal membership of the community of the Commonwealth of Australia, and Australian citizenship is a common bond, involving reciprocal rights and obligations, uniting all Australians, while respecting their diversity.
>
> The Parliament recognises that persons conferred Australian citizenship enjoy these rights and undertake to accept these obligations:
>
> (a) by pledging loyalty to Australia and its people; and
> (b) by sharing their democratic beliefs; and
> (c) by respecting their rights and liberties; and
> (d) by upholding and obeying the laws of Australia.

With the possible exception of the preamble, the statute provides a somewhat more prosaic legal framework for citizenship than can be offered by a constitutional base. And while a variety of statutory and discretionary mechanisms allow a degree of control over the granting of citizenship, the period of residence required before becoming a citizen, and the process itself, is less demanding than in some other developed countries.

Similarly, although the Constitution was clearly framed to enshrine representative government, it 'makes allowance for the evolutionary nature of representative government as a dynamic rather than purely static institution' and is not prescriptive either as to the processes by which this model of government should be put into effect, nor the extent of the franchise.[113] Sections 7 and 24 of the Constitution require that Senators and Members of the House of Representatives be 'directly chosen by the people'. The definition of 'the people' in this context has given rise to difficulties. In general the entitlement to vote attaches to citizenship.[114] A majority of the Court has rejected blanket disenfranchisement of all persons serving a sentence of imprisonment as not having a 'rational connection with the identification of community membership or with the capacity to exercise free choice'[115] or not being reasonably appropriate and adapted to serve an end compatible with the system of representative government for which the Constitution

[113] *Roach v Electoral Commissioner* (2007) 233 CLR 162, 186–87 (Gummow, Kirby and Crennan JJ); see also *McGinty v Western Australia* (1996) 186 CLR 140, 279–80; *Mulholland v Australian Electoral Commission* (2004) 220 CLR 181, 213–14. Accordingly, central features of the Australian electoral system, including compulsory voting, the secret ballot, preferential voting for members of the House of Representatives and proportional representation in the Senate, are creatures of statute only.

[114] Persons who were British subjects within the meaning of previous citizenship laws, and on the electoral roll as of 1984, are also entitled to enrol: Commonwealth Electoral Act 1918 (Cth) s 93(1)(b).

[115] *Roach v Electoral Commissioner* (2007) 233 CLR 162, 175 (Gleeson CJ).

provides.[116] Various members of the High Court have suggested that as a general principle it would not now be possible to move away from universal adult suffrage,[117] although the way has been left clear for exclusions, for example, for those guilty of treason or of unsound mind, both of which are factors going to the entitlement or capacity to exercise free choice.[118]

Similarly, although virtually all the mechanics of electoral process are contained in statute, changes to the statutory regime which have an adverse impact on opportunities to enrol and vote are likely to be scrutinised closely, and may be invalid unless they can be argued on balance to be reasonably appropriate and adapted to the achievement of an end compatible with the 'direct choice' for which the Constitution provides.[119] For those eligible to vote, voting is compulsory at national and state levels. Compulsory voting for federal elections was introduced in 1924 and, while not universally supported, seems likely to remain a central part of the Australian political landscape.

iv. Freedom/Independence

The Australian constitutional order, with its minimal explicit protection of rights, reflects a conception of individual freedom as 'negative liberty': a freedom from government constraint, rather than a freedom to do certain things. The existence of a substantial social safety net, which might in other countries be understood as nurturing certain freedoms to participate in society, is rarely understood in such terms in Australia.

The federal arrangements enshrined in the Constitution may be understood as protective of personal liberty, insofar as the separation of powers between federal and state government, and the existence of different states, limits the power that may be exercised by any one government over the individual (the territories are in a somewhat different position and subject to greater Commonwealth control). The Constitution also protects personal liberty insofar as the separation of powers, by checking excesses by any one branch of government, and protecting the independence of the judiciary and thus the integrity of court processes, may be thought to provide a general

[116] ibid 199 (Gummow, Kirby, Crennan JJ).

[117] See, eg, *McGinty v Western Australia* (1996) 186 CLR 140, 170 (Brennan J), 286–87 (Gummow J); *Roach v Electoral Commissioner* (2007) 233 CLR 162, 173 (Gleeson CJ); *Rowe v Electoral Commissioner* (2010) 243 CLR 1, 18 (French CJ).

[118] People who engage in acts of treason 'may be regarded as having no just claim to participate in the community's self-governance': *Roach v Electoral Commissioner* (2007) 233 CLR 162, 175 (Gleeson CJ).

[119] *Rowe v Electoral Commissioner* (2010) 243 CLR 1, 38-39 (French CJ), 59, 61 (Gummow and Bell JJ), 120–21 (Crennan J).

safeguard of individual freedom.[120] The Constitution also limits the power of the Parliament to acquire property to acquisition 'on just terms'.[121]

The High Court has implied from the provisions enshrining representative government a limited 'freedom of political communication' preventing statutes from burdening 'communication ... concerning political or governmental matters which enables the people to exercise a free and informed choice as electors', unless the burden is appropriate and adapted to a legitimate end.[122]

The common law itself carries within it a particular vision of freedom: that the individual is free to do anything not specifically prohibited, and that statutes purporting to restrict fundamental liberties should be strictly construed so as not to trammel freedom of movement,[123] freedom of association[124] or property rights,[125] unless there is a clear intention to do so. Substantive guarantees of physical freedom, or the freedom not to

[120] On the High Court's resistance to broad and self-defining executive power see, eg, *Australian Communist Party v The Commonwealth* (1951) 83 CLR 1, 182–86 (Dixon J), 211 (McTiernan J), 221 (Williams J), 236 (Webb J), 258–59 (Fullagar J), 281–83 (Kitto J). The Court has been explicit in linking the separation of powers to individual freedom. In *Wilson v Minister for Aboriginal and Torres Strait Islander Affairs* (1996) 189 CLR 1, the majority observed: 'The separation of the judicial function from the other functions of government advances two constitutional objectives: the guarantee of liberty and, to that end, the independence of Chapter III judges': ibid 11.

[121] Section 51(xxxi). It had been established since 1969 that guarantees such as s 51(xxxi) did not apply in the territories: that s 122 of the Constitution, providing a power to legislate for the territories, was so removed from the general distribution of powers between the Commonwealth and states in s 51 that the 'just terms' requirement did not apply to takings pursuant to s 122. This view was overruled in 2009, in part on the basis of the importance of the 'just terms' requirement in protecting rights: *Wurridjal v Commonwealth* (2009) 237 CLR 309, 359 (French CJ), 388 (Gummow and Hayne JJ), 419 (Kirby J).

[122] *Lange v Australian Broadcasting Corporation* (1997) 189 CLR 520, 559; *Coleman v Power* (2004) 220 CLR 1. The limit has been applied in recent years to invalidate, inter alia, state laws prohibiting political donations from corporations, other entities or individuals other than those enrolled to vote: *Unions NSW v New South Wales* [2013] HCA 58. In a case concerning letters sent to the families of Australian soldiers and officials killed in Afghanistant and Indonesia, insulting those who had died as part of a larger criticism of the war in Afghanistan, the High Court was evenly divided on the validity of criminal prohibitions of use of a postal service 'in a way ... that reasonable persons would regard as being, in all the circumstances, menacing, harassing or offensive': *Monis v The Queen* (2013) 249 CLR 92. The two subnational rights instruments contain express rights to freedom of opinion and expression, as well as to freedom of assembly and association: Human Rights Act 2004 (ACT) ss 16, 15; Charter of Human Rights and Responsibilities Act 2006 (Vic) s 15, 16.

[123] See, eg, *Potter v Minahan* (1908) 7 CLR 277, 305–06 (O'Connor J); *Melbourne Corporation v Barry* (1922) 31 CLR 174 at 206 (Higgins J).

[124] This was the subject of comment in *South Australia v Totani* (2010) 242 CLR 1 (concerning a legislative scheme targeted at motorcycle gangs and allowing for the making of control orders prohibiting individual members from communicating with other members of 'declared organisations'). The Court has rejected arguments that a freestanding freedom of association is implicit in the Constitution: *Wainohu v New South Wales* (2011) 243 CLR 181, 230 (Gummow, Hayne, Crennan and Bell JJ), 22 (French CJ, Kiefel J), 251 (Heydon J).

[125] *Clissold v Perry* (1904) 1 CLR 363, 373 (Griffith CJ).

be arbitrarily detained, also inhere within the common law.[126] The writ of habeas corpus, which provides a safeguard against arbitrary detention, is one such guarantee.[127] The writ has been invoked in a wide range of circumstances, from arrests of American deserters under legislative arrangements for cooperation between Australian and US military agencies,[128] to physical control exercised by military personnel over asylum-seekers trying to enter Australian waters.[129] However, despite the stated commitment to personal liberty and the availability of habeas relief, there have in fact been quite repressive, but legal, systems of non-punitive detention in Australia.[130] During both World War I and World War II the Minister for Defence had the power to order detention of individuals on broad and ambiguous grounds.[131] The current iteration of the Migration Act 1958 (Cth) provides for administrative detention of 'unlawful non-citizens' and has been held to permit indefinite detention of such individuals if they cannot be removed to another country.[132] Anti-terrorism provisions introduced in the wake of the September 11 attacks enable the Australian Federal Police (with the consent of the Attorney-General) to seek quite restrictive 'control orders' from federal courts in certain circumstances. Such control orders

[126] They are also explicit in the sub-national rights instruments: Human Rights Act 2004 (ACT) s 18; Charter of Human Rights and Responsibilities Act 2006 (Vic) s 18.

[127] The High Court has observed that '[m]any of our fundamental freedoms are guaranteed by ancient principles of the common law or by ancient statutes which are so much part of the accepted constitutional framework that their terms, if not their very existence, may be overlooked until a case arises which evokes their contemporary and undiminished force ... the common law of habeas corpus and the Habeas Corpus Act 1679 ... as extended by the Habeas Corpus Act 1816 ... are such laws': *Re Bolton & Anor, ex p Beane* (1987) 162 CLR 514, 520–21 (Brennan J); see also reference to 'the undisputed values securing the liberty of the individual that for centuries have illumined the common law' ibid 517 (Mason CJ, Wilson and Dawson JJ).

[128] *Re Bolton & Anor, ex p Beane* (1987) 162 CLR 514.

[129] See, eg, *Ruddock v Vadarlis* (2001) 110 FCR 491.

[130] This has recently been reiterated in *Thomas v Mowbray* (2007) 233 CLR 307, 330 (Gleeson CJ): 'It is not correct to say, as an absolute proposition, that, under our system of government, restraints on liberty, whether or not involving detention in custody, exist only as an incident of adjudging and punishing criminal guilt [though] It is true that the circumstances under which restraints on liberty may be imposed by judicial order other than as an incident of adjudging and punishing criminal guilt are carefully confined, both by the parliament and by the courts.'

[131] During WWI, detention could be ordered if the Minister had 'reason to believe that any naturalized person is disaffected or disloyal' (War Precautions Regulations 1915 (Cth) reg 55(1)); during WWII, if the Minister was 'satisfied with respect to any particular person that with a view to prevent that person acting in any manner prejudicial to the public safety or the defence of the Commonwealth it is necessary to do so [make an order for detention]' (National Security (General) Regulations 1939 (Cth) reg 26). These provisions were discussed in *Al-Kateb v Godwin* (2004) 219 CLR 562, 588–89 (McHugh J).

[132] *Al-Kateb v Godwin* (2004) 219 CLR 562. In a more recent case a unanimous five-judge bench emphasised that the purposes for which immigration detention is permitted 'must be pursued and carried into effect as soon as reasonably practicable': *Plaintiff S4-2014 v Minister for Immigration and Border Protection* [2014] HCA 34 (11 September 2014) [28].

may impose requirements (such as reporting at specific times and places, or wearing a tracking device) or prohibitions (such as upon being at specified areas or places, leaving Australia, communicating or associating with specified individuals, and accessing or using specified forms of telecommunication, including the internet) on named individuals.[133]

Insofar as freedom/independence refers to any sentiment at a national level, there has never been a strong desire in Australia to tidy up the institutional remnants of Australia's former colonial ties with Britain. The Queen is still an important part of the Australian constitutional order, and the Constitution itself remains an Act of the Imperial Parliament. Independence was achieved at a glacial pace and there is a sense in which the process is ongoing. In 1999, a referendum on whether Australia should become a republic (albeit on a less popular model, whereby the President was appointed by Parliament) failed to pass, attracting about 41 per cent support nationally. The Labor Party is formally committed to moving towards a republic, but neither party has actively pursued change in recent years. While becoming a republic is no doubt an important issue for many people, it does not arouse the passion and commitment that the cause of national independence inspires in many other countries.

v. Responsibility/Accountability and Integrity/Honesty

The Australian constitutional order is only really concerned with responsibility/accountability and integrity/honesty insofar as they affect the institutions of public life. In this limited sense, these values are very important in the Australian system.[134] At least in the Australian context, responsibility/accountability and integrity/honesty are fundamentally intertwined. Accountability of the executive to the legislature and of both to the people, are central elements of representative and responsible government. But they also serve to buttress and protect integrity in public office, defined broadly to encompass anything from the personal honesty of officeholders to broader issues about the proper performance of public functions, and respect for appropriate limits on the powers associated with office. Accordingly, these values are considered together.

Some accountability mechanisms arise directly or indirectly from the Constitution. The Constitution provides for a bicameral federal Parliament,

[133] Criminal Code (Cth) Div 104. A challenge to the constitutionality of these provisions, on the basis that they were not supported by the defence power, or alternatively breached the separation of powers, has failed: *Thomas v Mowbray* (2007) 233 CLR 307.

[134] Indeed, Australia has such extensive institutional and structural mechanisms enabling oversight of the conduct of those in public office that then-Chief Justice of New South Wales James Spigelman, writing extracurially, proposed that such mechanisms be understood as aspects of a fourth arm of government, the 'integrity branch': 'The Integrity Branch of Government' (2004) 78 *Australian Law Journal* 724.

with a Senate empowered to reject appropriation bills just as it may reject any other proposed laws.[135] Section 83 of the Constitution, said to reflect the 'fundamental rule of the constitutional law of the Anglo-Australian peoples ... that the Crown cannot expend money without the authorisation of Parliament',[136] provides that 'No money shall be drawn from the Treasury of the Commonwealth except under appropriation made by law'. The High Court in 2009 held that section 83 was not itself a power to spend money; spending pursuant to all appropriations must be supported by another head of legislative power or, where available, by the executive power of the Commonwealth, which in turn attracts the incidental legislative power.[137] Although this reading of section 83 asserts greater limits on federal power than were previously thought to exist, it arguably does not itself assist in improving oversight of the executive.[138] Annual appropriations now account for only approximately 20 per cent of all government expenditure; the balance arises from special appropriations, scattered across different statutes.[139] Departments are also able to use moneys transferred from other departments or retained as a surplus from previous years, without any real statement to Parliament of the purposes for which it will be expended. Even the annual appropriations bills now explain expenditure in terms of abstract outcomes, with no explanation, in some cases, of the specific policies or programmes that will be pursued. The High Court has ruled that the drawing of moneys pursuant to such general outcomes-based appropriations is valid, emphasising that it is for Parliament to specify the detail with which appropriations should be drafted.[140] After a further decision reinforced the potential implications of a narrow reading of the executive power for the constitutionality of a range of other programmes, the federal Parliament passed legislation crafted to try and ensure the constitutional validity of

[135] Triggering a process set out in s 57 of the Constitution. However, although the Senate may ultimately reject appropriation bills, s 53 provides that it may not amend them. If the Senate wishes to see the legislation amended, it must instead return it to the House of Representatives with a request for the amendments sought.

[136] *Combet v Commonwealth* (2005) 224 CLR 494, 535 (McHugh J); see also 522 (Gleeson CJ), 577 (Gummow, Hayne, Callinan and Heydon JJ), 596–604 (Kirby J).

[137] *Pape v Commissioner of Taxation* (2009) 238 CLR 1, 55 (French CJ), 73–74 (Gummow, Crennan and Bell JJ), 113 (Hayne and Kiefel JJ), 210–11 (Heydon J). In *Williams v Commonwealth of Australia* [2012] HCA 23 the executive power, insofar as it concerned the expenditure of moneys, was given a somewhat narrower ambit than it had previously been assumed to have.

[138] See submission by Harry Evans, then Clerk of the Senate, to the Democratic Audit of Australia, available at http://apo.org.au/node/2624.

[139] ibid 1.

[140] *Combet v Commonwealth* (2005) 224 CLR 494, 577 (by majority; strong dissents from Kirby and McHugh JJ in separate judgments). The majority reached their conclusion despite the fact that the funds in question were used to pay for advertising that was arguably partisan in nature, in support of controversial industrial relations legislation being opposed by the Opposition.

some 427 other spending programmes, worth billions of dollars in total, within a matter of days and with little detailed review.[141]

Section 97 of the Constitution foreshadowed a national audit function, stipulating that, until the Commonwealth otherwise provided, the laws then in force in the new states in relation to receipt and expenditure of government money apply to money received and expended in that state on the account of the Commonwealth Government. A Commonwealth audit function was established very quickly, under the Audit Act 1901 (Cth). The successor statute, the Auditor-General Act 1997 (Cth), establishes that the Auditor-General has power to audit, at his or her discretion, all Commonwealth agencies, authorities, companies and subsidiaries, with the exception of performance audits of government business enterprises.[142] The Auditor-General Act 1997 strengthened the independence of the office and, in particular, provides that the Auditor-General is an independent officer of the Parliament, has 'complete discretion in the performance or exercise of his or her functions or powers' and, subject to the Act itself and other laws, is not subject to direction from anyone in connection with the conduct of audits.[143] At the federal level, the Auditor-General's reports are provided to the Joint Committee of Public Accounts and Audit, a parliamentary committee established by statute and empowered to report to the Parliament on Commonwealth accounts, financial affairs, reports of the Auditor-General and 'any circumstances connected with them, that the Committee thinks should be drawn to the attention of the Parliament', the latter provision providing a capacity to instigate inquiries of its own independently of those referred by the Senate or House.[144]

Parliaments in Australia have a number of features designed to further accountability and integrity. At a structural level, the existence of a formally recognised Opposition and parliamentary procedures such as question time allow for some scrutiny of government conduct. The capacity to initiate parliamentary inquiries (albeit with a committee including members from both major parties) into specific subjects achieves similar ends. So-called 'estimates hearings', initiated in 1970 and now conducted before the Senate

[141] The Financial Framework Legislation Amendment Act (No 3) (Cth) was passed less than a week after judgment was delivered in *Williams v Commonwealth of Australia* (2012) 248 CLR 156. This legislation was later held invalid at least in its operation with respect to the funding arrangements in issue in that case: *Williams v Commonwealth of Australia* [2014] HCA 23 (19 June 2014).

[142] Sections 15–18.

[143] Section 8. All states and territories have their own Auditors-General, operating under state legislation, although a survey of factors contributing to independence of the respective Auditors-General has shown significant variation from state to state: Ken Coghill, 'Auditing the Independence of the Auditor-General', 14, available at http://apo.org.au/node/8889. State Auditors-General, like the Commonwealth Auditor-General, have been subject at various times to attempts to confine their inquiries, or to criticism of their reports, which can be highly embarrassing for executive governments.

[144] Public Accounts and Audit Committee Act 1951 (Cth) s 8(1)(d).

Finance and Public Administration Committee, have proved an effective means of overseeing executive agencies. While there has been debate about the proper scope of questioning in these hearings, consideration by the Procedure Committee in 1999 led to an acceptance that these hearings could range across all questions going to the operations and financial position of government departments and agencies, and the estimates hearings continue to function as a 'a general inquisition into the operations of government'.[145] However, these mechanisms are not infallible. The incomplete separation of the executive and legislative branches of government and the strong party discipline in Australia leave parliamentary processes vulnerable to manipulation by the executive. They are particularly weakened when one party holds a majority in both houses of Parliament, and is able to block the institution of inquiries, curtail debate,[146] and refuse to answer questions at estimates hearings, secure in the knowledge that the opposition will have little opportunity to take the matter further in the full chamber.[147]

Australia nominally has a convention of individual ministerial responsibility, whereby ministers are personally answerable to Parliament and thereby to the people for errors or misfeasance in the portfolios they oversee.[148] The scope of ministerial responsibility, and particularly whether it requires ministers to resign in connection with errors or misfeasance of which they were not aware at the time of commission, has never been entirely clear. In Australia, there has not been an instance in which a minister has resigned in connection with matters in which they were not involved, and of which they were not aware. Where resignations have occurred, they have arisen out of the personal involvement of ministers in wrongdoing (usually misleading Parliament, or personal impropriety concerning expenses or conflicts of interest).[149] The current federal *Statement of Ministerial Standards* does not

[145] Harry Evans, Clerk of the Senate, 'Senate Estimates Hearings and the Government Majority in the Senate: Address to the National Press Club' (April 2006), available at www.aph.gov.au/About_Parliament/Senate/Research_and_Education/The_Biographical_Dictionary_of_the_Australian_Senate/Papers_by_former_Clerk_of_the_Senate_Harry_Evans/Senate_Estimates.

[146] As occurred in 2005, when the government limited debate and sharply curtailed possible committee inquiries into controversial industrial relations and anti-terrorism legislation.

[147] See Evans, 'Senate Estimates Hearings' (n 145).

[148] The convention of ministerial responsibility appears, for example, in one of the 'Australian Public Service Values': 'the APS is open and accountable to the Australian community under the law and within the framework of Ministerial responsibility' (Public Service Act 1999 (Cth) s 10(1)(e)). The Public Service Commissioner's directions in respect of this value (made under s 11(1)) do not cast further light on the concept of ministerial responsibility.

[149] Roger Beale AM, 'Ministerial Responsibility for Administrative Actions: Some Observations of a Public Service Practitioner' (2002) 9 *Agenda* 291, 295. The issue of ministerial responsibility arose in 2005 following revelations of systemic incompetence and procedural flaws in the regime of immigration detention. Neither minister who had had responsibility for the immigration portfolio over the relevant period resigned. The position put by the Government was that, in light of the size and complexity of public administration today, if the minister was not personally involved or aware of wrongdoing, the convention did not require their resignation.

take a clear position on what the convention would require, but emphasises the importance of complete honesty and accuracy in statements made to Parliament and the public.[150]

Section 44 of the Constitution provides that any person who, inter alia, holds an office of profit under the Crown, or has any direct or indirect pecuniary interest in an agreement with the public service (other than as a shareholder in an incorporated company of more than 25 shareholders), is incapable of serving as a Senator or a Member of the House of Representatives. Section 45 provides that if a Senator or Member becomes subject to these disabilities, or '[d]irectly or indirectly takes or agrees to take any fee or honorarium for services rendered to the Commonwealth, or for services rendered in the Parliament to any person or State', their seat shall immediately be vacant. Senate and House orders and resolutions deal with the registration of pecuniary interests, and the declaration of gifts received, and all state and territory parliaments have adopted similar registers of pecuniary interests to address conflicts of interests. A number of Parliaments have adopted codes of conduct for all members, and some have codes for ministers.

Since 1983, there has been a mechanism at the federal level for the public funding of electoral campaigns, designed to ensure that differences in wealth do not distort the capacity of parties to secure public support for their policies, and to prevent the possible appearance or reality of corruption that might be fostered by a reliance on private donations. Post-election payments, calculated on the basis of the number of first preference votes received, are made to registered parties (subject to low thresholds for minimum party size and support). However, there are no limits to the private donations to political parties that may be made in addition to public funding, although there are requirements for the disclosure by parties of donations received.[151]

The executive branch, and public agencies, may be subject to a wide variety of other accountability mechanisms. Royal Commissions, themselves an executive body, have been established in the past to inquire into particular conduct of governments or agencies.[152] Some states have standalone commissions empowered to investigate corruption and abuse of

[150] *Statement of Ministerial Standards* (December 2013) [1.3(iv)], [5.1], available at https://www.dpmc.gov.au/sites/default/files/publications/Statement_of_Ministerial_Standards.pdf. This *Statement*, and previous codes covering similar matters, are drafted and promulgated by the executive and have no formal legal status.

[151] Commonwealth Electoral Act 1918 (Cth) Pt XX, div 4. A decision in 2005 to increase the threshold for disclosure of contributions, coupled with increasing reliance on non-donation contributions, and the possibility of undisclosed donations to entities associated with parties, may be weakening the ability of disclosure laws to provide meaningful information about parties' sources of financial support.

[152] A notable example is the Royal Commission established in 1992 to inquire into the questionable commercial and party political dealings of the Western Australian Government in the late 1980s.

office. Ombudsmen have a power to investigate complaints from the public and inquire into deficiencies in administration.[153] As noted above under 'Justice/Fairness', there is an extensive body of administrative law providing avenues for judicial review (and sometimes merits review) of administrative decisions—although there is also a history of attempts to exclude judicial review for particular classes of decision, particularly in the migration area. Statutory provisions now frequently require administrative decision-makers to provide written reasons,[154] or entitle individuals to seek reasons for certain classes of decision.[155] Additionally, at both federal and state levels there is freedom of information legislation providing a means of seeking access to government documents,[156] although the force of this legislation has been reduced by dilatory processing of requests,[157] deference to commercial-in-confidence protocols with private bodies and broad exemptions from disclosure on grounds such as the public interest.[158]

vi. Respect/Tolerance

There is no explicit recognition of the values of respect or tolerance in the Australian Constitution. There is some limited constitutional protection for freedom of religion, but most protection for minority groups, where it exists, lies in statutory regimes prohibiting discrimination and vilification.

Section 116 of the Constitution provides that:

> The Commonwealth shall not make any law for establishing any religion, or for imposing any religious observance, or for prohibiting the free exercise of any

[153] The office of Commonwealth Ombudsman was created by the Ombudsman Act 1976 (Cth). States and territories now all have ombudsmen too. Ombudsmen have been active in their roles and have initiated investigations into areas such as conditions for persons in police custody: see *Investigation into Deaths and Harm in Custody* (March 2014) 16–17, available at https://www.ombudsman.vic.gov.au/Publications/Parliamentary-Reports/Investigation-into-deaths-and-harm-in-custody.

[154] Provisions requiring decision-makers to provide reasons include, eg, Migration Act 1958 (Cth) s 368(1) (applying to decision on review by Migration Review Tribunal), s 430(1) (applying to decision on review by Refugee Review Tribunal) and Social Security (Administration) Act 1999 s 177(1)(a) (applying to decision on review by Social Security Appeals Tribunal).

[155] See, eg, Administrative Decisions (Judicial Review) Act 1977 (Cth) s 13; Administrative Appeals Tribunal Act 1975 (Cth) s 28.

[156] Freedom of Information Act 1982 (Cth); Freedom of Information Act 1982 (Vic); Government Information (Public Access) Act 2009 (NSW); Freedom of Information Act 1989 (ACT); Freedom of Information Act 1991 (SA); Right to Information Act 2009 (Tas); Right to Information Act 2009 (Qld); Freedom of Information Act 1992 (WA); Information Act 2002 (NT).

[157] For example, the Victorian Ombudsman has found that significant delay attends the processing of many FOI requests in Victoria: *Review of the Freedom of Information Act: Report of Ombudsman Victoria* (June 2006).

[158] For an example of the difficulty of overcoming such exemptions, see *McKinnon v Secretary, Department of Treasury* (2006) 228 CLR 423; FOI Independent Review Panel, *The Right to Information: Reviewing Queensland's Public Information Act* (2008) 138–45.

> religion, and no religious test shall be required as a qualification for any office or public trust under the Commonwealth.[159]

However, the High Court has held that section 116 does not effect a comprehensive separation of church and state, and does not prevent the Parliament from passing laws which, while falling short of recognising a religion as a national institution, may indirectly assist the practice of religion (such as laws providing funding for schooling and requiring states to distribute it to government and religious schools alike).[160]

At various points in history Australian governments have been patently intolerant and disrespectful of particular minorities, especially racial minorities. The founding of Australia as a British colony had a devastating and still contested impact on its indigenous people, and indigenous disadvantage persists today. Between the creation of the Australian Commonwealth in 1901 and the 1960s, the so-called 'white Australia policy', reflected in legislation and policy documents, sought to limit immigration of non-white people. Australia has now moved away from racism of the kind underlying previous treatment of indigenous peoples and non-white migrants, although such sentiments persist in pockets of the community.[161] However, there are only limited guarantees of tolerance for racial and other minorities, secured by means of statutory prohibitions on discrimination and intolerant conduct.

The two sub-national rights instruments include various rights and freedoms that would tend to ensure respect and tolerance for minority groups. Section 19 of the Victorian Charter, for example, provides:

> All persons with a particular cultural, religious, racial or linguistic background must not be denied the right, in community with other persons of that background, to enjoy his or her culture, to declare and practise his or her religion and to use his or her language.[162]

Laws on discrimination are discussed under the rubric of 'Equality' above. As well as providing for equal opportunity in employment and other aspects

[159] The Tasmanian Constitution contains a guarantee of freedom of religion, subject to 'public order and morality'.

[160] *Attorney-General (Vic) (Ex rel Black) v Commonwealth* (1981) 146 CLR 559. Most recently, the High Court unanimously dismissed arguments that a funding agreement between the Commonwealth and the Scripture Union of Queensland, under which the Commonwealth provided monies to fund salaries of chaplains in public schools that wished to offer such services, contravened s 116: *Williams v Commonwealth of Australia* (2012) 248 CLR 156. The chaplains were intended to support the spiritual wellbeing of students, and were required to be approachable by students and staff of all religious affiliations; students had no obligation to take up the services offered.

[161] Overt racism has been manifested, for example, in connection with the success of the anti-immigration platform of the 'One Nation' party (which won some 22% of the vote in a 1998 Queensland election, and some 10% of the primary vote in the 2001 federal election, before collapsing under the weight of internal divisions), and, in December 2005, in violent clashes in Sydney suburbs between white Australians and Lebanese migrants.

[162] An equivalent provision, although not applying to 'cultural' minorities, is found in s 27 of the Human Rights Act 2004 (ACT). Other relevant provisions include those ensuring freedom of religion: see s 14 of both instruments.

of life, these statutes often prohibit the vilification of minority groups.[163] However, such jurisprudence as there is under to date reflects a concern on the part of judges not to hinder political expression,[164] and the inevitable tension between anti-vilification provisions and freedom of speech has led to a great deal of debate in the parliament and media, but no principled resolution. In one prominent case, legal proceedings under a state provision allowed vilifiers of Islam as a religion to cast themselves as having their freedoms curtailed.[165]

In 2013, the federal Liberal Party undertook to radically curtain federal racial vilification provisions in order to correct for perceived burdens on freedom of speech. This initiative proved highly controversial,[166] and

[163] For example, following legislative amendments in 1995, s 18C(1) (together with s 18B) of the Racial Discrimination Act 1975 (Cth) renders it unlawful for a person to do an act, otherwise than in private, if the act is reasonably likely, in all the circumstances, to offend, insult, humiliate or intimidate another person or a group of people; and one of the reasons for which the act is done is the race, colour or national or ethnic origin of the other person or of some or all of the people in the group. There are limited exemptions under s 18C for artistic works, discussion or debate in the public interest, and the making or publishing of a fair report or comment.

[164] *Walsh v Hanson* [2000] HREOCA 8 (2 March 2000) concerned a publication associated with the leader of the 'One Nation' party (see above n 161) and elaborated by the respondents in various media comments. The publication and comments contained, among other statements, allegations that indigenous Australians had been cannibals, and now enjoyed, under 'reverse discrimination', a range of benefits not available to non-indigenous Australians. The Human Rights and Equal Opportunity Inquiry Commissioner commented: 'It is a concomitant of political freedom that political activists, especially those at the extreme ends of the political spectrum of ideas, will from time to time, even frequently, hurt and offend other members of society. It seems to me that we must be mature enough to accept that as a price that we must pay for the privilege of living in a society where political expression is to remain free and unfettered. This is so no matter how odious to the majority some of the fringe manifestations of that freedom may be.' The claims subject to complaint were found not to have been made *because of* the race of the complainants within the meaning of s 18C of the Racial Discrimination Act 1975 (Cth), and in any event the claims were found to form part of a genuine political argument and thus fall within the exception for discussion or debate in the public interest. See also *Australian Macedonian Advisory Council Inc v LIVV Pty Ltd* [2011] VCAT 1647 (30 August 2011) [70] (in which the material in question was held not to rise to the level prohibited by Victorian provisions): 'A commitment to free speech is an essential concept of all liberal democracies of which Australia is one. In this country we do not have a version of the USA's first amendment which protects the most rabid ideology in the name of free speech but the legislation under review here (and its federal and other state counterparts) serves to place some restriction on racist and other extreme expressions. That said I am firmly of the view that restrictions should only be placed on discourse in the most egregious of cases.'

[165] The first major case under the Victorian anti-vilification statute, the Racial and Religious Tolerance Act 2001 (Vic), concerning allegations that an evangelical Christian pastor had vilified Islam, was eventually resolved through mediation, but the initial hearing was used by the defendants as a forum for further negative comment on the Muslim faith, and perceived restrictions on freedom of speech inherent in the law attracted criticism in the media. Some later complaints made under the legislation seemed ill-founded and, following comments from judges about the risk of unmeritorious applications undermining public support for the legislation, a provision was inserted requiring applicants to obtain leave from the Tribunal before raising a claim under the Act.

[166] In response to questions about the potential for any amendment to 'facilitate vilification by bigots', the Attorney-General stated that 'People do have a right to be bigots, you know. In a free country, people do have rights to say things that other people find offensive, insulting

was ultimately dropped by the Government, although some variant of the proposed reform is still being pursued by a number of MPs.

vii. Participation/Inclusion

There is no recognition of the value of participation/inclusion as such in the Australian Constitution.

As discussed under 'Community' above, practices of majoritarian democracy (albeit limited by the bounds of citizenship and the franchise) guarantee, and indeed require, participation in public life through federal, state and sometimes municipal elections. To this end, the Australian electoral system is elaborate, involving strict protections for the integrity of the electoral rolls, procedural efforts to ensure that all those required to vote do so, and even prohibitions on the publication of material encouraging voters to submit 'informal', or invalid, ballot papers.[167] The preferential voting system ensures that each successful candidate has received preferences from more than 50 per cent of the voters in the relevant constituency. However, to the extent that participation as a value is reflected in features of the electoral process, this participation is procedural and comparatively passive,[168] largely confined to the acceptance or rejection of two main parties, whose platforms are, in some respects, quite similar.

At a practical level, anti-discrimination statutes and the social safety net function to facilitate social inclusion. The sub-national rights instruments contain statements of individual rights to take part in public life, but it is unclear what these provisions add to the status quo.[169]

viii. Security

Although there is no express recognition of the value of security in the Australian Constitution, security, at least insofar as it concerns the 'preservation of the existence of the Commonwealth and of the Constitution', has been acknowledged in constitutional jurisprudence as a paramount consideration.[170] However, this is not a valorisation of security as an end in

or bigoted'. Parliament of Australia, Senate, 24 March 2014 (Senator Brandis). It is not clear that this proposition was shared by all members of the caucus. On the other hand, it is difficult to understand whether the opposition aroused by this statement was a genuine objection to a priority of freedom of speech regardless of its effects on those insulted, or part of larger party political arguments.

[167] See *Langer v The Commonwealth* (1996) 186 CLR 302.

[168] Smith, *Australian Political Culture* (n 35) 22–45.

[169] Human Rights Act 2004 (ACT) s 17; Charter of Human Rights and Responsibilities Act 2006 (Vic) s 18.

[170] *Australian Communist Party v The Commonwealth* (1951) 83 CLR 1, 141 (Latham CJ). Chief Justice Latham was in dissent in this case, but the statement quoted is a basal assumption not particular to the dissenting reasoning.

itself, but a recognition that security in this sense is an essential prerequisite for constitutional government, 'a condition of the exercise of all the other powers contained in the Constitution'.[171] The jurisprudence on defence and security measures—largely dating from the period of the two world wars but also arising from more recent challenges to anti-terrorist provisions—reflects an ongoing tension between the purported imperatives of security and the need for measures taken in the name of security to remain within the confines of the Constitution.

The Constitution allocates to the federal Parliament power to make laws with respect to 'the naval and military defence of the Commonwealth and of the several States, and the control of the forces to execute and maintain the laws of the Commonwealth'. This power, being a power for a particular purpose rather than in respect of a subject matter, such as external affairs, permits the federal Parliament to make laws that are reasonably appropriate and adapted to achieving the purposes identified in the head of power. The scope of the laws supported by the power varies depending upon the prevailing circumstances:

> what the defence power will enable the Parliament to do at any given time depends upon what the exigencies of the time may be considered to call for or warrant. The meaning of the power is ... fixed but as, according to that meaning, the fulfilment of the object of the power must depend on the ever-changing course of events, the practical application of the power will vary accordingly.[172]

It is well established that the scope of the defence power does not depend only upon whether there is, in formal terms, a state of war. Moreover, in the context of a challenge to the constitutionality of certain anti-terrorist provisions, the High Court rejected arguments that the 'defence power' was limited to making laws with respect to defence against external aggression from a foreign nation, and a majority rejected arguments that the power was limited to making laws with respect to the protection of the Commonwealth or states as bodies politic, as opposed to protection of individuals within the body politic.[173]

Issues pertaining to security give rise to difficult questions not only with regard to the scope of Commonwealth legislative power, but also with regard to the relationship between the executive and judiciary. In some cases, security legislation has been declared invalid in part because it conferred extensive powers on the executive, and rendered the exercise of these

[171] ibid.

[172] *Australian Communist Party v The Commonwealth* (1951) 83 CLR 1, 195 (Dixon J); see also *Polyukhovich v The Commonwealth of Australia* (1992) 172 CLR 501, 593 (Brennan J, citing observations in *Richardson v Forestry Commission* (1988) 164 CLR 261, 326 (Dawson J)).

[173] *Thomas v Mowbray* (2007) 233 CLR 307, 324 (Gleeson CJ), 359–62 (Gummow and Crennan JJ); 457–58 (Hayne J); 504 (Callinan J); 511 (Heydon J); *cf* 393, 395 (Kirby J).

powers unreviewable by the courts.[174] In other cases, the complaint has been the reverse: that the security legislation implicated the courts in the exercise of powers that were not judicial in nature, thereby threatening the separation of powers.[175]

ix. Life

There is no recognition of the value of life in the Australian Constitution. There are a number of statutory provisions that concern life narrowly construed (rather than some more substantive conception of a fulfilling life), although it is not clear that such disparate issues as the death penalty, abortion and euthanasia are all conceptualised in terms of a position on 'life' as a value, rather than in terms of some more specific ethical framework.

The two sub-national rights instruments, the ACT Human Rights Act and the Victorian Charter, both identify a 'right to life' (applicable only from the time of birth).[176] All jurisdictions in Australia have now abolished the death penalty.[177] Abortion is reasonably accessible.[178] Legislation permitting euthanasia in certain circumstances was briefly in force in the Northern Territory, before being overturned by the Commonwealth.[179]

There is a rich vein of thinking within the common law about the value and sanctity of human life, probably influenced by a Christian heritage, but which has endured despite the fading of religious inclinations.[180]

[174] See *Australian Communist Party v The Commonwealth* (1951) 83 CLR 1.

[175] See *Thomas v Mowbray* (2007) 233 CLR 307 (although the legislation in this case was held, by majority, to be valid).

[176] Human Rights Act 2004 (ACT) s 9; this is also the effect of the Charter of Human Rights and Responsibilities Act 2006 (Vic) s 9, coupled with s 48 ('Nothing in this Charter affects any law applicable to abortion or child destruction ...').

[177] The last execution in Australia took place in 1967. The death penalty was abolished for federal crimes and in the territories in 1973 (Death Penalty Abolition Act 1973 (Cth)). The last state to abolish the death penalty was NSW, in 1985 (Crimes Amendment (Death Penalty Abolition) Act 1985 (NSW)), although by 1985 it only attached to some esoteric crimes such as piracy.

[178] Some jurisdictions (the ACT from 2002, Victoria from 2008, Tasmania from 2014) have largely decriminalised abortion. In each jurisdiction in which abortion remains subject to criminal prohibition the offences concerned are subject to exceptions: in South Australia, Western Australia and the Northern Territory there are statutory provisions that define circumstances in which an abortion is not unlawful, and in the remaining jurisdictions judicial interpretations of the legislation have had the effect of making lawful abortion available in circumstances where, speaking broadly, the continuation of the pregnancy would pose a risk to the health or wellbeing of the mother (interpreted loosely). There is little enthusiasm for the prosecution of unlawful abortion.

[179] Rights of the Terminally Ill Act 1995 (NT); Euthanasia Laws Act 1997 (Cth). At least two individuals procured death pursuant to the NT legislation.

[180] See remarks of Gleeson CJ in *Cattanach v Melchior* (2003) 215 CLR 1, 10: 'The common law has always attached fundamental value to human life; a value originally based upon religious ideas which, in a secular society, no longer command universal assent. ... Many people who now respect the same value, do so upon different grounds.' See also Heydon J at 130: 'The opinion that human life is of unique value, while it is shared by many religions, is

In Australia, this has emerged in the context of the criminal law[181] and, more recently, in tort actions claiming damages for 'wrongful life' (of a child born following a failed sterilisation)[182] and 'wrongful birth' (of a child born with disabilities who would not have been carried to term had the disabilities been diagnosed earlier).[183] However, these bodies of law are not part of the constitutional order, as defined for present purposes.

x. Dignity

There is little explicit recognition of the value of dignity in the Australian constitutional order.

The High Court has occasionally had cause to discuss dignity in connection with references to the concept in international conventions.[184] More significantly, a line of dicta identifying human rights and human dignity as the foundation of the privileges against self-incrimination and exposure to penalties[185] has attracted support, although dignity has not been seen as the exclusive rationale of these privileges.[186] Moreover, 'dignity' has from time to time been invoked as an ultimate goal of rights protection, or an ideal

not limited to them. Nor is it limited to particular moralities. It underpins much of the common law. And if a sedulous attempt were to be made to weed out of the common law every principle that rested on religious or moral values, it would be radically changed.'

[181] The High Court, in the course of exploring the scope of unlawful and dangerous act manslaughter, has identified 'the sanctity of human life' as '[o]ne principle which stands higher than all others in the criminal law': *Wilson v R* (1992) 174 CLR 313, 341 (Brennan, Deane and Dawson JJ). The offences of murder and manslaughter, and the serious sanctions attaching to them, were said to flow from the law's 'regard for human life': *Wilson*, 342; reference to 'respect for human life' also appeared in the majority judgment at 333 (Mason CJ, Toohey, Gaudron and McHugh JJ).

[182] Although a majority in the wrongful birth case found that damages could be awarded, the minority judgments evidenced, if not a respect for life in itself, an acknowledgment of the incommensurability of life and human relationships, and an aversion to weighing them as a monetary benefit or loss: *Cattanach v Melchior* (2003) 215 CLR 1, 24 (Gleeson CJ), 93 (Hayne J), 126 (Heydon J).

[183] Although the leading judgment in the wrongful life case explicitly disavowed any reliance on the value of life, and turned on the impossibility of any calculation of damages—a comparison between a life with disabilities and non-existence being 'impossible'—it is clear that members of the Court were troubled by the ethical implications of such an action being available. See *Harriton v Stephens* (2006) 226 CLR 52, 129–30 (Crennan J, with whom Gleeson CJ, Gummow and Heydon JJ were in agreement).

[184] See, eg, *Koowarta v Bjelke-Petersen* (1982) 153 CLR 168; *Gerhardy v Brown* (1985) 159 CLR 70.

[185] A series of dicta of Murphy J in *Rochfort v Trade Practices Commission* (1982) 153 CLR 134, 150; *Pyneboard Pty Ltd v Trade Practices Commission* (1983) 152 CLR 328, 346–47; *Controlled Consultants Pty Ltd v Commissioner for Corporate Affairs* (1985) 156 CLR 385, 395; see also, on legal professional privilege, *Attorney-General (NT) v Maurice* (1986) 161 CLR 475, 490 (Deane J).

[186] *Environment Protection Authority v Caltex Refining Co Pty Ltd* (1993) 178 CLR 477, 498 (Mason CJ and Toohey J), 514 (Brennan J), 546 (McHugh J), 532 (Deane, Dawson and Gaudron JJ).

that Australian society seeks to attain. For example, it has been said that all the express or implied guarantees of rights or immunities found in the Constitution 'are of fundamental importance in that they serve the function of advancing or protecting the liberty, the dignity or the equality of the citizen'.[187] However, even in these rare conceptual discussions, 'dignity' is referred to as a self-evident concept, and there is little exploration of its substantive content or implications.

Beyond the constitutional order, there has been occasional reference to human dignity in connection with an attempted tort claim for 'wrongful life',[188] with the conceptualisation of rape,[189] and with the sterilisation of a mentally disabled child.[190]

xi. Compassion/Caring

Australia has longstanding social welfare legislation, which at the national level is founded on a legislative power with respect to a wide range of social benefits,[191] and various aspects of the criminal and civil law evidence a particular regard for the needs of vulnerable or marginalised individuals. There is, however, no explicit recognition of the values of compassion or caring in the Australian constitutional order. As with many of the other values surveyed here, the place accorded to compassion in the nation's political discourse and in actual policies pursued varies enormously, depending on the mindset of individual leaders, the orientation of parties in government, and the extent to which individuals or communities in question are perceived as sympathetic by the electorate.

[187] *Street v Queensland Bar Association* (1989) 168 CLR 461, 522 (Deane J); see also *Australian Capital Television Pty Limited v The Commonwealth* (1992) 177 CLR 106, 169 (Deane and Toohey JJ); *Nationwide News Pty Ltd v Wills* (1992) 177 CLR 1, 78–9 (Deane and Toohey JJ); *R v Kearney, ex p Northern Land Council* (1984) 158 CLR 365, 383 (Wilson J).

[188] *Cattanach v Melchior* (2003) 215 CLR 1, 128 (Heydon J) ('It is contrary to human dignity to reduce the existence of a particular human being to the status of an animal or an inanimate chattel or a chose in action or an interest in land.')

[189] *R v L* (1991) 174 CLR 379 (abolition of common law doctrine according to which a husband could not rape his wife).

[190] *Department of Health and Human Services v JWB and SMB* (1992) 175 CLR 218, 266 (Brennan J).

[191] The Constitution originally granted power to the federal legislature to make laws with respect to 'invalid and old-age pensions'. Following a decision of the High Court that legislation establishing a system of pharmaceutical benefits to be paid out of a trust fund was not within the power of the federal Government (*Attorney-General (Vic); Ex rel Dale v Commonwealth* (1945) 71 CLR 237), a finding which cast doubt on the federal power to enact welfare legislation more broadly, a 1946 referendum approved the insertion of a new federal power (Constitution s 51(xxiiiA)) to make laws with respect to: 'the provision of maternity allowances, widows' pensions, child endowment, unemployment, pharmaceutical, sickness and hospital benefits, medical and dental services (but not so as to authorize any form of civil conscription), benefits to students and family allowances.'

xii. Family

Although the existence of the family as a mode of social organisation is recognised in many aspects of the legal system, and underpins a range of legislative regimes relating to matters such as immigration and welfare, there is very limited recognition of family within the constitutional order. The two sub-national rights instruments recognise that families merit special protection,[192] and there has been tacit recognition of the importance of family in the course of governmental responses to the 'Stolen Generations' of indigenous children removed from their families, pursuant to government policy, between about 1910 and 1970.[193]

xiii. Environment

Although Australia has a unique natural environment, and there is extensive regulation of environmental matters at both the federal and state level, there is no explicit recognition of the value of environment, or environmental sustainability, in the Australian constitutional order.

Environmental issues have played a major part in the jurisprudence on the scope of Commonwealth legislative power, particularly the power granted to the Commonwealth to make laws with respect to 'external affairs'. In the 1980s, the High Court held that the external affairs power supported various Commonwealth laws, said to implement Australia's obligations under the Convention for the Protection of the World Cultural and Natural Heritage, which had the effect of impeding proposals supported by the states for development and use of affected areas of land. However, the federal Government has not always aligned itself with international initiatives as against the states: in 2014 the federal Government sought unsuccessfully to delist a section of the Tasmanian Wilderness World Heritage Area.

Australia has been relatively active on aspects of environmental protection internationally, although this engagement has been selective. Australia has, for example, taken a leading role in efforts to curtail Japanese whaling in the Southern Ocean.[194] Of greater long-term significance is persistent

[192] Section 11(1) of the Human Rights Act 2004 (ACT) provides: 'The family is the natural and basic group unit of society and is entitled to be protected by society.' See also Charter of Human Rights and Responsibilities Act 2006 (Vic) s 17(1).

[193] See Human Rights and Equal Opportunity Commission, *Bringing Them Home: Report of the National Inquiry into the Separation of Aboriginal and Torres Strait Islander Children from their Families* (April 2007) (this inquiry, commissioned by the then Attorney-General, was the first major governmental investigation of the impact of forced removals), and the text of the federal Government's apology to the Stolen Generations (n 34).

[194] In May 2010 Australia instituted proceedings in the International Court of Justice ('ICJ') seeking orders that Japan cease operations under the Second Phase of its Japanese Whale Research Programme under Special Permit in the Antarctic ('JARPA II') until the programme had been brought into conformity with Japanese obligations under international law. The substance of Australia's complaint was that Japan was not observing prohibitions on commercial whaling. The ICJ decided that Japan must revoke JARPA II permits and refrain from granting further permits under that programme: *Whaling in the Antarctic (Australia/Japan)*, Judgment, 31 March 2014.

party-political division over the causes of, and appropriate responses to, climate change. The Liberal Party campaigned vigorously against an emissions trading scheme introduced by the Labor Government and has resisted any meaningful engagement in global climate change initiatives, even as countries with which Australia is usually in broad agreement on international issues (like the United States, the United Kingdom and Canada) move towards more serious commitments.

B. Priority of Values

As suggested earlier in this chapter, it is difficult to identify a precise hierarchy of values in Australian constitutional jurisprudence. Broadly speaking, it may be seen from the preceding analysis that the values which are most present across a range of different sources are those which serve to maintain Australia as a viable democratic polity and ensure the civil peace: justice and fairness, a limited community in the sense of majoritarian democracy, freedom from overweening executive power by means of a separation of powers and an independent judiciary, and a degree of accountability of the legislature and the executive to the people. Even these values, however, go primarily to *processes* of governance, not to substantive outcomes.

In the absence of constitutional protections for most rights, 'community', in the sense of majoritarian democracy, generally takes precedence over all other values, albeit within the bounds of the strict separation of judicial power from the executive or legislature. Democracy often trumps equality (for example in the 'intervention' in indigenous communities in the Northern Territory), liberty (in anti-terror laws, and administrative detention for asylum-seekers), and even justice/fairness (in provisions suppressing information in anti-terror trials). Filtered through the admittedly contingent preferences and orientations of political leaders and parties, majoritarian politics may also sharply curtail the resonance of appeals to compassion or human dignity.

The primacy of majoritarian democracy has the effect of creating a kind of two-tiered system: the majority of Australians benefit from various legal, procedural and practical (if not constitutional) safeguards of rights and freedoms, whereas those who for whatever reason are distant from the concerns of voters occupy a more precarious position. As the Consultation Committee described the views of participants at its roundtables, 'the protections afforded by majoritarian rule do not necessarily adequately take account of those who "fall through the cracks"'.[195] The vulnerability of these groups arises either because their legal status itself subjects them to particular curtailments of rights, or because their particular needs, perspectives or

[195] Consultation Report (n 4) 50.

everyday experience are remote to the political majority. The priority of majoritarian democracy over other values is not neutral in its political outcomes: it favours some sectors of the community over others. Moreover, the absence of a formal rights framework means that, once individuals find themselves remote from the sphere of majoritarian concern, there are few limits on the treatment that can be meted out to them.[196]

IV. CONGRUENCE

The issue of congruence might be considered in two distinct ways. The first concerns the relationship between constitutional law as laid out in relevant texts, and the law as it is applied in practice. The second concerns the relationship between the hierarchy of values reflected in the constitutional order and the values actually held by the population.

As to the first dimension—the relationship between law as written and law in practice—the degree of congruence in Australia is relatively high overall, at least for domestic law. Whether the laws themselves are supported or not, they are generally followed.[197] Governments, for example, often seek to avoid the full impact of various accountability mechanisms, but most instances of non-compliance involve attempts to rely on loopholes or exceptions, stretching the law for political or practical gain rather than flagrantly ignoring or confronting it in the course of some more principled opposition.

The picture with regard to international law is more complex. It has been suggested here that international human rights treaties will in future loom larger as a touchstone for domestic policy than they have done in the past, if only because Australia has opted to pay closer attention to international human rights conventions in the legislative drafting and review process as one alternative to formulating any domestic bill of human rights. However, Australia's frequently dismissive or indifferent response to the views of treaty bodies and special rapporteurs in recent years indicates a reluctance to assume the full scope of international commitments that have been formally accepted, at least insofar as they conflict with high-profile

[196] See, for example, Australian Human Rights Commission, *The Forgotten Children: National Inquiry into Children in Immigration Detention* (February 2014).

[197] The former Chief Justice has commented: 'This is a society which accepts the rule of law as the natural order of things. The decisions of courts are obeyed, even when they are unpopular, or offend powerful interests … Courts make decisions adverse to governments, sometimes in matters of great political importance. They may antagonise large sections of the community. Yet it would be beyond the contemplation of most citizens that those decisions might be not obeyed.' The Hon Murray Gleeson AC, then Chief Justice of Australia, 'Public Confidence in the Courts', Paper presented at the 'Confidence in the Courts' conference, Canberra, 9 February 2007, 3, available at www.hcourt.gov.au/assets/publications/speeches/former-justices/gleesoncj/cj_9feb07.pdf.

policies supported by both major parties.[198] The quintessential example is mandatory immigration detention, including of children, a practice which is heavily represented in complaints raised against Australia by and before international human rights bodies (and which has also given rise to multiple judicial challenges under domestic law). The reaction of the current federal Government to a 2015 report of the Australian Human Rights Commission on children in immigration detention shows little regard for either international human rights norms or for the role of domestic bodies, such as the Commission, charged with promoting human rights.[199]

Beyond the question of compliance, however, is a larger question about the relation between rights and entitlements encoded in the constitutional order, and the capacity of individuals to invoke these or enjoy their protections. It is perhaps inevitable that, in a system such as Australia's, which tends to privilege formal or procedural dimensions of values such as justice, there are very significant variations in individuals' likelihood of attaining protections and benefits formally open to all. Access to justice affords an excellent example. The National Human Rights Consultation Committee reported that it had been 'surprised by the extent of concern about access to justice throughout Australia: it was apparent at many community roundtables, and

[198] Some other aspects of Australia's foreign policy also sit uneasily with stated commitments to international law. Australia's de facto and then de jure recognition of Indonesian sovereignty over East Timor in connection with conclusion of the 1989 Timor Gap Treaty, arranging for joint Indonesian–Australian exploitation of oil resources in the so-called 'Timor Gap', without regard for any interests of the East Timorese in these resources, was widely criticised as violating the principle of self-determination. Australia avoided any formal adjudication of its conduct only as a result of the ICJ's decision that a case brought by Portugal against Australia was inadmissible (Indonesia, as a necessary third party, not being subject to jurisdiction). Australia subsequently played a more supportive role in relation to East Timorese independence, leading a UN peacekeeping mission deployed in 1999–2000 to stem pro-Indonesian militia violence unleashed in conjunction with a referendum on independence, and negotiating a new treaty giving East Timor a greater share of Timor Gap oil resources (however, Australia was unwilling to have the allocation of resources subject to formal adjudication, and shortly before East Timor attained statehood Australia amended its 'optional clause' declaration, setting out the matters in respect of which Australia accepted the jurisdiction of the ICJ, with a new declaration specifically excluding disputes concerning the delimitation of maritime zones or exploitation of disputed areas).

[199] See Australian Human Rights Commission, *The Forgotten Children: National Inquiry into Children in Immigration Detention* (February 2014). There are credible press accounts that, in the weeks prior to the Government's release of the report, an official conveyed to the President of the Human Rights Commission, on behalf of the Attorney-General, a request for her resignation and a promise to find her 'some other opportunity'. The President enjoys a statutorily fixed five-year term in order to protect the independence of the office. See Michael Gordon, 'Revealed: Abbott government tried to remove Gillian Triggs as head of the Australian Human Rights Commission', *The Age*, 14 February 2015, available at http://www.theage.com.au/federal-politics/political-news/revealed-abbott-government-tried-to-remove-gillian-triggs-as-head-of-the-australian-human-rights-commission-20150213-13du7s.html. Subsequent to the President's refusal to resign, and the release of the report, the Government attacked the report and the President, claiming that there was a partisan bias in the report's release under a Liberal Government when the previous Labor Government had presided over a similar system.

a large number of submissions raised the subject'.[200] Although Australia has a well-functioning judicial system, the cost of litigation, successive cuts to legal aid funding and the absence of any developed doctrine of protective costs orders in public interest cases have left many individuals without the means to pursue civil claims. Similarly, despite formal protections for fairness in criminal trials, circumstances of disadvantage still leave some groups vulnerable: the Committee noted, for example, concerns that a shortage of accredited interpreters may leave indigenous defendants at particular risk in the criminal justice system.

The second dimension of congruence—the relationship between values as manifested by the constitutional order and values held by the population—presents even more difficult questions. On one hand, the absence of any idealistic or abstract expression of values in the constitutional order means there is less likely to be a philosophical conflict of any kind between values reflected by the constitutional order and those professed by the population (although recent reforms to processes of legislative scrutiny may over time bring some conflicts into the realm of political debate). Moreover, in a system with few constitutionally entrenched rights one would expect at least statutory regimes to reflect the preferences of the population, albeit loosely and subject to the distorting effects of the electoral system and the effects of party discipline. However, it is difficult to say in any given case whether popular preferences genuinely mould political parties' platforms, or whether party leaders and platforms themselves shape popular discourse and expectations.

One way of determining the extent of, or limits to, congruence is to examine whether there is public pressure for change to the law, or public response (either laudatory or critical) to particular legal developments.

It may be noted that very few referenda for the amendment of the Constitution are successful, although again this may reflect disengagement from federal politics and the rather distant and formal nature of the Constitution, rather than public attachment to its current form. There are periodic debates over issues such as abortion and euthanasia, although for the present there is a more or less settled position permitting abortion in certain circumstances and prohibiting euthanasia (the Northern Territory's legislation permitting euthanasia having been overridden by the Commonwealth). Positions on these debates may reflect different values—life, (gender) equality, freedom, dignity, compassion—but it is difficult to discern any one of these dominant in the constitutional order, except perhaps the notion of democratic community, referred to earlier, by which the majoritarian preference prevails.

We have referred above to a perceived conflict between prohibitions of racial and religious vilification, on one hand, and freedom of speech, on

[200] Consultation Report (n 4) 203.

the other, but this debate has often been mired in party-political dynamics, making it hard to judge the extent to which a majority of the population perceive a tension in values and, if so, how they would resolve it.

There is currently considerable evolution on the issue of same-sex relationships, with pressure for change often couched in the language of equality or a 'fair go' for same-sex couples. As discussed earlier, there have been efforts to remove all discriminatory provisions on legislation governing matters such as taxation and pension entitlements, but access to adoption and fertility services, as well as marriage itself, have proven more contentious. The Australian Capital Territory enacted legislation providing for civil unions in 2006, but it was overridden by the Commonwealth, as were subsequent initiatives in the same vein. Several states and territories now have legislative schemes for 'registering' relationships, conferring on same-sex relationships all the benefits available to heterosexual de facto couples. Federal legislation still provides that 'marriage' must be between a man and a woman, but the Australian Labor Party platform in 2011 incorporated a commitment to remove this provision (although representatives will have a 'conscience vote', rather than being required to vote the party line). A number of private members' bills to remove these provisions and provide for the marriage of same-sex couples have failed, most recently in 2012. Although support for same-sex marriage is still a minority position in Parliament (the 2012 bill obtaining only 42 votes in the lower house, with 98 against), this is a higher level of support than that evident in previous years. A 2014 poll indicates that there is now majority support for legalisation of same-sex marriage in Australia, indicating that the general population may be in advance of the two major parties on this issue.[201]

The controversy surrounding some judicial decisions, or any movement for greater judicial involvement in rights protection, may also point to some divergence, or perceived divergence, between values in the constitutional order and in the population at large. The landmark native title cases aroused opposition from individuals concerned about the status of their own property rights following the decision, and from those (including the then federal Government) who felt that the High Court had, in reaching its decision, embarked on an politically-informed reinvention of the law that ought to have been left to the legislature.[202] Others, however, welcomed the decision.

The ongoing debate about 'judicial activism', which borrows many of its conceptual categories from the more developed discourse on constitutional interpretation in the US, flares up from time to time in Australia with controversial decisions. Critics charge that judges, including Justices of the

[201] Jim Reed, 'The tides have turned on same-sex marriage', 31 July 2014, available at http://www.abc.net.au/news/2014-07-31/reed-the-tides-have-turned-on-same-sex-marriage/5637770.

[202] See then Justice Michael Kirby, 'Attacks on Judges—A Universal Phenomenon' (1998) 72 *Australian Law Journal* 599, 601.

High Court, apply their own value judgements, rather than simply the law, to the cases before them. Although concerns about the appropriate locus of decision-making power in a democracy are, at a theoretical level, independent of any party political orientation, the underlying complaint of critics of 'judicial activism' in Australia is almost always that the values allegedly brought to bear by judges are too progressive or rights-oriented. The suggestion is that the values applied by judges are not reflective of the values of the rest of the population, or more specifically, that the population will always favour the value of majoritarian democracy over more individualistic, rights-oriented values. Views of this kind may have played some role in opposition to a national bill of rights, although it is difficult to tell how significant they are relative to a much more generalised acceptance of the existing system.

There is also, of course, major and ongoing debate in Australian society about many of the political issues mentioned in this chapter, but none of these responses is sufficiently marked, clear-cut or representative to found any general conclusions about the relationship between values reflected in the constitutional order and those held by private citizens.

Moments such as the National Human Rights Consultation offer a rare opportunity to glean some insights into the views of a cross-section of the community.[203] Comments made by attendees at round tables, many of whom had little exposure to legal understandings of human rights, provide some anecdotal evidence of the diversity of views held in Australia; public surveys and focus groups commissioned by the consultation to get at the opinions of the 'silent majority' throw the net even wider. Although the focus groups and surveys had a relatively small number of participants and no firm conclusions should be drawn from such limited materials about Australians' views as a whole, the findings are probably indicative of general trends. Participants in surveys and focus groups tended not to understand rights in the abstract, conceiving of rights instead in terms of particular benefits and services they already enjoyed. There was a widespread sense that the democratic system already protected 'rights'.[204] Questions about the relative priority of individual rights and community good elicited contradictory or conflicted responses, perhaps indicating a discomfort with the notion of trading one off for the other.[205] Participants showed little enthusiasm for more formal protection of rights, indeed a certain suspicion of formal

[203] Written submissions of course presented more elaborate discussions. The majority of the (35,000-odd) written submissions received by the consultation were in favour of a legislative bill of rights, but some three-quarters of the submissions in favour had been coordinated by pro-rights NGOs, and in any event those who were motivated enough to make submissions are probably not representative of public opinion more broadly. Consultation Report (n 4) 5–6.

[204] Final Report prepared by Colmar Brunton Social Research, September 2009, 18, 20, 28, 40, in Appendix B to the Consultation Report (n 4).

[205] ibid 26.

mechanisms and those who invoke them.[206] There was a strong aversion to differentiated rights being available to particular groups such as indigenous peoples,[207] and a sense, for more than half of participants, that 'minorities' of different kinds benefited from rights at the expense of 'mainstream' Australians.[208] Participants recognised that, even under a uniform regime of rights, some groups might need added protection, but differentiated between groups, seeing some (people with a mental illness or disability and the elderly) as in need of extra protection, and others (urban indigenous, gay and lesbians, asylum-seekers and recent arrivals) not in need of this.[209] Results of this kind tend to vindicate the observations made here concerning the pragmatism of Australian political culture, and suggest that the emphasis in the constitutional order on majoritarian democracy is broadly reflective of the values, whether articulated or not, of the Australian community. However, such results also indicate the serious implications of majoritarian politics for groups perceived as other to the 'mainstream', and the sense in which the reach of a value of 'equality' depends on perceptions of likeness with, or difference from, a majority population.

The social research also points to the fact that congruence is not only a matter of reconciling values and the legal order, but a much more dynamic process in which values themselves may change, or be articulated differently, as issues are subject to political debate and legal reform. In what is likely a response to increased awareness of environmental matters, participants rated the 'right' to a clean and healthy environment as one of the most important rights, although they recognised that its status as a 'right' was complex.[210] Tasmanians were quicker to understand environment in human rights terms and connect it to a right to protest, probably because of a history of contentious environmental politics in that state.[211]

[206] Although some 57% of participants supported a specific law defining the human rights to which all Australians are entitled, a much higher proportion supported the Government simply having to pay attention to rights in making laws, and 71% of survey respondents agreed or strongly agreed with the statement that 'People who know more about their rights tend to take advantage of the system': ibid 58, 66.

[207] ibid 25.

[208] ibid 53, 57–58 (this sense was stronger among older and less educated participants).

[209] Over 70% of respondents believed that those with mental illness or a disability, and the elderly, needed extra protection. For the other groups listed, the proportion of respondents believing that extra protection was required ranged from 25 to 33% (interestingly, while 28% believed asylum-seekers needed more protection, 30% believed they needed less protection). Indigenous people living in remote areas, all Australians in remote areas, and children, fell somewhere in the middle, with rates of 51–57% believing extra protection was warranted: ibid 60.

[210] 73% rated it 'very important' and a further 23% as 'important' (comparative figures for equality/ freedom from discrimination were 69% and 23%; for freedom of speech (subject to defamation laws) 57% and 31%; for social welfare services 40% and 37%): ibid 31, 35.

[211] ibid 35.

Although rights and values have always inhered in the common law, they are only now—with the adoption of sub-national bills of rights, and possibly some future constitutional change at the federal level—being brought into more open political and legal contestation. It may be that real conflict over rights and values, which would more clearly articulate priorities and cast more light on questions of congruence, is yet to emerge.

3

Global Values and Local Realities: Brazilian Constitutional Law

FÁBIO CARVALHO LEITE AND FLORIAN F HOFFMANN*

I. VALUES IN BRAZILIAN CONSTITUTIONAL HISTORY

SINCE GAINING INDEPENDENCE in 1822, Brazil has had no fewer than eight constitutions, including its present one, which makes any overview of the history of Brazilian constitutionalism problematic.[1] The reasons for such relatively frequent constitutional change during this period are varied and contested,[2] though underlying values are implicated in each transition. It is, therefore, fruitful to begin this survey with a brief look at the value framework adopted by each of these constitutions, not least so as to historically situate the values underlying Brazil's present constitution, which inaugurated the most democratic and stable phase in Brazilian political history.

The first constitution was promulgated in 1824 by Pedro I, the erstwhile Portuguese regent and then Emperor of independent Brazil. Having dissolved the originally convened constitutional assembly on account of its liberal tendencies, he then issued a constitution of his own design which 'balanced' strong centralising and power-concentrating elements with a number of civil and political rights of liberal inspiration. Although the 1824

* The authors wish to thank Mônica Campos de Ré, of the Rio de Janeiro Federal Prosecutors Office, for her very helpful comments; responsibility for error rests, of course, entirely with the authors.

[1] Particularly as some constitutions were in force for comparatively short periods, such as the 1934 Constitution, which was valid for only three years, and its 1937 successor, which was in force for nine years.

[2] See Vamireh Chacon, *Vida e Morte das Constituições Brasileiras* (Rio de Janeiro, Forense, 1987); Marcelo Cerqueira, *A Constituição na História: origem e reforma* (Rio de Janeiro, Editora Revan, 1993); Luís Roberto Barroso, *O Direito Constitucional e a Efetividade de suas Normas: limites e possibilidades da Constituição Brasileira*, 9th edn (Rio de Janeiro, Renovar, 2009); Paulo Bonavides and Paes de Andrade, *História Constitucional do Brasil*, 3rd edn (Rio de Janeiro, Paz e Terra, 1991).

Constitution is the first such document to enshrine individual rights,[3] their actual protection was not a constitutional priority. Both the institutional structure laid out in the constitutional text, with the judiciary subordinate to the emperor, an absence of constitutional judicial review, and an extensive royal prerogative (*poder moderador*), which effectively eclipsed all the other branches of government, as well as the actual distribution of political power, subverted the rights and the values they incorporated.

It was succeeded by the Constitution of 1891, which reflected the abolition of the monarchy and Brazil's becoming a republic in 1889. Explicitly modelled on the US Constitution, it set out a structure of government that would shape Brazil until modern days. It turned the country into a modern federal state and introduced a presidential system of government, the horizontal division of powers including an independent judiciary, and constitutional judicial review. It also contained an extensive Bill of Rights. However, as a modernising constitution, it confronted a conservative social and political reality which ultimately limited its reach; voting—by men only—was not secret, and, hence, was controlled by regional political elites, elections were frequently rigged, and there was no democratic public that would infuse the country with the republican spirit of its constitution. This period came, accordingly, to be referred to as the 'Republic of Colonels', or the 'Old Republic'.[4]

The next constitution was promulgated in 1934, as a result of the 'revolution' of 1930, effectively a *coup d'état* led by Getúlio Vargas, who would emerge as the defining figure of modern Brazil, against the 'Old Republic'. This constitution was meant to properly republicanise the country and to provide an appropriate framework for the rapid modernisation programme pursued by the Vargas government. Most importantly, it formally universalised the franchise and made the vote secret, thereby undercutting the stranglehold of traditional elites over the political machine. It also created a modern civil service, admission to which was by competitive exam, and the 'popular action' (*ação popular*) which empowered the ordinary citizenry to legally challenge public authorities. Moreover, inspired by the Weimar Constitution of 1918, it incorporated a number of social rights and established a national insurance scheme. It lasted, however, only for three years as the increasingly autocratic Vargas regime replaced it by the 1937 Constitution, which took its cues from the authoritarian Polish 'April Constitution' of 1935.[5] The 1937 Constitution permitted Vargas to remain in office and introduced heavy curtailments on civil and political liberties, censorship,

[3] José Afonso da Silva, *Curso de Direito Constitucional Positivo* (São Paulo, Malheiros, 1992).

[4] Boris Fausto, *História do Brasil* (São Paulo, EDUSP, 2004).

[5] Thomas Skidmore, *Brasil: De Getulio Vargas a Castelo Branco (1930–1964)*, 14th edn (São Paulo, Paz e Terra, 2007).

and the death penalty for subversion; the exercise of individual rights was made subject to security concerns, and while the social rights established in the previous document were largely retained, the right to strike and form unions was severely curtailed.

Vargas was toppled at the very end of the Second World War, as a result of which a constitutional assembly was convened which elaborated what, in 1946, would become Brazil's fifth constitution. Built on its grandparent, the 1934 Constitution, it re-established democracy and civil liberties, though it did not further adapt to the emerging post-war world. Indeed, it, arguably, rolled social rights back, making them 'programmatic', ie premised on implementation legislation left to the discretion of the legislature. The post-war period was marked by an increasingly volatile political situation reflecting international tension caused by the Cold War, and saw a number of right-wing attempts to overthrow successive democratic governments. In 1964, a military junta eventually managed to take and consolidate power and inaugurated a period of 20 years of military dictatorship. As would be expected, the regime scrapped the 1946 Constitution and, in 1967, replaced it with a document of its own making. This constitution underwrote many of the authoritarian structures created by the military government, and was additionally complemented by para-constitutional legislation—not subordinate to the Constitution—the Institutional Act No 5 (*Ato Institucional No 5* (AI 5)), which conferred wide-ranging powers to the general-president. In particular, it authorised the head of state to dissolve the Congress, state and municipal assemblies, and legislate in their place, to suspend civil and political rights, electoral mandates, and to institute censorship.

When, in 1969, the first military president stepped down, members of the military government carried out a coup within the coup, sidestepping the intended transition to a civilian vice-president and, instead, installed another general-president. The constitutional implications of this regime change were reflected in constitutional amendment no 1/69, which is today considered to represent a de facto new constitution on account of the profound changes it instituted. During the 1970s, resistance to the regime increased to the point when, in 1984, the junta was forced to allow a referendum on a proposed constitutional amendment reintroducing direct presidential elections. Although the referendum did not deliver the required qualified majority, the indirect elections to the presidency held in the following year produced a winning coalition that vowed to convene a constitutional assembly to draft a new—and democratic—constitution.

That assembly eventually convened in February of 1987 and lasted until October 1988 and was the most democratic and participatory such venture in Brazilian history. Its spirit was captured by the assembly's chairman, Congressman Ulysses Guimarães, when he commented that:

> [T]he enormous effort that has gone into the drafting process is evidenced by the 61,000 proposed amendments, in addition to the 120 popular amendments, some

> of which received more than a million votes, all of which have been submitted, published, distributed, reported, and voted on, from their first appearance in the assembly's subcomissions, to their final text. Participation also took place though pure physical presence, for, every day, around ten thousand petitioners roamed the long corridors of the parliamentary building, destined for meeting rooms, galleries, offices and lounges. There were all manner of people, from country and city, shanty town and factory, workers, cooks, poor children, indigenous peoples, leaseholders, businesspeople, students, senior citizens, civil servants and members of the military, all testifying to the currency and social authenticity of this text which hereby enters into force.[6]

Another feature which made the drafting process highly exceptional[7] was its deliberate break with the tradition of working from a set first draft, as had been the case with all previous constitution-making efforts.[8] Instead, the 559 members of the assembly[9] divided themselves into eight thematic commissions and numerous sub-commissions, instituting a bottom-up approach to drafting by which disparate bits of constitutional text would work their way up until, eventually, a consolidated draft emerged. The biggest challenge consisted of bringing together, in a single document, the manifold interests and ideas that came out of the drafting commissions, as well as from the considerable input by civil society.[10] The result was a lengthy and heterodox document, strongly reflective of different corporate interests, and more a grand compromise than a master plan for a newly democratic Brazil. Keith Rosenn aptly sums up the nature of this Constitution by pointing to five crucial factors:

> One was the confusion created by having the Congress double as Constituent Assembly. The second was the generalized concern about disrespect for law … The third was the widespread belief that a constitution can be a societal panacea and that Brazil's gargantuan economic and social problems could be miraculously cured by the choice of appropriate words in the constitutional text. The forth

[6] Ulysses Guimarães et al, *Estatuto do Homem, da Liberdade e da Democracia* (Brasília, Câmara dos Deputados, 1988) 9–10; and Adriano Pilatti, *A Constituinte de 1987–1988: Progressistas, Conservadores e Regras do Jogo* (Rio de Janeiro, Lumen Juris, 2008) 1.

[7] Pilatti (2008), ibid 2.

[8] As João Gilberto Lucas Coelho has observed, 'the rejection of a constitutional draft was rooted as much in widespread public sentiment as within the constitutional assembly. Left and right, conservatives and progressives, moderates and radicals, almost all had criticised the "commission of eminent persons" and the idea of a working draft, as a dangerous instrument of control over the assembly, emanating from the government, the members of said commission, or some other internal commission. Technically, a working draft would, of course, have helped considerably in organizing and streamlining the drafting process, and, for that reason, was common in previous constitution-making processes and in many other countries. However, politically, that approach had to be rejected, and, instead, the jump into the unknown had to be dared'; see 'O Processo Constituinte' in Milton Guran (ed), *O Processo Constituinte 1987–88* (Brasília, AGILA, 1988) 43.

[9] Notably 487 members of Congress and 72 senators.

[10] Bonavides and de Andrade, *História* (1991), above n 2, 456.

> was Brazil's prolix constitutional tradition ... Finally, there was the influence of the *dirigiste* model of the 1976 Portuguese Constitution, a lengthy, programmatic document.[11]

Nonetheless, and with all its shortcomings, the 1988 Constitution is considered a model of participatory law-making, and a symbolic turning point in Brazilian political history, besides having given rise to a vibrant constitutional culture that has played an important part in subsequent social and political developments. Indeed, some commentators see the present constitution as a paradigm change in that its principles and underlying values have radiated into all spheres of law and legal interpretation, unlike any constitution before it.[12]

II. FINDING VALUES IN CONSTITUTIONAL LAW

A. Legal Infrastructure and Legal Culture

The Brazilian legal system is a hybrid between the (north) American (common law) and the continental European (Roman-Germanic civil) legal systems. Whereas Brazilian constitutional law and, to some extent, its judicial institutions show considerable American influence, private law, as well as the general judicial *mentalité*, are firmly grounded in the civil law tradition. Perhaps the most important difference to the Anglo-American common law tradition is the lack of the doctrine of *stare decisis*, or binding precedent, which means that legal practice is not oriented towards case law, but rather to the Constitution, legislation, and law codes. It also means that, with few exceptions, courts cannot decide on a legal question in principle, but need to apply the relevant legal instruments to each case brought before them, with the core instrument being, of course, the Constitution itself.[13]

As in the United States, the administration of justice in Brazil has two tiers, namely a state and a federal one. At the apex of both systems stands the Federal Supreme Court (*Supremo Tribunal Federal*—STF), which has unlimited jurisdiction over all legal matters and across tiers. It is modelled after the US

[11] Keith Rosenn, 'Brazil's new constitutionalism: an exercise in transient Constitutionalism for a transitional society' (1990) 38 *American Journal of Comparative Law* 778.

[12] Luís Roberto Barroso and Ana Paula de Barcellos, 'O Começo da História. A Nova Interpretação Constitucional e o Papel dos Princípios no Direito Brasileiro' in Luís Roberto Barroso (ed), *A Nova Interpretação Constitucional: direitos fundamentais, ponderação e relações privadas* (Rio de Janeiro/São Paulo/Recife, Renovar, 2006).

[13] Eduardo CB Bittar, *História do Direito Brasileiro* (São Paulo, Editora Atlas, 2003); Luís Roberto Barroso, 'Dez anos da Constituição de 1988' in Ingo Sarlet (ed), *O Direito Público em tempos de crise: Estudos em homenagem a Ruy Ruben Ruschel* (Porto Alegre, Livraria do Advogado, 1999); Gilberto Bercovici, *Desigualdades regionais, estado e Constituição* (São Paulo, Max Limonad, 2003); José Adércio Leite Sampaio, *A Constituição Reinventada pela Jurisdição Constitucional* (Belo Horizonte, Del Rey, 2002).

Supreme Court, though it does not dispose of a *certiorari* procedure, and is, therefore, burdened with a comparatively large case load.[14] One reason for this is the manifold modes of access to the STF, which make it relatively easy to litigate up, or bring a case directly to the STF.

Next in the judicial hierarchy are the four federal superior courts, with the Superior Court of Justice (*Superior Tribunal de Justiça*—STJ) being the most important of these[15]—akin to the Supreme Court of Appeal in South Africa. It is the final court of appeal for all infra-constitutional matters, whether on the federal or on the state level. Then there are the ordinary courts on the federal and state levels: for the former, there are the Federal Courts of Justice (*Justiça Federal*—JF) of the first instance, and the Regional Federal Tribunals (*Tribunais Regionais Federais*—TRFs) of the second instance. The jurisdiction of these federal courts is complex, as they have formal competence to adjudicate all subject matters to which the Union (ie federal government) is a party but also all those which are defined, by the Constitution, to fall predominantly into the sphere of Union competence, as well as certain special (constitutional) interests such as the protection of fundamental rights and compliance with international legal obligations arising therefrom.[16] On the state level, there are the *Tribunais de Justiça* (TJs), which are divided into single-judge first instance, and multi-judge (ordinarily three to five) second instance chambers. It is important to note that while the Brazilian legal system contains specialised courts for labour, military and electoral matters, there are, unlike in most European civil law systems, no separate administrative tribunals, with most disputes concerning public administration being dealt with in the ordinary tribunals.

Next to the tribunals, there are a number of other relevant actors, namely the (state and federal) Prosecutor's Office (*Ministério Público*—MP), the Public Defender's Office (*Defensoria Pública*—DP), and the (municipal, state or federal) Solicitor's Office (*Procuradoria do Município/Estado* (PGM/PGE)/*Advocacia Geral da União* (AGU)). The MP is an independent judicial body present on both the state and the federal level and charged with the general 'guardianship of the legal order, the democratic system of

[14] The STF alone decided more than 110,000 cases in 2006 only; see http://www.stf.jus.br/portal/cms/vertexto.asp?servico=estatistica. In 2004, however, a constitutional amendment created the *súmula vinculante* by which the STF, by a two-thirds majority of its judges, can declare the bindingness of a certain precedent—a competence it has, so far, only used sparingly and the ultimate effect of which is no yet discernible; see Alfredo Canellas, *Constituição interpretada pelo STF* (Rio de Janeiro, Freitas Bastos, 2006); Gilmar Ferreira Mendes, 'O efeito vinculante das decisões do Supremo Tribunal Federal nos processos de controle abstrato de normas' (2007) 43 *Jus Navigandi; and Carlos Aurélio Mota de Souza, Segurança Jurídica e Jurisprudência, um enfoque filosófico jurídico* (São Paulo, LTr, 1996).

[15] The others are the Superior Electoral Court, the Superior Military Court, and the Superior Labour Court.

[16] See arts 108 and 109 of the Constitution as amended by Emenda Constitucional no 45 (30 December 2004).

government, and inviolable social or individual interests' (article 127). It has a wide range of competences, which include the supervision of compliance by public authorities on all levels with the rights guaranteed in the Constitution (article 129, section II), and the initiation of class action suits on virtually all issues of public interest. It has wide-ranging investigatory powers, and, most importantly, may act entirely on its own initiative, though it may receive, consider, and act upon complaints from the general public. The DP, in turn, is, like the MP, a public body of civil servant lawyers working as defence counsel in criminal, but, importantly, also as general counsel in certain civil actions for indigent defendants or plaintiffs. Lastly, the PGM/PGEs or, less frequently, the AGU, have the role, equivalent to that of disctrict attourneys in the United States, of arguing their respective public authority's case before the courts. The horizontal division of power in Brazil follows the Montesquieuean model adopted by most democratic constitutional states, notably into executive, legislative, and judicial branches. The system of government is presidential, though with parliamentarist overtones, notably in the form of the executive's need to rely on (more or less) stable multi-party coalitions in the Congress. The judiciary is independent, and fiercely safeguards its supervisory competences over governmental conduct. The main cause for disputes between the judiciary and the executive is the programmatic character of many constitutional norms, which are seen to serve as guidelines for government policy and the consequent uncertainty over how far judicial review of such public policy may go.

As regards legal culture in Brazil, a methodological distinction between the wide and the narrow legal cultures needs to be made. The narrow legal culture refers to the legal culture of the 'operators of the law', ie the judiciary, as well as public and private lawyers and the related institutions. The wide legal culture, in turn, refers to the way the general population thinks about and interacts with the law. As for the narrow legal culture, and especially the judiciary, it is still deeply imbued in the formalist tradition it absorbed from the continental European systems. This formalism has a substantive and a formal dimension: it is substantive in that it is, on the whole, positivist and 'black-letter law' oriented, with a notable aversion on the part of judges to the concept of judicial law-making, regardless of the fact that many of them effectively engage in it. And it has a formal dimension in that the law and lawyers perceive themselves as a close-knit community, with strict entry criteria (notably the general bar exam, as well as the difficult entrance exams to all (first-level) public legal offices), and a general culture of formality, as well as of corporatism. There are also undertones of the law being an expression of national sovereignty—which, in the Brazilian socio-political imaginary, continues to be perceived as a tender and continuously threatened good—as well as a 'native', as opposed to imposed, form of development. In addition, as in most late-modern societies, the law has become the predominant mode of public social interaction, elevating the legal profession to a central, perhaps the most central role in all public matters. This importance within the formal machinery of the state is clearly reflected in the attitudes of judges and lawyers.[17]

The wide legal culture is, essentially, a function of the heterogeneous nature of Brazilian society. Formal law and, in particular, fundamental rights, are still not seen as easily accessible, or even easily known remedies within poorer communities. However, significant inroads have been made, with a large number of NGOs providing basic legal services and basic legal education to such communities,[18] so much so that 'rights talk' has become commonplace across the social spectrum. This does not, however, mean that there would be any consensus as to what exactly (human) rights are, whether they are seen positively, or merely as 'bandit's rights', and what effects they are seen to have. The degree of rights consciousness, and the propensity to follow a judicial strategy is clearly dependent upon the level of socio-economic prosperity, and, in particular, education, as a recent survey on litigiousness rates across Brazil showed.[19] Knowledge of legal remedies and awareness of constitutional rights are highly dependent on social class, and on the level of education, even if the work of a well-organised civil society is beginning to diminish the class gap in legal and rights consciousness.

B. Values in the Constitutional Text and Jurisprudence

i. The Constitutional (Value) Architecture

The Constitution is divided into nine titles, of which the Preamble, as well as Titles I (Fundamental Principles) and II (Individual and Collective Rights

[17] See, inter alia, Antonio Carlos Wolkmer, *História do Direito no Basil*, 2nd edn (Rio de Janeiro, Forense, 2000); see also the separate (concurring) opinion by Judge Antonio Cançado-Trindade in the first-ever case against Brazil before the Inter-American Court of Human Rights, notably *Ximenes-Lopes v Brazil*, available at www.corteidh.or.cr/docs/casos/Art.iculos/Seriec_149_esp.pdf; see also Eliane Botelho Junqueira, *Faculdades de direito ou fábricas de ilusões?* (Rio de Janeiro, Letra Capital/IDES, 1999); Eliane Botelho Junqueira, 'Brazil, The road of conflict bound for total justice' in Lawrence M Friedman and Rogelio Pérez-Perdomo (eds), *Legal culture in the age of globalization, Latin America and Latin Europe* (Palo Alto CA, Stanford University Press, 2003); Eliane Botelho Junqueira, Josè Ribas Vieira, and MGP Fonseca, *Juízes, retrato em preto e branco* (Rio de Janeiro, Editora Letra Capital, 1997); Américo Bedê Freire Jr, *O controle judicial de políticas públicas* (São Paulo, Revista dos Tribunais, 2005); Luiz Werneck Viana et al, *A judicialiazação da política e das relações sociais no Brasil* (Rio de Janeiro, Revan, 1999).

[18] The probably best-known example is Viva Rio's *Balcão dos Direitos*, which provides legal assistance, as well as alternative dispute settlement to *favela* communities; see Fernando Lannes Fernandes, 'A representação das favelas no imaginário social e a "atualização" do "mito da marginalidade"' (2007) *Observatório de Favelas*, Rio de Janeiro.

[19] See Centro de Pesquisa de Opinão Pública (DATAUnB), 'Consultoria para Construção do Sistema Integrado de Informações do Poder Judiciário, '14. *Relatório, A Imagem do Judiciário Junto à População*,'available at http,//pyxis.cnj.gov.br/pages/downloads.jsp.

and Duties) set out the basic value scheme of the document. However, as is evident from the drafting history and constitutional jurisprudence, the Constitution is, as a whole, strongly informed by a host of different values, not all of which are, as will be seen, prima facie compatible. It is also one of the most detailed of its kind, with 250 articles, many of which are subdivided into a large number of sections such as article 5, on civil and political rights, which contains no fewer than 68 dispositions.[20]

As a consequence, the Constitution is very much a living document, with both the legislature and the judiciary playing a crucial role formulating and adjusting the constitutional text vis-à-vis the complex reality of Brazilian society. Indeed, even the strongest adjustment instrument, the constitutional amendment, has been used a staggering 91 times since the Constitution came into force, despite a stringent amendment procedure requiring two approving votes with a three-fifth majority in each house of Congress. Similarly, constitutional judicial review has played a significant role in forming a constitutional reality out of the ideal types and wish-lists of the original constitutional text. In fact, given both the breadth and abstractness of the values incorporated in that text, as well as the diffuse nature of (most) judicial review in Brazil, the courts are currently the primary articulators of these values.

ii. Jurisprudence

Brazil has a mixed system of judicial review, combining the American-inspired diffuse-concrete form with the continental European centralised-abstract one. The former allows all ordinary tribunals to pronounce on the constitutionality of legislation in concrete cases and is applicable only *inter partes*, whereas the latter is reserved to specialised constitutional tribunals judging on the constitutionality of laws in the abstract, and with an *erga omnes* effect. Within this mixed scheme of constitutional judicial review, the STF is both the equivalent of the US Supreme Court, ie the highest court of appeal in constitutional matters, as well as a specialised constitutional court actionable by a clearly delimited range of public actors, such as the President, the House and Senate—listed in article 103—and by means of three legal instruments, the 'direct action of unconstitutionality' (*Ação Direta de Inconstitucionalidade*), the 'direct action of constitutionality' (*Ação Direta de Constitucionalidade*) and the 'claim of non-compliance with a fundamental precept' (*Arguição de Descumprimento de Preceito Fundamental*).

Diffuse-concrete control of constitutionality remains, evidently, the more common form of judicial review, especially as STF decisions within this ambit are not binding beyond the decision in question. The already

[20] For an unofficial English version of the 1988 Constitution, see Political Database of the Americas, available at http,//pdba.georgetown.edu/Constitutions/Brazil/english96.html.

mentioned immense case load of this tribunal is, hence, a function of the fact that it is relatively easy to litigate up to STF-level. The STF has, however, developed a means by which it attempts to limit the influx of cases in the form of a quasi-*stare decisis*, notably the *súmula*. It is a declaration by the court that it considers the case law in a particular subject matter settled, and that it, hence, will judge any cases within that matter in one particular way. This does not formally preclude litigants from referring cases on the subject matter in question to the STF, but it aims to limit such referral in practice, as litigants, as well as lower courts, will know in advance how their case would be decided by the court. *Súmulas* have, hence, an influence beyond the STF, even if they are not formally binding *erga omnes*. In line with this development, Constitutional Amendment No 45 (2004), on judicial reform, additionally grants the STF the procedural means to pronounce certain decisions of *erga omnes* interest to have 'paradigmatic' force, that is, to effectively bind the inferior tribunals.

a. Fairness and Justice

The Constitution commits Brazil to being a social, though not a socialist, republic.[21] This transpires at various points in the document: article 3, Fundamental Principles, states as one of its objectives the 'eradication of poverty and social marginality, and the reduction of social and regional inequalities', a provision used to ground targeted social policies. This emphasis on the social dimension of the Brazilian polity is also evident in the economic constitution, which, despite its liberal, market-oriented focus[22]—and unlike many other liberal constitutions—gears economic activities explicitly to social values.[23] Hence, the commitment to 'free enterprise' (article 1(IV)) is explicitly associated with the 'social values' inherent in it, and the economic order is predicated on the '[valorisation] of human labour and free enterprise', which is to 'secure for all a dignified existence in accord-

[21] As Paulo Bonavides observes, 'the 1988 constitution is, in its basic orientation, the constitution of a social (welfare) state. This implies that the core constitutional issues, such as the separation of powers or fundamental rights, have to be interpreted in light of this fundamental orientation'; see Paulo Bonavides, *Curso de Direito Constitucional*, 7th edn (São Paulo, Malheiros Editores, 1997) 336.

[22] STF, ADIn no 1950 (3 November 2005): 'it is clear that the economic system espoused by the 1988 constitution points to a particular system, notably capitalism, in which free enterprise plays a central role. This does not, however, permit the conclusion that the state would only intervene in the economy in exceptional circumstances, on the contrary.' (Judgment of Justice Eros Grau, judge-japporteur).

[23] The Constitution defines as foundations of the state the 'social value of labour and of free enterprise' (art 1(IV)), which permits two interpretations, namely that the economic order is defined by two distinct but complementary values, or that labour and free enterprise are meant to be two facets of the same underlying value.

ance with social justice'.[24] Initially, however, doctrine and jurisprudence primarily recognised free enterprise, and less the social values component of this formula, though this stance has slowly given way to a more rigid view of the latter.[25] As the STF put it,

> Although the current constitution ... strongly emphasises free enterprise, in as much as it has not merely defined it as one of the general principles of the economic order, but as one of only two pillars of that order, and although competitive markets are, in the constitution, explicitly implied by free enterprise, it nonetheless also recognizes the limitations of the latter through its commitment to social justice. Hence, in Art. 1, where it declares the Brazilian republic to be democratic and based on the rule of law, it mentions, in para. IV, not the free enterprise of neo-classical economics, but the social values of free enterprise. Moreover, among the principles to be followed within the economic order, it lists consumer protection—which is also included in the Bill of Rights in Art. 5(XXXII)—as well as the reduction of social inequalities.[26]

In another decision, it added that 'on one hand, the constitutional text emphasises the social, and not the individual value of free enterprise; on the other hand, Art. 170 places side-by-side humane work and free enterprise, with the object of valorizing the former'.[27]

Justice, in general, is mentioned in the Preamble as the supreme value of a 'fraternal, pluralist and unprejudiced society', and it is again mentioned under the title on the economic and the social order. Free access to justice is, for instance, guaranteed in articles 5°, LXXIV, and 134, a significant step beyond all previous constitutional documents. As José Carlos Barbosa Moreira observed,

> the great innovation brought by the 1988 charter is that it is not limited to the courts, but comprises all legal dealings. The qualification of access to justice as being both free and comprehensive clearly points to this all-encompassing meaning of the stipulation [as a consequence] the indigent section of the population is now legally empowered also in relation to administrative and notarial acts, as much as in relation to simple legal advice. Similarly, the Constitution established gratuity for civil registry.[28]

[24] In this sense, see Maurício de Moura Costa: 'if there is not meant to be any contradiction between the foundation and the objective of the economic order, this does not mean that free enterprise could be taken, of its own, as the fulfillment of that objective. Hence, if free enterprise alone was taken to advance the common good, the specific mandate that the economic order be geared to assuring for everyone a dignified existence would be redundant and useless. Yet, Art. 170 is not useless, it predicates one value on another, notably by making free enterprise a function for the fulfillment of the common good'; in 'O princípio constitucional da livre concorrência' (2006) 5(1) *Revista do IBRAP* 11.

[25] See Fábio Carvalho Leite, 'Os Valores Sociais da Livre Iniciativa como Fundamento do Estado Brasileiro' in Manoel Messias Peixinho et al, *Os Princípios da Constituição de 1988*, 2nd edn (Rio de Janeiro, Lumen Juris, 2006) 721–53.

[26] STF, ADIn 319 (30 April 1993); STF, ADIn 1950 (3 November 2005).

[27] Replaced by the Civil Code of 2002.

[28] José Carlos Barbosa Moreira, 'O direito à assistência jurídica, evolução no ordenamento brasileiro de nosso tempo' in Sálvio de Figueiredon Teixeira (ed), *As garantias do cidadão na justiça* (São Paulo, Saraiva, 1993) 212.

Indeed, in a ground-breaking decision on the compulsory character of the establishment of state public defenders offices, Justice Celso de Mello derived access to justice from the 'right to have rights' and qualified it as an 'essential right, especially for those who have nothing and need everything.'[29]

b. Equality

Another important element is the role played by the principle of equality in the current constitution. *Prima facie*, equality before the law figured in the text of all previous Brazilian constitutions, but it was then always overshadowed by widespread discrimination in constitutional reality. Discrimination against women is exemplary in this respect. While the 1891 Constitution did not formally exclude women from the vote, the conservative interpretation that prevailed at the time effectively understood the vote to be only exercisable by men, a situation that only changed with the 'revolution' of 1930—first through a new electoral law in 1932, then, formally, through the 1934 Constitution. Similarly, the Civil Code of 1916[30] placed women in the category of 'relative incapacity, for instance, in relation to full contractual or property-holding capacity', a situation that only changed with the passage of the 1962 Married Women Act.[31] Until the 1988 Constitution, this and other legislation cohabited alongside successive constitutional regimes formally committed to equality 'without the stigma of unconstitutionality, as paradoxical as that may seem.'[32]

This history of inequality explains why the 1988 Constitution mentions equality in several places; it declares, in article 5, that 'all are equal before the law', that an objective of the Brazilian republic is 'to promote the common good without prejudice' (article 3, IV), and that 'men and women [are guaranteed] equal rights and obligations under this constitution'. Beyond these general provisions, equality is mandated in a number of specific areas, such as discrimination at the workplace, as with respect to salary, access to higher-level positions, or non-employment on grounds of sex, age, colour, or marital status (article 7, XXX). In addition, a number of positive discrimination measures are explicitly mandated or have been read to be implied in the constitutional text, such as the right to a 120 day maternity leave in order to 'protect women in the labour market through specific incentives, as determined by law' (article 7, XX),[33] or women's pension contributions

[29] ADI 2.903 (18 September 2008).

[30] See Lei no 3.071, of 1° de Janeiro de 1916.

[31] Lei no 4.121 of 27 August 1962.

[32] For various further examples, see Carlos Roberto de Siqueira Castro, *O Princípio da Isonomia e a Igualdade da Mulher no Direito Constitucional* (Rio de Janeiro, Forense, 1983) 94.

[33] In 2008, legislation was passed allowing for an extension of the 120-day limit up to 180 days; see Lei no 11.770, of 9 September 2008.

(article 201, I). On the basis of this constitutional mandate, a number of significant gender-based affirmative action laws have been enacted, such as the well-known *Lei Maria da Penha*, against domestic violence,[34] or legislation establishing a female quota for political parties.[35]

By far the most polemical issue, however, has been race-based affirmative action which has been instituted and gradually augmented since 2001 in both the public and the private sectors.[36] Its formal establishment was prefigured by a symbolic commitment on the part of the federal government to racial equality in the form of three unprecedented ministerial appointments and the nomination of the first Afro-Brazilian judge to the STF, Justice Joaquim Barbosa, in 2003. As the sociologist Rosana Heringer put it,

> even though there is intense debate, not only in Brazil, about the value of such symbolic measures as ministerial or judicial appointments—with critics pointing to the fact that, despite it, the great majority of the black population remain in poverty—for the majority of black activists, this is of considerable importance ... as it contributes to breaking artificial barriers that have historically excluded African Brazilians from political power. The importance of such measures was ironically illustrated when, at his first [informal] visit to the STF after having been appointed [as the tribunal's first Afro-Brazilian judge], Justice Joaquim Barbosa was stopped by court security and had to identify himself, unlike other visitors in similar circumstances.[37]

The most controversial issue in this context has been race-based quotas at public universities.[38] As Renato Emerson dos Santos observes,

> regardless of quota schemes in [other] sectors, the establishment of quotas [initially] in the State University of Rio de Janeiro provoked a veritable judicialization of the debate. This contrasts with the level of reaction to the principle of 'unequal treatment to unequal cases', which underlies affirmative action, [as] experienced in other areas.[39]

[34] Lei no 11.340, of 7 August 2006; the act was preceded by a successful complaint lodged against Brazil at the Inter-American Commission of Human Rights in 1998 (decided in 2001, case no 12.051) concerning a notorious case of intra-marital abuse which caused considerable discussion in Brazil; see the social network on the Act at www.leimariadapenha.com/.

[35] See Lei n° 9504 of 30 September 1996.

[36] Between 2001 and 2004, there were 69 affirmative action-oriented initiatives; see Rosana Heringer, 'Políticas de promoção da igualdade racial no Brasil, um balanço do período 2001–2004' in João Feres Jr and Jonas Zoninsein (eds), *Ação Afirmativa e Universidade—experiências nacionais e comparadas* (Brasília, Editora UnB, 2006) 83.

[37] ibid 86; Barbosa himself wrote his doctoral thesis on affirmative action, published as *Ação afirmativa e princípio constitucional da igualdade, o direito como instrumento de transformação social. A experiência dos EUA* (Rio de Janeiro, Renovar, 2001).

[38] See, generally and for opposite points of view, Angela R Paiva (ed), *Notícias e reflexões sobre discriminação racial* (Rio de Janeiro, Pallas, 2008); Peter Fry (ed), *Divisões Perigosas, Políticas Raciais no Brasil Contemporâneo* (Rio de Janeiro, Civilização Brasileira, 2007).

[39] Renato Emerson dos Santos, 'Políticas de cotas raciais nas universidades brasileiras, o caso da UERJ' in Feres and Zoninsein (2006) above n 36, 118.

Indeed, after the first entrance examination under new affirmative action rules, many unsuccessful candidates went to court on the basis of an alleged violation of the constitutional principle of equality.[40] Many of these actions were initially conceded, though subsequently suspended on appeal by the university, which alleged a threat to its security and public order.[41] There were also direct challenges to the constitutionality of the law on the state and federal level, though these were eventually withdrawn as the relevant legislation was repealed and substituted by one with changed quota percentages. The new law mandated 45 per cent of student places to be filled by quotas, of which 20 per cent would go to African Brazilians, 5 per cent to disabled students and members of other minorities, and 20 per cent to students coming from public schools. This law's constitutionality was successfully challenged on the state level, though, and in 2012, the STF unanimously upheld the quota policy in the test case involving the University of Brasília.[42] The judge-rapporteur, Justice Ricardo Lewandowski stated that:

> [I]n the case of the University of Brasilia, the reserving of 20 percent of its places for Afro-Brazilian and of a small[er] number for indigenous students constitutes, in my view, an adequate and proportional measure in relation to the desired objective. The affirmative action policy adopted by the University […] is, thus, neither disproportional nor unreasonable, in particular when considered with respect to its compatibility with the values and principles of the Constitution.[43]

c. Freedom and Independence

The Constitution enshrines a number of 'freedoms' within the fundamental rights chapter, notably the freedom of expression, which specifically mentions intellectual, artistic and scientific expression; the freedom of profession, which has, in a number of cases, been held to imply the unconstitutionality of certain qualificatory requirements where these exceeded reasonableness;[44] the freedom of movement; the freedom of assembly and association; and a number of freedoms relating to criminal law, such as the presumption of innocence, procedural due process, etc. The freedom of expression, in particular, has generally caused considerable discussion, with the best-known case concerning a habeas corpus action brought by

[40] In all, 263 preliminary injunctions were issued after the first entrance exam carried out under new affirmative action rules.

[41] See Renato dos Santos (2006), above n 39.

[42] See 'STF nega liminar contra cotas raciais da UnB', *Folha de São Paulo*, 31 July 2009.

[43] ADPF 186 (1 August, 2011).

[44] A recent STF decision confirmed this vision by declaring unconstitutional the section of the Press Act that stipulated that in order to exercise the profession of journalist, a university degree in journalism or a related discipline would be required; see Recurso Extraordinário no 511961 (8 June 2009).

a notorious author of anti-Semitic literature, Siegfried Ellwanger, whose defence had argued that his original condemnation for incitement of racism was unlawful, as the primary object of his writings, Jews, allegedly did not constitute a race according the meaning of that term. Here, the STF found, by majority vote, that the freedom of speech of an individual right could not be exercised through illicit conduct, analogous to cases involving offences to personal honour; human dignity and that the value of legal equality took precedence.[45] Interestingly, Justices Gilmar Ferreira Mendes and Marco Aurélio both filed separate opinions, explicitly referring to the value-balancing exercise in which the court had here engaged, though to opposite effects, with Mendes concurring on the basis of the majority's finding of human dignity as a precedent value, and Aurélio dissenting on account of freedom of expression as the precedent value in the particular case.[46] In another recent case, the decision of a judge of the Brasília Circuit Court to issue a preliminary injunction barring a São Paulo newspaper from publishing details of an ongoing fraud investigation against the son of former President José Sarney caused outrage among both the press and the wider judiciary.[47] The case was decided in 2009 by means of a declaration on part of the STF that the press law upon which the case was based and which preceded the 1988 Constitution had 'not been received' into the latter, a move amounting to a retroactive declaration of unconstitutionality.[48] Indeed, memories of widespread censorship during military rule are still fresh, and the role of the press in exposing corruption and political scandal is widely recognised and appreciated.

Furthermore, the Constitution lists as one of the fundamental values underlying the polity the freedom of private enterprise within a competitive marketplace. It, however, qualifies this by a specific provision granting preferred treatment to small and medium enterprises incorporated in Brazil. Likewise, is gives the safeguard of competition and anti-trust a formal constitutional mandate (articles 170 (IV) and 173 (4)).

[45] See STF, HC 82.424-2-RS. DJU (19 March 2004), Justice Moreira Alves.

[46] See Alonso Reis Freire, 'Evolution of Constitutional Interpretation in Brazil and the Employment of Balancing "Method" by Brazilian Supreme Court in Judicial Review' unpublished paper presented at the VIIth World Congress of the International Association of Constitutional Law—Workshop 15, *The Balancing and Proportionality in the Constitutional Review*, 2007, available at www.enelsyn.gr/papers/w15/Paper%20by%20Prof%20Alonso%20Reis%20Freire.pdf; Celso Lafer, 'O STF e o Racismo, o Caso Ellwanger', *Folha de S. Paulo*—30 March, 2004.

[47] See Felipe Recondo, 'Justiça censura Estado e proíbe informações sobre Sarney' *Estado de São Paulo*, 31 July, 2009, available at www.estadao.com.br/noticias/nacional,justica-obriga-grupo-estado-a-retirar-gravacoes-de-sarney,411711,0.htm.

[48] ADPF 130 (30 April 2009).

d. Respect for Life

The Constitution expressly affirms the inviolability of the right to life and, following common bill of rights practice, inaugurates with it the section on civil and political rights (article 5): 'Brazilians and foreigners resident in Brazil are assured of inviolability of the right of life.' It goes on to abolish the death penalty, except in times of war, which, given Brazil's historically scant record of belligerence, was always a mute addition. However, given the high incidence of crime, especially in urban centres, and the correlative climate of fear, spurred regularly by the news media, public debates about the reintroduction of the death penalty have been a regular feature since re-democratisation.[49] The clause is, however, entrenched, hence beyond the reach of regular constitutional amendment, a position firmly anchored in doctrine. The respective debates have, thus, largely been political posturing not accompanied by any deeper-seated popular sentiment.

The other big issue revolving around respect for life has been abortion and, connected to it, (embryonic) stem-cell research. In relation to the former, ordinary legislation stemming from the 1940s (!) criminalises abortion, with the exception of cases when the life of the mother is in danger or, significantly, when the pregnancy is the result of rape. Given the age of the legislation, these exceptions were certainly not based on concern for the women in question, but rather for the well-being and 'honour' of their husbands and fathers. A noteworthy case on this theme arose in 2004 when the National Confederation of Health Workers filed a complaint with the Supreme Court in relation to the abortion of anencephalic foetuses.[50] The preliminary injunction, issued by a sole judge-rapporteur, as the Court was then in recess, granted the complaint, though his decision was subsequently overturned, with the Court finding, in 2012 by a majority of eight to two that the case under review did not constitute (illegal) abortion. The case was preceded by a number of circuit court decisions on the matter, justifying their concession of an abortion on this particular case in words such as these:

> The pregnant woman cannot be expected to bear death in a situation when life is impossible ... the present case is exceptional and cannot be based on existing criminal law [but instead] on the supra-legal principle that no alternative conduct can be demanded, for not even the law ... can require people to be so heroic as to put at risk one's sanity and personal dignity.[51]

[49] However, see a recent poll which shows at most mid-level support for the death penalty, Mário Cesar Carvalho, 'Cai apoio à pena de morte e país fica dividido', *Folha de S. Paulo*, 6 April 2008, C1.

[50] ADPF—Ação de Descumprimento de Preceito Fundamental no 54.

[51] 'Continuidade de gestação de feto anencéfalo é "heroísmo" que não se pode exigir, diz magistrada, do TJ/RS', *Migalhas*, 28 August, 2008, available at www.migalhas.com.br.

Similarly, in relation to stem-cell research, the legislation on biosecurity,[52] which legalises the practice, was unsuccessfully challenged before the STF.[53]

e. Responsibility and Accountability

The Constitution sets Brazil up as a democratic republic with elective government renewed every four years. There is formal separation of powers (article 2), but the Constitution itself also establishes so-called crimes of executive responsibility. However, impeachment proceedings against a sitting president for a violation of executive responsibility, in which the head of state is tried and convicted, have only happened once, notably in relation to the first directly elected president after the transition, Fernando Collor de Mello. At the time, after a formal petition jointly submitted by the heads of the Brazilian Press Association and the Brazilian Bar Association, the House of Representatives, in accordance with article 52(I), authorised opening of proceedings relating to executive responsibility before the Senate (article 52(I)). When, subsequently, a legal debate on whether voting in the Senate proceedings was to be secret or public was decided in favour of a public vote, Collor resigned from the presidency in order to avoid a by then near-certain conviction. The trial, however, continued and resulted in Collor being stripped of his office—a merely nominal decision at that point—and barred from political activity for eight years. As Marcello Cerqueira observed, even though Collor's resignation frustrated the principal objective of the Senate trial, the process as a whole nevertheless resulted in the de facto impeachment of the president, which is how the episode has entered history.[54] Interestingly, two years later, the Supreme Court acquitted Collor of corruption charges, which, however, did not affect the Senate's judgment.

Besides this extraordinary judicial function, both Houses of Congress are also empowered to scrutinise government conduct in relation to potential violations of executive responsibility (article 51 and 52). Moreover, the Constitution prescribes 'probity' and 'morality for all public administration, and specifies, in its article 37, that 'the direct or indirect government administration of any of the Branches of the Republic of the States, of the Federal District and of the Municipalities, as well as any of their foundations, shall obey the principles of lawfulness, impersonality, morality, publicity.'

[52] Lei no 11.105, of 24 March 2005.

[53] ADIn 3510.

[54] Marcello Cerqueira, 'A Constituição e o Direito Anterior, o fenômeno da recepção' in Eros Roberto Grau and Sérgio Sérvulo da Cunha (eds), *Estudos de Direito Constitucional (em homenagem a José Afonso da Silva* (São Paulo, Malheiros Editores, 2003) 198.

f. Family and Community

The Constitution contains a chapter dedicated to the 'Family, Children, Adolescents, and the Elderly'. In fact, already the constitutional assembly operated a specific commission on this thematic cluster, highlighting the importance given to it from early on. The Constitution recognises religious marriages, in line with all previous constitutions with the exception of the 1891 Constitution, which only recognised civil marriage. As far as the family is concerned, the provision expands the traditional definition by recognising stable unions and any 'community formed by any parent and his or her descendants'. The text also grants the right to family planning to spouses, setting out, in article 226 (7), that

> based upon the principles of human dignity and responsible parenthood, family planning is a free option of the couple, it being incumbent upon the State to provide educational and scientific resources for the exercise of such right and any coercion on the part of official or private institutions being forbidden.

The constitutional text does not specifically mention same-sex marriage, and this has caused considerable controversy in terms of the latter's constitutionality. There are a number of decisions recognising certain legal effects deriving from same-sex unions, but no coherent line of jurisprudence has yet developed. Some of the more noteworthy cases have concerned the granting of standing to same-sex couples in divorce proceedings before family courts,[55] the recognition of civil obligations deriving from same-sex unions, notwithstanding marital status, as well as the possibility of adoption by same-sex couples.[56] Similarly, in four of the five regional federal courts,[57] as well as in the STJ,[58] the right of spouses in same-sex unions to receive public pension benefits upon the death of their spouse has been recognised.

Two cases relating to same-sex unions are currently before the STF, one concerning the application, in the state of Rio de Janeiro, of the legal regime established for stable unions to same-sex unions,[59] the other, by way of

[55] Agravo de Instrumento n° 599075496 (8ª Câmara Cível), decided 17 June, 1999; Agravo de Instrumento n° 598362655 (6ª Câmara Cível), decided 15 September; Conflito de competência n° 70000992156 (8ª Câmara Cível), decided 29 June, 2000.

[56] Apelação Cível no 70013801592 (7ª Câmara Cível), decided 5 April, 2006; and Apelação Cível n° 7000138892 (7ª Câmara Cível), decided 14 March, 2001.

[57] Apelação Cível no 70013801592 (7ª Câmara Cível), decided 5 April 2006; and Agravo de Instrumento no 2003.01.00.000697/MG (TRF—1ª Região, 2ª Turma), decided 29 April 2003; Apelação Cível no 2002.51.01.000777-0 (TRF—2ª Região, 3ª Turma), promulgated in the *Diário de Justiça* on 21 July 2003; Apelação Cível no 2000.04.01.073643-8 (TRF—4ª Região, 6ª Turma), decided 21 November 2000; Apelação Cível 2003.05.00.029875-2 (TRF—5ª Região, 3ª Turma), decided 15 June 2004.

[58] Recurso Especial no 395.904/RS, 6ª Turma, decided 12 December 2005.

[59] ADPF no 132 (5 May 2011).

abstract judicial review, on the mandatory recognition of same-sex unions as stable unions.[60] In the former, the then Solicitor-General of Brazil, José Toffoli—today an STF Justice-, affirmed that 'no hermeneutic effort short of prejudice ... could find a plausible justification for the differential treatment of homosexual couples. Without any doubt, they constitute a family.' The latter derived the positive obligation to recognise same-sex unions as family units from the principles of human dignity (article 1 (III)), equality and liberty (article 5), as well as from the prohibition of bad-faith discrimination (article 3 (IV) and the protection of legal certainty.[61]

g. Compassion and Caring

The Constitution does not explicitly mention compassion or caring, but, instead, employs the concept of solidarity. Among the purposes of the Brazilian republic listed in article 3 is the 'construction of a free and just society in solidarity', as well as the 'eradication of poverty and exclusion, and of social and regional inequalities'. This, however, the Constitution itself recognises as a gradual process when it specifies that such society is yet to be constructed. Under this programmatic umbrella, a number of more specific norms deal with solidarity, notably in relation to the poorer sections of society.

Furthermore, in article 6 it also lists a wide range of social rights, notably to education, health care, work, housing, leisure, security, social welfare, while article 7 deals in great detail with labour rights. The rights of the handicapped are also relatively prominent, with a specific non-discrimination clause embedded in article 7 on labour rights, and quota-based affirmative action established for the civil service (article 37(VIII)). The Constitution also mandates the social security system to help handicapped citizens integrate into society (article 203(IV)) and grants a minimum-wage pension to all handicapped and elderly unable to otherwise sustain themselves. Special mention is also made of handicapped children and adolescents, including such detailed stipulations as the mandatory provision of disabled access facilities in public spaces, and the gratuity of public transport.[62]

[60] The original action was filed as a 'Claim of Non-Compliance with a Fundamental Precept Deriving from this Constitution' (Argüição de Descumprimento de Preceito Fundamental (no 178)), as established in art 102 (III.1), but it was subsequently re-classified by the STF's President as a Direct Action of Unconstitutionality (Ação Direta de Inconstitucionalidade (ADI 4277)), as per art 102 (I.a).

[61] The eventual decision has been classified by the STF as setting binding precedent, and will, thus, have erga-omnes consequences.

[62] The latter was subject to several judicial disputes, all of which confirmed the constitutional provision; see, for instance, Mandado de Segurança no 13084/CE; Diário de Justiça of 1 July 2002, p 214); see generally, Carlos Roberto de Siqueira Castro, *A Constituição Aberta e os Direitos Fundamentais—Ensaios sobre o constitucionalismo pós-moderno e comunitário* (Rio de Janeiro, Editora Forense, 2003) 425.

h. Respect, Tolerance, and Spirituality

Since becoming a republic in 1889, Brazil has been a secular state, though the precise nature of its secularism has become the object of debate in the post-authoritarian period, as evidenced in recent discussion on the display of (Christian) religious symbols in public places, and, in particular, in virtually every courtroom in the country. The latter practice has come under attack through a submission to the National Judicial Council,[63] claiming its unconstitutionality. Although the submission was rejected,[64] in other instances, the controversial character of the issue has come to the fore more openly. Hence, two years earlier, the Rio Grande do Sul Council of Magistrates decided, by only one vote, to keep the crucifixes displayed in the state's courtrooms, a decision subsequently overturned by the Judicial Council of the Rio Grande do Sul Regional Tribunal.[65]

There is no constitutional provision which expressly establishes Brazil as a lay republic. Secularism rather emanates from article 19(I) which prohibits any federal entity to 'establish religious cults or churches, subsidize them, hamper their operation or maintain with them or their representatives relations of dependency or alliance, with the exception of cooperation for the public interest, as set forth by law.' This stipulation quite explicitly takes its cue from the US constitution's establishment clause in the First Amendment. As with its progenitor, the Brazilian clause has been considered too unspecific in its prohibitions for it to be clear as to what it permits. This certain lack of clarity is made worse by the seeming contradiction between the Constitution's overall commitment to secularism and its mention of God in its Preamble. There has been some discussion on the quality of the Preamble, notably whether it has some form of legal force, or whether it is a mere statement of 'ideology', with, however, even the proponents of it having legal force admitting that the mention of the deity is merely to express the religious character of Brazilian society and without prescriptive force.[66] Article 19, however, does permit an exception to the strict separation of state and religion, in that it allows for the state institutions to collaborate with religious establishments in 'the public interest' and as regulated by the law. This is, of course, a mere (constitutional) recognition that religious institutions can and do serve certain public interests, and that it is, therefore, licit for public authorities to interact with different religious communities to that end. The interest at hand must, however, be public and, therefore, subject to the principle of equality, and, hence, not confessionally biased.

[63] There were four separate claims: 1344, 1345, 1346 and 1362.

[64] Conselho Nacional de Justiça, decision of 6 June 2009.

[65] See, for instance, Aldir Soriano, *Liberdade religiosa no Direito Constitucional e Internacional* (São Paulo, Juarez de Oliveira, 2002).

[66] As confirmed by the STF in ADIn 2076 (15 August 2002).

The doctrinal point of view has been that such collaboration must remain an exception and is, therefore, subject to strict scrutiny. In a recent technical brief on the constitutionality of the transfer of public funds to religious entities, the Advisory Body for Budget and Oversight of the Brazilian Congress stated that legislation defining public interest is required for such transfers to be understood as falling under the exception of the prohibition stipulated in article 19(I). It affirmed that, although guidelines were in place regulating the transfer of public funds to private non-profit entities, this was not sufficient legal basis in relation to religious entities, for otherwise the equivalence of all such entities, whether religious or not, would be presumed, which would contradict the special—and exceptional—regime for religious entities foreseen in article 19. It further asserted that the fact that, in the past, such transfers had occurred, this could not establish precedent to the contrary.[67] Lastly, the Constitution also guarantees the exemption from taxation of religious communities.

In the Constitution's individual rights chapter, the rights to freedom of conscience and belief, to conscientious objection to mandatory military service, as well as to access to religious services in public (civil and military) establishments are guaranteed. Conscientious objection is provided for in article 5(VIII). This has been considered to be a complex provision, especially the second part, in which some form of alternative (public) service is presupposed in the event of the potential non-compliance with the obligation. The problem has been that there are a great many possibilities of conflict between certain religious prescripts and public obligations, and although the Constitution aims to minimise such conflicts, the constitutional formula only works when implementing legislation creating a specific alternative service is in place; currently, this is only the case with regard to mandatory military service. The most common issues on this front have concerned the sanctity of religious holidays. With no particular legislative reference point, nor any clear guidance from doctrine, courts have decided on this matter on a case-by-case basis, with a majority refusing to grant claims of this type.[68] Lastly, the Constitution also grants the right to optional religious instruction in public primary schools. The federal implementation legislation of this provision leaves it to the states to decide in what fashion this is to take place, with some (such as Rio de Janeiro) having decided to structure this by denomination, and others (such as São Paulo) inter-denominationally.

[67] Sérgio Tadao Sambosuke and Tarcísio Barroso da Graça, Estudo Técnico no 16/2007—Consultoria de Orçamento e Fiscalização Financeira, *Câmara dos Deputados*.

[68] A recent non-representative survey of several state jurisdictions has confirmed this picture; of a sample of 22 cases, 14 were decided against and five in favour of the claimants; see, seminally, Fábio Carvalho Leite, *Estado e Religião: a liberdade religiosa no Brasil* (Curitiba, Juruá Editora, 2014) 408.

III. CONCLUSION: VALUES BETWEEN CONSTITUTIONAL IDEAL AND REALITY

The preceding review of the range and application of constitutionally enshrined fundamental rights, seen as legal articulations of core values, shows how extraordinarily important 'rights talk' has become in Brazil under the present constitutional regime. However, beyond the mere affirmation that the 1988 Constitution commits the Brazilian polity to a logic of rights, and that this logic has increasingly pervaded constitutional jurisprudence, a number of tricky questions remain. The first and, perhaps, most obvious, concerns the assumed relationship between rights and values. For it is by no means obvious that the rights-oriented character of the Constitution is equivalent to a commitment to a 'concrete order of values' that (allegedly) springs directly from Brazilian society.[69] Indeed, in many ways, Brazilian constitutionalism has tended to be heavily influenced by both liberalism and positivism, both of which are averse to equating fundamental rights to substantive values. Yet, there has, arguably, also always been a communitarian streak in Brazilian constitutional thought, one that has lent itself to the abuses of authoritarian projects, but that has also repeatedly resurfaced, not least during the present constitutional regime, as a concern with national identity and the, perhaps, defining trait of Brazilian society, namely inequality.[70] There have certainly been strong indications that many a Brazilian judge, and not least the constitutional judiciary, see their task as essentially being about giving effect to the values the document purports, in their view, to enshrine. Hence, in his dissenting opinion in the above-mentioned *Ellwanger* case, Justice Marco Aurélio called fundamental rights the 'structural principles of the organization and functioning of the state, *objective values* which serve to orient state action on all levels'.[71]

On the face of it, this axiological vision of the Constitution conforms to a *dirigente* (directive) model of constitutionalism in which certain core values, as articulated in the constitutional text, are meant to provide the basic script for a government charged with 'concretising' these literally value-laden norms.[72] It is a model in part 'inherited' from the earlier Portuguese transitional

[69] The notion of the Constitution as a 'concrete order of values' stems from Portuguese and Spanish doctrinalists, such as JJ Gomes Canotilho, Jorge Miranda, José Carlos Vieira de Andrade, Pablo Lucas Verdú, or Perez Luño; exemplarily, see JJ Gomes Canotilho, Jose Joaquim Gomes, *Direito Constitucional e Teoria da Constituição* 2nd edn (Coimbra, Editora Almedina, 1998).

[70] See Giselle Citadio, *Pluralismo, Direito e Justiça Distributiva*, 2nd edn (Rio de Janeiro, Lumen Juris, 2000).

[71] Emphasis added. See dissenting opinion Justice Marco Aurélio Mello in the *Ellwanger* case, above n 45.

[72] See JJ Gomes Canotilho, *Constituição Dirigente e Vinculação do Legislador, Contributo para a Compreensão das Normas Constitucionais Programáticas*, 2nd edn (Coimbra, Coimbra Editora, 2001); and Alonso Reis Freire, 'Evolution of Constitutional Interpretation in Brazil

constitution-making effort, and one which focuses on the programmatic character of many of the Constitution's fundamental rights. However, whereas such 'directive constitutionalism' is traditionally premised on judicial restraint in the face of legislative and executive constitutional 'implementation', the current trend in Brazilian constitutional adjudication is towards highly proactive, intervening, and more or less openly law-making judicial activism. This shift from a 'programmatic' to a concrete interpretation of fundamental rights, that is, from negative to positive judicial review of the conduct of the other two branches of government, is, of course, linked to the (nearly) global epiphenomenon of the judicialisation of politics.[73] However, besides the sociological facts underneath judicialisation, there has been a much discussed shift in doctrine, too, away from traditional positivism, and towards openly axiological approaches linked to the 'principles vs rules' debate in Anglo-American (Dworkin) and continental European (Alexy) jurisprudence. Indeed, principles, seen as the legal embodiment of values, now figure as interpretative trump cards amply utilised by judges and doctrinalists all professing to 'post-positivism' as the new common (judicial) creed.[74] So much so that occasionally the courts, most notably the STF but also other judicial actors, such as the Public Prosecution Service, assume the role of substitute policy makers in a situation of perceived impasse and corruption of the ordinary political process.[75]

Yet, which and whose values are behind the current vogue of 'principiology'? Prima facie, it is, of course, the 'supreme values' recognised in the Constitution's Preamble, notably, social and individual rights, liberty, security, wellbeing, development, equality and justice which would form Brazil's axiological backbone.[76] Indeed, as was seen in the preceding review, fundamental rights, in particular, are seen as at once 'supreme values' in and of themselves, but also as the primary articulators of the concrete values that purportedly inhere in Brazilian society. Value-oriented jurisprudence is, hence, rights-based jurisprudence (and vice versa) in many a Brazilian

and the Employment of Balancing "Method" by Brazilian Supreme Court in Judicial Review,' unpublished paper presented at the VIIth World Congress of the International Association of Constitutional Law, Athens (Greece), 2007, available at www.enelsyn.gr/papers/w15/Paper%20by%20Prof%20Alonso%20Reis%20Freire.pdf.

[73] See, critically, Ran Hirschl, 'The New Constitutionalism and the Judicialization of Pure Politics Worldwide' (2006) 75 *Fordham Law Review* 721.

[74] Antonio Cavalcanti Maia, 'Nos Vinte Anos da Carta Cidadã, do Pós-Positivismo ao Neoconstitucionalismo' in Cláudio Pereira de Souza Neto, Daniel Sarmento, Gustavo Binenbojm (eds), *Vinte Anos de Constituição Federal de 1988* (Rio de Janeiro, Lumen Juris, 2009).

[75] See Florian Hoffmann and Fernando RM Bentes, 'Accountability for Social and Economic Rights in Brazil' in Varun Gauri and Daniel Brinks (eds), *Courting Social Justice, Judicial Enforcement of Social and Economic Rights in the Developing World* (Cambridge, Cambridge University Press, 2008).

[76] Andre Rufino do Vale, *A Estrutura das Normas de Direitos Fundamentais, Repensando a Distinção entre Regras, Princípios e Valores* (São Paulo, Saraiva, 2009).

jurist's mind. This is why many constitutional interpreters have not found it difficult to associate rights with principles, and to then engage in the sort of proportionality-informed balancing that is typical of the continental (European) constitutionalism from which it was derived. As one of Brazil's most influential contemporary constitutionalists, Luis Roberto Barroso, has put it,

> since no one abstract principle is supreme over another, in a concrete case, reciprocal concessions must be made, which produce a socially desirable result, while sacrificing as little as possible of the fundamental rights or principles in question. The legislator cannot arbitrarily choose one of the interests at stake and render the other void, risking a violation of the constitutional text.[77]

Hence, in judicial practice, the value-orientation implied in the 'principles approach' is really a procedural device to open up space for interest balancing. As such, it echoes the Constitution itself, which, as was seen, is a mixed bag of competing interests, as well as of Brazilian society at large, deeply imbued, as it is, with the spirit of balancing, as expressed in the notion of the *jeito*.[78]

Perhaps, this, then, is the key to understanding the role values play in Brazilian constitutional law. From one perspective, the Constitution is an artifice incorporating most if not all of the standard values present in most liberal (capitalist) democracies. Indeed, the constitutional text is so comprehensive and detailed, and aims so high with its extensive list of rights,[79] that it functions as a blueprint for an ideal Brazilian polity. Yet, that ideal stands in stark contrast to social reality 'on the ground' in which, despite very considerable progress during the present Constitution's (so far) 25-year reign, a sizeable part of Brazilian society is still marred by inequality, violence, and precarious living standards. As early as 1989, a year after the Constitution entered into force, the weekly newspaper *Veja* expressed this gap between ideal and reality in a comment on prison conditions in the notorious Carandiru facility in São Paulo: 'today, Brazil has one of the most beautiful constitutions in its history in all that it says with respect to fundamental human rights ... the problem is in the disturbing distance that separates the rights inscribed on paper from their effective exercise and, above all, in the guarantee of their exercise in practical life.'[80] Hence, from this perspective,

[77] Luís Roberto Barroso, *Interpretação e Aplicação da Constituição*, 6th edn (São Paulo, Saraiva, 2004) 330.

[78] See, for an early exploration, Keith Rosenn, 'The jeito, Brazil's institutional bypass of the formal legal system and its development implications' (1971) 19 *American ournal of Comparative Law* 514.

[79] STF President Gilmar Mendes called it 'one of the most extensive lists of fundamental rights'; see *New Challenges of Constitutional Adjudication in Brazil*, Woodrow Wilson International Center for Scholars, Brazil Institute Special Report, November 2008.

[80] *Veja*, 15 February, 1989, p 23.

the 'concrete order of values' is more an aspiration for than a ground of the Constitution, which is, arguably, why many constitutional jurists have turned to the 'principles approach' as a way to try to proactively imbue Brazilian social reality with the values of the Constitution. This, however, raises a related question, notably whether the values enshrined in the Constitution actually reflect the traditional values prevalent in Brazilian society, or whether they purport to constitutionally 're-valuate' the latter. This chicken and egg problem is, of course, inherent to all constitutional projects, but it is, arguably, of particular relevance in societies that are both diverse and asymmetric, as well as undergoing a post-authoritarian transition process. The answer, in the Brazilian case, is twofold: on one hand, a very conscious effort was made to produce an all-inclusive, bottom-up constitution-making process that would reflect virtually all different and potentially conflicting interests in society. In fact, the participatory nature of the drafting of what was meant to become a 'citizens' constitution' was considered to be of greater importance than conciseness, coherence, or even clarity. As such, the constitutional text can be said to accurately reflect the (value) aspirations of its multiple drafters. Yet, on the other hand, subsequent constitutional interpretation has, by and large, been in the hands of a comparatively small and professionally shielded judicial elite that has tended to act according to its own inner logic, rather than on behalf of any larger societal input. Their logic has traditionally been marked by benevolent paternalism, a (broadly) liberal value set, and, perhaps most importantly, a fierce sense of corporate independence that expresses itself in a formalist approach.

This, then, brings in another perspective, notably one in which constitutional values do not predominantly play a substantive, but a formal role. For, paradoxically, the 'principles approach' has not, by and large, been used to promote any particular value agenda,[81] but rather to advance constitutional, and, thus, judicial predominance. As was argued earlier, value-oriented constitutional interpretation by means of principles has enabled the courts to act as privileged fora for the mediation of diverse societal interests. Led by the STF, the 'operators of the law' have increasingly seen themselves as the primary articulators of a somewhat coherent meta-narrative, spun from the elements of the Constitution's 'supreme values', and in continuous need to be rebuilt in the face of the centrifugal effect of party and lobby politics. It is a particularly Brazilian version of the judicialisation of politics in which values serve as the hinge for an otherwise formalist judiciary to constitutionalise the political system. Whether this is for better or worse, and whether the other branches of government will, in fact, tolerate this

[81] At least by comparison to other jurisdictions, such as the United States, where the value orientation of Supreme Court nominees is the object of intense public scrutiny; see exemplarily, David O'Brien, *Storm Center, The Supreme Court in American Politics*, 8th edn (New York, NN Norton, 2008).

subtle revaluation of the balance of powers, is as yet an open question. A hint of irony can, thus, be discerned in former STF President Justice Gilmar Mendes' statement that:

> The intrinsic dialectical tension between democracy and the Constitution, between fundamental rights and people's sovereignty, between Constitutional Adjudication and the democratic legislator is what promotes the Democratic Rule of Law, making it possible for it to develop in the context of an open and pluralistic society, based on principles and fundamental values.[82]

[82] Mendes, above n 79.

4

Canada

LORRAINE E WEINRIB*

I. CONTEXT: HISTORICAL BACKGROUND AND PRE-CHARTER VALUES

AN ANALYSIS OF the values enshrined in Canadian constitutional jurisprudence necessitates a prior inquiry into the context in which the Charter of Rights and Freedoms of 1982 was introduced into Canada. The Canadian constitutional order was established in 1867 as a semi-autonomous, federal dominion within the British Empire. The foundational document was a constituent statute enacted by the British Parliament, acting as the Imperial Parliament. The Constitution Act 1867 made provision for a parliamentary system of government modelled on the unwritten Constitution of the United Kingdom, ie, based on parliamentary supremacy and the judicial protection of common law rights.[1] The Dominion of Canada was eventually to encompass the colonies in North America that had remained loyal to the British Crown after the American Revolution, including the former French colony of New France. It was also charged to carry out the fiduciary duties of the British Crown to a multitude of dispersed and disparate aboriginal peoples.

Canada did not acquire political and legal independence in 1867—the UK Parliament remained the supreme legislature for Canada. In addition, the UK executive acquired formalised authority to veto legislation passed by the federal Parliament and, through control over the federal executive, had the authority to veto provincial legislation as well.[2] It also had carriage of foreign affairs.[3] The Judicial Committee of the Privy Council continued

* I would like to thank Michael da Silva and Yale Hertzman for their editorial assistance.

[1] Constitution Act 1867, 30 & 31 Victoria, c 3 (UK) [Constitution Act 1867]. Until 1982, this Act was named the British North America Act 1867, 30 & 31 Victoria, c 3 (UK). The name was changed by the Canada Act 1982 (UK) 1982, c 11.

[2] ibid, ss 55, 56 and 57 and also s 90.

[3] ibid, s 132, enabled the British executive to enter into treaties that bound the federal government and the provinces. When this power was later assumed by the Canadian executive, the Privy Council determined that such treaties did not bind the provinces in their areas of legislative jurisdiction. See *AG Canada v AG Ontario (Labour Conventions)* [1937] AC 326, [1937] 1 DLR 673 (PC).

to function as Canada's highest appellate court. The constitutional arrangements for the new dominion therefore comprised a complex mix: colonial status; unwritten British constitutional norms, including common law rights and interpretation, constitutional principles and conventions; and the expansive but far from comprehensive supreme law dictates of the Constitution Act 1867. There was no bill of rights; there was no domestic capacity to amend the Constitution Act 1867 or to participate in the process of appointment of of judges to the highest appellate judicial authority.

These colonial arrangements outlived their legitimacy. Legislative independence came in the early 1930s.[4] Judicial and executive independence followed in the late 1940s. At Canada's request, the authority to amend the Constitution Act 1867 remained in the hands of the UK Parliament until 1982, due to repeated failures to meet the assumed standard of unanimity of the federal and all provincial governments to formalise a domestic amending formula. The Constitution Act 1867, along with earlier and later British and Canadian instruments, functions as Canada's non-comprehensive written Constitution.[5]

Canada's great size, challenging geography, and demographic diversity dictated a federal structure. Legislative jurisdiction was divided so as to create a strong federal government for national concerns and economic infrastructure, leaving the provinces authority over local matters and social life, including the liberties embedded in the common law. In stark differentiation to the US federal model, the federal government had a strong unifying influence over national values through its exclusive jurisdiction over the criminal law as well as marriage and divorce. In the final quarter of the twentieth century, this allocation of federal legislative jurisdiction facilitated important changes to national law, including the abolition of the death penalty, the decriminalisation of abortion, and the recognition of civil same-sex marriage.

The federal structure also made possible the creation of the francophone province of Quebec, which acquired the autonomy to govern according to its codified private civil law inherited from France and to forge public policy consistent with the population's Catholic religion. French and English became the official languages used in the federal Parliament to protect the minority anglophone population in Quebec and the minority francophone populations in the other provinces.[6]

[4] Statute of Westminster 1931, 22 & 23 Geo 5 c 4 (UK).

[5] Section 52(1) of Constitution Act 1982.

[6] Constitution Act 1867 (n 1), s 133. The French and English languages were designated official languages for debate and formal records of the national Parliament and of the province of Quebec. Either French or English could be used in the federally established courts or the courts in Quebec. Plans for other provinces with a francophone-Catholic majority did not materialise, largely due to the much stronger political power of the anglophone-Protestant elite on the national political stage.

Protection of minority religious education was crucial to the federal structure. Each province was required to establish and maintain a bifurcated public school system—the general segment would cater to its religious majority, Protestant in all provinces except Quebec, and a separate, smaller segment would serve the religious minority, Catholic in all provinces except Quebec.[7] In later years, as Canada diversified, some provinces extended partial or full funding to the private schools run by other religious minorities.[8]

The new federal government assumed exclusive legislative jurisdiction over the aboriginal peoples and their lands.[9] A treaty-making process secured the orderly transfer of usufructory aboriginal rights and title to the Crown to increase the land available for new settlers, carve out reserve areas for exclusive aboriginal occupation, and provide access to Crown lands for aboriginal hunting, fishing and other traditional uses. The intention was to facilitate the continuity of the traditional aboriginal way of life based on self-sufficient communities. Pervasive failure to carry out this policy resulted in deplorable disadvantage, isolation and despair. Having failed to establish a viable framework for the security of the aboriginal way of life, the federal government adopted a policy of assimilation. It undertook the peremptory removal of young aboriginal children from their families and communities to residential schools run by religious orders. These schools severed familial ties and cultural traditions, including aboriginal languages, as well as connection to ancestral lands. They provided no education or skills; physical and sexual abuse was rampant.

The restricted franchise prior to the early 1960s enabled the white Christian majority to impose its social values and moral code at the federal and provincial levels.[10] Laws restricted or permitted private restrictions on employment, higher education and professional training on the basis of race, religion and ethnicity. Restrictions also applied to access to public institutions, recreational and other services. Private legal arrangements reflected the same social hierarchies and prejudices; for example, restrictive covenants and discrimination in rental accommodations resulted in residential segregation.

Statutes and executive action suppressed political dissent and dealt harshly with dissenters, particularly those who advocated extensive change

[7] ibid, s 93.

[8] *Reference re Bill 30, An Act to Amend the Education Act (Ont)* [1987] 1 SCR 1148, 40 DLR (4th) 18.

[9] Constitution Act 1867, s 91(24).

[10] There were racial and some religious restrictions until after the Second World War. The federal franchise incorporated provincial exclusions of persons of Japanese, Chinese and East Indian origin. Aboriginal persons in all provinces acquired the franchise only by surrendering their special entitlements. Few accepted that trade-off. Members of the Doukhobor religious community in British Columbia were denied the vote as well. One member of Parliament, in expressing his support for the removal of the vote from Japanese internees during the War, stated, 'This is a white man's country, and we want it left a white man's country.'

to the political, social and economic arrangements. The federal criminal law punished the Christian ideas of sin and blasphemy. In some instances, it imposed Christian practices on the whole population, for example, the observance of Sunday as a day of rest. Basic legal protections were relaxed or removed in times of perceived emergency, often at the expense of members of minorities or marginalised individuals. Emergency powers often applied beyond the circumstances and continued beyond the duration of the conditions that prompted their adoption.

When the Supreme Court of Canada became Canada's highest court in 1949, it abandoned the Privy Council's more extreme decentralising approaches to the distribution of federal and provincial legislative jurisdiction. It also supported the development of the administrative state at the federal and provincial levels and in combined federal-provincial ventures.

After the Second World War, immigration from the far corners of the world weakened the existing social hierarchies and ushered in a wider range of public opinion and political aspirations. Many of the new Canadians were refugees; others immigrated hoping to build a society that was less authoritarian and repressive and more prosperous than their homelands. The result was an increase in the population of approximately 1 per cent per year, drawn increasingly from non-European origins. Canada is now one of the most diverse countries in the world.

These changes marked a new beginning for Canadian nationhood. Strong support developed for constitutional recognition of Canada's multicultural diversity, women's equality, the creation of modern administrative institutions at both the national and provincial levels, public welfare programmes and a more representative, accountable mode of governance. Quebec, which had opposed proposals for constitutional change in the past, experienced its Quiet Revolution in 1960. The strong influence of the Catholic Church abated. Quebec's desire to protect its distinctive language and culture fed a new nationalist movement that demanded enlarged legislative jurisdiction, reconfiguration of the federal structure of government or, in the extreme, independence from Canada.

The 1982 amendments to the Constitution may be understood as a delayed response to these post-WWII changes in that they embodied efforts initiated by civic society movements in the aftermath of the war. Canada finally acquired full legal independence from the United Kingdom, including the domestic capacity to amend its written Constitution. Aboriginal rights were constitutionalised. The Canadian Charter of Rights and Freedoms 1982 became part of the supreme law of Canada. The Charter reflected the desire of Prime Minister Pierre Trudeau to address Canadian diversity, in general, and Quebec's nationalist and separatist movements, in particular, by strengthening affiliation to the national community. He also wanted to bring Canada into conformity with the obligations it had undertaken in regard to international human rights. He had hoped to achieve comprehensive constitutional renewal. When the initial proposals faltered, he concentrated on the entrenchment of individual and some group rights. He insisted upon the inclusion of additional rights to use the official minority language in education and in dealings with the federal government to bolster national identity.

The Charter project floundered for years in federal-provincial deliberations. Eventually the public was invited to participate in televised public meetings of a committee of the national Parliament, marking the first time that 'ordinary Canadians' had had the opportunity to express their constitutional aspirations. Hitherto socially vulnerable and politically powerless groups and individuals insisted upon the constitutional entrenchment of a full range of substantive and procedural rights and freedoms, combined with the necessary reconfiguration of institutional roles to secure their enforcement.

This public support eventually broke the back of the opposition to the Charter, which was composed of social conservatives, most provincial premiers (who feared diminution of provincial powers) and those who preferred—and had benefitted by—the status quo.[11] The drafters then grafted elements of foreign national and international human rights law on to the basic framework of Canadian governance. The Charter in effect established a new social contract for Canada.[12] It protected the normative principles of governance that Canadians considered fundamental in the late twentieth century by terminating legislative supremacy, establishing access to the courts for judicial review, and reconfiguring the roles and interactions of the major institutions of governance.[13]

II. VALUES AND THEIR PRIORITISATION

Canada's distinctive path to nationhood did not produce a single, comprehensive constitutional text. As noted above, an important component

[11] *Re: Objection by Quebec to a Resolution to amend the Constitution* [1982] 2 SCR 783. Quebec was the only province to object to the final compromises. The 1982 amendments are nonetheless binding on that province, given that the prescribed degree of consensus was satisfied.

[12] *Vriend v Alberta* [1998] 1 SCR 493 [134]–[135]: '[I]t should be emphasized again that our Charter's introduction and the consequential remedial role of the courts were choices of the Canadian people through their elected representatives as part of a redefinition of our democracy ... So courts in their trustee or arbiter role must perforce scrutinize the work of the legislature and executive not in the name of the courts, but in the interests of the new social contract that was democratically chosen.' (Iacobucci J, for the majority.)

[13] Lorraine Weinrib, 'The Canadian Charter's Transformative Aspirations' (2003) 19 *Supreme Court Law Review* (2d) 17, reprinted in Joseph Magnet, Gerald-A Beaudoin, Gerald Gall and Christopher Manfredi (eds), *The Canadian Charter of Rights and Freedoms: Reflections on the Charter After Twenty Years* (Toronto, Butterworths, 2003) 17; Lorraine Weinrib, 'Trudeau and the Canadian Charter of Rights and Freedoms: A Question of Constitutional Maturation' in Andrew Cohen and JL Granatstein (eds), *Trudeau's Shadow: The Life and Legacy of Pierre Elliot Trudeau* (Toronto, Random House, 1998) 259.

of Canada's constitutional value structure derives from the 'unwritten Constitution' inherited from the United Kingdom.[14] A number of formal documents, including the Constitution Act 1867 and its amendments adopted over the years, make up the written Constitution.[15] The most important amendments are embodied in the Constitution Act 1982: the Charter, aboriginal rights, and the domestic amending formula.[16]

The values of the Canadian Constitution are not circumscribed by the unwritten Constitution or the written constitutional instruments. The judgments of the Supreme Court of Canada are most relevant, in that the courts are required to apply, interpret and develop these constitutional values in the adjudication of particular cases as well as in abstract review of questions referred by the provincial or federal executive. An important element of the Court's responsibility is to construct coherence and comprehensiveness out of the fragmented elements of Canadian constitutional law. The Court increasingly operates as both an appellate and constitutional court, ie, as guardian of the normative principles and values of the constitutional order at large.

A. The Normative Framework

In recent abstract review cases, the Supreme Court of Canada has set out a comprehensive and authoritative delineation of the foundational constitutional principles and values. The *Secession Reference* provides a luminous illustration thereof.[17] The Court had good reason to address the most basic principles and values of the Canadian constitutional in this abstract review case. It had under deliberation the strongest real threat to that order—the Quebec separatist movement's contention that the province of Quebec could unilaterally secede from Canada on the basis of a provincial referendum, ie without further negotiation or formal agreement or amendment to the Canadian Constitution. To assess these claims, the Court delineated four principles that structure Canadian governance: federalism, democracy, constitutionalism and the rule of law, and respect for minority rights.[18]

[14] Canada inherited these principles and their institutional arrangements in its first century by virtue of its colonial status and later dominion status within the British Empire. The Constitution Act 1867 expressly incorporated these norms and institutional arrangements through its preamble, which stated that the new Dominion would have a 'Constitution similar in Principle to that of the United Kingdom'.

[15] Constitution Act 1867, s 52(1) sets out a list of these formal constitutional documents, indicating that it is not complete.

[16] The Constitution Act 1982 constituted Sch B to the Canada Act 1982 (1982 c 11), enacted by the Parliament of the United Kingdom at Canada's request and consent. The Canada Act 1982 announced the termination of the UK's authority to legislate for Canada.

[17] *Reference re Secession of Quebec* [1998] 2 SCR 217, 161 DLR (4th) 385.

[18] ibid [49].

Through the prism of these principles, it then analysed the arguments supporting Quebec's claim to unilateral independence.

The Court began its analysis by focusing on the nature of Canadian federalism. It associated Canadian diversity to the constitutional arrangements for democratic participation, especially the provision for political participation in both the national and provincial political communities. The two modes of political participation, it stressed, operated to accommodate the self-government of a majority francophone province in an anglophone country, not to undermine the self-determination of a national minority, as alleged.

The Court then turned to examine democracy as a constitutional principle or value, in order to contrast the nature of democratic participation in ordinary electoral politics, on the one hand, and in referendum politics, on the other. The Court emphasised that democratic participation in Canada embraces more than the mechanics of voting, political representation and the production of legislation: it also establishes the right to governance characterised by participation, consent, political accountability and the rule of law. Democratic participation thus engages not merely those who share a language and cultural heritage; it also engages those who seek wider deliberation, compromise and negotiation attentive to moral values. These moral values include respect for individual identity, pluralism, and multiple allegiances. In making emotional appeals to ethnic identity, referenda undermine that which democracy requires—rational, fully informed deliberation.

The Court elaborated on these themes when it considered constitutionalism and the rule of law. These constitutional principles secure stable, predictable and orderly governance, rather than arbitrary state action. On this basis, the Court rejected the contention that a majority in a province-wide referendum might legitimately secure its collective goals at the expense of long-standing institutions, processes and rights established to protect vulnerable minorities.

While conceding that Canada had not always met current standards of equality and multicultural sensitivity, the Court noted the long-standing national preoccupation with demographic diversity. It emphasised that the constitutional order now recognises the special position of aboriginal peoples, historical linguistic minorities and immigrants, who together make up Canada's remarkable multicultural and pluralist fabric. These points drew attention to the voting patterns in the two separatist referenda held in Quebec, which revealed starkly different views on Quebec independence. While the francophone majority dispersed throughout the province strongly supported the separatist cause, the anglophone minority, the aboriginal peoples and other cultural minorities in the major urban centres did not.

The Court drew specific conclusions from its delineation of constitutional principles. It stipulated that the outcome of a referendum would precipitate political obligations only if the question posed and the support it garnered were clear. These strictures ruled out the opaque—bordering on deceptive—questions posed in Quebec's two separatist referenda. They also negated the legitimacy of any plan to seek immediate independence on the world stage in the aftermath of a vote in which the 'yes' side secured as little as 50 per cent plus one of the votes cast. The Court thus affirmed the primacy of the values of accountability, responsibility, rationality and fairness, all derived from fundamental constitutional principles.

The Court has, on numerous occasions, dealt with seemingly intractable political questions by setting out the applicable constitutional norms and leaving political institutions and officials to work out the details.[19] Its approach reflects a strong commitment to rationality and deliberation in a diverse and pluralist nation.

B. The Court and Nationhood: Respecting Diversity

The concern for multicultural vulnerability so evident in the *Secession Reference* extends beyond national and provincial minority communities delineated by language, culture and religion, to include minorities within minorities. Longstanding policies include support for established and recently arrived immigrant communities, such as family reunification preferences in immigration law, and support for cultural expression. More recently, protection has been extended to women and sexual minorities, who find their aspirations for personal freedom and equality frustrated within their families and identity communities. So too, the province of Ontario recently rejected proposals put forward by conservative elements in the Muslim community to mandate statutory arbitration, with judicial enforcement, in order to impose Sharia law upon the dissolution of marriages. The general public as well as members of the provincial legislature rejected these proposals when it became clear that they would undermine the preferences of Muslim women who preferred to have access to the entitlements under the generally applicable family law legislation and their enforcement in the regular court system. They were able to make their preferences clear, given the community organisation and communication skills they had developed thanks to long-standing federal funding supporting equality for women.

In *Syndical Northwest v Amselem*,[20] the Court developed what, in effect, is a doctrine of reasonable accommodation of minority religious beliefs:

> In a multiethnic and multicultural country such as ours, which accentuates and advertises its modern record of respecting cultural diversity and human rights and of promoting tolerance of religious and ethnic minorities—and is in many ways an

[19] See, eg, *Re: Resolution to amend the Constitution* [1981] 1 SCR 753, 125 DLR (3d) 1 and *Reference Re Remuneration of Judges* [1997] 3 SCR 3.

[20] *Syndical Northwest v Amselem* [2004] SCC 47 [87].

example thereof for other societies—the argument of the respondent that nominal, minimally intruded-upon aesthetic interests should outweigh the exercise of the appellants' religious freedom is unacceptable. Indeed, mutual tolerance is one of the cornerstones of all democratic societies. Living in a community that attempts to maximize human rights invariably requires openness to and recognition of the rights of others. In this regard, I must point out, with respect, that labelling an individual's steadfast adherence to his or her religious beliefs 'intransigence', as Morin JA asserted at para 64 [in his judgment in the Quebec Court of Appeal], does not further an enlightened resolution of the dispute before us.

This doctrine was enforced by the Court under somewhat controversial circumstances in *Multani v Commission Scolaire Marguerite-Bourgeoys*.[21] A Sikh boy contended that he had a constitutional right to wear a ceremonial dagger (*kirpan*) under his clothing at school. This contravened the school's code of conduct but a majority of the Court held that the wearing of the *kirpan* was constitutionally protected, subject to conditions set by the school.

The 1982 constitutional amendments also reconfigured the relationship between the federal government and the aboriginal peoples as a relationship based on enforceable constitutional rights. These changes bridge older and more modern values by affirming 'existing aboriginal and treaty rights' with a new proviso stipulating gender equality.[22] These communal entitlements do not pre-empt individual rights under the Charter; neither do individual rights displace the communal entitlements.[23] In addition, the Supreme Court has confirmed the constitutionality of special programmes designed to support the economic viability of aboriginal communities under the Charter's affirmative action clause.[24] By setting out the normative framework informing the various aboriginal constitutional entitlements, the Supreme Court has ushered in a period of intense negotiations, in effect reviving the neglected treaty-making commitments noted earlier. The purpose of these negotiations is to settle questions of land entitlement, aboriginal rights and self-government so that aboriginal communal life rests on a secure economic foundation. In addition, the Court has affirmed the political participation rights in the home communities of the many aboriginal men and women who now make their lives in Canada's urban centres.[25]

[21] *Multani v Commission Scolaire Marguerite Bourgeoys* [2006] SCC 37.

[22] Constitution Act 1982, s 35. But see *Native Women's Assn of Canada v Canada* [1994] 3 SCR 627, 119 DLR (4th) 224.

[23] Canadian Charter of Rights and Freedoms 1982 being Pt I of the Constitution Act 1982 (UK), which is Sch B of the Canada Act 1982 (UK), s 25.

[24] Section 15(2) of the Charter permits affirmative action. See *Lovelace v Ontario* [2000] 1 SCR 950, 188 DLR (4th) 193. See *R v Kapp* [2008] SCC 41, 294 DLR (4th) 1, [2008] 2 SCR 483.

[25] *Corbière v Canada (Minister of Indian and Northern Affairs)* [1999] 2 SCR 203, 173 DLR (4th) 1.

C. Language

The 1982 constitutional amendments affirmed a commitment to Canada's official language minorities. The Charter extended the entitlements to use French and English as official languages at the federal level and in the province of New Brunswick.[26] It also supports minority language education for the children of citizens.[27] Support for the two official languages protects the continued viability of these communities as originally situated, as well as the mobility of their members.

The Charter also preserved the pre-1982 constitutional arrangements laid down for minority religious education within the general public school systems in the provinces. The entitlements have become controversial. The Supreme Court permitted the province of Ontario to extend the 1867 entitlements to Catholic public schools to include secondary education, while other provinces have abandoned these arrangements, through constitutional amendment. The Court has rejected argumentation, based on the Charter's equality clause, to extend the entitlement to religious education to religious minorities other than those expressly protected in the Constitution Act 1867.[28] This position reflected its view of the vital importance of the diverse public school classroom as preparation for participation in a pluralistic, multicultural society. The Charter's treatment of faith and faith communities, which is discussed later in this essay, tracks this movement towards a pluralist and secular public sphere.

The historical continuity reflected in the constitutional provisions applicable to the aboriginal population, the official language communities and the religiously bifurcated public school system may appear incompatible with the Charter's strong commitments to individual autonomy, equality, multiculturalism and pluralism. The underlying idea is to bridge the particularities of history with the generic post-WWII commitment to the equal and inherent dignity of the human person. This tension is addressed by combining fidelity to Canada's historical commitments to minorities with respect for the more modern commitment to individual flourishing. Individual self-fulfilment is respected when the claim relates to the isolated individual; it is

[26] Charter (n 23), ss 21 and 16–19.

[27] ibid, s 23.

[28] ibid, s 29; *Reference re Bill 30, An Act to Amend the Education Act (Ont)* [1987] 1 SCR 1148, 40 DLR (4th) 18; *Adler v Ontario* [1996] 3 SCR 609, 140 DLR (4th) 385. The provinces of Newfoundland and Quebec have changed their structure of their education systems by way of amendments eliminating the entitlement to minority religious education. Quebec's public school system is now based on language. In *Waldman v Canada*, Communication No 694/1996, UN Doc CCPR/C/67/D/694/1996 (1999), the UN Human Rights Committee disapproved of the Supreme Court ruling in the Bill 30 case. It observed that the International Covenant on Civil and Political Rights does not obligate state parties to provide funding for religious schools. It then stipulated that if state parties choose to make funding to religious schools available, they must do so without discrimination.

also respected when the context is family life, chosen and given communities, and the public sphere in which all members of Canadian society stand as free and equal in their interactions with both each other and the state.[29]

The Charter stands as the centrepiece of the 1982 amendments because of its long gestation as well as the significant public contribution to its substantive values, principles and institutional arrangements. To elucidate these basic values and principles, it is important to note that the guarantees do not stand as isolated, disconnected absolutes. The Supreme Court has stipulated on many occasions that there is no hierarchy of rights, that the analysis focuses on the substantive principles and values underlying the rights claimed in the light of other relevant rights, principles and values.

D. Individual Protection

The Charter integrates the institutional roles often understood to stand in opposition in other systems of rights-protection—the so-called counter-majoritarian dilemma. The Charter's institutional arrangements were designed to discipline the democratic and executive process to substantive and procedural values that respect the inherent human dignity, liberty and equality of all members of Canadian society. Canadians would no longer find their civic engagement confined to the occasional opportunity to vote. Henceforth, they would be full-time, real-time rights holders; their political representatives would be constitutionally bound to respect their rights and freedoms in the exercise of all public authority.

This transformation in the relationship between the individual and the state is based on the application of the Charter to the federal and provincial governments alike. Any law, whether legislated or formulated under the common law, is 'of no force or effect' to the extent of any inconsistency with the Constitution.[30] By extension, state action carried out by public officials must comply with law, and that law must comply with the Constitution. The supremacy of the Charter requires the courts to vindicate rights claims against the state. When the courts find an unjustified infringement of these rights, they must provide 'appropriate and just' remedies.[31]

The Charter's short preamble presents two principles as foundational: the 'supremacy of God', and the rule of law. The reference to the 'supremacy of God' has had little effect because the specific clauses relating to freedom of

[29] See, eg, *R v Keegstra* [1990] 3 SCR 667, 61 CCC (3d) 1 [*Keegstra*]; *Ford v Quebec (Attorney General)* [1988] 2 SCR 712, 54 DLR (4th) 577 [*Ford*]; *Vriend* (n 12).

[30] Charter (n 23), s 52.

[31] ibid, s 24. The Supreme Court has broadened access to Charter claims beyond those directly injured to include public interest standing on the premise that the public at large has a right to constitutional behaviour by government.

religion, conscience, and equality as well as the affirmations of multiculturalism and gender equality take precedence. The second principle, the rule of law, marks continuity: Canadian constitutional law has always prioritised the rule of law. In recent rulings, the Supreme Court of Canada delineated some of its content, stipulating that the judiciary must enjoy independence; that law is supreme over officials of government and private officials; that the state must create and maintain an actual order of positive law that provides a norm-based order; and that law regulates the relationship between the individual and the state.[32]

Other Charter provisions reveal more of its basic value structure. Section 27 directs the judiciary to interpret the Charter text in conformity to 'the preservation and enhancement of the multicultural heritage of Canadians'.[33] Section 28 partially restricts the operation of section 27 by adding an overriding, substantive proviso to every Charter guarantee: 'notwithstanding anything in this Charter, the rights and freedoms referred to in it are guaranteed equally to male and female persons'.[34] Section 28 is best understood not as an interpretive directive but as an addendum to section 1, which both guarantees and lays down the exclusive justificatory criteria for limiting Charter rights and freedoms.

Section 28 thus precludes Charter interpretation or application that reflects traditional religious and cultural patterns of gender subordination or relegates women to biological roles.[35] For example, in *Morgentaler*, the major abortion case in the Supreme Court, the majority judgment focused on the ways in which unwanted pregnancy undermines a woman's 'priorities and aspirations'. The justices thus affirmed that women have a full range of life purposes and responsibilities during their fertile years, rather than presupposing procreation as their faith-based, familial, cultural or biological duty.[36] So too, the Court has rejected cultural defences by men charged with assault or murder of their intimate partners; it has also made clear that there is no implied consent to sexual assault in Canadian law.[37] To date, however, the judiciary has tended to temper claims to women's substantive

[32] *Reference re Remuneration of Judges of the Provincial Court (PEI)* [1997] 3 SCR 3,150 DLR (4th) 577; *Re Remuneration of Judges (No 2)* [1998] 1 SCR 3,155 DLR (4th) 1; *British Columbia v Imperial Tobacco Canada Ltd*, [2005] 2 SCR 473, 2005 SCC 49; *R v Big M Drug Mart Ltd*, [1985] 1 SCR 295, 18 DLR (4th) 321 [*Big M*].

[33] Charter (n 23), s 27.

[34] ibid s 28.

[35] Penny Kome, *Taking of 28* (Toronto, The Women's Press, 1983). This clause should operate to restrict the permitted limits on the Charter's guarantees in s 1. The notwithstanding clause in s 28 is further strengthened by its exclusion from the reach of the s 33 override power.

[36] *R v Morgentaler* [1988] 1 SCR 30, 82 NR 1, 44 DLR (4th) 385 [27], [38] and [59] [*Morgentaler*], Dickson CJC.

[37] See, eg, *R v Tran* [2010] 3 SCR 350 [34] and *R v Ewanchuk*, [1999] 1 SCR 330.

equality to avoid impact on the marketplace as well as economic and fiscal policy.[38]

E. Democracy and Rights

The Charter's entrenchment of fundamental rights and freedoms beyond the reach of temporarily elected majorities is encapsulated in the term 'free and democratic society', which section 1 sets out as the sole justificatory consideration for limitation of Charter rights.[39] In a formative early statement, Chief Justice Dickson delineated some of the values and principles essential to such a society:

> [T]he inherent dignity of the human person, commitment to social justice and equality, accommodation of a wide variety of beliefs, respect for cultural and group identity, and faith in social and political institutions which enhance the participation of individuals and groups in society. The underlying values and principles of a free and democratic society are the genesis of the rights and freedoms guaranteed by the *Charter* and the ultimate standard against which a limit on a right and freedom must be shown despite its effect, to be reasonable and demonstrably justified.[40]

This formulation stipulates that the Charter requires the state to respect the autonomy and equality of the individual, not to negate the power of the state to govern for the common good of all members of Canadian society. The Charter right holder is accordingly not regarded as a self-sufficient atomistic person resistant to regulation or redistribution of wealth. On the contrary, Charter right holders may be embedded in a family or identity community; may be engaged in social or political activity; and may be self-reliant or vulnerable and disadvantaged.

While the Constitution does not guarantee specific, enforceable social and economic rights, Canada's political tradition has supported redistribution of wealth among the provinces to ensure comparable levels of basic public services—such as healthcare, post-secondary education, old age pensions and welfare—across the country. The Canadian dream, if there is one, is for public provision of public services, such as health care, education and basic welfare, to support individual, familial and identity group flourishing. It is important in this context to note that the Charter does not protect property,

[38] *Symes v Canada* [1993] 4 SCR 695, 110 DLR (4th) 470; *Newfoundland (Treasury Board) v NAPE* 2004 SCC 66, [2004] 3 SCR 381.

[39] Section 1 of the Charter (n 23) reads: 'The *Canadian Charter of Rights and Freedoms* guarantees the rights and freedoms set out in it subject only to such reasonable limits prescribed by law as can be demonstrably justified in a free and democratic society.'

[40] *R v Oakes* [1986] 1 SCR 103, 26 DLR (4th) 200 [64].

either held for the benefit of the individual or for general social welfare. The Supreme Court accordingly avoids recognition of economic interests in its interpretation of the scope of Charter rights and favours remedies that are fiscally neutral.

F. Dignity: The Core Value

The Court has consistently identified the core value informing its Charter analysis as respect for human dignity. This elusive concept was delineated in a leading equality judgment in the following terms:

> Human dignity means that an individual or group feels self-respect and self-worth. It is concerned with physical and psychological integrity and empowerment. Human dignity is harmed by unfair treatment premised upon personal traits or circumstances which do not relate to individual needs, capacities or merits ... It is harmed when individuals and groups are marginalised, ignored, or devalued and is enhanced when laws recognize the full place of all individuals and groups within Canadian society.[41]

Iacobucci J developed this key concept of dignity as follows:

> What is human dignity? There can be different conceptions of what human dignity means. For the purpose of analysis under s. 15(1) of the Charter, however, the jurisprudence of this Court reflects a specific, albeit non-exhaustive, definition ... [T]he equality guarantee in s. 15(1) is concerned with the realisation of personal autonomy and self-determination. Human dignity means that an individual or group feels self-respect and self-worth. It is concerned with physical and psychological integrity and empowerment ... Human dignity within the meaning of the equality guarantee does not relate to the status or position of an individual in society per se, but rather concerns the manner in which a person legitimately feels when confronted with a particular law. Does the law treat him or her unfairly, taking into account all the circumstances regarding the individuals affected and excluded by the law?[42]

The Charter's first set of guarantees, set out in section 2 under the heading 'fundamental freedoms', reflects this understanding of the role of constitutional rights. Protection extends to freedom of conscience and religion; freedom of thought, belief, opinion and expression as well as of the press and media; peaceful assembly; and freedom of association.

The guarantees of freedom of religion and conscience support the flourishing of individuals (in their adherence to or rejection of any and all religious precepts), the privacy of the family, and the integrity of faith-based communities and institutions. The guarantee of freedom of conscience emphasises

[41] *Law v Canada (Minister of Employment and Immigration)* [1999] 1 SCR 497, 530.
[42] ibid [53].

individual liberty in directing one's life based on one's personal values. More generally, these freedoms promote respect and tolerance for pluralism in the public sphere, and facilitate full participation in social and political dimensions of Canadian life. Limitations on these guarantees affirm the same values. The state may permissibly restrict these guarantees when their exercise imposes harm or restricts the freedoms of others to exercise their own equal rights.

On this basis, the courts invalidated legislation mandating prayer and religious indoctrination in the component of the public school system that caters to the general public, even when exemptions were available to teachers and students, and rejected sectarian prayer in legislative bodies.[43] The courts also invalidated state imposition of religious belief or practice in the public sphere, eg by laws promoting Christian Sabbath observance. In contrast, the judiciary upheld state designation of public days of rest for secular purposes on days having religious significance.[44] Also rejected were faith-based arguments invoked to justify limiting rights, eg, to retain arbitrary restrictions on access to therapeutic abortion, in one instance,[45] and to restrict marriage to opposite-sex couples, in another.[46] The Court initially validated the criminal prohibition of assisted suicide. It stressed the sanctity of life, but rested its analysis on the need to protect the vulnerable. It later overruled that approach, on the basis of a much expanded factual record that included the affidavits of many persons afflicted with grievous and irremedial physical and psychological suffering caused by disease or disability, as well as expert scientific and medical opinion from Canadian and international sources. On this basis, it concluded that administrative arrangements designed to examine informed consent and decisional capacity on a case by case basis would suffice to exclude vulnerable applicants.[47]

Many cases pertaining to the freedom of religion and conscience have involved children. The Supreme Court justified state intervention to provide medically necessary treatment to a baby despite the religious objections of the parents and restricted parental imposition of physical punishment on their children. The Court has also ruled that the public school classroom must afford a secure place for children of minority faiths to express their religious faith, eg, wear a *kirpan*; impose no religious indoctrination and suggest no hostility based on race or religion; and provide educational

[43] *Zylberberg v Sudbury Board of Education (Director)* (1988) 52 DLR (4th) 577, 65 OR (2d) 641 (CA); *Freitag v Penetanguishene (Town)* (1999), 125 OAC 139 (Ontario CA).

[44] *Big M* (n 32); *Edwards Books and Art Ltd v The Queen* [1986] 2 SCR 713, 35 DLR (4th) 1.

[45] *Morgentaler* (n 36) Wilson J.

[46] *Halpern v Canada* [2003] OJ No 2268 (Ont CA) [*Halpern*].

[47] *Rodriguez v British Columbia (Attorney General)* [1993] 3 SCR 519 [*Rodriguez*], overruled by *Carter v Canada* [2015] SCC 5, http://scc-csc.lexum.com/scc-csc/scc-csc/en/item/14637/index.do?r=AAAAAQAYY2FydGVyIGFzc2lzdGVkIHN1aWNpZGUgAAAAAAE.

material that reflects Canadian public policy, such as readers on families with same-sex spouses.[48]

G. Expression

The Charter's expansive guarantee of freedom of expression protects the non-violent expression of meaning. Given the expansiveness of this protection, most of the judicial analysis relates to examples of justified limitation of the right. The Supreme Court upheld the narrowly drawn crime of public, wilful promotion of hatred to protect the human dignity and equality of members of vilified minority groups, and, by extension, to support their political participation and social engagement beyond their identity communities.[49] The high threshold for the protection of freedom of expression is well illustrated in *Saskatchewan (Human Rights Commission) v Whatcott*:[50]

> As explained in *Irwin Toy Ltd v Quebec (Attorney General)*, freedom of expression was guaranteed in the Charter 'so as to ensure that everyone can manifest their thoughts, opinions, beliefs, indeed all expressions of the heart and mind, however unpopular, distasteful or contrary to the mainstream'. If the repugnancy or offensiveness of an idea does not exclude it from Charter protection under s. 2(b), they cannot, in themselves, be sufficient to justify a limitation on expression under a s. 1 analysis. A blanket prohibition on the communication of repugnant ideas would offend the core of freedom of expression and could not be viewed as a minimal impairment of that right.

When the Court upheld obscenity laws that prohibited the possession, sale and distribution of sexually explicit material deemed degrading and dehumanising to women and children, it provided exemptions for privately created, closely held sexually explicit writings and depictions.[51] The Court also invalidated Quebec legislation that banned the use of any language other than French in commercial signs, while indicating its openness to regulation designed to promote French as the predominant language in Quebec. The province of Quebec eventually took up the Court's suggestion.[52]

[48] *Ross v New Brunswick School District No 15* [1996] 1 SCR 825; *Multani c Marguerite-Bourgeoys (Commission scolaire)* 2006 SCC 6 [2006] 1 SCR 256; *Trinity Western University v British Columbia College of Teachers* [2001] 1 SCR 772, 199 DLR (4th) 1; *Chamberlain v Surrey School District No 36* 2002 SCC 86 [2002] 4 SCR 710; *Congrégation des témoins de Jéhovah de St-Jerome-Lafontaine v Lafontaine (Village) v Commission scolaire des Chenes* [2012] 1 SCR 235; *Canadian Foundation for Children, Youth and the Law v Canada* [2004] 1 SCR 76.

[49] *Keegstra* (n 29). The offence is narrowly drawn in order to permit open discussion of religious topics and repudiation of racism.

[50] *Saskatchewan (Human Rights Commission) v Whatcott* 246 CRR (2d) 270 [50].

[51] *R v Butler* [1992] 1 SCR 452, 89 DLR (4th) 449. But see *R v Sharpe* [2001] 1 SCR 45, 194 DLR (4th) 1, validating the legislation prohibitions against child pornography generally, but protecting the private exercise of freedom of thought and its expression.

[52] Initially, the separatist government used the legislative override power to reinstate its ban. Later, in light of strong disapproval within and beyond Canada, a Liberal government legislated to promote the French language without a ban on other languages.

The Supreme Court was originally cautious in its reading of the right to freedom of association. Two recent judgments have departed from that caution. In one, the Court affirmed the right of Canadian workers to form and join unions and in the other it affirmed the right to strike.[53]

H. Political Rights

The Charter's political guarantees endorse full and effective political participation by citizens in choosing their representatives, to support the diversity of opinion within a multicultural, pluralist society. Section 3, for the first time in Canada, sets down the basic guarantee of the citizen's right to vote and stand for political office, an entitlement that the Supreme Court applied to invalidate the legislated disenfranchisement of prisoners.[54] The basis of this ruling was the recognition that the laws laying down the prosecutorial process and modes of punishment depend on the universality of the franchise for their legitimacy, most of all in their application to those whose most personal liberties these laws restrict, day in and day out over extended periods. The Court also expressed concern that the prison population includes disproportionate numbers of racial minorities, whose political participation should not be undermined.

The Charter directly supports democratic governance in a number of ways. It stipulates the frequency of elections and legislative sessions under normal circumstances and in times of emergency.[55] In addition, the Supreme Court has formulated standards for the regulation of political parties. For example, it invalidated a legislative stipulation that denied registered political party status and related benefits that facilitate fund-raising for parties that do not nominate candidates in at least 50 electoral districts. In a country as large, pluralistic and diversified as Canada this stipulation favoured established parties and stifled participation in the political process of new parties introducing new issues and perspectives.[56] The Court has also upheld regulation of the electoral process to secure democratic governance, eg, restrictions on third party advertising expenses that might tilt election results in favour of wealthy individuals and organisations.[57]

Beyond the franchise, the Charter's citizenship entitlements include the right to enter, remain in and leave Canada.[58] These rights provide a degree

[53] *Mounted Police Association of Ontario v Canada (Attorney General)* [2015] SCC 1, http://scc-csc.lexum.com/scc-csc/scc-csc/en/item/14577/index.do?r=AAAAAQAPcmlnaHQgdG8gc3RyaWtlAAAAAAE; *Saskatchewan Federation of Labour v Saskatchewan* [2015] SCC 4, http://scc-csc.lexum.com/scc-csc/scc-csc/en/item/14610/index.do?r=AAAAAQAPcmlnaHQgdG8gc3RyaWtlAAAAAAE.

[54] *Sauvé v Canada (Chief Electoral Officer)* [2002] SCC 68, [2002] 3 SCR 519.

[55] Charter (n 23), ss 4–5.

[56] *Figueroa v Canada (Attorney General)* 2003 SCC 37, [2003] 1 SCR 912.

[57] *Harper v Canada (Attorney General)* 2004 SCC 33, [2004] 1 SCR 827.

[58] See *Divito v Canada* [2013] 3 SCR 157.

of security to planning one's life. In addition, citizens and permanent residents are entitled to take up residence and work in any province subject to non-discriminatory restrictions. Similar to the protections afforded to the two official languages, these entitlements affirm attachment to a national community to complement the strong attachment many Canadians feel to their provinces and identity communities.

I. Rights to Life

The Charter offers a long list of legal rights under sections 7 to 15, which commence with a general protection of life, liberty and security of the person, subject to deprivation only according to the 'principles of fundamental justice'. These entitlements have generated extensive litigation.

Several leading cases address the right to life. When the Supreme Court invalidated Canada's criminal abortion prohibition on the grounds that its therapeutic exemption was arbitrary and unfair to pregnant women, the three judgments in the majority indicated that restrictions would be justified in the advanced stages of pregnancy as the foetus developed towards human personhood.[59] Consistent with its insistence upon the individual liberty of women in respect to reproduction, the Court denied the claim of a biological father to prevent his estranged partner from terminating a pregnancy. These cases make clear that the Charter does not recognise the right to life of a foetus in early pregnancy.[60]

When the Court validated the criminal prohibition against assisted suicide in 1993, it affirmed the common law liberty of individuals to refuse or discontinue treatment necessary to support life. On the primary issue, it based its ruling on the possibility that the prohibition against assisted suicide protected the lives of those who might be vulnerable due to physical pain and suffering, as well as mental illness or undue influence.[61] Strong dissenting opinions emphasised individual autonomy and equality as the dominant considerations, leaving the protection of the vulnerable to the criminal law and to the regulation of the medical profession. As noted above, the Supreme Court of Canada recently overturned this ruling, relying instead on a first instance judgment.[62]

The Supreme Court accepted the argument submitted based on the right to life: that an individual's right to life is impaired by the blanket prohibition

[59] *Morgentaler* (n 36).

[60] *Borowski v Canada (Attorney General)* [1989] 1 SCR 342, 57 DLR (4th) 231; see lower court judgments in *Borowski v Canada (Attorney General)* (1987) 39 DLR (4th) 731 (Sask CA) and *Borowski v Canada (Attorney General)* (1983) 4 DLR (4th) 112 (Sask QB); *Tremblay v Daigle* [1989] 2 SCR 530.

[61] *Rodriguez* (n 47).

[62] *Carter v Canada* (Attorney General) 2012 BCSC 886. This section has now been appealed to the Supreme Court, which has accepted the appeal.

against assisted suicide when he or she considers it necessary to commit suicide, unaided, at a point in time earlier than when he or she would seek out and consent to an assisted suicide. In this situation the individual's life is shortened by the effect of the prohibition against assistance. The Court did not insist upon proof of terminal illness. And it left the deliberation on specific arrangements to Parliament.[63]

Two other important decisions impinge on the right to life in contexts when death may occur as a result of state conduct or in the absence of state conduct, suggesting that the Court understands the right to life to encompass positive content.

The Court invalidated three federal criminal prohibitions relating to prostitution: the offence of keeping or being found in a common bawdy-house, living on the avails of prostitution, and communicating in public for the purposes of prostitution. It rejected the government's claim that the prohibitions protected prostitutes and avoided public nuisance. It deferred to the arguments and supporting factual material, found to be reliable in extensive reasons by the trial judge. She had found that the prohibitions increased the dangers present in a legal activity. These dangers included preventing recourse to indoor spaces and other safety measures, such as working in groups and securing the assistance of body guards. The Court also pointed out that those who engage in street prostitution are often marginalised individuals—without education or vocational skills, poor, addicted to drugs, controlled by pimps, and members of groups subject to racial discrimination. Accordingly, it was inappropriate to assume, from their participation in risky activity, that they had voluntarily taken responsibility for all the dangers inherent in that activity.[64]

So too, in the context of epidemic levels of HIV/AIDS and hepatitis C following crisis levels of drug injecting in downtown Vancouver, the Supreme Court ordered the federal Minister of Health to renew an exemption, from the federal prohibitions relating to the possession and trade in illegal drugs, to shield a medically supervised safe injection site for addicts (based on models in Europe and Australia) from prosecution. The Court's ruling indicates that it is shifting away from the idea that the criminal law is the best or only way to deal with drug trafficking and addiction, given the protection of life and security of the person that the Charter affords.[65]

J. Death Penalty

Canada's Parliament abandoned the death penalty in 1976, affirming that decision in the House of Commons in an open vote in 1987. The last

[63] *Carter* (n 47).
[64] *Canada v Bedford* [2013] 3 SCR 1101.
[65] *AG Canada v PHS Community Services Society* [2011] 3 SCR 134.

executions occurred in 1982. The Supreme Court recently considered the propriety of extraditing persons accused of capital crimes to countries that impose the death penalty. Departing from an earlier ruling, it concluded that, subject to exceptional circumstances, Canadian officials must obtain assurances that the death penalty will not be imposed (or, if imposed, will not be carried out) prior to extradition. Support for this conclusion derived from Canada's advocacy against the death penalty on the international stage as well as the practices of other countries that Canada regards as models in the protection of fundamental rights.[66]

K. Liberty

The Charter's guarantees of liberty and security of the person in section 7 have had wide application: protected interests include the impact on health of waiting periods under the public health care system;[67] the physical integrity of children within the family in the context of assessing reasonable physical discipline administered by parents;[68] personal autonomy to make decisions on matters pertaining to health;[69] and the stress and challenges entailed when a parent must engage in a legal proceeding in which the state seeks custody of his or her children.[70] These cases demonstrate the intertwining values of autonomy, personal security, familial privacy as well as the best interest of the child. These cases and others confirm that section 7 does not protect pure economic interests.

The rights set out in section 7 are conditioned on an inquiry as to whether their deprivation conforms to the principles of fundamental justice. The Court has derived these principles from common law norms and international conventions which, like the Charter, prioritise respect for the dignity and worth of the human person and the rule of law. These principles have deep roots in the justice system. They include the following precepts: the state must prove *mens rea* for the most serious crimes; the state must provide fair disclosure of its case to the accused; statutes may not be arbitrary or unfair; criminal defences must not be illusory; punishment must accord with the law at the time of the commission of the offence; trial process includes a right to cross-examine and a right against self-incrimination. These principles, which

[66] *United States v Burns* [2001] 1 SCR 283.

[67] *Chaoulli v Quebec* [2005] SCC 35, [2005] 1 SCR 791.

[68] *Canadian Foundation for Children, Youth and the Law v Canada (Attorney General)* [2004] SCC 4, [2004] 1 SCR 76.

[69] *Morgentaler* (n 36); *Rodriguez* (n 47).

[70] *New Brunswick (Minister of Health and Community Services) v G (J)* [1999] 3 SCR 46, 177 DLR (4th) 124. This is the rare case where the Court issued a remedy with financial implications, ruling that the state must pay for legal services for an indigent parent to participate in custody proceedings under child welfare legislation.

are both procedural and substantive, assure the fairness and legitimacy of the criminal justice system.

In the criminal law context, the Charter's legal guarantees have been invoked to restrict reverse onuses[71] and to predicate incarceration on proof of moral guilt.[72] These provisions were successfully invoked to challenge some of the more rigorous features of Canada's post-9/11 anti-terrorism laws, such as indefinite detention for non-citizens who cannot be deported due to reasonable apprehension of torture.[73] Special sentencing considerations operate to reduce incarceration for aboriginal Canadians, who are over-represented in the prison population due to historical deprivation and disadvantage resulting to a great extent from state neglect and discrimination.[74]

L. Equality

Canada's equality clause, section 15, protects against state discrimination, whether intentional or not, based on a number of grounds: race, national or ethnic origin, colour, religion, sex, age or mental or physical disability. The Charter deems these characteristics suspect considerations for state imposition of benefits or burdens, because they are not chosen, lie beyond the ability of individuals to alter without unreasonable financial or personal burden, and stand as important indicia of identity. Many relate to associations and choices that the state should neither control nor influence. The list of prohibited grounds of discrimination is open-ended. The Supreme Court has added a number of grounds analogous to those listed, including citizenship, marital status, sexual orientation and aboriginal place of residence.

The Charter's equality guarantee has precipitated a number of important rulings in regard to the family and sexuality, areas of social policy that reflected faith and culture in the pre-Charter period of legislative supremacy controlled by majoritarian politics. For example, the courts have equated common law relationships to marriage in most circumstances;[75] established equal treatment for gays and heterosexuals as individuals[76] and in

[71] *Oakes* (n 40).
[72] *BC Motor Vehicle Reference* [1985] 2 SCR 486.
[73] *Charkaoui* v *Canada* (*Citizenship and Immigration*) [2007] 1 SCR 350.
[74] *R v Gladue* [1999] 1 SCR 688.
[75] *Miron v Trudel* [1995] 2 SCR 418, 124 DLR (4th) 693. For qualifications that ensure that individuals remain at liberty to order their private lives as long as they do not impose disadvantage on their partners, see *Nova Scotia (Attorney General) v Walsh* [2002] 4 SCR 325, [2002] SCC 83; *Hodge v Canada (Minister of Human Resources Development)* [2004] SCC 65, [2004] 3 SCR 357.
[76] *Vriend* (n 12); *Canada (Attorney General) v Hislop* [2007] SCC 10, [2007] 1 SCR 429 [*Hislop*].

their intimate relationships and familial roles,[77] including civil marriage;[78] and rejected differential rules for the acquisition of citizenship based on the gender of the Canadian parent.[79]

Equality litigation has worked incrementally to eliminate religious morality, historical social privilege and arbitrary distinctions from public policy. The underlying principle or value of the equality guarantees is to ensure that every exercise of public power treat all citizens and residents as deserving of equal concern, respect and consideration, without stereotype, prejudice or exacerbation of vulnerability. Consistent with this objective is the Charter's recognition of the permissibility of affirmative action, which has legitimated programmes designed to provide special economic opportunities for aboriginal communities and for segments of these communities.

III. CONGRUENCE AND INCONGRUENCE

Within the framework of unwritten constitutional principles, the judiciary delineates fundamental norms and values applicable to the exercise of public power, often leaving the execution of particular policies to public bodies and officials. This approach vests enormous responsibility in the executive and the legislature to deliver the basic norms of the constitutional order. Unfortunately, the inherited norms of British parliamentary government do not ensure that legislatures operate free of the control of the executive. Canadian parliamentary government increasingly operates under executive control at both the federal and provincial levels of governance, including control over the sittings of the legislative bodies. In recent years, this power appears to have been abused by the federal government. It has adjourned Parliament in order to evade a vote of no confidence, in one instance, and to avoid debate on highly controversial exercises of state power, in another instance. The government of the province of Ontario, following this example, adjourned the legislature's proceedings to avoid the need to defend its controversial positions in labour negotiations with teachers' unions. Unfortunately, there is no recourse to the courts to object to such developments.

Under the Charter, enforcement of constitutional norms lies with the judiciary, which provides principled direction and remedies when it identifies an infringement of guaranteed rights and freedoms. Affected individuals and/or public interest groups litigate claims alleging that legislatures or state officials have failed to conform to their positive and negative duties under the Constitution. The judiciary also considers questions relating to constitutionality referred directly by the federal government and on appeal

[77] *M v H* [1999] 2 SCR 3, 171 DLR (4th) 577.
[78] *Halpern* (n 46).
[79] *Benner v Canada (Secretary of State)* [1997] 1 SCR 358.

from appellate court rulings of concern to provincial governments. In both concrete and abstract cases the courts may permit public interest groups to contribute perspectives and arguments that reflect the wider significance of the issues than presented by the parties to the litigation. The public interest group participation, as parties and interveners, helps to ensure that the judiciary remains attentive to the interests of the vulnerable, marginalised and disadvantaged sectors of Canadian society.

This is not to say that the judiciary is the sole guardian of constitutional principles and Charter guarantees. The ministries of justice at the federal and provincial levels vet all amendments and new legislation for conformity to the Constitution. These ministries respond to constitutional concerns by revising old and proposed legislation and defending or conceding constitutional challenges in the courts. Legislative bodies are also attentive to constitutional strictures. Their committees often invite constitutional experts to comment on draft legislation and legislative debate demonstrates the internalisation of constitutional strictures.

Nonetheless, while the Constitution frames the political system and constrains the exercise of public authority, Canadians in public and private life have differing views as to the meaning of constitutional text, the roles and duties of public institutions and the nature of fundamental constitutional norms. This divergence reflects differing views on the transformational purposes and effects of the Charter. National survey data indicates that the public supports the Constitution, the Charter and the constitutional work of the judiciary. The public has repudiated constitutional amendments to undermine the 1982 amendments. In contrast, the current Conservative majority government is critical of the Charter and the judicial role thereunder.

A key difficulty in determining the question of congruence with the Canadian text, as 30 years of Charter litigation reveals, is that there are significant divergences in the methodological approaches of various justices on the Supreme Court to the scope of the rights and freedoms, the justification of limitations on rights, and remedial measures. Justices who embrace the Charter's transformative purposes insist upon a normative reading of the rights; narrow, principled strictures for limitation that endorse the principles that inform the guarantees; and strong remedial orders. Other justices have introduced deference and reasonableness considerations—in effect reviving elements contained in rejected drafts of the Charter's text. The case law reproduced in the previous section does however, reveal certain clear instances of fidelity to the values of the text as divined in the early jurisprudence.

A. A Particular Canadian Solution

The final stages of the drafting of the Charter, which included public interest group participation and public support, produced the strongest formulations of the guarantees and the most principled version of the limitation clause under section 1. It also introduced a notwithstanding clause permitting legislative override of certain Charter rights. Section 33 embodied the views of the provincial premiers who had successfully blocked the Charter project to that date. Some premiers opposed the Charter project altogether, preferring to retain the British inheritance of legislative supremacy and the common law. Others protested at what they deemed to be excessive encroachment on the prerogatives of elected legislatures generally, or provincial legislatures in particular. There was also concern that rights protection would undermine legislative promotion of social and economic well-being.

Canada adopted a specific measure to respond to these concerns. Section 33 of the Charter empowers the federal and provincial legislatures by simple majority to expressly suppress the operation of selected rights and freedoms for a maximum, renewable period of five years. This duration coincides with the frequency of elections. This power applies to the fundamental freedoms, the legal rights and the equality rights, which were considered politically contentious, but not rights considered fully judiciable, ie the legal and mobility rights, language rights and aboriginal rights. The Supreme Court has added another caveat: retroactive invocation of the override power is impermissible.[80]

These features trigger so high a political price that politicians no longer consider the override a feasible option. It has only been invoked in a handful of instances, and has never been used by the federal government. In the aftermath of controversial judgments that radically altered social policy, such as the invalidation of Canada's criminal abortion prohibition and the legalisation of same-sex civil marriage, there was no invocation of the override power. This may be a sign that ordinary Canadians have internalised the Charter's values, principles and judicial mode of analysis, and expect their political representatives to do likewise.

The dormant override power is not without significance, however. It protects the institutional structure of rights protection by undermining criticism of judicial review as the usurpation of the prerogative of democratically representative and accountable legislatures. It is difficult for Charter rejectionists and critics to castigate judicial usurpation of the democratic function when our political representatives possess the authority by a simple majority to legislate prospectively to suppress the most controversial Charter guarantees for the duration of their term in office.

As one would expect, the judiciary's work under the Charter has displeased those who opposed its adoption or some of its more transformative elements, whether based on political ideology, cultural affiliations or religious beliefs. They support a conservative reading of rights and reasonableness-based

[80] *Ford* (n 29) [37]. See Lorraine Weinrib, 'Learning to Live With the Override' (1990) 36 *McGill Law Journal* 541.

deferential approaches to limitation on rights. It is difficult to determine the extent to which these views have affected the judiciary. Time will tell whether they have politicised the procedure for appointing senior justices.[81]

Charter supporters also register dissatisfaction with judicial review under the Charter. Some express disappointment in the Supreme Court's tendency to afford rights protection only prospective effect in the form of suspended declarations of invalidity that give governments time to remedy infringements. Prospective remedial orders undermine the incentive that governments would otherwise have to proactively amend legislation in the light of Supreme Court rulings, choose which challenges to defend, and concede positions within litigation. Others find fault with the judicial preference that Charter rulings have minimal impact on fiscal and budgetary planning. Still others express disappointment in the judiciary's failure to protect social and economic rights. Perhaps the most bitter of Charter supporters are those who find fault with the Supreme Court's failure to accord women's equality the priority that the hard-won strictures of section 15 and section 28 were designed to secure. In addition, a few cases suggest judicial reluctance to acknowledge blatant failings of governments to live up to their duties under the Charter.[82]

Charter litigation is the process by which the Constitution's basic norms are affirmed. Many of the leading Charter cases derived funding from the Court Challenges Program, a federally funded programme that gave small amounts of money to individuals and public interest groups to prepare and argue meritorious Charter cases asserting equality and language rights. Some of this funding supported interventions by public interest groups. The total annual budget of this programme was about $6 million. It was cancelled once by a Conservative government, and then reinstated when an election returned to power the Liberal Party, which had championed the adoption of the Charter in 1982. Recently, the incumbent Conservative government cancelled the programme again. The Liberals have promised to re-establish it, but are unlikely to form a government in the near future.

There are other ways to fund Charter litigation, such as preliminary orders placing the financial burden of meritorious litigation on the government. The Court does not regard this type of funding as a means of supporting Charter litigation. Since Charter rights do not favour the rich, the political

[81] *Reference re Supreme Court Act, ss 5 and 6* [2014] SCR 433. The Supreme Court invalidated the appointment of Marc Nadon, a justice of the Federal Court, to the Supreme Court of Canada, to one of the seats designated for Quebec. The reasons for the judgment are based on statutory interpretation, but the context of the appointment included strong criticism that the Conservative Government was using its appointing power to ensure greater success in Charter litigation.

[82] *Little Sisters Book and Art Emporium v Canada (Minister of Justice)* [2000] SCC 69, [2000] 2 SCR 1120; *Little Sisters Book and Art Emporium v Canada (Commissioner of Customs and Revenue)* [2007] SCC 2, [2007] 1 SCR 38; *Hislop* (n 76).

elite or the socially powerful, it seems appropriate for the state to fund cases of high merit where funding is unavailable. After all, the state uses public funds to defend these cases, brought to ascertain the extent to which the state has complied with its duties under the supreme law of the land. Given the Charter's transformative agenda, it makes sense for the judiciary to impose costs on the government to ensure that it is proactive in constitutional compliance and reluctant to defend cases where the challenge is meritorious.

In summary, constitutional litigation has effected an intensive transformation of the Canadian political and legal landscape. As time passes, it appears that the general public as well as the political class have internalised the constitutional norms that underpin the Charter as well as the larger framework of the Canadian constitutional order. It is to be hoped that this process of internalisation will continue, eventually rendering the executive and legislative branches of government as important as the judiciary in the affirmation and development of constitutional norms.

5

Constitutions and Values in Three Chinese Societies

ALBERT HY CHEN

I. INTRODUCTION

IN THIS BOOK, the lens of constitutions and constitutional jurisprudence is used to enquire into the values of different societies and the possible existence of universal values. Conversely, and at the same time, the lens of values is also being used to view constitutional texts and constitutional jurisprudence. This chapter focuses on the constitutional texts of three Chinese societies—mainland China, Taiwan, and Hong Kong. The constitutional texts concerned are the Constitution of the People's Republic of China (1982, with subsequent amendments), the Constitution of the Republic of China (1946, with subsequent amendments) that is in force in Taiwan today, and the Basic Law of the Hong Kong Special Administrative Region of the People's Republic of China (1990). Given space limitations, the Basic Law of the Macau Special Administrative Region (the only other special administrative region in China with its own Basic Law, or 'mini-constitution') will not be covered, but it may be noted that it is very similar in content to the Hong Kong Basic Law.[1]

This chapter consists of the following sections. In section II, we examine the historical and ideological contexts in which the three constitutional texts were enacted. The political system of the three societies concerned will be then be described, with particular reference to the roles of legislative and judicial institutions in the implementation of the Constitution in each respective society. Section III briefly describes the nature of the political systems of the three Chinese societies concerned. In section IV, we explore how each of the relevant values covered in this book project is expressed, embedded or reflected in each of the constitutional texts. Section V deals with the questions of the prioritisation of different values and the degree

[1] See, eg, Yash Ghai, 'The Basic Law of the Special Administrative Region of Macau: Some Reflections' (2000) 49 *International and Comparative Law Quarterly* 183.

of congruence between constitutionally proclaimed values and social and political reality. Finally, section VI provides some concluding reflections on constitutions and values in mainland China, Taiwan and Hong Kong.

II. HISTORICAL AND IDEOLOGICAL CONTEXTS

In this section, we shall study the historical and ideological contexts in which the three constitutional texts were originally enacted and subsequently revised. Following the chronological order of the original enactments, we shall begin with the Constitution of the Republic of China (ROC) that was originally enacted in 1946 and that is still largely in force in Taiwan today. Then we shall move to the Constitution of the People's Republic of China (PRC), and then to the Basic Law of the Hong Kong Special Administrative Region (HKSAR).

A. The ROC Constitution

The historical origins of the ROC Constitution can only be understood in light of modern Chinese constitutional history,[2] which begins with the collapse of the Qing Empire—the last dynasty of imperial China—in the 1911 Revolution.[3] The establishment of the new Republic of China (ROC) was proclaimed in 1912. In the first one and a half decades of the republican era, China was beset by warlordism and civil strife. In 1928, Chiang Kai-shek, leader of the Chinese Nationalist Party (Kuomintang, or KMT), founded by Dr Sun Yat-sen, succeeded in defeating the warlords and established a national government of the ROC with its capital in Nanking. However, civil war continued between the KMT and the Chinese Communist Party (or CCP, founded in 1921), until the 'Xi'an Incident' of 1936, after which Chiang and the Communists (who had by that time retreated to the remote town of Yanan, in Shaanxi Province) entered into an alliance in order to face the threat of Japanese invasion.

The KMT's approach to constitutional development was based on Sun Yat-sen's three-stage programme for China's political transformation.[4] The first stage was military government (*junzheng*), for the purpose of ending

[2] See generally Pan Wei-tung, *The Chinese Constitution: A Study of Forty Years of Constitution-Making in China* (Westport CT, Hyperion Press, 1983); Ch'ien Tuan-sheng, *The Government and Politics of China 1912–1949* (Cambridge MA, Harvard University Press, 1950).

[3] On modern Chinese history, see, eg, John K Fairbank, *The Great Chinese Revolution 1800–1985* (New York, Harper & Row, 1987); Immanuel CY Hsü, *The Rise of Modern China* (Oxford, Oxford University Press, 2000).

[4] See, eg, ECY Tseng, 'Democratic and Authoritarian Elements in Twentieth-Century Chinese Political Thought' (unpublished PhD thesis, New York University, 1968) 72ff; CC Tan, *Chinese Political Thought in the Twentieth Century* (Newton Abbot, David & Charles, 1972).

warlordism and unifying the country. The second was preparation for constitutional democracy under the KMT's political tutelage (*xunzheng*). The third and final stage would be constitutional government (*xianzheng*). Thus Chiang's government promulgated a provisional constitution in 1931 known as the Constitution of the ROC in the Period of Political Tutelage (*Zhonghua minguo xunzheng shiqi yuefa*), which expressly vested political power in the KMT.[5]

After the end of the Second World War and before civil war erupted again between the KMT and the CCP, a formal Constitution of the ROC was adopted by a constituent assembly convened by the KMT in December 1946.[6] The original purpose of this Constitution was to move China from the stage of political tutelage by the KMT, to full liberal constitutional democracy with a constitutional government based on the separation of powers, elected by free multi-party election and respectful of civil liberties and human rights. Article 1 of this Constitution declares: 'The Republic of China, founded on the Three Principles of the People, shall be a democratic republic of the people, to be governed by the people and for the people.' The Three Principles of the People, developed by Dr Sun Yat-sen, represented the KMT's ideology. They are the Principle of People's National Consciousness (*minzu*), the Principle of People's Rights (*minquan*) and the Principle of People's Livelihood (*minsheng*).[7]

Although the 1946 ROC Constitution contains provisions on separation of powers, checks and balances, free elections and the guarantee of human rights, these provisions were largely suspended as a result of the ensuing events.[8] China descended into a state of civil war, and in April 1948 the KMT-led National Assembly introduced a constitutional amendment known as the 'Temporary Provisions for the Period of National Mobilisation to Suppress the Communist Rebellion' (the 'Temporary Provisions'), which expanded the emergency powers of the President. *Jieyan* (which may be translated as a state of siege, or martial law) was declared by the KMT government in December 1948 in mainland China, and in May 1949 in Taiwan (Taiwan was recovered from the Japanese at the end of the Second

[5] See Pan (n 2 above). For the original Chinese text of this consitution and other twentieth-century Chinese constitutions up to 1978, see Chen Hefu (ed), *Zhongguo xianfa leibian* (*Collection of Chinese Constitutions*) (Beijing, Chinese Academy of Social Sciences Press, 1980).

[6] See generally Jing Jiren, *Zhongguo lixian shi* [*History of Chinese Constitutionalism*] (Taipei, Lianjing, 1984) ch 16; Chen Xinmin, *Xianfaxue shilun* [*Constitutional Law*], 5th edn (Taipei, Sanmin, 2005) ch 1.

[7] See the works cited in n 4 above, and Hsü (n 3 above) 459.

[8] See generally Hungdah Chiu, 'Constitutional Development in the Republic of China in Tawian' in Steve Tsang(ed), *In the Shadow of China: Political Developments in Taiwan Since 1949* (Hong Kong, Hong Kong University Press, 1993) ch 1; Chi-tung Lin and Herbert HP Ma, 'The Republic of China (Taiwan)' in Lawrence W Beer (ed), *Constitutional Systems in Late Twentieth Century Asia* (Seattle WA, University of Washington Press, 1992) 88ff; Chen (n 6 above) ch 14.

World War, after the island had experienced half a century of Japanese colonial rule). After its defeat by the Communist forces in the mainland, the KMT government retreated to Taiwan in 1949.[9]

It was not until July 1987 that the *jieyan* (martial law) decree was finally lifted by President Chiang Ching-kuo, son of Chiang Kai-shek. A new era of liberalisation and democratisation was thus inaugurated in Taiwan.[10] In 1991, the National Assembly repealed the Temporary Provisions, and introduced the first of a series of constitutional amendments known as the additional articles to the ROC Constitution. Since then, a total of six sets of further amendments have been introduced, in 1992, 1994, 1997, 1999, 2000 and 2005 respectively,[11] with the 1999 amendment invalidated by Taiwan's constitutional court, the Council of Grand Justices.

B. The PRC Constitution

After defeating the KMT forces, the CCP established the new People's Republic of China (PRC) in October 1949.[12] For the first few years of the regime, China was governed by a provisional constitution known as the 'Common Programme of the Chinese People's Political Consultative Conference'. The first Constitution of the PRC was adopted by a new National People's Congress in 1954[13] and was to a considerable extent modelled on the 1936 Constitution of the USSR,[14] although the ROC Constitution was included among the reference materials compiled for some of those involved in the drafting exercise.[15] The second Constitution was enacted in 1975 at a time when the PRC was under the 'ultra-leftist' rule that began with the

[9] On the history of Taiwan, see generally Murray A Rubinstein (ed), *Taiwan: A New History* (Armonk NY, ME Sharpe, 1999); John F Copper, *Taiwan: Nation-State or Province?*, 3rd edn (Boulder CO, Westview Press, 1999); Denny Roy, *Taiwan: A Political History* (Ithaca NY, Cornell University Press, 2003).

[10] See the works cited in n 9 above, and Linda Chao and Ramon H Myers, *The First Chinese Democracy: Political Life in the Republic of China on Taiwan* (Baltimore MD, Johns Hopkins University Press, 1998).

[11] See generally Chen (n 6 above) ch 14; Xie Zhengdao, *Zhonghua minguo xiuxian shi* [*The History of Constitutional Revisions in the Republic of China*], 2nd edn (Taipei, Yangzhi wenhua, 2007).

[12] On the history of the PRC, see generally the works cited in n 3 above, and Jonathan Fenby, *The Penguin History of Modern China: The Fall and Rise of a Great Power, 1850–2008* (London, Allen Lane, 2008).

[13] On the constitutional history of the PRC, see Xu Chongde, *Zhonghua renmin gongheguo xianfa shi* [*Constitutional History of the People's Republic of China*](Fuzhou, Fujian People's Press, 2003).

[14] Albert HY Chen, 'Socialist Law, Civil Law, Common Law, and the Classification of Contemporary Chinese Law', in JM Otto et al (eds), *Law-Making in the People's Republic of China* (The Hague, Kluwer Law International, 2000) 55, 57.

[15] Cai Dingjian, *Xianfa jingjie* [*Commentary on the Constitution*], 2nd edn (Beijing, Law Press, 2006) 33.

launch of the 'Great Proletarian Cultural Revolution' in 1966. The third Constitution, introduced two years after Mao Zedong's death in 1976, was a product of the period of transition between the ultra-leftist ideology and the new orientation of 'socialist modernisation' and 'reform and opening'. The fourth Constitution, which (subject to several amendments) is still in force today, was enacted in 1982 and has since served as the constitutional embodiment of Deng Xiaoping's ideology of 'socialism with Chinese characteristics'.

The 1982 Constitution was drafted using the 1954 Constitution as the baseline and seeking to improve upon it. The 'Four Cardinal Principles' advocated by Deng Xiaoping were often referred to as forming a key ingredient of the guiding ideology behind the 1982 Constitution.[16] Deng had stated that adherence to these four principles was essential for the purpose of pursuing China's economic modernisation.[17] The four principles are insisting on the socialist path, insisting on the people's democratic dictatorship, insisting on the CCP's leadership, and insisting on Marxism-Leninism-Mao Zedong Thought (subsequently revised to include Deng Xiaoping Theory and the idea of the 'three represents').[18] These principles may be discerned from a passage in the Preamble to the 1982 Constitution.[19]

Article 1 of the PRC Constitution states that 'The PRC is a socialist state under the people's democratic dictatorship led by the working class and based on the alliance of workers and peasants. The socialist system is the basic system of the PRC.' 'People's democratic dictatorship' is a term coined by Mao Zedong for the purpose of the indigenous application of the Marxist concept of 'proletarian dictatorship' which is to be practised after the socialist revolution overthrowing capitalism. The leadership of the working class mentioned in article 1 of the Constitution is an implicit reference to the leadership of the CCP, as under the Leninist theory of the communist party, this party consists of the vanguard of the proletariat (ie, the working class) and shall exercise leadership on behalf of the proletariat in building a socialist society.

Since the 1982 Constitution was enacted, four sets of amendments to it have been introduced, in 1988, 1993, 1999 and 2004 respectively. The amendments reflect the deepening and strengthening of the policy of 'reform and opening', and include, for example, the introduction of the following terms and concepts into the Constitution: the preliminary stage of socialism, socialism with Chinese characteristics, the socialist market economy, protecting the private sector of the economy, ruling the country according to

[16] Cai (n 15 above) 73, 81, 84, 99; Xu (n 13 above) 878 (citing Peng Zhen's speech to the National People's Congress when the draft constitution was presented to it).

[17] Cai (n 15 above) 73.

[18] Albert HY Chen, *An Introduction to the Legal System of the People's Republic of China*, 4th edn (Hong Kong, LexisNexis, 2011) 57–58.

[19] See the para 7 of the Preamble.

law, and building a socialist *Rechtsstaat* (*fazhiguojia* in Chinese, or a state based on the rule of law), and protecting human rights and private property rights.

C. The Basic Law of the HKSAR

The Basic Law of the HKSAR is sometimes called Hong Kong's 'mini-constitution':[20] it is a constitutional instrument providing for what legal, political, economic and social systems the HKSAR should practise under the framework of 'one country, two systems' (OCTS) for the autonomy of Hong Kong as part of the PRC. The concept of OCTS was developed by Deng Xiaoping in the late 1970s, originally for the purpose of achieving peaceful reunification with Taiwan.[21] However, the PRC decided to apply this concept as a solution to the question of Hong Kong's future constitutional status when the question was raised by British Prime Minister Margaret Thatcher before Chinese leaders when she visited Beijing in 1982. After nearly two years of strenuous negotiations between the two governments, the Sino-British Joint Declaration on the Question of Hong Kong was concluded in September 1984.[22]

This treaty provided for the return of the colony of Hong Kong—created and subsequently expanded in three stages by three treaties between the Qing Empire and the British Empire in the nineteenth century[23]—to the PRC in July 1997. In the treaty, the PRC made various undertakings as regards how Hong Kong would be governed as a Special Administrative Region of the PRC after 1997. For example, the HKSAR would enjoy a high degree of autonomy, with 'Hong Kong people ruling Hong Kong'. Hong Kong would be allowed to retain its existing social and economic systems. The existing laws of Hong Kong would remain basically unchanged; civil liberties, human rights and private property rights would continue to be respected and protected.

The Joint Declaration also provided that the PRC's policies towards the HKSAR, as stated in the Joint Declaration, would be stipulated in a Basic

[20] See Peter Wesley-Smith and Albert Chen (eds), *The Basic Law and Hong Kong's Future* (Hong Kong, Butterworths, 1988).

[21] See generally Albert HY Chen, 'The Concept of "One Country, Two Systems" and Its Application to Hong Kong' in C Stephen Hsu (ed), *Understanding China's Legal System: Essays in Honor of Jerome A Cohen* (New York, New York University Press, 2003) ch 9.

[22] See generally Steve Tsang, *Hong Kong: An Appointment with China* (London, IB Tauris, 1997).

[23] On Hong Kong's history, see GB Endacott, *A History of Hong Kong*, 2nd edn (Hong Kong, Oxford University Press, 1964); Frank Welsh, *A History of Hong Kong* (London, HarperCollins, 1993); Steve Tsang, *A Modern History of Hong Kong* (Hong Kong, Hong Kong University Press, 2004).

Law of the HKSAR and would remain unchanged for 50 years. Such a Basic Law was enacted by the National People's Congress of the PRC in 1990.[24] It came into force on 1 July 1997, when the colony finally achieved reunification with China, and the HKSAR was formally established.

III. THE POLITICAL SYSTEMS CONCERNED

Constitutional documents of states establish the political systems of the states concerned. At the same time, they function within and in the context of, and depend on, such political systems which determine to what extent a constitution is meaningful and significant in practice—for example, whether it is, in Loewenstein's words, a 'nominal', 'semantic' or 'normative' constitution.[25] A nominal constitution does not even correspond to the reality of the political system at all and is no more than words on paper. A semantic constitution does tell us something about the political system and how it operates, but plays no significant role in controlling the behaviour of political actors. A normative constitution determines who holds power, and truly regulates the exercise of power and the relationship between the holders of power; their normative force is internalised by political actors who take the rules stipulated in the constitution seriously, respect them and abide by them. In this section, we shall describe briefly the nature of the political systems of the three Chinese societies concerned.

A. Taiwan

Since the island's liberalisation and democratisation in the late 1980s and 1990s, Taiwan's political system has come close to systems in Western liberal constitutional democratic states.[26] There has been free electoral competition for the office of the Presidency and for seats in parliamentary institutions among different political parties and activists. A two-party system has emerged, with the KMT and the Democratic Progressive Party (DPP) being the dominant parties. The KMT, which had ruled Taiwan ever since the island's return from Japan to the ROC in 1945, handed over power peacefully to the DPP after its defeat in the presidential election of 2000. In 2008, the KMT was back in power, with its leader Ma Ying-jeou elected as President of the ROC.

[24] See generally Yash Ghai, *Hong Kong's New Constitutional Order: The Resumption of Chinese Sovereignty and the Basic Law*, 2nd edn (Hong Kong, Hong Kong University Press, 1999).

[25] Karl Loewenstein, *Political Power and the Government Process* (Chicago IL, University of Chicago Press, 1957) 147–53.

[26] See n 10 above.

The ROC Constitution of 1946 established a constitutional court known as the Council of Grand Justices (CGJ) of the Judicial Yuan, charged with the task of issuing authoritative interpretations of the Constitution. Following the ROC government's retreat to Taiwan, the CGJ gradually built up a record of judicial interpretations and thus also of institutional capacity and judicial authority.[27] Most of the early judicial interpretations dealt with technical jurisdictional issues of separation of powers, rather than citizens' rights. Although the CGJ had the power of constitutional review of laws, regulations and decrees, it did not exercise this power in practice until 1980.[28] Before the late 1980s, the CGJ, because of its unimpressive record in dealing with several politically sensitive cases, was not perceived as a strong and independent guardian of constitutional norms and rights, but was regarded by some as an accomplice of the authoritarian regime, merely giving constitutional legitimacy to it.[29]

The image of the CGJ began to change for the better in the second half of the 1980s. The CGJ became more activist and more willing to exercise its power of constitutional review of legislative and administrative acts.[30] In 1990, the CGJ had the opportunity to prove its importance and establish its authority when it considered the question of the re-election of the parliamentary institutions[31] (the majority of whose members were still those elected in mainland China in the late 1940s, and whose seats had not been subject to periodic elections because in theory the parliamentary institutions still represented the whole of China and yet it had not been possible to hold elections on the mainland since 1949). In the famous and celebrated Interpretation No 261,[32] the CGJ in effect ordered fresh elections in Taiwan for the whole of the parliamentary institutions. Since this interpretation, the CGJ has issued many more interpretations on questions of citizens' rights

[27] See generally Chang Wen-chen, 'Transition to Democracy, Constitutionalism and Judicial Activism: Taiwan in Comparative Constitutional Perspective' (unpublished SJD dissertation, Yale University, 2001).

[28] See Albert HY Chen, 'A Tale of Two Islands: Comparative Reflections on Constitutionalism in Hong Kong and Taiwan' (2007) 37 *Hong Kong Law Journal* 647, 676.

[29] See, eg, Jau-yuan Hwang and Jiunn-rong Yeh, 'Taiwan' in Cheryl Saunders and Graham Hassall (eds), *Asia-Pacific Constitutional Yearbook 1995* (Melbourne, Centre for Comparative Constitutional Studies, University of Melbourne, 1997) 279, 282–86; Tsung-fu Chen, 'The Role of Law in Taiwan: Culture, Ideology, and Social Change' in Hsu (n 21 above) 374, 383–84.

[30] See generally Lawrence Shao-liang Liu, 'Judicial Review and Emerging Constitutionalism: The Uneasy Case for the Republic of China on Taiwan' (1991) 39 *American Journal of Comparative Law* 509; Jyh-pin Fa, 'Constitutional Developments in Taiwan: The Role of the Council of Grand Justices' (1991) 40 *International and Comparative Law Quarterly* 198.

[31] The major parliamentary institutions included the National Assembly and the Legislative Yuan.

[32] For the CGJ's interpretations, see its website www.judicial.gov.tw/constitutionalcourt.

and separation of powers that have collectively rebuilt the CGJ's reputation as a credible, respected and activist constitutional court.[33]

B. The PRC

Unlike the case of Taiwan, the PRC in mainland China is still a one-party state. Since the Dengist era of 'reform and opening' began in the late 1970s, China has moved a long way from a totalitarian communist system in which the Party-State controlled all social and economic domains and all aspects of citizens' lives, to an authoritarian political system that has committed itself to certain standards of legality[34] and has fostered the development of a vibrant 'socialist market economy' or 'socialism with Chinese characteristics' (or what some outside observers have called 'capitalism with Chinese characteristics'),[35] which in turn has sustained the rapid growth of domains of private and economic life outside the direct control of the Party-State.

In theory, the 'supreme organ of state power'[36] in the PRC is the National People's Congress, which is elected by the provincial people's congresses, which in turn are elected by municipal people's congresses. The municipal people's congresses are elected by the county-level people's congresses, and these are directly elected by the people. In practice, candidature of the higher-level people's congresses is determined by CCP bodies, and the National People's Congress is largely a rubber-stamp body under the leadership of the CCP.[37]

In the PRC, the principal means by which the Constitution is implemented is the making and enforcement of laws in accordance with the Constitution.[38]

[33] See generally Chen (n 28 above); Thomas Weishing Huang, 'Judicial Activism in the Transitional Polity: The Council of Grand Justices in Taiwan' (2005) 19 *Temple International and Comparative Law Journal* 1; Wen-chen Chang, 'The Role of Judicial Review in Consolidating Democracies: The Case of Taiwan' (2005) 2 *Asia Law Review* 73; Sean Conney, 'A Community Changes: Taiwan's Council of Grand Justices and Liberal Democratic Reform' in Kanishka Jayasuriya (ed), *Law, Capitalism and Power in Asia: The Rule of Law and Legal Institutions* (London, Routledge, 1999) ch 11; Tom Ginsburg, *Judicial Review in New Democracies: Constitutional Courts in Asian Cases* (Cambridge, Cambridge University Press, 2003) ch 5.

[34] See, eg, Albert HY Chen, 'Toward a Legal Enlightenment: Discussions in Contemporary China on the Rule of Law' (1999) 17 *UCLA Pacific Basin Law Journal* 125; Randall Peerenboom, *China's Long March Toward Rule of Law* (Cambridge, Cambridge University Press, 2002).

[35] Yasheng Huang, *Capitalism with Chinese Characteristics: Entrepreneurship and the State* (Cambridge, Cambridge University Press, 2008).

[36] Constitution of the PRC (1982), art 57.

[37] See generally Jiang Jinsong, *The National People's Congress of China* (Beijing, Foreign Languages Press, 2003), esp ch 7; Li Fan (ed), *Renda daibiao xuanju caozong neimu* [*Insider Story of Manipulation of Elections of Deputies to People's Congresses*] (Hong Kong, Xiafei'er Press, 2009); Yang Guangbin and Li Yuejun, *Dangdai Zhongguo zhengzhi zhidu daolun* [*Introduction to the Contemporary Chinese Political System*](Beijing, China Renmin University Press, 2007), esp ch 4.

[38] Zhang Qianfan (ed), *Xianfa* [*Constitutional Law*] (Beijing, Peking University Press, 2008), ch 3.

In the era of 'reform and opening', the court system has developed rapidly in terms of size, case load and the educational qualifications and professionalisation of judges,[39] but it has also been beset with problems of corruption, political interference in judicial decision-making and failure to enforce court judgments in civil cases.[40] The constitutional function of the Chinese courts is to try cases in accordance with the law.[41] They have no role to play in interpreting the Constitution or reviewing the constitutionality of legal norms and administrative actions.[42] In 2001, the Supreme People's Court's interpretation in the much publicised *Qi Yuling* case seemed to suggest that Chinese courts may apply constitutional provisions directly in adjudicating cases,[43] but the repeal by the Supreme People's Court itself of this interpretation, in December 2008,[44] signalled that courts would no longer be permitted to rely on or refer to provisions of the Constitution in their adjudicative work.

C. The HKSAR

English common law, together with the English tradition of the rule of law and judicial independence, was transplanted to Hong Kong in the colonial era.[45] However, British parliamentary democracy was never exported to the colony of Hong Kong, which until 1997 was governed by Governors appointed directly by London.[46] Before democratisation began in the mid-1980s,

[39] See, eg, Bin Liang, *The Changing Chinese Legal System, 1978–Present* (New York, Routledge, 2008) ch 3; Zhu Jingwen (ed), *Zhongguo falü fazhan baogao* [*Chinese Legal Development Report*] (Beijing, China Renmin University Press, 2007) chs 1, 4.

[40] See, eg, Chen (n 18 above) ch 7; Hualing Fu, 'Putting China's Judiciary into Perspective, Is It Independent, Competent, and Fair?' in Erik G Jensen and Thomas C Heller (eds), *Beyond Common Knowledge, Empirical Approaches to the Rule of Law* (Stanford CT, Stanford University Press, 2003) ch 6; Benjamin L Liebman, 'China's Courts, Restricted Reform' (2007) 191 *China Quarterly* 620; Xin He, 'The Recent Decline in Economic Caseloads in Chinese Courts, Exploration of a Surprising Puzzle' (2007) 190 *China Quarterly* 352.

[41] See art 126 of the PRC Constitution (1982).

[42] Tong Zhiwei, 'The Constitution Should be Applied in Accordance with the Provisions of the Constitution Itself' [2008] 6 *Zhongguo faxue* [*Chinese Legal Science*] 22; Zhang (n 38 above) 464–66; Hu Jinguang and Han Dayuan, *Zhongguo xianfa* [*Chinese Constitutional Law*], 2nd edn (Beijing, Law Press 2007) 162–66.

[43] See Kui Shen, 'Is It the Beginning of the Era of the Rule of the Constitution? Reinterpreting China's "First Constitutional Case"' (2003) 12 *Pacific Rim Law and Policy Journal* 199; Qianfan Zhang, 'From Administrative Rule of Law to Constitutionalism? The Changing Perspectives of the Chinese Public Law' (2006) 3 *Asia Law Review* 47, esp 70–73.

[44] See the forum on this subject in [2009] 3 *Faxue* [*Legal Science Monthly*] 3–35. For discussion in English, see Thomas E Kellogg, 'The Constitution in the Courtroom: Constitutional Development and Civil Litigation in China' in Margaret Y K Woo and Mary Gallagher (eds), *Chinese Justice*: *Civil Dispute Resolution in Contemporary China* (Cambridge, Cambridge University Press, 2011) ch 11.

[45] See generally Peter Wesley-Smith, *An Introduction to the Hong Kong Legal System* (Hong Kong, Oxford University Press, 1987); Peter Wesley-Smith, *Constitutional and Administrative Law in Hong Kong* (Hong Kong, Longman Asia, 1995).

[46] On the political system of colonial Hong Kong, see Norman Miners, *The Government and Politics of Hong Kong*, 4th edn (Hong Kong, Oxford University Press, 1986).

the political system of Hong Kong might be described as an 'administrative no-party state',[47] a 'bureaucratic polity',[48] or a benign and enlightened authoritarianism.[49] After the Sino-British Joint Declaration was signed in 1984, the British began efforts to introduce a 'representative government' in Hong Kong.[50] This was done mainly by introducing elected seats in the colonial legislature—the Legislative Council.[51] In 1991, in response to the crisis of confidence in Hong Kong's future, resulting from China's brutal suppression of the student movement in Beijing in spring 1989, the colonial government introduced the Hong Kong Bill of Rights Ordinance, which basically reproduced and imported into Hong Kong's domestic law the provisions of the International Covenant on Civil and Political Rights that Britain had already made applicable to Hong Kong in 1976.[52] The Hong Kong Bill of Rights Ordinance, when read together with the corresponding amendment to Hong Kong's colonial constitution introduced at the same time as the enactment of the Bill of Rights, empowered the courts to review and to strike down laws that were inconsistent with the human rights guarantees in the Hong Kong Bill of Rights. The era of constitutional judicial review thus began in Hong Kong.[53]

Since 1997, the Hong Kong courts have continued to exercise the power of constitutional review, which in the post-1997 era has been based on the Basic Law of the HKSAR instead of the colonial constitution. The Basic Law contains elaborate provisions on the protection of civil liberties and human rights. It also incorporates by reference the International Covenant on Civil and Political Rights (ICCPR) and the International Covenant on Economic, Social and Cultural Rights. The Hong Kong judiciary, led by its new Court of Final Appeal, established in 1997 to replace the Privy Council in London as the final appellate court for Hong Kong, has been fairly liberal and has practised

[47] Peter Harris, *Hong Kong, A Study in Bureaucracy and Politics* (Hong Kong, Macmillan, 1988) ix.

[48] Lau Siu-kai, *Society and Politics in Hong Kong* (Hong Kong, Chinese University Press, 1984) 25.

[49] Lau Siu-kai and Kuan Hsin-chi, *The Ethos of the Hong Kong Chinese* (Hong Kong, Chinese University Press, 1988) 28.

[50] See generally Lo Shiu-hing, *The Politics of Democratization in Hong Kong* (Basingstoke and London, Macmillan Press, 1997); Alvin Y So, *Hong Kong's Embattled Democracy* (Baltimore MD, Johns Hopkins University Press, 1999).

[51] See Kathleen Cheek-Milby, *A Legislature Comes of Age, Hong Kong's Search for Influence and Identity* (Hong Kong, Oxford University Press, 1995).

[52] See, eg, Albert HY Chen, 'The Interpretation of the Basic Law, Common Law and Mainland Chinese Perspectives' (2000) 30 *Hong Kong Law Journal* 380, 418–20.

[53] See generally Yash Ghai, 'Sentinels of Liberty or Sheep in Wolf's Clothing? Judicial Politics and the Hong Kong Bill of Rights' (1997) 60 *Modern Law Review* 459; Andrew Byrnes, 'And Some Have Bills of Rights Thrust Upon Them, The Experience of Hong Kong's Bill of Rights' in Philip Alston (ed), *Promoting Human Rights Through Bills of Rights, Comparative Perspectives* (Oxford, Oxford University Press, 2000) ch 9.

a certain degree of judicial activism in constitutional review.[54] The Hong Kong courts are well respected and trusted by the people of Hong Kong.

As regards the political system of the HKSAR, it may be described as a 'semi-democracy'.[55] Half of the seats in the Legislative Council are now returned by universal suffrage in free elections in which all political parties and actors may participate. The other half are elected by functional constituencies, consisting largely of business and professional groups (such as members of chambers of commerce and of industrialists' federations, banks, lawyers, doctors, teachers, etc). The Chief Executive of the HKSAR (the most senior political office, equivalent to the Governor in colonial times) is elected by a 1200–member electoral college (whose members are largely elected from the functional constituencies) and appointed by Beijing. The political spectrum in the HKSAR consists of 'pro-China' political parties (such as the Democratic Alliance for the Betterment and Progress of Hong Kong, and the Liberal Party) and 'pro-democracy' political parties (such as the Democratic Party and the Civic Party). The 'pro-democracy' parties constitute the 'political opposition' in the legislature, in which there has been a majority of pro-government members since the establishment of the HKSAR in 1997.[56]

IV. VALUES IN THE THREE CONSTITUTIONAL TEXTS

We now begin to explore the values in the constitutional texts of Taiwan, mainland China and Hong Kong. The approach used here is to discuss each relevant value in the context of the three constitutional texts, drawing comparisons between them where appropriate. The focus in this section of the chapter is on the language and provisions of the constitutional texts. Questions of the actual implementation of the provisions in practice will be addressed in section V.

A. Life

There is no express provision on the value of life in the PRC Constitution (PRCC).[57] By contrast, the ROC Constitution (ROCC) provides that the

[54] See generally Albert HY Chen, 'Constitutional Adjudication in Post-1997 Hong Kong' (2006) 15 *Pacific Rim Law and Policy Journal* 627.

[55] William H Overholt, 'Hong Kong, The Perils of Semidemocracy' (2001) 12(4) *Journal of Democracy* 5; Ma Ngok, *Political Development in Hong Kong, State, Political Society, and Civil Society* (Hong Kong, Hong Kong University Press, 2007) 226.

[56] See generally Albert HY Chen, 'Development of Representative Government' in Johannes Chan and C L Lim (eds), *Law of the Hong Kong Constitution* (Hong Kong, Sweet & Maxwell, 2011) ch 8.

[57] The relatively widespread use of the death penalty in mainland China has long been of concern to human rights activists in the international community. See, eg, Liang (n 39 above) 92–95. The PRC government has not released any figures regarding capital punishment cases.

people's right to life (*shengcunquan*, alternatively translated as the 'right of existence') shall be protected. The right to life is not mentioned in the Hong Kong Basic Law (HKBL), but is provided for in the ICCPR[58] which, as mentioned above, has been incorporated by reference into the HKBL. In the following discussion of values in the HKBL, the ICCPR will be referred to where relevant as if it were part of the HKBL.

B. Dignity

The term 'dignity' (*zunyan*) appears in both the PRCC and ROCC, and also in the ICCPR (as applied in the HKSAR). The PRCC provides that the 'personal dignity' (*renge zunyan*, alternatively translated as 'the dignity of the human personality') of citizens shall not be violated.[59] The ROCC (in its additional articles) refers to dignity in the context of the protection of women's rights, and provides that the state shall protect the personal dignity of women.[60] The ICCPR in its preamble affirms 'the inherent dignity of the human person' as the source of human rights.

C. Security

Security as a value affirmed in the three constitutional texts is reflected in provisions on the maintenance of social order and its protection from external aggression. The PRCC provides that the state shall maintain public order and punish crimes,[61] and that the armed forces shall be responsible for national defence;[62] citizens are under a duty to safeguard the security of the motherland,[63] to defend the motherland against invasion and to perform military service in accordance with law.[64] Similarly, the ROCC provides that the objective of the ROC's national defence is to safeguard national security;[65] the people are under a duty to perform military service in accordance with law.[66] It may also be noted that the ROCC in additional

[58] Art 6 of the ICCPR.

[59] This provision did not exist in the previous constitutions of the PRC and was introduced for the first time in 1982. It was largely a response to the trauma of the Cultural Revolution, in which countless persons were purged as rightists and counter-revolutionaries, cruelly treated physically and publicly humiliated; see Cai (n 15 above) 261. The second sentence of art 38 provides illustrations of how personal dignity may be violated: 'Insult, libel, false accusation or false incrimination directed against citizens by any means is prohibited.'

[60] Additional articles, art 10(6). The provisions goes on to say that women's personal safety shall be safeguarded.

[61] Art 28.

[62] Art 29.

[63] Art 54.

[64] Art 55.

[65] Art 137.

[66] Art 20.

article 5(5) provides that a political party shall be deemed unconstitutional (and ordered to be dissolved by the GGJ)[67] if its objective or behaviour is such as to endanger the existence of the ROC or its liberal democratic constitutional order.[68] In the case of the HKBL, it is provided that the central government shall be responsible for the defence of the HKSAR, while the government of the HKSAR shall be responsible for the maintenance of public order in the HKSAR.[69] HKSAR residents are not under any legal duty to perform military service.

D. Freedom (or Liberty)

Freedom or liberty is undoubtedly one of the most influential values of the modern age. For present purposes, it may be understood to include both (a) the freedom of the human individual, which should be protected against infringement by the state, and (b) the freedom of the community or nation-state from foreign domination, which in the case of China is often expressed in the terms 'national liberation' (*minzu jiefang*), and the 'independence' (*duli*) and 'autonomy' (*zizhu*) of the nation-state.

Both the PRCC and the ROCC stress the importance of the independence and autonomy of the nation-state, although this is not mentioned in the HKBL. In addition, the PRCC also uses the term 'national liberation'. The preamble to the PRCC states, among other matters, that after 1840, 'feudal China was gradually turned into a semi-colonial and semi-feudal country', and that the Chinese people have struggled for 'the independence of the nation-state, national liberation, democracy and freedom'.[70] The preamble also points out that since the PRC was established, the independence and security of the nation-state have been secured.[71] It is also stated that the PRC's foreign policy is independent and autonomous.[72] Similarly, the ROCC provides that the ROC's foreign policy shall be based on a spirit of independence and autonomy.[73]

We now turn to the freedom of the human individual or individual citizen. Freedom as a value may be formulated at a high level of abstraction and generality, and as we descend to a lower level, freedom may be seen as concretised in various rights to specific freedoms. We therefore look at what rights relating to civil liberties are included in the constitutional texts. All three constitutional texts mention the following rights or freedoms: freedom

[67] Additional articles, art 5(4).
[68] Additional articles, art 5(5).
[69] Art 14.
[70] Preamble, para 2.
[71] Preamble, para 6.
[72] Preamble, para 12.
[73] Art 141.

of the body of the person, freedoms of speech, publication, assembly and association, and freedom of religion.[74] The ROCC contains particularly elaborate provisions (relating to arrest, detention and trial) regarding the freedom of the body of the person.[75] It also mentions the freedoms of teaching (*jiangxue*, alternatively translated as 'academic instruction') and writing (*zhuzuo*, alternatively translated as 'composition'),[76] and the freedoms of residence and change of residence (or migration).[77] Both the PRCC and the HKBL mention the freedoms of procession and demonstration.[78] The HKBL also mentions the freedom of the press,[79] the freedom of conscience (*xinyang de ziyou*),[80] the freedom (in addition to that of religious belief) to preach and to conduct and participate in religious activities in public,[81] freedom of movement within the HKSAR and of emigration, freedom to travel and to enter or leave the HKSAR,[82] the right and freedom to form and join trade unions and to go on strike,[83] freedom of choice of occupation,[84] and freedom to engage in academic research, literary and artistic creation and other cultural activities.[85]

Furthermore, all three constitutional texts contain a general provision on people's rights and freedoms. The ROCC states in its preamble that one of the purposes of the enactment of this constitution is to secure the rights of the people (*minquan*). The PRCC (after its amendment in 2004) provides that 'the State shall respect and protect human rights'.[86] The HKBL declares that the rights and freedoms of HKSAR residents and of other persons in the HKSAR shall be safeguarded.[87]

E. Privacy

As in the case of freedom, the value of privacy is recognised in constitutional texts mainly by provisions on certain rights and liberties. The privacy of

[74] The PRCC, arts 35–37; ROCC, arts 8, 11, 13, 14; HKBL arts 27, 28, 32.
[75] Art 8.
[76] Art 11.
[77] Art 10. There was a similar provision on the freedom of residence and of change of residence (or migration) in the PRC Constitution of 1954 (art 90), but this does not exist in the 1982 Constitution. See the discussion in Cai (n 15 above) 263.
[78] The PRCC, art 35; HKBL, art 27.
[79] Art 27.
[80] Art 32.
[81] Art 32. This freedom was expressly provided for in the HKBL mainly because it was not fully recognised in mainland China. See also art 141 of the HKBL.
[82] Art 31.
[83] Art 27. The freedom to go on strike was provided for in the PRC Constitution of 1978 but not in the PRCC 1982. See the discussion in Cai (n 15 above) 249–50.
[84] Art 33.
[85] Art 34.
[86] Art 33.
[87] Art 4.

personal communication or correspondence is provided for in all three constitutional texts covered by this chapter, and two of them also recognise the privacy of the home. The ROCC declares that the people shall have the freedom of privacy of correspondence.[88] The provisions on privacy in the PRCC and HKBL are almost identical in content.[89] They provide that homes are inviolable and shall not be subject to unlawful search or intrusion. They also affirm the freedom and privacy of communication, and stipulate conditions under which interception of communication is permissible.[90]

F. Equality

Like freedom, equality is one of the most powerful values of modernity. All three constitutional texts concerned affirm the equality of all citizens or persons before the law. In addition, two of the texts make references to the equality of all ethnic groups in China, and to the equality of women and men.

The ROCC provides that 'All citizens of the ROC, irrespective of sex, religion, race, class, or party affiliation, shall be equal before the law.'[91] The PRCC[92] and HKBL[93] provide respectively that all PRC citizens and all HKSAR residents are 'equal before the law'.

As regards China's ethnic groups (of which there are 56, according to official figures, the Han Chinese being the majority), both the ROCC[94] and the PRCC[95] provide in almost identical language for the equality of all such ethnic groups. The preamble[96] to the PRCC also states that the PRC is a unified multi-ethnic state jointly created by its ethnic groups, and that socialist relations of equality, solidarity and mutual assistance have been established among the ethnic groups.

As regards the status of women, the PRCC[97] provides that 'Women in the PRC enjoy equal rights with men in all spheres of life', including 'political, economic, cultural, social and family life'. The principle of 'equal pay for equal work' done by men and women is expressly mentioned. It is also stated that the state shall 'train and select cadres from among women'.[98]

[88] Art 12.

[89] The PRCC arts 39, 40; HKBL, arts 29, 30. This provides a rare example of the direct influence of the PRCC on the drafting of the HKBL.

[90] It may also be noted that art 17 of the ICCPR provides that 'No one shall be subjected to arbitrary or unlawful interference with his privacy, family, home or correspondence ...'.

[91] Art 5.

[92] Art 33.

[93] Art 25.

[94] Art 5.

[95] Art 4.

[96] para 11.

[97] Art 48

[98] Art 48(2).

The ROCC provides that in various elections to political offices, 'quotas of successful candidates shall be assigned to women'.[99] The additional articles to the ROCC provide for a quota for women in elections to the Legislative Yuan (Taiwan's legislature),[100] and require the state to eliminate gender discrimination and promote substantive equality between the sexes.[101]

Interestingly, the ROCC also mentions equality in two other contexts. One is the equality of opportunities among all citizens to receive education.[102] The other concerns economic policy: 'The national economy shall be based on [Sun Yat-sen's] Principle of People's Livelihood and shall seek to effect equalisation of land ownership and restriction of private capital in order to attain a well-balanced sufficiency in national wealth and people's livelihood.'[103]

G. Justice and Fairness

The Constitution and the law should try to achieve justice; the fair trial is a central notion of the administration of justice. In all three constitutional texts concerned, the values of justice and fairness are reflected in provisions on the constitutional, legal and judicial systems. They all affirm the supremacy of the Constitution or basic law, the authority of the law and the principle of judicial independence or independent adjudication of cases by courts in accordance with the law.

The PRCC states in its preamble that this Constitution is 'the fundamental law of the State and has supreme legal authority', and that all people, state organs, political parties and social organisations have a duty to 'uphold the dignity of the Constitution and ensure its implementation'. The main text of the PRCC goes on to provide that no law or regulation may contravene the Constitution;[104] all state organs, political parties and social organisations must abide by the Constitution and the law;[105] the state upholds the unity and dignity of the socialist legal system;[106] the state shall practise 'ruling the country according to law' and construct a socialist state based on the rule of law (*Rechtsstaat*);[107] citizens shall abide by the Constitution and the law.[108] It is also provided that trials should normally be held in public;[109]

99 Art 134.
100 Additional articles, art 4(2).
101 Additional articles, art 10(6).
102 Art 159.
103 Art 142.
104 Art 5(3).
105 Art 5(4). This implies that the Chinese Communist Party itself is subject to the law. See Cai (n 15 above) 182–87.
106 Art 5(2).
107 Art 5(1). This provision was added to the PRCC by the 1999 amendment.
108 Art 53.
109 Art 125.

the accused has the right of defence;[110] the courts shall exercise adjudicative power independently in accordance with law;[111] the procuratorates shall exercise procuratorial power independently in accordance with law;[112] the courts, procuratorates and public security (police) organs shall, in handling criminal cases, practise a division of labour, coordinate their efforts and check against one another so as to ensure the correct and effective implementation of the law.[113]

The ROCC affirms the supremacy of the Constitution by providing that laws or decrees that are in conflict with the Constitution shall be invalid.[114] It empowers the Council of Grand Justices (CGJ) of the Judicial Yuan to interpret the Constitution[115] and to determine whether any law or decree is inconsistent with the Constitution.[116] It also provides that 'Judges shall be above partisanship and shall, in accordance with law, hold trials independently, free from any interference',[117] and that judges have security of tenure.[118] Interestingly, the ROCC is the only constitutional text among all three texts covered by this chapter that expressly uses the term 'justice' (*zhengyi*), which it uses in the context of the ROC's foreign policy. It is provided that one of the objectives of the ROC's foreign policy is to promote 'international justice'.[119]

We now turn to the HKBL. The supremacy of the HKBL over other laws in the HKSAR is guaranteed by a provision that no law enacted by the HKSAR legislature shall contravene the HKBL.[120] The courts of the HKSAR are empowered to interpret the HKBL as they try cases, subject to the overriding power of China's National People's Congress Standing Committee to issue interpretations of the HKBL.[121] The HKBL contains provisions on the judicial system and judicial process that are more detailed than those in the PRCC and ROCC.[122] Judicial independence,[123] judges' security of tenure,[124] trial by jury,[125] the right to confidential legal advice,[126] access

110 Art 125.
111 Art 126.
112 Art 129.
113 Art 135.
114 Arts 171, 172.
115 Arts 78, 79, 173.
116 Art 171.
117 Art 80.
118 Art 81.
119 Art 141.
120 Art 11. See also art 8.
121 Art 158.
122 See particularly s 4 (on the judiciary) of ch IV of the HKBL.
123 Arts 19, 85.
124 Art 89.
125 Art 86.
126 Art 35.

to courts[127] and litigants' rights[128] are all provided for. These provisions are further supplemented by the relevant provisions in the ICCPR.[129]

H. Respect and Tolerance

The value of respect for human beings and human dignity is partly reflected in the constitutional provisions on freedoms, privacy and equality mentioned above. As regards tolerance, this is mainly reflected in constitutional provisions on freedom of religion (also mentioned above), on respect for the ways of life and culture of ethnic minorities, and on the equality of different ethnic groups (mentioned above). This section will cover provisions on ethnic and other minorities that have not been covered above.

The PRCC declares that the state protects the lawful rights and interests of ethnic minorities, and upholds and develops a relationship of equality, solidarity and mutual assistance among China's ethnic groups.[130] It further provides that the state shall promote the economic and cultural development of areas inhabited by the ethnic minorities;[131] they may practise regional autonomy and establish organs of self-government;[132] they have the freedom to use and develop their own oral and written languages and to preserve or reform their folkways and customs.[133] The PRCC in a separate section of 11 articles[134] contains elaborate provisions on the institutional features of the regional autonomy of ethnic minorities. At the national level, it is provided that there shall be an appropriate quota for ethnic minorities in the membership of the National People's Congress Standing Committee—the top parliamentary body of the PRC.[135]

The ROCC provides that the state shall safeguard the status of the ethnic groups in China's frontier region, support their regional autonomy,[136] and promote and support the development of their education, culture, transportation, water conservation, public health and other economic and social enterprises.[137] It is further provided in the additional articles that the state affirms cultural pluralism, and shall preserve and foster the development of the languages and culture of the aboriginal people in Taiwan, safeguard the status and political participation of the aboriginal people in Taiwan,[138] and

[127] Art 35.
[128] Art 35.
[129] See particularly arts 14–15 thereof.
[130] Art 4(1).
[131] Art 4(2).
[132] Art 4(3).
[133] Art 4(4).
[134] Arts 112–22.
[135] Art 65.
[136] Art 168. The autonomy of Mongolia and Tibet is expressly mentioned in arts 119–20.
[137] Art 169.
[138] Additional articles, art 10(11).

safeguard and promote the development of their education, culture, transportation, water conservation, health and medical care, economy, land and social welfare.[139]

Hong Kong has no indigenous ethnic minorities, but the HKBL affords special protection to the descendants of the indigenous (Han Chinese) inhabitants of the New Territories—that part of the colony of Hong Kong acquired by Britain in 1898 pursuant to a 99-year lease from the Qing Empire.[140] The HKBL provides that their 'lawful traditional rights and interests' shall be protected.[141]

I. Family

The family or family life as a value may be discerned in all three constitutional texts. The PRCC provides that 'marriage, the family and mother and child are protected by the State'; 'violation of the freedom of marriage is prohibited'; 'parents have the duty to rear and educate their children who are minors, and children who have come of age have the duty to support and assist their parents.'[142] The PRCC is unique among the three constitutional texts in providing for family planning: 'Both husband and wife have the duty to practise family planning';[143] 'the State promotes family planning so that population growth may fit the plans for economic and social development.'[144]

The policy of family planning is not applicable to the HKSAR. The HKBL provides for both the freedom of marriage and the 'right to raise a family freely'.[145] In the ROCC, marriage or family are not expressly mentioned, but it is provided that 'the State, in order to consolidate the foundation of national existence and development, shall protect motherhood and carry out a policy for the promotion of the welfare of women and children.'[146]

J. Work

Work as a value is reflected in all three constitutional texts. The PRCC is however unique in providing that work (*laodong*, alternatively translated as 'labour') is both a right and a duty of citizens.[147] It also declares that 'work

[139] Additional articles, art 10(12).
[140] The two other parts of the colony were ceded to Britain in 1842 and 1860 respectively, and had few inhabitants at the time of cession. See generally the works cited in n 23 above.
[141] Art 40.
[142] Art 49.
[143] Art 49(2).
[144] Art 25.
[145] Art 37.
[146] Art 156.
[147] Art 42(1).

is an honourable responsibility of all citizens who are able to work'.[148] It further provides that the state shall create and improve conditions for employment.[149] The ROCC provides for the right to work in the same article which provides for the right to life and the right of property.[150] It further provides that the state shall provide opportunities to work for people who are able to work,[151] and shall legislate to protect labour.[152] The HKBL does not expressly mention the right to work,[153] but provides for the freedom of choice of occupation.[154]

K. Property

The emphasis on public ownership of property or the means of production has traditionally distinguished socialism or communism from capitalism. Private property rights and private property as a value have been recognised in the ROCC and HKBL from the time of their enactment. The PRC originally emphasised public ownership, but has given increasing recognition to private property rights as economic reform has deepened.

The ROCC provides that the people's right to property shall be protected.[155] The HKBL protects 'the right of private ownership of property',[156] including the right to compensation for lawful deprivation of property[157] and the right of inheritance.[158] The 'ownership of enterprises' and 'investments from outside' the HKSAR are also expressly protected.[159] Land and natural resources in the HKSAR are technically 'state property' but the HKSAR government may lease or grant them to other persons for use or development.[160]

The PRCC declares that socialist public property is 'sacred and inviolable'.[161] As a result of the 2004 amendment, it is provided that citizens'

148 Art 42(3).
149 Art 42(2).
150 Art 15.
151 Art 152.
152 Art 153.
153 The right to work is provided for in art 6 of the International Covenant on Economic, Social and Cultural Rights, which is applicable to Hong Kong under art 39 of the HKBL.
154 Art 33. This provision was probably introduced to highlight the fact that Hong Kong's practice in this regard was different from that in mainland China, which at the time still practised the socialist planned economy in which there was little freedom of choice of occupation for many people.
155 Art 15. The same article also provides for the right to life and the right to work.
156 Art 6.
157 It is also provided that such compensation shall correspond to the real value of the property (art 105(2)).
158 Art 105(1).
159 Art 105(3).
160 Art 7.
161 Art 12.

lawful private property is also inviolable; citizens' right to private property and right of inheritance shall be protected in accordance with law; the state may take or requisition citizens' private property upon payment of compensation.[162] There are other provisions in the PRCC which deal with the ownership system in the economy and land. It is provided that 'the basis of the socialist economic system of the PRC is socialist public ownership of the means of production';[163] in the 'preliminary stage of socialism' (which the PRC is in), public ownership shall be the main body of the economy, while other forms of ownership may also exist within the economic system.[164] Urban land is state-owned, while rural land is collectively owned;[165] the right to use land may be transferred;[166] the state may take or requisition land for the purpose of the public interest subject to payment of compensation.[167]

L. Community

The value of community may be understood as the good of individuals living together and engaging in social cooperation in a community or nation-state. It may be reflected in constitutional provisions on national unity, territorial integrity, the security of the nation-state,[168] and the interests of the community or the public interest which may sometimes be distinguished from individuals' interests.

The PRCC provides that citizens have a duty to safeguard 'national unity' and 'the solidarity of all ethnic groups within the nation'.[169] Furthermore, in exercising their freedoms and rights, citizens 'may not infringe upon the interests of the State, of society or of the collective, or upon the lawful freedoms and rights of other citizens'.[170] As regards economic policy, it is provided that 'the State shall reasonably organise accumulation and consumption, taking into account the interests of the State, the collective and individuals, and shall, on the basis of the development of economic production, gradually improve the material and cultural life of the people.'[171]

162 Art 13.
163 Art 6(1).
164 Art 6(2).
165 Art 10. Collective ownership means that the land is collectively owned by the peasants of the area concerned. See Cai (n 15 above) 195–96; Xu Chongde (ed), *Xianfa* (*Constitutional Law*) (Beijing, China Renmin University Press, 1999) 91–92.
166 Art 10(4).
167 Art 10(3).
168 In this regard, see the section IVC 'Security'.
169 Art 52.
170 Art 51.
171 Art 14(3).

As regards territorial integrity, the preamble to the PRCC states that 'Taiwan is part of the sacred territory of the PRC. It is the sacred duty of all Chinese people, including our compatriots in Taiwan, to accomplish the great task of reunifying the motherland.'[172]

The ROCC refers to the communitarian values of social order and public interest in the context of limitations on freedoms and rights. It is provided that apart from freedoms and rights expressly protected in the ROCC, other freedoms and rights of the people shall also be protected insofar they are not detrimental to the social order or the public interest.[173] And the freedoms and rights enumerated in the ROCC shall not be restricted by law except where necessary for the purpose of preventing infringement upon others' freedoms, averting an emergency or crisis, maintaining the social order or advancing the public interest.[174] As regards territorial integrity, the ROCC[175] and its additional articles[176] stipulate the procedures for introducing a change in the territory of the state.

The HKBL states in its preamble that Hong Kong has been part of China since ancient times, and the resumption of the exercise of Chinese sovereignty over Hong Kong in 1997 fulfilled 'the long-cherished common aspiration of the Chinese people for the recovery of Hong Kong'. 'Upholding national unity and territorial integrity' is cited in the preamble as one of the reasons for the establishment of the HKSAR.

M. Compassion and Solidarity

The values of compassion and solidarity, or those of a caring society, are mainly reflected in constitutional provisions on social and economic rights and social welfare. There are ample provisions in this regard in the three constitutional texts, particularly in the PRCC and ROCC.

The PRCC provides that citizens who are elderly or sick or who have lost their capacity to work have the right to receive material assistance from the state and society.[177] The state shall develop social insurance, social relief and medical and health services for this purpose.[178] The state and society shall assist in making arrangements for the work, livelihood and education of the blind, deaf, mute and other disabled citizens.[179] There is also a

172 Para 9 of the preamble.
173 Art 22.
174 Art 23.
175 Art 4.
176 Arts 1, 4(5).
177 Art 45(1).
178 Art 45(1). See also art 21 regarding the development of medical and health services.
179 Art 45(3).

special provision on disabled members of the armed forces and family members of martyrs.[180] In view of the shift from the socialist planned economy (in which most workers were employed by state-owned enterprises and taken care of by such enterprises after retirement) to the socialist market economy, the 2004 constitutional amendment provides that the state shall develop a social security system that corresponds to its level of economic development.[181]

The ROCC provides that 'the State, in order to promote social welfare, shall establish a social insurance system. The State shall provide appropriate assistance and relief to the old, the infirm, the disabled, those who are unable to make a living and victims of unusual calamities.'[182] 'The State, in order to improve national health, shall establish extensive services for hygiene and health, and a system of public medical service.'[183] Interestingly, it is also provided that in order to promote balanced economic development among provinces and counties, the central government shall provide assistance to poorer provinces, and the provincial government assistance to poorer counties.[184] The additional articles make special provisions for national health insurance,[185] care of and support for the physically and mentally disabled,[186] priority in budgetary allocations for purposes of social welfare and assistance,[187] and support for retired soldiers.[188]

The HKBL provides for residents' 'right to social welfare'.[189] The government of the HKSAR shall formulate policies on the development and improvement of the social welfare system in the light of economic conditions and social needs.[190] It may also be noted that the International Covenant on Economic, Social and Cultural Rights (ICESCR), applicable to the HKSAR under article 39, contains more detailed provisions on various economic and social rights.

N. Education

Under the influence of Confucianism, the importance of education has long been recognised in the Chinese tradition. There are fairly elaborate provisions on education in all three constitutional texts.

[180] Art 45(2).
[181] Art 14(4).
[182] Art 155.
[183] Art 157.
[184] Art 147.
[185] Additional articles, art 10(5).
[186] Additional articles, art 10(7).
[187] Additional articles, art 10(8).
[188] Additional articles, art 10(9).
[189] Art 36.
[190] Art 145.

Under the ROCC, the people have both the right and the duty to receive education.[191] Citizens shall have an equal opportunity to receive education.[192] 'All children from 6 to 12 years of age shall receive free primary education. Those from poor families shall be supplied with books by the Government.'[193] 'The national, provincial and local governments shall extensively establish scholarships to assist students of good scholastic standing and exemplary conduct who lack the means to continue their school education.'[194] To promote the balanced development of education in different regions, the state shall give special support to the funding of education and culture in the frontier regions and low-income areas.[195] The state shall safeguard the livelihood of those who work in the fields of education, science and the arts.[196] There are also provisions on the purpose of education (which is to 'develop among citizens the national spirit, the spirit of autonomy, morality, bodily health, scientific knowledge and capacities for life'),[197] the funding of education,[198] state supervision of educational institutions,[199] and state support for private educational enterprises.[200]

Interestingly, the PRCC contains a provision almost identical to its counterpart in the ROCC, declaring that citizens have both the right and the duty to receive education.[201] The state shall develop 'the educational enterprise of socialism', establish various types of schools, seek to eliminate illiteracy, and 'provide political, cultural, scientific, technical and vocational education for workers, peasants, state functionaries and other working people.'[202] The state shall train specialised personnel in various fields who serve socialism, expand the team of intellectuals and create conditions to enable them to fully fulfil their role in socialist modernisation.[203] The state shall 'strengthen the construction of socialist spiritual civilisation' by promoting 'education in ideals, ethics, general knowledge, discipline and legality'.[204] 'The State shall promote the public morality and civic virtues of love of the motherland, of the people, of labour, of science and of socialism. The State shall

[191] Art 21.
[192] Art 159.
[193] Art 160.
[194] Art 161.
[195] Art 163.
[196] Art 165.
[197] Art 158.
[198] Art 164; Additional articles, art 10(10).
[199] Art 162.
[200] Art 167.
[201] Art 46.
[202] Art 19.
[203] Art 23. This provision was intended to put an end to the practice of discrimination against and persecution of intellectuals in the earlier period of PRC history, Cai (n 15 above) 220–21.
[204] Art 24(1).

conduct education among the people in patriotism, collectivism, internationalism and communism, and in dialectical and historical materialism, and shall oppose capitalist, feudal and other decadent ideas.'[205]

The HKBL provides that the HKSAR shall formulate policies on the development and improvement of education.[206] Community organisations and individuals may run educational undertakings.[207] Educational institutions may retain their autonomy and enjoy academic freedom.[208] They may continue to recruit staff and use teaching materials from outside Hong Kong.[209] Schools run by religious organisations may continue to provide religions education.[210] Students shall enjoy freedom of choice of educational institutions and freedom to pursue their education outside the HKSAR.[211] The right to education is provided for in the ICESCR,[212] which is applicable to the HKSAR under article 39 of the HKBL.

O. Environment

Environmental protection as a value is recognised in the PRCC and ROCC, but not expressly provided for in the HKBL. The PRCC states that 'the State shall ensure the reasonable use of natural resources and protect rare animals and plants. Appropriation of or damage to natural resources by any organisation or individual by any means shall be prohibited'.[213] 'The State shall protect and improve the living environment and the ecological environment, and prevent and control pollution and other public hazards. The State shall organise and encourage afforestation and the protection of forests.'[214]

The ROCC touches upon the environment in the context of the development of agriculture. It is provided that 'the State shall, by the use of scientific techniques, develop water conservation, increase the productivity of land, improve the agricultural environment, plan the use of land and develop agricultural resources so as to achieve the industrialisation of agriculture'.[215] The additional articles provide that 'in pursuing economic and technological development, equal consideration shall be given to environmental and ecological protection'.[216]

205 Art 24(2).
206 Art 136(1).
207 Art 136(2).
208 Art 137(1).
209 Art 137(1).
210 Art 137(1).
211 Art 137(2).
212 Art 13.
213 Art 9(2).
214 Art 26.
215 Art 146.
216 Additional articles, art 10(2).

P. Peace

Peace as a value is recognised in both the PRCC and ROCC, but not in the HKBL (which is understandable, as the HKBL is not a constitution of a sovereign state). The PRCC states in its preamble that peaceful coexistence with other states is one of the five principles that form the basis of the PRC's foreign policy.[217] Securing world peace is mentioned in the ROCC as one of the objectives of the ROC's foreign policy.[218]

Q. Responsibility and Accountability

Responsibility or accountability as a value is recognised in the constitutional texts mainly in the context of the responsibility or accountability of political institutions and checks and balance between organs of government. The PRCC also provides for responsibility in socialist economic production and in the work of civil servants.

Under the PRCC, the people's congresses at the national and local levels are elected by the people, responsible to the people and supervised by the people.[219] The administrative, judicial and procuratorial organs of the state are all created by, responsible to and supervised by the people's congresses.[220] The National People's Congress Standing Committee (the standing body of the PRC's parliament) is responsible to the National People's Congress (NPC) and reports to it.[221] The State Council (the highest administrative organ in the PRC) is responsible to the NPC and the NPC Standing Committee and reports to them.[222] Deputies to the NPC have the right to submit questions to (or interpellate) the State Council, which is obliged to respond.[223] Local governments are simultaneously responsible to the local people's congress at the same level and the administrative organ at the next higher level.[224] Deputies to people's congresses are subject to the supervision of their electors who have the right to recall them.[225] Citizens have the right to criticise and make suggestions regarding any state organ or functionary, and the right to lodge petitions, complaints or charges in respect of violations of the law or dereliction of duty by any state organ or functionary.[226] Victims of violations of citizens' rights by state organs or

[217] Para 12 of the preamble.
[218] Art 141.
[219] Art 3(2).
[220] Art 3(3).
[221] Art 69.
[222] Art 92.
[223] Art 73.
[224] Art 110.
[225] Arts 77, 102.
[226] Art 41(1).

functionaries have the right to compensation.[227] It is also provided that state organs shall implement 'a system of responsibility for work';[228] in the context of economic management and the management of enterprises, the state shall implement various forms of 'the system of socialist responsibility'.[229]

The main provision in which the term 'responsible' is used in the ROCC is that stating that the Executive Yuan (the highest executive organ of the ROC) shall be responsible to the Legislative Yuan (the legislature).[230] The Executive Yuan is under a duty to present to the Legislative Yuan statements of policies and reports on its work.[231] Members of the Legislative Yuan have the right to interpellate the Executive Yuan.[232] The Legislative Yuan may propose a vote of no confidence in the President of the Executive Yuan.[233] As in the PRCC, the ROC government's accountability to the people is also evidenced in some provisions on citizens' rights. It is provided that the people have 'the rights to petition, to lodge a complaint [*suyuan*] and to litigate'.[234] 'Any public functionary who, in violation of law, infringes upon the freedom or right of any person shall, in additional to being subject to disciplinary measures in accordance with law, assume criminal and civil liability'; victims have the right to claim compensation.[235]

Under the HKBL, 'the Chief Executive of the HKSAR shall be accountable to the Central People's Government [in Beijing] and the HKSAR in accordance with the provisions of' the HKBL.[236] The executive branch of the HKSAR government is 'accountable' to the Legislative Council of the HKSAR.[237] For example, the executive shall present regular policy addresses to the Legislative Council, and answer questions raised by members of the Council.[238] It is also expressly provided that 'Hong Kong residents have the right to institute legal proceedings in the courts against the acts of the executive authorities and their personnel'.[239]

R. Participation

The value of participation is recognised in all three constitutional texts in the context of provisions on democratic participation in elections, politics

227 Art 41(3).
228 Art 27.
229 Art 14(1).
230 Art 57 as amended by additional articles, art 3.
231 Additional articles, art 3(2)(i).
232 Additional articles, art 3(2)(i).
233 Additional articles, art 3(2)(iii).
234 Art 16.
235 Art 24.
236 Art 43.
237 Art 64.
238 Art 64.
239 Art 35.

and public affairs, which overlap to some extent with the provisions on political accountability covered by the preceding section. In the following, the provisions mentioned above will not be repeated.

The preamble to the PRCC states that since the establishment of the PRC, the Chinese people have gained control of state power and have become masters of the nation-state.[240] The main text of the PRCC provides as follows. 'All power in the PRC belongs to the people. The NPC and the local people's congresses at various levels are the organs through which the people exercise state power. The people administer state affairs and manage economic, cultural and social affairs through various channels and in various ways in accordance with the law.'[241] All citizens aged 18 or above have the right to vote and to stand for election, except those who have been deprived of their political rights in accordance with law.[242] 'Deputies to the NPC should maintain close contact with the units which elected them and with the people, hear and reflect the opinions and demands of the people and work hard to serve them.'[243] The people have the right to elect directly the people's congresses of counties, towns and townships.[244]

Under the ROCC, the sovereignty of the ROC vests in all citizens.[245] The people have the right of election, recall, initiative and referendum.[246] All elections, unless otherwise specified in the Constitution, shall be by universal, equal and direct suffrage and by secret ballot.[247] According to the additional articles, the President and Vice-President of the ROC are directly elected by the people of Taiwan;[248] bills for constitutional amendment and change of territory of the state must be voted upon at a referendum.[249] The Legislative Yuan is also elected by the people.[250] Furthermore, the ROCC provides for the people's right to take public (civil service) examinations and to hold public offices.[251] The recruitment of civil servants shall be based on a system of open competitive examinations.[252]

The HKBL provides that permanent residents of the HKSAR have the right to vote and to stand for election.[253] It is stated that the 'ultimate aim' of the political development of the HKSAR is the selection of the Chief

[240] Para 5 of the preamble.
[241] Art 2.
[242] Art 34. Deprivation of political rights is one form of punishment under PRC criminal law. See the Criminal Code of the PRC, Arts 54–58.
[243] Art 76.
[244] Art 97.
[245] Art 2.
[246] Art 17.
[247] Art 129.
[248] Additional articles, art 2(1).
[249] Additional articles, art 1.
[250] Art 62; additional articles, art 4(1).
[251] Art 18.
[252] Art 85.
[253] Art 26.

Executive of the HKSAR by universal suffrage[254] and the election of all members of the Legislative Council by universal suffrage.[255] HKSAR residents who are PRC citizens have the right to participate in the management of PRC state affairs, mainly through a system of election of deputies of the HKSAR to the NPC.[256]

S. Honesty and Integrity

Turning finally to the value of honesty and integrity, it may be noted that this value is not directly reflected in the PRCC and ROCC. The HKBL does affirm this value in its provision that 'the Chief Executive of the HKSAR must be a person of integrity, dedicated to his or her duties'.[257]

V. PRIORITISATION AND CONGRUENCE

Having surveyed the values reflected in the three constitutional texts in section IV above, we now proceed to explore the issues of prioritisation of values and congruence between proclaimed values and social and political reality.

A. Prioritisation of Values in the Constitutional Texts

The manner in which different values are prioritised in the PRCC, ROCC and HKBL may be investigated by looking at the constitutional texts themselves and taking into account the historical and ideological background of their enactment as reviewed in section II of this chapter, as well as the views of the judiciary where relevant.

Among the three constitutional texts, the PRCC most clearly prioritises the values of community (particularly the collective interests of the community or the nation-state) and security (particularly social order and national security) over the freedom of the individual. This is understandable, as the guiding ideology behind the PRCC is socialism and communism. Various provisions in the PRCC reflect such prioritisation. For example, in its first article on citizens' rights, the PRCC reminds citizens that 'every citizen is entitled to the rights, and at the same time must perform the duties, prescribed by the Constitution and the law'.[258] 'When citizens of the PRC

[254] Art 45.
[255] Art 68. For the existing political system of the HKSAR, see section II above.
[256] Art 21.
[257] Art 47.
[258] Art 33. This is known as the principle of correspondence between rights and duties. See Cai (n 15 above) 245–46.

exercise their freedoms and rights, they may not infringe upon the interests of the State, of society or of the collective'.[259] In its provision on freedom of religious belief, the PRCC states that 'no one may make use of religion to engage in activities that harm public order, impair the health of citizens or hinder the educational system of the State. Religious bodies and religious affairs shall not be subject to foreign domination.'[260] The value of community also has priority over that of family to some extent, as evidenced by the constitutional requirement on family planning.[261] Furthermore, the emphasis on socialist public ownership and public property reflects the value of community and of course follows from socialist ideology.

The ROCC also gives a certain degree of priority to the value of community in its provisions on property and the economy. 'The national economy shall be based on the Principle of People's Livelihood and shall seek to effect equalisation of land ownership and restriction of private capital in order to attain a well-balanced sufficiency in national wealth and people's livelihood.'[262] 'If the value of a piece of land has increased, not through the exertion of labour or application of capital, the State shall levy thereon an increment tax, the proceeds of which shall be enjoyed by the people in common.'[263] 'Public utilities and other enterprises of a monopolistic nature' shall be state enterprises except where permitted by law.[264] It is also provided that 'the State shall restrict private wealth and private enterprises by law if they are deemed detrimental to a balanced development of national wealth and people's livelihood'.[265]

Since the era of liberalisation and democratisation began in Taiwan in the late 1980s, and particularly with the Council of Grand Justices (CGJ) actively interpreting the constitutional provisions on individuals' freedoms and rights and striking down laws and regulations inconsistent with them since the 1990s, the values of individuals' freedom, equality, justice, participation and accountability have become prioritised. In Interpretation No 499 issued in 2000,[266] the CGJ declared that certain principles in the ROCC are so fundamental and essential for a liberal democratic constitutional order that no constitutional amendment contravening such principles can be valid. These principles include the ROC being a democratic republic, the sovereignty of the people, the protection of the rights of the people, separation of powers and checks and balance.

[259] Art 51.
[260] Art 36.
[261] Arts 25, 49(2).
[262] Art 142.
[263] Art 143.
[264] Art 144.
[265] Art 145.
[266] See n 32 above.

In the case of the HKSAR, it should be noted that one of the raisons d'être for the establishment of the HKSAR as a part of the PRC practising a different 'system' from that in mainland China in accordance with the concept of 'one country, two systems' was to ensure, in the words of the Sino-British Joint Declaration of 1984, that the existing 'social and economic systems in Hong Kong will remain unchanged, and so will the life-style', and that existing 'rights and freedoms' and 'private property' would continue to be respected.[267] Unlike the PRCC, therefore, the HKBL accords priority to individuals' freedoms and private property. Indeed, the Court of Final Appeal—the highest court of the HKSAR—has declared when giving judgment in several leading cases that the rights and freedoms of individuals that receive constitutional protection in the HKSAR stand at the heart of Hong Kong's separate system: 'one country, two systems'.[268]

B. Congruence Between Constitutionally Proclaimed Values and Social and Political Reality

The degree to which values affirmed and proclaimed in constitutional texts correspond to social and political reality depends partly on whether such values do represent the prevailing values in society, partly on the nature and institutional features of the political system (as discussed in section II of this chapter), and also partly on the effectiveness of the legal system in ensuring that the law in the books is translated into law in action.

Of the three constitutional texts discussed in this chapter, the PRCC is probably most problematic in terms of the congruence between proclaimed values and social and political reality. Since the era of 'reform and opening' began in the late 1970s, China has undergone rapid change, economically, socially, culturally as well as politically. It is a society and economy in transition, from a totalitarian communist system with a command economy to an unknown destination. Values are in flux, as far-reaching social changes unfold. As mentioned above, the 1982 Constitution has undergone several series of amendments, which have contributed significantly to the constitutional expression of values such as justice, freedom and property.

As mentioned in section III, the PRCC is not justiciable or enforceable by the courts. This, particularly when compared with the cases of the ROCC and HKBL, constitutes an inherent limitation of the PRCC, and makes it more difficult to ensure that the values proclaimed in the PRCC are put into practice. In recent years, particularly since the case of *Qi Yuling* mentioned

[267] Para 3(5) of the Joint Declaration.
[268] Chen (n 28 above) 687, esp fn 187 thereof.

above, a body of scholarship[269] has developed in the PRC focusing on how the Chinese courts have directly or indirectly applied constitutional provisions, particularly those on individuals' freedoms and rights and on equality, in particular cases. However, these cases are of more theoretical than practical interest, as their impact upon society at large and upon laws and policies has been minimal. And no Chinese court has the power to give an authoritative interpretation of any provision of the PRCC.[270] With the repeal in late 2008 of the *Qi Yuling* interpretation,[271] the prospects for judicial enforcement of constitutionally proclaimed values appear uncertain.

In the absence of judicial enforcement, legislation is the principal means for the implementation of the PRCC. The progress made in Chinese law-making in the three decades of 'reform and opening' has indeed been enormous, but the problems of ineffective enforcement of the law and the weaknesses of the Chinese courts are also well-known.[272] While these problems are not unique to China, being common to the legal systems of developing countries, the PRC suffers from a particularly serious incongruence between certain constitutionally proclaimed values, and social and political reality, because of the peculiar nature of its political system.

The values in question here are those of responsibility (accountability) and participation. There are provisions in the PRCC that create the impression that the PRC is a democratic republic ruled by a National People's Congress elected by provincial people's congresses, which are elected by municipal people's congresses, which are themselves elected by county-level people's congresses that are directly elected by the people.[273] In practice, organs of the Chinese Communist Party (CCP) determine who may be candidates in the elections, particularly elections to the people's congresses at higher levels.[274] There is actually a tension between those provisions in the PRCC on elections, participation and accountability on the one hand, and those on the leadership of the CCP and on the PRC as a 'people's democratic

[269] See, eg, Han Dayuan (ed), *Zhongguo xianfa shili yanjiu* [*A Study of Chinese Constitutional Law Cases and Incidents*], vol 1 (Beijing, Law Press, 2005); Hu Jinguang (ed), *Zhongguo shida xianzheng shili yanjiu* [*A Study of Ten Major Chinese Constitutional Law Cases and Incidents*] (Beijing, China Renmin University Press, 2009); Hu and Han (n 42 above).

[270] See n 42 above.

[271] See n 44 above.

[272] Some of these problems have been acknowledged by the government itself. See, eg, the Chinese Government's White Paper on *China's Efforts and Achievements in Promoting the Rule of Law* (2008), www.china.org.cn/government/news/2008-02/28/content_11025486.htm. According to the World Bank's 'Rule of Law' indicator (as part of its Governance Indicators for countries in the world), the PRC in 2008 was on the 25–50 percentile rank, as compared to Germany, Britain, the USA and France (on the 90–100 percentile rank), Japan (on the 75–90 percentile rank), and India (on the 50–75 percentile rank). See http://info.worldbank.org/governance/wgi/mc_countries.asp.

[273] See the PRCC, ch 3.

[274] See the works cited in n 37 above.

dictatorship' led by 'the working class' on the other hand. And there is a lack of congruence between the constitutionally affirmed values of participation and accountability and the political reality of rule by the top Party leadership which appoints the Party leaders at the provincial and local levels.

In the case of Taiwan, there was also a lack of congruence between constitutionally proclaimed values of freedom, participation and accountability and the social and political reality during the period of one-party authoritarian rule by the KMT. However, since the era of liberalisation and democratisation began in the late 1980s, these values in the ROCC, which had to a considerable extent been 'frozen' for nearly four decades, have gradually been put into practice. The Council of Grand Justices as a constitutional court and interpreter and guardian of the ROCC has issued hundreds of interpretations, many of which touch upon the values of freedom, equality and justice, leading to major reforms of many areas of law in Taiwan.[275]

In the HKSAR, the rule of law and the values of freedom, equality and justice that have been inherited from colonial Hong Kong have continued to flourish in the post-1997 era. The courts of the HKSAR have played a role more significant than ever before in interpreting the constitutional text and in judicial review of laws and administration actions.[276] The legal and judicial systems of the HKSAR have a good reputation, and are generally regarded as effective.[277] And the values proclaimed in the HKBL correspond largely to the values upheld by the people of Hong Kong.

VI. CONCLUSION

It is remarkable that despite the differences between the political, economic and social systems of mainland China, Taiwan and Hong Kong, and despite the very different historical and ideological origins of the three constitutional texts discussed in this chapter, there is a fairly high degree of convergence between the values affirmed or reflected in these constitutional texts. The following table demonstrates this ('yes' refers to the relevant value being affirmed in the constitutional text; in the case of the HKBL, reference is also made to the ICCPR which, as mentioned above, has been incorporated by reference into the HKBL).

275 See generally the works cited in n 33 above.

276 See generally Chen (n 54 above).

277 According to the World Bank's 'Rule of Law' indicator (as part of its Governance Indicators for countries in the world) (see n 272 above), Hong Kong in 2008 was on the 90–100 percentile rank; Taiwan was on the 50–75 percentile rank with a score close to 75; while the PRC was on the 25–50 percentile rank.

	PRCC	ROCC	HKBL
Life		Yes	Yes [in ICCPR]
Dignity	Yes	Yes (context: women's rights)	Yes [in ICCPR]
Security	Yes	Yes	Yes
Freedom	Yes	Yes	Yes
Privacy	Yes	Yes	Yes
Equality	Yes	Yes	Yes
Justice	Yes	Yes	Yes
Respect/tolerance	Yes	Yes	Yes (context: New Territories indigenous inhabitants)
Family	Yes	Yes (context: motherhood)	Yes
Work	Yes	Yes	Yes
Property	Yes	Yes	Yes
Community	Yes	Yes	Yes
Compassion	Yes	Yes	Yes
Education	Yes	Yes	Yes
Environment	Yes	Yes	
Peace	Yes	Yes	
Responsibility	Yes	Yes	Yes
Participation	Yes	Yes	Yes
Integrity			Yes

Despite the convergence in the values affirmed, there are, as discussed in section V above, differences in the manner of prioritisation. In the case of the PRCC, community and security are accorded priority relative to freedom. In the ROCC, the value of community is also emphasised in the domain of the economy and property, but otherwise freedom, equality, responsibility (of government) and participation are prioritised. In the HKBL, freedom and private property are emphasised.

In terms of the congruence between constitutionally proclaimed values and social and political reality, the ROCC (since the era of liberalisation and democratisation began in the late 1980s) and the HKBL seem to have achieved better records than the PRCC. In the case of the PRC, institutional and practical limitations exist with regard to the effective enforcement of the Constitution and laws. The non-democratic nature of the political system also constitutes an obstacle to the realisation of values such as freedom, responsibility (of government) and participation.

Despite differences in the prioritisation of values and problems of lack of congruence between proclaimed values and reality, the affirmation of the relevant values in the constitutional texts and the convergence of such values in the three constitutional texts may, I think, give us hope and provide some ground for optimism regarding the possibility of universally recognised values of humankind and global constitutional values. In particular, the case of the PRCC does not, I think, furnish a counter-example regarding convergence of values. On the contrary, this chapter shows that the set of values affirmed in the PRCC is largely the same set as that affirmed in the ROCC, the HKBL, and, indeed, many other contemporary constitutional texts. How to prioritise them, and how to put them into practice, are questions which the Chinese people need to answer for themselves, just as they are questions which the people of every country in the contemporary world need to answer for themselves.

6

Human Dignity, Individual Rights and Equality: The Core Values of the Finnish Constitutional Act

MARTTA OCTOBER AND RIIKKA SALONEN

I. INTRODUCTION

TO UNDERSTAND AND interpret the values behind a modern constitutional act, it is essential to first study the historical background of the granting state. In its first section this chapter aims to give an overview of the political and historical experiences of the Finnish nation, on which the relatively modern Constitutional Act of the present century was built. The second section goes beyond the law described in the Constitutional Act and addresses the morals, values and principles of the constitution. In the third section, the chapter briefly examines the constitutional principles as they are currently applied, and points out some challenges and inconsistencies. The fourth section draws conclusions.

The Finnish Constitutional Act,[1] as we know it today, is the outcome of a journey of first autonomy, then independence and then finally maintaining that independence—a long and difficult process that has lasted for over 200 years. The complexity of the path to independence meant that some creativity was required from the lawyers and statesmen who crafted the early constitutional documents.

The constitution-building process in Finland has consisted of three main threads. First, many of the early reforms were limited to balancing state powers and regulating the political system. The second main path has been the rather slow development of the individual citizen's position under the law, including reform of basic rights. Thirdly, and most recently, there has been Finland's adaptation to international developments, primarily European integration and the ratification of international human rights conventions. It is necessary to note that many of these changes have taken place

[1] The full text of the Finnish Constitutional Act (Act 731 of 1999, amended in 2011 by Act 1112) is available at www.finlex.fi/en/laki/kaannokset/1999/en19990731.pdf.

outside the legal framework of the Constitution.[2] Hence, a juridical constitution includes not only the founding Constitutional Act itself, but also lower-ranked provisions that govern state powers and individual rights, as well as norms and principles which come from repeated applications of the law. Politically, a constitution refers to the concrete system in which the state's decisions are made, and sometimes practices can occur that do not fully comply with the written Constitutional Act.

In the early Finnish legal tradition, values were excluded from the positivistic view on law, which is why jurists often found themselves amidst constitutional paradoxes.[3] For example, the nurturing of localised politics of identity growing into independency; and the history of Swedish rule giving way to Russian takeover. The paradox of constitutionalism, especially in an unseasoned legal culture such as Finland had at the time, was the tension that put constituent power into constitutional form.

A. Constitutional Processes at the Gaining of Independence 1809–1917

The Russian Empire gained control of Finland following the War of Finland in 1809.[4] Under Swedish rule, Finland had been governed by the Swedish Kingdom, where a Form of Government was passed in 1772. This law, afterwards referred to as 'Gustavian' after the ruling Swedish King Gustav the Third, was accepted by the Finns as their own constitution. The new ruler, Russian Emperor Alexander the First, made Finland an autonomous Grand Duchy of the Russian Empire—and paradoxically, the emerging Finland preferred to adhere to its Swedish constitution. Perhaps the attachment explains some of the traditionally strong respect for proper legal forms in Finnish legal culture, characteristic of both the authorities and the citizens of Finland for centuries.[5]

However, the century that Finland spent under the rule of the Russian Empire was crucial to the emergence of the Finnish state. Luckily, the Tsar did not specify in any way which laws or rights should remain in force, allowing Finland to maintain its own[6] legislature, and remaining essentially in charge of its own domestic affairs. The development of Finnish national

[2] Pekka Hallberg's speech of 18 July 1999, '80 years of the Finnish Constitution'; see: www.kho.fi/21897.htm.

[3] Kangas, U, *Oikeustiede Suomessa 1900-2000* (Juva, WSLT, 1998).

[4] A brief but descriptive article about the Finnish war was published by the main Finnish newspaper, *Helsingin Sanomat*, see www.hs.fi/english/article/War+of+Finland+1808-1809+/1135234369020.

[5] Nousiainen, J, *The Finnish system of government: From a mixed constitution to parliamentarism* (Vammala, Vammalan Kirjapaino, 2001).

[6] Despite mainly having inherited it from the Swedish Crown and maintaining it for about a century.

identity promoted the quiet but persistent constitutional aspirations of autonomy. Thus, even under near-revolutionary conditions in 1906–07, Finland managed to change its legislature from a four-chamber estate assembly to a unicameral parliament, to be elected by universal suffrage. It is worth noting that, in doing so, Finland was the first state in the world to grant women full political rights.[7]

B. The Development of Finnish Constitutionalism 1917–90

The February and October Revolutions of 1917 led to Russia's collapse. The chaos that ensued in mainland Russia induced the collapse of the Grand Duchy of Finland and breakdown of the Finnish government, military force, economy and society. By 1917 the Finnish people had experienced a rapid population growth, industrialisation, and the rise of a comprehensive labour movement, as well as rapid modernisation in terms of the creation of the Parliament. The power vacuum of 1917 led to a bitter contest for the leadership of the Finnish state between the left-leaning labour movement and the more right-wing Conservatives. Finally, Finland declared independence on 6 December 1917. Although the majority of Finns supported sovereignty, the declaration occurred in the context of the power struggle. Therefore, it neither unified nor pacified the nation and society. Finland was still socio-economically a divided nation. At the critical stage of political liberation, the class divide descended into a civil war in 1918, eventually escalating into one of the most brutal in the history of Europe.[8]

The 1919 Form of Government Act provided for a semi-presidential regime in the newly founded independent state of Finland. The 1928 parliamentary statute was also considered part the constitution. It embraced a tension between strong presidential powers and parliamentarianism, which remained nearly untouched until the 1980s. The system formed a 'flexible but rigid' constitution. For about 60 years, the written constitutional text was interpreted in a variety of different ways. It was capable of resolving national crises and offered a strange continuity in political affairs, despite the changing conditions. Even the questionable proceedings of the post-World War II cabinets were seen as fitting within its framework.[9] The adaptive constitution was itself a paradox in the strictly legalist jurisprudence.

[7] An article about women's electoral rights in Finland written by the former minister of Social Affairs and Health, Tuula Haatainen, see: www.afaemme.org/studies/11%20CM_100%20Years%20Political%20Rights%20Women%20Finland_Haatainen.pdf.

[8] Finland's civil war lasted from 27 January to 15 May 1918, during which out of a population of three million, 37,000 lost their lives.

[9] For a brief summary of the Cabinet proceedings of post-war trials, see: http://motherearthtravel.com/history/finland/history-7.htm.

Finally, during the presidential term of Mauno Koivisto (1982–94), the constitutional balance took a significant swing towards parliamentarianism. A series of reforms between 1987 and 1995 changed the form of presidential elections and abolished the president's autonomous right to dissolve Parliament.

In terms of basic rights of the people, the 1919 Form of Government Act, which remained in force for over 70 years, provided protection of only the rights that traditionally were included in the Western, liberalistic constitutional tradition. Such rights were the protection of life and honour, personal liberty and property, freedom of religion, speech and movement, including the freedom of assembly and right to join unions. Freedom of movement and secrecy of communications were also protected. These rights were only protected in the case of Finnish nationals; foreigners on Finnish soil were not included within their ambit. These basic rights were only seen as binding on state entities and public authorities—they had no horizontal applicability between private individuals. Furthermore, the legislature was granted by the Constitution the ability to ignore these basic rights, if certain emergency conditions were at hand. This ability ensured the political flexibility of the written law.

C. The Reformed Finnish Constitution 1995–2000

A complete constitutional reform took place between 1995 and 2000. Building on the three decades of constitutional debate and committee work by experts, a commission composed of parliamentarians produced a report that was formulated into a Government Bill to the Parliament in 1998. The constitutional reform was a milestone in the political culture of Finland, since the opposing party ideologies were able to conclude in the process. The time had come to strengthen the position of the Parliament vis-à-vis that of the president in the division of state powers.

A new list of protected rights was incorporated based on the fundamental values of individual freedom, democratic participation and personal security. The most significant changes, with respect to the rights included in the 1919 Form of Government, widened the scope of these basic rights and liberties. Since 1995, basic rights provisions pertain to all persons under the jurisdiction of the Finnish legal system, regardless of citizenship, not just Finnish nationals, as had been the case hitherto. In addition, it included for the first time economic, social and cultural rights.

The reformed list of basic rights supported the protections of equality with new protections: the prohibition of segregation, equal treatment of children, and gender equality. And now, the aperture of prior basic liberties was widened and simultaneously made more specific. A provision regarding the right to a clean environment was inserted. Procedural rights concerning the use of law and good governance were also included in the renewed list.[10]

For political reasons, Finland only joined the Council of Europe in 1989, well after its Nordic counterparts. Thus, constitutional reform was strongly influenced by international legal instruments that had become binding on Finland.[11] The interpretation of basic rights already had international precedents. As a general rule, the new list of basic rights was intended strengthen the binding force of human rights norms within the Finnish legal system. However, many provisions of Finnish Constitution provided even stronger protection of individual rights.

Finland's new Constitution entered into force in 2000 and is based on the four earlier constitutional statutes. The provisions of the new Constitution are generally more modern and have evolved towards greater democracy. The new Constitution defines the Parliament as a central actor in the process of government formation, leaving the president with a largely ceremonial role. The reform completes Finland's path into a parliamentary form from the previous, somewhat peculiar, semi-presidential system.

The reform was also influenced by the Europeanisation of constitutional law in Finland. The legal consequences of the direct effect of Community law have internationalised the source of values of Finnish jurisprudence. A process of constitutionalisation within the European Union has recently led to the drafting of the Constitutional Treaty. The Treaty coexists with national constitutions and has its own justification and its autonomy. Today, the constitutions are regarded as intertwined. From the standpoint of the Finnish legal system, the relationship between the different levels of protection of human rights and the Charter's fundamental rights is not as contradictory as perhaps in some other Member states.[12]

Following the constitutional reforms of 1990–2000, state powers have been transferred and Parliament strengthened vis-à-vis the presidency. In conclusion, the amended Constitution in force today is a carefully drafted and unanimously adopted document. For the citizens, the Constitution is seen as quite neutral with strong legitimacy and fitted for application. Politically, the Constitution has been adopted into already established state practices, but due to history, Finnish cnstitutionalism includes a long tradition of party interrelations and governing coalitions.[13]

[10] See the Constitutional Committee Statement 25 of 1993, regarding the Government Bill 309 of 1993.

[11] At the time, Finland had signed and ratified about 40 internationally binding Conventions, mainly within the UN, ILO and the European Union, such as the European Convention on Human Rights.

[12] Nieminen, L, *Eurooppalaistuva valtiosääntöoikeus—Valtiosääntöistyvä Eurooppa* (Vammala, Suomalaisen Lakimiesyhdistyksen Julkaisuja, 2004) A-sarja 259.

[13] Nousiainen, J, *The Finnish system of government: From a mixed constitution to parliamentarism* (Vammala, Vammalan Kirjapaino, 2001).

II. EXPLICIT AND IMPLICIT CULTURAL VALUES OF THE FINNISH CONSTITUTIONAL ACT

The first chapter of the Finnish Constitutional Act embodies the three core values that form the framework for the entire Constitution: human dignity, individual rights, and equality. The first section states that Finland is a sovereign republic and that the Constitution shall guarantee the inviolability of human dignity, the sanctity of individual freedoms and rights, and the promotion of justice in society. This section explores the basis of values to which the further sections can be compared, but it has also independent interpretational value.[14]

The second reference to individual rights and freedoms highlights the central position of basic rights in the Finnish Constitution. This includes the right to self-determination, which underlies and precedes other rights. The third reference to justice denotes equality but also economic, social and educational rights specified later in the Constitutional Act. In short, the Finnish way of thinking underlies the lawfulness of the exercise of power, the separation of powers and the protection of fundamental rights of the individual.

A. Human Dignity, Democracy and Rule of Law

The concept of formal equality under law was the starting point of the first constitution of independent Finland. When the new Constitution of 2000 was being drafted, *human dignity* was included as one of the fundamental provisions[15] that the Constitution now rests upon. Its fundamental value is highlighted by the fact that human dignity is mentioned in the first section of the whole Constitution. This formulation was borrowed from the German Constitution, where human dignity has a special position as the most important and invariable basic right.

The inviolability of human dignity as a core value expresses the general humane fundamentals the Finnish legal conception of 'basic rights'. According to the Government Bill, the most basic rights of individuals are seen as independent from the state and its current legal order.[16] This 'natural justice-like' reasoning of the Bill has ignited controversy among Finnish legal scholars, who traditionally tend to cling to the legalistic reasoning of law. In addition, the concept refers to the principal idea of equality between all human beings. The more specific list of basic rights in Chapter 2 of the Constitution is built on the concept of protection of human dignity along

[14] See pp 40 to 41 of the Bill referred to in n 10.

[15] Section 1 of the Finnish Constitution, second para: 'The constitution shall guarantee the inviolability of human dignity and the freedom and rights of the individual and promote justice in society.'

[16] See p 42 of Government Bill 309 of 1993.

with the fundamental values of individual freedom, democratic participation and personal security. When interpreting the basic rights listed in Chapter 2, the provision on the inviolability of human dignity can be seen as also having general interpretational value.

Section 2 of the Constitution highlights the values of *democracy* and the *rule of law*. It states that the powers of the state in Finland are vested in the people, who are represented by the Parliament. *Democracy* entails the right of the individual to participate in and influence the development of society, whereas *rule of law* implies the principle of legality, a traditional and continuous characteristic of Finnish legal thinking. According to KJ Ståhlberg, the first President of Finland and one of the writers of the early Constitution, 'democratic progress founded on law' was included in his conception of the rule of law.[17] This principle was further developed in the new Constitution, where all exercise of public power must be based on law.

The value of *participation* is protected by section 14, which governs the electoral and participatory rights of Finnish nationals. Every Finnish citizen who has reached 18 years of age has the right to vote in national elections and referendums. Specific provisions govern the eligibility to run for office in national elections. Every Finnish citizen and every other citizen of the European Union residing in Finland, having attained 18 years of age, has the right to vote in European Parliamentary elections. Also, every Finnish citizen and every foreigner permanently residing in Finland, having attained 18 years of age, has the right to vote in municipal elections and municipal referendums. The public authorities must promote the opportunities for the individual to participate in societal activity and to influence the decisions that concern him or her.

Thus, from protecting merely the formal legalism, Finland has progressed towards protecting human dignity and in the process, has become a truly participatory *democracy*. It is important to note, that despite a few raised eyebrows among the jurists, this process of renewing basic rights was unanimous and amicable in the Finnish Parliament. The lowest common denominator of Finnish society, protection of human dignity, now lies at the core of the Constitution.

B. Equality and Equity

Hofstede[18] has conducted extensive research about the national cultural values and their impact on society, workplace, education and families. According to Hofstede, Finnish culture values *equality* and has a small 'power distance', meaning that all individuals in societies are fundamentally

[17] Hallberg, P, *The rule of law* (Helsinki, Edita Publishing, 2004).

[18] See: http://geert-hofstede.com/finland.html.

equal and social attitudes reflect that. Lewis,[19] a cross-cultural expert on Finnish culture, also identifies equality as one of the core Finnish values.

Section 6 of the Constitution, entitled 'Equality', states that everyone is equal before the law. The second paragraph enumerates various qualities, on the grounds of which discrimination or different treatment is forbidden. According to the Non-discrimination Act,

> nobody may be discriminated against on the basis of age, ethnic or national origin, nationality, language, religion, belief, opinion, health, disability, sexual orientation or other personal characteristics. The prohibition of discrimination based on gender is covered by the provisions of the Act on Equality between Women and Men (609/1986).[20]

Since the passing of the equality provision in the Finnish Constitution, Finland has also adopted the Charter of Fundamental Rights of the European Union.[21] Chapter 3 on Equality in many ways goes beyond the notion of 'equality before the law' as described in the Finnish Constitution. The main differences or additions can be seen in the European articles that highlight respect for cultural, religious and linguistic diversity (article 22), the rights of the elderly (article 25), as well as the inclusion of people with disabilities (article 26). The promotion of 'diversity' goes beyond the mere prohibition of discrimination. Respecting plurality of language, religion and conviction requires more from a state than simply protecting its citizens from discrimination.

According to the legislative proposal of the Constitution,[22] the prerequisite of equality does not exclude positive discrimination, but in fact allows it, provided that there is 'an acceptable reason' for the differential treatment. The Constitution supports equity. Equity can be defined as the principle of treating people fairly according to their different needs. The terms equity and equality are often used interchangeably, yet they have conceptually different meanings. Equality can be defined as the 'state of being equal, especially in status, rights or opportunities'.[23] Equity and positive discrimination, 'the practice or policy of favouring individuals belonging to groups which suffer discrimination',[24] may involve distributing a resource equally or unequally, depending upon what the fairness requires in a given situation. The following section discusses how Finnish law supports both equality and equity.

[19] Lewis, RD, *Finland, cultural lone wolf* (Yarmouth ME, *Intercultural Press/Nicholas Brealey*, 2005).

[20] Non-discrimination Act, see: www.finlex.fi/en/laki/kaannokset/2004/en20040021.

[21] 2007/C 303/01.

[22] See p 40 of the Government Bill 1 of 1998.

[23] Definition by *Oxford English Dictionary*, see: http://oxforddictionaries.com/definition/english/equality.

[24] Definition by *Oxford English Dictionary*, see: http://oxforddictionaries.com/definition/english/positive%2Bdiscrimination?q=positive+discrimination.

An Act on Equality between Women and Men prohibits discrimination on the basis of sex or gender.[25] The Act is applied in the contexts of recruitment, work-life balance, equal pay, education, social welfare and healthcare services. Employers are accountable for promoting gender equality by conducting equitable recruitment of women and men, creating equal opportunities for career advancement, promoting equality between women and men in terms of employment and pay, developing working conditions to ensure gender equality, and facilitating work-life balance. The composition of public administration bodies and entities exercising public authority or crafting legislation must maintain a minimum 40 per cent representation of women in government committees and advisory boards, unless there are special reasons to the contrary.

The Finnish Constitution protects the language and cultural heritage of certain ethnic groups in Finland, such as the Sami and Roma. The Sami people are entitled to receive services in Sami language when dealing with the authorities. A similar right is guaranteed to both Finnish- and Swedish-speaking individuals. According to the Act, the public authorities are required to provide services for the Finnish-speaking and Swedish-speaking populations on an equal basis. Sign language services and necessary accommodations for people with disabilities are also explicitly articulated in the Constitution.

Section 11 of the Constitution assures freedom of religion and conscience, including the right to practise a religion, to express one's convictions and to be a member of or decline membership of a religious community.

The Constitution guarantees freedom of opinion and speech. However, one is not allowed to violate basic rights or human dignity of others by claiming their right to freedom of speech. Hate speech and other offensive statements towards particular ethnic groups or other minority groups are considered violations of the law. In Finland, crimes related to prejudice or hostility towards others, based on ethnicity, nationality, religion, conscience, sexual orientation, gender identity, gender expression or disability, are considered hate crimes.[26] Distribution of racist material is prohibited[27] and is monitored by Finnish law enforcement.

Section 19 of the Constitution highlights equality based on socio-economic status. Everyone is guaranteed adequate social, health and medical services and the right to basic subsistence in the event of unemployment, illness, disability, ageing or at the birth of a child. Discrimination on the

[25] The Act on Equality between Women and Men, see: http://www.refworld.org/docid/3ae6b51c0.html.

[26] Hate crime definition in Finnish, see: www.polamk.fi/poliisi/poliisioppilaitos/home.nsf/webprint/C52B9C8FE74D48C9C2257936002553CB?OpenDocument.

[27] The former Ombudsman for Minorities addresses these issues at their website, see: www.vahemmistovaltuutettu.fi/intermin/vvt/home.nsf/pages/02D68EB7EF560127C22573A200335C90?opendocument.

grounds of pregnancy, childbirth, parenthood or family obligations is prohibited. Finnish society values and supports families by offering maternity, paternity and parental paid leave following childbirth. Either one of the parents may take parental leave. In Finland, the combined maternity and parental leave amounts to around 280 weekdays. One of the parents may stay at home to care for their children, and they are entitled to financial support in the form of home care allowance until the child reaches the age of three. If they choose to use day care services, those fees are determined on the basis of the family's income. For low-income families day care is free of charge.[28]

Section 16 outlines everyone's right to free basic education, including instruction, school materials, meals, healthcare, dental care, commuting, special needs education and remedial teaching. There is equal access for everyone, regardless of gender, economic situation, linguistic or cultural background. Higher education is also free, and there are no tuition fees in universities. Students are expected to pay for their books, housing, travel and meals.[29]

Finland's equalising educational system achieves high standards. A global survey, the Programme for International Student Assessment (PISA),[30] evaluated the skills of Finnish 15-year-old students as being among the best in the world. PISA assessed literacy in three domains: reading, mathematics and science. Differences between the strongest and weakest students and between schools and regions are remarkably small in Finland. Also differences based on language or socio-economic background have a lower impact on students' performance in Finland than in the other PISA countries. It is interesting that Finnish students spend less time per week studying than other students in OECD countries, and the annual expenditure on education is the OECD average. The reason for Finland's success can be found in the underlying values of quality, efficiency, equity and internationalism.

C. Justice and Freedom

According to the Finnish Constitution, the judicial power in Finland belongs to independent courts, with the Supreme Court and the Supreme Administrative Court exercising ultimate jurisdiction. The independence of the judiciary means that the courts are under the sole obligation to apply the law in force, without any restrictions or instructions from authorities. The Constitution also guarantees that cases are heard appropriately and without undue delay. Moreover, the public status of he hearings is guaranteed under

[28] Equality in Finland, see: www.vahemmistovaltuutettu.fi/intermin/vvt/home.nsf/files/sm_tasaarvo_engl_low/$file/sm_tasaarvo_engl_low.pdf.

[29] Funding structure of Finnish education system, see: www.minedu.fi/OPM/Koulutus/koulutuspolitiikka/rahoitus/?lang=en.

[30] Programme for International Student Assessment (PISA), see: www.oecd.org/pisa/.

the Constitution. This is thought to provide the citizen with an opportunity to supervise the functioning of the courts, and increases confidence in the justice system.

Personal freedom is protected and the legality of decisions on deprivation of liberty is guaranteed in section 7. According to this section, no one shall be sentenced to death, tortured or otherwise treated in a manner violating human dignity. The personal integrity of the individual shall not be violated, nor shall anyone be deprived of liberty without a reason specifically indicated in Parliament. A penalty involving deprivation of liberty may be imposed only by a court of law. The lawfulness of other cases of deprivation of liberty may be submitted for review by a court of law. The rights of individuals deprived of their liberty shall be guaranteed by an Act. Furthermore, the principle of legality in criminal cases is outlined by section 1, which states that no one shall be found guilty of a criminal offence or be sentenced to a punishment on the basis of a deed, which has not been determined punishable by an Act of Parliament at the time of its commission. Also, the legalistic notion is present in the Acts governing the criminal procedure. Two key principles of regular criminal procedures are orality and immediacy. Therefore, it is to a large degree the duty of the prosecutor, and not of the Court, to conduct the proceedings in the main hearing. This aims to provide a fair trial to the parties. Traditionally, the true legal tenet of the Finnish criminal procedure has followed the contradictory principle: no judgment may be passed until all the parties have been given the opportunity to be present at the trial and to express their views concerning the case.

Personal rights and freedoms of individuals prevail in Finland through constitutional sections 9 to 15. These sections include the right to free movement (section 9) and privacy (section 10), which protects everyone's private life and honours the sanctity of the home. Furthermore, the secrecy of correspondence, telephony and other confidential communications is inviolable. Everyone has freedom of expression, which entails the right to express, disseminate and receive information, opinions and other communications without obstruction by anyone. More detailed provisions on the exercise of the freedom of expression are laid down by an Act. Provisions on restrictions relating to pictorial programmes that are necessary for the protection of children may be laid down by an Act. Also according to section 10, documents and recordings in the possession of the authorities are public, unless their publication has for compelling reasons been specifically restricted by an Act. Everyone has a right of access to public documents and recordings.

Section 13 concerns the freedoms of assembly and of association. Everyone has the right to arrange meetings and demonstrations without a permit, as well as the right to participate in them. Freedom of association entails the right to form an association without a permit, to be a member or not to be a member of an association and to participate in the activities of an association. The freedom to form trade unions and to organise in order to look after other interests is likewise guaranteed. Under section 15, the property of everyone is protected.

Secularism is not a value that is widely recognised within the Constitution. Despite allowing everyone the freedom to choose his or her religious beliefs or the lack thereof (section 11), the Finnish state still grants legislative powers to the Finnish Evangelical Lutheran Church, which has sole jurisdiction regarding the Church Code. The Evangelical Lutheran Church holds a very special position within the Constitution.

D. Inclusion and Community

Apart from the protection of human dignity, equality, individual rights and freedoms, the Constitution obligates the public authorities to integrate and include individuals into society. Many of the protected individual rights actually demand from the authorities both negative and positive measures.[31] The equality provision, prohibition of discrimination and requirement of inclusion form a constitutional trinity, which strongly directs the public authorities' functions in safeguarding basic and human rights. However, as an EU member state and a signatory party of many human rights conventions, Finland already has established a minimum level of protection of basic rights.

The Finnish welfare state is based on the belief that providing equal opportunities for all prohibits exclusion in itself. The means of inclusion contains measures of social, labour and educational politics. For example, in the case of education, inclusion is seen as an integral part of legal norms governing education. At the constitutional level[32] the value of inclusion is integrated in the provisions.[33] The lower-ranked norms and laws governing education include a wide interpretation of exclusion. Exclusion does not only mean lack of finances and problems related to poverty, but also other kind of marginalisation. The problem is, however, that the minimum requirements set by laws and regulations often tend to turn into maximum levels of services. This creates pressure for legal instruments to become more and more detailed.

The goal of Finnish society is to achieve a balance where everyone's human dignity is recognised and secured, and where the different minorities are included within the society and its functions. This means that society needs to be flexible and support sufficiently the manifold identities of

[31] See s 22 of the Finnish Constitution: Protection of Basic Rights and Liberties.
[32] Section 16 of the Constitution provides the right to free basic education for everyone.
[33] Pajukoski, M, *Koulutuksen osallisuuden edellytykset—inkluusio ja lainsäädäntö at University of Joensuu* (Joensuu, Joensuu University Press, 2008).

individuals, namely its diversity. Possessing a background that deviates from the norm should not mean exclusion or marginalisation. However, this goal is not always met in practice.[34] The actualisation of the values expressed in the Constitution is examined through the following examples.

The value of diversity is expressed by section 17, which provides for the right to one's language and culture. Finland is officially a bilingual country, so both national languages of Finnish and Swedish are mentioned. The public authorities must provide for the cultural and societal needs of the Finnish-speaking and Swedish-speaking populations of the country, on an equal basis. The Sami, as an indigenous people, as well as the Roma and other groups, have the right to maintain and develop their own language and culture.

The constitutional basic rights are primarily rights of the individual, not of groups. On the other hand, for example the freedom of assembly can only be realised in a community, and the above-mentioned linguistic and cultural rights only gain significance through a community.

E. Peace, Life, Integrity and Security

The promotion of peace is mentioned in the first section of the Constitution as an international obligation: 'Finland participates in international co-operation for the protection of peace and human rights and for the development of society.' In the individual sphere, section 7 of the Constitution protects the personal rights to life and security, according to which everyone has the right to life, personal liberty, integrity and security. In more detail, no one shall be sentenced to death, tortured or otherwise treated in a manner violating human dignity. Thus, the Constitution protects individuals from any form of cruel and unusual punishment. This means both mental and physical treatment. The personal integrity of the individual shall not be violated, nor shall anyone be deprived of liberty arbitrarily or without a reason prescribed by an Act. Penalties physically or mentally violating human dignity are forbidden. The protection of personal integrity prevents acts such as forced medical examinations. The right to security emphasises the government's obligation to protect citizens' lives. Freedom also includes the freedom not to act or make commitments, and security is a prerequisite for this. However, the definition of the right to life excludes human life in the early stages of its development, and abortion of a foetus is not considered contradictory to this section. Full command of these individual rights is seen to begin at the moment of birth.

[34] Committee on the Elimination of Racial Discrimination examines report of Finland: www.ohchr.org/EN/NewsEvents/Pages/DisplayNews.aspx?NewsID=12457&LangID=E.

F. Compassion and Environment

The relatively strong commitment to social rights echoes the value of compassion behind the Nordic welfare model and the Finnish Constitution. The chapter on economic, social and cultural fundamental rights is far-reaching. This was a conscious decision by the Constitution's drafters. The aim was to capture the concrete and applicable social and economic norms on the constitutional level to highlight and protect these norms as core values of the state.

The right to social security is protected under section 19. The public authorities guarantee for everyone adequate social, health and medical services. Moreover, the public authorities must support families and others responsible for providing for children so that they have the ability to ensure the well-being of their children. Public authorities must promote the right of everyone to housing. Section 19 reveals a strong sense of responsibility on the part of the state to provide the basic necessities for its citizens. This section is perhaps at the core of the Nordic constitutional tradition that places great emphasis on the common cultural traditions of solidarity and compassion.

According to Hofstede,[35] Finland is a 'feminine society' that cares for its members and supports a high quality of life for everyone. Whereas masculine societies value competition, achievement, assertiveness and material reward, the focus in a feminine society is on general well-being of its members. Feminine societies prefer cooperation, modesty and caring for the weak.

The only responsibility laid on the individual citizen, apart from naturally respecting the rights of other individuals, is responsibility for the environment. According to section 20, nature and its biodiversity, the environment and the national heritage are the responsibility of everyone. The public authorities will endeavour to guarantee for everyone the right to a healthy environment and the ability to influence the decisions that concern their own living environment. This responsibility for a clean environment makes future generations a party to this basic right.

The only explicit requirement of honesty is directed at the members of the Government. According to section 60, the Government consists of the Prime Minister and the necessary number of Ministers. Ministers shall be Finnish citizens known to be honest and competent. According to Piispanen-Krabbe and Hovemyr,[36] Finns value honesty, and it takes the form of a moral obligation to be open and direct toward others. At the macro level, this takes the form of an absolute intolerance of corruption and dishonesty among public

[35] See: http://geert-hofstede.com/finland.html.

[36] Piispanen-Krabbe, T and Hovemyr, A, *Cultural Detective Finland*, 2nd edn (Laredo, TX, Nipporica Associates, LLC, 2011). See: www.culturaldetective.com/package.html#FIN.

officials. Finns are law-abiding and tend to respect community rules and company policies to the letter. Common good is prioritised over individual gain. According to Hofstede,[37] Finland has a medium-high preference for avoiding uncertainty. A culture with high uncertainty avoidance has high expectations for its members to follow normative behaviours. These cultures follow rules and people desire security and certainty.

Over recent years there has been a wave of protest and outcry about corruption and the lack of transparency of leaders in different societies. The Corruption Perceptions Index[38] evaluates 183 countries and territories according to their perceived levels of public sector corruption. Finnish commitment to the values of honesty and transparency is evidenced by Finland being among the top three least corrupted nations, according to the Corruption Perceptions Index.

III. LAW IN ACTION—DO THE VALUES EXPRESSED IN THE TEXT CONFORM WITH REALITY?

A. Supervision of the Compliance with the Constitution

The purpose of the Constitution is to provide citizens with a reliable idea about the way the political system works, and what the legal status of the individual is based upon. However, compliance with the Constitution requires efficient supervision.

The Constitution conveys to public authorities the responsibility for guaranteeing basic rights and liberties as well as the full spectrum of human rights. When legislation is drafted, it is the duty of the Constitutional Law Committee of Parliament to ensure the constitutionality of legislative proposals. This abstract control takes place before the law is applied on any concrete case. This abstract form of control is at the centre of Finnish constitutional compliance supervision, and has replaced the need for a national Constitutional Court. As it stands, the strong supervising position of Finland's Constitutional Committee is unique among nations.[39]

After a law has been passed and is applicable, it should be in conformity with the Constitution. In individual cases, the courts must take the constitutional provisions into consideration and apply the law in a manner favouring basic rights. This means that the courts may not enforce an act that is in obvious contradiction to the Constitution. It is the duty of the Chancellor of Justice and the Parliamentary Ombudsman to oversee public authorities' respect of basic rights. In concrete individual cases, courts are required

[37] Hofstede, G, *Culture's Consequences: Comparing Values, Behaviors, Institutions, and Organizations Across Nations*, 2nd edn (Thousand Oaks, CA, Sage Publications, 2001).
[38] The Corruption Perceptions Index, see: http://cpi.transparency.org/cpi2011/results/.
[39] Saraviita, I, *Suomalainen perusoikeusjärjestelmä* (Helsinki, Talentum, 2005).

by the constitution to overrule a law if its application in that specific context would clearly not be in compliance with basic rights conferred by the Constitution.[40] This model was copied from Swedish practice. So far, this provision has rarely been applied in practice.

The full realisation of basic rights often calls for a variety of measures. For example, guaranteeing legal protections not only requires up-to-date legislation, but also efficient government mechanisms and judicial system. Thus the fulfilment of many basic rights, for example the right to a fair trial, requires major financial input by society.

Despite a relatively modern constitutionally protected list of basic rights and liberties, the Finnish human rights culture is still surprisingly undeveloped. Finland regularly receives convictions from the European Court of Human Rights.[41] It seems as if the Finnish Courts interpret the basic rights protected by the European Convention on Human Rights to some extent differently from the European Court of Human Rights. This has happened especially in cases concerning the speed of judicial processes and those of freedom of speech, versus the Finnish relatively strictly interpreted limitation of honour and reputation.

B. Challenges of the Present Practice of National Basic and Human Rights Policies

Violence against women is a global human rights problem that affects the wellbeing and equality of individuals and undermines human dignity. Violence causes physical, sexual, emotional and psychological disadvantage and suffering. Violence does not only mean physical assault; it also occurs in the form of control over another human being. In Finland, violence against women is about twice as common as the EU average.[42] According to a national study, 43.5 per cent of all Finnish women have been subjected to physical or sexual violence, or the threat of violence, at least once after the age of 15.[43]

In its recommendations to Finland in 2008, the Committee on the Elimination of Discrimination against Women (CEDAW) remained concerned about the high incidence of violence against women, including a high number of

[40] See s 106 of the Finnish Constitution: Primacy of the Constitution.

[41] Over the past 15 years, the ECHR has decided cases against Finland twice as often as cases against all other Nordic states together. Decisions where the Court ruled against the Nordic states during years 1959–2009 total as following: Finland 103, Sweden 43, Norway 20, and Denmark 13.

[42] A Eurobarometer Report on Domestic Violence, 2010. See: http://ec.europa.eu/public_opinion/archives/ebs/ebs_344_en.pdf.

[43] A comprehensive study on the matter was made by Piispa, Heiskanen, Kääriäinen and Sirén: *Naisiin kohdistunut väkivalta* (Helsinki, The European Institute for Crime Prevention and Control, 2006).

women killed in domestic violence and sexual harassment. CEDAW was also concerned that Finnish policy on violence against women is couched in gender-neutral language, which undermines the notion that such violence is a clear manifestation of discrimination against women. CEDAW regretted that the number of shelters, many of which have been established and are operating on the initiative of NGOs, is insufficient to meet the needs of women, both in numbers and in their mode of operation.[44] While welcoming the adoption of the national Programme on the Prevention of Violence Against Women in 2010, the Committee Against Torture (CAT) recommended that Finland should redouble its efforts to prevent and eradicate all forms of violence against women, and adopt legislation with a view to increasing the number of shelters for victims, with appropriate funding and specialised staff. These recommendations are yet to be fully realised by the Government.

As the national rapporteur on trafficking in human beings, the Ombudsman for Minorities, monitors phenomena relating to human trafficking, oversees action against human trafficking and issues proposals, recommendations, statements and advice relevant to developing anti-trafficking work and promotes the status and rights of victims of human trafficking. According to the Ombudsman for minorities, trafficking of human beings is a serious crime and a grave violation of human rights. It violates the dignity and integrity of individuals. Finland is a transit and destination country of victims of trafficking. In Finland, human trafficking manifests itself in at least two ways: prostitution and procuring. The exploitation of foreign workers and immigrants in sectors such as domestic work, the service industry, the construction industry and the berry-picking field, can meet the statutory definition of a human trafficking offence. So far, no cases of organ trafficking have been reported in Finland. Finnish citizens may also fall victim to human trafficking. Lately, also foreigners begging on the streets, of Roma background, have been thought to be victims of traffickers. In Finland, human trafficking is an offence which carries a severe penalty.[45]

C. Equality Provisions in Action

During the most recent Universal Periodic Review of Finland by the United Nations Human Rights Council in May 2012, Finland received a number of recommendations to improve its human rights situation.[46] One of the

[44] See: http://lib.ohchr.org/HRBodies/UPR/Documents/Session1/FI/Finland.pdf.

[45] Trafficking in Finland, see: www.vahemmistovaltuutettu.fi/intermin/vvt/home.nsf/pages/1B936BA99455F674C22576C500386A8A.

[46] The Universal Periodic Review (UPR) involves a review of the human rights records of all 192 UN Member States every four years. The ultimate aim of this new mechanism is to improve the human rights situation in all countries and address human rights violations wherever they occur. The national report of Finland of 2012, see: http://daccess-dds-ny.un.org/doc/UNDOC/GEN/G12/116/11/PDF/G1211611.pdf?OpenElement.

most frequent recommendations given to Finland concerns the value of equality in practice. The recommendations raised concerns that, despite the equality provisions of the Constitution and other laws, de facto discrimination against persons of foreign origin persists in a number of areas. Concrete examples include the lower employment rate among people of immigrant origin.

At the end of 2011, non-Finnish citizens represented 3.4 per cent of the Finnish population. Of the general population, 4.5 per cent speaks a language other than Finnish, Swedish or Sami as their first language. The largest of these groups spoke Russian, Estonian, Somali, English or Arabic as their first language.[47] The largest groups experiencing unemployment spoke the following first languages: Somali (12.3 per cent unemployed), Kurd (10.8 per cent) or Farsi (9.9 per cent).[48] Immigrants and refugees continue to face difficulties when trying to access services and to procure contractual services. These examples concern not only discrimination based on ethnic origin, but on other grounds as well.

On the legislative level, some fragmentation of the law persists, although the recently updated Non-Discrimination Act has significantly strengthened the legislative framework on non-discrimination and equality in several areas. The updated Non-Discrimination Act entered into force on 1 January 2015 after almost seven years of preparation. The scope of the improved Act is very broad as it covers all public and private activities, with the exception of private and family life and the right to practise religion. The protection against discrimination is now equal regardless of the reason for discrimination.[49] Up to now, the possibilities for a discriminated person to get advice or legal aid have been different depending on the discrimination ground. Still, despite the equality norm in the Constitution and the improved Act, other provisions concerning equality in Finland are somewhat incoherent. The biggest challenge remains with the interpretation of the Non-Discrimination Act and awareness of the rights included both in public and private spheres of life.[50]

Similar to the Finnish Constitution's equality provision, based on a limited list of reasons, the applicable national and EU non-discrimination law does not allow for the extension of these grounds through case law. The only possible approach, and indeed the one taken by the national courts

[47] Finnish vital statistics, see: www.stat.fi/til/vaerak/2011/vaerak_2011_2012-03-16_tie_001_en.html.

[48] Statistics Finland, *Työttömäksi joutumisen riski suurin vieraskielisillä* (2012); www.stat.fi/til/tyokay/2011/01/tyokay_2011_01_2012-06-05_tie_001_fi.html.

[49] For more information on the renewed Act please see the Ministry of Justice press release in English: http://oikeusministerio.fi/en/index/currentissues/tiedotteet/2014/12/uusiyhdenvertaisuuslakivoimaanensivuodenalusta.html.

[50] For more information on the renewed Act please see the Ministry of Justice press release in English: http://oikeusministerio.fi/en/index/currentissues/tiedotteet/2014/12/uusiyhdenvertaisuuslakivoimaanensivuodenalusta.html.

and the Court of Justice of the EU, is that of interpreting an already existing basis widely; for example, to include discrimination based on gender reassignment under the category of discrimination based on gender identity. However, this approach remains very limited as it covers only a small group of people who suffer from discrimination on grounds of gender identity and gender expression. This also does not include discrimination against intersex people, even though the basis on which intersex people suffer discrimination is biological sex itself. This is primarily because national, and indeed also EU law, is based on the male/female binary sex model. People who do not easily fit these gender norms, such as transgender and intersex people, encounter numerous difficulties, both at the practical level of everyday life and at the legal level. Obviously, this is not acceptable under the European Union's founding Treaty. Article 2 of this treaty is founded on respect for human dignity and human rights, including the rights of persons belonging to minorities.[51]

However, it should be remembered that the existing EU non-discrimination law sets out *minimum* rules only. Member states are not prevented from providing higher levels of protection against discrimination. This can be done through a broader interpretation of the terms in favour of victims of discrimination, or a broader material scope of the national legislation, including the inclusion of additional discrimination grounds. In fact, from the point of view of the victims of discrimination on grounds of gender identity and gender expression, good regulations at the national level are probably the most beneficial approach. Given this situation, Finland could make the most of the flexibility inherent in EU non-discrimination law, and go well beyond the minimum established at the common EU level when redrafting its national Non-discrimination Act. In fact, the Ombudsman for Equality has insisted that the currently prevailing Equality Act of Men and Women needs to be amended to include provisions for the protection of gender minorities against discrimination and the promotion of their equality in society. Recently, provisions on prohibition of discrimination based on gender identity or gender expression were added to the Equality Act and entered into force on 1 January 2015.

D. More to be Done on Inclusion

Finland has very high global rankings on freedom of expression and press freedom listings. However, a recent increase in hate speech in social media has become a problem. In order to strengthen inclusion in Finland, government efforts in the fight against discrimination, racism and xenophobia,

[51] For a thorough study on the discrimination of trans- and intersex people on the European level, see: http://ec.europa.eu/justice/discrimination/files/trans_and_intersex_people_web3_en.pdf.

should be increased. More work is needed to increase respect for foreigners and members of ethnic minorities. Additional restrictions on hate speech in social media should be considered. While cases of discrimination continue to be reported, actual complaints alleging discrimination or hate speech are rarely brought to court. Convictions for racist crimes remain rare.[52] Racism and xenophobia are phenomena that require more stringent monitoring of actions of prosecutors and police, to ensure that racially motivated crimes are promptly detected, investigated and punished.

Despite the right to education being included in the basic values of the Finnish Constitution, the current legislation does not provide for compulsory basic education for asylum-seeking or refugee children that are not permanently living in the municipality. In order to do so, the law should be amended to provide equal rights and access to basic education for every child living in Finland. Furthermore, specific attention should be given to ensure that all children are treated equally, regardless of ethnic background or special needs.

According to a 2011 study, child poverty has grown significantly.[53] In Finland, the poverty of families with children tripled between 1990 and 2009. This increases the risk of social exclusion of children and young people. Minorities tend to suffer disproportionally from societal inequalities. However, the cycle of social marginalisation is also linked to the decreased time spent with the family, which may result in disturbed behaviour among children and adolescents. Therefore, reducing child poverty and social marginalisation should be a key concern for policy-making in order to improve inclusion in Finnish society.

IV. CONCLUSION

Finland's geographical location between the East and the West has strongly influenced its constitutional development, first, as a part of Sweden and later as an autonomous part of Russia. This historical passage has resulted in a unique mixture of constitutional principles, including the duty of the state to protect the rights of the citizen.

The current Constitutional Act is an emblem of the long tradition of hard work towards achieving equality, especially between men and women. Finnish women were the first in the world to be granted full political rights, over a hundred years ago. Women have commonly been working outside the house ever since the Second World War, when most men were occupied

[52] Hate crimes statistics, see: www.polamk.fi/poliisi/poliisioppilaitos/home.nsf/webprint/C52B9C8FE74D48C9C2257936002553CB?OpenDocument.

[53] For an overview on a recent study in child poverty in Finland, see: www.tarki.hu/en/research/childpoverty/child_poverty_session2_finland_m_jantti.pdf.

by military responsibilities. This has given Finnish women early and wide access to the labour market. Social security benefits and labour laws were crafted to take these realities into account. For example, a public day care system was created half a century ago to enable women to have full-time jobs when their children were small. Also, the constitutional requirement providing access to free education has meant that individuals of both genders, regardless of their socio-economic background, have had access to high-quality education free of charge. All of these factors have kept Finnish society relatively equal with respect to gender.

However, the interpretation of the value of equality, before mainly concentrated on improving the equal rights of the genders, has recently widened as a result of demographic changes. Finland's immigrant population has increased significantly during recent decades. Between 1990 and 2009, the number of foreign citizens legally residing in Finland increased six-fold, from 26,300 to 155,700 individuals. Today, out of the total population of around 5.4 million, over 300,000 people in Finland, or roughly 5 per cent, claim a foreign background.[54]

While the proportion of foreigners to native Finns has increased steadily since 1990, it is still considerably lower than in other western European countries, such as Germany, Sweden, or even Switzerland, where the percentages of the foreign-born are above 10 per cent. Recent developments have led to legislative norms being passed to ensure integration and equal treatment for foreign-born adults and their children. The Integration Act went into force in 2006[55] and was modified in 2011. It was established to promote the integration, equality and freedom of choice of immigrants through measures that help them acquire the essential knowledge and skills they need to function in society. It also ensures the livelihood and welfare of asylum-seekers.

However, Finland still struggles with xenophobia, and according to a relatively recent poll,[56] the groups that suffer most from racism and intolerance are Somalis, Muslims in general, and the Roma. According to the survey, 75 per cent of the participants in this poll felt that there is a large or at least a moderate amount of racism in Finland. This shows the practical gap between the values of equality enshrined in the Constitution and the real-life experiences of exclusion and intolerance.

Another core value expressed by the Constitution is human dignity. This is embedded in article 1, whereby the constitution guarantees the inviolability of human dignity and the freedom and rights of the individuals to

[54] Statistical facts of the population of Finland, see: www.stat.fi/tup/suoluk/suoluk_vaesto_en.html.

[55] The original text of the Integration Act, see: www.finlex.fi/en/laki/kaannokset/1999/en19990493?search%5Btype%5D=pika&search%5Bpika%5D=integration.

[56] The summary of a poll commissioned by Helsingin Sanomat, 12 November 2011; see: www.hs.fi/english/article/Poll+Majority+of+Finns+see+Finland+as+racist+country/1135269860316.

promote justice in society. The Finnish understanding of human dignity not only covers personal freedom and integrity, but also the scope of its meaning goes as far as defining social and financial protection to those who cannot obtain the means necessary for a life with dignity. Thus, everyone has the right to receive basic subsistence and care, as defined by article 19 of the constitution. The strong emphasis on the rights related to social security is a result of the political developments and the development of the 'Nordic Welfare State Model', which was implemented in Finland following the example of other Scandinavian states. The Nordic Welfare State Model aims to provide inclusion and a substantial standard of living for those who, for one reason or another, cannot work.

When critically observing Finnish society, there are still numerous challenges to the fulfilment of the value of human dignity in practice. Currently, a discussion of elderly care minimum standards is an expression of human dignity within institutionalised care. Another very vulnerable group includes people with disabilities or mental health problems living in institutions, where the realities do not always meet with constitutional ideals. Also, European Roma travelling as beggars have indicated another grey area of the conformity between values and reality.

Social justice and a sense of responsibility have traditionally been fundamental values of Finnish society. In the process of globalisation, implementing inclusivity in the face of the visible inequalities of the world is becoming increasingly difficult. The challenge ahead lies in aligning the law and the practices of the society. This calls for wide cooperation between states and organisations such as the United Nations on the international level. Nationally, a strong political focus is necessary on integrating the values of human dignity and equality into action.

7

Constitutional and Legal Framework for Rights Protection in France

MICHEL TROPER

FIRST OF ALL, it seems necessary to describe some specific characteristics of the French constitutional system that will explain the way rights and values are protected. These characteristics include the system of sources of law and the use of the terms 'values', 'principles' and 'rights' in the language of constitutional law.

I. SOURCES

The first and most important source of law regarding Human Rights is the Declaration of the Rights of Man and the Citizen, adopted on 26 August 1789.

For a very long time, the Declaration was not considered a part of positive law, in spite of its historical importance. There were two main reasons for this opinion. The first lies in the title of the document. A 'declaration' is not a set of prescriptions that ought to be obeyed, but a statement of the fundamental principles of natural law, or a list of political principles that lawmakers ought to follow. The second reason is that the Declaration was later promulgated as part of the Constitution of 1791 but this constitution was short lived. Scholars still debate whether the Declaration was originally meant to be binding, but the question is moot, since the Constitution of 1791 ceased to be applied after the proclamation of the Republic in 1792. Thus, after 1792, the courts did not enforce the Declaration of the Rights of Man, and although the principles it contained were a source of inspiration for lawmakers and for judge-made law, it was not in itself applied as law.

Moreover, even if it had been part of positive law, it would not have been part of constitutional law, since it still would not have been binding on the legislative power, for lack of judicial review of legislation.

The same can be said of the Preamble of the Constitution of 1946, which mentions new principles and new rights, particularly social and economic rights.

This does not mean that there was no rights protection in France, but that the rights protected were not constitutional rights. These rights were first granted by statutory law. Some derived from the civil and the criminal code and, after the inauguration of the Third Republic, several very important laws were passed by acts of Parliament, for example in 1881 on freedom of information, in 1884 on freedom to establish trade unions, in 1901 on freedom of association, in 1905 on the separation of Church and state. These laws and others were enforced by the courts. In addition to those acts the courts, particularly the Council of State, developed, very much in the manner of the common law, a very important and complex system of protection mainly based on 'general principles of Law' that the Council claimed to have discovered and constructed. Naturally, both statutory law and judge-made law could be derogated by new statutes according to the principles *lex posterior derogat priori* and *lex superior derogat inferiori*. Thus, rights were not entrenched. Yet, according to a general opinion, this did not mean that they were limited. This opinion was linked to the French conception, going back to the Revolution, that men do not hold rights *against* the state but through the state, namely through statutes that are the expression of the general will. Thus a statute limiting freedom of expression in certain cases, for example punishing slander, was not and still would not be considered a real limitation but a mere definition or redefinition of freedom of expression.

Everything changed with the Fifth Republic after 1958, because the new constitution established a Constitutional Council of nine members with the power to review the constitutionality of statutes. The question whether the Council is a constitutional court became the focus of a long debate, now made largely irrelevant after the last constitutional amendment in 2008. In any case it is certainly very different in several respects from other European constitutional courts such as those of Italy or Germany. And it was even more different in the first period of the new Republic. The members of the Council are appointed by the President of the Republic, the President of the National Assembly and the President of the Senate for a nine-year term, the appointments of one-third of the nine members taking place at three-year intervals. When appointing new members, the three presidents have complete discretion and the persons appointed need not even be competent lawyers. Moreover ex-Presidents of the Republic become members for life as soon as they leave the presidency. During the first 50 years of the Constitution, statutes could only be deferred to the Council during a period of 15 days after their adoption by Parliament, and at first only the President of the Republic, the Prime Minister and the presidents of the two Houses of Parliament had access to the Council and could challenge the constitutionality of a statute. Even more important, for the first 13 years the Council could only confront the statute on the basis of provisions within the document called 'Constitution' and therefore not the Preamble or the Declaration of the Rights of Man. Thus the most fundamental principles, which were outside the Constitution properly speaking, still were not really part of positive law.

A first revolution took place in 1971, when the Council imposed a new interpretation to the provision defining its own powers. According to article 61 of the Constitution, Acts of Parliament could be deferred to the Council 'that shall rule on their conformity to the constitution'. In a decision comparable to *Marbury v Madison,* the Council ruled that the word 'constitution' referred not only to the numbered articles of the document, but also to the Preamble. Thus, the Council suddenly had the power to review statutes by referring to the Preamble. This opened a new and immense space to the Council. The first and most important paragraph of the Preamble reads: 'The French people solemnly proclaim their attachment to the Rights of Man and the principles of national sovereignty as defined by the Declaration of 1789, confirmed and complemented by the Preamble to the Constitution of 1946.'[1] Suddenly there was scope for the Council to make reference both to the Declaration of the Rights of Man and to the Preamble to the Constitution of 1946. However, the new dimension of the Constitution was even wider, because the Preamble to the Constitution of 1946 not only stated many new principles in rather vague terms, leaving considerable scope for interpretation, but also referred to 'fundamental principles recognised by the laws of the Republic'. This provision of the Preamble of 1946, which had been adopted as a political compromise, and which was considered at the time to be without any legal consequence, was interpreted by the Constitutional Council in 1971 in an entirely new way. This new interpretation meant that some of the most important statutes adopted under the previous republics were not mere unilateral expressions of the will of the legislative power of the time, but recognition of pre-existing principles. Therefore, the Council decided that these principles had a value superior to that of the statutes that 'recognised' them, and were part of the Constitution. It is easy to see that since there is neither a pre-established list of those fundamental principles nor a pre-established list of the statutes that 'recognised' them, it falls to the Council to decide what they are and to make those lists.

Thus in its decision of 1971 the Council considered that a statute of 1901 on associations had not merely established but 'recognised' the constitutional principle of freedom of association, and on that basis decided that a new statute, that established some limitations on the right to form a new association of citizens, was unconstitutional.

[1] All English excerpts of constitutional documents are taken from translations on the official websites of the Presidency, the National Assembly or the Constitutional Council.

Another major step was taken in 1974 when the Constitution was amended to give access to the Constitutional Council to 60 members of the National Assembly or 60 members of the Senate, in addition to the four government authorities who originally had the power to refer a statute. The predictable consequence was that the number of statutes reviewed by the Constitutional Council increased significantly. Between 1974 and 2008, almost all important statutes were referred to the Council by the minority of one or the other house immediately after having been adopted. However, after 15 days following the vote in Parliament, the law could not be challenged and obviously neither could old laws, even when they were thought to be grossly unconstitutional.

On the other hand, while neither the Constitutional Council nor ordinary courts could review the constitutionality of statutes, every single court had the power to disapply statutes contrary to international treaties and to European law.

The realisation that international and European law enjoyed better protection than the national Constitution, plus the ideology of the rule of law, led to what a majority of scholars view as the most decisive development in the history of the Council. A 2008 constitutional amendment created an *ex post* review named the 'priority issue of constitutionality'.[2] Today, one of the parties in a case before any court may challenge a statute on the ground that it infringes on the rights and freedoms guaranteed by the Constitution. The court cannot decide on its own on the issue of the constitutionality of the statute, but must refer the question to the highest court of its jurisdictional order (the Court of Cassation or the Conseil d'État), which acts as a filter. These high courts must verify that the issue of constitutionality is decisive for the case, that it has not been frivolously challenged, that it bears on rights and freedoms, and that it has not already been previously decided by the Council. Once these conditions have been met, they must refer the question to the Constitutional Council. The Council however is not a supreme court of appeal. It does not decide the case, but only the issue of constitutionality. The case itself is then decided by the lower court.

This new procedure has proved highly successful and, in spite of the initial reluctance of the Court of Cassation to refer cases to the Council, the number of cases decided by the Constitutional Council has increased enormously: between March 2010 (when the amendment was first implemented) and March 2013 the Conseil d'État and the Court of Cassation referred 314 cases to the Constitutional Council, while only 60 were referred by 60 members of Parliament. This will obviously have far-reaching consequences for the protection of rights and liberties.

[2] The 2008 amendment introduced a new art 61-1: 'If, during proceedings in progress before a court of law, it is claimed that a statutory provision infringes the rights and freedoms guaranteed by the Constitution, the matter may be referred by the Conseil d'État or by the Court of Cassation to the Constitutional Council, within a determined period.'

The Constitution does not require that members of the Council have received any legal training, and a significant proportion are actually not professional lawyers. Nevertheless, they have the assistance of highly qualified judges either from the Court de Cassation or of the Council of State (the supreme administrative court). Drawing from a great variety of texts and principles the Constitutional Council was thus able to create a very comprehensive and structured system of constitutional law.

It should be noted that the influence of the Council of State on the jurisprudence of the Constitutional Council explains the continuity of the French conception of rights and its basis in the fundamental values of the Republic.

However, rights are granted not only by the constitutional documents mentioned above, but also in statutes and in the jurisprudence of the courts.

Statutes are a particularly important source because of the specific conception of rights in the French system. From a liberal perspective, rights are viewed as protection of individuals from interference by the state into the private sphere. This has never quite been the case in the French system. The Declaration of Human Rights of 1789 defines most rights by referring to statutory law. For instance article 11 reads:

> The free communication of ideas and opinions is one of the most precious of the rights of man. Every citizen may, accordingly, speak, write, and print with freedom, but shall be responsible for such abuses of this freedom as shall be defined by law.

This does not mean that freedom of expression is first recognised, and then limited by statute. On the contrary, it means that freedom exists only in a situation where there is no prior control, but only sanctions for abuses, and where these abuses are defined by law (and not by arbitrary decisions). This results from the prevailing conception of political liberty, defined by Montesquieu and Rousseau, as the fact of being subject to the law.

Combined with the absence of judicial review of the constitutionality of statutes, this explains why many rights have been defined not by constitutional documents but by statutes. To continue with the example of freedom of expression, it has been detailed in an important act in 1881, in the same way that freedom of association was defined by a statute of 1884 and separation of state and religion in a statute of 1905.

The jurisprudence of the courts is also an extremely important source of rights. It should be stressed that France, like a few other continental countries, has not one, but two court systems. One is the system of judicial courts, with the Court of Cassation at its head, enforcing what is called here 'private law', which includes civil, commercial, labour, but also criminal law. Another is the system of administrative courts topped by the Council of State. These courts do not differ only by the substantive law that they are enforcing, but also by the types of sources. Whereas judicial courts adjudicate by applying statutes, which are largely codified, there are no codes and few statutes dealing with administrative law. The consequence has been that, from the nineteenth century onwards, administrative law has been mostly judge-made law, produced by the Council of State, mainly by claiming to apply general unwritten principles. The Constitutional Council is not part of either one of the court systems but its methods of reasoning have been largely inspired by the Council of State and its jurisprudence also rests on principles.

One should add that the European Convention of Human Rights is another very important source. This is due first to the fact that, because France may be condemned if the European Court finds that the Convention has been violated, French courts tend to interpret the French Constitution in the light of the Convention and the jurisprudence of the European Court of Human Rights. Secondly, following article 55 of the Constitution of 1958, international conventions prevail over statutes. Thus if a court, even a trial court, finds that a statute violates a treaty, it ought to refuse the application of the statute. Parties to a dispute frequently raise an exception and claim that a statute applicable to their case violates the European Convention. This means that even though courts may not review the constitutionality of statutes they enjoy a power that is in many ways comparable, since the law that they enforce is substantially constitutional.

II. THE TERMS 'VALUES' AND 'PRINCIPLES'

The term 'values' is very rarely used in French jurisprudence. It cannot be found in any of the founding documents, the Declaration of the Rights of Man and the Citizen, the Constitution of 1958 or the Preamble of the Constitution of 1946, nor in most writings by legal scholars, or in court opinions. It is almost never listed in the index of books on human rights. Naturally, there were philosophical discussions on 'values', but they had almost no impact on legal language.[3]

One of the reasons for the reluctance to use the word may have been its association with Catholic philosophy between the two world wars, while the republican tradition was deeply secular and at times even anti-Catholic. Indeed the only French constitutional document to use the word 'values' has been Petain's constitutional project: 'liberty and dignity of the human person are supreme values and intangible goods'.

Instead of 'values', we find a very wide use of 'principle', with at least two very different meanings. First, a principle was a philosophical or moral basis for legal rules expressed in statutes or case law. For instance 'liberté, égalité, fraternité' were 'principles', or it was said that the civil code was based on the 'principle' of the autonomy of the will. The 'principles' themselves were

[3] One exception in legal philosophy is Grzegorczyk, C, *Théorie générale des valeurs et le droit* (Paris, LGDJ, 1982).

not rules and only served to justify rules. Thus, the term was more or less a synonym of what we now call 'values'. Nevertheless, there was another meaning where a principle simply referred to a general rule conferring rights and duties.

Recently, though, the term 'value' has surfaced partly because of the vocabulary of the European Treaties. Thus the Treaty on the European Union as amended by the Treaty of Amsterdam (1997) reads:

> The Union is founded on the principles of liberty, democracy, respect for human rights and fundamental freedoms, and the rule of law, principles which are common to the Member States.

In the Treaty establishing a Constitution for Europe (2004), these same principles are now called 'values':

> The Union is founded on the values of respect for human dignity, freedom, democracy, equality, the rule of law and respect for human rights, including the rights of persons belonging to minorities. These values are common to the Member States in a society in which pluralism, non-discrimination, tolerance, justice, solidarity and equality between women and men prevail.

But we can already find this use of 'values' as a synonym for 'principles' in the first sense in the European Charter (2000), where the Preamble reads:

> Conscious of its spiritual and moral heritage, the Union is founded on the indivisible, universal values of human dignity, freedom, equality and solidarity; it is based on the principles of democracy and the rule of law.

There are several reasons for the growing popularity of the word 'values'. One is the influence of Anglo-Saxon culture, and of an anthropology that understands that each culture is defined by a number of values, and since the Constitution is increasingly viewed as expressing the legal and moral culture of the land, scholars use it more often.[4] This idea is in conformity with the departure on the Continent from the purely formal Kelsenian definition of the Constitution, whereas there is a growing influence of material conceptions. The Constitution is not only a set of norms whose rank in the hierarchy of the legal order is the highest but also a system of norms that express a common political morality with the highest degree of generality and the highest importance for the wellbeing of society.

Another is precisely that it is easier to refer to values that are often extremely vague and sometimes not even specified—politicians frequently swear that they will be faithful to 'our values', without telling what they are—rather than to legal principles which confer rights and obligations.

This helps to explain why the courts resist the term 'values': by using 'principles' (in the second sense) they can convey the idea that they are not

[4] See for instance, Pierre-Caps, S, *La constitution comme ordre de valeurs, ds. Mélanges en l'honneur de Dimitri-Georges Lavroff* (Paris, Dalloz, 2005) 283–96.

creating legal rules justified on the basis of some very general philosophical idea, but are merely applying legal rules, rules that are binding not because they are substantially justified but because they happen to be part of the legal system.

Yet, another explanation for the use in contemporary scholarly works of the term 'values', as distinct from 'principles' in the second sense, is the need to provide a basis for comparison. If we counted as values all the principles that are mentioned under that name in some legal document we would probably find it very difficult to compare them with principles valid in different legal systems. For example, in France the principle of freedom of communication implies the right of the readers of daily newspapers to access a sufficient number of publications reflecting different tendencies, and therefore the right of the lawmaker to place a limit to the number of newspapers that can be owned by one person. It would make little sense to note that the constitutional law of other countries also mentions the principle of freedom of communication or freedom of the press and conclude that they are similar to French constitutional law, if in these countries freedom of communication does not imply in the same way pluralism of the press. On the contrary, we should conclude that French law has a different principle and, if 'value' is a synonym for 'principle', that French law embodies different values from those of other countries. On the other hand, if we distinguish between values and principle and speak not of the 'principle' of freedom of the press but of the 'value' of freedom of expression, then we can say that French law is based on the same values as most other legal systems from democratic countries.

It is therefore useful to understand, by 'value', not a legal 'principle' implying rights and obligations, but a very general and abstract moral or political principle asserting the quality of something that is considered fundamentally good and can therefore be used to justify a legal principle. Values are the basis of legal principles, but the relationship between values and principles is not a logical one and very different principles can be justified by referring to the same values. Thus, if freedom of the press is a value in that sense, we can very well say that France, which has a limitation on the number of newspaper that may be owned by one person, nevertheless has the same value as other countries where it serves as a justification to the right of anyone to own and publish as many newspapers as they might wish to. Focusing on values taken in that sense thus allows us to find some common characters in the constitutional law of various countries.

Identifying values with moral or political principles has another advantage, that of avoiding the philosophical problem of the relationship between norms and values. Some authors believe that norms are justified by values whereas others insist that values are created by norms. Since values are defined as moral or political principles, which are nothing other than norms, the problem simply does not arise.

The difficulty with this notion of 'values' is that they are not easy to identify precisely because they are not mentioned as such. This comes from the fact that not only can one value serve to justify different principles, but also that one same principle can be justified by referring to several values. For example the principle that schools ought to be neutral can be justified because it serves the values of education, liberty, equality, order and so on. It is therefore only the scholar's interpretation that will suggest the references to various values and there is no possibility of determining if the references are correct.

The task is even harder in France, because of the variety of authorities that are capable of expressing legal principles. We find them not only in the constitutional documents mentioned in the first section of this paper but also in statutes and in the jurisprudence of the courts.

III. VALUES

> Which of the following values is explicitly articulated in your country's bill of rights or your country's constitution, common law practice or court interpretation?

This question can only be answered in the French context by distinguishing between four categories:

- Some of the values are mentioned in constitutional documents in terms identical or analogous to those of the list.
- Some of the values mentioned in constitutional documents relate to or are comparable to some of the list.
- Some of the values on the list are never mentioned in constitutional documents or in court interpretations.
- Some values, which are not in the list, are mentioned frequently either in constitutional documents or in court interpretations.

A. Values Mentioned in Constitutional Documents in Terms Identical or Analogous to those of the List

Freedom or *liberty* appear several times in the Declaration of Human Rights of 1789. It is one of 'the natural and imprescriptible rights of man', the preservation of which is one the aims of all political association (article 2). We even find in that document a definition of 'liberty': 'Liberty consists in the freedom to do everything which injures no one else' (article 4).

Liberty thus is clearly the autonomy of the individual. However, the word also had other meanings and other provisions of the Declaration are based on another conception of liberty, political liberty, as defined by Montesquieu, and other thinkers of the Enlightenment, ie, the right to be subject to the law.

This is the conception that is expressed in article 16: 'A society in which the observance of the law is not assured, nor the separation of powers defined, has no constitution at all.'

In the Constitution of 1958, liberty is used with these two meanings. The latter in the motto of the Republic proclaimed in article 2, 'Liberty, Equality, Fraternity', the former in article 66, 'The judicial authority, guardian of individual liberty, shall ensure the observance of this principle as provided by statute'. Here we can see that the word 'principle' is used in the sense of 'value', because article 66 does not imply any precise rights and duties. When liberty is a principle *stricto sensu,* it is generally specified as 'freedom of' expression, of education, etc…

The second of the values, mentioned in the preamble of the 1946 constitution is family:

> The Nation shall provide the individual and the family with the conditions necessary to their development.

That 'family' is a value and not a mere principle appears clearly from the fact that the provision does not create rights or obligations but serves as a justification for future principles. In particular first the State Council, then the Constitutional Council, have recognised the right to a normal family life that includes the right for a foreign resident in France to bring in his family.

One should note however that 'family' here is not considered as a group. French constitutional law does not recognise group rights—this is the reason why 'community' is never mentioned—but only individual rights, such as the right to live a normal family life.

Thirdly, ' tolerance' is not mentioned in any constitutional document, but we find freedom of religion in the Declaration of 1789:

> Art 10. No one shall be disquieted on account of his opinions, including his religious views, provided their manifestation does not disturb the public order established by law. It shall respect all beliefs.

Similarly, the preamble to the 1946 Constitution prohibits discrimination, notably on the basis of race or religion, and we find the word 'respect' in the formulation of article 1 of the 1958 Constitution: 'France … shall respect all beliefs'. Moreover, freedom of religion and tolerance are implied by *laïcité*, or 'secularism', which is guaranteed by the Constitution of 1958 (article 1).

Nevertheless, it should be noted that the word 'respect' can be used in French with different meanings. It can refer to a feeling of veneration or admiration, or simply to toleration or to duty to refrain from interfering with some behaviour. Here it is clearly respect in the second sense.

Finally, we find 'education' in the Preamble to the Constitution of 1946:

> The Nation guarantees equal access for children and adults to instruction, vocational training and culture. The provision of free, public and secular education at all levels is a duty of the State.

However, there is no provision regarding life. A constitutional amendment is presently being discussed by Parliament prohibiting the death penalty and has been justified as a means to further the sacred and inviolable character of human life,[5] but this inviolable character is not proclaimed in the amendment itself.

B. Values that Relate or are Comparable to Some of the List, Although Formulated in Different Words

The list mentions 'fairness/justice'. There is no occurrence of these words, but of course *equality* is repeatedly mentioned in every single document, starting with the Declaration. It is interpreted by the courts in the sense of fairness, since equality means that like situations ought to be treated alike, and different situations differently.

It also mentions 'compassion/caring'. Such words cannot be found, but of course, we have 'fraternity', which does not have the connotation of an emotion, but can be the basis for similar principles, particularly 'solidarity'. 'Fraternity' is not part of the Declaration of 1789 because it is only in 1848 that it was adopted as part of the motto of the Republic, since when it has been one of the most fundamental values. It is in the Preamble of the 1946 Constitution that we find explicit and implicit reference to solidarity:

> [The Nation] shall guarantee to all, notably to children, mothers and elderly workers, protection of their health, material security, rest and leisure. All people who, by virtue of their age, physical or mental condition, or economic situation, are incapable of working, shall have the right to receive suitable means of existence from society.

The nation proclaims the solidarity and equality of all French people in bearing the burden resulting from national calamities.

More generally, it is assumed that the social character of the Republic proclaimed in article 1 of the Constitution of 1958 relates to *fraternity:*

> France shall be an indivisible, secular, democratic and social Republic. It shall ensure the equality of all citizens before the law, without distinction of origin, race or religion.

C. Values that Never Appear either in Fundamental Documents or in Court Interpretations

This can happen either because they go without saying, they are too broad to be worth mentioning, or it is hard for the courts to create principles on

[5] Projet de loi constitutionnelle relatif à l'interdiction de la peine de mort, présenté au nom de M Jacques Chirac, Président de la République, par M Dominique De Villepin, Premier Ministre.

the basis of these values, without any intervention by the legislative power. This is the case with 'integrity/honesty'.

But it can also happen because they are completely alien to the French legal culture of secularism, like spirituality.

D. Values which are not on the List, but are Mentioned Very Frequently in Constitutional Documents

These are extremely important and we can make a tentative list, starting with the Declaration of Human Rights of 1789, which 'among the natural and imprescriptible rights of man' enumerates in article 2, in addition to liberty, 'property, security, and resistance to oppression'.

Property is mentioned again in article 17, where it is termed 'inviolable and sacred'.

Security has several meanings. First, it is understood as 'legal security' and serves to justify the prohibition of retroactive laws and more generally the preservation of situations that have been lawfully acquired. But it can also refer to physical security, respect for privacy, or the right not to be deprived of one's liberty or property without an order from a judge.

But the list would also comprise national sovereignty, democracy, and the Republic. These values are the basis for the principle of universal suffrage and for the right to form political parties. Article 4 of the Constitution of 1958 reads:

> Political parties and groups shall contribute to the exercise of suffrage. They shall be formed and carry on their activities freely. They must respect the principles of national sovereignty and democracy.

Democracy and national sovereignty justify the primacy of the Constitution and of statutory law. For example in a recent decision, the Constitutional Council struck down statutes that were written in very vague language. According to the Council, vagueness would leave too much discretion to the courts in the process of interpretation, which would constitute a denial of democracy, since the rule would have its source in the court and not in the statute, that is the expression of the general will.

Since 1946, work has also been a very important constitutional value. Reflecting the historical circumstances, whereby left wing parties dominated the national constituent assembly, the Preamble devotes several paragraphs to several principles implied by this value: the right and the duty to work, the right to form unions and to strike, and the right to participate in the management of the firm:

> Each person has the duty to work and the right to employment. No person may suffer prejudice in his work or employment by virtue of his origins, opinions or beliefs.

> All men may defend their rights and interests through union action and may belong to the union of their choice.
>
> The right to strike shall be exercised within the framework of the laws governing it.
>
> All workers shall, through the intermediary of their representatives, participate in the collective determination of their conditions of work and in the management of the work place.

Laïcité, or 'secularism' has been a key element in French political and legal culture since at least the Act of 1905, separating Church and state. The various rules governing the relations between religion and state and also the rules on education were justified by the idea that the state—and more generally the public sphere—is entirely secular. In 1905, secularism was considered a fundamental value of the Republic, but this was only expressed in statutory law and was not constitutionalised until 1946. At that time, the Preamble mentioned it indirectly by referring to the fundamental principles recognised by the laws of the Republic and in the statement that 'The provision of free, public and secular education at all levels is a duty of the State'.

In the Constitution of 1958 the word appears in article 1: 'France shall be an indivisible, secular, democratic and social Republic', and this value plays a very important role in the jurisprudence of the courts, where it is used as a principle. For example, the Constitutional Council balances the principle of freedom of religion or the principle of freedom of education with the principle of *laïcité*.

The importance of this value is illustrated by the fact that it was one of the major issues in the debate over the European constitutional treaty. One of the provisions in the treaty proclaimed the liberty to manifest one's religious beliefs in public, and it was uncertain whether this was compatible with the value of *laïcité*. The answer given by the Constitutional Council was in the affirmative.

This is a sign that this value is being interpreted in a very liberal fashion. It is certainly true that the wearing by women of the Islamic veil was banned from elementary and secondary public schools in the name of secularism, but on the other hand, the same value does not prohibit public subsidies to private schools, even religious schools. In effect, an Act of 1959 organises these subsidies.

Secularism is sometimes construed as merely implying that the state should treat all religions alike. Some scholars and politicians stress that the Catholics, the Protestants and the Jews were permitted after 1905 to make use of religious buildings that were public property in the nineteenth century, at a time when religion was a public service. However, there were no Muslims in France in 1905. There are now claims that secularism combined with equality requires today that the state should help to build mosques and train imams.

Another value that plays a similar role in the balancing of principles is the 'general interest'. This is translated by several different expressions in constitutional documents. We find for instance in the Declaration of the Rights of Man and the Citizen, 'the general good' (article 1: 'Men are born and remain free and equal in rights. Social distinctions may be founded only upon the general good'), the good of all (article 13: 'public military forces are ... established for the good of all', public necessity (article 17: 'Since property is an inviolable and sacred right, no one shall be deprived thereof except where public necessity'). In the language of the courts it is more often called 'the general interest', and it justifies exceptions to strict equality or to specific liberties.

At the time when the Declaration was not legally binding, the general interest has been construed as a general principle of law by the State Council in the field of administrative law. However, the Constitutional Council adopted it later by referring, as it always does, to a constitutional document.

The same applies with another value that lately has become very important, dignity. Dignity is not mentioned as such in the Constitution, but on several occasions, when the Constitutional Council referred to it yet was unwilling to appear to have created that value, it referred to a provision of the Preamble of 1946:

> In the morrow of the victory achieved by the free peoples over the regimes that had sought to enslave and degrade humanity, the people of France proclaim anew that each human being, without distinction of race, religion or creed, possesses sacred and inalienable rights.

It can logically serve to justify every one of the fundamental rights, but the Constitutional Council does not make such a broad use of it, and reserves it for cases when no other principle or value is available, as in the field of bioethics.

Another example of such an attitude is *service public*. The French expression involves more than the English 'public utilities' does. *Service public* is everything that functions for the general interest and that should be ruled by public law. The concept was widely used in the twentieth century to justify the existence of administrative courts and the specificity of the law they make. It is mentioned in the Preamble of the 1946 Constitution: 'All property and all enterprises that have or that may acquire the character of a public service or de facto monopoly shall become the property of society.' This value had to be reconciled with other constitutional values, especially property and today with European law. Nevertheless, one can still derive from it several principles, such as that of 'Equality before the public service or continuity of the public service.' 'Equality before the public service' means the right of every person to benefit equally from every public service, from education to electricity, the post office or clean water. 'Continuity of the public service' means that it ought to be organised in order to guarantee that there will be no interruption in the service. This also justifies restrictions on the right to strike.

More generally it seems reasonable to count as a 'value' every idea or objective that justifies a temporary suspension or softening of the pursuit of other values. Among such values, one of particular importance in the French context is 'the state'. We have previously mentioned the French conception of rights that makes the state, rather than a possible threat to rights or liberties, instead the very instrument and guarantor of rights. It is therefore no wonder that the state itself can be considered a value. This is the reason why preserving the existence and integrity of the state—or the nation, which in this context is an equivalent concept—justifies the temporary limitations of rights, and why a danger for the state is part of the definition of exceptional circumstances.

Finally, the environment has also become a fundamental value. It has been incorporated into the Constitution, through an amendment to the Preamble that now reads:

> The French people solemnly proclaim their attachment to the Rights of Man and the principles of national sovereignty as defined by the Declaration of 1789, confirmed and complemented by the Preamble to the Constitution of 1946, and to the rights and duties as defined in the Charter for the Environment of 2004.

Through the Charter, the Constitution indirectly refers to a 'precautionary principle'.

IV. PRIORITISATION

The Constitution itself does not prioritise these values either explicitly or implicitly into any kind of hierarchy.

The main reason is formal: all constitutional sources have the same legal value. French scholars write that they are all elements of one 'block of constitutionality'. Thus, the values mentioned in the Declaration of Human Rights of 1789 are considered neither superior nor inferior to those in the Constitution itself. One could neither argue that it is more respectable because it is an older and more prestigious rule, nor that the Constitution, being the expression of a later will of the sovereign, should therefore prevail.

In the specific context of French constitutional history, it is not possible to say that the various documents were adopted at different moments in time or that the Constitution of 1958 is posterior to the Declaration of 1789. This is because the validity of the Declaration of 1789, like that of the Preamble of 1946, is based not on votes that took place in 1789 or in 1946, but only on the preamble of the Constitution of 1958. It is the Constitution of 1958 that gives binding force to the Declaration of 1789, and it could not make it binding over itself. In other words, the Constitution alone cannot create super-constitutional principles.

Such a debate effectively took place in 1982 after the left, which had just won presidential and general elections, legislated to nationalise a large number of public corporations, and two different provisions seemed to be applicable. One was article 17 of the Declaration, already cited: 'Since property is an inviolable and sacred right, no one shall be deprived thereof except where public necessity, legally determined, shall clearly demand it, and then only on condition that the owner shall have been previously and equitably indemnified.' According to some authors, this implied that the Constitutional Council should examine whether public necessity clearly demands nationalisation. But others claimed that article 17 expressed an outdated conception of property that had been superseded by the victory of progressive forces in the Second World War.

However the Constitutional Council reconciled the provisions of 1789 with that of 1946: property is still a fundamental right, but this does not prohibit the legislative power to freely appreciate whether public necessity demands nationalisation and decide that it does, provided that owners of nationalised corporations be equitably compensated.[6]

Moreover, unlike the German Constitution, which makes some fundamental rights intangible, no provision of the French Constitution is protected against possible constitutional amendments. There is no limit to the power of amendment, except the prohibition on changing the republican form of government. It is thus theoretically possible to imagine an amendment abridging the right to life or liberty, since these rights do not enjoy a special status.

However, the Constitutional Council has decided that it could review the conformity of constitutional amendments to the limits set by the amending clause (article 89 of the Constitution), and it is not inconceivable that it could construe the expression 'the republican form of government', to mean 'fundamental values of the republic'.

This last phrase 'fundamental values of the republic' is not part of the language of the Constitution, but is used quite frequently in political language and although vague, it is not difficult to find in it some minimum content. Indeed, whereas the word 'value' itself is never used in the Constitution and very rarely by the courts, it is a sort of code word in political discourse. This minimum content would include the values of liberty, equality, fraternity and secularism.

If this were the case, we could conclude that the Constitution organises a formal hierarchy of values, with fundamental values of the republic at a super-constitutional level. However, that hierarchy would have been created not by the Constitution itself but by the judge. Since the Constitutional Council has not taken that road, we must consider for the time being that all values are on the same level.

Nevertheless, it is inevitable that courts encounter situations where two or more values conflict.[7] The absence of a formal hierarchy does not exclude

[6] Conseil constitutionnel, Décision n° 81-132 DC du 16 janvier 1982.

[7] Champeil-Desplats, V, 'Raisonnement juridique et pluralité des valeurs: les conflits axio-téléologiques de normes' (2002) *Analisi e Diritto* 59s.

a substantive hierarchy or order of preference between values. In case of a conflict, one can think of two possible types of solution: on a case-by-case basis, or by establishing a permanent order of preferences between values.

When the courts decide on a case-by-case basis in the presence of conflicting values, they can either let one value prevail over another, or they can try to reconcile them. In practice however it is difficult to distinguish these two types of attitude, because even when the court mentions only one value in its published opinion, it is still possible that it has taken another value into account, without letting its reasoning appear in the justification. This is particularly true in the French context where traditionally court opinions are written in a deductive style and are extremely brief. Thus if some kind of balancing has taken place it will not always be noticeable.

Yet, trying to reconcile and to balance is more frequent in contemporary constitutional law, at least in the context of justification, in part under the influence of foreign courts. For example, the Constitutional Council, as we have seen, sees the lawmaker as under an obligation to reconcile the sacred value of property with the duty to nationalise corporations that have the character of a public service. The Constitutional Council also tries to reconcile (or imposes the duty to reconcile on the lawmaker) the necessity of public order with the respect of fundamental liberties,[8] or freedom of expression with respect for privacy, or individual liberty and the need for cultural pluralism.[9] Since the reconciliation is operated on a case-by-case basis, the solution may be different in another concrete situation.

Courts can also establish a permanent supremacy of one value over others. One should stress that this supremacy is not a consequence of the formal value of the document that expresses them. They prevail because they are considered more important.

Sometimes the prevalence has a textual basis: we have already noted that the Declaration of the Rights of Man lets public order prevail over other rights. For example, following article 7,

> No person shall be accused, arrested, or imprisoned except in the cases and according to the forms prescribed by law. Any one soliciting, transmitting, executing, or causing to be executed, any arbitrary order, shall be punished. But any citizen summoned or arrested in virtue of the law shall submit without delay, as resistance constitutes an offence

or article 10:

> No one shall be disquieted on account of his opinions, including his religious views, provided their manifestation does not disturb the public order established by law.

[8] Conseil constitutionnel, n° 96-378 DC du 23/07/1996, loi de réglementation des telecommunications; 97-389 DC du 22/04/1997, loi portant diverses dispositions relatives à l'immigration.

[9] Conseil constitutionnel, n° 86-217 DC du 18 septembre 1986, Loi relative à la liberté de communication.

However, more frequently, it is the courts that decide that some values always prevail over others. Among the values that are the most important, we find, beside public order, the general interest, the preservation of democracy and the republic. They always justify exceptions to equality and limitations to the exercise of fundamental rights. The degree to which these limitations are acceptable may of course vary according to circumstances. The most severe limitations are only acceptable in case of an emergency, and only if they are strictly necessary to end the situation. Another value that is put forward more and more frequently is that of dignity, and it is used to justify limitations of freedom of expression or personal liberty. One emblematic case was that of a show with a game consisting in throwing a dwarf as far as possible. The show was suspended, and the administrative courts upheld the suspension on the ground that it jeopardised human dignity, although the dwarf, who made a living by participating in the show, had not complained and did not feel that his personal dignity was jeopardised.[10]

V. CONGRUENCE

Values are not isolated but are combined as elements of systems of values. In a pluralist society, the different groups hold different systems of values. Some elements may be common but others will be present in one system and not the other. Moreover, the relative importance attached to each element in the various systems of values will also be different.

In spite of permanent efforts by the state, first under the absolute monarchy, then during the Revolution and again under the various republics, to unify and homogenise the nation around common practices and common values, French society has been deeply divided. At times, different systems of values have dominated, some of which were not easily accepted by some sectors of society. For example at the beginning of the twentieth century, secularism was imposed by the left and faced strong resistance by the Catholics. In the 1930s, there were sharp conflicts between left and right over several issues, particularly social and economic rights, the role of the state, and immigration. When the left wing Popular Front, an alliance between the Socialists, the Radical Party and the Communists, won the elections in 1936, there was again strong resistance from the right. The end of the Second World War saw the victory of the left after the brief period of the reactionary regime of Vichy. This time the left included an important group of Christian Democrats, Catholics who had fought in the Resistance and accepted secularism as well as most of the values of the left, especially social and economic rights. Three political parties, the Socialists, the Christian Democrats and the Communists, were able to adopt the Constitution of 1946 with its

[10] Conseil d'État, 27 octobre 1995—Commune de Morsang-sur-Orge—Rec Lebon, p 372.

Preamble that is still in force since it was referred to in the Preamble of the 1958 Constitution. However, before 1971 and the emergence of a sort of judicial review of statutes, the conflict between conflicting systems of values did not take place on a constitutional level, and decisions taken in the name of values that were not accepted by part of the population took the form of statutes and were contested as statutes.

Naturally, in modern society pluralism and conflicting values have not disappeared. However, because of the particularities of the French constitutional system, such opposition rarely takes the form of a reaction to court decisions. The role of the French Constitutional Court is not comparable to that of the American Supreme Court, and most important decisions are made by statutes. As previously mentioned, prior to 2008 the Constitutional Council's intervention could take place only during the short period between adoption of a statute by Parliament and its promulgation by the President of the Republic.

Because a debate has already taken place in Parliament and the values justifying the statute have been discussed in that arena, if the Council decides that the statute is constitutional, that decision has rarely been perceived by the public as the source of the new norm, and there was usually little reaction. If a reaction did occur, it was directed against Parliament, as we shall see.

Nevertheless, if the Council decides that the statute is unconstitutional, then a reaction can happen. However, the reaction will be not from the public but from the parliamentary majority or the executive who introduced the bill. They will usually say on such occasions that the Council's motives were not legal but political, and that the institution is abusing its power. However, sometimes it goes further and the Constitution can be amended in order to overturn the doctrine of the Constitutional Council. In 1982, a statute on local authorities had a provision stating that the list of candidates for the municipal council could not contain more than 75 per cent candidates of one sex. The Council decided that this was contrary to the principle of equality of all citizens, and that no categories could be established on the basis of sex.[11] Nevertheless a few years later, because of the very small proportion of women in politics and in high office, it was considered necessary to remove this constitutional obstacle and a new clause was added by amendment to article 3 of the Constitution: 'Statutes shall promote equal access by women and men to elective offices and positions.'

It should be stressed that such amendments can be apprehended in two different ways. They can be viewed as a change in the interpretation of fundamental values—here the value of equality—and in the proper means to promote them. They can also be seen as a promotion of the value of democracy and of the rule of law. In particular, it has been argued that the

[11] 82-146 DC—18 novembre 1982—Quotas par sexes.

Constitutional Council cannot be legitimate if it opposes the will of the sovereign people. The constituent power expresses that will. Therefore, a constitutional amendment is proof of the supremacy of the people's will and the silence of the constituent power is the sign of a tacit assent of the sovereign.

However, such conflicts have not been frequent, because of the Council's general attitude of deference to Parliament. This attitude partly reflects the possibility of constitutional amendment, partly the fact that most members of the Council are former politicians and are not directly opposed to the political majority, and partly also the possibility that, instead of deciding that a statute is unconstitutional, it can be declared constitutional provided it is interpreted in a certain way. Thus by giving these interpretive guidelines the Council is able to avoid direct confrontation and at the same time to redraft the statute. The introduction of the priority issue of constitutionality in 2008 has so far not changed the relation of public opinion to the Council, mainly because the Council itself has not departed from its policy of restraint and still leaves decisions about fundamental values to the political authorities.

Differences between constitutional values and the 'lived' values of the community can also be felt when a statute is contested because it is based on an interpretation of fundamental values by a parliamentary majority.

There are many examples of such reactions against statutes. One is that of private schools. Because of the separation between religion and state, the state could not subsidise private schools, the majority of which were Catholic. Catholic schools were funded only with private money. Nevertheless, when, after 1958, the Gaullists came into power, they passed a statute authorising such subsidies, in spite of the constitutionally avowed secular character of the republic, but no court was competent at the time to review the constitutionality of that statute. Under the new law, the salaries of teachers in private schools would be paid by the state. However, there were strong feelings against this law on the part of the socialists, who were in the opposition, who announced that they would nationalise private schools. Indeed after they won the elections in 1981, the Minister of Public Education, Alain Savary introduced, in the name of secularism, a bill that unified private and public schools into one public service of education. Supporters of private schools, in the name of freedom of education, organised a huge demonstration in Paris of more than a million people, and Mitterrand, then President of the Republic, decided to abandon the bill. The fact that the initial decision had been made by a legislative act rather than by a court should not lead us to believe that it was political and not constitutional and that the debate was not over values. In Parliament and on the streets, arguments were based on constitutional values. The event was thus emblematic not only because it showed a clash of values, secularism versus freedom of education, but also because, when a compromise proved impossible, this led to the decision to keep the status quo, a decision paradigmatic of the Fifth Republic.

Several events of this kind took place during the Fifth Republic. One of them happened in the spring of 2006 when the Prime Minister introduced a bill to reform labour law and create the possibility of a first employment contract, which would have allowed employers to dismiss employees without giving a reason and at any time during a probationary period of two years. The bill was passed as a law, but it fuelled huge demonstrations in the name of job security, related to the social rights mentioned in the 1946 Preamble. Again, the solution was the status quo and the law was abrogated.

8

Values in German Constitutional Law

DIETER GRIMM

I. CONSTITUTIONS AND VALUES

CONSTITUTIONS USED TO be value-based documents. Most constitutions emerge from a deep break in a country's history, be it a successful revolution against an oppressive regime, or a national catastrophe from which a country wants to recover by aspiring to better aims. The upheaval against or the break with the previous order is conducted in the pursuit of values better than those of the old system. The function of a constitution is to give these values legally binding force and to organise the political system in a way that guarantees them continuous respect. A value-neutral constitution has yet to be invented. Even a constitution without a bill of rights, limited to organisational and procedural provisions, establishes the political structure and organises the political process in view of certain values. Behind institutional arrangements like separation of powers, uni- or bicameral parliament, judicial review, etc, value considerations can be discovered. The fact that constitutions are value-based has to be distinguished, however, from the question whether the text of the constitution uses value language or whether those who want to ascertain the meaning of the text by way of interpretation use a value-oriented approach.

II. VALUES IN THE GERMAN CONSTITUTION

A. General Survey

Germany's post-war Constitution, the Basic Law, which was adopted by West Germany in 1949 and extended to the unified Germany in 1990, does not use the term 'value'. Even so, it is a constitution based on, and established in order to promote values, the underlying implication being that the values on which the previous order had been based did not deserve this name. The spirit in which the Basic Law was elaborated can be best described in two words: 'Never again!' This 'Never again' had a double point of reference. It meant first: never again the self-destruction of a democracy as happened during the final years of the Weimar Republic, culminating in Hitler's rise to power in January 1933. Hitler, as is well known, did not come to power by a revolution against the Weimar democracy, but by using the democratic means provided in the Weimar Constitution of 1919, only to abolish the democratic system as soon as he had gained a majority. 'Never again' meant secondly: never again the atrocities committed by the National Socialists, the worst of which are today known as the Holocaust, enabled by a total neglect of human rights and by the abolition of all the mechanisms to control and restrain power that the Weimar Constitution had established.

The Weimar Constitution had certainly been a value-based constitution, emerging as it did from a revolution against the Bismarck Empire. It regarded democracy as a value in comparison to the pre-democratic character of the Empire and its Constitution of 1871. It enlarged the traditional bills of rights, which had been in force in Germany long before 1919, by a number of social and economic rights, realising that many classical liberties had been no more than empty shells for those lacking the material means to make use of them. It extended the suffrage to women, thereby recognising equality between men and women. However, as usual in constitutions, all this was formulated in terms not of values, but of legal principles and rules. More importantly, the dominating methodological approach to the value-inspired norms of the Weimar Constitution was itself not value-oriented. With the foundation of the Second German Empire in 1871 (the first having been the Holy Roman Empire of the German Nation which was dissolved in 1806 after almost 1000 years of existence) a methodological school had gained ground that tried to eliminate all subjective influences, in particular all political influences, from the interpretation of the law, and favoured a strictly legalistic approach: legal positivism. For this school the only object of interpretation was the text of the law, and the only instruments to ascertain the meaning of the text were grammar and logic.[1] This meant that the legislative history and the values by which the framers were driven belonged to the sphere of politics, and were thus irrelevant for the interpretation of the texts. Equally irrelevant for determining the meaning of a norm was its purpose, which remained outside the text and therefore was not part of the norm. It followed that the social reality in which the norm was to take effect could play no role in its interpretation.

This is not the place to discuss the merits and shortcomings of positivism in its capacity as a method of interpretation. But it seems noteworthy that the text of the 1919 Constitution was understood and interpreted in the old fashion of 1871. A younger generation of constitutional law scholars soon

[1] The approach found its classical expression in the preface to the second edition of Paul Laband, *Das Staatsrecht des Deutschen Reiches*, vol I (Tübingen, Mohr, 1888).

started to rebel against this attitude, but were overtaken by the collapse of the Weimar Republic in 1933.[2] The consequence was a formalistic understanding of the Constitution's guiding principles. Democracy was identified with majority rule. Hence, whatever political initiative found the necessary majority in the prescribed process, gained the force of law. The rule of law was identified with legality of state action. In particular, any infringement of a fundamental right needed a legal basis. But the rule of law was indifferent to the content of the law. Fundamental rights, in this formalistic view, did not bind the legislature. Since the legislature was constitutionally entitled to limit fundamental rights, it was considered to be above them. Fundamental rights mattered only to the extent that the law recognised and implemented them. Given these circumstances, it will come as no surprise that the courts applied the ordinary law, but not fundamental rights. Social and economic rights were not regarded as law at all. Since they were not directly applicable, but depended on legislative implementation, they were understood as mere proclamations of political intentions. The Constitution's distinctive feature in the positivistic view was not its foundational and legitimating role. It differed from ordinary law only in that amendments to it required a supermajority. As a consequence, any law that was passed with a two-thirds majority could set aside the Constitution without any formal amendment. Furthermore, any amendment gaining a two-thirds majority in parliament could alter the Constitution, even to the extent of abolishing majority rule. It is clear that from this value-neutral understanding of the Weimar Constitution no protection of the values enshrined in it could be expected. Interpreted in this way, the Constitution was helpless against Hitler's attack.

The Basic Law of 1949 reacted to these experiences in many ways, all of them value-oriented, albeit not expressed in terms of values, but rather of legal principles and rules. The most important of these are as follows.

(1) The Basic Law starts with the Bill of Rights; this in itself is symbolic of the enhanced importance the framers wished to attribute to fundamental rights, in contrast to their minor role in the Weimar Constitution, where they had been placed at the end of the text. The Bill of Rights starts with a guarantee of human dignity. This is not the first time that a constitution mentioned dignity, but constitutions before World War II that contained the term used it in a different sense, namely in the context of social policy directives or social and economic rights: everybody shall be able to lead a dignified life. In a broader, more philosophical sense, it appeared first in the post-war state constitutions adopted in Germany in 1946 and 1947. It then appeared in the Universal Declaration of Human Rights of the

[2] For a very good account of the constitutional theory of the Weimar Republic, see Arthur J Jacobson and Bernhard Schlink (eds), *Weimar* (Berkeley CA, University of California Press, 2000).

United Nations. The Basic Law gave dignity a particularly prominent position, and coined it in very strong language. Article 1 I BL refers to human dignity as *unantastbar*. The term is often translated as 'inviolable'. However, the German equivalent for inviolable is *unverletzlich*, which appears several times in connection with the liberties enumerated in the Bill of Rights, whereas *unantastbar* will be found only as an attribute to dignity. Perhaps 'sacrosanct' gives a better impression of the term's connotation. Article 1 continues with the assertion that the state must not only respect, but also protect human dignity, this again being a singular formulation in the Basic Law. It follows in article 1 II that therefore, namely because of human dignity, the German People acknowledges inviolable and unalienable human rights as the basis for every community as well as for justice and peace in the world. The text recalls the natural law language of the Rights Declarations of the late eighteenth century, and indeed natural law theory enjoyed a short renaissance in Germany after the perversion of positive law during the Nazi era.

(2) Article 1 III BL then reacts directly to the formalistic and minimising interpretation of fundamental rights during the Empire and the Weimar Republic by saying that the following rights bind the legislature, the executive and the judiciary as directly applicable law.

(3) Again in reaction to previous practice, article 19 II BL states that, where the Constitution allows for limitations of fundamental rights, they may not touch their very essence.

(4) In the following Bill of Rights some liberties are added to the classical rights, in response to the Nazi experience. On the other hand, the Weimar experiment with social and economic rights is not repeated, except for a very few exceptions (social care for mothers in article 6, right to form unions and to conclude collective agreements with the employers in article 9). Instead, the principles on which the state is based: democracy, rule of law, federalism, republicanism, are enlarged by the principle that Germany is a social state (articles 20 and 28).

(5) In reaction to the self-destruction of the Weimar Republic in 1933, dignity as well as these basic principles and the existence of fundamental rights are exempted from amendment insofar as their substance, rather than the wording, is concerned. Political parties and associations that undertake to destroy the free and democratic order can be banned, and individuals who attempt to overthrow the order can forfeit some of their fundamental rights such as freedom of speech and freedom of assembly (the so-called 'militant democracy' concept).

(6) Finally, in order to enforce the Constitution, and particularly the fundamental rights the Federal Constitutional Court was established and endowed with ample powers of review.

This being said, I turn now to the questions in the protocol.

III. VALUES IN THE BASIC LAW

The following values have found expression in the Basic Law:

Fairness, justice: Justice in connection with dignity: recognition of dignity as precondition of justice; fairness indirectly in connection with the procedural guarantees in articles 101, 103.
Equality: article 3 I: general equality clause, equal protection of the law. Article 3 II: gender equality combined with a duty of the state to promote substantive equality. Article 3 III: anti-discrimination clause. Article 6 V: equal conditions for legitimate and illegitimate children. Article 33 I: equal citizenship in every state. Article 33 II: equal access to public office. Article 38 I: equal suffrage.
Honesty, integrity: integrity as physical integrity (article 2 II).
Community: in some limitation clauses of fundamental rights, when limitations are permitted in the general or public interest (eg article 11—free movement, article 14—property and expropriation).
Family: special protection of marriage and family in article 6.
Freedom, independence, liberty: freedom/liberty in connection with the rights of the individual throughout the Bill of Rights (articles 1–19), in particular in article 2 I (right to free development of one's personality), and elsewhere (e.g. article 38—free elections, article 104—habeas corpus); independence in connection with the judiciary (article 97).
Responsibility, accountability: in connection with protection of the environment and the responsibility for future generations (article 20a), frequently in connection with government, political parties etc.
Compassion, caring: in the special protection for the disabled (article 3 III); in social care for mothers and an improvement of the status of illegitimate children (both article 6); in the principle of the social state.
Respect, tolerance: respect in the form of honour, reputation, which figure as justification for limitations of freedom of speech and media (article 5); tolerance, if at all, in the recognition of religious freedom to all faiths (article 4).
Life: article 2 II; prohibition of death penalty (article 102).
Security: in connection with the permission to join systems of collective security (article 24 II).
Learning, education: educational system under the control of the state (article 7). More is to be found in the state constitutions, education being a matter of the states, not of the federation.
Dignity: as the highest principle of the whole constitutional order, in article 1.
Environment: Protection of the environment as task of the state, in article 20 a.
Participation: in elections—article 38.

If no or only a remote constitutional provision is mentioned in connection with one of these items, this does not mean that it does not play a role in constitutional theory and practice (eg security, in many decisions of the Federal Constitutional Court concerning anti-terror laws; participation in connection with procedural due process or as a right of citizens to participate in administrative procedures that may affect their fundamental rights; tolerance in connection with freedom of religion (article 4).

IV. UNDERSTANDING THE TEXT

As described earlier in connection with the Weimar Constitution, the value-orientation of a constitution does not guarantee that the values will guide its interpretation and application. Even if they do, there will always be room for more than one definition of their meaning. The text cannot fully determine the application to concrete cases. The social reality in which the norms are to take effect does not play a merely passive role. Legal norms are formulated in view of a certain state of social reality to which they shall apply, and a change of this reality may have an impact on their meaning. If not adapted to new challenges, the norm may fail to reach its end or even produce dysfunctional effects. Because of the genuine contribution of interpretation, the comparison of legal texts can only be a first step in comparative legal analysis. The way the texts are interpreted, the change of meaning over time, the general and legal culture in which they are embedded, and the effects they produce must all be considered if a deeper understanding is to be reached.

Although the determination of the meaning of constitutional provisions takes place in a process in which many actors participate, I concentrate here on the contribution of the German Constitutional Court, because it has become the most important actor.[3] The Constitutional Court is the most salient novelty among the many novelties that were introduced into German constitutionalism by the Basic Law. The Court's impact on the relevance of the Basic Law in German political and social life can hardly be overestimated. In the spirit of 'Never again' the framers were convinced that a

[3] For an excellent collection of decisions in English language (excerpts), see Donald P Kommers and Russell A Miller (eds), *The Constitutional Jurisprudence of the Federal Republic of Germany*, 3rd edn (Durham, NC, Duke University Press, 2012). See also: *Decisions of the Bundesverfassungsgericht—Federal Constitutional Court—Federal Republic of Germany*, (Baden-Baden, Nomos, 1992). Six volumes, organised according to subject matter, have appeared. For a general introduction into German constitutional law, see David P Currie, *The Constitution of the Federal Republic of Germany* (Chicago, The University of Chicago Press, 1994), and Kommers and Miller, above, pp 1–76. For the function of the Constitutional Court, see Ralf Rogowski and Thomas Gawron (eds), *Constitutional Courts in Comparison. The U.S. Supreme Court and the German Federal Constitutional Court* (New York, Berghahn Books, 2002), in particular the contribution by Alfred Rinken, pp 55–90.

constitution, as good as it might be, is of little value if it is not accompanied by an independent institution that enforces constitutional law in cases of conflict. So a court with a very wide range of powers was foreseen in the Basic Law of 1949, and established in 1951. The doors to the Court are wide open: everybody has access to the Court without need for representation by an attorney, and free of costs. The Court has some 20 competences, the most important ones being to adjudicate: (1) disputes among the various branches of government; (2) disputes between the Federal Republic and the states; (3) disputes about the constitutionality of laws (judicial review in the narrower sense or norm control), in two forms: (a) abstract, ie without case and controversy, on application of either the Federal Government, the governments of the states, or one third of the members of the Federal Parliament; (b) concrete, ie arising out of case and controversy: ordinary courts, if they believe that a norm that applies in a specific case is unconstitutional, are obliged to refer the question to the Constitutional Court; (4) individual complaints concerning alleged violations of fundamental rights by state actors (the vast majority of cases, around 6000 per year).

The Court treats fundamental rights as expressions of values. It started to do so explicitly in the *Lüth* case of 1958, the landmark case for fundamental rights theory.[4] The problem presented by Lüth was the horizontal effect of fundamental rights (*Drittwirkung*). Lüth, a prominent figure in German-Jewish reconciliation after 1945, had called for a boycott of a movie, with which Veit Harlan, the infamous director of anti-Semitic films during the Third Reich, reappeared on the post-war movie scene. The film companies sought an injunction against Lüth, ordering him to cease the call for boycott. The civil law courts issued the injunction, based on paragraph 826 of the Civil Code (BGB), which holds a person liable for damages caused by behaviour that contradicts good morals. Entirely in line with the then accepted doctrine and jurisprudence, the courts decided that calling for a boycott fulfils the requirements of paragraph 826. Lüth's defence that he had made use of the right to free speech guaranteed in article 5 of the Basic Law was not accepted by the civil courts since, in their view, again in line with contemporary understanding, fundamental rights did not apply in private law relationships, ie horizontally, but only vertically, in the relationship between citizen and state. Lüth filed an individual complaint with the Constitutional Court.

In order to resolve the issue the Constitutional Court had to determine the nature of fundamental rights. It arrived at the decision that they are in the first place what everybody agreed they were, namely subjective rights meant

[4] BVerfGE 7, 198 (1958). ('BVerfGE' refers to the official collection of the judgments of the Federal Constitutional Court. The first number designates the volume, the second the page on which the decision begins). An English version of the *Lüth* case appears in *Decisions of the Bundesverfassungsgericht*, Vol 2, Pt I, p 1; Kommers and Miller (n 3) 442–50.

to protect individual self-determination against the state. But this classical function, as it is sometimes called, was not the only one. According to the Court they are also objective principles, expressions of values that society regards highly. This is why they were entrenched in the country's Constitution. The Court even said that, taken together, these rights form a system of values. From this premise, the Court drew the conclusion that their application is not limited to the vertical dimension. As highest values, they rather permeate the whole legal order, including private law. However, this does not mean that they apply directly to individuals. The addressee of the rights is the state, and no one else. The relationship of private persons remains regulated by private law. But private law not only has to be compatible with fundamental rights, it must also be interpreted in the spirit of the values that have found their legal expression in fundamental rights. As a consequence, wherever the interpretation and application of a provision of private law results in a limitation on someone's fundamental right, the ordinary courts have to take this right into account and interpret the ordinary law in its light. The Court called this a 'radiating effect'. An ordinary court that fails to do so not only violates objective law, but the subjective right of the individual as well.

In the *Lüth* case this interpretation of paragraph 826 BGB in the light of article 5 BL led to a reversal of the lower courts' judgments. Viewed in the light of freedom of speech, this particular call for boycott could not be regarded as contradicting good morals. Lüth had not pursued any self-interest, but raised his voice in a matter of high public concern. Compared to the film companies' economic interests, which had found recognition in paragraph 826 BGB, the free speech interests prevailed. The *Lüth* case itself remained within the realm of subjective and negative rights limiting state action. But the Court had to resort to rights as objective values in order to extend their scope to the horizontal dimension.

Lüth had a tremendous effect. It revolutionised fundamental rights thinking in Germany.[5] Compared to the traditional understanding it brought three changes:

1. Fundamental rights are not only subjective rights of the individual, but also objective principles (nature).
2. As such, they are not limited to public law relationships, but extend to private law relationships as well (scope).
3. They do so not directly, but indirectly as guidelines for the interpretation of the clauses and provisions of ordinary law (effect).

If the intention of this move was strengthening of fundamental rights, the effect was a considerable gain of power for the Constitutional Court as

[5] *Cf* Dieter Grimm, 'Human Rights and Judicial Review in Germany' in David M Beatty (ed), *Human Rights and Judicial Review* (Dordrecht, Martinus Nijhoff Publishers, 1994) 267; Dieter Grimm, 'The Role of Fundamental Rights after Sixty-Five Years of Constitutional Jurisprudence in Germany' (2015) 13 *International Journal of Constitutional Law* (forthcoming).

the agent of constitutional values. Before *Lüth*, the Constitutional Court could examine a law as to its constitutionality. If the law was found to be constitutional, the influence of the Constitution ended. Its interpretation and application to concrete cases was exclusively a matter of ordinary law, and hence of the ordinary courts. Now the whole interpretation of ordinary law and the functioning of the whole judiciary came under the control of the Constitutional Court, at least as far as fundamental rights were affected.

Lüth was not the end of the fundamental rights revolution, but the beginning. The value approach allowed the Court a dynamic interpretation of constitutional rights, totally different from the positivistic approach in earlier periods of German constitutionalism. The result was in many cases a modernisation of the law by way of the radiating effect. This was particularly true for the great codifications of civil, criminal, commercial and procedural law, which all dated from pre-democratic times. But in addition, the value (or objective principle) approach proved to be very productive in generating further enlargement of the scope and effect of fundamental rights.

The first is the proportionality test. Proportionality had already been in use in the jurisprudence of the famous Prussian Administrative Law Tribunal in the late nineteenth century. It applied to police actions. According to the jurisprudence of the administrative court, a police action was legal only when it had a basis in the law, and was suitable and necessary to reach its end. The Constitutional Court introduced it into constitutional law where it serves as an additional, judge-made, limitation on the legislature, supplementing the limitations that are contained in the limitation clauses of the various rights and in article 19 II BL (the essence clause). The Court further added a third step to the test that had remained rudimentary in nineteenth-century administrative law: the law (and its application in a concrete case) has to strike a reasonable balance between the competing interests and goods affected by it. The Court never justified the introduction of the proportionality principle. It more or less crept into constitutional adjudication, case by case.[6] But the Court could hardly have developed it without the background of the value orientation. A number of fundamental rights, among them rights as important as that to life and health, have an unqualified limitation clauses: 'This right may be limited by law or pursuant to law.' Hence, the mere text would allow any limitation that stops short of the very essence of the right. Yet, if fundamental rights give expression to the highest values of society, and laws are no longer above fundamental rights but subordinated to them, only a limitation that stands the muster of the proportionality test can be regarded as constitutional. It seems fair to say that today the principle of proportionality bears the main burden of

[6] Starting with BVerfGE 3, 383 (1954); fully developed in BVerfGE 7, 377 (1958). For a brief account of the development see Dieter Grimm, 'Proportionality in Canadian and German Constitutional Jurisprudence' (2007) 57 *University of Toronto Law Journal* 383.

fundamental rights protection against restrictions, be they by law or by acts of the executive or judgments of courts.[7]

The second enlargement flowing from the value-based approach was the understanding of fundamental rights, not only as negative, but also as positive rights. If they are not just subjective rights protecting the individual against the state, but also objective values it cannot be left to the legislature whether it is willing to protect these values against threats emanating not from the state but from private actors. Beginning with the first abortion decision of 1975, the Court developed the idea that the state is under a constitutional duty to intervene when the values to which fundamental rights give legal expression are endangered by private parties or societal forces.[8] This duty is fulfilled in the first place by the legislature, which has to take adequate steps to eliminate or minimise the danger. In the abortion decision of 1975 the Court declared a reform law of the Penal Code unconstitutional that had reduced an existing protection of unborn life, which, according to the Court, enjoys the protection of article 2 II BL. But it soon turned out that this was not the typical field of application for the new dimension of fundamental rights. Currently, the notion of a duty to protect is mostly used in cases of risks created by scientific and technological progress and its commercial use.[9] If the legislature remains inactive or renders a degree of protection that seems inadequate in comparison to the magnitude of the risk, the Court obliges the legislature to take action in order to protect the endangered value. While in their classical negative capacity fundamental rights oblige the legislature to refrain from certain actions in the interest of individual freedom, in their capacity as positive rights they oblige the legislature to take action in the interest of freedom. Freedom remains the point of reference, but the theory acknowledges that government may not be the only foe of individual freedom. Consequently, the Court often declares laws unconstitutional, not because they went too far in restricting a fundamental right, but because they did too little in order to protect it.

Both the proportionality principle and the duty to protect increase the number of conflicts between fundamental rights and the values behind them. The proportionality test applies to laws that restrict fundamental rights. But they mostly do so in the interest of another fundamental right

[7] Although the proportionality principle is widely accepted, there is some criticism, mainly concerning the last step; see, eg Bernhard Schlink, 'Der Grundsatz der Verhältnismäßigkeit' in *Festschrift 50 Jahre Bundesverfassungsgericht*, vol II (Tübingen, Mohr, 2001) 445; see, from a philosophical point of view, Jürgen Habermas, *Faktizität und Geltung* (Frankfurt, Suhrkamp, 1992) (in English: *Between Facts and Norms* (Cambridge, MA, MIT Press, 1996) 256 et seq). There is a critique of Habermas in Robert Alexy, 'Constitutional Rights, Balancing and Rationality' (2003) 16 *Ratio Juris* 131.

[8] BVerfGE 39, 1 (1975); Kommers and Miller (n 3) 336.

[9] For an example see BVerfGE 49, 89 (1978); Kommers and Miller (n 3) 177. *Cf* Dieter Grimm, 'The Protective Function of the State' in Georg Nolte (ed), *European and US Constitutionalism* (Cambridge, Cambridge University Press 2005) 137.

or constitutionally protected interest. The duty to protect requires laws that take adequate measures against risks for constitutionally protected values that emanate from private actors' activities. But since these activities are frequently protected themselves by fundamental rights, such as freedom of scientific research, freedom of profession, of property etc, different rights of the same rank collide. These collisions are solved by balancing, both by the legislature and by the applicants. Balancing requires a threefold operation: the first is to determine the importance of the fundamental right that is subject to a limitation by law or to a risk created by a private actor, and what loss this right would suffer if the countervailing right prevailed. The second is to determine how important the aspect of the right is in whose interest the law was enacted or which was exercised by the risk-creating actor, and what loss it would suffer if the other right prevailed. After this filling of the two scales, the balancing takes place in step three.

Finally, the value approach determines the method of interpretation that the Constitutional Court applies. The value behind a fundamental right inspires the interpretation. In order to determine the meaning of a fundamental right in an individual case, the Court asks what the value is that found expression in the text of the right. The question can also take the form of a functional approach. What is the function that, say, the freedom of the media is intended to fulfil? Is it, to stick to this example, to give media owners a privileged position to disseminate their ideas and promote their political interests? Or is it a purely economic right allowing the owners to make as much profit as possible? Or is this freedom constitutionally protected in order to guarantee that persons or democratic societies receive the range and quality of information they need in order to form an opinion and to be able to conduct their own affairs?[10] Different consequences flow from each solution. The value or the function determines the purpose of the law. Value-oriented interpretation is purposive interpretation.

In addition, when the Constitutional Court says that the various rights form a 'system of values', it means that the rights should not be seen and interpreted in isolation, but in connection with one another. The idea of a system had been formulated one year before *Lüth*, when the Court had set out to bridge the gaps between the various rights by ruling that any state act that prohibits or hampers individual behaviour not protected by a specific constitutional guarantee falls under the scope of article 2 I BL, according to which everybody has the right to free development of his personality.[11] There is no longer a zone void of fundamental rights protection. The Court thus

[10] *Cf* BVerfGE 57, 295 (1981) (in English in *Decisions* (n 4) vol 2/I, p 199); Kommers and Miller (n 3) 514.

[11] BVerfGE 6, 32 (1957); Kommers and Miller (n 3) 401. The decision remains contested, see my dissenting opinion in BVerfGE 80, 164 (1989); Kommers and Miller (n 3) 404. Yet, the dissent did not undermine the value approach.

turned article 2 I into a general freedom right whose scope is only limited by the specific liberties enumerated in the Basic Law. The system is complete.

The basis of this system is human dignity, as stated in article 1 BL. The Court often calls it the highest or the foundational principle or value.[12] Unlike the following rights, it is regarded as absolute, ie subject neither to limitation nor to balancing.[13] The Court derives this from the qualification of dignity as *unantastbar*, regarded as an inherent quality of every human being. This means that it can neither be earned by leading a good life, nor forfeited by leading an evil life. Everyone is in possession of dignity, regardless of age, physical or mental condition etc. It protects against any inhuman, degrading, humiliating treatment. The Court, in trying to explain its meaning, several times referred to the Kantian formula that no person may be treated as a mere object.

The idea of a system is also behind the practice of the Court to combine certain rights and thus produce an enriched definition of their meaning or scope. Very often the precise meaning of a right is determined in connection with article 1 BL (dignity). For example, in the absence of a specific guarantee of privacy, a comprehensive right to privacy was developed by combining articles 2 I and 1 I BL.[14] Article 2 I BL, with its extremely broad scope, appears to be particularly productive in generating new rights that protect the individual against new types of dangers for individual freedom, such as the protection of personal data (the so-called right to informational self-determination)[15] or very recently a guarantee of the confidentiality of modern electronic communication systems.[16]

The same is true for other constitutional principles. Democracy, rule of law, social state inform the interpretation of fundamental rights. The close link between freedom of the media and democracy shapes the understanding of article 5 BL: as commercial TV seems unable to provide a democratic society with the range and quality of information it needs, the private sector with its deficits can only be tolerated if there is a strong, competitive, but still independent public TV.[17] Since some of the guarantees of due process or a fair procedure apply only to criminal law (eg the principle of non-retroactivity of laws, in article 103 II) the Court finds them rooted in the rule of law and turns them into a subjective right by combining the rule of law with article 2 I.[18] The right to life and health in combination with the social state principle gives everybody the positive right to the bare necessities

[12] BVerfGE 5, 85 at 204 (1956).

[13] BVerfGE 93, 266 at 293 (1995); Kommers and Miller (n 3) 470. See Dieter Grimm, 'Dignity in a Legal Context. Dignity as an Absolute Right' in Christopher McCrudden (ed), *Understanding Human Dignity*. Proceedings of the British Academy (Oxford: Oxford University Press 2013) 381.

[14] Beginning with BVerfGE 27, 1 (1969); Kommers and Miller (n 3) 356.

[15] BVerfGE 65, 1 (1983); Kommers and Miller (n 3) 408.

[16] BVerfGE 120, 274 (2008); Kommers and Miller (n 3) 417.

[17] BVerfGE 73, 118 (1986); BVerfGE 74 , 297 (1987); Kommers and Miller (n 3) 517 et seq.

[18] BVerfGE 97, 67 (1997).

of a decent living, including a minimum of participation in the societal, cultural and political life.[19]

In sum, the Court's maxim of interpretation can be described as giving the utmost effect to the purpose of a constitutional norm under given conditions. The latter shows that this interpretation would not work if the segment of social reality to which a certain constitutional provision applies were ignored. What the utmost effect is can be determined only if the current conditions are taken into account. If this is so, social change will not leave the interpretation of a norm unaffected. Changed conditions may require a change of interpretation if the purpose of the norm otherwise would be missed. This is why the Court's judgments always contain a careful analysis of the conditions to which the norm applies. In a value-oriented approach, the meaning of a norm is constituted by text, purpose and reality.

Students of decisions of the Federal Constitutional Court will notice that the term 'value' has appeared less frequently in its opinions over the last 30 years. The reason may be that the value-orientation at times found considerable criticism. The concerns were partly methodological and institutional, partly substantive in nature.[20] Some commentators feared that positive constitutional provisions were relativised by a supra-positive order of values. As a consequence, the specific rationality of the law would be undermined since the value orientation opened the door to subjective preferences of the law applicants. Institutionally, the authoritative interpreter of the Constitution, the Constitutional Court, would change its function from that of guardian of the Constitution, to its master. For some commentators the value orientation endangered the liberal character of fundamental rights and turned them from liberties into duties. Fundamental rights would no longer protect individual self-determination, but require value-conforming behaviour.

Meanwhile this criticism has diminished. As the jurisprudence of the Court shows, it was not well founded.[21] If fundamental rights are indeed legal expressions of values, it cannot be regarded as a deviation from positive constitutional law when they are understood as such and when their interpretation is guided by the value that the law wants to protect. After all, it is the value behind a certain fundamental right that inspires its interpretation, not some other value that has not found constitutional expression. Moreover, the values behind fundamental rights are themselves freedom values. The value orientation did not initiate a shift from rights to duties, but a fuller understanding of freedom. The Court turned away from the purely formal understanding that identified freedom with the absence of state

[19] BVerfGE 40, 121 at 133 (1975); BVerfGE 1, 97, 104 (1951); BVerfGE 125, 175 (2010).

[20] See in particular Ernst Forsthoff, *Rechtsstaat im Wandel*, 2nd edn (München, Beck, 1976) 130 et seq; Helmut Goerlich, *Wertordnung und Grundgesetz*, (Baden-Baden, Nomos, 1973).

[21] See Robert Alexy, *Theorie der Grundrechte* (Baden-Baden, Nomos, 1985) 125 et seq (English edition: *A Theory of Constitutional Rights* (Oxford, Oxford University Press, 2002)).

intervention. Rather, the Court developed a substantive or material understanding of freedom that included the preconditions necessary to make use of a constitutionally protected right, and took into account that individual freedom is not only endangered by government but also by private actors or societal forces.

The value orientation thus served as a basis for developing the so-called objective dimension of fundamental rights. The more this dimension found its doctrinal contours, the less were the values invoked by the Court. Fully in line with the theoretical assertion that for all practical reasons the term 'value' can be replaced by 'principle' without a loss in meaning[22] the Court now uses a principle, rather than a value language. However, no change in substance went along with this change in terminology.

V. PRIORITISATION

The general assumption is that all fundamental rights are of the same rank. The only exception is dignity. Since the Constitutional Court regards dignity as an absolute right, the usual two-tier approach in dealing with fundamental rights (step 1: Has the right been infringed by some state action?; step 2: Does the infringement violate the right, or is it constitutionally justified?) does not apply. Every infringement is a violation. Furthermore, it means that dignity is not subject to balancing. In a conflict between dignity and another constitutionally protected value, dignity always trumps the other value. This heightening of dignity has a price. If dignity is subject neither to limitation nor to balancing, it must be defined narrowly and held in reserve for instances of major assaults on human beings such as the Nazi atrocities, which are indeed frequently invoked when it comes to determining what sort of behaviour would violate dignity. The consequence is that in German constitutional jurisprudence, not many cases exist where a decision was based directly on article 1 BL. The leading case for a long time concerned the constitutionality of lifelong imprisonment.[23] Quite recently, dignity became more important as a directly applied criterion, namely in connection with the so-called fight against terror.[24] The Court defined the limits of covert surveillance by invoking dignity, and it declared the Aviation Security Act, which allowed the German Air Force to shoot down a hijacked aircraft when necessary in order to save the lives of potential victims, incompatible with article 1 BL.[25]

[22] See Alexy, *Grundrechte* (n 21) 125.

[23] BVerfGE 45, 187 (1977); Kommers and Miller (n 3) 363.

[24] BVerfGE 109, 279 (2004); BVerfGE 113, 29 (2005); BVerfGE 113, 348 (2005); BVerfGE 115, 166 (2006); BVerfGE 115, 320 (2006); BVerfGE 120, 378 (2008); BVerfGE 120, 274 (2008).

[25] BVerfGE 115, 118 (2006), English version available at www.bundesverfassungsgericht.de/en/decisions/rs20060215_1bvr035705en.html. Kommers and Miller (n 3) 396.

All other fundamental rights are regarded as being of equal rank. As a consequence, the question of which right prevails in cases of conflict is to be answered case by case. However, there may be some sort of a clandestine hierarchy. The right to life as a presupposition to all other rights enjoys a certain priority, as for instance in abortion cases, when it is balanced against the freedom of the pregnant woman.[26] But it does not take the status of an absolute right. The Constitution itself allows for limitations. In the case of the president of the German Industrial Association, Hanns Martin Schleyer, who had been kidnapped by terrorists in 1977 and was threatened with death unless the government fulfilled certain conditions, the Constitutional Court refused to order the government to concede these conditions in order to save Schleyer's life.[27]

Sometimes, however, the Court distinguishes between certain 'spheres' of protection within one fundamental right, a core or intimacy sphere, a private sphere and a more social sphere. These spheres correspond with different degrees of protection and consequently with different degrees of scrutiny by the Court. Thus, the Court tends to exercise a rather loose control over laws regulating the economy.[28] The rights affected by such laws are usually freedom of profession (article 12) and freedom of property (article 14). But this practice should not be confused with a prioritisation among different rights. The Court is prepared to exercise a strict control when personal aspects of these rights are concerned, as opposed to the more anonymous rights of corporations or their shareholders.

VI. CONGRUENCE

In general, one can say that the Basic Law is held in high esteem in Germany. The Constitutional Court enjoys solid support in society.[29] The compliance rate with court orders is exceptionally high, in international comparison. Politicians have to a large extent internalised the primacy of the Constitution, and attempts to openly disobey court orders would not leave the citizens indifferent. This does not mean that the Court is not subject to criticism. This is often the case, but despite criticism of certain judgments, the general support for the Court remains largely unaffected. Incidents where this has not been so (such as following the well-known 'Crucifix' judgment)[30] have not had lasting impact. Of course, Germany is a pluralistic society, and

[26] BVerfGE 39, 1 (1975); BVerfGE 88, 203 (1993); Kommers and Miller (n 3) 374, 387.

[27] BVerfGE 46, 160 (1977); Kommers and Miller (n 3) 394.

[28] BVerfGE 50, 290 at 332 ss (1979); Kommers and Miller (n 3) 660.

[29] See Georg Vanberg, *The Politics of Constitutional Review in Germany* (Cambridge, Cambridge University Press, 2005).

[30] BVerfGE 93, 1 (1995); Kommers and Miller (n 3) 577.

increasingly so. But fundamental opposition to the values enshrined in the Basic Law are limited to very small groups of extremists. Some immigrant communities live at some remove from those values, yet not in open rebellion against them. And it may also play a role that the Constitutional Court, although much more active than the US Supreme Court, seems less politicised than its American counterpart.

9

Crafting Constitutional Values: An Examination of the Supreme Court of India

MENAKA GURUSWAMY

THE INDIAN CONSTITUTION and the Indian Supreme Court are both remarkable for having redefined an ancient country, whose history and existence are thought to find their origins as early as 200 BC.[1] India's extraordinary diversity—in terms of religions observed, languages spoken, and cultures practised—makes for fascinating study. However, its society was also long characterised by stark inequalities, perpetuated by exclusionary practices based on caste and gender. This together with long experiences of colonisation left grave scars on its people.

After much struggle, India won its independence from its British colonisers in 1947. But, its truly momentous reconception only emerged with the drafting and adoption of a Constitution, in 1950. The values that this chapter will discuss are the values of this Constitution, and their interpretation by the Supreme Court. The crafting of constitutional values like access to education for all Indians, equality between all citizens, and even a conception of 'one people' by the Supreme Court has enabled the re-imagination of Indian society. The Constitution's idea of an egalitarian nation, defined by equality, fraternity and liberty have been given effect by the Supreme Court in ways that are unique to this court. Its exposition of rights that are justiciable have included both political and civil rights, as well as rather unusually socio-economic rights. It is possibly the only apex court that has evolved its own appointment procedure, routinely assessed governmental policy, and also evolved relaxed *locus standi* requirements enabling rather radical public interest litigation.

Section I will provide an overview of the Constitution of India, 1950 and the Supreme Court. Section II discusses the formulation of constitutional

[1] R Thapar, *Early India: From The Origins To AD 1300* (Oakland CA, University of California Press, 2004) 25 and 31.

values—by examining creation of constitutions, conceptions of 'the people' and the Preamble to the Indian Constitution. The Preamble, adopted by 'We the People' of India, is important since it has been utilised by the Supreme Court to interpret and craft constitutional values.

Section III is entitled 'Fundamental Rights' and is the heart of this chapter. It includes a discussion of the Directive Principles of State Policy. It then proceeds to examine some core Indian constitutional values that have arisen from first: the rights to life, second: education, third: family and community, fourth: freedom and independence, fifth: sustainable development and environment, sixth: tolerance and education, seventh: justice, eighth: democracy and ninth: secularism. Section IV discusses 'prioritisation' by the Supreme Court in the context of two clear jurisprudential strands. First is the 'basic structure doctrine or the unamendable core of the Indian constitution. The second is the use of Fundamental Rights to interpret Directive Principles of State Policy.

I. THE CONSTITUTION OF INDIA, 1950

On 26 January 1950, after almost three years of debate and drafting by the Constituent Assembly, India adopted its Constitution.[2] The Indian Constituent Assembly had acted as both India's parliament and constituent assembly. On 29 August 1947 it decided to operate as a legislature in the morning, and as a constituent assembly in the afternoons.[3]

The Constitution adopted was rather detailed, originally having 395 articles and eight schedules. Today, after being amended more than a hundred times, it now has 444 articles and 12 schedules, and is believed to be longest constitution ever. The spirit of the nationalist movement for change which resulted in independence is most reflected in the Preamble and the Fundamental Rights and Directive Principles of State Policy in the Constitution.

Fundamental Rights, which are contained in Part III of the Constitution, are broadly civil and political rights akin to human rights internationally, and also those similarly protected in many other democratic constitutions. Directive Principles of State Policy, contained in Part IV of the Constitution, consist mostly of traditional socio-economic and cultural rights. The difference between the two is set out in article 37 of the Constitution, which specifies that while the Directive Principles are fundamental in the governance of the

[2] SP Sathe, 'India From Positivism to Structuralism' in J Goldsworthy (ed), *Interpreting Constitutions* (Oxford, Oxford University Press, 2006) 215.

[3] *Official Reports Of The Constituent Assembly Debates*, Vol VI, Lok Sabha Secretariat, Fifth Reprint (2009) 330.

country, and the state is duty-bound to apply them in making law, they shall not be enforceable in court.

Mostly, the discussion of global constitutional values comes up in the context of either the fundamental rights or the directive principles of state policy. These values are either expressly provided for by the text of the constitutional provisions, or have been introduced by the 'activist' judges of the Supreme Court.[4] In a few rare instances a constitutional amendment, approved by the parliament, has added them to the Constitution.[5]

At independence in 1947, the Indian judiciary was thought to be a conservative institution, by virtue of having been established by the colonial power. In contrast many of the executive and members of the Constituent Assembly and subsequently parliament had been part of the nationalist struggle. Often these members had been at the receiving end of judicial decisions during the colonial era. The judiciary, like the military, was viewed with some scepticism.

This is evident when Nehru, the first Prime Minister of independent India, said in the Constituent Assembly,

> no Supreme Court and no judiciary can stand in judgment over the sovereign will of Parliament representing the will of the entire community. If we go wrong here and there, it can point it out but in the ultimate analysis, where the future of the community is concerned, no judiciary can come in the way.[6]

There is some irony that the Constitution's drafters were apprehensive about a conformist judiciary standing in the way of the social change that parliament would seek to bring. Far from being conservative, the Supreme Court has emerged as a rather dynamic institution, committed to crafting progressive values. This shall be examined in detail in later sections.

A. The Power of the Supreme Court Under the Constitution

The Constitution provides specific powers that can be exercised by the Supreme Court. Article 32 states that the Supreme Court shall have the power to issue directions, or orders or writs, including writs in the nature of habeas corpus, mandamus, prohibition, quo warranto and certiorari, whichever may be appropriate for the enforcement of rights conferred by Part III, the fundamental rights segment of the Constitution.

[4] See SP Sathe, *Judicial Activism In India: Transgressing Borders and Enforcing Limits* (New Delhi, Oxford University Press, 2002). Also see, Upendra Baxi, 'The Avatars of Indian Judicial Activism: Explorations in the Geographics of Injustice' in SK Verma and K Kusum (eds), *Fifty Years Of The Supreme Court Of India: Its Grasp and Reach* (New Delhi, Oxford University Press, 2003).

[5] The Constitution can be amended by a vote of two-thirds of the members of the legislature.

[6] *Official Reports Of The Constituent Assembly Debates*, Vol IX, Lok Sabha Secretariat, Fifth Reprint (2009) 1195.

Dr Ambedkar called this provision the 'very soul of the Constitution and the very heart of it.'[7] He explained that the various writs were specifically listed, since this would prevent such writ powers from being taken away by the executive. He observed that the legislature could take it away only by an appropriate constitutional amendment.[8] The writs were clearly meant to be instruments that the court could use to rein in the executive.

The Constitution mandates that the law declared by the Supreme Court shall be binding on all other courts within the country.[9] Thereby the Supreme Court was established as the pinnacle of the hierarchy of courts. Article 142 is an even more fascinating provision of power for the Supreme Court. It states that the Supreme Court, in the exercise of its jurisdiction, may pass such decree or make such order as is necessary for doing complete justice in any cause or any matter pending before it. Since the article was adopted without any discussion in the Constituent Assembly, we have no way of truly discerning the intention of the founders.[10] However, both these constitutional provisions have been invoked by the court to craft an extraordinary range of rights, reliefs leading to the cultivation of values.

B. The Emergence of the Supreme Court as a Value Crafter

The articulation of the global values that this book seeks to discern, in the context of India, is not only a function of constitutional text, but is mostly a creation of interpretative strategies by a creative or activist, or 'exasperated'[11] judiciary—bolstered by its own carving-up of a very indigenous style of judicial independence. This Indian style of judicial independence extends to the court not only crafting for itself an independent role in the matter of judicial appointments and transfers, but has also resulted in a robust review of executive action (and inaction), and declaration of a 'basic structure' of the Constitution or the core part of the Constitution that cannot be amended by the legislature, and finding many constitutional amendments unconstitutional.

The Court has also negated major social and economic policies of the government, including nationalisation of banks, land reform (or land redistribution);[12] upheld legislation providing free and compulsory elementary

[7] *Official Reports Of The Constituent Assembly Debates*, Vol III, Lok Sabha Secretariat, Fifth Reprint (2009) 953.

[8] ibid.

[9] Art 141 of the Constitution of India.

[10] Art 142 was then art 118 of the draft Constitution of India.

[11] Pratap Bhanu Mehta, 'Just Impatient—Can a jurisprudence of exasperation sustain the court's authority?' *The Telegraph*, 17 October 2005 (www.telegraphindia.com/1051017/asp/opinion/story_5303862.asp).

[12] *Golak Nath v State of Punjab*, AIR 1967 SC 1643.

education for children,[13] supervised the public distribution of food after first declaring the right to food a fundamental right,[14] and held certain counter-insurgency policies of the state to be unconstitutional.[15] This unelected body of now 30 judges, without fear of elections or opposition parties, or of being censured in parliament, and subject to far less of criticism by the press or other institutions, seems to be have crafted constitutional values in an unparalleled fashion.

Further, the Indian Supreme Court does not sit *en banc*, or as a full court. Judges sit in benches or panels of two, three or more unusually five or more judges. Therefore, at present in 2015, on a daily basis, there are 12 functioning courtrooms in the Supreme Court. Each court consisting of usually two or three judge panels, hear a variety of cases, and often are unaware of what the panel in the neighbouring court is laying down as jurisprudence. Hence, the jurisprudence of the Court as a whole is not always cohesive. Given the relatively short terms of the judges, of usually three to five years, prior to retiring at the age of 62 years old, the Court witnesses a high turn-over of judges.[16] Therefore, the Supreme Court often functions as many courts, and not necessarily one court.

The sheer volume of cases that reach the Supreme Court of India is unprecedented. And this, along with the ideological and proactive role that the Court has ascribed to itself, has ensured that that this institution wields an enormous amount of power. Let us locate the number of cases it hears in a comparative perspective. The American Supreme Court typically hears about 75 to 80 cases a year.[17] The South African Constitutional Court decided about 30 cases between 1 April 2010 and 31 March 2011, and 115 new cases were filed during this period.[18] Meanwhile, the House of Lords hears around 80 to 90 appeals a year.[19] In contrast, the Supreme Court of India disposed an astonishing 79,621 cases between May 2010 and April 2011.[20]

In contemporary India, Pratap Bhanu Mehta says that 'unelected judges have effectively replaced the notion of separation of powers among three governmental branches with a unitarian claim of formal judicial supremacy.'[21]

[13] *Society for Unaided Private Schools of Rajasthan v Union of India* (2012) 6 SCC 102.

[14] *People's Union for Civil Liberties v Union of India and Others*, Writ Petition (Civil) 196 of 2001, Supreme Court of India [still pending].

[15] *Nandini Sundar v State of Chhattisgarh* (2011) 7 SCC 547.

[16] See also the website of the Supreme Court of India, http://supremecourtofindia.nic.in.

[17] The Supreme Court of United States, www.supremecourt.gov/faq.aspx.

[18] The Constitutional Court of South Africa, *Annual Performance Report: 2010/2011*, www.constitutionalcourt.org.za/site/Admin/constitutional-court-annual-report-2010-11.

[19] The House of Lords, *House of Lords Briefing: Judicial Work*, www.parliament.uk/documents/lords-information-office/hoflbpjudicial.pdf.

[20] Supreme Court of India, *Monthly Pending Cases*, www.supremecourtofindia.nic.in/pendingstat.htm.

[21] Pratap Bhanu Mehta, 'The Rise of Judicial Sovereignty' (2007) 18 (2) *Journal of Democracy* 70.

Mehta seems to suggest that the Indian courts have vitiated the boundaries of separation of powers as understood in a parliamentary democracy, and adopted a role indicative of supremacy of the judiciary. We shall examine the trajectory of this journey made by the courts and examine the veracity of this perception of a self-created supremacy by the judiciary over the executive and the legislature.

Nowhere are these global values more widely articulated and expanded upon, with unrestrained judicial merry-making, than through the Supreme Court's 'greatest judicial innovation and the most important vehicle for the expansion of its powers—the institution of Public Interest Litigation (PIL)'.[22]

As Pratap Bhanu Mehta explains:

> In PIL cases, the Court relaxes the normal requirements of 'standing' and 'pleading', which requires litigation be pressed by a directly affected party or parties, and instead allows anyone to approach it seeking correction of alleged evil or injustice. Such cases also typically involve the abandonment of adversarial fact-finding in favor of Court-appointed investigative and monitoring commissions. Finally, in PIL matters the Court has expanded its own powers the point that it sometimes takes control over the operation of executive agencies.[23]

In terms of global values, this chapter will discuss notions of fairness, justice, tolerance, reverence for life, dignity, education, family, freedom or independence, sustainable development, environment, tolerance, democracy and inclusion. The peculiarly Indian constitutional value of 'secularism' is also discussed. To say that India's jurisprudence on equality is vast would be to understate the situation. Given the number of cases that the Supreme Court hears, the length of arguments (cases are heard for months on end), the number of benches (the courts never sits en-banc) and the size of the judgments, the identification of cases and values is rendered difficult. The difficulty is due to the magnitude of the case law, and the multiplicity of decisions on the same facet of a value in any court term. Therefore, in order to keep the length of this chapter to a manageable size, the value of equality will not be discussed.

II. CONSTITUTIONS, VALUES AND THE PEOPLE

The vesting of power of the people in a constitution is symbolic. For instance, the Preamble to the Indian Constitution declares that the Constitution is adopted by 'We the People'. This preamble shall be discussed in detail in the next section. However, the common citizen (as opposed to the

[22] Pratap Bhanu Mehta, 'The Rise of Judicial Sovereignty' (2007) 18(2) *Journal of Democracy* 70, 71.

[23] ibid.

elite citizen) is rarely involved or allowed to participate in either the making of the Constitution or even adoption of the final product. What then establishes the Constitution as occupying a moral, legal and in the popular imagination, an enhanced standing—a higher ground? It is the legitimacy that the Constitution is accorded by the people. Such legitimacy is derived not necessarily via a referendum, but through the respect that is accorded to the values of the Constitution, and the internalisation of the Constitution as being that which is fundamental to a nation. And therefore, Hanna Lerner says that constitution-writing has been described as an attempt to identify and articulate the fundamental norms and values that are shared by 'the people' in whose name and for whom the Constitution is drafted.[24]

Who are the people that the constituent power is meant to belong to? Habermas calls them 'perhaps a community of fate, shaped by common descent, language and history'.[25] Alternatively, as Preuss writes, the people could be viewed as a 'political construction, a voluntary association of rational individuals acting on the basis of shared principles'.[26] Preuss denies that one needs factors like a common religion or language to come together as the people. What is needed, according to him, is a 'common sphere of public debate and reasoning.'[27]

Preuss located the notion of a people then in non-ethnic or religious factors. He elucidates further, that the people are illuminated by the values of that which is constituted, and in fact can be defined by that cosmopolitan notion of a common sphere of public debate and reasoning. In other words, perhaps it is common values, common challenges, and the common idea of nation that may constitute a country. As we proceed further, this might well unpack the secrets of when constitutionalism endures. Quite surprisingly it is not located in the sameness of language, religion, race or ethnicity of a population. It is located in the ingredients of the dialogue that permeates their consciousness and the expectations that constitute them.

Finally, Murphy highlights Aristotle's sweeping definition of the constitution later in Book 4, as being a 'way of life', thereby ensuring competition between politics and religion.[28] It is exactly this phenomenon of the constitution becoming a 'way of life', and its values permeating through a nation,

[24] Hanna Lerner, *Making Constitutions In Deeply Divided Societies* (Cambridge, Cambridge University Press, 2011) 30.

[25] Jurgen Habermas, 'Why Europe Needs A Constitution' (2001) 11 (2nd Series) *New Left Review* 5, 15A.

[26] Ulrich Preuss, 'Constitutional Power Making For the New Polity: Some Deliberations on the Relations Between Constituent Power and the Constitution' (1993) 14 *Cardozo Law Review* 639, 644–47, cited by Richard Kay, 'Constituent Authority' (2011) 59(3) *American Journal of Comparative Law* 740.

[27] Preuss, ibid, 648, cited by Kay, ibid 741.

[28] Walter Murphy, *Constitutional Democracy, Creating And Maintaing A Just Political Order* (Baltimore MD, The Johns Hopkins University Press, 2007) 13.

or at least defining the ethos of significant political institutions, that seems to account for enduring constitutionalism. India's Constitution and its values seem to have defined many of the country's institutions—including the jurisprudence evolved by the courts, respect for parliament being accorded by its people, and consistently held elections. Robust voting turn-outs, in a country with substantial poverty, and governments both at the state and central levels that have lost elections, respecting the Constitution and making way for the winner of the elections, have been defining features of Indian constitutional democracy.

The constituent power has been appreciated by many, ascribing to it varied manifestations and effects. Preuss describes it most beautifully as the secularised version of the divine power to create the world, to create an order without being subject to it.[29] This is indicative of the notion that whereas previously the monarch or a religious entity was considered to be the source of power to create values that manifested themselves in models of governance or morality, that which is now represented to be the people through a constitution now do so.

According to Preuss, the will of the constituent power aims at transforming itself into an objective and enduring incarnation, a constitution, but it cannot simultaneously submit itself to its own creation without losing its character as the supreme secular power.[30] Whereas the constituent power may not be able to submit to itself (though this is a illusionary distinction), the product of that will—through the people's agents a constituent assembly—the constitution in contemporary times is expected to conform to certain core values, or even to be certified by the judiciary.

A. The Preamble of the Indian Constitution—Values of We the People

The Preamble to the Indian Constitution declares that

> We the People of India, having solemnly resolved to constitute India into a sovereign, socialist,[31] secular,[32] democratic republic and to secure to all its citizens: Justice—social, economic and political; Liberty of thought, expression, belief, faith and worship; Equality of status and opportunity; and to promote among them all fraternity assuring dignity of the individual and the unity and integrity[33] of the nation.

[29] Ulrich K Preuss, 'Constitutional Powermaking for the New Polity: Some Deliberations on the Relations between the Constituent Power and the Constitution' (1993) 14 *Cardozo Law Review* 639, 640.

[30] ibid 640

[31] Inserted by the Constitution (42nd Amendment) Act, 1976

[32] ibid.

[33] ibid.

The symbolic importance of 'We the People' in according legitimacy to the Constitution as being adopted by the people has been discussed above.

The Preamble also establishes that the people of India are united by the common values they share. These values are initially identified in the Preamble itself and then subsequently in greater detail in the constitutional provisions that follow. Such articulation by the Preamble of these common shared values, and the adoption of the Constitution by the people of India, whose commonality is those shared values, sets up the Constitution as having a higher status, and therefore accords it great legitimacy. It also locates the conception of India in the common core values that her people share—of a socialist, secular democracy, amongst others.

These common core values identified by the Preamble include social, economic and political justice, liberty of thought, belief, faith and worship, and equality of opportunity. Fraternity would also be a core value that binding the people of India.

The Supreme Court has also consciously crafted jurisprudence that has utilised the Preamble and the core values that it lists as being influential in interpreting fundamental rights (or the bills of rights) and many other provisions of the Constitution. For instance the Supreme Court has held that the Preamble contains ideals and aspirations,[34] or the objects which the Constitution's drafters intended to be realised.[35] The Supreme Court of India has been described by the scholar Durga Das Basu as being inclined to take cognisance of the Preamble to 'determine the ambit of Fundamental Rights[36] and the Directives,[37] because it is the ideals of socialism, secularism and democracy, which are elaborated by the enacting provisions'.[38]

The Preamble is also unique in that it has been amended post the adoption of the Constitution, as recently as the 1980s, to insert words like 'socialist' and 'secular'.[39] These additions have had a substantial influence in facilitating the nationalisation of private property.[40] The words 'social justice' have also been elucidated upon, as meaning removal of social imbalance by the law,[41] to provide facilities and opportunities to remove the handicaps

[34] *Atam Prakash v State of Harayana*, AIR 1986 SC 234 (864), (1986) 2 SCC 249.

[35] *Golaknath IC v State of Punjab* AIR 1967 SC 1643 (1655), 1967 2 SCR 249.

[36] *Kesavananda Bharti v State of Kerala* AIR 1973 SC 1461 [292], [599], [62], [1164, [1437]. (1973) 4 SCC 225.

[37] Its full form is the Directive Principles of State Policy, or Part IV of the Constitution. Durga Das Basu, *Commentary on the Constitution of India*, Vol III (New Delhi, Lexis Nexis/ Butterworth, 2008).

[38] Durga Das Basu, *Shorter Constitution Of India*, 13th edn (New Delhi, Wadhwa and Company, 2002) 2.

[39] The words socialist and secular were added by the Constitution (Forty-second Amendment) Act, 1976, s 2 (w.e.f. 31-1-1977).

[40] 'Article 19(1)(f), the fundamental right to property, was deleted by the Constitution (Forty-fourth Amendment Act, 1978). See also *Excel Wear v Union of India* AIR 1979 SC 25 [24], (1978) 4 SCC 224. See Durga Das Basu (n 37) 2.

[41] *Dalmia Cement (Bharat) Ltd v Union of India* (1996) 10 SCC 104 [13].

and disabilities of the poor,[42] and to enact positive measures for the protection of tribal and weaker sections of society.[43] The apex court has declared that social justice means distributive justice, and may also take the form of forced redistribution of wealth as a means of achieving a fair division of material resources among the members of society.[44] A concrete example of using the Preamble and its social justice aim was when the Supreme Court utilised this conception of social justice to ensure maternity leave for 'casual' or non-permanent or 'muster roll' women workers.[45]

The Supreme Court has also engaged the notion of 'democracy' as stated in the Preamble, and observed that the state in a democratic society derives its strength from the cooperative and dispassionate will of its free and equal citizens,[46] and that social and economic democracy is the foundation on which political democracy would be a way of life in the Indian polity.[47]

III. FUNDAMENTAL RIGHTS

The fundamental rights which comprise Chapter 3 of the Constitution are India's Bill of Rights. They are rather detailed and specific. In this section these fundamental rights shall be briefly listed. Each right in turn has been interpreted in detail by the Supreme Court. This shall be discussed in detail subsequently.

The fundamental rights in the Indian Constitution include the rights to equality,[48] to non-discrimination on grounds of religion, race, caste, sex, or place of birth,[49] freedom of speech, to peacefully assemble, to form associations, to movement and residence in any part of India, and the practice of any profession, trade or business. Fundamental rights also include the right not to be discriminated against in public employment; the right not to be subject to retroactive penal legislation, to punishment more than once for the same offence, or to compulsion to give evidence against oneself;[50] the right not to be deprived of life or personal liberty except according to procedure established by law;[51] and the rights for an arrested person to be

42 *Consumer Education and Research Centre v Union of India* (1995) 3 SCC 42 [19], AIR 1995 SC 992.

43 *Lingappa Pochanna Appelwar v State of Maharashtra* AIR 1985 SC 389 [14], [16], [18], [20], (1985) 1 SCC 479; *Indra Sawhney v Union of India* (1992) Supp (3) 217 [23], [26], [416], AIR 1993 SC 477.

44 ibid.

45 *Municipal Corporation of Delhi v Female Workers (Muster Roll)* (2000) 3 SCC 224 [32] and [33], AIR 2000 SC 1274.

46 *State of Punjab v G S Gill* (1997) 6 SCC 129 [8], AIR 1997 SC 2324.

47 *Samatha v State of AP* (1997) 8 SCC 191 [76].

48 Art 14.

49 Art 15.

50 Art 20.

51 Art 21.

given grounds for her arrest, and opportunity to be defended by a lawyer of her choice.[52]

The Constitution provides for the rights of person held in preventive detention,[53] the right to freedom of religion,[54] rights of religious denomination,[55] the rights not to be compelled to receive religious instruction in educational institutions,[56] the right to sustain cultural diversity,[57] the right not to be denied admission, on grounds of religion, race, caste or language, to an educational institution maintained by the state,[58] the right of religious and linguistic minorities to establish and administer educational institutions of their choice,[59] and the right to move the Court for the enforcement of fundamental rights.[60]

The fundamental right to property which was part of the original text of the constitution was amended away in 1978.[61] In its stead was inserted a constitutional right to property[62]—a lower level right than a fundamental right. This enabled the government to initiate and implement widespread land reform programmes. At present, article 300A of the Constitution only provides 'that no person shall be deprived of property save by authority of law'.

A. The Directive Principles of State Policy

The Indian Constitution has a section that pertains to development goals of the country. This rather unusual and uncommon section, which marries development goals to constitutionalism, is called the Directive Principles of State Policy (DPSPs). The DPSPs have been described by the eminent scholar Upendra Baxi as 'defining and prescribing minimal indices for development',[63] while the Constitution in turn 'defines development as a series of governance obligations.'[64] In short, according to Baxi, the DPSPs define 'constitutional essences of good governance'.[65]

[52] Art 22(1) and (2).
[53] Art 22(4)–(7).
[54] Art 25.
[55] Art 26.
[56] Art 28.
[57] Art 29(1).
[58] Art 29(2).
[59] Art 30.
[60] Art 32. For an excellent and concise introduction to Fundamental Rights, see SP Sathe (n 4) 218i–20.
[61] Constitution (44th Amendment Act) 1978, s 2.
[62] Constitution (44th Amendment Act) 1978, s 34. See *Bishamber v State of Uttar Pradesh* AIR 1982 SC 33.
[63] Upendra Baxi, in Zoya Hassan, E Sridharan and R Sudarshan (eds) *India's Living Constitution* (Delhi, Permanent Black, 2002) 37.
[64] ibid 38.
[65] ibid 43.

The Constituent Assembly debates on the Directive Principles indicate that they were meant to 'give directions to the Legislatures and to the Executive as regards the manner in which they should exercise their power'.[66] Further, it seems to be the intent that these powers should be channelled towards the simultaneous achievement of a political democracy and an economic democracy,[67] which would ostensibly bring about equitable development.

Articles 36 to 51 in Chapter IV the Constitution deal with the DPSPs. These include free legal aid, equal justice, right to work, a living wage for workers, maternity relief, and just and humane conditions for workers, amongst others. Interestingly, whereas the text of the Constitution provides that these DPSPs shall not be enforceable in a court of law.[68] The Supreme Court through creative interpretation over the years has systematically ensured that DPSPs would be taken in account when characterising rights and remedies. Therefore, as subsequent sections shall show, DPSPs were used in interpreting fundamental rights. Consequently, what the Constitution did not allow directly, the Court ensured indirectly.

B. The Right to Life: A Right that Encompasses All

The text of the Constitution provides for a fairly conventional right to life. Article 21 provides that 'no one shall be deprived of his life or personal liberty, except according to procedure established by law.' Textually, there are no hints of the all-encompassing right to life that it would become—at least constitutionally, in India.

India's Supreme Court has created an extensive jurisprudence spanning all the fundamental rights. However, it is in the right to life that the Court has been at its most creative and activist. The Court has read in and provided for an array of subsidiary rights that it was sure flowed from the right to life. Within this right the Court also found ways to make DPSPs justiciable. The commentator R Sudarshan termed the jurisprudence evolved by the Supreme Court in the context of the right to life as 'creative'—whereby interpretation has been adopted that has enabled social, economic, cultural and environmental rights into the realm of justiciable issues.[69] This mode of making Directive Principles justiciable was done by 'reading into them' the right to life and personal liberty.[70] In essence, the object of Article 21 was

[66] 7 Constituent Assembly Debates 476.

[67] MP Jain, *Indian Constitutional Law* (Nagpur, Wadhwa and Company, 2005) 1363.

[68] Art 37.

[69] R Sudarshan in Roberto Gargarella, Pilar Domingo and Theunix Roux (eds), *Courts and Social Transformation in India* (Hampshire, Ashgate Publishing, 2006) 157.

[70] *Minerva Mills v Union of India* (1980) 3 SCC 225.

to prevent the encroachment upon personal liberty by the executive save in accordance with the law, and in conformity with the provisions thereof.[71]

In its sheer range and magnitude, the India Constitution's right to life is unparalleled. The Supreme Court has observed that the right means more than survival or animal existence.[72] It went onto say that this right would include the right to live with human dignity,[73] and a life meaningful, complete and worth living.[74] Subsequently, the Court would find that life includes the rights to food, water, a decent environment, education, medical care and shelter.[75] The right to life would also include culture and protection of heritage,[76] not to be subjected to unfair conditions of labour,[77] and the right to livelihood.[78] Conversely, rape has been declared to violate the right to life, since this right includes that of dignity.[79] According to the Court, chronic exposure to polluted air also violates this right.[80] The all-encompassing view of the right to life is illustrated in more recent times, by the orders passed by the Supreme Court in what is now called the 'right to food' case.[81]

More traditionally, the right to life was also litigated in the context of the right not to live and/or suicide. In *Gian Kaur v State of Punjab*,[82] the Court grappled with whether section 309 of the Indian Penal Code, which punished the abetting of suicide, was constitutional. In deciding that such protection did not extend to those who abetted suicide, the Court upheld the constitutionality of the penal provision that criminalised such action.

Finally, the right to privacy though not specifically provided for in the text of the Constitution, has been read into Article 21 via the right to life. Privacy has been recognised as having two components: one a constitutional right to privacy which protects personal privacy from unlawful governmental intrusion, and a general law of privacy which affords a tort action for damages upon a violation being committed.[83] A significant departure from

[71] *Gopalan AK v State of Madras* 1950 SCR 88, AIR 1950 SC 27; see DD Basu (n 37) 258.

[72] *State of Maharashtra v Chandrabhan* AIR 1983 SC 803 [1] and [20] (1983) 3 SCC 387.

[73] *Francis Coralie Mullin v Union Territory Delhi, Administrator* AIR 1981 SC 746 [3]; *Olga Tellis v Bombay Corporation* AIR 1986 SC 180 [33]-[34], (1985) 3 SCC 545; *DTC v Mazdoor Congress Union DTC* AIR 1991 SC 101 [223], [234], [259], 1991 Supp (1) SCC 600; *Consumer Education and Research Centre v Union of India* (1995) 3 SCC 42 [22].

[74] *Maneka Gandhi v Union of India* AIR 1978 SC 597, (1978) 1 SCC 248.

[75] *Chameli Singh v State of UP* (1996) 2 SCC 549 [8], AIR 1996 SC 1051.

[76] *Ramsharan Autyanuprasi v Union of India* AIR 1983 SC 549 [13]-[14], 1989 Supp (1) SCC 251.

[77] *People's Union v Union of India* AIR 1982 SC 1473, (1982) 3 SCC 235.

[78] *Olga Tellis v Bombay Corpn* AIR 1986 SC 180 [33]-[34]; (1985) 3 SCC 545; *DTC v Mazdoor Congress Union DTC* AIR 1991 SC 101 [223], [234], 259], 1991 Supp. (1) SCC 600.

[79] *Boddhisatwa Gautam v Subhra Chakraborthi* (1996) 1 SCC 490 [10], AIR 1996 SC 922.

[80] *MC Mehta v Union of India* (1996) 6 SCC 9 [9].

[81] *People's Union of Civil Liberties v Union of India and Ors* (2013) 2 SCC 688.

[82] *Gian Kaur v State of Punjab* (1996) 2 SCC 648.

[83] *R Rajagopal v State of Tamil Nadu* (1994) 6 SCC 632.

the expansive right to life jurisprudence of the Court has been with regard to the rights of Indian citizens who are lesbian, gay, bisexual and transgendered (LGBT). In *Suresh Kumar Kaushal v Naz Foundation,*[84] Justice Singhvi in a poorly reasoned judgment, held that section 377 of the Indian Penal Code 1860 that also criminalised consensual sexual acts between same-sex partners did not violate the right to life and the right to privacy of LGBT Indians.[85] Justice Singhvi also held that this criminal law provision did not violate the equality or non-discrimination protection of LGBT Indians.[86]

This judgment saw the Court falling short of the standard of application of law and reason expected from an apex court. Apart from relying on incorrect statutes, the Judge displayed a great hostility towards foreign case law—from jurisdictions including the United States, the European Union, South Africa and even Nepal.[87] The Judge eventually upheld the constitutionality of this penal provision on flimsy grounds including that only 200 people had been prosecuted under the section since 1860 when the Indian Penal Code was adopted by India's British colonial rulers.[88] He reasons that the Delhi High Court which had 'read down' this section to exclude consensual sexual relations between adults was wrong since it

> had overlooked that a miniscule fraction of the country's population constitutes lesbians, gays, bisexuals and transgendered and in the last more than 150 years less than 200 persons had been prosecuted for committing offence under section 377 IPC and this cannot be made a sound basis for declaring section 377 IPC ultra vires the provisions of Articles 14, 15 and 21 of the Constitution.[89]

This judgement is a grave departure from the Court's constitutional trajectory of expanding rights, and never disempowering or disenfranchising minorities of any kind. The animus of the Judge, evidenced by references to LGBT Indians as a 'miniscule fraction' and the poor legal reasoning, makes *Suresh Kumar Kaushal* an institutional embarrassment for the Court. The decision is in desperate need of being overturned.

Outside of cases like *Suresh Kumar Kaushal,* the Court has rendered the right to life all-encompassing. The Supreme Court has evolved into India's most strident author of an ever-growing list of rights. Given its own sense of authority, the Court has been prolific in the jurisprudence and crafting of new constituents to each right guaranteed by the text of the constitution. The right to life was easy to marry to the twin self-adopted mandates of the Court—to further a welfare-oriented socio-economic rights jurisprudence

[84] *Suresh Kumar Kaushal v Naz Foundation* (2014) 1 SCC 1.
[85] See Menaka Guruswamy, 'Making Criminals of Us All', *The Indian Express*, 13 December 2013.
[86] Above n 84 [65].
[87] ibid [77].
[88] ibid [66] and [67].
[89] ibid [66].

to harness benefits from the state while guaranteeing traditional civil and political rights against the state. Life, with its constituents of fair procedure and liberty, would also speak for the ability to achieve maximum potential of that life. Thence, the provision of health, roads, sanitation, food amongst other to enhance the ability to exercise the right to life.

C. Right to Education

Initially, the fundamental right to education was specifically provided to religious and linguistic minorities. The Constituent Assembly drafting the Constitution obviously did so to ensure that while minority communities protect their culture, they would not be discriminated while accessing education on grounds of their religion or language. Hence the text of the Constitution provided that no citizen could be denied admission into any educational institution maintained by the state or recently receiving aid out from state funds on grounds only of religion, race, caste, language, or any of them.[90] Again in the context of religious minorities, the Constitution provided that all linguistic and religious minorities has the right to establish and administer educational institutions of their choice,[91] and that the state could discriminate while giving aid to educational institutions run by such minorities.[92]

The individual right to education was provided for only in the DPSPs. The DPSPs provided that the state in general must, within its economic capacity and development, make effective provision for securing the right to education,[93] and that it was expected to take 'specific care' of the educational interests of weaker sections of people like Scheduled Castes and Scheduled Tribes.[94] An original Directive Principle provided that the state shall provide free education for all children to the age of 14 years, and that this would be provided for within 10 years of the commencement of the Constitution.[95] It has been noticed that, being the only Directive Principle with a 'built-in time limit', this shows the seriousness with which the Constitution framers viewed this need.[96] Even so, in December 2002, by the Constitution (Eighty-sixth Amendment) Act 2002, education was explicitly made a fundamental right for those between the ages of six and 14.[97]

[90] Art 29(2).
[91] Art 30(1).
[92] Art 30(2).
[93] Art 41.
[94] Art 46.
[95] Art 45.
[96] Vijayashri Sripathi and Arun K Thiruvengadam, 'Constitutional amendment making the right to education a Fundamental Right' (2004) *International Journal of Constitutional Law* 148, 150.
[97] For more about the right to education, see ibid.

The Court began its engagement with education quite conventionally by explaining the importance of education for children—in the context of children enslaved the carpet industry and therefore deprived of the right to education. In *Bandhua Mukti Morcha v Union of India*[98] a public interest litigation was filed to ask the government to take steps to stop employment of children in the carpet industry in the State of Utter Pradesh; to appoint a committee to investigate into their conditions of employment; and to issue such welfare directives as are appropriate for total prohibition on employment of children below 14 years and directing the respondent to give them facilities such as education, health, sanitation and nutritious food. This case took well over 18 years to resolve, and is considered one of the classic public interest litigations. Many years later, in this same litigation, the Court provides its justification for the crafting of the right to education as a fundamental right is provided by the importance that the Court attached to literacy. It explained that:

> Illiteracy has many adverse effects in a democracy governed by rule of law. A free educated citizen could meaningfully exercise his political rights, discharge social responsibilities satisfactorily and develop spirit of tolerance and reform. Therefore, education is compulsory. Primary education to the children, in particular, to the child from poor, weaker sections, Dalits and Tribes and minorities is mandatory. Compulsory education, therefore, to these children is one of the principal means and primary duty of the State for stability of the democracy, social integration and to eliminate social tensions.[99]

It is believed the Supreme Court was the catalyst for this constitutional amendment that transformed the right to education from a non-enforceable Directive Principle to a fundamental right for children.[100] The Supreme Court in the 1990s had already laid the groundwork for a dramatic shift in the status of this right to education, going arguably well beyond what was necessary to adjudicate two cases that concerned higher education, and the levy of excessive capitation fees by private higher educational institutions, in *Mohini Jain v State of Karnataka*[101] and *Unni Krishnan J v State of Andhra Pradesh.*[102]

In *Unni Krishnan v State of Andhra Pradesh,*[103] private professional educational institutions challenged the ability of the government to fix tuition fees for them as well. In a much-heralded judgment written by Justice Jeevan Reddy, the Court made far-reaching inroads into the policy arena:

> The citizens of this country have a fundamental right to education. The said right flows from Article 21. This right is, however, not an absolute right. Its content

[98] *Bandhua Mukti Morcha v Union of India* (1984) 3 SCC 161.
[99] *Bandhua Mukti Morcha v Union of India* (1997) 10 SCC 549 at para 11.
[100] ibid.
[101] *Mohini Jain v State of Karnataka* AIR 1992 SC 1858.
[102] *Unni Krishnan J v State of Andhra Pradesh* (1993) 1 SCC 645.
[103] ibid.

> and parameters have to be determined in the light of Articles 45 and 41. In other words, every child/citizen of this country has a right to free education until he completes the age of 14 years. Thereafter his right to education is subject to the limits of economic capacity and development of the State. The admission of students and the charging of fee in the private educational institutions shall be governed by the scheme evolved herein set out in Part III of the judgment.[104]

The immediate effect of the *Unni Krishnan* decision was that any child below the age of 14 who was denied facilities for primary education could approach the court for a writ of mandamus directing the state to initiate appropriate action.[105] In time this led to civil society launching a movement spanning a large assortment of activists and NGOs spanning numerous issues, who began to lobby the government to make the right to education a fundamental right through a constitutional amendment.[106]

What is extraordinary about the role of the Court in crafting and enhancing the right to education was the detail pertaining to administration and allocation of resources to the institutions that is dealt with in the judgments. For instance, in *Islamic Academy v State of Karnataka*,[107] the Supreme Court was not simply content with finding that each minority institution is entitled to have its own fee structure subject to the condition that there can be no profiteering and capitation fees cannot be charged. It went further, to declare that a provision for reasonable surplus can be made to enable future expansion (ranging from 6 per cent to 15 per cent).[108] It explained that the relevant factors which would go into determining the reasonableness of a fee structure, in the opinion of majority, are (i) the infrastructure and facilities available, (ii) the age of the institution, (iii) the investments, (iv) salaries paid to the teachers and staff, and (v) future plans for expansion and betterment of the institution.[109]

The Court cemented its position as the author of an expansive fundamental right to education by upholding the constitutionality of the Right to Children to Free and Compulsory Education Act 2009. While finding in favour of the constitutionality of this statute, which provides that up to 30 per cent of seats in every private school across the country would be set aside for disadvantaged children, the Court located its rationale in the importance of education and the fabric of social democracy. It was education that provided for equal opportunities and therefore strengthened the

[104] ibid [226].
[105] Sripathi and Thiruvengadam (n 96) 153.
[106] ibid 154.
[107] *Islamic Academy v State of Karnataka* (2003) 6 SCC 697. In *TMA Pai Foundation v State of Karnataka* (2002) 8 SCC 481 the Supreme Court laid down that art 30(1) gives religious and linguistic minorities the right to establish and administer professional and non-professional educational institutions of their choice.
[108] ibid [156].
[109] ibid [154].

social fabric of democracy.[110] This case was also significant since it enabled the state to ensure that private institutions were also subject to the state policies of integration and compensation for historical and social disadvantage experienced by some quarters of society.

D. Family/Community

The cases that went to the Supreme Court with regard to the family and community involved definitions of the family itself, and within that the role played by members as recognised by the state. While grappling with the problem of an ever-growing Indian populace (the country now comprising approximately 1.2 billion people), the state formulated policies to encourage a maximum of two children per family.

In *Javed v State of Haryana*[111] the Supreme Court was confronted with the Haryana Panchayati Raj Act 1994 which had, as one of its objectives, the disqualification of persons for election of Panchayats (village or small town level) at each level, having more than two children after one year of the date of commencement of this Act, to popularise the Family Welfare/Family Planning Programme. The Court upheld this disqualification since it felt that the number of children—two—was based on legislative wisdom and therefore was a policy decision that is not open to judicial scrutiny.

A further point had been raised by the parties to the litigation about whether the law violated the freedom of religion, since Muslim personal law allowed a man to marry up to four women, and this therefore presumably did not allow that man to have a child with each of his four wives. The Court however rejected this contention, as no religious authority had been presented to it to show that marrying less than four women, or abstaining from procreating with each wife, would be offensive to the dictates of that religion.

The Supreme Court confronted the issue of the presumed higher standing accorded to a father as compared to a mother and their child, in *Githa Hariharan v Reserve Bank of India*.[112] Traditionally, the father was presumed to be the legal guardian of his child. In December 1984 the petitioner, the mother, applied to the Reserve Bank of India for a 9% rate of interest return bond instrument, to be held in the name of her minor son Rishab, along with an intimation that the petitioner being the mother, would act as the natural guardian for the purposes of investments. However, the application was sent back to the petitioner by the bank advising the mother to

[110] *Society of Unaided Private Schools of Rajasthan v Union of India* (2012) 6 SCC 1.

[111] *Javed v State of Haryana* (2003) 8 SCC 369. Followed in *Khurshid Ahmed Khan v State of UP and Ors*, CA No 1662 of 2015, dated 9 February 2015.

[112] *Githa Hariharan v Reserve Bank of India* (1999) 2 SCC 228.

produce the application signed by the father, and in the alternative a certificate of guardianship from a competent authority in her favour. The mother challenged the relevant law that was being relied on by the bank to insist on the signature of the father. The mother argued that such law was opposed to article 14 (right to equality) and article 15 (prohibition on discrimination on grounds of sex)[113] of the Constitution.

The Court accepted that the statute relied on by the Bank 'depicts that the mother's right to act as a natural guardian stands suspended during the lifetime of the father and upon the death of the father, the mother obtains a right to act as a natural guardian of a Hindu minor'. The Court further held that 'normal rules of interpretation shall have to bow down to the requirement of the Constitution since the Constitution is supreme and the statute shall have to be in accordance therewith and not de hors the same'.[114] Therefore, the Court interpreted the law as allowing the mother to sign the paperwork for the bond application and hence ensured that the law was in consonance with the constitutional values of equality and non-discrimination on the grounds of sex alone.

E. Freedom/Independence

The Supreme Court has been somewhat conservative in the area of 'freedom'—especially in the context of speech and expression. This section will establish that the Court is more amenable to protecting speech in the course of activities that it believes are important to the functioning of a political democracy. For instance, the ability of established newspapers to operate out of offices where they have long been located, or the flying of the national flag by a private citizen. But the Court is less amenable to protecting the rights of artists when they question the state of affairs in society though their work—especially if such may be seen to be provocative. The Court was also less than amenable to protecting the conduct of missionaries who sought to convert citizens from one religion to another. The Court appears to believe that private citizens must be protected from provocative films and conduct that is oriented to persuading them to change their religion. The Court's jurisprudence appears to indicate that it may be somewhat paternalistic when confronted by issues of personal choice and expression of private citizens, and apparently more progressive when it involves activities traditionally perceived as being political.

In *KA Abbas v Union of India,*[115] the petitioner made a film called *A Tale of Four Cities* which attempted to portray the contrast between the life of

[113] Art 15 of the Constitution.
[114] Supra n 112 at para 45.
[115] *KA Abbas v Union of India* (1970) 2 SCC 780.

the rich and that of the poor in the country's four largest cities. The film included certain shots of the red light district (areas where sex workers live and work) in Bombay. Consequently, the Board of Film Censors granted the film an A (adult) certificate. The central government issued a direction on 3 July 1969 that a U certificate (which allowed for viewing by all) might be granted provided certain specified cuts were made in the film. The petitioner claimed that his fundamental right of free speech and expression was denied by the order of the central government, since it was premised on certain cuts to the original film. The petitioner who was the maker of the film argued that he was entitled to a U certificate for the film as of right.

In upholding the act of censorship by the state, the Court declared, these alleged restraints on liberty were justified by their absolute necessity. The Supreme Court felt that the larger interests of the community required the formulation of policies and regulations to 'combat dishonesty, corruption, gambling, vice and other things of immoral tendency and things which affect the security of the State and the preservation of public order and tranquillity.'

In *Express Newspapers Pvt Ltd v Union of India,*[116] the petitioners, a reputed Indian newspaper known to criticise the government, challenged the constitutional validity of two notices, first, a notice of re-entry upon forfeiture of lease on the basis of violation of some of the provisions of the lease deed. The second was an earlier notice seeking demolition of the buildings. Both were challenged on the grounds that the location—Bahadurshah Zafar Marg, in New Delhi—was the nerve centre of the newspaper industry, and the government's actions were wholly mala fide and politically motivated. They further alleged that the impugned notices constituted acts of personal vendetta against the Express Group of Newspapers in general, and against Ramnath Goenka, chairman of the board of directors, in particular, and consequently violated the right to equality,[117] freedom of speech[118] and freedom of association.[119]

The Court stressed that freedom of thought and expression, and freedom of the press, are not only valuable freedoms in themselves but are basic to the democratic form of government.[120] The Court stated that the test for permissible limitation on the freedom of speech and expression was whether the impugned actions had a direct and immediate impact on these rights. The Court deduced that the impugned notices of re-entry upon forfeiture of lease, and of the threatened demolition of the Express Buildings, were intended to silence the voice of the *Indian Express.*[121] Therefore, these

[116] *Indian Express Newspapers v Union of India* (1986) 1 SCC 133.
[117] Art 14.
[118] Art 19(1)(a).
[119] Art 19(1)(g).
[120] ibid [75].
[121] ibid [76].

impugned notices constituted a direct and immediate threat to the freedom of the press and therefore violated the rights to freedom of speech and expression.

The Supreme Court was confronted with the quest of a wealthy Indian citizen who wanted to fly the national flag at the premises of his corporation, in *Union of India v Naveen Jindal*.[122] The government sought to prohibit this on the grounds that this practice violated the Flag Code, whereas Mr Jindal contended that this affected his right to freedom of speech and expression guaranteed by article 19(1)(a). The Court felt that as long as the flag was respected and not mutilated in any way, the freedom of expression of a private citizen included the right to express one's nationalism and therefore this encompassed the right to fly the national flag.

Rev Stainislaus v State of Madhya Pradesh[123] involved the constitutional validity of the Madhya Pradesh Dharma Swatantraya Adhiniyam 1968 and Orissa Freedom of Religion Act 1967 which prohibited forcible conversion and make the offence punishable. The Orissa High Court had held that article 25(2) of the Constitution guarantees propagation of religion and that conversion was a part of Christian religion. However, the Supreme Court upheld the validity of the impugned Acts. The Court declared:

> It has to be remembered that Article 25 (1) guarantees 'freedom of conscience' to every citizen, and not merely to the followers of one particular religion, and that, in turn, postulates that there is no fundamental right to convert another person to one's own religion because if a person purposely undertakes the conversion of another person to his religion, as distinguished from his effort to transmit or spread the tenets of his religion, that would impinge on the 'freedom of conscience' guaranteed to all the citizens of the country alike.[124]

The Court does appear to believe that citizens must be protected from being led astray or their sentiments being hurt—whether such apparent injury is caused by conversion to another religion or by art that provokes. Freedom that may be ascribed to conduct in the more public and political arena—through acts like flying the flag or publishing a newspaper—the Court feels must be absolutely protected, even though the flag was to be flown at the corporate headquarters of an elite private citizen, and the publication of the newspaper might not have been directly influenced by the location of the offices of the newspaper. The Court sees freedom as a more complicated value, less straightforward for instance than the right to life.

[122] *Union of India v Naveen Jindal* (2004) 2 SCC 510.
[123] *Rev Stainislauparavs v State of Madhya Pradesh* (1977) 1 SCC 677.
[124] ibid [20].

F. Sustainable Development/Environment

The values of sustainable development and protection of the environment are often in conflict with economic growth, all the more so in a country which experiences the grave poverty that India does. In *Intellectuals Forum v State of Andhra Pradesh*[125] the Court was faced with resolving the often competing needs of development/economic growth as opposed to the environment. As Justice Lakshmanan, who wrote the judgment, observed:

> this court has often faced situations where the needs of environmental protection have been pitched against the demands of economic development. In response to this difficulty, policy makers and judicial bodies across the world have produced the concept of 'sustainable development'.[126]

The Court then explained this concept of sustainable development by referring to the earlier case of *Essar Oil v Halar Utkarsh Samiti,*[127] where in it was declared that 'there need not necessarily be a deadlock between development on the one hand and the environment on the other. The objective of all laws on environment should be to create harmony between the two, since neither one can be sacrificed at the altar of the other.'

The Court noted that article 48A, a Directive Principle of State Policy, mandates that the state shall endeavour to protect and improve the environment to safeguard the forests and wildlife of the country. Article 51A also a Directive Principle, enjoins that it shall be the duty of every citizen of India, inter alia, to protect and improve national environment including forests, lakes, rivers, wildlife and to have compassion for living creatures. According to the Supreme Court, these two articles were not only fundamental in the governance of the country, but it was also the duty of the state to apply these principles in making laws.[128] The Court also stated that these two articles were to be kept in mind in understanding the scope and purport of the fundamental rights guaranteed by the Constitution, including articles 14, 19 and 21 of the Constitution of India and also the various laws enacted by the parliament and the state legislature.

This case is indicative of the interpretive technique that the apex court appears to use to ensure that DPSPs are rendered enforceable—through their marriage within the construction of applicable fundamental rights. By using the fundamental rights to equality, occupation and life to illuminate the DPSPs that seek to protect forests and wildlife, the Court is ensuring that governmental policy and action as it pertains to these two areas can be challenged by citizens and adjudicated upon by the courts.

[125] *Intellectuals Forum v State of Andhra Pradesh* (2006) 3 SCC 549.
[126] ibid [68].
[127] *Essar Oil v Halar Utkarsh Samiti* 2004 (2) SCC 392 [27].
[128] ibid [82].

G. Tolerance and Education/Spirituality

In *Aruna Roy v Union of India*[129] a public interest litigation was filed where it was contended that the National Curriculum Framework for School Education published by the National Council of Educational Research and Training was against the constitutional mandate, being anti-secular. The Court decided that whereas there is a prohibition against imparting religious instructions, by article 28, there is no such obstacle to a value-based education. Such values would include the notion that the essence of every religion is common. According to the Court, the present curriculum seeks to teach self-discipline, courage, love for social justice, truth, peace and non-violence. The Court felt that such values were not anti-secular, and in fact gave effect to article 51(A)(e) which seeks 'to promote harmony and the spirit of common brotherhood amongst all the people of India transcending religious, linguistic and regional or sectional diversities; to renounce practices derogatory to the dignity of women.'

The Court in *Aruna Roy* appears to have distinguished the impartation of values from the instruction of religion via the education curriculum. The Court found that the values of self-discipline, courage, love for social justice, truth, peace, non-violence that the curriculum sought to impart to school children were not specific to any one religion and were common to all. Therefore, such a curriculum could not be unconstitutional as violating the mandate that religious instruction in schools. The Court here appears to have distinguished between religious values that are specific to believers of one faith and those values that should be common to all citizens. The Court used a fundamental duty—that of promoting common brotherhood—to ground its understanding of secular or non-religious values.

H. Justice

In *Zahira Sheikh v State of Gujarat,*[130] the petitioner Zahira Sheikh, claimed to be an eye-witness to the gruesome mass killing of Muslims in the state of Gujarat. She made statements and filed affidavits after completion of trial and judgment, alleging that during the trial she was forced to depose falsely and to turn hostile on account of threats and coercion. Ms Sheikh felt that this raised important questions pertaining to witness protection, and in the absence of which, the credibility or otherwise of the evidence before the court. She also highlighted the improper conduct of the trial by the public prosecutor, and further alleged that the investigating authority itself was not impartial. Therefore, Ms Sheikh contended that the trial was not a fair one.

[129] *Aruna Roy v Union of India* (2002) 7 SCC 368.
[130] *Zahira Sheikh v State of Gujarat* (2004) 4 SCC 158.

In his judgment for the Court, Justice Parsayat commented that 'right from the inception of the judicial system it has been accepted that discovery, vindication and establishment of truth are the main purposes underlying [the] existence of Courts of justice.' He further elucidated the concept of fair trial by declaring that it entails a familiar triangulation of the interests of the accused, the victim and the society, and it is the community that acts through the state and prosecuting agencies. He also clarified the role of the judge, if the criminal court was to be an effective instrument in dispensing justice, by stating that the presiding judge must cease to be a spectator and a mere recording machine, by becoming a participant in the trial evincing intelligence, active interest and elicit all relevant materials necessary for reaching the correct conclusion, to find out the truth, and administer justice with fairness and impartiality both to the parties and to the community.

The Supreme Court used this case to illuminate its understanding of the business of doing justice. The Court located this in the requirement, for a fair trial, of an active judge who displays intelligence and interest in arriving at the truth. The Court showed that in its opinion justice is done by the court through a fair and impartial trial conducted by an inquisitive and committed judge.

I. Democracy

Interestingly, the concept of 'democracy' has been used by the Supreme Court to prevent the judicial review of policy decisions by the executive. In *BALCO Employees' Union (Regd) v Union of India,*[131] a case that concerned the disinvestment (or the government selling its share in an entity either partly or entirely to private parties) by the government in Bharat Aluminium Company Ltd, a public sector undertaking, the Supreme Court refused to evaluate this wisdom of this governmental action. This move reflected the larger wave of liberalisation of the Indian economy, and the government of India allowing the privatisation of erstwhile public sector entities.

The Court, citing the *Narmada Bachao Andolan* case,[132] which had concerned the building of a large dam and the consequent displacement of the inhabitants of the area, observed:

> in a democracy welfare of the people at large, and not merely of a small section of the society, has to be the concern of a responsible Government. If a considered policy decision has been taken, which is not in conflict with any law or is not mala fide, it will not be in public interest to require the court to go into and investigate those areas which are the function of the executive.[133]

[131] *BALCO Employees' Union (Regd) v Union of India* (2002) 2 SCC 333, 380.
[132] *Narmada Bachao Andolan v Union of India* (2000) 10 SCC 664, 763.
[133] ibid [234].

The Court appears to suggest that in a democracy, the welfare requirements of larger society will trump those of a small section of citizens, and that such a decision by the state through a concerted policy will not be adjudicated upon by the courts. It is interesting that the Court locates the reasoning for its refusal to assess governmental policy due to the requirements of democracy and public interest. Such a refusal is not simply located in a political question doctrine or one whereby the court does not possess the expertise to assess socio-economic policies.

J. Secularism

Secularism, along with other values like separation of powers and equality, has been held to be part of the fundamental or basic structure of the Constitution. This means that secularism cannot be amended out of the constitutional text.[134] Given the presence of the Hindu right in the country, there has been increasing litigation around cases concerning hate speech, which in turn then look to the content of 'secularism'.

In *State of Karnataka v Praveen Bhai Thogadia*,[135] the Additional District Magistrate of Dakshin Kannada restrained the respondent, a well-known Hindu-right-wing ideologue, from entering an area where, two months earlier, he had delivered an inflammatory speech which had incited communal feelings, greatly affecting communal harmony with neighbouring area. The ADM feared that the respondent would deliver a similar speech and further raise communal tensions. The Supreme Court, while upholding the order prohibiting Thogadia from entering the area, discussed the content of 'secularism'. It declared that

> secularism is not to be confused with communal or religious concepts of an individual or a group of persons. It means that the State should have no religion of its own and no one could proclaim to make the State have one such or endeavour to create a theocratic State. Persons belonging to different religions live throughout the length and breadth of the country. Each person, whatever be his religion, must get an assurance from the State that he has the protection of law freely to profess, practise and propagate his religion and freedom of conscience. Otherwise, the rule of law will become replaced by individual perceptions of one's own presumptions of good social order.[136]

[134] See *IR Coelho v State of TN* (2007) 2 SCC 1, 104.
[135] *State of Karnataka v Praveen Bhai Thogadia* (2004) 4 SCC 684, 690.
[136] ibid [6].

IV. PRIORITISATION

A. Prioritisation: Creation of the Basic Structure Doctrine by the Supreme Court

The Supreme Court created the doctrine of the 'basic structure' of the Constitution. Such doctrine is unprecedented in any constitutional dispensation, and is a feature that truly sets Indian constitutional law apart from all other jurisdictions. The basic structure doctrine was first carved out in the landmark case of *State of Kerala v Kesavananda Bharati*[137] decided by 13 judges of the highest court in India. This constitutional bench heard the case to reconsider its previous decision *Golak Nath v Union of India*,[138] where it had ruled that a constitutional amendment under article 368, which takes away or abridges a fundamental right, would be void.

The background to these cases, and amendments, were the conflict between the executive and legislature on one side, and the judiciary on the other. The ruling government, led by Prime Minister Indira Gandhi, was committed to pushing through a number of popular economic measures, and felt that the judiciary was an impediment to this. Therefore, the government, through parliament, made a number of amendments to the Constitution. Article 368 grants parliament the power to amend the Constitution, and lays down the procedure to do so. In *Kesavananda*, the Supreme Court decided that whereas parliament has the power to amend the Constitution, it cannot through these amendments destroy the basic features of the Constitution. In *Kesavananda Bharati*, the question was whether article 31C violated articles 14, 19 and 31.

B. The Content of this 'Basic Structure' was Considered and Crafted on a Case-by-Case Basis

The content of basis structure has included the supremacy of the Constitution,[139] the democratic nature of the government,[140] secularism,[141] separation of powers,[142] and the federal character of the Constitution.[143] Subsequently, 'unity and integrity', 'equality'[144] and independence of the

137 *State of Kerala v Kesavananda Bharati* (1973) 4 SCC 225.
138 *Golak Nath v Union of India* AIR 1967 SC 1643.
139 See n 1.
140 *Indira Gandhi v Raj Narain* (1975) Supp SCC 1.
141 *SR Bommai v Union of India* (1994) 3 SCC 1.
142 *Indira Gandhi v Raj Narain* (1975) Supp SCC 1.
143 ibid.
144 *Raghunath Rao v Union of India* AIR 1993 SC 1267.

judiciary[145] and judicial review[146] have been brought under it. Only some of the fundamental rights, however, constitute the basic structure of the Constitution, as held in *Kesavananda Bharati* and subsequently in *Minerva Mills*.[147] Thus, a fundamental right itself may be amended or altered, but in a manner that does not contravene other fundamental rights which form a part of the basic structure and other features of the Constitution forming part of the basic structure.

However, the conflict between the parliament/executive and the courts did not quite end here. By the 39th Amendment to the Constitution in 1975, parliament sought to remove from judicial scrutiny the election of the Prime Minister, and to declare void the High Court decision declaring Indira Gandhi's election to the Lok Sabha. Further, the Supreme Court was not to hear any appeals relating to these matters.

The Supreme Court eventually did hear a challenge to the election of the Prime Minister, Mrs Indira Gandhi. In *Indira Gandhi v Raj Narain*[148] Justice Mathew held that free and fair elections in a democracy were an essential feature of the Constitution, and that under article 329(b), judicial oversight of this process is provided for. This cannot be taken away by amending the Constitution. Justice Chandrachud in his judgment in this case opined that such a creation of a 'privileged regime' for the Prime Minister would violate the basic feature of Constitution, which was equality of status and opportunity. And finally Chief Justice Ray wrote that deciding that the election as valid without applying any law was held to be contrary to the rule of law.

C. Prioritisation: Directive Principles and Fundamental Rights

The Supreme Court has used fundamental rights to determine the contours of DPSPs. The text of the Constitution makes it clear that fundamental rights are prioritised over DPSPs. For instance, article 32 provides for writ remedies in the event of their violation. Article 37, on the other hand, imposes a 'duty' on the state to make efforts towards these goals, but does not make them enforceable. Moreover, article 13 says that any law that contravenes fundamental rights is void, while a similar provision for the Directive Principles is absent.

[145] *Supreme Court Advocates on Record Association v Union of India* AIR 1994 SC 268.

[146] *L Chandra Kumar v Union of India* (1997) 3 SCC 261. The Court held in this case that: 'The jurisdiction conferred upon High Courts under Articles 226 and 227 and upon the Supreme Court under Article 32 of the Constitution is part of the inviolable basic structure of the Constitution. While this jurisdiction cannot be ousted, other courts and tribunals may perform a supplemental role in discharging the powers conferred by Articles 32, 226 and 227 of the Constitution.'

[147] *Minerva Mills Ltd v Union of India* (1980) 3 SCC 625.

[148] *Indira Gandhi v Raj Narain* (1975) Supp SCC 1.

However, the Supreme Court has taken it upon itself to ensure that the DPSPs are rendered effective. For example, the Supreme Court opines in the context of a labour dispute in *Workmen of Meenakshi Mills Ltd v Meenakshi Mills*:[149]

> Ordinarily, any restriction so imposed which has the effect of promoting or effectuating a Directive Principle can be presumed to be a reasonable restriction in public interest.[150]

The jurisprudence of the Court with reference to DPSPs has evolved over time. It has also changed with the institutional self-conception of the Court, and the legitimacy that the Court feels it enjoys with regard to a more activist role.

i. The Literal Approach

In the early years post-independence, and soon after the adoption of the Indian Constitution, the Supreme Court adopted a more formalistic reading of the Constitution. Therefore, it was categorical that DPSPs could not infringe upon fundamental rights. For instance, *State of Madras v Champakam Dorairajan*[151] is typical of this approach. With regard to the admission of students to the engineering and medical colleges of the state, the province of Madras issued an order (known as the Communal GO) that seats should be filled by the selection committee strictly on the basis that out of every 14 seats, six were to be allotted to non-Brahmin (Hindus), two to Backward Hindus, two to Brahmins, two to Harijans, one to Anglo-Indians and Indian Christians, and one to Muslims. This was held to be in pursuance of article 46 of the Constitution, which asks the state to provide educational facilities to protect the interests of the weaker sections of society. However, the petitioners argued that this was a violation of their fundamental rights under article 15(1) that prohibited discrimination only on grounds of caste, sex, religion amongst other grounds and article 29(2) that prohibited such discrimination in the context of admissions to educational institutions.

Justice Das speaking for the Constitution Bench of seven judges declared that:

> The Directive Principles of State Policy, which by article 37 are expressly made unenforceable by a Court, cannot override the provisions found in Part III (Fundamental Rights added) which, notwithstanding other provisions, are expressly made enforceable by appropriate Writs, Orders or directions under article 32.[152]

[149] *Meenakshi Mills Ltd v Meenakshi Mills* (1992) 3 SCC 336 [27].
[150] ibid [27].
[151] *State of Madras v Champakam Dorairajan* AIR 1951 SC 226.
[152] ibid [10].

ii. Harmonious Construction

Soon afterwards, the Supreme Court in *Re Kerala Education Bill*[153] shifted to an understanding of the Directive Principles as 'determining the scope and ambit' of the fundamental rights. In using this approach, the Court used the principle of harmonious construction as used in statutory interpretation to say that the Directive Principles '[m]ay not be completely ignored'.[154]

iii. Equally Important—The Balancing Act

As the judiciary took on a more activist attitude, the emphasis shifted to regarding the fundamental rights and directive principles as equally important. The case of *Kesavananda Bharati v State of Kerala*[155] noted that there was no 'antithesis' between the Directive Principles and fundamental rights, and that they were 'supplementary' to each other.[156] The lack of a priority, according to the Court in this case, was deemed necessary to assert the 'dignity of the individual'.

In *Pathumma v State of Kerala,*[157] the Court went a step further and said that the Constitution envisaged a synthesis between the Directive Principles and the fundamental rights. The Court in this case was dealing with section 20 of the Kerala Agriculturists' Debt Relief Act 1970, which allowed debtors to recover properties sold to purchasers in execution of decree passed in liquidating the debt owed by the agriculturist. The question was whether this was a reasonable restriction on the right to property. Holding that it was indeed reasonable, the Court stated that:

> In interpreting the constitutional provisions for judging the impact of an enactment on the fundamental rights of the citizens the approach of the Courts is to interpret the constitutional provisions against the social setting of the country so as to show a complete consciousness and deep awareness of the growing requirements of the society, the increasing needs of the nation, the burning problems of the day and the complex issues facing the people which the legislature in its wisdom, through beneficial legislation, seeks to solve. The judicial approach should be dynamic rather than static, pragmatic rather than pedantic and elastic rather than rigid. It must take into consideration the changing trends of economic thought, the temper of the times and the living aspirations and feelings of the people. *This Court must strike a just balance between the fundamental rights and the larger and broader interests of society.*[158]

[153] *Re Kerala Education Bill* AIR 1958 SC 956.
[154] ibid [14].
[155] *Kesavananda Bharati v State of Kerala* AIR 1973 SC 1461.
[156] ibid [759].
[157] *Pathumma v State of Kerala* AIR 1978 SC 771.
[158] ibid [5] (emphasis supplied).

This approach perhaps finds its clearest elucidation in the case of *Minerva Mills v Union of India*.[159] Minerva Mills, a company that dealt with textiles, was to be nationalised by the government. On the basis of a report submitted, Minerva Mills was to be taken over by the National Textile Corporation Ltd. It was subsequently nationalised and taken over by the central government under the Sick Textile Undertakings (Nationalisation) Act 1974. The constitutional validity, inter alia, of some of the provisions of this Act, the order of the government regarding the nationalisation, and the 39th Amendment to the Constitution placing the said Act in the Ninth Schedule, was challenged. To this the Court declared that:

> In fact Directive Principles of State Policy are fundamental in governance of the country and there is no sphere of public life where delay can defeat justice with more telling effect than the one in which the common man seeks the realisation of his aspirations.[160]

The Supreme Court further explained that:

> Parts III and IV are like two wheels of a chariot, *one no less important than the other.* Snap one and the other will lose its efficacy. They are like a twin formula for achieving the social revolution which is the ideal which the visionary founders of the Constitution set before themselves. In other words, the Indian Constitution is founded on the bed-rock of the balance between Parts III and IV. *To give absolute primacy to one over the other is to disturb the harmony of the Constitution. This harmony and balance between fundamental rights and directive principles is an essential feature of the basic structure of the Constitution.*[161]

The Supreme Court, as it grew in stature, slowly shifted its views on the status of the DPSPs with regard to the fundamental rights. With increased standing, and with it slowly beginning to occupy a more central space in the imagination of urban India, the Court feels confident to use interpretative techniques to ascribe a more dominant position to DPSPs. And by doing so the Court steadily commences upon a path of passing judgment on governmental policies.

V. CONCLUSION

The Supreme Court, since the Constitution came into force, has steadily undertaken a more active role in shaping and implementing values that it has perceived to be important to the welfare of the people, and also significant in shaping the ethos of the nation. Whereas courts in liberal democracies do not usually adopt such a role for themselves, the Indian Supreme Court

159 *Minerva Mills v Union of India* AIR 1980 SC 1789.
160 ibid [47].
161 *Minerva Mills*, n 147 [61] (emphasis supplied).

certainly seems to see its position as a significant value-making institution in the shaping of a social democracy, not just one premised on civil and political rights, but also one that seeks to enforce social and economic ones.

The jurisprudence of the Supreme Court of India shows three remarkable trends. First, the interpretation of fundamental rights, or the Bill of Rights like life, equality, non-discrimination, free speech etc, to be mandated to impose on the state the necessity to take positive action to realise these seemingly conventional constitutional rights. Within this trend the evolution of jurisprudence by the Court to expand the right to life to make it an all-encompassing value that has enabled social, economic, cultural and even environmental rights (all typically non-justiciable rights in most constitutional courts), to enter into the realm of justiciable issues.

Second the prioritisation of certain values or crafting of almost a grund norm in the form of the 'basic structure' of the Constitution. This basic structure has included the democratic nature of government (including free elections), secularism, separation of powers, federal character of the constitution, independence of the judiciary amongst others. This basic structure as per court jurisprudence can never be amended out of the Constitution and was crafted to act as an impermeable wall against belligerent parliaments and executives, who may command large enough majorities in parliament to amend away these basic values. This creation of the 'basic structure' has enabled the core essence of the Constitution to remain protected, and perhaps is a major reason why the world's largest democracy, despite poverty and a host of other impediments, functions as a stable and well-oiled democracy.

Within the prioritisation of certain values, the Supreme Court used the Directive Principles of State Policies, or the non-justiciable constitutional essences of good governance or governance obligations to influence the interpretation of the content of fundamental rights. This has ensured the crafting of these obligations in the form of justiciable values.

The final trend concerns the court's greatest creation—the institution of 'public interest litigation', or expanded standing. While this expanded notion of standing has ensured that many of the poor and disenfranchised who otherwise would never have been able to access the court system, and perhaps justice, were able to do so. The number of PILs appears to add to the backlog of about 20 million cases (across the various levels of courts) that permeates the Indian judicial system.[162] And this all-permeating and somewhat unpredictable reliance of the casting of all disputes, or injustices as constitutional issues, might lead to the 'neglect of the legal system overall'.[163] This unprecedented expansion of judicial power and lack of a

[162] See also Mehta (n 21).

[163] Donald L Horowitz, 'Constitutional Courts: A primer for Decision Makers' (2006) 17(4) *Journal of Democracy* 125, 135.

coherent and tightly developed jurisprudence has rendered decision-making sometimes unpredictable. And it has been well argued that the rule of law depends 'as much on ordinary law and the predictability and regularity of its application as it does on constitutional law.'[164] It remains to be seen whether the Supreme Court will recast itself institutionally, clear its backlog, and create a more refined jurisprudence around the constitutional values that it has crafted.

A more cohesive and refined jurisprudence will depend on the Court restructuring itself as an institution. A permanent constitutional bench or panel of judges who will only hear matters of constitutional interpretation and evolution may bring consistency in legal and philosophical reasoning. It may also lead to judgments with more clarity in reasoning. For now the judges of the Court are over-burdened by being a multi-faceted court—with original and appellate jurisdiction, which on a daily basis hears hundreds of cases. The Supreme Court must refashion itself as more of a constitutional court and less of a court of appeals. However, the role of the Court in ensuring that India has developed into an enduring constitutional democracy is undisputed and unparalleled. Along with Parliament, the Supreme Court has ensured that the country has affirmed constitutional values and aspirations located in an egalitarian conception of society, with a firm commitment to addressing historical and social disadvantage.

[164] ibid.

10

Values in Iranian Constitutional Law

NAZILA GHANEA

I. CONTEXT OF IRANIAN CONSTITUTIONAL VALUES

A. Constitutions and Values

Discussing values in Iranian constitutional law within a comparative context gives rise to fairly unique challenges. The Islamic Republic of Iran's Constitution has received little sustained analysis in the English language,[1] and legal studies of its constitutional values are hard to locate. Yet values, freedom, and rights take a very particular and nuanced form in the case of the Iranian Constitution, and these lend themselves to fairly sharp observations.[2]

B. Historical Context

Iran's 1979 Constitution is the second such constitution, the first having been adopted in 1906–07. It is 'the most important and superior legislative document in Iran, and at present, the contents ... have priority over all other legal sources'.[3]

[1] Major discussions of the Iranian Constitution include the monograph by Asghar Shirazi, *The Constitution of Iran: Politics and the State in the Islamic Republic* (London, IB Tauris, 1997). The Iranian Constitution is discussed as part of a study of Islam and human rights in: Anne Elizabeth Mayer, *Islam and Human Rights: Tradition and Politics* (Boulder CO, Westview Press, 1991) 66–73. There is an interesting account of the extent of the involvement of the three recognised religious minorities in the drafting of the Iranian Constitution in: Eliz Sanasarian, *Religious Minorities in Iran* (Cambridge, Cambridge University Press, 2000) 58–72.

[2] The translation of the Constitution being used is that provided by Dr Alexander Aghayan and Associates, and available online at www.aghayan.com/iranconst.htm. An English translation along with the original Persian can also be found in: Adineh Abghari, *Introduction to the Iranian Legal System and the Protection of Human Rights in Iran* (London, British Institute of International and Comparative Law, 2009), Appendix 4, 163–90; and also at http://www.wipo.int/wipolex/ea/details.jsp?id=7697.

[3] Adineh Abghari, *Introduction to the Iranian Legal System and the Protection of Human Rights in Iran* (London, British Institute of International and Comparative Law, 2009) 9.

The first Constitution of Iran is said to have had a 'double personality' in that '[whereas] in the West constitutionalism developed after the Reformation and acceptance of separation of the state from religion, in the Islamic nations it took a different shape as it harmonized itself with a set of Islamic laws that had permeated every facet of life.'[4] The second Constitution of the Islamic Republic of Iran (IRI) emerged from a very particular historical episode—the country's break with monarchy and new experiment with the concept of 'Islamic democracy'.

The Islamic revolution emerged from growing public protests during 1978 and 1979. Its intellectual nucleus was based on the work of Ali Shariati,[5] who is credited with overturning the millennium-long Shia position of political quietism[6] with the actual possibility of holding political power. Iranian Shia clergy, who had utilised all their political ambitions in extensive behind-the-scene manoeuvrings since Shia Islam had been established in Iran in the Safavvid era,[7] now came to the fore, 'unambiguously' subordinating 'the state to Shi'ism'.[8]

Ayatollah Khomeini built on the foundation offered by Shariati's work and set out the *velayat-i faqih* construct (guardianship or rulership of the Juriconsult)[9] which was set to become 'the soul of the republic'.[10] What made this concept unique was that the *faqih* (or Juriconsult) 'should be not

4 Mohsen Milani, 'Shi'ism and the State in the Constitution of the Islamic Republic of Iran' in Simin K. Farsouri and Mehrdad Mashayekhi, ed, London: Routledge, 1992 134.

5 Shariati has, in turn, been criticised for 'ideologising Islam'. Schirazi holds this as the position of 'Abdolkarim Sorush', but also concurs with this criticism himself. Asghar Schirazi, *The Constitution of Iran: Politics and the State in the Islamic Republic* (London, IB Tauris, 1997) 287.

6 Olivier Roy, *The Failure of Political Islam* (London, IB Tauris, 1994) 168. The Shia cleric Hasan Yousefi Eshkevari holds that 'Ultimately, in any time or place, Muslims create their desired government and choose properly qualified people to rule them; the legitimacy and acceptability of the government and the rulers comes from their election by the people, from nowhere else. Thus the responsibility for this election is with the people themselves, not with God, the Prophet or religion.' See Ziba Mir-Hosseini and Richard Tapper, *Islam and Democracy in Iran: Eshkevari and the Quest for Reform* (London, IB Tauris, 2006) 90.

7 Shah Ismail I (1501–24) of the Safavid Dynasty established Shia Islam as the religion of Iran.

8 Mohsen Milani, 'Shi'ism and the State in the Constitution of the Islamic Republic of Iran' in Simin K Farsouri and Mehrdad Mashayekhi (eds) *Iran: Political Culture in the Islamic Republic* (London, Routledge, 1993) 134. Enayat refers to the Safavid state of the sixteenth and seventeenth centuries as 'an obvious precursor to the Islamic republic ... with its avowed intention of making a particular vision of Islam (Twelver Shi'ism) the official creed of the Iranians'. Hamid Enayat, 'Iran: Khumayni's Concept of the "Guardianship of the Juriconsult"' in James P Piscatori (ed), *Islam in the Political Process* (Cambridge, Cambridge University Press, 1983) 160.

9 See: Hamid Enayat, 'Iran: Khumayni's Concept of the "Guardianship of the Juriconsult"', in James P Piscatori (ed), *Islam in the Political Process* (Cambridge, Cambridge University Press, 1983).

10 Mohsen Milani, 'Shi'ism and the State in the Constitution of the Islamic Republic of Iran' in Simin K Farsouri and Mehrdad Mashayekhi (eds) *Iran: Political Culture in the Islamic Republic*, (London, Routledge, 1993) 143.

just one high official among the many who form the top echelon of the state administration, but its supreme overseer, judge, and guardian'.[11] Two weeks after Muhammad Reza Shah left Iran, Ayatollah Khomeini returned triumphant from exile, with millions blocking the road to the airport to welcome him. The 2,500-year history of monarchy in Iran was brought to an end and the *velayat-i faqih* model received assent in the referendum approving the new IRI Constitution. Just before the passing of Ayatollah Khomeini in 1989, the IRI Constitution was changed once again in order to allow for the continuity of the system beyond the Ayatollah, by the creation of the post of 'Supreme Leader' or just 'Leader'. The 'novel construct' was passed on intact.[12]

The revolution had brought together a whole range of unlikely suspects[13]—secularists, Muslim leaders, feminists, communists—and the crafting of the Constitution itself was carried out over a number of stages during 1979. The story of which actors survived, which were sidelined and which dominated is one that can be detected in part within the actual text of the Constitution. Further details emerged in the years to come, in the first of Iran's cultural revolution[14] and in the political purges of the early 1980s and beyond.

C. Religious Context

The Iranian Constitution is invested with loaded value-language which attempts to marry Islamic ascendance with republican government—with the former enjoying clear supremacy.[15] This Islamic supremacy is particularly evident in the Constitution's text, where the revolution is underlined as being 'religious and Islamic', Iranians as 'Muslim' and 'united in faith',

[11] Hamid Enayat, 'Iran: Khumayni's Concept of the "Guardianship of the Juriconsult"', in James P Piscatori (ed), *Islam in the Political Process* (Cambridge, Cambridge University Press, 1983) 161.

[12] George Linabury, 'Ayatollah Khomeini's Islamic legacy', in H Amirahmadi and N Entessar (eds), *Reconstruction and Regional Diplomacy in the Persian Gulf* (London, Routledge, 1992) 34.

[13] Schirazi expresses it in these terms: 'Iranian society had risen against the Pahlavi monarchy under a constellation of contradictory social, economic, political and cultural interests of its classes, strata and other segments which interacted to some extent with international factors.' Asghar Schirazi, *The Constitution of Iran: Politics and the State in the Islamic Republic* (London, IB Tauris, 1997) 291.

[14] 1980–83. For a discussion of some aspects of this cultural revolution see: Reza Razavi, 'The Cultural Revolution in Iran, with Close Regard to the Universities, and its Impact on the Student Movement' (2009) 45(1) *Middle Eastern Studies* 1–17.

[15] In contrast, the Shia cleric Eshkevari holds that 'Our basic argument and claim is that the democratic method has so far been the most effective, the most logical and the most Islamic way of administrating society. And Islam teaches us to make the best use of common sense, in life and in social and political organizations.' Ziba Mir-Hosseini and Richard Tapper, *Islam and Democracy in Iran: Eshkevari and the Quest for Reform* (London, IB Tauris, 2006) 94.

the nation's conscience as 'Islamic', and the nation itself as 'Muslim', its revolutionary movement supported by 'Muslim combatants' who 'opened up the true path for the religious fight of Islam' and its leadership as presided over by its Islamic Government. 'The Mission of the Constitution is to identify itself with the basic beliefs of the movement [of the revolution] and to bring about the conditions under which the lofty and worldwide values' of Islam will flourish' (Preamble).

As the final article of the Constitution, addressing revisions to the Constitution asserts, there are nine elements of the Constitution that are 'unalterable'; seven of these safeguard its Islamic credentials:

[1] the Islamic character of the political system;
[2] the basis of all the rules and regulations according to Islamic criteria;
[3] the religious footing;
[4] the objectives of the Islamic Republic of Iran;
[5] the democratic character of the government;
[6] the *wilayat al-'amr* the Imamate of *Ummah*;
[7] and the administration of the affairs of the country based on national referenda, official religion of Iran [Islam] and the school [Twelver Ja'fari].[16]

The two additional elements are the democratic character of the government and the role of national referenda. The Islamic overtures are so overshadowing that little room, if any, remains for Iranians who are not, or who do not wish to define themselves as, Muslim. In contrast with this reality, Eshkevari's vision of an Islamic democratic government—for example—is one where there is the permanent right to dismiss representatives and where all enjoy equal rights.[17]

In the comparative typology of different state policies of religion outlined by Hallencreutz and Westerlund, the IRI model clearly fits in the strict confessional category. In Iran's case, 'religious institutions and values' are 'regarded as sources of inspiration for the state' and government policies are subordinated 'to the specific truth-claims, norms and structures of one

[16] Art 177; numbers added for ease of consideration.

[17] 'Like any other government, Islamic government depends on the people, thus it is accountable to the stakeholders, that is to say the people; and the rulers cannot say "we are the representatives of God and religion and we are only accountable to God for our actions" (though they too must answer to God. For this reason people consider they have the permanent right to dismiss the rulers and change the government and regime. Free-thinkers (whether Muslim or non-Muslim) enjoy equal rights with others within the framework of law, and all can be present and participate in the state and legislative and political activities; in such a system there are no second-class citizens. This is so because an Islamic government is necessarily "national", that is to say, when people live within defined geographical boundaries and enjoy common rights to the land, this means that all are members of one nation and all enjoy equal social rights.' Ziba Mir-Hosseini and Richard Tapper, *Islam and Democracy in Iran: Eshkevari and the Quest for Reform* (London, IB Tauris, 2006) 99.

religious tradition'.[18] Of Iran, these authors state: 'here the state apparatus is subordinate to Islam and religious leaders have a decisive say in political affairs'.[19]

In his doctoral research on law and religion in constitutional law, Temperman explores the various ways in which states reference religion in their constitutional laws in particular. Such acknowledgement takes many forms, ranging from a historical acknowledgement to the acknowledgement of: a predominant religion, of religious phenomena such as God or specific characteristics of God. Such acknowledgement, in some cases, also spills over to a particular religion-law nexus and accommodation for a religion or a number of religions or beliefs—whether political, in the shape of an advisory role, financial support or other cooperation. His study holds that

> most of the states that are officially entangled with a single religion fail to fully comply with the principle that no one should be treated differently because of one's religion or belief (or lack therefore) ... Forms of establishment of religion in many cases negatively affect the 'equal religious rights of others'.[20]

This is examined in relation to discrimination in the context of support for religions, free speech, freedom of association, employment and education. Temperman also establishes the distinction of the religion-state relationship, as upheld in the Iranian Constitution. 'The constitutional provisions regarding Islam as the state religion of the constitutions of Iran and Brunei are unique in that they expressly establish a specific branch of Islam as the state religion'.[21] In the case of Iran this is the Twelver Ja'fari school of Shia Islam, while in the case of Brunei it is the Shafi'i school of Sunni Islam. The human rights implications of this and other state-religion relationships receive careful consideration in Temperman's study.

D. Political Context

The language of fury, of an explosion or volcano of public anger, which proved 'decisive and dramatic', permeates the early paragraphs of the Constitution. Schirazi refers to the 'series of crises'[22] that framed the historical emergence of the Constitution. It is only after painting this picture of the

[18] Carl F Hallencreutz and David Westerlund, 'Introduction' in David Westerlund (ed), *Questioning the Secular State: The Worldwide Resurgence of Religion in Politics* (London, Hurst & Company, 1996) 2.

[19] ibid 3.

[20] Jeroen Temperman, 'State-Religion Relationships and Human Rights Law: Towards a Right to Religiously Neutral Governance', PhD submitted January 2009 at the Irish Centre for Human Rights, National University of Galway, Ireland, p 359.

[21] ibid, 50.

[22] Asghar Schirazi, *The Constitution of Iran: Politics and the State in the Islamic Republic* (London, IB Tauris, 1997) 291.

dramatic shift brought about by the revolution that there is mention of the affirmation of a 'final and categorical decision to set up an exalted new republican and Islamic order' through a referendum[23] for the Islamic Republic which, the Constitution states, enjoyed a majority vote of 98.2 per cent.

This revolution, in the language of the Constitution, overturns idolatry, foreign ideological influence, arrogance, and all despotic systems; thereby signalling 'the victory of all the oppressed over the arrogant' and allowing a system that entrusts 'men's destiny to their own hands' (Preamble).

It is worth recalling that the slogans and protests that brought an end to monarchy in Iran, sought also to overturn western interference in domestic affairs—whether through direct intervention or in the cultural sphere—as well as injustice (especially the Savak secret police), the sharp rich/poor and urban/rural divide, lack of political freedom, and enforced election for the Shah's Rastakhiz one party rule. The 'extraordinary break between the Shah and civil society'[24] represents the ashes on which the Islamic revolution built itself, and still draws credence from. This context helps us understand the strong and loaded overtures in the constitution for independence, freedom and self-representation.

II. VALUES AND THEIR PRIORITISATION

A. Values Contained in the Constitution

The following values, highlighted and examined by this project, find explicit expression in the Iranian Constitution.

i. Fairness, Justice

The term 'justice' is utilised in the Constitution in a range of contexts. Competent courts are referred to as 'courts of justice' (articles 34, 61, 140, 156, 159, 168, 170); 'just' is utilised as the description of the *faqih* and Supreme Leader, Islamic scholars, members of the parliament (*majlis*), head of the judiciary, judges, Minister of Justice, Chief of the Supreme Court and Prosecutor-General; the 'support of justice' included in the oath of the

[23] Three referenda have been held in Iran since the revolution: 'April 1979 for determining the system of the government; in 1979 for ratification of the Constitution; and then for its revision in 1989'. Adineh Abghari, *Introduction to the Iranian Legal System and the Protection of Human Rights in Iran* (London, British Institute of International and Comparative Law, 2009) 9.

[24] Nikki R Keddie, 'Can Revolutions be Predicted? Can their Causes be Understood?', in Rosemary HT O'Kane (ed), *Revolution: Critical Concepts in Political Science*, Vol VI, (London, Routledge, 2000) 378.

President (Preamble, articles 5, 67, 109, 121, 157, 158, 160, 162); and 'justice' is used interchangeably with dignity and to be obtained on the basis of the Quran and Sunnah and attained through a just economic system (articles 2, 3).

However, in terms of 'justice' as a value, the term is regularly prefixed by 'Islamic'. 'Islamic justice', 'Qura'nic justice', the 'justice of God' are said to underpin the role of almost every actor and every objective stated in the Constitution (Preamble, articles 1, 2). 'Islamic justice' must inform even the utilisation of the army (article 147) and the duty to treat non-Muslims with such justice (article 14) is also emphasised.

The most significant mention of 'justice' as a value, however, is the upholding of the 'rule of justice' as a right of all people of the world. In this context, the Constitution upholds the Islamic Republic of Iran's objective of supporting just struggles 'in every corner of the globe' whilst refraining 'scrupulously' from 'all forms of interference in the internal affairs of other nations' (Article 154). The promotion of justice in this sense therefore is situated within a global rather than domestic context, and juxtaposed with interference. How the tension between the two is to be managed, however, is far from clear from this text.

ii. Freedom, Independence

Freedom and independence were rallying calls for the Islamic revolution itself, and hence are core to the very rationale behind the establishment of the IRI regime. This finds expression in the Constitutional guarantee 'to struggle for freedom from the despotic system' (Preamble, article 154). This independence and freedom is claimed for the Islamic Republic of Iran itself, in the sense of its territorial integrity and unity (articles 3, 9, 143, 152), and its economic and cultural independence (articles 43, 67, 78, 121).

When it comes to the values of independence and freedom for public authorities, the Constitution claims freedom for those in authority to express their views, and for the various branches of government to serve in a free and independent manner (articles 57, 86, 156). Freedom and human dignity are projected in the Constitution as key pillars of the public media; freedom of expression for publications and the press, limited by the tenets of Islam and public rights; freedom of association for political parties and other societies and associations, limited by Islamic standards (Preamble, articles 24, 26, 27, 175).

Individual freedoms are expressed in fairly limited terms of ensuring social and political freedoms within the framework of the law, of choosing one's occupation (articles 3, 43) and the freedom and dignity of citizens (article 121). Freedoms are also claimed for minorities of other Islamic schools of thought, and the three recognised religious minorities (Zoroastrians, Jews and Christians),[25] to act in accordance with their own canon in matters of personal law, in performing their religious rites and in particular matters such as education (articles 12, 13).

In all these contexts, 'freedoms' are tempered with reference to the cross-cutting importance of balancing rights with Islamic justice in a way that ensures freedom from 'any kind of unhealthy relationship' and the coupling of freedom with responsibility before God in a way that upholds cultural independence (Preamble, article 2).

iii. Community, Family

The Iranian Constitution recognises the family as 'the basis of society, and the true focus for the growth and elevation of mankind'—the 'fundamental unit of Islamic society'—thereby outlining the duties of the Islamic Government towards it (Preamble, article 10). Women are encouraged to focus on the 'precious duty of motherhood', mothers are to be protected, and 'worthy' mothers awarded guardianship of children (Preamble, article 21). In order to uphold this value, the Constitution suggests the importance of laws, regulations and programmes to facilitate the formation of a family and its stability 'on the basis of law and the ethics of Islam'. Courts are to be established to protect and preserve the family, and citizens are to be provided the basic necessities of 'housing, food, clothing, hygiene, medical treatment, education, and the necessary facilities for the establishment of a family' (articles 10, 21, 43).

When it comes to the 'community', the term is used interchangeably with the Islamic *Ummah* and the importance of its unity (or prevention of its 'deviation'). The very duty of the IRI leadership is said to be to the *Ummah* (articles 11, 57, 109). The Constitution does not appear to offer recognition to either the national community (irrespective of religious or belief affiliations) nor to the international community beyond the *Ummah*.

iv. Responsibility, Accountability

The Constitution asserts that the responsibility of Islamic Government is vested in 'devout men'[26] (Preamble), who in turn are charged with being responsible to God, to the *faqih*, the Supreme Leader, representatives of the *Majlis* and the *Majlis* as a whole, the President, the Guardian Council,

[25] For a discussion, see: Eliz Sanasarian, *Religious Minorities in Iran* (Cambridge, Cambridge University Press, 2000). See also: Nazila Ghanea, *Human Rights, the UN and the Bahá'ís in Iran* (The Hague, Kluwer, 2002).

[26] Discussion of whether the Arabic term used, *rejal*, is a generic term that refers to both men and women, or is intended to mean only men, has been very lively and contested in Iran. It is tested every time female candidates put themselves forward for selection for Presidential elections, most recently in the tenth Presidential elections of June 2009.

the Exigency Council and other councils (articles 5, 84, 85, 89, 99, 106, 107, 112).

'Responsibility' and 'accountability' to the people as values, however, find no mention in the Constitution.

v. Integrity, Honesty

'Integrity' only finds mention in the Constitution in the context of the territorial integrity and independence of the Iranian nation, and not as a value to be upheld by those in office. 'Honesty' finds no mention. Neither are considered as values in the Constitution.

vi. Compassion, Caring

'Compassionate' is only used in praise of God in the Constitution (Preamble, article 67, 121). 'Care' is only used in relation to health care. Neither are considered as values in the Constitution.

vii. Respect, Tolerance

Islamic schools other than the Ja'fari Twelver school are to be accorded full respect regarding their own laws and rites, and the human rights of non-Muslims[27] are to be respected as long as they 'refrain from engaging in conspiracy or activity against Islam and the Islamic Republic of Iran' (articles 12, 14).

The Constitution notes that the dignity of persons arrested, detained or exiled by law should be respected (article 39), as should legitimately acquired private ownership, as determined by law (article 47). 'Tolerant' and 'tolerance' find no mention at all.

viii. Reverence for Life

The only mention of human life in the Constitution is that of the life of the individual being inviolate 'except in cases sanctioned by law' (article 22). The limitations are not outlined any further and the exceptions not stipulated exhaustively. Where the term 'life' is used, it is in the context of other terms such as the creation of Islamic society and the putting into effect of

[27] For a discussion see: UN Doc E/CN4/Sub2/AC5/2003/WP8, Nazila Ghanea, 'Ethnic and Religious Groups in the Islamic Republic of Iran', Working Groups on Minorities, May 2003, available at www.unhchr.ch/Huridocda/Huridoca.nsf/(Symbol)/E.CN.4.Sub.2.AC.5.2003.WP.8.En?Opendocument. See also: International Federation for Human Rights (FIDH), 'Religious Minorities in Iran', August 2003, available at www.fidh.org/IMG/pdf/ir0108a.pdf, and *Iran, Religious and Ethnic Minorities, Discrimination in Law and Practice* (New York: Human Rights Watch, 1997), available at www.hrw.org/legacy/reports/1997/iran.

Islamic ordinances and regulations as 'laying the foundations for the ultimate goal of life' (Preamble); and the claim of any form of foreign control compromising national life being forbidden (article 153).

ix. Spirituality

'Spirituality' as such is not mentioned in the Constitution, but 'Islam', 'Islamic' and 'Muslim' are mentioned 227 times. In contrast, 'Iran' is mentioned 61 times, and 'religion' just 11 times. This imbalance between 'Islamic' rather than 'Iranian' is indeed very telling, even though the record of the Islamic revolution has suggested Islam's clear centrality, along with Persian chauvinism.[28]

x. Learning, Education

The Iranian Constitution asserts free education at all levels, but later specifies this to be free only to the close of the secondary stage. It states that the facilitation and expansion of free facilities for higher education 'within the limits of the country's own capacity' should be seen as one of the binding duties of the IRI Government (articles 3, 30, 43, 100).

With regards to minority education, Islamic schools other than the Twelver Ja'fari school are to enjoy official status in matters pertaining to religious education, while the three recognised religious minorities have freedom to act according to their own canon regarding religious education, 'within the limits of the law' (articles 12, 13). There has been a whole-scale exclusion of Bahá'ís from tertiary education, for students and academics alike.[29]

B. Understanding these Values Conceptually

The dominant value expressed in the Constitution is clearly the assertion of Islam. Other values that find mention are circumscribed and limited in accordance to Islamic criteria. Considering the three central pillars of the Constitution: Islam, independence, and the role of public opinion, it is clear that the former dominates. Independence is subsumed under, and constrained by 'Islamic' criteria; and though public opinion brought the revolution into being, its role now can only be considered as subsidiary. This

[28] For further discussion see: UN Doc E/CN4/Sub2/AC5/2003/WP8, Nazila Ghanea, 'Ethnic and Religious Groups in the Islamic Republic of Iran', Working Groups on Minorities, May 2003, available at www.unhchr.ch/Huridocda/Huridoca.nsf/(Symbol)/E.CN.4.Sub.2.AC.5.2003.WP.8.En?Opendocument.

[29] See Friedrich W Affolter, 'Resisting Educational Exclusion: The Baha'i Institute of Higher Education in Iran' (2007) 1(1) *Diaspora, Indigenous, and Minority Education: Studies of Migration, Integration, Equity, and Cultural Survival* 65–77.

is because when public opinion is mobilised at elections—whether for the *Majles* (parliament) or Presidency—the choice is only in relation to a heavily edited list of candidates.

A number of safeguards are operational in order to ensure the fulfilment of Islamic criteria and, indeed, further Islamic credentials are required of those in office. The Constitution asserts the Islamic Republic's belief in divine revelation, whose 'fundamental role in setting forth the laws' it recognises (article 2.2). Article 4 makes the all-encompassing scope of this criterion—and its absolute nature—quite clear. It holds that:

> All civil, penal, financial, economic, administrative, cultural, military, political, and other laws and regulations must be based on Islamic criteria. This principle applies absolutely and generally to all articles of the Constitution as well as to all other laws and regulations, and the fuqaha' of the Guardian Council are judges in this matter.

As Mayer notes, article 4 serves to establish that 'Islamic principles are to be considered not only superior to ordinary laws but also as overriding provisions in the constitution itself'. She goes on to describe this as 'the policy of using Islam to deny rights'.[30] Elsewhere in the Constitution, even the individual's choice of employment cannot be 'contrary to Islam' (article 28). There is no clear definition, scope or objective delimited with regards to this criterion; but the decision-makers on this matter are very clearly designated.

The Constitution is certainly shaped by the official recognition of Twelver Ja'fari Shia Islam (article 12), and by the events that led to the creation of the Islamic Republic of Iran (Preamble). Its sources and governance structure are also spelt out: 'Legislation which is to set out the codes for the management of society will have as its central axis the Koran and tradition. Therefore there is great necessity for exact and serious supervision by just and virtuous and dedicated Islamic scholars' (Preamble). This section goes on to introduce the role of the Executive, the public media and the representatives in the *Majlis* in realising the goal of creating Islamic society.

Shia perspectives on Islamic law are notable in that they allow for continued *ijtihad*, in contradistinction with most Sunni schools, which consider the 'doors of *ijtihad*' to have been closed in the tenth century.[31] Many critics consider that the opening of these doors would allow for more liberal interpretations of Islamic law, enabling obstacles between Islamic conceptions

[30] Ann Elizabeth Mayer, *Islam and Human Rights: Tradition and Politics* (Boulder CO, Westview Press, 1991) 30.

[31] 'By the tenth century it was thought that the established schools of jurisprudence had fully exhausted all the possible questions of law and that the necessary material sources of Islamic law were fully formed. The utilization of the doctrine of independent reasoning *(ijtihad)* consequently diminished and this led, by the thirteenth century, to what was termed as "closing the gate of legal reasoning *(ijtihad)* and opening that of legal conformism *(taqlid)*".' Mashood Baderin, *International Human Rights and Islamic Law* (Oxford, Oxford University Press, 2003) 38.

on, for example, women's rights, minority rights and Islamic criminal punishments to be adapted towards harmonisation with international human rights standards. The presumption of human rights academics and activists is that this would lead to reason, and hence harmonisation with international human rights norms.[32] In the case of Iran, though, such potential for dynamism is structurally constrained. Islamic law's official acceptance in the Iranian Constitution not only means that it 'plays the main role in legislation, but also has a complementary role for judges in issuing judgments'.[33] Recourse to 'continuous *ijtihad* of the *fuqaha'* possessing necessary qualifications, exercised on the basis of the Qur'an and the Sunnah' (article 2.6.a) is recognised as enabling security freedom, justice and other objectives. The Constitution imposes many restrictions on the flexibility and responsiveness of Islamic law, as it conceives of it. It is suggested that just judges should be 'well acquainted with the exact rules of the Islamic code', that it is vital that 'localised deviation within the Islamic community' be prevented with regard to safeguarding people's rights (Preamble, The Judiciary of the Constitution).

The interpretation and application of 'Islamic criteria' in itself, insofar as this limits other rights, values and freedoms, and the operation of all structures within the Islamic Republic and those that serve within its ranks therefore constitutes a dominant value that needs to be addressed. It will be seen below that this is not just theoretically challenging, but has taken a dominant role in challenging the reality of the whole context within which the IRI Government operates and constitutional law is interpreted, called upon and applied to society. *All* actors have a role to ensure compliance with 'Islamic criteria'—everyone: judges, the President, the *Majlis*, the Guardian Council, the Supreme Leader, various ministries, the Revolutionary Guards (article 150) and the Army (article 144). Should the extensive protections within the formal machinery fall short, two further safeguards generalise this responsibility. One requires judges to refrain from enforcing governmental laws that 'are in conflict with the laws or the norms of Islam', and the second is that 'everyone' is empowered with the 'right to demand the annulment of any such regulation from the Court of Administrative Justice' (article 170).

In discussing 'Islamic criteria' throughout the rhetoric and mechanisms of the IRI, there are many benefits of interpreting such references as leaning

[32] Schirazi characterises this as Abdolkarim Sorush's conclusion on the matter of a democratic religious state becoming possible with *ijtihad*, quoting him as follows: 'In this manner, liberalism is denied but democracy based on social reason, is connected to a rational and leaned faith. Thus, one of the preconditions for a religious democratic state is created.' Asghar Schirazi, *The Constitution of Iran: Politics and the State in the Islamic Republic* (London, IB Tauris, 1997) 287.

[33] Adineh Abghari, *Introduction to the Iranian Legal System and the Protection of Human Rights in Iran* (London, British Institute of International and Comparative Law, 2009) 67.

towards the political and ideological, rather than as elements of religious belief. After all, the Constitution makes 'Islam the basis of law and of the state'.[34] The fact that the Iranian governmental system 'uses Islam as a legitimating device'[35] and means of expanding its political base is plainly discernible. In fact Mayer simply holds that 'in the post-revolutionary Iranian environment, Islam is interpreted to be an ideology—much as communism used to be in the East Bloc countries'.[36] She also uses the Iranian Constitution as a prime example of the 'ideologization of Islam'.[37] In the context of foreign policy, for example, and as Chubin and Tripp note, '[d]espite its use of Islamic vocabulary and imagery, revolutionary Iran has shown no tendency to forswear national interest for Muslim solidarity ... when constrained, Iran will readily drop the Islamic emphasis'.[38] Rather charitably, the authors of this paper argue that it does not necessarily follow from this that 'the selective use of Islam' suggests that 'Iran uses ideology opportunistically ... Iran's clerical leaders doubtless believe their own utterances. Depending on the issue at hand, Islam is accordingly exploited or played down'.[39] As George Linabury concludes, 'That Islam is firmly embedded in Iran seems assured for the foreseeable future.'[40]

C. Realising these Values—The Balance of Powers System

One reason for Iranian conservatism has been the tortuous balance of powers system envisaged in the IRI Constitution. The system has proved deeply hierarchical, with many having argued that it was indeed designed to be so. Schirazi asserts that

> The fact that the hierocratic legalists tolerated the inclusion of democratic elements in the constitution did not mean that they were prepared to regulate their behaviour accordingly. Nor did it mean that the Islamic state was conceived in a way that would guarantee the promotion or the enforcement of these elements.

[34] Mohsen Milani, 'Shi'ism and the State in the Constitution of the Islamic Republic of Iran' in Simin K Farsouri and Mehrdad Mashayekhi (eds), *Iran: Political Culture in the Islamic Republic* (London, Routledge, 1992) 144.

[35] Shahram Chubin and Charles Tripp, *Iran-Saudi Arabia relations and Regional Order: Iran and Saudi Arabia in the balance of power in the Gulf*, Adelphi Paper no 304, IISS (Oxford, Oxford University Press, 1996) 63.

[36] Ann Elizabeth Mayer, *Islam and Human Rights: Tradition and Politics* (Boulder CO, Westview Press, 1991) 133.

[37] ibid 134.

[38] Shahram Chubin and Charles Tripp, *Iran-Saudi Arabia relations and Regional Order: Iran and Saudi Arabia in the balance of power in the Gulf*, Adelphi Paper no 304, IISS (Oxford, Oxford University Press, 1996) 64.

[39] ibid 64.

[40] George Linabury, 'Ayatollah Khomeini's Islamic legacy' in H Amirahmadi and N Entessar (eds), *Reconstruction and Regional Diplomacy in the Persian Gulf* (London, Routledge, 1992) 42.

> The intention was to get rid of the constitution's democratic elements as quickly as possible. Since it was not necessary or advisable to change the text, the process of elimination was carried out in the practical running of the state, in particular by concentrating power in the hands of the leader, undermining and disempowering representative institutions, suppressing fundamental democratic rights and carrying the implementation of the *velayat-e faqih* to its logical conclusion.[41]

Articles 57 to 176 of the Constitution, over two-thirds of the Constitution, are dedicated to the balance of power. The articles spelling out the powers of government—and the functions of the legislature, executive and judiciary—are preceded by these words in Article 56:

> Absolute sovereignty over the world and man belongs to God, and it is He who has made man master of his own social destiny. No one can deprive man of this divine right, nor subordinate it to the vested interests of a particular individual or group. The people are to exercise this divine rights in the manner specified...

It is therefore for the purposes of the facilitation of the sovereignty of the people that the balance of powers system is crafted. Human sovereignty, though, is subordinate to 'the sovereignty of truth and Qur'anic justice', with the Islamic Republic itself being a system which is based on belief in God, divine revelation and an afterlife (article 2).

The first thing to be noted is that along with the assertions of democratic credentials come numerous limitations to representation in the balance of power system. Popular elections take placve at three levels: (i) village, district, regional, city and provincial; (ii) parliamentary (or *Majlis*); and (iii) Presidential. Candidature, for example for the Presidency, is subject to screening by the Guardian Council on the basis of the criteria set out in article 115:

> The President must be elected from among religious and political personalities possessing the following qualifications: Iranian origin; Iranian nationality; administrative capacity and resourcefulness; a good past record; trustworthiness and piety; convinced belief in the fundamental principles of the Islamic Republic of Iran and the official religion of the country.

This screening is certainly not nominal. In the 10th Presidential elections of June 2009, for example, of 475 candidates who came forward, just four were approved to take part in these Presidential elections. All 42 female candidates were rejected. In the 9th Presidential elections of 2005, only five candidates were approved, but after a public uproar in the press the Supreme Leader intervened in order to allow a further two candidates to be included.

Once the formidable obstacle of screening is overcome, the next question is that of decision-making powers. The Constitution outlines that parliamentary legislation needs to be examined as to its compatibility with Islam

[41] Asghar Schirazi, *The Constitution of Iran: Politics and the State in the Islamic Republic* (London, IB Tauris, 1997) 294.

by the Guardian Council (articles 72 and 94). The Guardian Council is a body composed of six *fuqaha* selected by the Supreme Leader, and six jurists elected by the *Majlis* from the jurists nominated by the Head of the Judiciary (himself appointed by the Supreme Leader) (article 91) and then approved by the President (article 123). Indeed the Constitution notes that the *Majlis* 'does not hold any legal status' if there is no Guardian Council in existence (article 93). The reason given for subjecting the decisions of the *Majlis* to Guardian Council approval is 'With a view to safeguard the Islamic ordinances and the Constitution, in order to examine the compatibility of the legislation passed by the Islamic Consultative Assembly with Islam' (articles 91 and 96). Furthermore, the very 'authority of the interpretation of the Constitution is vested with the Guardian Council' (article 98); the President's duty is merely that of 'implementing the Constitution' (article 113). In cases where the Guardian Council deems decisions of the *Majlis* to be unconstitutional or against the principles of *sharia*, and where the *Majlis* does not accept the Guardian Council's decision, the body entrusted to intervene to resolve the deadlock is the National Exigency Council—a body all of whose members are appointed by the Supreme Leader. In exceptional circumstances the Supreme Leader himself may intervene. It is worth noting that the Supreme Leader is appointed or elected by the Leadership Council. In theory the Leadership Council can dismiss the Supreme Leader (article 111), who is equal to all people in the eyes of the law (article 110); however, considering the scope of his powers, this would appear to purely a chimera. In addition to the extensive powers accorded to the Supreme Leader, therefore, almost all other authorities in the Iranian system are beholden to him in the final analysis.

It is interesting to note that in fact the powers entrusted to the Supreme Leader in the 1989 revision to the Iranian Constitution increased[42] those originally invested in the *faqih* himself in the 1979 constitution. Whilst the ideal of a checks and balances system is one of state bodies keeping each other in check by limiting one another's powers, in the Iranian system the Supreme Leader's powers are not effectively checked or limited. He determines the direction of policy, his is the only position for life. His nominee as the Head of the Judiciary determines the nominees for the Guardian Council, which in turn check the power of those who stand for election and the *Majlis* in passing legislation, which in turn reduces the little scope for developments instigated by the Presidency. The checks are therefore on the representative elements of the system, elements whose power differential with the Supreme Leader is already marked. This is even before one takes into account the notable 'unofficial' actors in the system that amplify the

[42] Mohsen Milani, 'Shi'ism and the State in the Constitution of the Islamic Republic of Iran' in Simin K Farsouri and Mehrdad Mashayekhi (eds), *Iran: Political Culture in the Islamic Republic* (London, Routledge, 1992) 150–53.

powers of the Supreme Leader yet further—the powerful and rich religious foundations, or *Bonyads*, the *Basij* forces and non-uniformed armed forces—to name just a few. The League of the Militant Clergy of Tehran, the Revolutionary Guards and the daily newspapers are amongst the 'institutions of the revolution' Schirazi refers to as bodies that 'defend the hierocracy against its opponents and at the same time are an instrument through which the distribution of power can be influenced'.[43]

Of the three arms of government, the judiciary's operation has been described by many as the weakest of the branches. It is also the most 'overshadowed' and constrained of the branches. Majid Mohammadi offers this critical assessment of the Iranian judiciary:

> [The] Iranian judiciary is formally independent (Article 156 of the 1989 Constitution) but merely from the elected bodies of government. All the high-ranking officials of the judiciary including its head are directly and indirectly appointed by the leader (Article 157 of the 1989 Constitution) without any formal input from the elected President or Parliament; the minister of justice is chosen by the President from among the candidates nominated by the head of the judiciary (Article 160 of the 1989 Constitution); the parliament cannot draft judicial laws (Article 156 of the 1989 Constitution); the Parliament has really no power of oversight over the judiciary and all the judicial policies are dictated by the leader; and judges are regularly removed from the post they occupy, transferred or re-designated without their consent when their decrees in political files are not satisfying for the establishment.[44]

Insofar as constitutional values are concerned, and the numerous conditionalities on the vague criteria of 'Islam', one has to conclude that it is the interpretation of the Supreme Leader that in cases of conflict of laws, constitutional values and conflict between the various branches of government, and alleged violations of fundamental rights by state actors, will hold sway. This reality serves to reduce the problematic degree of transparency and legal certainty offered within the Iranian system. A few instances in Iran have illustrated this, for example, regarding the commutation of the sentence of the trumped up charges against journalist Roxanna Saberi from eight years' imprisonment to a two-year suspended sentence and the possibility to leave the country;[45] the question of stoning of women;[46] and the screening of election nominees as discussed above.

[43] Asghar Schirazi, *The Constitution of Iran: Politics and the State in the Islamic Republic* (London, IB Tauris, 1997) 299.

[44] Majid Mohammadi, *Judicial Reform and Reorganization in 20th Century Iran, State Building, Modernization and Islamicization* (London, Routledge, 2007) 197–98.

[45] See: Farnaz Fassihi, 'Iran Frees US Reporter from Prison' *Wall Street Journal*, 12 May 2009, available at http://online.wsj.com/article/SB124204072586206361.html.

[46] The Iranian NGO Maydan-e Zanan's 'Stop Stoning Forever' Campaign (www.meydaan.net/english/aboutus.aspx) has noted: 'For the last three years ago, the Head of the Iranian Judiciary has repeatedly stated that although the punishment of stoning remained under Iranian law, the execution of such sentences were [*sic*] not enforced; at the same time, a moratorium

D. 'Human Rights' in the Constitution?

The Iranian Constitution states: 'In the creation of Islamic foundations, all the human forces which had been in the service of general foreign exploitation will recover their true identity and human rights' (Preamble). No commitment to universal rights is indicated in the text. The above statement is in the context of women, the vindication of whose rights is then elaborated in a discussion of the family and motherhood. The past is condemned for having drawn women away from the family unit 'in the service of consumerism and exploitation', and deflecting them from the 'serious and precious duty of motherhood', which is loftier from an Islamic point of view (Preamble, Women in the Constitution; see also article 21). This illustrates the dedication to a particular 'Islamic' point of view of human rights, rather than human rights as developed and upheld in international human rights instruments. These particular Islamic foundations and outlook on human rights can be discerned from other contexts in the Constitution as well. For example, in addressing 'The Judiciary of the Constitution', the Preamble notes that people's rights are to be safeguarded along the lines adopted by 'the Islamic movement with the object of preventing localized deviation within the Islamic community'. Mayer holds that the Iranian government is able to 'override rights protections at will' simply by invoking vague Islamic qualifications.[47]

Duties and responsibilities, in the context of discussion of rights, also come up on a number of occasions in the Constitution. Article 2 couples responsibility with rights, recognising this as one of the beliefs on which the Islamic Republic is predicated: 'the exalted dignity and value of man, and his freedom coupled with responsibility before God' (Articles 2.6). A complex triangular set of duties is founded regarding the Qur'anic injunction of enjoining good and forbidding evil *al'-amr bilma'ruf wa al-nahy 'an al-munkar* as a 'universal and reciprocal duty that must be fulfilled by the people with respect to one another, by the government with respect to the people, and by the people with respect to the government' (article 8). Furthermore, the upholding of freedom, independence, unity and territorial integrity of the country is recognised as a duty not only of the government but also of all individual citizens (article 9).

on stoning has been in effect for the entire country. Nevertheless, we have witnessed at least 6 cases of stoning in the last 3 years. Clearly, as long as the penalty of stoning remains under the Penal Code and sanctioned by Iranian law, such words by the Head of the Judiciary are worthless.' Press Release of the Stop Stoning Forever Campaign: 'Stoning Continues in Iran: At least 10 More People are at Risk of Death by Stoning', 10 January 2009, available at http://meydaan.net/English/showarticle.aspx?arid=733.

[47] Ann Elizabeth Mayer, *Islam and Human Rights: Tradition and Politics* (Boulder CO, Westview Press, 1991) 30.

The fulfilment of this 'universal duty' by the government with respect to the people can in no way be compared to its fulfilment by the people with respect to the government, given the power imbalance regarding the two. Furthermore, it should not be presumed that the majority vote of 98.2 per cent for the revolution in 1979 per se gives democratic credence to either the 'Islamic criteria' embedded immutably in the Constitution, nor to its authorisation of the army of officials determining that final criterion of the whole system.

Ultimately then, human rights in the Iranian Constitution are hierarchical, limited and conditional. They are hierarchical because they recognise the rights of Muslims, non-Muslims and 'others' differently (See for example: articles 12, 13, 14 and 23); and also those of men and women differently (See for example: articles 20 and 21). They are limited according to undefined—but institutionally constrained and complex—criteria of 'Islamic'. Rights can only be enjoyed as limited by unspecified Islamic criteria, hence leaving 'virtually unlimited discretion to states in deciding what the scope of the affected rights should be'.[48] They are also further conditional on compliance with 'law' and duties on multiple levels.

In other contexts, it has been noted that '[d]uties of rulers and individuals' alone or 'duties that are not correlative to rights'[49] do not amount to a concept of human rights. Further privileges should be distinguished from human rights. Khadduri's claim that 'Human rights in Islam, as prescribed by the divine law, are the privilege only of persons of full legal status. A person with full legal capacity is a living human being of mature age, free, and of Moslem faith',[50] is used by Donnelly to observe that Islam's 'strong concern for human good and human dignity … is important in itself, and even a prerequisite for human rights notions. But it is in no way equivalent to a concern for, or a recognition of, human rights.'[51] Fundamental concerns arise in the Iranian Constitutional context regarding '(i) freedom from religion; (ii) equality before the law; and (iii) transparency, legal certainly and checks and balances'.[52]

III. CONGRUENCE AND PRIORITIES?

The Iranian Constitution makes reference to freedom, to republicanism, to representation and to rights. Yet the adjective and precursor 'Islam' has

[48] ibid 64.

[49] Jack Donnelly, *Universal Human Rights in Theory and Practice* (Ithaca NY, Cornell University Press, 1989) 51.

[50] Khadduri as quoted in ibid 51.

[51] Khadduri as quoted in ibid 52.

[52] Jeroen Temperman, 'State-Religion Relationships and Human Rights Law: Towards a Right to Religiously Neutral Governance', PhD submitted January 2009 at the Irish Centre for Human Rights, National University of Galway, Ireland, p 356.

a dominant social and cultural, political and legal implication. Whilst the open interpretation of the requirements of 'Islam' has had multiple and diverse historical and contemporary manifestations on a global scale, the structural constraints within which it operates in the Iranian governmental system hinders pluralism, dynamism, and value-based interpretations in all but the most specialist areas,[53] or where self-interest dictates dramatic shifts.[54]

'Islam' is not merely a matter of belief in the Islamic Republic of Iran, it is an ideologically supreme value in its system of constitutional and other law, politics and policy. It has a whole machinery of government dedicated to its realisation. It is *the* immutable factor in the Constitution, to which the IRI governmental machinery is dedicated, and its predominant value.

In sum, the Iranian Constitution offers a mirage of values which in reality concede to 'Islamic criteria' as officially designated to the hierarchical yet dynamic system ultimately answerable to the Supreme Leader. The full flexibility of 'Islam' is not realisable within its political schema, and all other values—such as fairness, justice, freedom, compassion and tolerance—when tested and challenged, are finally limited by reference to this framework. The asymmetrical nature and impact of this dominant value in the Iranian Constitutional was being tested from time to time. Its fundamental values are becoming evident for all to witness.

[53] For an overview of flexibility and concession to change in the area of assisted reproductive technologies, see: Soraya Tremayne, Guest Editorial (2006) 22(3) *Anthropology Today* 2.

[54] The devastating Iran-Iraq war of 1980–89 was considered a 'holy war', until pragmatism decided the agreement to a ceasefire by Ayatollah Khomeini.

11

Global Values and Local Realities: The Case of Israeli Constitutional Law

AEYAL M GROSS*

I. INTRODUCTION: VALUES IN ISRAELI CONSTITUTIONAL LAW

ISRAEL CONSTITUTIONAL HISTORY is rather unique. The country's 1948 Declaration of Independence stipulated that a Constitution would be adopted that year, but this promise has yet to be fulfilled. In 1950, after a stormy Knesset debate, a compromise measure was adopted: the Knesset would enact a series of Basic Laws that would eventually be united into a Constitution, with each Basic Law as a prospective chapter. The first of these Basic Laws was enacted only in 1958, and dealt with the legislative branch—the Knesset. Other Basic Laws dealing with the structure of government (eg Basic Law: The President, Basic Law: The Government, and so forth) followed. By the early 1990s, two Basic Laws were needed to complete the Constitution-making process: Basic Law: Legislation was supposed to determine the supremacy of Basic Laws and set the terms for judicial review, and Basic Law: Human Rights was supposed to add the rights dimension, missing from Basic Laws that until then had dealt only with institutional issues.

The enactment of these two Basic Laws and the completion of the Constitution-making process were hindered in the extant political reality, which forestalled the legislation of a complete Bill of Rights touching on sensitive and controversial issues such as equality, religion, land and more. Knesset member Amnon Rubinstein, a constitutional law scholar and author of the leading treatise on Israeli constitutional law, submitted a motion to duplicate the 1950 compromise. Just as the Constitution was fragmented into individual Basic Laws that would serve as chapters within it, Rubinstein

* I am grateful to Daphne Barak-Erez for her helpful comments, to Batya Stein for her excellent editing work, and to Hedi Viterbo, Adar Grayvesky and Yehuda Goor for their excellent research work.

put forward the idea of fragmenting the proposed Basic Law: Human Rights into smaller laws dealing with clusters of rights, which would be easier to enact than a complete Bill of Rights.

This idea led to the legislation of two Basic Laws in 1992, the first in Israel's history to deal explicitly with human rights. Basic Law: Human Dignity and Liberty (hereinafter 'the Basic Law') included rights that were perceived as relatively consensual. Thus, the Basic Law explicitly protects the following rights: (1) preservation of life; (2) of body; (3) of dignity; (4) protection of property; (5) of liberty; (6) freedom to leave Israel (and for Israeli citizens also to enter), which may be read as a partial protection of freedom of movement; (7) right to privacy and intimacy, including a general declaration of these rights and specific provisions that prohibit entry to private premises, restrict searches in the private sphere, and protect the privacy of a person's conversations, writings, or records. Another Basic Law was also enacted at the same time, protecting freedom of occupation and stating the right to engage in any occupation, profession or trade.[1]

Israel's Basic Laws thus explicitly protect eight rights. Beside this written Bill of Rights, however, Israel has an unwritten one, with its history split into before and after the enactment of the 1992 Basic Laws. Constitutional values, including local values and global values with local reach, have consistently played a key role in the development of the unwritten Bill of Rights and in the interpretation of the newly developed, written one. Because no written Bill of Rights had existed until 1992 and a very limited one became available after it, the turn to values has always been a central feature of Israeli constitutional law. Values derived from different sources have served to explain and legitimise the judicial development of the unwritten Bill of Rights.

Section II of this chapter will trace sources for the values in Israel's constitutional order. Section III will examine several key values in Israeli constitutional law. Finally, section IV will deal with the interaction between global values and local realities and consider clashes and connections between global values within the Israeli constitutional order. I will argue in this chapter that Israeli constitutional discourse does turn to values, but only selectively, and, at times, engages in an analysis that ignores these values altogether. No less significantly, values often serve as a vehicle for various ideological projects, when ideas such as 'human dignity' are flexible enough to often be interpreted as supporting the entrenchment of a neo-liberal order, and in exactly the opposite direction in other cases. I will also argue that the turn to global values often obscures the particular circumstances of

[1] For a discussion of the legislation of the 1992 Basic Laws and the process that led to them, see also Daphne Barak-Erez, 'From an Unwritten to a Written Constitution: The Israeli Challenge in American Perspective' (1995) 26 *Columbia Human Rights Law Review* 309; Aeyal Gross, 'The Politics of Rights in Israeli Constitutional Law' (1998) 3 *Israel Studies* 80.

Israeli constitutional law, specifically the constitutional entrenchment of the ethno-national definition of the state and the reality of a long-term occupation eroding democracy's most basic tenets.

II. SOURCES OF VALUES

A. The First Channel for Values: 1948–92

Israel's unwritten Bill of Rights, as noted, developed in two tracks. Before 1992, Israel lacked not only a Constitution but also a statutory listing of civil and human rights. Over the years, however the Israeli Supreme Court developed a judicial, unwritten Bill of Rights, and exercised judicial review invoking civil rights. The Supreme Court, however, confined itself to the judicial review of administrative actions,[2] and explicitly held that it could not exercise judicial review over primary legislation.[3] Regarding legislation, then, the effect of the unwritten Bill of Rights was considered only interpretive.

Despite this limitation, the judicial Bill of Rights significantly affected the interpretation of existing statutes. By incorporating a 'normative umbrella'[4] that affects the interpretation of all legislation, the Court developed a theory about overarching values that are the basis of civil rights norms and affect the interpretation of all statutes. The seminal 1953 *Kol-Ha'am* decision not only established this type of judicial review building upon some earlier precedents, but also set the terms for the idea of 'values' as central to Israeli constitutional law. In *Kol-Ha'am*, two Communist newspapers challenged a temporary closing order issued by the Minister of the Interior based upon the Press Ordinance, a piece of legislation dating back to the British Mandate that, like most mandatory legislation, remained in force after the creation of the state of Israel. The Ordinance determined that a newspaper may be shut down if the minister determines that something it had published is 'likely' to endanger public peace. The minister held that an item about Israel's policy on American-Soviet relationships that was critical of a purported plan whereby Israel would supply soldiers to assist the US if it were at war with the Soviet Union met the danger criterion. The paper sued the government and the Supreme Court held for it, determining that

[2] Except for matters pertaining to equal participation in general elections, given that the Basic Law: Knesset included a specific entrenched clause on this question. See HCJ 98/69 *Bergman v Minister of Finance and State Comptroller* [1969] 23(1) PD 693, the leading case in this regard.

[3] See HCJ 450/70 *Rogozinski v the State of Israel* [1971] 26(1) PD 129.

[4] This term was coined at a later stage in the development of the judicial Bill of Rights by then Supreme Court Justice Aharon Barak. See HCJ 165/82 *Kibbutz Hatzor v Rehovot Assessment Officer* [1985] 39(2) PD 70.

'likely' in the Press Ordinance requires 'near certainty' that risk to public safety would actually occur, and mere likelihood is not sufficient to issue a closing order.

The Court held that this interpretation was warranted by Israel's status as a democracy. Israel's Declaration of Independence, stating 'it will be based on freedom' and will guarantee freedom of conscience, the Court held, make it a democracy. The Declaration, continued the Court, represents the people's credo and vision, and should be taken into account when interpreting statutes. As Pnina Lahav notes, in *Kol-Ha'am* the Israeli Supreme Court used the Declaration of Independence as a 'normative mediator between society's vision of its values and the notion of rights protected by law.' The Court thereby established that statutes would be interpreted in accordance with a national value system that incorporates the notion of rights, allowing the Court judicial review in the name of rights.[5] In this case, the Court could recognise a right to freedom of the press, which does not appear in the Declaration of Independence or, for that matter, in any constitutional or statutory text. 'The law of a people', determined the Court, 'must be studied in the light of its national way of life'.[6] The idea of unwritten values allowed the Court to develop the judicial Bill of Rights and to determine, in another case, that values such as equality are part of the system:

> We do not have such an express provision, neither in a written constitution nor in an 'entrenched' provision of a basic law. Nevertheless, this unwritten principle is the soul of our entire constitutional regime.[7]

In the 1980s, the Court expanded the judicial Bill of Rights even further, and issued crucial opinions on freedom of speech, freedom of religion, and more.[8] From this perspective, the lines between 'values', 'unwritten principles', and 'rights' in Israeli constitutional discourse are blurred, and some ideas can be placed under either of these categories.

The *Kol-Ha'am* decision, however, is only one side of the coin of values affecting constitutional interpretation. Only eight months before this famous judgment, the Supreme Court denied a similar petition by the same *Kol Ha'am* newspaper on a similar case, stating that the question of whether a publication was likely to endanger public peace was within the discretion of the Minister of Interior and not of the Court.[9] As Lahav shows, this decision

[5] Pnina Lahav, *Judgment in Jerusalem: Chief Justice Simon Agranat and the Zionist Century* (Berkeley and Los Angeles CA, California University Press, 1997) 111. See also A Barak, 'Chief Justice Agranat: "Kol ha-Am": The People's Voice' in Barak et al (eds), *Gvurot le-Shimon Agranat* [Essays in Honor of Shimon Agranat] (Jerusalem, Graf Press, 1986) [Hebrew].

[6] HCJ 73/53 *Kol Ha'am v Minister of Interior* [1953] 7 PD 884.

[7] *Bergman*, above n 2.

[8] Aeyal Gross, above n 1, 80; Pnina Lahav, 'Rights and Democracy: The Court's Performance' in Ehud Sprinzak and Larry Diamond (eds), *Israeli Democracy Under Stress* (Boulder CO, Lynne Reiner, 1993).

[9] HC 25/53 *Kol Ha'am v The Minister of Interior* [1953] 7(1) PD 165.

invoked no values, and relied on a formalist legal analysis to enable broad governmental discretion without protecting rights.[10]

This comparison, however, need not lead to the conclusion that turning to values necessarily implies broader protection of rights, as another decision shows. In its 1965 *Yerdor* decision, the Supreme Court returned to the logic it had relied upon in *Kol-Ha'am*, interpreting statutes in light of the values stated in the Declaration of Independence. This time, however, it did so in order to restrict rather than expand rights. The Central Election Committee disqualified an Arab nationalist party from running in the general election, despite the absence of any statutory provisions authorising the Election Committee to take such steps. Ruling on this issue, the Court cited the determinations in *Kol-Ha'am* on the need to interpret the law in accordance with national values, including those derived from the Declaration of Independence. Citing the Declaration, the Court stated that Israel had been founded as a Jewish state, and that its establishment was, in the words of the Court, an expression of Jewish self-determination. The Court held that the value of Israel's existence and sovereignty enshrined in the Declaration of Independence justifies the disqualification of political parties that deny this 'fundamental constitutional' fact.[11]

In its rationale of the decision to disqualify the party, the Court wavered between reasons based on the existence and sovereignty of Israel, and reasons based on its ethno-national character. The Court emphasised that Israel was established as a Jewish state and pointed to its background in Jewish history, noting that the Arab party negated Israel and its sovereignty. Basic Law: The Knesset was amended in 1985 to explicitly prohibit political parties denying the existence of Israel as a Jewish and democratic state. By contrast, the Court had in 1965 allowed the restriction of rights in the name of competing constitutional values, without any textual source. In this case, the issue at stake was not the existence of the state but, as is apparent from the Court's rationale, the values of ethnic nationalism. Together, these two cases tell the dual story of global universal and particular nationalist values. The interaction, and indeed the tension, between these two types of values may be typical of all constitutional regimes. In Israel, however, its unique ethno-national definition as a Jewish state, together with specific issues pertaining to the religion and state relationship, the Middle East conflict and, since 1967, the occupation of the West Bank and Gaza, have all added unique elements to this tension.

[10] Pnina Lahav, 'The Jurisprudence of Chief Justice Simon Agranat' in A Barak et al (eds), *Essays in Honour of Shimon Agranat* [Hebrew]. For a comparison of the two cases see Avraham Shapira, 'Judicial Self Restraint in the Supreme Court and the Protection of Civil Rights' (1973) 3 *Tel-Aviv University Law Review* 640 [Hebrew].

[11] HCJ 1/65 *Yerdor v Chairman of the Central Elections Committee for the Sixth Knesset* [1965] 19(3) PD 365.

B. The Second Channel for Values: Since 1992

The 1992 Basic Laws changed the landscape of Israeli constitutional law. Not only did they explicitly include a limited number of rights, but they paved the way for the judicial review of primary legislation in the name of rights. Chief Justice Aharon Barak heralded the new Basic Laws as a 'constitutional revolution',[12] and defined the right to human dignity as a 'canopy' encompassing other 'non-enumerated rights' deriving from it. How should the scope and content of this right and of its derivatives be determined? Barak's position and subsequent Supreme Court opinions relied on the two opening clauses of Basic Law: Human Dignity and Liberty. Article 1 of the Basic Law states:

> Fundamental human rights in Israel are founded upon recognition of the value of the human being, the sanctity of human life, and the principle that all persons are free; these rights shall be upheld in the spirit of the principles set forth in the Declaration of the Establishment of the State of Israel.

Article 1(a) determines as follows the purpose of the Basic Law:

> to protect human dignity and liberty, for the purpose of anchoring in a Basic Law Israel's values as a Jewish and democratic State.

These determinations have been the subject of much debate, especially over the definition of Israel as a 'Jewish and democratic' state, focusing on whether a state can harmoniously be both, or whether this is an oxymoron.[13] Resonating in these debates are echoes of controversies in social and political science concerning the relationship between ethnicity and democracy in Israel, discussing whether Israel's ethnic version of nationalism and citizenship is compatible with democracy.[14]

In the constitutional debate surrounding these two articles of the Basic Law, Barak took the position that the Basic Laws include rights 'objectively' derived from the values of a Jewish and democratic state. Based on this analysis, Barak suggested that the right to human dignity should be interpreted as encompassing civil and political rights intertwined with the concept of dignity, including equality, freedom of speech, freedom of religion, and freedom of association. In his analysis, at the foundation of Basic Law: Human Dignity and Liberty is a vision of free individuals, a concept including the

[12] See Aharon Barak, 'The Constitutional Revolution: Protected Human Rights' (1992) 1 *Mishpat Umimshal* 9 [Hebrew].

[13] Ruth Gavison, *Israel: A Jewish and Democratic State* (Jerusalem, VanLeer and Hakibutz Hameuhad, 1999) [Hebrew]; Aeyal Gross, 'Democracy, Ethnicity and Constitutionalism in Israel: Between the "Jewish State" and the "Democratic State"' (2000) 2 *Israeli Sociology* 647 [Hebrew]; Daphne Barak Erez (ed), A *Jewish and Democratic State* (Tel Aviv, Ramot, 1996).

[14] See Aeyal Gross, 'Democracy, Ethnicity and Constitutionalism in Israel', above n 13, for an overview of these debates.

protection of the autonomy of free will. Freedom of contract, therefore, is also part of human dignity.[15]

Barak's conception has been criticised on several fronts, two of which warrant discussion in this context. First, Barak's articulation of the right to human dignity has been criticised for being inclusive of a broad range of civil rights, but not of welfare (or social) rights. In his initial discussion on the concept of human dignity, his proposed index of 'non-enumerated' rights that should be included in the right to human dignity on the basis of the value oriented interpretation he suggested, did not include any social right.[16] Several legal scholars have rejected this position, and Ruth Ben-Israel noted that, from this perspective,

> the values of the State of Israel as a Jewish and democratic state seem to be anchored in a neo-liberal, individualistic approach where individual values reign supreme, as evident in labor relationships and in freedom of contract, and as translated into support for a market economy and in the rejection of any state involvement.[17]

Ben-Israel emphasised that this view of Israel's values contradicts the socio-economic foundations of the country's labour legislation, pointing out what she called the 'ideological breakdown' that followed the replacement of a Zionist-socialist ideology, essentially collectivistic, egalitarian, and upholding social solidarity, with one supporting a competitive free market economy. This ideological breakdown, claimed Ben-Israel, was most prominent within social affluent elites although, in her view,

> the great majority of Israel's million laborers ... or the hundreds of thousands who do not earn even a minimum wage ... or the hundreds of thousands ... living below the poverty line ... continue to adhere to another ideology ... that seeks state involvement so as to correct the distortions created by a competitive free market economy, anti-egalitarian by definition.[18]

These people represent a majority, said Ben-Israel, that is silent not only because its voice is not heard but because its opinions are not considered relevant in the discourse on Israel's values as a Jewish and democratic state.

[15] Aharon Barak, 'Protected Human Rights: Scope and Limitation' (1992) 1 *Mishpat Umimshal* 253, 261 [Hebrew]. For a later articulation by Barak of the content of 'human dignity', see Aharon Barak, *The Judge in a Democracy* (Princeton NJ and Oxford, Princeton University Press, 2006) 85–88.

[16] Aharon Barak, *Protected Human Rights: Scope and Limitation*, above n 15.

[17] Ruth Ben-Israel, 'The Impact of Basic Laws on Labour Law and Industrial Relations' (1994) in Ruth Ben-Israel (ed), 4 *Labour Law Yearbook* 31 [Hebrew].

[18] ibid 33. See also criticism by Guy Mundlak, 'The Right to Work, The Value of Work' in Daphna Barak-Erez and Aeyal Gross (eds), *Exploring Social Rights: Between Theory and Practice* (Oxford, Hart Publishing, 2007); Aeyal Gross, 'The Israeli Constitution: A Tool for Distributive Justice, or A Tool Which Prevents It?' in Menachem Mautner (ed), *Distributive Justice in Israel* (Tel Aviv, Ramot, 2000) [Hebrew].

In later writings, Barak expanded the right to human dignity to include a modicum of material and mental conditions as falling within the scope of the right.[19] Even in his revised position, he set a much lower threshold than that recognised in international law, making social rights secondary to civil and political rights. Barak's revised position was adopted by the Israeli Supreme Court in several decisions.[20] For instance, in *Commitment*, the Court rejected a petition challenging the constitutionality of a significant decrease in state support for a guaranteed income, which led to an average reduction of in excess of 30 per cent. In rejecting the argument that these cuts violated the right to live with dignity, Chief Justice Barak, writing for the Court, held that the right to human dignity encompasses a positive right to a minimum level of living, but no more. This right is only activated when material deficiency precludes subsistence, which the petitioners in this case had failed to demonstrate. A dissenting opinion in this case argued that the right to human dignity should be interpreted as including a right to adequate conditions of living, as opposed to the minimum approach adopted by the court. Based on this approach, the dissenting judge determined that the petitioners had proved that the legislative measures in question had violated their right to human dignity, as clear from an affidavit submitted by one of the petitioners showing that the reduced allowance together with the rest of her income failed to cover the cost of her most basic needs.[21]

Emptying the idea of social rights from content, and reducing it to the minimal approach, may reflect the subjection of social rights to the concept of human dignity, which became the overarching value of Israeli constitutional law. As a result, the current constitutional discourse in Israel concerning 'a dignified existence' has shifted from questions of distribution and social equality to a humiliation-based model, with only blatantly degrading violations warranting constitutional intervention. This model will only protect persons whose access to welfare, education, health, social security, housing, and food humiliates them, and does not allow any discussion of these rights beyond the mere minimum.

This interpretation of the Basic Law in general, and of the concept of 'dignity' in particular, reflects an ideological choice to prefer civil to social rights. The ideological choice is apparent in the very decision to divide rights into different sets, as if significant differences prevailed between them, even

[19] Aharon Barak, 'Human Dignity as a Constitutional Right' (1994) 41 *Hapraklit* 271, 275 [Hebrew].

[20] HCJ 4905/98 *Gamzu v Yeshayau* [2001] 55 (3) PD 360; HCJ 366/03 *The Commitment to Peace and Social Justice Foundation v the Minister of Finance* (Decision from 12 December 2005).

[21] For a broader discussion see Daphne Barak-Erez and Aeyal Gross, 'Social Citizenship: The Neglected Aspect of Israeli Constitutional Law' in Daphne Barak-Erez and Aeyal Gross (eds), *Exploring Social Rights* (Oxford, Hart Publishing, 2007) 250–52.

though the current understanding of rights indicates that both rights traditionally understood as 'civil' and rights traditionally understood as 'social' impose 'positive' and 'negative' obligations on states.[22] But in a decision issued in 2012 by Barak's successor, Dorit Beinisch, the Supreme Court retreated from the distinction between sets of rights: in *Hassan*,[23] for the first time, it struck down a statute based on the determination that it violated the right to exist in human dignity. The Court held that the statutory determination that a person who owns or uses a car will be denied income support by the state violates the right to exist in human dignity. Writing for the Court in this case, President Beinisch accepted the argument that no distinction prevails between civil and political rights on the one hand and social rights on the other, pointing to the 'positive' and 'negative' elements required for the protection of both.[24] However, while this decision could signal a breakthrough in the Court's case law on social rights, the scope of the Court's recognition of the right was limited to minimal (rather than adequate) conditions of existence in dignity, and its implications on further case law is yet to be seen.

The decision to interpret the right to 'human dignity' in light of values, as noted, though apparently describing a supposedly objective study of 'values' may actually mask ideological choices and biases. Ben-Israel's critique resonates here and, in a book on global values, the place of human dignity in Israel's constitutional order may provide an opportunity for examining the use of values as a purportedly objective cover for ideological decisions and prejudices,[25] even if these may shift over time.

A second major controversy in the interpretation of Basic Laws and value choices ensued from the 'Jewish and democratic' clause. Barak's view that the term 'Jewish values' should be interpreted at a 'high level of abstraction' to enable its co-existence with democratic values was criticised for diminishing the role of Jewish values and Jewish law in judicial interpretation.[26] One case illustrating this divide involved a petition by a burial society demanding that inscriptions on tombstones should be only in Hebrew, and all dates should follow the Hebrew calendar. Justice Barak ruled that this stipulation in a contract signed between the burial society and a widower

22 Barak-Erez and Gross, 'Introduction: Do we need social rights', ibid 1–17; Stephen Holmes and Cass R Sunstein, *The Cost of Rights: Why Liberty Depends on Taxes* (New York, WW Norton and Co, 1999).

23 HCJ 10662/04 *Hassan v National Insurance Institute* [2012] The Judicial Authority Website (Isr) (Hebrew).

24 ibid [28].

25 On the role of ideology in adjudication, see Duncan Kennedy, *A Critique of Adjudication: Fin de Siècle* (Cambridge MA, Harvard University Press, 1997).

26 See Barak, above n 12. But see Menachem Elon, 'Law by Constitution: The values of a Jewish and democratic state in the light of the Basic Law: Human Dignity and Freedom' (1992) 17 *Tel-Aviv University Law Review* 654 [Hebrew].

was void, because it violated the right to dignity. Barak emphasised the values of human dignity and the rights to freedom of speech and freedom of conscience, and the value of tolerance in a democracy. He discussed the conflict between the perception of the Hebrew language as a social value in Israel and the human dignity of the deceased and her family. He concluded that the burial society's demand was genuinely injurious to the right to human dignity, and that this right should prevail. In a dissenting opinion, Justice Elon, who was Justice Barak's leading critic concerning the interpretation of 'Jewish values' in this equation, pointed to the Hebrew language as a national value, and determined that this value should prevail. Both judges rested their argument on the Basic Law, with Barak deriving from it the central place of human dignity as an individual right, and Elon pointing to the need to interpret the right in light of Israel's values as a 'Jewish and democratic state'.

The debate on the values that should frame the interpretation and development of Israeli constitutional law is crucial in Israel's constitutional discourse, especially given the incomplete Constitution and the prime role of the judiciary in filling gaps and lacunae. The values discourse is extremely well-suited to a situation where free-floating ideas have long served as a 'canopy' from which the courts can derive what they need to fill what is missing. But at least since 1992, these values and the constitutional debates where they have come into play have been taking place within a set of concrete circumstances: first, a growing shift to neo-liberal policies at the expense of the welfare state, a shift that eventually instigated a mass social protest that erupted in Israel in 2011 under the banner 'the people demand social justice'; second, an ongoing debate about the Jewish nature of the state bearing implications for the religion and state conflict (as illustrated by the burial society case), but also for the status of non-Jews in Israel, especially the large Arab minority; third, the persistent Arab-Israeli conflict, especially the occupation of Palestinian territories; and fourth, the implication of the long-term tensions concerned with the conflict for democracy within Israel itself. In the next section, I examine the presence and the effect of some values we may consider global on Israeli law.

III. EXAMINING VALUES

A. Declaration of Independence

The values and principles that are now part of the discourse on Israeli constitutional law originate in a variety of sources. Some of them have evolved from the Declaration of Independence that, as noted, has played a significant role in this regard since Israel's early years, and has now been integrated into the Basic Laws. Others are part of the Basic Laws per se, and yet others are derived from numerous judicial decisions, especially from the Supreme Court. An often-quoted passage from the Declaration of Independence reads:

> The State of Israel ... will foster the development of the country for the benefit of all its inhabitants; it will be based on freedom, justice and peace as envisaged by the prophets of Israel; it will ensure complete equality of social and political rights to all its inhabitants irrespective of religion, race or sex; it will guarantee freedom of religion, conscience, language, education and culture; it will safeguard the Holy Places of all religions; and it will be faithful to the principles of the Charter of the United Nations.[27]

This paragraph lists fundamental principles of human rights and emphasises democratic values. At the same time, the Declaration speaks of establishing a 'Jewish State', hence the dual role it has played over the years.[28]

B. Basic Laws

Another source is the text of the Basic Laws, which list a number of rights and also the oft-cited reference to values in articles 1 and 1(a) noted above. The Basic Law, however, also includes a 'limitation clause' in article 8, as follows:

> There shall be no violation of rights under this Basic Law except by a law befitting the values of the State of Israel, enacted for a proper purpose, and to an extent no greater than is required.

The courts tend to join the 'values of the State of Israel as a Jewish and democratic state' in Article 1(a) and the 'values of the state of Israel' in Article 8, thus in effect reading Article 8 as follows:

> There shall be no violation of rights under this Basic Law except by a law befitting the values of the State of Israel, as a Jewish and democratic state, enacted for a proper purpose, and to an extent no greater than is required.

Both the focus on human dignity and the limitation clause suggest similarities between Israel's Basic Laws and other recent constitutions. The limitation clause invites comparison with the rights structure and the inherent limitation clause in the Canadian Charter. Dan Avnon, however, points out

[27] Published in the *Official Gazette*, no 1 of the 5th, Iyar, 5708 (Jerusalem, 14 May 1948) www.mfa.gov.il/MFA/Peace%20Process/Guide%20to%20the%20Peace%20Process/Declaration%20of%20Establishment%20of%20State%20of%20Israel.

[28] See section II above, on the contrasting use of the Declaration's principles in *Kol Ha'am* and *Yerdor*. See also Orit Kamir, 'The [Israeli] Declaration [of Independence] Has Two Faces: The Zionist Declaration and the Democratic Declaration' (1999) 23 *Tel-Aviv University Law Review* 473 [Hebrew].

the significant difference with section 1 of the Canadian Charter of Rights and Liberties:[29]

> The Canadian Charter of Rights and Freedoms guarantees the rights and freedoms set out in it subject only to such reasonable limits prescribed by law as can be demonstrably justified in a free and democratic society.

Whereas the Canadian Charter allows the restriction of rights only to reasonable limits and uses as its benchmark what is justified in a *free and democratic society*, the Israeli Basic Law, as Avnon points out, deals with a limitation befitting *the values of the state as Jewish and democratic*. The demand of the Basic Law that rights should not be violated beyond requirement is interpreted as a call to incorporate a proportionality demand similar to that assumed to derive from the Canadian Charter.[30] The focus on the *values of the state* as Jewish and democratic rather than on the *values of the society* as *free and democratic* is a significant touchstone of the gulf between these two constitutional orders.

C. Case Law

Constitutional case law often resorts to the discourse of values. In the Israeli context, this discourse served as a justification for the development of rights jurisprudence, given the lack or limited presence of constitutional texts. The following discussion will point to some of the values noted in the Court's jurisprudence, especially after the legislation of Basic Law: Human Dignity and Liberty in 1992. These values draw on the two previous sources, but also on the Court's invocation of values *ex cathedra*, sometimes anchoring its determinations in comparative and international law.[31] This reference to comparative and international law attests to the Court's attempt to see itself as part of an international judiciary that enforces common global values. Rather than offering an exhaustive survey of Israeli constitutional case law, this review identifies the more significant values in the constitutional discourse, be they from the list of global values suggested by the editors of this book, or from a range of others that recur in Israeli case law.

i. Human Dignity

Dignity is considered the overarching value in Israel's constitutional order, partly due to a formal reason: the term's presence in the title of

[29] Dan Avnon, 'The Israeli Basic Laws (Potentially) Fatal Flaw' (1998) 32(4) *Israel Law Review* 535, 544.

[30] The Canadian Supreme Court articulated the demands of proportionality in *R v Oakes* [1986] 1 SCR 103. The Israeli Supreme Court adopted the Canadian three-prong test in HCJ 6821/93 *United Mizrahi Bank v Migdal Cooperative Village* [1993] 49(4) PD 221.

[31] On the role of international human rights law in Israeli constitutional law, see Daphne Barak-Erez, 'The International Law of Human Rights and constitutional Law: A Case Study of an Expanding Dialogue' (2004) 2 *ICON—International Journal of Constitutional Law* 611.

Basic Law: Human Dignity and Liberty, and its status in this law as a right from which many others can be derived. The meaning of dignity in the context of social rights, however, was noted in the above discussion of *Commitment*,[32] which showed how this value can be depleted of any meaningful content. An interesting contrast emerges from the comparison of this ruling with another decision that also involved budgetary considerations. *Nof*[33] addresses the policy of supplying Israeli citizens with gas masks for protection in the event of chemical warfare. Mr Nof petitioned against the supply of the special—and more expensive—gas masks fitting bearded men only to people growing a beard for religious reasons. The Court held for Mr Nof, determining that his beard was part of his identity and thus his human dignity, and found the regulation in question was discriminatory. Although invoking the right and the value of dignity in this case would not be troubling per se, against the background of *Commitment* it shows that the concept of human dignity as developed and interpreted by the Court extends to the protection of identity but not, beyond the modicum noted above, to material conditions of existence. Human dignity is considered crucial to a person's identity insofar as a decision about facial hair is concerned, but ensured only minimal scope when material conditions of existence are concerned, although *both* cases involve a demand of positive action from the state and the investment of resources to protect the right in question.

Not only do the limits of the concept of dignity thereby become evident, but so does the ideological shift setting an arbitrary limit between so-called 'civil' and 'social' rights, despite the lack of any conceptual distinction between them, as these two cases demonstrate. In the Israeli constitutional order, human dignity may become part of a neo-liberal regime that treats individuals as if they were free-floating subjects who are not embedded in material conditions and power relationships. This order respects a personal choice to grow a beard and the need for a suitable gas mask, but not the daily survival needs of a large group of individuals. But the Court, as noted, retreated from this distinction in *Hassan,* where it held that '[t]he apparent gaps between these [classes of] rights, are mainly the product of historic evolution, and not of genuine differences between the rights themselves.' Holding that the right to a minimum dignified existence is at the heart of human dignity, Beinisch determined that '[w]ithout minimal material conditions, man cannot create, aspire, make choices and exercise his freedoms.' At the time of writing, it is still hard to tell whether this decision will mark a shift in the Court's jurisprudence. It remains limited to the notion of 'minimal' rather than 'adequate' material conditions, yet includes a rejection of the civil vs social rights distinction which the Court had adhered to until *Hassan*. The value of human dignity, famously anchored in article 1(1) of

32 *Commitment to Peace*, above n 20.

33 HCJ 205/94 *Nof v Ministry of Defence* [1997] 50(5) PD 449.

the German *Grundgeseszt*[34] and now considered a global value, serves in the Israeli context to legitimise a neo-liberal rights order.[35] As *Hassan* illustrates, however, it can also potentially serve to criticise this order. Although it is a significant value, with great potential to affect people's lives, different meanings may be attached to human dignity, contingent on ideological choices.

These caveats notwithstanding, the value of human dignity has featured prominently in several decisions of the Israeli Supreme Court. Together with the right to liberty, it served as grounds for forbidding the holding of Lebanese prisoners in Israel as 'bargaining chips' for Israeli MIAs and POWs,[36] and was invoked to specify state duties concerning conditions in detention facilities used to hold Palestinian prisoners.[37] It also featured, alongside the right to liberty, in the Court's decision holding that the privatisation of prisons was unconstitutional: in this case, the Court held that incarceration in a for-profit prison turns the prisoners into a means for making profits and thus violates their dignity.[38] The choice as to what falls within the ambit of this value and what does not is critical to an understanding of the ideological biases at the root of constitutional law.

True, the Court has not always endorsed a neo-liberal outlook in its opinions. Constitutional law cannot be reduced to a single perspective or interpretation, and the Court's jurisprudence has proposed alternatives to this option by granting limited recognition to social rights and developing doctrines in other fields of the law. In private law, for instance, the Court has proposed notions of contractual justice that recognise contractual inequality

[34] Art 1 of the *Gruedgeszest* determines: '(1) Human dignity shall be inviolable. To respect and protect it shall be the duty of all state authority.'

[35] On the constitutional order in Israel and other countries as part of a neo-liberal order, see Aeyal Gross, *The Politics of Rights*, above n 1; Ran Hirschl, *Towards Juristocracy: The Origins and Consequences of the New Constitutionalism* (Cambridge, MA, Harvard University Press, 2004); Ran Hirschl, 'Negative Rights vs Positive Entitlements: A Comparative Study of Judicial Interpretations of Rights in an Emerging Neo-Liberal Economic Order' (2000) 22 *Human Rights Quarterly* 1060s; Ran Hirschl, 'The Judicial Interpretation of Entrenched Civil Liberties in an Emerging Neo-Liberal Economic Order' (1998) 46 *American Journal of Comparative Law* 427; Ran Hirschl, 'The "Constitutional Revolution" and the Emergence of a New Economic Order in Israel' (1997) 2 *Israel Studies* 136.

[36] HCJ 7048/97 *Anonymous v Minister of Defence* [2000] 54(1) PD 721.

[37] HCJ 5591/02 *Yasin v The Commander of the Ktzi'ot Military Camp* [2002] 57(1) PD 403; HCJ 3278/02 *Centre for the Defence of the Individual v IDF Commander in the West Bank* [2002] 57 (1) PD 385. However, these are somewhat peculiar cases, in both of which the HCJ rejected the petitions after noting changes that took effect in the conditions in the scrutinised facilities while the cases were pending, but mentioning that some of the conditions still required change. While one cannot dismiss the important contribution of the HCJ to the change of conditions in the facilities that happened under its supervision while the cases was pending, the question remains of why the HCJ rejected the petitions, and did not accept them in the sense of giving an explicit order requiring changing the conditions it still found faulty.

[38] HCJ 2605/05 *Academic Center for Law and Business v Minister of Finance*, paras 34–39 (decision from 19 November 2011).

and justify restrictions of 'contractual freedom';[39] in labour law, the Court has intervened in the labour market for various purposes, such as imposing equality based on sexual orientation,[40] in addition to *Hassan* and to the prison privatisation case discussed above. Thus, although constitutional rights and its concept of dignity make the Court part of the neo-liberal order, understanding the Court's jurisprudence as corresponding to a libertarian approach would be misleading, as these examples show.[41]

ii. Fairness

Fairness is a central principle of Israeli administrative law, and features in several Supreme Court decisions. Whereas the government's duty to act fairly is well established, a more controversial question has been whether the citizen has a corollary duty toward the government. This position was taken by Justice Zamir in *Kontram*, when he held for a citizen's expanded duties of disclosure to provide all relevant information when applying to a government authority. The majority, however, held that the government owes all citizens procedural and substantial fairness, but the individual has no such corollary duty toward the government—the government is a trustee charged with the citizens' welfare, but not vice-versa.[42]

iii. Equality

Equality is not synonymous with fairness. In Israeli public law, equality is identified with a general conception that must guide the behaviour of the public administration, and fairness is a more specific principle that may trigger constitutional rights. Although equality can largely be considered a manifestation of fairness, due to the Israeli constitutional structure it has recently been linked mostly to human dignity. This linkage allows the recognition of equality as a constitutional right, paving the way for the judicial review of not only administrative action but also of statutes.[43]

[39] See, eg, HCJ 1195/95 *The Inheritors of Milgrom v Mishaan & The Attorney General* [1998] 52(4) PD 145; HCJ 8163/05 *Hadar Security Company v Anonymous* (decision from 6 August 2007).

[40] See HCJ 721/94 *El-Al Israel Airlines v Danilowitz* [1994] 48(5) PD 749.

[41] For additional discussions of the concept of human dignity in Israeli constitutional law see also: Judith Karp, 'Basic Law: Human Dignity and Liberty—A Biography of Power Struggles' (1993) 1(2) *Mishpat Umimshal*; Amnon Reichman, 'Human Dignity as Membership in the Community of Moral Agents' (2005) 7 *Mishpat Umimshal* 323 [Hebrew]; Orit Kamir, 'Honour and Dignity Cultures: the Case of kavod (honour) and kvod ha-adam (dignity) in Israeli Society and Law' in David Kretzmer and Eckart Klein (eds), *The Concept of Human Dignity in Human Rights Law* (Amsterdam, Kluwer Press, 2002).

[42] HCJ 164/97 *Kontram Ltd v Ministry of Finance—Custom and VAT Department* [1998] 52(1) PD 289.

[43] See, eg, HCJ 7052/03 *Adalah et al v Minister of Interior* (decision from 14 May 2006); HCJ 3267/97 *Rubinstein v Minister of Defense* [2000] 52(5) PD 481; HCJ 6298/07 *Resler v the Knesset* (decision from 21 February 2012).

Equality in the constitutional order came to mean decisions that expanded the protection of women,[44] gays,[45] and Palestinian-Arabs who are Israeli citizens.[46] Again, however, when inequality is economic, the result is different. While recognising that restricting supply of a vital service to paying customers may trigger a decision that equality was violated when the poor cannot meet payments,[47] this declaration was not translated into practice. A prominent case involved a woman who was gradually going deaf. An operation to install a cochlear implant in her ear could have saved her hearing. This operation was included in the service basket of the national health insurance, subject to a 70 per cent contribution by the patient amounting to 70,000 NIS (about 20,000 USD in current values). The patient, a low-salaried teacher and a single parent, based her petition on both a right to equality and on a right to health. The Court refused to intervene, stating that the matter had been carefully considered by the appropriate committee.[48] Although the government eventually retreated from any contributions to this procedure,[49] and this litigation certainly contributed to the decision, the ruling decision demonstrated a refusal to expand the notion of equality to the social-economic sphere.

Contrast this decision with a Court opinion holding that making permission for a demonstration contingent on the organisers covering security expenses of 100,000 NIS (about 30,000 USD in current values) is illegal because it violates the right to freedom of speech.[50] The comparison points to the link between the value of equality and the exercise of other rights. When the state conditions access to these rights on excessive payment, the problem concerns both the equal enjoyment of the right (hence equality) and the access to the right per se. The court rejected the petition bearing on access to health but accepted the one concerning access to a demonstration, although both involved a similar sum, again pointing to the arbitrary division between civil and social rights. Note that this is not merely the

[44] See eg, HCJ 453/94 *Israel Women's Network v Government of Israel* [1994] 48(5) PD 501; HCJ 4541/94 *Alice Miller v Minister of Defence* [1995] 49(4) PD 94.

[45] See, eg, *Danilowitz*, above n 40; *APA 343/09 Jerusalem Open House for Pride and Tolerance v Muncipality of Jerusalem* (decision from 14 September 2010).

[46] See, eg, HCJ 6698/95 *Kaadan v Israeli Land Authority* [2000] 54(1) PD 258; HCJ 11163/03 *High Follow-up Committee for Arab Citizens in Israel v Prime Minister of Israel* [2006] (decision from 17 June 2007). These cases stand in contradiction to the court's previous deference when it came to such issues. See David Kretzmer, *The Legal Status of the Arabs in Israel* (Boulder CO, Westview Press, 1990); Ilan Saban, 'Minority Rights in Deeply Divided Societies: A Framework for Analysis and the Case of the Arab-Palestinian Minority in Israel' (2004) 36 *New York University Journal of International Law & Politics* 885.

[47] See HCJ 5394/92 *Hupert v Yad Vashem Memorial Authority* [1994] 48(3) PD 353.

[48] HCJ 2974/06 *Israeli v Committee for the Expansion of the Health Basket* (decision from 11 June 2006).

[49] Government Decision 406, 27 August 2006.

[50] HCJ 2557/05 *Majority Headquarters v Israeli Police* (decision from 12 December 2006).

preservation of a libertarian social order, limiting state duties to 'negative rights.' Both the case of the gas masks and the case of the demonstration show that courts resort to a values and rights analysis to demand positive action and investment to protect rights, but only when these rights are associated with civil liberties. Hence, although equality is a central value in Israel's constitutional order, its interpretation and implementation often suffer from the same ideological biases affecting the value of human dignity.[51]

iv. Freedom

Against this background, it may not be surprising that freedom and liberty have often been invoked in Israeli constitutional law, often in the direct context of protecting individual freedom in the narrowest sense of the word. Recall that the central Basic Law dealing with human rights is called Basic Law: Human Dignity and Liberty and that, in Hebrew, the same word denotes both 'liberty' and 'freedom'. Based on this constitutional guarantee, the Court held against regulations that allowed soldiers' detention for up to 96 hours before bringing them before military judicial bodies, and determined that this statute violated the right to liberty enshrined in the Basic Law.[52] Based on the same provision, the Court also restricted the arrest of indebted individuals.[53] It also held that a statutory provision allowing courts to conduct hearings regarding the extension of detention for detainees suspected of security offences was unconstitutional and violated the right to fair trial, which the Court held to derive from the constitutional rights to both liberty and dignity.[54] The central role that freedom and liberty played in these contexts attests to the importance of these values for the expansion of due process in Israeli law. Another major decision invoking the right to liberty was the decision concerning the privatisation of prisons, discussed above. The Court emphasised that the legitimacy of denying liberty depends, inter alia, on the type of organisation denying it and on the manner in which this is done: the legitimacy of the denial of liberty by the state is undermined when the state transfers one of its most basic powers to private hands.[55]

[51] Of course there are other ideological biases which can be detected in case law concerning equality. See eg HCJ 1213/10 *Eyal Nir v. Speaker of the Knesset* (decision from 23 February 2012), where the Court upheld a collective pardon given to people committed offences while protesting Israel's 'disengagement' from Gaza, rejecting the petition of left-wing protesters indicted in other contexts who argued they were discriminated against. The dissenting opinion by Justice Jubran pointed to the way the statute in question gave preference to certain ideologies over others.

[52] HCJ 6055/95 *Tzemach v Minister of Defense* [1999] 53(5) PD 241.

[53] HCJ 5304/92 *Perah Association v Minister of Justice et al* [1993] 47(4) PD 715.

[54] MRC 8823/07 *Anonymous v State of Israel* (decision 11 February 2010).

[55] *Academic center for law and business*, above n 38, paras 20–34.

Freedom and liberty were also invoked in a ruling accepting a petition that challenged a policy making work visas to foreign citizens contingent on their commitment to a specific employer. This policy allowed employers to exploit migrant workers, who risked losing their visa unless they remained in their jobs. The Court invoked the rights to individual freedom and human dignity, as well as freedom of occupation.[56] While this case marked a victory in the protection of migrant workers, the Court was asked to protect the workers' 'negative liberties', by holding that government regulations restricting the workers' mobility were illegal. This case, then, is as much about the protection of workers' rights as about the protection of 'free markets', and does not deviate from the Court's general reluctance to extend protection to positive welfare rights beyond the minimum.

Last, freedom played a major role in the HCJ's twice striking down legislation that allowed detention of asylum-seekers without trial.[57] The reason for the two judgments was that, following the first case, a new law was passed that, as the HCJ held in the second case, suffered from the same constitutional flaws of the first one. While these two judgments are among the HCJ's most important decisions concerning the Basic Law: Human Dignity and Liberty, the Knesset in 2014 legislated yet a third, amended, version of the statute in question, the constitutionality of which is at the time of writing pending before the HCJ.[58] Following this judgment, it was also proposed that an 'override' clause be introduced into the Basic Law that will allow the Knesset to legislate, under special conditions, statutes that contradict it. If this amendment is passed, the power of the Basic Law will be significantly decreased.[59]

v. Tolerance

Tolerance has prevailed in Supreme Court decisions mostly in freedom of speech cases. Faced with attempts to limit free speech, the Court emphasised the value of tolerance to justify the protection of controversial speech. Several of these cases have dealt with gay and lesbian speech. In one case, the Court dealt with an instruction of the Minister of Education forbidding the educational television channel to broadcast an episode on gay and

[56] HCJ 4542/02 *Worker Line Association v Government of Israel* (decision from 30 March 2006).

[57] HCJ 7146/12 *Adam v The Knesset* (decision from 16 September 2013); HCJ 7385/13 *Eytan v Government of Israel* (decision from 22 September 2014).

[58] See Aeyal Gross, 'Israel's Human Rights Record is No Source of Pride' *Haaretz* (30 Oct 2014), www.haaretz.com/opinion/.premium-1.623452. HCJ8665/14 *Desta v The Knesset* (pending).

[59] See Aeyal Gross, 'Knesset Bids to Override Those Pesky Human Rights' *Haaretz* (27 Oct 2014), www.haaretz.com/news/national/.premium-1.622896.

lesbian youth in a series on teenagers' dilemmas. In holding this decision was illegal,[60] the Court held:

> Knowledge about a phenomenon does not make it desirable and acceptable ... and is particularly necessary to those wishing to obstruct it. Today's era fosters individual rights and bears the banner of understanding, patience, and tolerance of minorities and nonconformists ... and as long as no special reason justifies hindering their course and limiting their right to introduce the public to their way of life and to their experiences, this right should not be denied.

Justice Kedmi, who wrote this opinion for a unanimous court, had forcefully dissented in a previous holding granting spousal rights to same-sex couples.[61] 'Tolerance', then, is a value in Israel's constitutional order, but this case is a paradigm of the value's limits and of how far removed it can be from including respect for the tolerated.[62]

A decade later, the Court again considered tolerance in the context of gay speech when dealing with individual petitions demanding that the Court instruct the police to prohibit a gay pride parade in Jerusalem.[63] The petitioners relied on the doctrine developed in the context of petitions against censorship concerning limitation on freedom of speech. They argued that this case passed the tests set in this doctrine—'near certainty' of a serious and harsh violation of public safety and profound, grave, and harsh injury to public feelings, factors which case law had previously recognised as justifications for limiting freedom of speech. The Court rejected this petition and decided that holding the parade would not imply risks that would justify limiting freedom of speech. The tolerance question emerged in the discussion on the potential injury to 'public feelings.' The Court held that even if the parade were truly injurious to religious feelings, and even if most of the public in Jerusalem were against the parade due to the affront to their feelings, violating the rights to freedom of speech and demonstration would still be unjustified. Only the near certainty of profound, grave, and harsh injury to public feelings, only unusual and exceptional circumstances that 'essentially shatter the very foundations of mutual tolerance' could justify such limitations. Given the location, length, and character of the planned event, the injury to religious feelings did not pass the high level of endurance required to justify infringing the freedoms of speech and demonstration.

[60] HCJ 273/97 *The Society for the Protection of Personal Rights v Minister of Education* [1997] 51(5) PD 822.

[61] *Danilowitz*, see above n 40. For a discussion see Aeyal Gross, 'Challenges to Compulsory Heterosexuality: Recognition and Non-Recognition of Same-Sex Couples in Israeli Law' in Robert Wintemute and Mads Andenas (eds), *Legal Recognition of Same-Sex Partnerships: A Study of National, European and International Law* (Oxford, Hart Publishing, 2001).

[62] For a critique of this case along these lines see Alon Harel, 'The Rise and Fall of the Israeli Gay Legal Revolution' (2000) 31 *Columbia Human Rights Law Review* 443, 465–67.

[63] HCJ 5277/07 *Marzel v the police commander of Jerusalem district* (decision from 20 June 2007).

This holding involves a problem in its theoretical, even if limited, approval of the idea that rights could be limited adducing injury to the feelings of others. Such an idea again points to the limitations of the underlying basis of tolerance—not respect for others appears but rather the opposite. Invoking 'injured feelings' as a possible justification for limiting the rights of others is a dangerous and unsustainable idea. My feelings are very frequently hurt by views people express publicly on a variety of issues. Can that be a justification to limit their freedom of speech? My discussion here does not deal with the question of whether speech can indeed harm others by inciting violence or by perpetuating and reinforcing their subordinate status (as argued in the racism and pornography debate) and should therefore be restricted. The idea that 'mutual tolerance' can, albeit in extreme cases, justify limiting rights in the name of others' injured feelings may warrant consideration of the dark side of the tolerance discourse in constitutional law.

vi. Respect for Life

The right to life is explicitly stated in Basic Law: Human Dignity and Liberty. Though invoked in various contexts, it generally appears as a right that may generate restrictions on government behaviour, rather than one requiring positive action to guarantee material conditions. In one case, the Court addressed the government policy of crop-dusting Bedouin fields in the Negev. The state considered these crops illegal because they lacked permits, but the Court accepted the petition arguing that this government action was illegal because it endangered the life and health of the local residents.[64] But although the petitioners expressly relied on the right to life, and the Court did discuss the health risks entailed by this action, the Court did not explicitly address the right to life beyond citing the petitioners' arguments.

This is yet another instance of a pattern: although many cases involve human life, the right to life has not been developed in Israeli constitutional discourse. In another case, the Court mandated the government to install an effective protective system in Israeli schools exposed to missiles fired from Gaza. The Court cited the petitioners' arguments invoking the right to life, but articulated its decision in terms of the right to education, noting that parents should not have to chose between the right to education and the protection of the children's lives.[65]

The right to life was cited in the Court's decision in a petition that challenged Israel's declared policy of targeted killings of Palestinians it holds to be terrorists. Although citing the right to life, the Court did allow the policy

[64] HCJ 2887/04 *Abu Mdieghem v Israel Land Administration* (decision from 15 April 2007).

[65] HCJ 8397/06 HCJ 8397/06 *Eduardo v The Minister of Defence* (decision from 13 November 2007).

in principle stating that specific cases must be determined individually in accordance with international humanitarian law, focusing on the distinction between civilians and combatants and on the principles of proportionality in humanitarian law. Relying on the legitimacy that international law grants to the killing of combatants and civilians who partake in hostilities, the Court did not recognise those targeted in these assassinations as protected by this right. The others' right to life, however, follows from the Court's discussion of proportionality, which would restrict such assassinations if it led to disproportional damage to civilian bystanders. The complex questions raised by this case exceed the scope of this chapter, and I will only note that the occupation brings to the surface several anomalies of Israeli law. Palestinians live under Israeli occupation, which owes them duties of protection. Yet, when participating in hostilities against Israel, they are viewed as enemy combatants or as civilians who participate in hostilities, displacing an analysis focused on the value of life to a war setting where killing is the norm. While this may indeed be the right setting for this question, my point is that this case was not examined through a constitutional perspective.

vii. Accountability and Integrity

Since the 1990s, government accountability and integrity have featured prominently in decisions of the Israeli Supreme Court. The Court has invoked the principles of fairness, integrity, faith, and public trust in government in holdings concerning various issues, including the topic of coalition agreements, mandating their publicity, and restricting their content.[66] Other decisions invoking these values were cases where the Court held against the appointment or continuing service of public officials involved in criminal proceedings. In one case, the Court held that a minister could not continue serving in the cabinet when indicted although not yet convicted for serious crimes.[67] In two other cases, it stopped the appointment to high positions in the civil service of individuals who had been involved in the killing of two Palestinian terrorists after they had been caught, and in a subsequent cover-up of the affair.[68] These individuals had not been convicted in court since they had been pardoned before their trial, but the Court held that their appointment

[66] See, eg, HCJ 1601/90 *Shalit v Peres* [1990] 44(3) PD 353; HCJ 1523/90 *Levy v Prime Minister of Israel* [1990] 44 (2) PD 213.

[67] See *Deri's case*: HCJ 3094/ 93 *Movement for Quality Government in Israel v Government of Israel* [1993] 47(5) PD 404.

[68] On the affair in question, see Pnina Lahav, 'A Barrel without Hoops: The Impact of Counter-Terrorism on Israel's Legal Culture' (1988) 10 *Cardozo Law Review* 529; see also HCJ 7195/08 *Abu-Rahma v MAG* (decision from 1 July 2009) where the Court overturned the *MAG* decision to prosecute an officer and a soldier who had shot at a Palestinian prisoner only for 'conduct unbecoming', holding that this offence did not reflect the gravity of the event.

would jeopardise the values of fairness, integrity and public faith in the public service.[69]

viii. Education

Shortly after the 1992 Basic Laws were passed, a petition was filed against a government decision to stop funding for an educational programme for children from underprivileged socio-economic backgrounds. The Court rejected the petition, with the presiding judge maintaining that the right to education cannot be recognised as a constitutional right since it has no foundation in the Basic Law: Human Dignity and Liberty.[70] The Court nevertheless emphasised the importance of the value of education, but this remained only dictum. In later decisions involving judicial review of administrative actions, the Court reiterated the importance of this value and held for the petitioners on several occasions.

In one case, the Court recognised the right to education as a basic right, inspired by international conventions and by the Constitutions of various countries. The Court did not state whether the right is to be read into the Basic Law (thus warranting judicial review of primary legislation) because this case involved judicial review of an administrative decision. The petition involved the right of children with Down's syndrome who are interested in receiving mainstream education to receive government assistance. The Court's decision to accept the petition rested on the right to education, thus recognising the value of education in the Israeli legal order, and on specific provisions in the Special Education Law 1988, which acknowledges the right to mainstreaming for children with disabilities.[71] Despite subsequent legislation that later explicitly recognised the right to mainstreaming for children with disabilities, litigants were required to petition the Court again in order to implement it.[72] The Court also invoked the right to education in other cases, pointing to the need for equality in education, and disqualifying demands for payment from students that it held limited education and equal access.[73] None of these cases,

[69] HCJ 6163/92 *Eisenberg v Minister of Building and Housing* [1993] 47(2) PD 229; HCJ 4668/01 *Sarid v Prime Minister* [2001] 56(2) PD 265.

[70] HCJ 1554/95 *Friends of GILAT Association v Minister of Education, Culture and Sport* [1996] 50(3) PD 2.

[71] HCJ 2599/00 *YATED v Minister of Education* [2002] 56(5) PD 834.

[72] HCJ 6973/03 *Marciano v the Minister of Finance* [2003] 58(2) PD 270.

[73] See, eg, HCJ 7374/01 *Anonymous v Director of the Ministry of Education* [2003] 57(6) PD 529; HCJ 4363/00 *Poriya Ilit Committee v Minister of Education* [2004] 56(4) PD 203; For other significant cases where the Court invoked the right to education in the context of discriminatory practices in education, emphasising the importance of equality in this context, see HCJ 5373/08 *Abu Labda v Minister of Education* (decision from 6 February 2011); HCJ 7426/08 *Tabeka Law and Justice to Immigrants from Ethiopia v Minister of Education* (decision from 31 August 2010); HCJ 1067/ 08 *'Noar KeHlacha' v Ministry of Education* (decision from 6 August 2009).

however, challenged the growing inequalities in Israeli society due to privatisation and disparities between different municipalities.[74] Hence, although the Court's decisions in these cases may reflect a consensus on the importance of education and, to some extent, a departure from its general stand on social rights, their limited reach must also be noted.

ix. Family

The Israeli Supreme Court recognised the right to family life and even elevated it to the level of a constitutional right in the Basic Law. The majority position in the case granting this recognition, however, interpreted this right in such narrow terms that this recognition becomes questionable.

In a landmark case, the Court upheld a statute that prohibited granting visas and residence permits in Israel to Palestinian residents of the occupied territories even if they are married to Israeli citizens, with few exceptions.[75] This legislation adduced security grounds, claiming that Palestinians married to Israeli citizens who had obtained Israeli IDs had been involved in terrorist actions. The extent of this involvement remained controversial even during the litigation, and opponents of this legislation as well as two of the dissenting judges claimed it had been motivated by demographic rather than by security concerns.[76]

All judges in the panel agreed that family life is a constitutional right and embraced the value of family, but a controversy arose concerning its scope. In his dissent, Barak determined that the right includes the right to common family life: Israeli citizens have a right to maintain a family life in Israel with their foreign spouses. Cheshin held in his majority opinion that citizens do not have a constitutional right to the immigration of their foreign spouses to Israel following marriage, and questioned a state's constitutional duty to allow entry to foreigners married to its citizens. Specifically, Israel does not have such a duty, held Cheshin, given its conflict with the Palestinians. The family served here as a battleground between different concepts of this right, which actually reflect different concepts of the relationship between rights, security, and nationality in Israel's complex realities. It thus involves the value of family but on the other hand illustrates the central role of security as a value of itself in the Israeli legal culture. Cheshin's opinion is especially interesting—and troubling—in its claim that rights can be limited because of

[74] For a discussion see Barak-Erez and Gross, above n 21. On inequalities in education, see Yishai Blank, 'Decentralized National Education: Local Government, Segregation, and Inequality in the Public Education System' (2004) 28 *Tel Aviv University Law Review* 347 [Hebrew]; Yishai Blank, 'Brown in Jerusalem: A Comparative Look on Race and Ethnicity in Public Schools' (2006) 38(3) *The Urban Lawyer* 367.

[75] *Adalah et al v Minister of Interior,* above n 43.

[76] See Aeyal Gross, 'In Love with the Enemy: Justice, Truth, Integrity and Common Sense: Between Israel and Utopia in the Citizenship Law' (2007) 23 *Hamishpat* 79, 84 [Hebrew].

security interests without having to pass the hurdle of the limitation clause, since these interests can influence the very definition of rights. His position indeed paves the way for the unrestricted limitation of rights.[77]

The different conceptions of family that appear in this judgment also deserve note. Judge Cheshin notes in his ruling: 'We shall all agree—how could we not—that a person, every person, has a right to marriage and to family life.' He further explains:

> The covenant between man and woman, family life, was agreed before the state and before rights and obligations came into being … a man needs a woman and a woman needs a man … A covenant was thus signed between man and woman, and, when children were born, the extended family emerged. In this constellation, love is forged. Concerning the family, then, the state merely extended its protection to what already existed according to nature's dictates. Society and the state sanctified the covenant between man and woman through marriage … Whatever philosophers and intellectuals may say … the family's existence came from God above, from nature, from the human genetic makeup … This is the way it is in the man-woman relationship, and in the parents-children relationship.

From Cheshin's perspective, then, the family that deserves protection is the traditional nuclear family: man, woman, and children. Only this structure, ostensibly based on a natural and genetic order, is a family. Only there is love kindled. This view conveys belief in a pre-legal and pre-discursive natural order as to what is a family, and perhaps also what is love. This belief, which disregards the fact that the family is a social institution assuming different forms in various places and at various times, echoes the minority view of Justice Kedmi in *Danilowitz*, where the Israeli Supreme Court recognised the duty of employers to provide spousal benefits for same-sex couples. In his dissent, Kedmi ruled that two people of the same sex cannot be a 'couple', because this is contrary to the meaning that life and nature had accorded to this term. Cheshin's ruling is indeed adorned with biblical quotations similar to those featured in Kedmi's ruling, and he sometimes draws from the same sources. This conception obviously leaves no room for many other types of families, such as single-parent families, families of same-sex couples, families with adopted children, and others not necessarily built on a couple-based relationship.

[77] A slightly revised version of the same statute was upheld by the Court in HCJ 466/07 *Galon v Attorney General* (decision from 11 January 2012), with the majority judges once again giving preference to the security concerns. However in a specific case concerning family reunification rights, the Court, citing the centrality of the right to family life, accepted a petition against a decision to revoke the license the Palestinian petitioner in this case already had to live in Israel, where her husband and children, all of them Israeli citizens, resided. The Court in this case held that the government did not strike the right balance between the right to family life and the security concerns involved. See HCJ 7444/03 *Daka v Minister of Interior* (decision from 22 February 2010).

Beside Cheshin's disregard for the broad spectrum of family life ('… whatever philosophers and intellectuals may say'), we hear Justice Salim Joubran's voice, who joined the minority opinion of Chief Justice Barak. Unlike Cheshin, Joubran notes: 'It is man's nature … to search for a [male] partner or [female] partner for himself.' This neutral language, though limited to the couple model, validates a spectrum of relationships. Whereas Cheshin relies on quotations from Genesis, Joubran turns to one of the philosophers that Cheshin might have been hinting at and cites Aristophanes in Plato's *Symposium*:

> For if we are friends of God and at peace with him we shall find our own true loves … and I believe that if our loves were perfectly accomplished, and each one returning to his primeval nature had his original true love, then our race would be happy. And if this would be best of all, the best in the next degree must in present circumstances be the nearest approach to such a union; and that will be the attainment of a congenial love.[78]

Commenting on this passage, Joubran notes that only for very few choices do people exercise their free will as they do in the choice of the person with whom they wish to share their lives. Indeed, Aristophanes addresses three forms of love: love between men and women, love between women and women, and love between men and men. Although Joubran elided Aristophanes' reference to a loving male couple in the passage he quoted, the spirit of the passage does not change and the phrase about 'all of the men and women' remained.

In its gender-neutral language and its reference to *Symposium*, Joubran's ruling opens up a possibility for many types of love and families, at least those based on a couple. By contrast, Cheshin's ruling precludes any option other than normative heterosexuality. This case highlights the strong connection between Cheshin's heteronormativity, which limits the term family to the nuclear patriarchal version, and his decision to reject the petition challenging the constitutionality of the law. Joubran's ruling, both in its use of broad and neutral language regarding couples and family relationships and in its rationale, recognises choice as a key variable. The meaning attached to the value of family thus remains in dispute, when different ideologies may lead to different results.

In another case, the Court ordered that same-sex couples married in Canada should be registered in Israel as married.[79] Although the petition rested inter alia on the right to family life, the Court's reasoning was formally anchored in case law precedents, which require clerks at the population

[78] Plato, *Symposium* in (Benjamin Jowett, tr) *Dialogues of Plato* (New York, Pocket Books, 1956) 193.

[79] HCJ 3045/05 *Ben Ari v The Director of Population Administration in the Ministry of Interior* (decision from 21 November 2006).

registry to note details as they appear in public certificates from abroad. This determination has long been useful to opposite-sex couples who married in nearby Cyprus because only religious marriage is available in Israel. This formal justification illustrates how legal changes in the definition of what is a family often evolve in Israel through a kind of 'back-door' procedure, transforming the family without explicit discussion of what is changing.

D. The Elephant in the Room: A Jewish Democratic State—Questions of Community, Participation and Inclusion

The case of the Citizenship Law discussed in the previous section and the shadow of demographic considerations looming over it bring us back to the question of Israel's self-understanding and constitutional definition as 'Jewish and democratic.'

Case law is obviously not sufficient to understand the implications deriving from Israel's identification as a Jewish state and various practices, including informal ones, should also be considered. When discussing issues within the realm of constitutional law, the Court often turned to Israel's values as a Jewish state. These cases include one dealing with the partial closure of a road on the Sabbath in an area populated by Orthodox Jews. The Court held that taking into account religious feelings and ways of life befits the values of the state as a Jewish state, and that keeping the Sabbath is a central value in Judaism. The Court's analysis went on to discuss the demands of democracy and tolerance, which it defined as the basis of democracy, holding it should protect the right to freedom of movement but also limit it to protect religion. On these grounds, the Court held that although closing the road during prayer times was a valid decision that reasonably balanced the competing interests, it did not provide solutions for the area's secular residents and ordered the government to reconsider and reach a new decision.[80]

Whereas this decision illustrates a course usually followed on issues of religion and state, the 'Jewish and democratic' compound emerges on another front as well—the rights of the Palestinian-Arab citizens of Israel. The understanding of Israel as a 'Jewish state' is pervasive, as evident in discriminatory practices tied to the identification of the state with the dominant ethnic group, especially in the allocation of such resources as land and education.[81]

In one notable case, the Court accepted a petition to disqualify a practice whereby the state had transferred the function of allocating state land for

[80] HCJ 5016/96 *Horev v Minister of Transportation* 51(4) PD 1.

[81] See Kretzmer, above n 46; Adalah—The Legal Center for Arab Minority Right in Israel, *Report to the UN Committee on the Elimination of Racial Discrimination* (March 1998) Geneva. www.adalah.org/eng/intladvocacy/cerd-adalah-report1998.htm; Saban, above n 46.

the purpose of establishing new population centres to the Jewish Agency, a non-state body, thereby evading responsibility on this count toward the country's Arab citizens. The Court held that Israel's values as a Jewish state not only do not justify discrimination against its Arab citizens but require it to act equally toward everyone.[82] While the potential of this decision to redress the extensive history of discrimination in access to land is limited, it served, in the Court's words, as 'a first step in a difficult and sensitive road'.[83] It also demonstrated the importance of global values, since this case had been highly publicised and subject to international scrutiny.[84] Although practices of the kind challenged in this case had strong roots in Zionist tradition, reconciling them with the desire to be perceived as part of a universal human rights community committed to values of equality was proving increasingly hard.

The remedy awarded to the petitioners in this case, however, was quite modest. Rather than ordering that they should be allowed to buy a plot in the village in question, the Court held that their application should be considered on an equal basis, but the final decision could take into account the interests of the village's current residents. Indeed, only after six years and a second petition to the Supreme Court were the petitioners able to implement their right.[85]

The issue that spurred the Court's deepest engagement with the core meaning of 'Jewish and democratic state' is the disqualification of political parties. Already in the 1965 *Yerdor* judgment, as noted, the Court accepted without statutory provision a petition to disqualify a party for what was perceived as the denial of Israel as a Jewish state. A 1985 amendment to Basic Law: The Knesset codified this issue, and determined that political parties may be banned from participating in parliamentary elections for several reasons, including the negation of the existence of Israel as a democracy and as the 'state of the Jewish people'. In 2002, this section was amended to conform to the 1992 Basic Law, to read that a person or a party could not stand as a candidate for Knesset election, if it could be inferred from their goals or acts that they deny the existence of Israel as a Jewish and democratic state. The Basic Law as it stands today allows the Central Elections Committee to disqualify a party or a specific candidate from a party list.

The Court developed criteria for the implementation of this amendment in a case relating to a 2003 decision by the Central Elections Committee. This case had sought to disqualify the candidacy of an Arab nationalist

[82] HCJ 6698 *Ka'adan v the Israel Land Administration* [2000] PD 54 (1) 258.

[83] ibid. See Sandy Kedar, 'A first step in a sensitive road: Preliminary observations on *Kaadan v Katzir*' (2000) *16 Israeli Studies Bulletin* 3.

[84] The case was reported on the front page of the *New York Times*: Serge Schmemann, 'Israeli Learns Some Are More Israeli Than Others', *New York Times*, (New York, 1 March, 1998) query.nytimes.com/gst/fullpage.html?res=9C0DE4DB1631F932A35750C0A96E958260.

[85] HCJ 8060/03 *Ka'adan v the Israel Land Administration* (decision from 26 April 2006).

party and two individual Arab candidates for negating Israel as a Jewish state and supporting armed conflict against it, which is a further reason for disqualification in the Basic Law.[86] The Court heard the appeal of the party and the individuals the Committee had banned, together with an appeal against a decision of the Central Elections Committee's to disqualify a candidate from an extremist Jewish right-wing party for negating Israel as a democracy and incitement to racism. The Court overturned the disqualification ruling and rejected the petition to disqualify a candidate. In deciding this case, the Court determined that individuals and parties should be disqualified only if they negated the core components of each of the disqualification causes. Regarding the 'Jewish state' component, the Court held that the state's characteristics include Zionist elements and elements of tradition. At their core is the right of every Jew to immigrate to Israel, a state where Jews will be a majority, Hebrew will be the main language, and the calendar and symbols will reflect the national revival of the Jewish people. The core components of the state as 'democratic' are the recognition of the people's sovereignty as manifest in free and equal elections, the recognition of a core of human rights including dignity and equality, the separation of powers, the rule of law, and an independent judiciary.

In deciding this case, the Court analysed article 7(a) of Basic Law: The Knesset, which allows the disqualification of parties as part of the 'democratic paradox'. The paradox relates to the need to sustain an open democracy while ensuring its protection—'defensive democracy', a term adopted by the Court in *Yerdor* and since then ensconced in Israeli legal and public discourse. The Court compared the Israeli legislation to parallel legislation in Germany, Italy, France, Spain and other countries, but overlooked the differences between them. Israeli law prohibits not only political parties that threaten democracy, as in cases fitting the model of the 'democratic paradox', but also parties that deny the ethno-national character of Israel as a Jewish state, a principle unparalleled in the democracies mentioned in the ruling. This principle, contra the Court's discourse since 1965, does not represent 'defensive democracy', but rather an attempt to defend Israel's Jewish character at the price of limiting democracy. By framing this issue as part of the 'democratic paradox', the Court 'normalised' Israel's ethnic character and ensured its entrenchment as a constitutional value that cannot be revoked, since political parties and individual candidates wishing to rescind it may be disqualified from running for election.

The identification of the terms 'Jewish and democratic' in the 'values' clause of Basic Law: Human Dignity and Liberty and Basic Law: The Knesset suggests that a discussion of basic constitutional values must take into account how values construed as universal fare in a state defined in ethno-national

[86] EDA 11280/02 *Central Elections Committee for the Sixteenth Knesset v Tibi* [2003] IsrSC 57 (4) 1.

terms. The disqualification cases are further evidence of the tangle obscuring the distinction between Israel's Jewish and democratic character. No party has been disqualified on these grounds since 1965, and the Supreme Court reversed the decisions of the Central Elections Committee in 2003. In a subsequent decision, which reiterated the same principles of the 2003 decision, it also reversed the disqualification of two Arab parties in 2009.[87] In 2012 and 2015, it reversed decisions to disqualify Hanin Zuabi, who is a member of one of the Arab parties previously disqualified.[88] Nonetheless, the chilling effect of the legislation and the disqualification on the political scene can hardly be exaggerated, especially since the Court was divided on the reversal of the Committee's decision. Thus, these cases attest to tensions between a concept that identifies the political community with one ethnic group, and between the values of democracy, inclusion and participation.

E. The Elephant Outside: The Occupation and the Role of the Security Discourse

The previous section addressed the dissonance between the global discourse of democratic values of rights and Israel's constitutional definition as a 'Jewish state', including the reference to these values as constitutional. The dissonance between the discourse of constitutional democracy prevalent in the opinions of the Court[89] and the reality of Israel's ongoing occupation of the Occupied Palestinian Territory since 1967 is even greater. Addressing the legal structure of the occupation in detail is beyond the scope of this article,[90] but we cannot discuss the role of values in Israeli constitutional adjudication, including the central role of the security discourse, without addressing this discrepancy. The gap between Israel's self-understanding and constitutional definition as a democracy and the reality of long-term control over millions of Palestinians who do not participate in the election of the government that effectively rules their life is unbridgeable. In this context, we should note the extension of Israel's Election Law on a personal basis, allowing Israeli settlers residing in the Occupied Territories to vote in their places of residence.[91] This provision is significant, especially since Israel has no absentee ballot voting.[92] Its effect is to allow Israeli settlers in the

[87] EA 561/09 *Balad and Raam-Taal v Central Election Committee for 18th Knesset* (decision from 7 March 2011).

[88] AA 9225/12 *Central Election Committee for the 19th Knesset v Haneen Zoabi* (decision from 12 December 2012; Reasoning published 20 August 2013). AA 1095/15 Central Election Committee for the 20th Knesset v Haneen Zoabi (decision from 18 February 2015).

[89] See, eg, *United Mizrahi Bank*, above n 30.

[90] See Orna Ben-Naftali, Aeyal Gross and Keren Michaeli, 'Illegal Occupation: Framing the Occupied Palestinian Territories' (2005) 23 *Berkeley Journal of International Law* 551.

[91] Election Law (Consolidated Version) 1969, art 147.

[92] Israeli law does not allow Israeli citizens, with the exception of diplomats and other officials and special groups, to vote outside the country's geographical boundaries. See ibid art 6.

Occupied Territories to be part of the people electing the government ruling these territories as an occupying power, when Palestinians residing in the very same territories who are also subject to the actions of this government are not.[93]

The Court's involvement in the many petitions pertaining to the Occupied Territories, especially those filed by Palestinians arguing that their rights have been violated, deserves special note. I cannot address this case law in detail here,[94] and will confine myself to noting some patterns in the Court's jurisprudence.

The characteristic mode of the Court's case law regarding the Occupied Territories in recent years has been to transplant to these areas the discourse of rights and the search for balance typical of its jurisprudence in general. The price of this process has been the normalisation of the occupation and the veiling of its non-democratic features. Some cases illustrating it come from the city of Hebron, home to about 150,000 Palestinians—35,000 of them living in the H-2 area where about 800 Israeli Jews have also settled.[95] About 7,000 Jewish settlers live in the adjacent settlement of Kiryiat Arba.[96]

In *Hass*,[97] the Court dealt with a petition challenging the Israeli army's land seizures and the destruction of several structures in Hebron to widen the road that Kiryiat Arba's Jewish settlers use to access the Cave of the Patriarchs in Hebron. The military commander decided on these steps after several attacks against the settlers and against members of the security forces guarding them, when several soldiers were killed. After the petition was submitted and after the Court asked the military commander to examine alternative options for achieving its security goals, the army revised its plans, reduced the number of buildings to be demolished, and also made other changes.[98] But since the army insisted on these plans, the decision on these measures remained pending before the Court. In many ways, *Hass* illustrates the legal working of the occupation. The Court noted that the houses the army set out to destroy were 'vacant,' a fact that supposedly alleviates

[93] For an analysis of the Israeli legislation applying Israeli law on a personal basis to Israelis in the territories, see Amnon Rubinstein, 'The Changing Status of the "Territories" (West Bank and Gaza): From Escrow to Legal Mongrel' (1988) 8 *Tel Aviv University Studies in Law* 59, 68–72. For a discussion of the significance of the difference in suffrage, see Oren Yiftachel, '"Ethnocracy": The Politics of Judaizing Israel/Palestine' (1999) 6 *Constellations* 364, 377.

[94] For a discussion of the case law until 2000, see David Kretzmer, *The Occupation of Justice: The Supreme Court of Israel and the Occupied Territories* (Albany NY, State University of New York Press, 2002).

[95] Ofir Feuerstein, 'Ghost Town: Israel's Separation Policy and Forced Eviction of Palestinians From the Center of Hebron', *B'Tselem: The Israeli Information Center for Human Rights in the Occupied Territories* and *Association for Civil Rights in Israel* (May, 2007). www.btselem.org/english/publications/Index.asp?YF=2003&image.x=10&image.y=4.

[96] The Central Bureau of Statistics Israel (2010), www.cbs.gov.il/publications12/local_authorities10/pdf/676_3611.pdf.

[97] HCJ 10356/02 *Hass v Commander of the IDF forces in the West Bank* [2004] 58(3) PD 443.

[98] ibid [5].

the gravity of the rights violations. For their part, the petitioners argued that the purported security reasons were a cover for a political motive: creating territorial continuity between Kiryiat Arba and Hebron to enable the eventual expansion of Jewish settlement in the area. They also challenged the army's security arguments by pointing out that the area in question had already been declared a closed military zone and had been abandoned by its residents,[99] possibly explaining why the buildings in question were already empty.

The petitioners' arguments rested both on applicable norms of international humanitarian law (the Hague Convention on the Law and Customs of War 1907, and the Fourth Geneva Convention Relative to the Protection of Civilian Persons in Time of War 1949) and on rights guaranteed within Israeli constitutional law.[100] The Court examined the issue based on these sources, following its previous determination that the military commander's actions are subject not only to the rules of international law but also to Israeli public law, by which he is bound as an agent of the Israeli government.[101] The Court noted that any violation of civilian property thus needs to balance military needs against damage to the property owner. It further noted that, in addition to the rules of international law, the Israeli law binding on the military commander requires him not to violate the property of residents in the area unless for a purpose within his authority and as required by critical necessity. The Court then proceeded to examine the balance struck between the exercise of the Jewish settlers' right to pray in a holy place within relative security and the private property rights of the Palestinian residents. Disregarding the question of the legality of the settlers' residence, which the Court said was not before it, it held that the very fact of their residence gives rise to the military commander's duty to maintain their security and their human rights as part of the humanitarian dimension of the military force in belligerent occupation. This concerns all aspects of life, including the constitutional human rights—freedom of movement, freedom of religion, and property rights—of the area's residents, both Jews and Arabs. Sometimes this protection will require balancing conflicting human rights and, in this context, violating the right to private property is reasonable and proportional.[102]

Hass illustrates problems in the 'convergence' of international humanitarian law and human rights law.[103] In the present context, however, its importance lies in the use of human rights analysis to normalise the context of occupation. The supposed balancing act in *Hass* is in fact an imbalance,

[99] ibid [3].
[100] ibid
[101] ibid [8].
[102] ibid [15]–[21].
[103] See Aeyal Gross, 'Human Proportions: Are Human Rights the Emperor's New Clothes of the International Law of Occupation' (2007) 18 *European Journal of International Law* 1.

since it places the burden of the settlers' security on the people living under occupation, conceptualises the need for balance between the rights involved as if they were the rights of equal parties, and allocates the rights to be balanced in a way that predetermines the results. This decision highlights the problems involved in the use of constitutional values in the context of the occupation, while ignoring their context.

Another example is a petition of two Palestinians who were prevented from returning to homes they had left because of harassment from neighbouring Jewish settlers. The Court ruled that the arrangement for their return suggested by the army was satisfactory and was required from a security perspective. In rejecting the petition, the Court accepted the paradigm that Palestinian rights can be restricted to protect the settlers and that only settlers can invoke 'security' arguments. It also ruled that the suggested arrangement, requiring the residents to co-ordinate every entry to their home with the occupying army so as to protect the security of settlements whose legality was never questioned, was acceptable.[104]

These examples show that, even when the Court resorts to a values discourse, it often does so in a way that abstracts it from the occupation context and justifies distorted results. In some cases, the Court has ruled for Palestinian petitioners, again in the name of a value-rich analysis and ordered, for instance, a re-routing of the wall separating Israel from the West Bank because of excessive, non-proportional violation of rights. In these very cases, however, the Court legitimised the building of the wall in the occupied territories and justified the violation of Palestinian rights to protect Israeli settlers residing there.[105] These decisions are problematic not only because of the illegality of the settlements under international law, but because of the inherent inequality between the Jewish settlers and the local Palestinian residents in their access to resources and in the protection of their rights.[106] In another decision, the Court upheld the decision of the Israeli army to reduce or limit the supply of fuel and electricity to Gaza in response to missiles fired from Gaza to Israel. The Court noted that, unlike its enemies, Israel is 'a democratic state fighting for its life with the means the law places at its disposal.'[107] This invocation of democracy seems hard to reconcile with the undemocratic reality of the occupation.

[104] HCJ 4547/03 *Chlabi v The Prime Minister* (Decision from 30 May 2005). Some of the facts of this case are not detailed in the HCJ's verdict but in the petition itself. Significantly, the HCJ did not mention in its decision that while the petitioners were outside the house they could not enter, their house was set on fire and destroyed.

[105] See Aeyal Gross, 'The Construction of a Wall between The Hague and Jerusalem: The Enforcement and Limits of Humanitarian Law and the Structure of Occupation' (2006) 19 *Leiden Journal of International Law* 393.

[106] See Ben-Naftali, Gross and Michaeli, above n 90.

[107] HCJ 9132/07 *Jaber al-Basyouni Ahmed v The Prime Minister of Israel* (Decision from 30 January 2008).

IV. CONCLUSION: GLOBAL VALUES IN A LOCAL CONTEXT

Menachem Mautner published a book in 1993 called *The Decline of Formalism and the Rise of Values in Israeli Law*.[108] The turn to values has indeed been a central feature of Israeli constitutional discourse in recent decades, but the persistence of 'formal' judgments beside those involving a 'values' analysis deserves note. As is apparent from the two *Kol Ha'am* cases, both types of analysis existed in 1953, and as the cases discussed in the previous section illustrate, both types are still found today. The proportions have indeed changed, but the persistence of decisions involving no discussion of global human values, and the variant interpretations and ideological underpinnings when values do appear, deserve attention.

A values discourse, as noted, has become inherent in Israeli constitutional law and informs Supreme Court judgments. Its content, however, is subject to a judicial interpretation often appearing to reinforce neo-liberal conceptions and neglecting social concerns. Moreover, the definition of Israel as a 'Jewish and democratic state' has at times blurred the distinction between these two terms, as illustrated by the election cases discussed above. The application of constitutional analysis to the context of the occupation may have served to justify the ongoing dispossession of Palestinians, presenting these cases as if they dealt with conflicts between equal citizens or between citizens and the state in an accountable democracy. Recent attempts at constitution-making 'by consensus', both by the Israel Democracy Institute and in the Knesset, seem to have reinforced prevailing biases by suggesting constitutional formulas that will give little if any protection to social rights and reinforce the ethno-national nature of the state.[109] As long as Israel has no defined borders of territory and citizenship, and with the occupation undermining its democracy, any such attempts are obviously questionable. The Supreme Court has recently been attacked for what some consider its over-involvement in public and political matters. In these circumstances, the conflict between global values and local realities will only deepen when the Court, facing threats of limitation to its authority due to unjustified accusations of interventionism, deals with value questions. The recent wave of anti-democratic bills in the Knesset, some of which actually became law,[110] attests to the irresponsible nature of the tension between occupation and

[108] Menachem Mautner, *The Decline of Formalism and the Rise of Values in Israeli Law* (Tel Aviv, Maagali Daat, 1993) [Hebrew].

[109] For a discussion see Aeyal Gross, 'A Constitution for Israel: With Whose Consent and at Whose Expense?' (2005) 9 *Adalah's Newsletter*. www.adalah.org/newsletter/eng/jan05/ar2.pdf; Aeyal Gross, 'The Paradox of "Constitution by Consensus": A Perspective through the Lens of Equality, Sexual Orientation and Social Rights Issues' (2007) 49(2) *Hapraklit* 333 [Hebrew].

[110] See:www.acri.org.il/en/category/democracy-and-civil-liberties/anti-democratic-legislation.

democracy.[111] In another context, the mass social protest of the summer of 2011, which was also part of a global movement that challenges the hegemony of market economy, points to the way neo-liberal policies touch upon the daily life of the citizenry in ways that undermine the substantive meaning of human dignity and could be part of the background that led to the Court's embrace of social rights in *Hassan*.[112] The Court may thus be confronted with both these issues in years to come, and value discourse is likely to continue playing a major role in its reasoning.

Drawing on Benjamin Barber's suggestion that globalisation is encapsulated in the image of 'McWorld versus Jihad',[113] Uri Ram suggested that globalisation has triggered in Israel a dialectical process that simultaneously generates neo-liberalism and neo-fundamentalism. According to Ram, this McWorld-Jihad dialectic is the source of the confusing situation in which Israel is both a stable parliamentary democracy and a Western-style consumer society, but also a state of occupation and a place where separation between religion and state hardly obtains. Globalisation splits the 'Jewish-democratic' unison into a Jewish-Jihad trend he calls 'neo-Zionism' and an Israeli-McWorld trend he labels 'post-Zionism'.[114] In this analysis, the Court and constitutional values are part of 'McWorld' rather than of 'Jihad'.

When considering the interaction of global values with local realities within constitutional law, Israel may be viewed as attesting to the bifurcation but also the composition of 'McWorld' and 'Jihad'. Israeli constitutional law is the arena for a struggle over the relevance and meaning of values and over the nature of the polity. Although the Declaration of Independence ensures 'complete equality of social and political rights', constitutional law prefers political and civil rights at the expense of 'social rights', thus reflecting the McWorld of neo-liberalism. The value of freedom (even in the most restricted neo-liberal meaning of the term) promised by McWorld, clashes with the fundamentalism and ethno-nationalism Ram calls 'Jewish-Jihad' that can, to some extent, seek anchor in the constitutional definition of a 'Jewish state'. Although fundamentalism and ethno-nationalism are somewhat contained and restricted by the global values purportedly originating in 'McWorld', these global values have not challenged the basic structure of the anti-universalist tendencies epitomised in the occupation, dispossession, and discrimination of Palestinians.

[111] See Aeyal Gross, 'Democracy, Delegitimization and Denial in Israel', +972 (15 Jan 2011), 972mag.com/democracy-delegitimization-and-denial-observing-a-sea-change-in-israel; Amos Shocken, 'The Necessary Elimination of Israeli Democracy', *Haaretz* (25 Nov 2011), www.haaretz.com/opinion/the-necessary-elimination-of-israeli-democracy-1.397625.

[112] See Aeyal Gross, 'High Court Rules for Social Justice', *Haaretz* (29 Feb 2012), www.haaretz.com/print-edition/news/legal-analysis-high-court-rules-for-social-justice-1.415438.

[113] Benjamin Barber, *Jihad vs McWorld: Terrorisms Challenge to Democracy* (New York, Ballentine Books, 2001).

[114] Uri Ram, *Globalization of Israel: McWorld in Tel Aviv, Jihad in Jerusalem* (Tel Aviv, Resling, 2005).

The coexistence of 'McWorld' and 'Jihad', and of neo-liberal policies and the occupation, require further exploration. As Gadi Algazi has shown, Israeli capitalism often benefits from different aspects of the occupation.[115] Over 60 years after Israel's Declaration of Independence and after the Universal Declaration of Human Rights, the search for constitutional values that reflect and implement the commitment to freedom, justice, peace, and the equality of social and political rights to all formulated in the former, and the ideas of universality formulated in the latter, is still under way.

[115] Gadi Algazi, 'Offshore Zionism' (2006) 40 *New Left Review* 27. See also Algazi, 'The Upper-Class Fence' in Haim Ya'acobi and Shelly Cohen (eds), *Separation: The Politics of Space in Israel* (Tel Aviv, Xargol, 2007) [Hebrew].

12

Japan

YASUO HASEBE

I. CONTEXT

THE CONSTITUTION OF Japan 1946 was imposed by the Allied occupying forces after the Second World War. Immediately after the war, the Japanese government had been preparing a more conservative, lukewarm proposal to amend the then-current 1889 Constitution of the Empire of Japan, but after learning of this proposal, General Douglas MacArthur, Supreme Commander for the Allied Powers (SCAP), decided to propose his own version of a draft Constitution, prepared by his staff in the Government Section at the General Headquarters (GHQ) of the occupation, which he pressed the government to adopt as the basis of an amended Constitution. Both the contents and the underlying values of the Constitution underwent profound changes in the course of its amendment on this basis. The resulting constitutional bill of rights is quite similar to those standard in Western constitutions. Equipped with an American-style judicial review system, post-war Japan was to be reborn as a normal constitutional democracy.

II. VALUES IN THE CONSTITUTION OF JAPAN

A. Fairness/Justice

The Constitution of Japan does not expressly mention 'fairness'. The term 'justice' appears twice (in the Preamble and article 9(1)), but on both occasions it refers to the ideal basis of international order. The idea of fairness (or justice) seems to underlie more specific guarantees of rights to fair or just treatment, such as the guarantee of equality under the law in article 14 (see section IIB below).

The Constitution of Japan provides extensive protection for rights relating to criminal procedure. The officers at the GHQ who prepared the draft

Constitution insisted that these clauses were necessary in light of problematic aspects of the criminal justice system of pre-war Japan.[1]

Thus, article 31 states: '[n]o person shall be deprived of life or liberty, nor shall any other criminal penalty be imposed, except according to procedure established by law.' Apparently, this clause derives from the due process clauses of the American Constitution. Although this clause, on its face, demands only that any criminal penalties be imposed 'according to procedure established by law', most legal scholars, as well as case law, have held that the clause requires that criminal penalties be imposed in accordance not only with '*due* procedure established by law', but also with '*substantive* law the contents of which should be due'. The clause is also thought to imply the precept that there can be no offence without a law that the offence violates.[2]

In contrast to the American due process clauses, this article has not been understood to entail 'implied' or 'unenumerated' constitutional rights. Instead, the judiciary has relied upon the 'right to the pursuit of happiness', guaranteed in article 13, as the source of implied rights such as the right to privacy.[3]

Other constitutional rights relating to due process include the right to a 'speedy and public trial by an impartial tribunal' (article 37); the prohibition of torture and cruel punishment (article 36); and the prohibition of detention without informing the detainee of charges and the immediate privilege of counsel (article 34).

B. Equality

Article 14 (1) stipulates that: '[a]ll of the people are equal under the law and there shall be no discrimination in political, economic or social relations because of race, creed, sex, social status or family origin.' According to case law of the Supreme Court, differential treatment of people is constitutional as far as it has a 'reasonable' basis. To be reasonable, the treatment should have a legitimate purpose, and also the content of the differential treatment should be proportionally related to the purpose. While, under the influence of American jurisprudence, the dominant academic view argues that classifications based on 'race, creed, sex, social status or family origin' are inherently 'suspect', and strict scrutiny should be applied to them, case law has not clearly adopted such a view.

[1] Kenzo Takayanagi, Ichiro Otomo, and Hideo Tanaka, *Nihonkoku Kenpō Seitei no Katei* [*The Making of the Constitution of Japan*], Vol II Comments (Tokyo, Yūhikaku, 1972) 183.

[2] The Supreme Court held in its decision of 28 November 1962, 16 KEISHÛ 1593, that it is unconstitutional to confiscate goods without giving their owners a hearing; in its decision of 10 September 1975, 29 KEISHÛ 489, the Court held that wording used in penal laws should be clear and precise enough to be understood by ordinary citizens.

[3] The Supreme Court held in its decision of 24 December 1969, 23 KEISHÛ 1625, that the right not to be photographed arbitrarily is protected by art 13. The Court held, furthermore, in its decision of 6 March 2008, 62 MINSHÛ 665, that art 13 guarantees anyone the right of not having their personal information disseminated or divulged without good cause.

In a decision of 4 July 2008, 62 MINSHŪ 1367, the Supreme Court struck down the treatment of an illegitimate child born to a foreign mother and recognised by a Japanese father after the birth. According to the then Nationality Act, such a child could receive Japanese nationality only when his or her parents got married. Taking into account the fact that Japanese nationality is a necessary condition for a child to receive basic social services like education in Japan, as well as the fact that a child is not accountable for whether her parents get married, the Court held that the constitutionality of such a differential treatment should be 'carefully reviewed'. While the law has a legitimate purpose to accord Japanese nationality only to a child whose living is closely related to Japanese society, the Court said, marriage of parents is not a necessary condition for a child to acquire a close relationship to Japanese society.

As described below at section IIIA, the Court has tried vigilantly to guarantee the equality of voting rights in malapportionment cases.

C. Honesty/Integrity

The Constitution does not explicitly mention either 'integrity' or 'honesty' in its text. From the individualist viewpoint of the Constitution, whether a person should be honest or maintain her integrity is a question left for the person herself.

On the other hand, clauses relating to the judiciary obviously presume respect for its integrity and for the autonomy of judges. A basic ideal underlying the Freedom of Information Act 1999 is the accountability of the government to the sovereign people; the Act is understood to ensure the honesty of the government, which is implied by the obligation of accountability.

D. Community

The Constitution makes no mention of the concept of community. A movement has recently arisen calling for the Constitution to be amended so as to require respect for traditional communal values. Constitutional scholars are generally sceptical of the efficacy of such amendments. Whether one respects communal values or not is beyond the control of the law. As the law cannot incur upon one's mind-set, they argue, such revisions can have no more than symbolic effect.

E. Family

Article 24 (1) stipulates that: 'marriage shall be based only on the mutual consent of both sexes and it shall be maintained through mutual cooperation with equal rights of husband and wife as a basis.' This clause can be traced back to the draft Constitution prepared by General MacArthur's staff at GHQ,[4] who intended to raise the social status of woman and specifically to reform traditionally accepted ideas regarding the subservient relationship of wife to husband.

Article 24(2) stipulates that: 'with regard to choice of spouse, property rights, inheritance, choice of domicile, divorce and other matters pertaining to marriage and family, laws shall be enacted from the standpoint of individual dignity and the essential equality of the sexes'.[5] After the enactment of the Constitution in 1947, clauses of the Civil Code relating to family were fundamentally rewritten on the basis of these two constitutional clauses. This newly enacted part of the Code is generally called 'the New Civil Code'.

However, some scholars maintained that certain pre-modern ideas persisted in the laws pertaining to family matters. For example, according to article 900 of the Civil Code, an illegitimate child could inherit by intestate succession from his or her parent's estate only half of the portion of a legitimate child. In its decision of 5 July 1995, 49 MINSHÛ 1789, the Supreme Court upheld this clause on the grounds that this apportionment protects not only the interests of legitimate family members but to some extent those of illegitimate children as well. If desired, the majority reasoned, the parents of illegitimate children could either adopt them (making them legitimate), or specify a larger bequest to them in a will. A minority opinion supported by five justices[6] argued that this unequal treatment of illegitimate children unreasonably punishes and stigmatises them on grounds for which they are not themselves accountable.

In a recent decision of 4 September 2013, the Grand Bench completely changed its former doctrine and held the unequal treatment of illegitimate heirs under article 900 to be unconstitutional. The Court held that taking into consideration the changing social perceptions about marriage and family, recent trends of foreign laws, as well as the recent transformation of relevant legal statutes, and so on, the notion that every child should be respected as an equal individual has become firmly established in Japanese society; and this notion entails that inflicting disadvantages to an illegitimate child on the ground that her parents are not formally married to which fact she herself is totally unaccountable is without reasonable basis and unjustifiable despite the broad discretion of the legislature. The Court concluded that the relevant clause had become unconstitutional at the latest in July 2001, when the disputed inheritance commenced.

[4] Takayanagi et al, above n 1, 169–70.

[5] Apparently this text does not assume the existence of same-sex marriages, though this does not necessarily mean that the legalisation of same-sex marriage would be unconstitutional under the current Constitution.

[6] The Grand Bench of the Supreme Court is composed of 15 justices.

F. Freedom/Liberty/Independence

The guarantee of fundamental rights, along with popular sovereignty and pacifism, is a fundamental pillar of the Constitution of Japan.[7] The most widely recognised individual freedoms are all enumerated in the Constitution, including freedom of conscience (article 19), freedom of religion (article 20), freedom of expression (article 21), freedom of occupation (article 22), and the right to property (article 29). These rights typically protect individuals from the interference of public authorities. Since the Constitution endows inland corporations with the same rights as individuals, as far as the nature of the rights allows,[8] they also enjoy these rights. For example, newspapers can assert their freedom of expression, and religious associations can assert their freedom of religion.

Both the dominant academic view and case law recognise that these constitutional rights have so-called horizontal effects. For example, in the well-known *Nissan Motors* case, the Supreme Court of Japan voided an employment regulation of a major corporation that stipulated different retirement ages for male and female employees.[9] When the privacy of an individual is infringed by a media company, to offer another example, the constitutional right to privacy is understood to apply indirectly through the tort clause in the Civil Code. The Court has seen to it that through its horizontal-effects control the dignity and autonomy of each citizen is duly protected.

As indicated above in section IIA, article 13 is regarded as the fall-back clause guaranteeing 'implied' constitutional freedoms, including privacy.[10]

G. Responsibility/Accountability

The Constitution of Japan makes three references to 'responsibility' in its text. Two of these references concern the political responsibilities of the Cabinet. As the Constitution establishes a parliamentary system, the Cabinet is politically accountable to the Diet, and ultimately to the sovereign people of Japan. The transition from the traditional imperial sovereignty

[7] According to the dominant academic view, these three principles are immune from constitutional revision.

[8] The Supreme Court held in its decision of 24 June 1970, 24 MINSHÛ 625, that inland corporations are endowed with the freedom to pursue political activities like contributing to political parties. *Cf* Yasuo Hasebe, 'Rights of Corporations, Rights of Individuals: Judicial Precedents' in Yoichi Higuchi (ed), *Five Decades of Constitutionalism in Japanese Society* (Tokyo, University of Tokyo Press, 2001).

[9] The Supreme Court decision of 24 March 1981, 35 MINSHÛ 300.

[10] Some controversy has surrounded the issue of whether the right to pursue happiness stipulated in art 13 implies licence to do anything one likes to do. Most constitutional scholars disagree with this counter-intuitive conclusion.

to popular sovereignty, confirmed and promulgated in the Constitution of Japan 1946, was the product of the 'regime change' brought about by Japan's surrender to the Allied Powers in 1945.[11] The Constitution makes it clear that the Emperor has forfeited all political authority, and that his every juridical act, such as the proclamation of legislation, must conform strictly to the proposals of the Cabinet (article 3). The position of the Emperor as symbol of the state derives 'from the will of the people with whom resides sovereign power' (article 1).[12] The principle of popular sovereignty is one of the three pillars of the Constitution, as mentioned above in section IIB.

The Constitution is generally understood as adopting not direct but rather representative democracy. The preamble to the Constitution states that the Japanese people act through their 'duly elected representatives in the National Diet', and article 41 provides that 'the Diet shall be the sole law-making organ of the State'. In other words, the people cannot act through referendum in everyday politics; they can participate directly only in the case of constitutional amendments (article 96).

The Supreme Court has used the idea of political responsibility to avoid making decisions in highly political cases on the grounds that the judiciary is not accountable to the people. Thus, the Court avoided dealing with the constitutionality of the Japan-US security treaty,[13] as well as the constitutionality of the dissolution of the Lower House.[14]

The third reference to responsibility in the Constitution occurs in article 12, which specifies the responsibility of the Japanese people to utilise the freedoms and rights guaranteed to them by the Constitution 'for the public welfare'. The meaning of this clause is ambiguous, and constitutional scholars generally view it as merely a political statement, that is, as having no legal significance.

The Constitution furthermore mentions that the people have three obligations. First, the people 'shall be liable to taxation as provided by law' (article 30); secondly, all 'people shall have the right and the obligation to

[11] It is generally accepted that a kind of revolution from the legal point of view occurred when the Japanese government agreed to the Potsdam declaration, which prescribed the conditions of Japan's surrender in August 1945. See my 'The August Revolution Thesis and the Making of the Constitution of Japan' (1997) Beiheft 17 *Rechtstheorie* 335–42.

[12] Some scholars have argued that since the Constitution provides that the Emperor is a symbol of the state, he should be regarded so (eg, Shiro Kiyomiya, *Kenpō I* [*Constitutional Law I*], 3rd edn (Tokyo, Yūhikaku, 1979) 155). However, whether or not any person is a symbol depends on the socio-psychological fact that people do or do not actually regard that person as a symbol; the law cannot direct anyone's thought. At most, the law can command that the Emperor be treated as if he were a symbol of the state. Whether the Emperor actually symbolises the state depends upon 'the will of the people with whom resides sovereign power'. Art 1 should not be viewed as a prescription. Rather, it should be understood to describe how things are concerning the Emperor's status as a symbol of the state.

[13] The Supreme Court decision of 16 December 1959, 13 KEISHÛ 3225.

[14] The Supreme Court decision of 8 June 1960, 14 MINSHÛ 1206.

work' (article 27); and third, all 'people shall be obligated to have all boys and girls under their protection receive ordinary education as provided by law' (article 26 (2)).[15]

However, scholars find little juridical significance in these clauses. Article 30 merely states that people should pay taxes in accordance with the law, and thus might be understood as a protection against taxation without a legal basis, rather than as an obligation to pay taxes; in any case, generally speaking, people have various reasons to obey laws, but there is no particularly good reason why people should above all respect tax laws. The obligation to work does not imply that the government can coerce people to work, which would amount to an infringement of the prohibition against 'involuntary servitude' in article 18. Finally, the obligation to provide children with an education is less a duty of the people to the government, than of parents to their children; in this case too, the obligation (of parents) is imposed only by means of law.

H. Compassion/Caring

The Constitution does not explicitly refer to compassion or caring. However, article 25(1) guarantees 'the right to maintain the minimum standards of [a] wholesome and cultured life'. The Supreme Court has held that the idea of 'minimum standards of [a] wholesome and cultured life' does not indicate any specific obligation of the government to provide welfare benefits, and that the legislature has wide discretion in the design of welfare benefit programmes.[16]

Under article 25(2), the state is obliged to 'use its endeavours for the promotion and extension of social welfare and security, and of public health'. The obligation of the government to provide welfare benefits is regarded as subsidiary to the obligation of family members to support one another.[17]

I. Respect/Tolerance

Article 13 of the Constitution, in its first sentence, states that: 'all of the people shall be respected as individuals'. This clause states the fundamental principle that provides the justification for all of the freedoms and rights guaranteed by the Constitution. The precept that every person should be

[15] According to the *Gakkō Kyōiku Hō* (School Education Act), school attendance is required for nine years, until age 15.

[16] The Supreme Court decision of 7 July 1982, 36 MINSHŪ 1235.

[17] The *Seikatsu Hogo Hō* (Welfare Benefit Act), art 4.

treated as equal (article 14) is thought to derive directly from this principle.[18] Both judicial precedent and legal scholarship supports the view that the right to autonomy also derives from article 13.[19]

However, as mentioned above in section IIF, case law has established that corporations also enjoy constitutional freedoms and rights as far as their natures allow it. Since corporations cannot be respected as individuals, a different justification is required for their enjoyment of constitutional rights. Some scholars argue that corporations enjoy constitutional rights because, and to the extent that, such enjoyment furthers the public welfare of society as a whole. For example, when media companies enjoy freedom of speech, people receive varied and abundant information; this state of affairs is conducive to a well-functioning democratic process and fosters a spirit of tolerance among the people. One discerns in this argument the clear resonance of Ronald Dworkin's argument on policy for a free press.[20]

J. Life

Article 13, in its second sentence, states that the 'right to life ... shall, to the extent that it does not interfere with the public welfare, be the supreme consideration in legislation and in other governmental affairs'. As the qualification concerning the public welfare indicates, this right is not considered absolute. Article 31 provides that a person may be deprived of life as a criminal penalty. The Supreme Court has held that capital punishment is not a 'cruel punishment' prohibited by article 36, if it is executed by hanging.[21]

One judicial precedent[22] indicates that the right to autonomy deriving from article 13 may override the obligation to respect life. The plaintiff, a Jehovah's Witness suffering from liver cancer, asked her doctor not to make any blood transfusions during her operation. Although the doctor accepted the patient's request, he actually made a blood transfusion when he thought it absolutely necessary to save the patient's life. The Tokyo High Court held

[18] Art 13 has been mentioned rarely in relation to the value of respect for, and tolerance of, minority groups. One district court decision held that the first sentence of art 13 required the government to respect traditional cultures of aboriginal *Ainus*, because such cultures were essential for them to lead autonomous lives (Sapporo district court decision of 27 March 1997, 1598 HANREI JIHÔ 33). The court said that the Minister of Construction had paid insufficient respect to these cultures when approving a plan to construct a dam, which submerged a religious site sacred for *Ainus* under water. Apparently this holding is influenced by communitarian liberalism.

[19] See section IIJ below.

[20] See Ronald Dworkin, *A Matter of Principle* (Cambridge MA and London, Harvard University Press, 1985) Ch 19.

[21] The Supreme Court decision of 12 March 1948, 2 KEISHÛ 191.

[22] The Tokyo High Court decision of 9 October 1998, 1629 HANREI JIHÔ 34.

that the doctor had infringed the patient's religious autonomy, and awarded her consolatory compensation. The Supreme Court rejected the defendant's appeal, confirming that the plaintiff's right to autonomy must be respected under tort law.[23] This line of reasoning seems to imply that if the doctor had not made a blood transfusion and the patient had died, the doctor would not have been legally responsible for her death. Moreover, it also seems to imply that what must be respected is not life itself, or the state of being alive, but the value of autonomous life, which may be violated when others rewrite an agent's life-plan.

The legality of abortion is not as controversial an issue in Japan as in some Western countries. According to article 14 of the *Botai Hogo Hō* (Maternity Protection Act), officially designated doctors may artificially terminate pregnancy when continuing pregnancy is 'unusually harmful to the mother for physical or *economical* reasons' (emphasis added).

K. Security

Article 18 of the Constitution stipulates that: '[n]o person shall be held in bondage of any kind. Involuntary servitude, except as punishment for crime, is prohibited'. This article is regarded to have a direct horizontal effect. Judicial courts have the power to issue habeas corpus to ensure a speedy relief from all unlawful imprisonment. As to the protection for rights relating to criminal procedure, see section IIA above.

The Constitution itself does not have any provision granting the government special power in the case of emergency. According to the so-called 'National Emergency' legislation, in the case of emergency, constitutional rights are to be restricted, to accord the Self-Defence Forces more scope of action.

As to the security of the country, see sections IIP and IIIB below.

L. Learning/Education

Article 26(1) of the Constitution states that: 'all people shall have the right to receive an equal education correspondent to their ability, as provided by law'. As indicated above in note 15, every child is to be given an equal basic education for nine years. There has been controversy about the extent of the authority of the government to determine the content of basic education. Some scholars have argued that this should be determined by parents as well

[23] The Supreme Court decision of 29 February 2000, 54 MINSHÛ 582.

as the teachers, who have fiduciary duties to fulfil the parents' obligation to educate their children, and that the role of the government is to be limited to providing the material conditions for education, such as school facilities. The Supreme Court has held that due to the interest of society in the proper development of children, as well as the interests of children themselves, not only parents and teachers but also the government are obliged to ensure that children receive a sufficient education; and moreover that the government must assure that an equal education is universally provided to children throughout the country.[24] The Court also noted that no one may dictate the contents of basic education such that they inhibit the development of free and autonomous individuals.

Article 26(2) of the Constitution states that 'compulsory education shall be free'. The Supreme Court has long held that this clause means that parents do not have to pay any education fees for the nine years of basic education.[25] To date, school textbooks for basic education at primary and junior high schools have also been provided free of charge.

M. Dignity

As described in section IIE, article 24 states: 'matters pertaining to marriage and the family, laws shall be enacted from the standpoint of individual dignity and the essential equality of the sexes'. This is the sole occasion the Constitution explicitly refers to dignity. According to the dominant academic view, the first sentence of article 13, which states '[a]ll of the people shall be respected as individuals' presupposes the 'dignity of individual', though what this actually means is ambiguous.

N. Environment

The Constitution makes no explicit reference to environment. Though many scholars argue that article 13, which protects the right to 'the pursuit of happiness', implies that people are equipped with the right to live in a comfortable environment, it is uncertain whether we can deduce from this argument any enforceable legal right against the state. As to the proposal to amend the Constitution to include the right to a comfortable environment, most constitutional scholars are sceptical. The stipulation of an abstract right to an environment is of no use without specifying the legal mechanism. And when such a legal mechanism already exists, we can dispense with the stipulation of abstract principles.

[24] The Supreme Court decision of 21 May 1976, 30 MINSHÛ 615.
[25] The Supreme Court decision of 26 February 1964, 18 MINSHÛ 343.

O. Participation/Inclusion

As to political participation, article 15 of the Constitution guarantees the Japanese people 'the inalienable right to choose their public officials and to dismiss them'. The Supreme Court has been vigilant to maintain fair democratic process, as described in section IIIA below.

The Court has been also progressive in promoting the gender equality in the social context, having recourse to the horizontal effects of constitutional rights, in particular the right of equal protection. As described in section IIF above, in the *Nissan Motors* case of 24 March 1981, the Supreme Court of Japan held void an employment regulation of a big corporation stipulating different retirement ages for male and female employees. The Court made recourse to the so-called 'indirect application of the Constitution', a technique to realise the horizontal effects of the Constitution. In *Nissan Motors* the Supreme Court held that the working regulation was in conflict with the 'public order' clause of the Civil Code interpreted in accordance with the spirit of the equal protection clause of the Constitution. The public order clause of the Civil Code, its article 90, stipulates that any juristic act which is against public order or good morals is null and void. The 'indirect application of the Constitution' strategy has been widely adopted in other similar cases as well.

P. Peace

Pacifism, along with the guarantee of fundamental rights and the principle of popular sovereignty, is the third pillar of the Constitution of Japan. Its enshrinement as a central constitutional principle originated in Douglas MacArthur's instructions to the staff in the Government Section at General Headquarters as they began to prepare the draft Constitution.[26] His memorandum specified several conditions that he insisted be included in the document. The memorandum states:

> War as a sovereign right of the nation is abolished; Japan renounces it as an instrumentality for settling its disputes and even for preserving its own security; it relies upon the higher ideals which are now stirring the world for its defence and its protection.
>
> No Japanese Army, Navy or Air Force will ever be authorised and no rights of belligerency will be conferred upon any Japanese force.

The staff at the Government Section regarded this instruction as overly idealistic. They therefore, first, deleted the words 'and even for preserving its own security' to afford the possibility of defensive warfare. They furthermore tried to graft in the two clauses in the Preamble of the draft Constitution in

[26] Takayanagi et al, above n 1, 133–36.

order to make salient their non-juridical, political character;[27] however, at General MacArthur's insistence, the clauses were included in the draft as an article, and eventually became article 9 of the Constitution.

During deliberations in the Lower House of the Diet, the following phrase was added at the beginning of the second of the two clauses:

> In order to accomplish the aim of the preceding paragraph

Since the first clause implies that Japan may defend its own security, this amendment can be understood as meaning that military forces may be maintained for defensive purposes. The staff at GHQ recognised this implication.[28] The occupying forces therefore demanded an amendment specifying that members of the Cabinet must be 'civilians'. This amendment eventually became article 66(2).

Nonetheless, a layman reading article 9 understands it as clearly prohibiting the government from maintaining any military forces. There has long been a glaring gap between the layman's understanding of article 9 as imposing absolute pacifism and the interpretation of the government that an 'indispensable minimal force' may be maintained to defend the country.[29] Although Japan has the lowest level of military expenditure as a percentage of GDP (around 1 per cent) among the major powers, its military budget is nevertheless one of the largest in the world (around $46 billion in 2012).

No authoritative judicial precedent has been established on this issue. One of the main arguments of the recent movement to amend the Constitution to close this gap is that such an estrangement between the text of article 9 and the actions of the government undermines respect for the law. However, there is also strong support for the contrary view that article 9 in its current form functions as an effective bar on the possibility of Japan undertaking adventurous military conflicts.[30]

III. CONGRUENCE

A. Judicial Review: Gap Between Text and Law

The Constitution does not detail the judicial review process. To address the question of how judicial review is to be exercised, a number of Japanese constitutional scholars have introduced American doctrines concerning

[27] ibid.

[28] ibid, 140.

[29] In the view of the government, factors such as Japan's international relations and the state of military technology must be taken into consideration to determine what constitutes 'indispensable minimal forces'.

[30] As to UN peacekeeping operations by the Self-Defence Forces, see my 'War Powers' in Michel Rosenfeld and András Sajó (eds), *The Oxford Handbook of Comparative Constitutional Law* (Oxford, Oxford University Press, 2012) 478–79.

the protection of individual rights, particularly those bearing on tests of constitutionality.[31] In particular, many have introduced the doctrine set forth in the famous footnote 4 to *United States v Carolene Products Co*,[32] which established that the courts must use their review powers to sustain democratic political processes. According to this doctrine, the courts must protect freedom of speech vigilantly, using stricter standards of review than the lenient 'rational basis' test used to review governmental acts restricting economic liberties. According to this doctrine, the constitutional review powers of the judiciary are justified as supportive of the principles of democracy. The purpose of judicial review is not to override democratic decisions taken by the political branches, but to sustain and reinforce the democratic process itself. Thus, freedom of speech is accorded a 'preferred position' not because it is intrinsically more valuable, but because it is an indispensable component of fair democratic processes.[33]

In several important decisions, the Supreme Court has affirmed its responsibility in reviewing the constitutionality of governmental acts to exercise vigilance in maintaining democratic political processes.[34] The rulings of the Court on the electoral system clearly reflect this stance. In 1998, the Diet amended the *Kōshoku Senkyo Hō* (Public Offices Election Act) to make possible the participation of Japanese nationals living overseas in elections for both Houses of the Diet. However, the Act stipulated in article 8 of its Supplementary Provision that voters living abroad could vote only for members elected by proportional representation.

In its ruling of 14 September 2005, 59 MINSHÛ 2087, the Supreme Court held that this limitation of access to the ballot was unconstitutional. According to the Court, restrictions on the right to vote are not allowed without compelling reason for them. The Court further stipulated that the reason for a restriction may be characterised as compelling only when the fair execution of elections becomes extremely difficult without the restriction. While the government asserted that it could not provide overseas voters with the information necessary for them to participate effectively in elections in single-member constituencies of the Lower House and prefectural

[31] *Cf* Hidenori Tomatsu, 'Judicial Review in Japan: An Overview of Efforts to Introduce U.S. Theories' in *Five Decades of Constitutionalism in Japanese Society*, above n 8, 251–92.

[32] *United States v Carolene Products Co* 304 US 144 (1938).

[33] A few scholars have argued that freedom of speech is intrinsically more valuable than economic freedom, since the former is more essential to individual autonomy, which is the most fundamental value underlying the Constitution. See, for example, Koji Sato, 'Rikkenshugi to iwayuru niju-no-kijun-ron' ['Constitutionalism and the so-called "double standard doctrine"'], in *Gendai Rikkenshugi no Tenkai* [*The Development of Modern Constitutionalism*] (Tokyo, Yūhikaku, 1993) 3–35.

[34] In its decision of 11 June 1986, 40 MINSHÛ 872, the Supreme Court held that interlocutory injunctions against disseminating information about electoral candidates are to be granted only in exceptional circumstances, where the contents are clearly false and cause unrecoverable damage to claimants.

constituencies of the Upper House, the Court found this assertion to be implausible in this global information society. The Court also held that the Diet was negligent in failing to make it possible for Japanese citizens living abroad to participate in national elections until 1998, and that this denial of access to the ballot constituted a 'gross error' that required the state to compensate the disenfranchised overseas citizens.

The orientation of the Court toward vigilantly protecting the fairness of democratic processes is also reflected in its rulings in malapportionment cases. For example, the Supreme Court in 1976 heard a case in which the weighting of some votes in an election for the Lower House was as much as five times greater than others; that is, in the least populated district, an MP represented one-fifth the number of voters as an MP in the most populated one. The Supreme Court held that the Constitution requires that each vote be accorded equal value, and that while the Diet may take into account factors such as administrative boundaries, demographics, convenience for traffic, and geographical features in drawing up constituencies, so gross a difference in weighting as five to one was unconstitutional, since there was no conceivable mitigating rationale for it.[35]

With regard to the role of judicial review in protecting freedoms of speech, conscience, and religion, however, the predominant academic view is that the Court has not been sufficiently activist in upholding its commitment to vigilance. Several explanations might be offered for the apparent reluctance of the Court to use its review powers more effectively; one is that the constitutionality of most laws enacted by the Diet is meticulously scrutinised in advance by the Cabinet Legislation Bureau, which is modelled on the French *Conseil d'Etat*.[36]

B. Constitutional Pacifism: Gap Between Value and Reality

The most glaring incongruity between the values enshrined in the Constitution and those in the actual constitution of the state appears to be evident in the issue of Japan's constitutional pacifism, as discussed above in section IIP. Deriving from MacArthur's draft Constitution and the deliberations of the Diet, the text of article 9 provides for a pacifist state as follows:

> Aspiring sincerely to an international peace based on justice and order, the Japanese people forever renounce war as a sovereign right of the nation and the threat or use of forces as a means of settling international disputes.

[35] The Supreme Court decision of 14 April 1976, 30 MINSHÛ 223.

[36] Mutsuo Nakamura and Teruki Tsunemoto, 'The Legislative Process: Outline and Actors' in *Five Decades of Constitutionalism*, above n 8, 195, 199, and 200. For other possible explanations, see my 'Constitutional Borrowing and Political Theory' (2003) 1 *International Journal of Constitutional Law* 236–40.

> In order to accomplish the aim of the preceding paragraph, land, sea, and air forces, as well as other war potential, will never be maintained. The right of belligerency of the state will not be recognised.

The current position of the Japanese government on this article is that, despite its apparently pacifist message, it recognises a national right of self-defence even as it prohibits the initiation of violence to settle international disputes. This position is sometimes characterised as 'modest pacifism'.[37] Given the detrimental effects of militarism on both international relations and civil society in pre-war and war era Japan, the position of the government can be understood as a prudent, constitution-based pre-commitment to minimising the potential of the state for militarism; as such, this position is a prerequisite for the development of a healthy liberal democracy and peaceful, positive relationships with neighbouring countries.

However, most constitutional scholars in Japan take a contrasting, pure-pacifist view of article 9. According to this dominant view, the text of the article must be read literally; the article prohibits the government from maintaining any military forces whatsoever. Most people view the protection of their lives and property against the possibility of foreign aggression as an essential function of government, and as it is highly doubtful that a national territory can be defended from foreign aggression without the presence of an armed force, the only reasonable understanding of the pure-pacifist view of article 9 is that the article represents a kind of moral imperative, specifically, an assertion that renouncing military force is the only good and virtuous way to live. From this perspective, the moral imperative of pure pacifism—however perilous it may be—comprises a necessary demonstration of penitence for crimes committed by the Japanese against other Asian peoples during the Second World War.

In the New Testament, Jesus Christ teaches a similar sort of pure pacifism, saying that if an evil man strikes you on the right cheek, you should turn the other cheek to him (Matthew 5:39). He does not mean to suggest that if you turn the other cheek, the evil man will stop hitting you; rather, you should turn the other cheek whether he stops hitting you or not, because to do so is virtuous.

Although this teaching may be a praiseworthy guide for personal behaviour, to impose such a comprehensive conception of goodness upon an entire society is contrary to constitutionalism in a fundamental sense. That is, constitutionalism presupposes that individuals within a society hold diverse, even mutually incommensurable conceptions of the good; different religious

[37] See my *Kenpō to Heiwa o Toinaosu* [*Rethinking Constitutionalism and Pacifism*] (Tokyo, Chikuma-Shobō, 2004). According to the Japanese government's established view, only the right of individual self-defence was admitted under art 9. The government was prohibited from not only exercising its right of collective self-defence but also participating in military measures taken in accordance to art 42 of the UN charter. The Abe administration changed this official stance in July 2014, and stated that the right of collective self-defence can be exercised when Japanese people's rights to life, liberty, and pursuit of happiness are jeopardised because of military attacks against foreign countries, which are in close relationship with Japan.

doctrines, each purporting to teach the 'truth', exemplify such comprehensive conceptions.

Although the members of a society may embrace a plurality of values, however, constitutionalism supposes them nonetheless to want to participate in the wider life of society, sharing in its benefits and burdens on fair terms.[38] To fulfil the potential of constitutionalism to provide for such participation, a clear division must be drawn between people's lives in the private and public spheres. In the private sphere, an individual is free to live in accordance with his or her own comprehensive conception of the good. On the other hand, the individual must wear the mantle of equal citizenship in the public sphere, particularly in participating in public deliberation concerning the interests of society as a whole. In such public deliberation, the individual must reason independently of his or her private conception of goodness, for collisions between incommensurable values have the potential to destroy the fragile, artificial public sphere. In the absence of public reasoning that is independent of privately held values, ideological warfare will break out, and society will fragment into camps of friends and foes. The imposition of pure pacifism on an entire society would constitute an exercise in such a failure of public reasoning.

The pure-pacifist view that predominates among constitutional scholars in Japan is thus disturbing, not least because it reveals that most Japanese constitutional scholar fail to recognise the serious tension between this viewpoint and constitutionalism itself.[39]

IV. CONCLUSION

Any genuinely universal value should be compatible with the immensely wide variety of ways of life. In other words, values specific to a particular worldview or value-system that is indicative of one 'good way of life' cannot be universally accepted. The Japanese experience of constitutional law seems to corroborate this mundane truth.

It is difficult to say that the observation so far indicates any prioritisation of specific values in Japan. Japanese case law and academic views have been much influenced by American constitutional law, but the Supreme Court has seen to it that through its horizontal-effects control the dignity and autonomy of each citizen is duly protected.[40] While the Court confirms the 'preferred

[38] See, for example, John Rawls, *Political Liberalism* (New York, Columbia University Press, 1993).

[39] For more on the incompatibility of pure-pacifism and constitutionalism, see my 'Constitutional Borrowing and Political Theory', above n 36, 240–43, from which this argument is adapted.

[40] See section IIF above.

position' of freedom of speech, it has also taken care of the protection of economic freedoms.[41] Although the value for respect for minority groups is not mentioned in the text of the Constitution, such a value is still taken into consideration in solving concrete issues.[42] Despite article 9's apparent declaration of pure pacifism, the government has maintained that to maintain the nation's Self-Defence Forces is within its constitutional power.[43] Rather, given the actual situation of value pluralism, both the Court and the political branch have tried to strike a delicate balances between various conflicting values. While some scholars think that the Supreme Court has been too deferential to the political branch in using (or not using) its power of constitutional review,[44] I find it difficult to perceive any clear tendency in its striking balances in deciding concrete cases.

One prominent former justice says that the primary task of the Court is not wielding power of constitutional review or constructing coherent academic doctrines, but giving an appropriate solution to each case at hand. It strikes down a statute only when it is necessary to give justice to the case.[45] In the end we may say that Japan is a normal constitutional democracy without any conspicuous characteristic.

[41] The Supreme Court decision of 22 November 1972, 26 KEISHÛ 586, upheld a regulation prohibiting setting up a new marketplace for small retailers was as rationally related to its purpose of protecting retailers from excessive competition; The Supreme Court held in its decision of 30 April 1975, 29 MINSHÛ 572 that a regulation restricting entry to the pharmacy market was unnecessarily stringent in view of its purpose of protecting public health. See my 'The Supreme Court of Japan: Its adjudication on electoral systems and economic freedoms' (2007) 5 *International Journal of Constitutional Law* 305–07.

[42] See, for example n 18.

[43] See section IIIB above.

[44] *Cf* my 'The Supreme Court of Japan', n 41 above, 297–300.

[45] Tokiyasu Fujita, 'The Supreme Court of Japan: Commentary on the Recent Work of Scholars in the United States' 88 *Washington University Law Review* 1508, 1521–22.

13

Values in the South African Constitution

CATHERINE ALBERTYN

I. INTRODUCTION

FOR CENTURIES, SOUTH Africa was subject to colonial and apartheid rule in which black people were oppressed and denigrated on the basis of race. Successive white parliaments enacted laws that entrenched inequality and exclusion, with little possibility of judicial review. A lengthy national liberation struggle ended when the white National Party government sat down with the African National Congress and other stakeholders to negotiate a transition to 'majority' power in the early 1990s. At that stage, the legacy of apartheid was huge:

> In 1996 when the Constitutional Assembly adopted a Constitution for South Africa we were one of the most unequal societies in the world. We had recently emerged, almost miraculously, from a repressive and undemocratic legal order, and had embraced democracy. The past hung over us and profoundly affected the environment in which we were living. The great majority of our people had been the victims of a vicious system of racial discrimination and repression which had affected them deeply in almost all aspects of their lives. This was seen most obviously in the disparities of wealth and skills between those who had benefited from colonial rule and apartheid and those who had not. In the contrast between those with land, and the millions of landless people; between those with homes and the millions without access to adequate housing; between those living in comfort and the millions without access to adequate health facilities, clean water and electricity, between those with secure occupations and the millions who were unemployed or had limited employment opportunities.[1]

The new 'interim' Constitution constituted a political and legal revolution.[2] It established universal suffrage in a multi-party democracy, the structures

[1] Arthur Chaskalson, 'Equality as a Founding Value of the South African Constitution' Oliver Schreiner lecture, University of the Witwatersrand, February 2001.
[2] Constitution of the Republic of South Africa Act, 108 of 1993.

of a democratic state and a justiciable Bill of Rights. The Constitution was declared supreme, and henceforth all laws and state conduct had to comply with the rights and values of that Constitution. A new Constitutional Court was established and given final authority over the Constitution, including the power to strike down policies and laws found to be unconstitutional. The 'final' Constitution, written by the new Parliament sitting as a Constitutional Assembly, was passed in 1996.[3] One of its more innovative features was the introduction of justiciable social and economic rights.

A notable feature of the South African Constitution is the extent to which it is recognised as a transformative document, a 'bridge' from an unjust past to a democratic future.[4] In the words of the Constitutional Court, a 'commitment ... to transform our society ... lies at the heart of the new constitutional order':[5]

> We live in a society in which there are great disparities of wealth. Millions of people are living in deplorable conditions and in great poverty ... These conditions already existed when the Constitution was adopted and a commitment to address them, and to transform our society into one in which there will be human dignity, freedom and equality, lies at the heart of our new constitutional order.[6]

The idea of 'transformation' is an important theme in South Africa's democratic project. At the heart of this is the nature of its democracy and new society based on 'dignity, equality and freedom'. This is a contested vision, animated by different readings of the text, and different understandings of the trajectory of change in South Africa. Reading and interpreting the text, therefore, can never be a narrowly formalist enterprise. On the contrary, it requires legal, political and philosophical concerns to be made visible and interrogated. In doing so, judges (and all participants in the democratic debate of meaning) need to give substance to the values within the Constitution that form the basis of its vision and provide meaning to the text.

[3] Constitution of the Republic of South Africa Act, 1996.

[4] The interim Constitution is explicit about this constitutional role: see the post-amble 'National Unity and Reconciliation'.

[5] *Soobramoney v Minister of Health* 1998 (1) SA 765 (CC), 1997 (12) BCLR 1696 (CC) [8]; *Minister of Finance v Van Heerden* 2004 (6) SA 121 (CC), 2004 (11) BCLR 1125 (CC) [22]. See also Arthur Chaskalson, 'The Third Bram Fischer Lecture: Human Dignity as a Foundational Value of Our Constitutional Order' (2000) 16 *South African Journal on Human Rights* 193, 199; Pius Langa, 'Transformative Constitutionalism' (2006) 17 *Stellenbosch Law Review* 351, 351.

[6] *Soobramoney v Minister of Health* 1998 (1) SA 765 (CC), 1997 (12) BCLR 1696 (CC) [8] (whether the right of access to healthcare includes the right to be given kidney dialysis treatment against the rules of the scheme).

II. VALUES

A. Values in the South African Constitution

Constitutional values play a central role in South Africa's democracy. Marking the transition from an authoritarian, repressive and racist past to a democratic future, the South African Constitution[7] establishes South Africa as

> one, sovereign, democratic state founded, inter alia, on the … values [of]:
>
> (a) Human dignity, the achievement of equality and the advancement of human rights and freedoms.
> (b) Non-racialism and non-sexism.
> (c) Supremacy of the Constitution and the rule of law.
> (d) Universal adult suffrage, a national common voters roll, regular elections and a multi-party system of democratic government, to ensure accountability, responsiveness and openness.[8]

Section 1 suggests that values are constitutive of democracy in South Africa, and that they are present within the Constitution at differing levels of abstraction. While interpretations of dignity, equality and freedom can differ quite fundamentally across different political and philosophical viewpoints, and require considerable interpretative work, this is less true of ideas of constitutional supremacy and the rule of law. Accountability, openness and responsiveness are flexible concepts, but are given more certain content in section 1 and the Constitution as whole. Section 1 is also not the only source of values. Further values are explicit and implicit within the text, and may be identified and developed through judicial interpretation. Values may also originate outside the Constitution in common or customary law, although they must be consistent with the Constitution in order to be sustained.[9]

The new constitutional dispensation places values at the centre of the post-apartheid democratic project in a number of important and interrelated ways. First, values form the basis of constructing the constitutional vision of a new society, representing the goals or aspirations of a future democratic society. It is by engaging and debating the meaning of these values that South Africans participate in a 'democratic dialogue' over the shape and form of their society and state.[10] Here values are linked to the idea of a transformative constitution, constituting a process or journey from an

[7] All subsequent reference are to the 'final' Constitution: the Constitution of the Republic of South Africa, 1996.

[8] Section 1. See also Preamble.

[9] Section 39(3). *Alexkor Ltd v Richtersveld Community* 2004 (5) SA 460 (CC), 2003 (12) BCLR 1301 (CC) [53] (recognising that a customary or indigenous right to ownership founded a claim under the Restitution Act).

[10] Several scholars have pointed to this. See for example, Dennis Davis, *Democracy and Deliberation* (Cape Town, Juta and Co, 1999); Sandra Liebenberg, *Socio-economic Rights. Adjudication under a Transformative Constitution* (Cape Town, Juta and Co, 2010); Stu

authoritarian past to a more just future.[11] It is in the contestation over the meaning of values in relation to the nature and pace of political, social and economic change that the democratic project is given substance.

Second, values have significant legal purchase. They 'inform and give substance to all the provisions of the Constitution',[12] but are particularly important with respect to the Bill of Rights. Section 7(1) confirms that the Bill of Rights is to be applied and interpreted to give effect to the 'democratic values of human dignity, equality and freedom'. Section 39(2) expresses this slightly differently: 'when interpreting the Bill of Rights, a court ... must promote the values that underlie an open and democratic society based on human dignity, equality and freedom'. This widens the ambit of possible values to be considered and debated in interpreting rights.

Third, values also play a central role in justifying the limitation of rights.[13] Here again, dignity, equality and freedom are determinative: section 36 allows rights to be limited only 'to the extent that the limitation is reasonable and justifiable in an open and democratic society based on human dignity, equality and freedom'.

Finally, constitutional values inform the interpretation and development of all law.[14] Hence the Constitutional Court has described the Constitution as embodying an 'objective normative value system' that guides the development of the law,[15] and the actions of the state as a whole.[16] All courts are expected to take account of values in interpreting and applying all law: common, customary and statutory.

B. Value Hierarchies?

The values of equality, dignity and freedom enjoy particular prominence in the South African Constitution. The Court has described them as 'conjoined,

Woolman and Henk Botha, 'Limitations: Shared constitutional interpretation, an appropriate normative framework and hard choices' in S Woolman et al, *Constitutional Conversations* (Pretoria, Pretoria University Law Press, 2008) 149.

[11] The idea of transformative constitutionalism follows the influential work of Karl Klare, 'Legal Culture and Transformative Constitutionalism' (1998) 12 *South African Journal on Human Rights* 146.

[12] *Minister of Home Affairs v NICRO* (2004) 2005 (3) SA 280 (CC), 2004 (5) BCLR 445 (CC) [21].

[13] Sections 7(3) and 36 of the Constitution.

[14] Section 39(1) of the Constitution requires the courts to '[p]romote the values that underlie an open and democratic society based on human dignity, equality and freedom' when interpreting the Bill of Rights, while s 39(2) requires courts, tribunals and other forums to 'promote the spirit, purport and objects of the Bill of Rights' in 'interpreting any legislation, and ... developing the common law or customary law'.

[15] *Carmichele v Minister of Safety and Security* 2001 (4) SA 938 (CC), 2001 (10) BCLR 995 (CC) [54], referring to the development of the common law.

[16] ibid [54] (quoting the German Constitutional Court, Ackerman J referred to this value system as 'a guiding principle and stimulus for the legislature, executive and judiciary').

reciprocal and covalent values' that are foundational to this country.[17] Their role in the interpretation of rights, the limitations analysis and in the development of the legal system as a whole means that '[t]he starting and end point of analysis must be to affirm the democratic values of dignity, equality and freedom'.[18] This trio of values also gives rise to a range of derivative values that are present in the Constitution directly or through judicial interpretation,[19] but whose meaning and existence depends upon the prior value of dignity, equality or freedom. A fourth, and interrelated, foundational value might be construed to be democracy, as many of the ideas and values in the preamble and section 1 are constitutive of a deeper idea of democracy.[20]

The next section considers which values on the 'universal list' are present in the South African Constitution, as developed by the jurisprudence of the Constitutional Court. First up are the foundational values of human dignity, equality and freedom. Next is a discussion of those values which do not have the same textual status as dignity, equality and freedom, but are nevertheless 'foundational' to the Constitution, either by their place in the text or through constitutional interpretation: accountability, participation and life. Accountability and participation, of course, are also constitutive of the value of democracy. Community is addressed next as a value that has a strong presence within the text, although is not directly mentioned as such. The values of justice, honesty/integrity, family, compassion/caring and respect/tolerance are discussed briefly as they are derivative of, or dependent upon, other primary values (dignity, equality, freedom and accountable, open and responsive government). Learning/education and respect for the environment are present in the Constitution as rights rather than values, whereas (state) security is absent from the South African Constitution. Important values that are not on the 'universal list', namely the values of the supremacy of the constitution and the rule of law,[21] are discussed throughout the chapter.

[17] *S v Mamabolo (E TV Intervening)* 2001 (3) SA 409 (CC), 2001 (5) BCLR 449 (CC) [41].

[18] *Port Elizabeth Municipality v Various Occupiers* 2005 (1) SA 217 (CC), 2004 (12) BCLR 1268 (CC) [15].

[19] See s 39(2).

[20] See, for example Halton Cheadle and Dennis Davis, 'Structure of the Bill of Rights' in Halton Cheadle, Dennis Davis and Nicholas Haysom (eds), *South African Constitutional Law: The Bill Of Rights* (London, Butterworths, 2002) ch 1; Theunis Roux 'Democracy' in S Woolman et al (eds), *Constitutional Law of South Africa*, 2nd edn (Cape Town, Juta and Co, 2006) ch 10.

[21] Section 1(c).

III. THE 'UNIVERSAL LIST' OF VALUES

A. Dignity

Dignity is the first, and some argue the most important, of the triumvirate of foundational values.[22] As with equality and freedom, it is an abstract and contested concept capable of serving both individual and collective interests that has been used to support a wide variety of norms and standards in the international community.[23] The dignity jurisprudence of the South African Constitutional Court has developed over its 15-year history, moving from history to transformation, and from more individual notions to occasionally embrace collective and material concerns. As such it has developed into a multi-faceted and robust, if sometimes unwieldy or unarticulated, concept. The value of dignity was initially developed in relation to the abolition of the death penalty and equality jurisprudence. As will be discussed below, the Kantian idea of individual human worth is particularly influential in these cases. A more collective and materially based notion of dignity, first apparent in references to *ubuntu* in *S v Makwanyane*[24] (the death penalty abolition judgment) and extra-curial statements on poverty and inequality, subsequently emerged in the Court's socio-economic rights jurisprudence. This section tracks the various manifestations of the Court's interpretation of the value of dignity as it addresses the interpretation of different rights, as well as academic debate and critique.[25]

Dignity is said to be particularly significant in South Africa, in the light of its apartheid past:

> Respect for the dignity of all human beings is particularly important in South Africa. For apartheid was a denial of a common humanity. Black people were refused respect and human dignity and thereby the dignity of all South Africans was diminished.... [R]ecognition and protection of human dignity is the touchstone of the new political order and is fundamental to the new Constitution.[26]

This past is the impetus for invoking the Kantian notion of dignity referring to the infinite human worth of each individual:

> The state did its best to deny that which is definitional to being human, namely the ability to understand or at least define oneself through one's own powers and

[22] See *S v Makwanyane* 1995 (3) SA 391 (CC), 1995 (6) BCLR 665 (CC) [144] (Chaskalson CJ), [328] (O'Regan J); *Dawood v Minister of Home Affairs* 2000 (3) SA 936 (CC), 2000 (8) BCLR 837 (CC) [35] ('dignity is a value that informs the interpretation of many, possibly all, other rights').

[23] Suzannah Cowen, 'Can dignity guide our equality jurisprudence?' (2001) 17 *South African Journal on Human Rights* 34, 49–50.

[24] *S v Makwanyane* 1995 (3) SA 391 (CC), 1995 (6) BCLR 665 (CC).

[25] For a detailed discussion of the many manifestations of dignity, see Stu Woolman, 'Dignity' in S Woolman et al (eds), *Constitutional Law of South Africa*, 2nd edn (Cape Town, Juta and Co, 2005) ch 36.

[26] 1995 (3) SA 391 (CC), 1995 (6) BCLR 665 (CC) [329] (O'Regan J).

> to act freely as a moral agent pursuant to such an understanding of self-definition. Blacks were treated as a means to an end and hardly ever as an end in themselves; an almost complete reversal of the Kantian imperative and concept of priceless inner worth and dignity.[27]

In *S v Makwanyane*, the Court adopted the idea that respect for human dignity meant that people should not be treated as a means to an end (or as an object to be eliminated by the state), but rather should be accorded recognition of their individual human worth.[28] This view of dignity is also apparent in *Christian Education South Africa v Minister of Education*,[29] where the prohibition of corporal punishment in schools was confirmed. In considering the place of dignity in relation to the equality right, the Court emphasised an idea of dignity requiring that human beings be treated with (equal) concern and respect. Thus in *President of the RSA v Hugo*[30] the Court explained equality as follows:

> At the heart of the prohibition of unfair discrimination lies a recognition that the purpose of our new constitutional and democratic order is the establishment of a society in which all human beings will be accorded equal *dignity* and respect regardless of their membership of particular groups.[31]

The meaning of dignity that emerges from this is consistent with the Court's earlier statements—the idea of intrinsic human worth, requiring people not to be treated in a demeaning or dehumanising manner, but with concern and respect. It was given particular substance in a series of cases brought by gay and lesbian groups for recognition of their identity and relationships.[32]

[27] Laurie Ackermann, 'Equality and the South African Constitution: The Role of Dignity', Bram Fischer lecture delivered at Rhodes House, Oxford, 26 May 2000.

[28] 1995 (3) SA 391 (CC), 1995 (6) BCLR 665 (CC) [26] (Chaskalson CJ), [271], [281] (Mahomed J), [313]-[316] (Mokgoro J) and [328] (O'Regan J). See also *S v Dodo* 2002 (3) SA 382 (CC) [38]: Human beings are 'creatures with inherent worth and infinite worth; they ought to be treated as ends in themselves, never as merely as means to an end'.

[29] *Christian Education South Africa v Minister of Education* (2000) 4 SA 757 (CC), 2000 (10) BCLR 1051 (CC) [44].

[30] *President of the RSA v Hugo* 1997 (4) SA 1 (CC), 1997 (6) BCLR 708 (CC) (finding the exclusion of fathers of young children from a general amnesty for mothers of the same, to be fair sex/gender discrimination).

[31] ibid [41]. In this case, the Court drew on L'Heureux-Dube J's judgment in *Egan v Canada* (1995) 29 CRR (2d) 79, who analysed the purpose of the Canadian equality right as 'recognising each person's equal worth as a human being, regardless of individual differences' and preventing them being treated in a manner that would 'offend fundamental human *dignity*' (104–05).

[32] *National Coalition for Gay and Lesbian Equality v Minister of Justice* 1999 (1) SA 6 (CC), 1998 (1) BCLR 1517 (CC) (criminalisation of sodomy is unfair discrimination); *National Coalition for Gay and Lesbian Equality v Minister of Home Affairs* 2000 (2) SA 1 (CC), 2000 (1) BCLR 39 (CC) (failure to confer immigration benefits provided to spouses on permanent, same-sex life partners unfairly discriminatory); *Satchwell v President of the RSA* 2003 (4) SA 266 (CC), 2002 (9) BCLR 986 (CC) (unfair exclusion of same-sex couples from the provisions of the Judges Remuneration and Conditions of Employment Act 88 of 1989); *Du Toit v Minister for Welfare and Population Development* 2003 (2) SA 198 (CC), 2002 (10) BCLR 1006 (CC) (finding provisions of the Child Care Act 74 of 1983 unconstitutional for limiting

In the first case, *National Coalition for Gay and Lesbian Equality v Minister of Justice* (decriminalising sodomy) Justice Ackermann acknowledges the difficulty of capturing dignity in precise terms, but finds 'at the very least … [it] requires us to acknowledge the value and worth of all individuals as members of society', to enable the self-identification and fulfilment of gay men and to prohibit laws that build insecurity and vulnerability in day-to-day life, that criminalise and stigmatise their intimate sexual conduct and that degrade and devalue them in society.[33] The recognition of the right of same-sex couples to marry in *Minister of Home Affairs v Fourie* saw dignity form the main support in the justificatory framework for full moral and social citizenship of gays and lesbians, overcoming the ongoing denial of their inherent worth as human beings.[34]

The Court's identification of dignity as individual human worth, and as equal concern and respect, in its equality jurisprudence attracted substantial criticism at the time both for its apparently indeterminate nature[35] and for its narrow, individualist focus on individual personality issues rather than a group-based understanding of material disadvantage and the systemic nature of inequality.[36] In both instances, it was suggested that limiting the value of dignity to an abstract and individualised concept would not meet the transformative imperatives of the Constitution for more fundamental socio-economic change.

However, as the Court moved from equality jurisprudence to socio-economic rights, the value of dignity was developed substantially. In *Soobramoney v Minister of Health* (turning down a claim for state-funded dialysis treatment) the Court spoke of the commitment to transform our society from one in which '[m]illions of people are living in deplorable conditions and in great poverty … into one in which there will be human dignity, freedom and equality'.[37] In the next socio-economic rights case, *Govt of the RSA v Grootboom*, the Court commented that '[t]here can be no doubt that human dignity, freedom and equality, the foundational values of our constitution, are denied those who have no food, clothing or shelter'[38] and

joint adoption to married people to the exclusion of same sex couples); *J v Director-General, Department of Home Affairs* 2003 (5) SA 621 (CC), 2003 (5) BCLR 463 (CC); *Minister of Home Affairs v Fourie; Lesbian and Gay Equality Project v Minister of Home Affairs* 2006 (1) SA 524 (CC), 2006 (3) BCLR 355 (CC).

[33] *National Coalition for Gay and Lesbian Equality v Minister of Justice*, ibid [28].

[34] *Minister of Home Affairs v Fourie* 2006 (1) SA 524 (CC), 2006 (3) BCLR 355 (CC).

[35] Dennis Davis has argued that the indeterminate meaning of dignity meant that it was inappropriate as the dominant conceptual tool for interpreting the equality right. 'Equality: The majesty of Legoland jurisprudence' (1999) 15 *South African Law Journal* 398. See also Dennis Davis, *Democracy and Deliberation* (Cape Town, Juta and Co, 1999) 69–95.

[36] See Catherine Albertyn and Beth Goldblatt, 'Facing the Challenge of Transformation: Difficulties in the Development of an Indigenous Jurisprudence of Equality' (1998) 14 *South African Journal on Human Rights* 248, 257–58.

[37] *Soobramoney v Minister of Health* 1998 (1) SA 765 (CC), 1997 (12) BCLR 1696 (CC) [8].

[38] *Govt of the RSA v Grootboom* 2001 1 SA 46 (CC), 2000 11 BCLR 1169 (CC) [23].

that '[a] society must seek to ensure that the basic necessities of life are provided to all if it is to be a society based on human dignity, freedom and equality'.[39] Although registered in abstract terms, these cases speak to the connections between the Constitution's foundational values and the constitutional imperative to reduce inequality and provide basic needs to those living in poverty, and thus point to an idea of dignity that takes account of people's material well-being.

In *Khosa v Minister of Social Development*, the Court found the exclusion of destitute permanent residents from certain social assistance grants to be unfair discrimination as well as a violation of the right of adequate social assistance.[40] In weighing up whether this exclusion impaired the dignity of the applicants, the Court found that 'decisions about the allocation of public benefits represent the extent to which poor people are treated as equal members of society'. Where they are excluded from such benefits, the applicants were forced into 'relationships of dependency upon families, friends and community', 'relegated to the margins of society' and 'cast in the role of supplicants'.[41] The exacerbation of material disadvantage, even destitution, reflected an absence of equal concern and respect and impaired the applicants' dignity. This absence was not merely a concern of the state, but of society as a whole:

> Sharing responsibility for the problems and consequences of poverty equally as a community represents the extent to which wealthier members of the community view the minimal well-being of the poor as connected with their personal well-being and the well-being of the community as a whole.[42]

In this case, the Court found the impairment of dignity a strong justification for overturning the government's budgetary concerns.[43]

Finally, the Court has tied the value of dignity to ideas of political participation. In *August v Electoral Commission*, (a case concerning the right of prisoners to vote), Sachs J speaks of the importance of the 'universality of the franchise' in which '[t]the vote of each and very citizen is a badge of *dignity* and of personhood'.[44] In *Doctors for Life v Minister of Health*, the Court struck down laws that failed to comply with constitutional requirements for public participation. In addressing the political rights set out in section 19 of the Constitution, the Court noted participation 'enhances the civic dignity of those who participate by enabling their voices to be heard and taken account of'.[45]

[39] ibid [44].
[40] *Khosa v Minister of Social Development* 2004 6 SA 505 (CC), 2004 6 BCLR 569 (CC).
[41] ibid [74], [76], [77].
[42] ibid [74].
[43] ibid [82]. See also *Hoffman v SAA* 2001 (1) SA 1 (CC); 2000 (11) 1235 (CC) [33].
[44] *August v Electoral Commission* 1999 (3) SA 1 (CC); 1999 (4) BCLR 636 (CC) [17].
[45] *Doctors for Life v Minister of Health* 2006 (6) SA 416 [115]. See also ibid [234].

As seen above, the Court has infused the value of dignity with diverse meanings in response to what Chaskalson referred to as the 'evolving demands of human dignity in our [transforming] society'.[46] However, much of this remains fragmented or abstract. Rather than one idea of dignity, there are many ideas, often inextricably bound up with the ideas of equality and freedom and not yet given full conceptual consistency. If dignity clearly implicates a measure of intrinsic human worth in which one is not treated as a means, but an end in oneself, deserving of equal concern and respect; it has also embraced a measure of a collective well-being and (possibly) redistributive justice. It is not clear whether the latter necessarily derives from an idea of respect for intrinsic human worth requiring that the state provides basic goods in manner that does not stereotype—or from more utilitarian ideas of dignity that requires redistribution for particular purposes. It remains a challenge for the Court to fully articulate a concept of dignity (even a multi-faceted one) that can meet the demands of transformation.

B. Equality

The value of equality is the second of three foundational values of the Constitution. The importance of equality as an 'organising principle' of the Constitution was noted in the 1997 case of *President of the RSA v Hugo* by Kriegler J:

> The South African Constitution is primarily and emphatically an egalitarian Constitution. The supreme laws of comparable constitutional states may underscore other principles and rights. But in the light of our own particular history, and our vision for the future, a Constitution was written with equality at its centre. Equality is our Constitution's focus and its organising principle.[47]

Equality is most visibly present in the Constitution as a detailed right[48] that embraces positive measures and provides substantive protection against unfair discrimination on a range of prohibited grounds. Here, the Constitutional Court has developed a jurisprudence that requires a contextual enquiry into the impact and effects of the alleged unfair discrimination on the complainant and his or her group, paying particular attention to the kind of disadvantaged suffered by the group.[49] However, the right to be free

[46] Arthur Chaskalson, 'The Third Bram Fischer Lecture: Human Dignity as a Foundational Value of Our Constitutional Order' (2000) 16 *South African Journal on Human Rights* 193, 204.

[47] *President of the RSA v Hugo* 1997 (4) SA 1 (CC) [74] (Kriegler J). See Catherine Albertyn and Janet Kentridge, 'An Introduction to the Right to Equality' (1994) 10 *South African Journal on Human Rights* 149 for a discussion of equality in the interim Constitution.

[48] Section 9 of the Constitution.

[49] See *Harksen v Lane NO* 1998 (1) SA 1300 (CC), discussed in detail in Catherine Albertyn and Beth Goldblatt, 'Equality' in S Woolman et al (eds), *Constitutional Law of South Africa*, 2nd edn (Cape Town, Juta and Co, 2007) ch 35.

from unfair discrimination has been interpreted through the value of dignity, establishing the 'impairment of dignity' as the standard against which unfair discrimination is measured, This has generated some critical debate as the Court's use of thin notions of dignity and a formalist approach to adjudication has resulted in a denial of rights to particularly vulnerable groups, such as sex workers, co-habiting couples and refugees.[50]

In identifying the value of dignity as the lodestone of unfair discrimination, the Court has paid little theoretical attention to the value of equality. Of course, this is a complex issue, given the deep, pervasive and material nature of inequality in South Africa. Potential answers to the question 'equality of what?' pose difficult challenges to courts tasked with enforcing the Constitution, especially in relation to separation of powers concerns.

As a value, however, equality is less constrained by questions of institutional boundaries. It has an aspirational and interpretative quality, but does not directly give rise to enforceable claims. In the absence of substantive debate on the meaning of equality, the Court has given it descriptive content. In a public lecture, (then) Chief Justice Chaskalson noted that the Constitution does not contemplate 'equality of goods or wealth', but that it does recognise the need to achieve a level of 'basic needs, such as housing, health-care, food, water and social security'.[51] In *Grootboom*, the Court stated that equality, together with dignity and freedom, required that the 'basic necessities of life [be] provided to all'.[52] In *Bannatyne v Bannatyne*, the Court stated that the founding value of the achievement of gender equality was undermined by gendered economic inequalities suffered by divorced or separated women left to bear the full financial burden of childcare.[53] These statements suggest that the meaning attributed to the founding value of the achievement of equality is captured by the movement from socio-economic inequality to equality, through the application of positive measures and the

[50] *Volks NO v Robinson* 2005 5 BCLR 446 (CC); *The State v Jordan* 2002 6 SA 642 (CC) and *Union of Refugee Women v The Director: The Private Security Industry Regulatory Authority* 2007 4 SA 395 (CC); 2007 4 BCLR 339 (CC). A proper application of the test requires courts to recognise that the adjudication of context, impact and values are closely bound up with each other. Failure to engage context disables the court from engaging values in a substantive manner, resulting, for example, in statements about dignity that amount to mere assertion, rather than a concern with the actual effects of the discrimination. For a detailed discussion, see Catherine Albertyn, 'Constitutional Equality' in Ockert Dupper and Christoph Gerbers (eds), *Equality and Labour Law: Reflections from South Africa and Elsewhere* (Cape Town, Juta and Co, 2009) ch 5.

[51] Arthur Chaskalson 'The Third Bram Fischer Lecture: Human Dignity as a Foundational Value of Our Constitutional Order' (2000) 16 *South African Journal on Human Rights* 193, 202.

[52] *Government of the Republic of South Africa v Grootboom* 2001 (1) SA 46 (CC), 2000 (11) BCLR 1169 (CC) [44].

[53] *Bannatyne v Bannatyne (Commission for Gender Equality, as* Amicus Curiae) 2003 (2) SA 363 (CC), 2003 (2) BCLR 111 (CC) [29] and [30]. This case concerned problems in the enforcement of the system of private maintenance in South Africa.

'progressive realisation' of socio-economic rights.[54] This view is partly echoed in a public address by Langa CJ, where he suggests that substantive equality includes socio-economic transformation, the reduction of inequality and poverty, the eradication of authoritarianism and violence and freeing persons to live according to full human potential.[55] Given the commitment to 'non-racism and non-sexism' in section 1 of the Constitution, race and gender equality are highlighted in seeking an 'evolution of society in which women and men are equally able to fulfil their potential'.[56]

The case law on positive measures gives further content given to the value of equality. In *Bato Star v Minister of Environmental Affairs and Tourism*, a case concerning positive measures within the fishing industry, Ncgobo J speaks of equality as a fundamental goal that both mandates and guides transformation to a more equal society.[57] He describes the systemic and entrenched nature of inequality in South Africa, noting that the commitment to overcoming such inequalities requires positive measures that address the ongoing effects of past discrimination.[58] Undoing the past is no easy task and 'profound difficulties' may be encountered in the process of achieving equality.[59]

> The measures that bring about transformation will inevitably affect some members of the society adversely, particularly those coming from previously advantaged communities. It may be that other considerations may have to yield in favour of achieving the goal we fashioned for ourselves in the Constitution, What is required though, is that the process of transformation must be carried out in accordance with the Constitution.[60]

In this sense the achievement of equality is both a process and an end. The process involves addressing the 'ongoing negative consequences' of past discrimination in a manner that balances the harm caused to those were previously advantaged against the constitutional imperative of addressing past disadvantage. This balancing process was considered in more detail in *Minister of Finance v Van Heerden*,[61] in which the Court found a scheme

[54] Arthur Chaskalson, 'The Third Bram Fischer Lecture: Human Dignity as a Foundational Value of Our Constitutional Order' (2000) 16 *South African Journal on Human Rights* 193, 202–03.

[55] Pius Langa, 'Transformative Constitutionalism' (n 5) 2–3, citing Catherine Albertyn and Beth Goldblatt, 'Facing the Challenge of Transformation' (1998) 14 *South African Journal on Human Rights* 248, 249.

[56] *Government of the Republic of South Africa v Grootboom* 2001 (1) SA 46 (CC), 2000 (11) BCLR 1169 (CC) [23].

[57] *Bato Star Fishing (Pty) Ltd v Minister of Environmental Affairs and Tourism* 2004 (4) SA 490 (CC); 2004 (7) BCLR 687 (CC) [73]–[74] (footnotes omitted) (Ncgobo J concurring, with agreement of all judges). This case concerned the allocation of fishing quotas to previously disadvantaged individuals, within the overall transformation of the fishing industry.

[58] ibid [74]–[75].

[59] ibid [76].

[60] ibid [76].

[61] *Minister of Finance v Van Heerden* 2004 6 SA 121 (CC), 2004 11 BCLR 1125 (CC) [31].

to subsidise the pension contributions of post-1994 parliamentarians to be constitutional. The case suggests that, in measuring the competing moral claims of prejudice (and potential harm to dignity) caused to individuals by positive measures against the collective benefit of these measures to society in overcoming past discrimination and disadvantage, the constitutional commitment to achieving equality enables the balance to be tipped in favour of redressing group-based disadvantage. Here the value of substantive equality can be prioritised over a more individualised version of dignity.

If the achievement of equality is a process of redressing historical imbalance and disadvantage, what is its end? Here the absence of theoretical or philosophical discussions of equality means that one has to infer meaning from the descriptive content of the Court's decisions. Different interpretations exist. Ngcobo J suggests that the value of equality coheres with the goal of creating a society in which 'all people have equal access to economic opportunities'.[62] Moseneke DCJ refers to remedial or restitutionary equality and the achievement of social justice.[63] Chaskalson CJ speaks of achieving a level of basic needs[64] and of

> action ... to enable people who lack the capacity to do so alone, to be able to lead a life of value to themselves and to the society of which they are a part and to enjoy the benefits of the Constitution's promise of dignity and freedom.[65]

While there is evidence of a concern with material ends—especially in references to meeting people's basic needs, it seems as if the Court is more likely to emphasise capacity and opportunities rather than material ends in themselves. While equality involves redistribution, it is through expanding opportunities and capacities of people rather the provision of than actual goods. Any theory of equality is thus more likely to focus on equality of opportunity rather than equality of outcome.

In the end, while the Court recognises its role in transforming South African society, it stops short of a full commitment to redistributive justice, even if its jurisprudence might enable this. This is largely attributable to its recognition of institutional boundaries:

> In interpreting and applying the Constitution there is a need for the courts to be sensitive to the difficult task confronting the legislature and the executive in giving effect to the positive obligations existing in our society. A balance has to be struck between the role of the Court as interpreter and upholder of the Constitution and the role of government in a democratic society. This is not easily done; nor are

[62] ibid [92].
[63] ibid [30] and [73]–[74] (Mokgoro J).
[64] Arthur Chaskalson, 'The Third Bram Fischer Lecture: Human Dignity as a Foundational Value of Our Constitutional Order' (2000) 16 *South African Journal on Human Rights* 193, 202.
[65] Arthur Chaskalson, 'Equality as a Founding Value of the South African Constitution' Oliver Schreiner lecture, University of the Witwatersrand, February 2001, 12.

> there accepted principles for determining where this line should be drawn. It is, however, what the courts have to do for it is their duty to uphold and enforce the Constitution, including its commitment to the transformation of our society.[66]

The Court adopts a variety of mechanisms to manage its separation of powers concerns. The idea of equality as encompassing positive, remedial action to overcome previous disadvantage and redistribution is more likely to be present where the Court is asked to defend positive or transformative measures.[67] The Court tends to make its most affirmative statements of transformative equality either outside court—in public lectures—or in cases where it is asked to defend remedial government action. In cases on socio-economic rights, this translates into a concern with the reasonableness of government action (in progressively realising socio-economic rights) rather than the provision of, for example, housing or water in itself.[68] When asked to act positively by extending rights and benefits to particular groups, the Court is more circumspect, relying on mechanisms such as the determination of the context of the dispute and the relevant issues, as well as the value of dignity, to negotiate concerns over institutional security and separation of powers.

C. Freedom/Independence/Liberty

Although freedom appears consistently alongside dignity and equality in the South African Constitution, it is perhaps the least developed of the three founding values. It is also manifested in a range of political rights and freedoms[69] and in a self-standing right—the right to freedom and security of person. A detailed right, section 12 includes protection against deprivations of physical liberty[70] and from violence and torture,[71] as well as an affirmation of bodily and psychological integrity.[72]

[66] ibid 13.

[67] See *Minister of Finance v Van Heerden* 2004 6 SA 121 (CC), 2004 11 BCLR 1125 (CC) and *Bato Star Fishing (Pty) Ltd v Minister of Environmental Affairs and Tourism* 2004 (4) SA 490 (CC), 2004 (7) BCLR 687 (CC). The Constitutional Court had previously emphasised the remedial and restitutionary aspects of substantive equality in passing in several cases: *Pretoria City Council v Walker* 1998 (3) BCLR 257 (CC) [45]–[48]; *National Coalition for Gay and Lesbian Equality v Minister of Justice* 1998 (12) BCLR 1517 (CC) [60]–[62].

[68] See eg, *Government of the Republic of South Africa v Grootboom* 2001 (1) SA 46 (CC), 2000 (11) BCLR 1169 (CC); *Mazibuko v City of Johannesburg* 2010 (4) SA 1 (CC), 2010 (3) BCLR 239 (CC).

[69] Including freedom of religion, belief and opinion (s 15); freedom of expression (s 16); rights to assembly, demonstrate, picket and petition (s 17); freedom of association (s 18); freedom of political choices and activity and vote (s 19).

[70] Section 12(1)(a) and (b).

[71] Section 12(1)(c), (d), (e).

[72] Section 12(2).

A primary tension in the interpretation of freedom exists between negative concepts of non-interference by the state and positive ideas of the state acting to protect one's freedom. Underlying this tension are different philosophical approaches to the individual, her place in society and her ability to act and make choices, as well as the nature of state and its duties towards its citizens. On the one hand, are classical conceptions of an abstract, autonomous individual, freely able to make choices about her life, and thus thriving in a 'laissez-faire' state that refrains from interfering with her individual freedom and protects her autonomy through this 'non-interference'.[73] On the other, are less abstract notions of the individual living within a society whose structural inequalities constrain her choices in a variety of ways and limit her ability to live to her full human potential. Rather than mere non-intervention, she also requires the state to act positively to ensure her autonomy and freedom, and to create the conditions that enhance her choices to improve her situation.[74]

The Court has not engaged with the value of freedom in a substantive manner. Most of its freedom jurisprudence focuses on negative conceptions of physical liberty in the context of criminal law and procedure. However, as discussed below, there is textual evidence and some jurisprudence that points towards a largely unarticulated, but nevertheless more positive and substantive idea of freedom.

Ferreira v Levin[75] saw the Court's first extensive foray into freedom jurisprudence in the context of section 11, the freedom right in the interim Constitution. Ackerman J suggested that section 11 contained a residual right to freedom that protected 'the area within which ... a person ... is or should be left to do or be what he is able to do or be without interference from other persons'.[76] In reaching this conclusion, Ackerman J relies on the work of Isaiah Berlin to support a negative idea of freedom: the right not to have obstacles placed in one's way by the state.[77] A majority of the Court rejected the idea that section 11 incorporated a residual right,[78] stating that it was only concerned with deprivations of physical liberty, but accepted the narrow, negative idea of freedom. In subsequent cases on deprivation of physical liberty under section 11 of the interim Constitution and section 12 of the 1996 Constitution, the Court has read substantive and procedural protections into

[73] This is epitomised by the work of Isaiah Berlin, *Four Essays on Liberty* (Oxford, Clarendon Press, 1969) 121.

[74] See, for example, Jennifer Nedelsky, *Laws Relations. A Relational Theory of Self, Autonomy and Law* (Oxford, Oxford University Press, 2011).

[75] *Ferreira v Levin* 1996 (1) SA 984 (CC); 1996 (1) BCLR 1 (CC). This concerned a Companies Act, 61 of 1973, provision that compelled a person in an enquiry into winding up a company to answer potentially incriminating questions, and allowed the answers to be used in evidence in subsequent criminal proceedings against such person.

[76] ibid [52].

[77] ibid [54].

[78] ibid [182] (Chaskalson P).

this aspect of the right: The state must have good reasons ('just cause') for a deprivation of liberty and must do so with fair procedures.[79]

Despite this limited jurisprudence, there are strong textual indications for a wider idea of freedom. For example, section 12(1)(c) guarantees the right 'to be free from all forms of violence from public and private sources'. The positive idea of freedom underpinning this right was recognised by the Court in a series of cases dealing with the state's duties in relation to violence against women. In *S v Baloyi*,[80] the Court defended a law that required a person charged with breaching a family violence interdict to prove an absence of guilt (reverse onus), noting that 'the specific inclusion of private sources emphasises that serious threats to security of the person arise from private sources' and that the state is obliged 'directly to protect the right of everyone to free from private or domestic violence'.[81] In several cases concerning the duty of the police to protect the public from violence in general, and to protect women in particular,[82] the Court has again confirmed both the duty of the state not to infringe the right to freedom and security of the person, as well as the 'positive component' which 'obliges the state and its organs to provide appropriate protection to everyone through laws and structures designed to afford such protection'.[83] The constitutional value of freedom, together with dignity and equality, as well as the right to freedom and security of the person, have thus seen the development of the law of delict to expand the state's responsibility to act to protect its citizens and ensure their freedom from violence, including freedom from sexual violence.[84] In several cases concerning the duties of the state to protect

[79] See *Bernstein v Bester NNO* 1996 (2) SA 751 (CC), 1996 (4) BCLR 449 (CC) [145]; and the cases discussed in *De Lange v Smuts NO* 1998 (3) SA 785 (CC); 1998 (7) BCLR 779 (CC) [17]–[22]. For a longer discussion on the jurisprudence of deprivations of physical liberty, Michael Bishop and Stu Woolman, 'Freedom and Security of the Person' in Woolman et al (eds), *Constitutional Law of South Africa*, 2nd edn (Cape Town, Juta and Co, 2003) ch 40, 26–48.

[80] *Sv Baloyi* 2000 (2) SA 425 (CC); 2000 (1) BCLR 86 (CC).

[81] ibid [11].

[82] These included the duty, in certain circumstances to arrest dangerous people (where complaints had been made to police about a person's violent behaviour and the person was known to police), to oppose bail (where the prosecutor had information of a previous charge of rape) in *Carmichele v Minister of Safety and Security* 2001 (4) SA 938 (CC), 2001 (10) BCLR (CC) [39]; and to remove a firearm (where man known to be dangerous and where consequently shot wife and daughter, and injured neighbour) *Minister of Safety and Security v Van Duivenboden* 2003 (1) SA 389 (SCA) and to prevent escape (where police failed to close a gate and a dangerous prisoner escaped and raped a young woman) *Van Eeden v Minister of Safety and Security* 2003 (1) SA 389 (SCA).

[83] *Carmichele*, ibid [39].

[84] In *Carmichele*, the Court said that 'in meeting obligations to dignity and freedom and security of the person, few thing scan be more important than freedom from sexual violence'. See also *K v Minister of Safety and Security* 2005 (6) SA 419 (CC), 2005 (9) BCLR 835 (CC)—liability of state for rape of women by three uniformed, but off-duty police officers and *F v Minister of Safety and Security* 2012 (1) SA 536 (CC), 2012 (3) BCLR 244 (CC), (2012) 33 ILJ 93 (CC)—liability for rape by a police officer on stand-by duty.

people from violence, the Court has developed common law delictual duties of public officials to embrace a positive idea of freedom. Disappointingly, this has not been done in the context of any theoretical development of the value of freedom in the Constitution.

Section 12(2) of the Constitution relates to bodily and psychological integrity—the right to make decisions concerning reproduction and to security in and control over one's body.[85] Although this right has been important in rejecting challenges to the 1996 Choice on Termination of Pregnancy Act,[86] it has also seen little theoretical development in the Court. It is clearly a strong assertion of women's rights to reproductive autonomy—enabling reproductive choice and the removal of barriers that impede the free exercise of that choice. Arguably, this right is also underpinned by a positive idea of freedom that imposes duties on the state to make safe and accessible reproductive health-services available to all women.[87]

The Constitutional Court has claimed that socio-economic rights are closely related to the founding values of dignity, freedom and equality,[88] and has often spoken of how freedom, as well as dignity and equality, are denied to those who do not have the basic necessities of life.[89] Yet it has not yet spelt out what this means for an understanding of the freedom value within the South African Constitution. There is much to be said for a positive view of freedom, and for an exploration of its social and material dimensions.[90] Fredman argues that 'from a human rights perspective, it is difficult to see why freedom should only be seen as an absence of deliberate state interference'.[91] She argues for a view of freedom that 'emphasizes the importance of facilitating individuals' ability to fulfil their choices' and suggests that the state has a positive duty to 'ensure the provision of a range of options,

[85] Sections 12(2)(a) and (b).

[86] *Christian Lawyers Association v Minister of Health* (1998) 4 SA 113 (T), (1998) 11 BCLR 1434 (T), concerning a challenge to the right to choose to have an abortion on the basis that it violated the right to life of a foetus; *Christian Lawyers Association v Minister of Health* 2005 (1) SA 309 (T), 2004 (10) BCLR 1086 (T), concerning the right of minors to obtain abortions without parental consent.

[87] See for example, Joanna Birenbaum, 'Contextualising Choice: Abortion, equality and the right to make decisions concerning reproduction' (1996) 12 *South African Journal on Human Rights* 485, 485–86, 489–90, 502; Jonathan Berger, 'Taking Responsibilities Seriously: The Role of the State in preventing HIV Transmission from Mother to Child' (2001) 5 *Law, Democracy and Development* 163, 165–66; Michelle O'Sullivan, 'Reproductive Rights' in Woolman et al, *Constitutional Law of South Africa*, 2nd edn (Cape Town, Juta and Co, 2005) ch 37, 23–24. See also Marius Pieterse, 'The Interdependence of Rights to Health and Autonomy in South Africa' (2008) 125 *South African Law Journal* 553, 560–63.

[88] *Khosa v Minister of Social Development* 2004 (6) 505 (CC), 2004 (6) BCLR 569 (CC) [40].

[89] *Government of the RSA v Grootboom* 2001 1 SA 46 (CC), 2000 11 BCLR 1169 (CC) [23], [44]; *Khosa* [52].

[90] See Marius Pieterse, 'The Interdependence of Rights to Health and Autonomy in South Africa' (2008) 125 *South African Law Journal* 553 for an exploration of this in relation to health rights.

[91] Sandra Fredman, *Human Rights Transformed* (Oxford, Oxford University Press, 2008) 11.

of public goods and the framework within which human relationships can flourish'.[92]

The positive dimensions of freedom seem to cohere with South Africa's constitutional vision of a society seeking to escape its unequal and unjust past and secure a future based on 'democratic values, social justice and fundamental human rights'.[93] However, other than a few minority judgments by Sachs J that recognise the social nature of autonomy,[94] the Court has directly and indirectly adopted a more negative view. For example, in equality cases concerning personal relationship and lifestyle choices, the majority of the Court has adopted a narrow, libertarian view of choice.[95] In *Ferreira*, Ackerman's minority judgement actively distinguished the idea of freedom from the material conditions of its existence.[96] The majority's rejection of his interpretation of section 11 as a residual right was partly justified by institutional boundary issues: 'We should not … construe section 11 so broadly that we overshoot the mark and trespass upon terrain that is not rightly ours'.[97] However, concern with the ambit of the rights is not a reason to limit the meaning of the value. Indeed, the Court has subsequently demonstrated its ability to address separation of powers concerns through a variety of interpretative tools and remedial options.

More so than the other fundamental values, therefore, freedom requires particular development both in relation to the nature and role of the state and the rights and responsibilities of the individual. Not only does the Constitution appear to envision a more proactive, and protective state, but it also suggests that individuals bear some responsibility for others. The possibility for the horizontal application of the Constitution, as expressed in section 8(2), suggests that South Africa's notion of freedom is one in which society is concerned about its relationships with others (this is reinforced by the notion of *ubuntu*).[98]

[92] ibid 14, 18.

[93] Preamble, Constitution.

[94] See *National Coalition for Gay and Lesbian Equality v Minister of Justice* 1999 (1) SA 6 (CC) [117]; *Soobramoney v Minister of Health* 1998 (1) SA 765 (CC), 1997 (12) BCLR 1696 (CC) [54]; *Volks NO v Robinson* 2005 5 BCLR 446 (CC) [155]–[156] (O'Regan; Mokgoro dissenting).

[95] The failure to address freedom in a consistent and theoretical manner in seen in the libertarian ideas of autonomy and choice that have surfaced in some judgments of the Court, such as *Volks NO v Robinson* 2005 5 BCLR 446 (CC) and *S v Jordan* 2002 6 SA 642 (CC). See further Catherine Albertyn, 'Substantive Equality and Transformation in South Africa' (2007) 23 *South African Journal on Human Rights* 253; Elsje Bonthuys, 'Institutional Openness and Resistance to Feminist Arguments: The Example of the South African Constitutional Court' (2008) 20 *Canadian Journal of Women and the Law* 1; Marius Pieterse, '"Finding for the Applicant" Individual Equality Plaintiffs and Group-based Disadvantage' (2008) 24 *South African Journal on Human Rights* 397.

[96] *Ferreira v Levin* 1996 (1) SA 984 (CC), 1996 (1) BCLR 1 (CC) [182] (Chaskalson P).

[97] ibid [183].

[98] In *Minister of Safety and Security v Van Duivenboden* 2003 (1) SA 389 (SCA) [19] (concerning the duty of the state to remove firearms from certain dangerous categories of persons), the Supreme Court of Appeal suggested that the protection of freedom rights might bolster the duties of citizens as well as public officials, to intervene, and thus to assume liability for omissions.

In the end, however, freedom remains an undeveloped value, promising much, but limited in current constitutional jurisprudence.

D. Responsibility/Accountability

Etienne Mureinik famously described the interim South African Constitution as a bridge from a 'culture of authority' to a 'culture for justification', namely, 'a culture in which every exercise of public power is expected to be justified; in which the leadership given by government rests on the cogency of the case offered in defence of its decisions, not the fear inspired by the force of its command'.[99] The importance of accountability or a 'culture of justification' has been endorsed many times by the Constitutional Court[100] and is present in the Constitution in many ways—in the text, in the structure of the state and in the quality of its constitutional democracy.

The 1996 Constitution lists 'accountability, openness and responsiveness' amongst the founding values of the new democratic state. All organs of state and public enterprises are bound by the value of accountability in the Constitution,[101] both individually and under the idea of 'co-operative government', requiring all levels of government to work together to 'provide effective, transparent, accountable and coherent government for the Republic as a whole'.[102] Accountability exists within and between the different structures of the state,[103] and to the public as a whole.[104] In relation to the latter, O'Regan J speaks of the 'constitutional value of accountability, in terms of which government and those exercising public power should be held accountable to the broader community for the exercise of their power'.[105]

Accountability is central to South Africa's constitutional democracy. The ideas of constitutional supremacy and the rule of law require the state to act in accordance with the Constitution, and to account in terms of its provisions. The structural provisions are given further substance by a justiciable Bill of Rights, including the right to just administrative action clause[106]

[99] Etienne Mureinik, 'A Bridge to Where? Introducing the Interim Bill of Rights' (1994) 10 *South African Journal on Human Rights* 31, 32.

[100] *S v Makwanyane* [156]; *Prinsloo v Van der Linde* 1997 (3) SA 1012 (CC); 1997 (6) BCLR 759 (CC) [25]; *PMA v President of the RSA* 2000 (2) SA 674 (CC); 2000 (3) BCLR 241 (CC) [85].

[101] Section 195(2).

[102] Section 41(1)(c).

[103] For example, s 55(2) deals with accountability of the executive to the legislature; the security services are accountable to parliamentary committees to promote the principle of accountability and transparency (s 199(8)).

[104] See s 195(1) relating to public administration and s 152(1)(a) which requires local government to promote democratic and accountable government for local communities.

[105] *Rail Commuters Action Group v Transnet Ltd t/a Metrorail* 2005 (2) SA 359 (CC), 2005 (4) BCLR 301 (CC) [73].

[106] Section 33.

and justiciable socio-economic rights.[107] Under section 36 of the Constitution, the 'process of justifying limitations [of rights] ... serves the value of accountability in a direct way by requiring those who defend limitations to explain why they are defensible.'[108] The state is bound to justify any incursion into the rights of the public.

The application of the Constitution to the common law—requiring the courts to 'promote the spirit, purport and objects of the Bill of Rights' when interpreting and developing the common law[109]—expands the idea of accountability and responsibility throughout the legal system. This has been particularly visible in the expansion of delictual liability.[110] There is also an explicit, but undeveloped, sense of individual responsibility in the Constitution. For example, private persons are bound by the Bill of Rights 'to the extent that it is applicable, taking into account the nature of the right, and the nature of any duty imposed by it'.[111] In addition, the equality right[112] and the rights to freedom and security of the person[113] have explicit horizontal application.

E. Participation/Inclusion

Ideas of participation and inclusion are present within South Africa's Constitution and form part of its overarching commitment to democracy. The preamble lays 'the foundations of a democratic and open society in which government is based on the will of the people', and section 1 identifies 'a multi-party system of democratic government, to ensure accountability, responsiveness and openness' as a founding value of the new state. In

[107] See *Mazibuko v City of Johannesburg* 2010 (3) BCLR 239 (CC); 2010 (4) SA 1 (CC) [160]. The purpose of litigation concerning the positive obligations imposed by social and economic rights should be to hold the democratic arms of government to account through litigation. In so doing, litigation of this sort fosters a form of participative democracy that holds government accountable and requires it to account between elections over specific aspects of government policy.

[108] *Rail Commuters Action Group v Transnet Ltd t/a Metrorail* 2005 (2) SA 359 (CC); 2005 (4) BCLR 301 (CC) [75].

[109] Section 29(2).

[110] In *Metrorail* (para 78), O'Regan J notes that 'the principle of accountability will not always give rise to a legal duty whether in public or private law. In determining whether a legal duty exists, either in private or public law, careful analysis of the relevant constitutional provisions, any relevant statutory duties, and the relevant context will be required. It will be necessary too to take account of other constitutional norms, important and relevant ones being the principle of effectiveness and the need to be responsive to people's needs.'

[111] Section 8(2).

[112] Section 9(3).

[113] Section 12(1)(c).

addition, various provisions require public involvement and participation in the proceedings of the legislature.[114]

The idea of participatory democracy came under scrutiny in *Doctors for Life International v Speaker of the National Assembly*, a case concerning the nature of the National Council of Provinces (constitutional obligation to ensure public involvement).[115] The Court noted that:

> our democracy includes as one of its basic and fundamental principle, the principle of participatory democracy. The democratic government that it contemplated is partly representative and partly participatory, is accountable, responsive and transparent and makes provision for public participation in the law-making processes.[116]

The Court proceeded to strike down two laws on the basis that Parliament had failed to comply with its constitutional obligations to facilitate public involvement, and the laws had accordingly not been passed in a manner that was consistent with the Constitution.[117] This was the first time that a law had been declared unconstitutional for procedural rather than substantive reasons. The Court's willingness to do so affirms a deep commitment to the principle of participation in South Africa's democracy.[118]

F. Life

South Africa's Constitution has a strong commitment to the right to life,[119] most visibly present in the Court's rejection of the death penalty in *S v Makwanyane*.[120] This case saw the rejection of the death penalty as unconstitutional, based on the right to be free from cruel, inhuman and degrading punishment, as well as the rights to life and dignity. Significantly, Chaskalson P confirmed that 'the rights to life and dignity are the most important

[114] Section 57 enables the National Assembly to make rules for its internal arrangements, proceedings and procedures with due regard to 'representative and participatory democracy, accountability, transparency and public involvement'. Section 59 mandates the National Assembly to facilitate public involvement and public access. Similar provisions exist for the National Council of Provinces (the second house of parliament) in ss 70 and 72.

[115] *Doctors for Life International v Speaker of the National Assembly* 2006 (12) BCLR 1399 (CC), 2006 (6) SA 416 (CC). In this case, the failure of the National Council of Provinces to hold public hearings was found to violate a constitutional obligation to hold public hearings.

[116] ibid [116]. See also *Matatiele Municipality v President of the RSA* (2) (2007) 1 BCLR (CC) 47.

[117] ibid [125]. The declaration of invalidity was suspended for 18 months to enable Parliament to enact the law in a procedurally correct manner.

[118] See Theunis Roux, 'Democracy' in Woolman et al (eds), *Constitutional Law of South Africa*, 2nd edn (Cape Town, Juta and Co, 2006) ch 10, esp 69–77, for a discussion of how the Court had previously refrained from adopting a deep principle of democracy. This chapter was written before the *Doctors for Life* judgment.

[119] Section 11.

[120] *S v Makwanyane* 1995 (3) SA 391 (CC); 1995 (6) BCLR 665 (CC).

of all human rights and the source of all other personal rights'.[121] They are also non-derogable in a state of emergency.

The normative content of the right to life in the South African Constitution includes the outlawing of the death penalty,[122] but goes beyond the protection of mere corporeal life. Thus O'Regan wrote in *Makwanyane* that:

> the right to life was included in the Constitution not just to enshrine the right to existence. It is not life as mere organic matter that the Constitution cherishes but the right to human life: the right to live as a human being, to be part of a broader community, to share in the experience of humanity.[123]

Beyond the cognitive, intellectual and communitarian aspects of humanity, the Constitution shows concern for the quality of life, life in its material aspects, both in the preamble's concern 'to improve the quality of life of all citizens and free the potential of each person' and in the inclusion of a number of socio-economic rights. In *Grootboom v President of the RSA*, the Court stated that '[a] society must seek to ensure that the basic necessities of life are provided to all if it is to be a society based on human dignity, freedom and equality'.[124]

Does this pervasive concern with all aspects of life in the South African Constitution signify a reverence for life that amounts to a foundational value of the Constitution, beyond its presence as a right or as a derivative principle of the primary value of human dignity? The evidence seems to suggest this is the case. The Court has elevated the rights to life and dignity as the source of all other rights. In *S v Walters*,[125] a case concerning the use of lethal force in effecting an arrest, Kriegler J noted that the rights to life, dignity and bodily integrity were 'individually essential and collectively foundational to the value system prescribed by the Constitution'.[126] Given the Court's consistent equation of life and dignity, even if it is in the context of rights rather than values, it is clear that the deep respect for life that emerges in our constitutional text gives life a particular status above many other rights, that is not primarily founded on the value of human dignity.

[121] ibid [144].

[122] The Court has also placed a positive duty on the state to act to protect life, for example by requiring the state to secure an undertaking that any person extradited or deported to another country will not face the death penalty in that country. See *Mohamed v Government of the RSA* 2001 (3) SA 893 (CC); *Minister of Home Affairs v Tsebe* 2012 (5) SA 467 (CC), 2012 (10) BCLR 1017 (CC).

[123] *S v Makwanyane* [326].

[124] *Government of the Republic of South Africa v Grootboom* 2001 (1) SA 46 (CC), 2000 (11) BCLR 1169 (CC) [44]; see also *Khosa v Minister of Social Development* 2004 (6) 505 (CC), 2004 (6) BCLR 569 (CC) [53].

[125] *Ex Parte Minister of Safety and Security: In Re S v Walters* 2002 (4) SA 613 (CC); 2002 (7) BCLR 663 (CC).

[126] ibid [28].

The elevated status of life within the Constitution's value system has particular traction in relation to what might be called the core meaning of 'life', namely, physical existence. Hence (the right to) life has been foundational to the development of the state's delictual liability in relation to its duties to protect the public from harm,[127] as well as the state's responsibilities towards those who face egregious violations of human rights, including the death penalty in other countries.[128] However, as one moves towards material and communitarian notions of life or 'quality of life', as prescribed by socio-economic rights, reverence for life is not influential.[129] Here, the driving force of dignity, as well as the values of equality and freedom, are determinative. It is also worthy of note that reverence for life does not prevent reproductive choice and termination of pregnancy.[130] To the extent that the state might have an interest in protecting foetal life, Meyerson has argued that this derives from value of human dignity.[131] The question of euthanasia has not been directly addressed under the Constitution, but it is likely that the values of dignity and freedom (autonomy) will play a primary role in determining the boundaries of 'the right to die'.[132]

Under the South African Constitution, therefore, reverence for life has some independent status within the Constitution's value system, but it also merges into the value of dignity especially as its meaning moves beyond the protection of physical existence.

G. Community

Although not a foundational value, the idea of community is present in the constitutional text and its jurisprudence in several ways. It has perhaps been most visible in the Court's discussion of *ubuntu*, a value included in the 'post-amble' to the interim Constitution,[133] but left out of the final text.

[127] See the cases discussed in nn 82 and 84 above.

[128] See *Mohamed v President of the Republic of South Africa* 2001 (3) SA 893 (CC); *Kaunda v President of the Republic of South Africa* 2005 (4) SA 235 (CC).

[129] Marius Pieterse, 'Life' in Woolman et al (eds), *Constitutional Law of South Africa*, 2nd edn (Cape Town, Juta and Co, 2006) ch 39, 18–21.

[130] Section 12(2) guarantees the right to reproductive decision-making, rights enshrined in the Choice on Termination of Pregnancy Act, 94 of 1996. A constitutional challenge to this Act based on the right to life of a fetus failed in *Christian Lawyers Association v Minister of Health* (1998) 4 SA 113 (T); (1998) 11 BCLR 1434 (T).

[131] Denise Meyerson, 'Abortion: The Constitutional Issues' (1999) 15 *South African Law Journal* 50, 56–57. Meyerson applies the limitations analysis to the Choice on Termination of Pregnancy Act and suggests that it probably strikes the right balance between the values of dignity, equality and freedom.

[132] See for example Pieterse 'Life' (n 129) 6–8.

[133] The post-amble, entitled 'National Unity and Reconciliation' speaks of the movement from an unjust past to a democratic future, and sets the tone for the Truth and Reconciliation Commission that was address the human rights violations of apartheid: 'there is a need for understanding, but not for vengeance, a need for reparation but not for retaliation, a need for ubuntu but not for victimisation'.

Ubuntu is an idea that one's humanity is defined by one's relationship with others. Mokgoro J describes it thus in *S v Makwanyane*:[134]

> *ubuntu* ... metaphorically, ... expresses itself in *umuntu ngumuntu ngabantu*, describing the significance of group solidarity on survival issues so central to the survival of communities. While it envelops the key values of group solidarity, compassion, respect, human dignity, conformity to basic norms and collective unity, in its fundamental sense it denotes humanity and morality. Its spirit emphasises respect for human dignity, marking a shift from confrontation to conciliation.[135]

Mokgoro J emphasises the communitarian nature of *ubuntu* as well as its connections to other rights and values, especially dignity. In this sense, it also resonates with her discussion of dignity in *Khosa* as concerned with the collective well-being of all.[136]

Despite its absence from the 1996 Constitution, the Court has continued to evoke *ubuntu* in its judgments. In the 2003 judgment of *Bhe*, in which the customary rule of male primogeniture was outlawed, Ncgobo J emphasised the communitarian and reciprocal nature of *ubuntu*, especially in attending to those in need:

> A sense of community prevailed from which developed an elaborate system of reciprocal duties and obligations among the family members. This is manifest in the concept of *ubuntu—umuntu ngumuntu ngabantu*—a dominant value in African traditional culture. This concept encapsulates communality and the interdependence of the members of a community. As Langa DCJ put it, it is a culture which 'regulates the exercise of rights by the emphasis it lays on sharing and co-responsibility and the mutual enjoyment of rights'. It is this system of reciprocal duties and obligations that ensured that every family member had access to basic necessities of life such as food, clothing, shelter and healthcare.[137]

However, the Court's articulation of *ubuntu* remains generally undeveloped.[138] It has not formed the basis of a new jurisprudence based on the values of community and solidarity,[139] nor has its relationship with the value

[134] 1995 (3) SA 391 (CC), 1995 (2) SACR 1 (CC), 1995 (6) BCLR 665 (CC).

[135] ibid [308] (footnotes omitted). *Ubuntu* was taken up by several of the Constitutional Court judges in *Makwanyane* in rejecting the death penalty. See the judgments of Chaskalson P [130]–[131]; Langa J [223]–[227]; Madala J [237]–[260]; Mohamed DP (para 263); Mokgoro J [307]–[313]; Sachs J [374].

[136] *Khosa v Minister of Social Development* 2004 (6) 505 (CC), 2004 (6) BCLR 569 (CC) [74]. See also Mahomed DP's description of *ubuntu*, which also speaks to dignity: 'the ethos of an instinctive capacity for and enjoyment of love towards our fellow men and women; the joy and the fulfilment involved in recognizing their innate humanity' (*Makwanyane* [263]).

[137] *Bhe v Magistrate, Khayelitsha* 2005 (1) SA 580 (CC), 2005 (1) BCLR 1 (CC) [163] (footnotes omitted).

[138] *Ubuntu* has been invoked in a series of cases concerned with criminal justice (eg, *Makwanyane* on the death penalty); customary law (*Bhe v Magistrate, Khayelitsha*) and evictions (*PE Municipality v Various Occupiers*).

[139] See eg, Drucilla Cornell and Karin Van Marle's argument that *ubuntu* could form an indigenous value basis for a radical communitarian vision in the Constitution: 'Exploring Ubuntu: Tentative Reflections' (2005) 5 *African Human Rights Law Journal* 195. But see also the absence

of dignity been fully interrogated. In the end, however, it remains present as an important constitutional value, independent of the value of dignity, and is evoked, inter alia, to affirm the spirit of community and solidarity.

Other than its presence in the values of *ubuntu* and dignity, a sense of community is also manifest in the Constitution's affirmation of the rights of religious and cultural communities to enjoy their culture, practise their religion and speak their language, albeit in a manner consistent with individual rights guaranteed in the Bill of Rights.[140] The Constitution also promotes a strong sense of a 'local community' through its expectation of community involvement in local government,[141] policing matters[142] and its provisions relating to participatory democracy.[143]

A concern with community is thus present through the invocation of *ubuntu* and in the protection of certain community-based rights. It is visible, although undeveloped, in a third sense, and that is the manner in which invocations of 'community' influence the understanding of the rights bearer as a person living within a network or relationships or a community, rather than an autonomous individual. The resolution of the relationship between individual and community would take considerable theoretical work, but might find some support in an incipient value or principle of community in the constitutional text.

H. Fairness/Justice

The value of justice in the South African Constitution is inextricably bound up with the Preamble's invocation of a society 'based on human dignity, the achievement of equality and the advancement of human rights and freedoms'. 'Social justice', together with democratic values and human rights, are interrelated aspirations made possible, inter alia, by the promotion and protection of fundamental human rights.[144] The meaning of (social) justice thus derives substantially from our understanding of human dignity, equality and freedom and is a principle of democracy.

of a fully fledged *ubuntu* jurisprudence, discussed in Helen Keep and Rob Midgley, 'The Emerging Role of *Ubuntu-Botho* in Developing a Consensual South African Legal Culture' in Fred Bruinsma and David Nelken (eds), *Explorations in Legal Culture* (The Hague, Elsevier, 2007).

140 Section 31. See also provisions concerning traditional leaders (s 26 in the Schedule) and protection of communal land tenure (s 25).

141 Sections 151(3), 152(1)(e), 153(3), 185(1)(c).

142 Section 206(3) and (5) promote relations between the police and the community.

143 See section IIIE above.

144 In *Kaunda v President of the Republic of South Africa* 2005 (4) SA 235 (CC), 2004 10 BCLR 1009 (CC) [220] O'Regan J identifies the promotion and protection of fundamental human rights as the *leitmotif* of the Constitution, and as part of the quest for social justice. See also *Bato Star Fishing (Pty) Ltd v Minister of Environmental Affairs and Tourism* 2004 (4) SA 490 (CC), 2004 (7) BCLR 687 (CC) [73]–[74].

Fairness is not a primary value in the Constitution, although it is an important principle that assists in determining the scope of protection of several rights, including equality (protection against unfair discrimination),[145] the right to fair labour practices,[146] the right to a fair hearing or trial[147] and just administrative action.[148]

I. Family

Family, or the right to family life, is not mentioned in the constitutional text, a fact that was challenged during the certification hearings of the Constitution. In response, the Constitutional Court found that the provisions of the Constitution 'met the obligations imposed by international human rights law to protect the rights of persons freely to marry and to raise a family'.[149]

In *Dawood v Minister of Home Affairs*, a case concerning the rights of foreign spouses to live with their families while awaiting the outcome of residency applications, O'Regan J found that the right to establish and maintain a family was protected by the right to dignity. Legislation that prohibited the establishment of such a relationship, or that prevented partners living together as a family, 'impaired the ability of the individual to achieve personal fulfilment in an aspect of life that is of central significance'.[150] O'Regan also discussed the importance of the family as a social institution and the need to 'take care not to entrench particular forms of family at the expense of other forms'.[151] The recognition of a variety of family forms in South African law derives from the values of dignity and equality.[152]

[145] Section 9(3) and (4). For a discussion of the meaning of fairness in this context, see Catherine Albertyn and Beth Goldblatt, 'Equality' in Woolman et al (eds), *Constitutional Law of South Africa*, 2nd edn (Cape Town, Juta and Co, 2007) ch 35, 75–79.

[146] Section 23(1). For a discussion of fairness in this context, see Carole Cooper, 'Labour Relations' in Woolman et al (eds), *Constitutional Law of South Africa*, 2nd edn (Cape Town, Juta and Co, 2006) ch 53, 11–12, 15–19.

[147] See s 34 on access to courts and s 35(3).

[148] Section 33 of the Constitution and the Promotion of Administrative Justice Act, 3 of 2000.

[149] As stated by O'Regan J in *Dawood v Minister of Home Affairs* 2000 (3) SA 936 (CC), 2000 (8) BCLR 837 (CC) [28]. In the certification judgment, the Court found that the Constitution 'would clearly prohibit any arbitrary state interference with the right to marry or to marry and raise a family', and that it 'prohibits the kinds of violations of family life produced by the pass laws or the institutionalised migrant labour system, just as it would not permit the prohibitions on the free choice of marriage partners imposed by laws such as the prohibition of Mixed Marriages Act, 55 of 1949'. *Ex Parte Chairperson of the Constitutional Assembly: In re Certication of the Constitution of the Republic of South Africa 1996* 1996 (4) SA 744 (CC), 1996 (10) BCLR 1253 (CC) [100].

[150] *Dawood v Minister of Home Affairs* 2000 (3) SA 936 (CC); 2000 (8) BCLR 837 (CC) [37].

[151] ibid [31].

[152] See eg, *Minister of Home Affairs v Fourie; Lesbian and Gay Equality Project v Minister of Home Affairs* 2006 (3) BCLR 355 (CC) (summarising the jurisprudence on gay and

Family is thus present in the South African Constitution in a derivative sense, and is not a primary value.

J. Integrity/Honesty

The value of integrity as 'honesty', rather than integrity as wholeness or completeness, is not directly present in the Constitution.[153] However, the idea is generally present in describing the conduct of the judiciary and public institutions.

For example, section 165(2) requires the courts to apply the law 'impartially and without fear, favour or prejudice'. In section 195, the public services is required to exercise 'a high standard of professional ethics', make 'efficient, economic and effective use of resources' and act 'impartially, fairly and without bias'.[154] The security and police forces must act within the law, and may not be partisan or further the interests of a political party.[155]

In general, the quality of being honest can be seen to be a sub-set of the foundational values of accountable, responsive and open government.[156]

K. Compassion/Caring

The idea of compassion and caring is not a primary constitutional value, but is manifest within the purpose and commitment of the Constitution. In *S v Makwanyane*, Mahomed J memorably wrote of the Constitution's 'vigorous identification of and commitment to a democratic, universalistic, caring and aspirationally egalitarian ethos'.[157] The idea that the Constitution commits South Africa to a compassionate and caring society is expressed through the jurisprudence in a number of ways.

First, it emerges from the articulation of other values. The collective notion of dignity, as expressed in *Khosa v Minister of Social Development*,

lesbian relationships); *Amod* (Muslim marriages). But also see *Volks NO v Robinson*, a case concerning cohabitation, in which the majority of the Court agreed that marriage could be privileged over other family forms, and the minority judgments of O'Regan J and Sachs J for the opposite view.

[153] The idea of integrity as 'wholeness or completeness' is captured in the South African Constitution in the right to freedom and security of the person (see above section on 'Freedom/independence/liberty') and in s 41: 'All spheres of government must … exercise their powers and perform their functions in a manner that does not encroach on the geographical, functional or institutional integrity of government in another sphere'.

[154] Section 195(1)(a), (b), (d)

[155] Section 199(7).

[156] Section 1(d)

[157] *S v Makwanyane* [262].

demonstrates the need for compassion for the poor. In the words of Mokgoro J:

> Sharing responsibility for the problems and consequences of poverty equally as a community represents the extent to which wealthier members of the community view the minimal well-being of the poor as connected with their personal well-being and the well-being of the community as a whole.[158]

The value of *ubuntu* is said to 'envelop ... the key values of group solidarity, compassion, respect, human dignity, conformity to basic norms and collective unity, in its fundamental sense it denotes humanity and morality'.[159] Equality and dignity affirm the commitment of the preamble 'to restore and protect the equal worth of everyone, to heal the divisions of the past and to establish a caring and socially just society'.[160]

Secondly, it is present in the adjudication of rights. Rights to equality are concerned with redressing disadvantage, ensuring that vulnerable and excluded groups are bought into the constitutional community. The Court speaks of the need to treat outsider groups, such as refugees, people living with HIV and those who are destitute and in need, with compassion.[161] Socio-economic rights jurisprudence identifies the need for government policy to address those who are poor and in most desperate need, in order to be reasonable, and thus constitutional.[162]

Compassion and caring thus emerge from the constitutional text as characteristics of the new society and constitutionally mandated ways of being. While not self-standing values, they are present in many of the foundational values, including the idea expressed in the preamble to the Constitution of a 'society based on democratic values [dignity, equality and freedom], social justice and fundamental human rights'.

L. Respect/Tolerance

The ideas of respect and tolerance are most clearly stated through the values of dignity and equality, and do not exist as separate values. The court's interpretation of equality, as informed by the value of dignity, involves 'equal

[158] ibid [74].

[159] ibid [308] (footnotes omitted).

[160] *Minister of Finance v Van Heerden* 2004 (6) SA 121 (CC), 2004 (11) BCLR 1125 (CC) [23].

[161] *Hoffman v SAA* 2001 (1) SA 1 (CC); 2000 (11) 1235 (CC) [38]; *Khosa v Minister of Social Development* 2004 (6) 505 (CC), 2004 (6) BCLR 569 (CC) [65]; *Union of The State v Jordan* 2002 6 SA 642 (CC) and *Union of Refugee Women v The Director: The Private Security Industry Regulatory Authority* 2007 4 SA 395 (CC), 2007 4 BCLR 339 (CC) [28].

[162] See *Government of the Republic of South Africa v Grootboom* 2001 (1) SA 46 (CC), 2000 (11) BCLR 1169 (CC) [36].

concern and respect across difference', requiring a society that 'embraces everyone and accepts people for what they are'.[163] It thus asserts difference as a positive characteristic of South African society, which is strengthened by its pluralism and diversity: 'South Africa belongs to all who live in it, united in our diversity.'[164]

Respect for difference has been particularly prominent in cases relating to the removal of unfair discrimination based on sexual orientation and in those concerned with religious and cultural diversity. In a series of cases addressing unfair discrimination on the basis of sexual orientation, the Court has affirmed the need to accord equal concern and respect to gay and lesbian relationships, noting that the Constitution represents a 'radical rupture' from a 'past based on intolerance and exclusion' to the 'need to develop a society based on equality and respect by all for all'.[165]

The Court has also identified language, religious and cultural diversity, as 'an important feature of our constitutional democracy'[166] and has addressed several cases involving legislative failures to acknowledge and accommodate religious diversity.[167] In *Christian Education South Africa v Minister of Education*[168] (finding against a religiously based challenge to the prohibition of corporal punishment in schools):

> There are a number of other provisions designed to protect the rights of members of communities. They underline the constitutional value of acknowledging diversity and pluralism in our society and give a particular texture to the broadly phrased right to freedom of association contained in section 18. Taken together, they affirm the right of people to be who they are without being forced to subordinate themselves to the cultural and religious norms of others, and highlight the importance of individuals and communities being able to enjoy what has been called the 'right to be different'. In each case, space has been found for members

[163] *Minister of Home Affairs v Fourie* 2006 (1) SA 524 (CC), 2006 (3) BCLR 355 (CC) [60].

[164] Preamble, Constitution.

[165] *Fourie* [59]. This judgment is an excellent summary of the Court's jurisprudence on sexual orientation discrimination and demonstrates the centrality of the concept of respect and tolerance.

[166] *Bhe v Magistrate, Khayelitsha* 2005 (1) SA 580 (CC), 2005 (1) BCLR 1 (CC) [234] (Ncgobo J, concurring on this point).

[167] *Christian Education of South Africa v Minister of Education* 2000 (10) BCLR 1051 (CC). This concerned a challenge to the South African Schools Act 84 of 1996, in that the prohibition of corporal punishment therein offended against religious and cultural rights protected in ss 15 and 31 of the Constitution. The court found that the provision did violate the religious rights of parents, but that this was justified under s 36. See also *S v Lawrence, S v Nagel, S v Solberg* 1997 (4) SA 1176 (CC), 1997 10 BCLR 1348 (CC) (on the question of restricted liquor sales on Sundays); *Prince v The President of the Law Society of the Cape of Good Hope* 2000 (7) BCLR 823 (SCA) (the refusal of the Law Society to register Prince as an attorney was not a violation of his freedom of religion); *Prince v The President of the Law Society of the Cape of Good Hope* 2001 (2) BCLR 133 (CC) (on whether the blanket criminalisation of marijuana in the Drugs and Drug trafficking Act violated the freedom of religion of Rastafarians, for whom the smoking of marijuana was an essential part of their religion).

[168] 2000 (4) SA 757 (CC), 2000 (10) BCLR 1051 (CC).

> of communities to depart from a general norm. These provisions collectively and separately acknowledge the rich tapestry constituted by civil society, indicating in particular that language, culture and religion constitute a strong weave in the overall pattern.[169]

The affirmation of different communities is based on the idea of equality as 'equal concern and respect': '[T]he essence of equality lies not in treating everyone in the same way, but in treating everyone with equal concern and respect.'[170]

M. Security

If the protection of state security was a primary value of the apartheid state, justifying its authoritarian and repressive nature,[171] then post-apartheid democracy places government 'based on the will of the people' at its centre.[172] The Constitutional Court has recognised that a 'collective pursuit of national security is integral to the primary constitutional object of establishing a constitutional state based on democratic values, social justice and fundamental human rights', and notes that national security in the Republic is subject to constitutional principles and provisions.[173] Thus section 198(a) of the Constitution states that: 'National security must reflect the resolve of South Africans, as individuals and as a nation, to live as equals, to live in peace and harmony, to be free from fear and want and to seek a better life.'

Thus while state security or national security is present in legislation and in some constitutional jurisprudence as a limit on the exercise of rights, such as access to information, it is not a constitutional value. It is rather a function of the state that is subject to the democratic values of the Constitution and the rule of law.[174]

N. Learning/Education

The Constitution guarantees the right to education in section 29. The Constitutional Court has noted that right to a basic education, including adult education, in section 29(1)(a) is 'immediately realisable' and may 'only be limited only in terms of a law of general application which is reasonable and justifiable in an open and democratic society based on human dignity, equality

[169] ibid [24] (footnotes omitted).

[170] ibid [42].

[171] See John Dugard, *Human Rights and the South African Legal Order* (Cape Town, Juta and Co, 1978) esp 325–65.

[172] Preamble, Constitution.

[173] *Masetlha v President of the RSA* 2008 (1) SA 566 (CC), 2008 1 BCLR 1 (CC) [32].

[174] *Masetlha* [33].

and freedom'.[175] The right to further education is subject to progressive realisation. Whilst an important right, learning/education is not a constitutional value. However, the courts have increasingly recognised its importance within our democracy. Thus the Constitutional Court has noted the 'significance of education, in particular basic education for individual and societal development in our democratic dispensation in the light of the legacy of apartheid'[176] and that 'basic education is an important socio-economic right directed, among other things, at promoting and developing a child's personality, talents and mental and physical abilities to his or her fullest potential.'[177] Although Constitutional Court jurisprudence is currently limited, several High Court cases have begun to explore the substantive content of the right.[178]

O. Environment

The South African Constitution also addresses the issue of the environment as a right, not a value. Section 24 provides that '[e]veryone has the right (a) to an environment that is not harmful to their health and well-being; and (b) to have the environment protected for the benefit of present and future generations through reasonable legislative and other measures'. Substantial legislation thus seeks to enforce this right.[179]

IV. VALUES, TRANSFORMATION AND COURTS

The transformative nature of the South African Constitution and the aspirational quality of its values presuppose a gap between the values and reality, between the inheritance of the past and the imperative for a better future. Fifteen years into the new democracy, that gap remains, for many, as wide as ever. Great disparities of wealth persist, with significant income inequalities manifest in a rising Gini co-efficient.[180] Increased wage inequality is only

[175] *Governing Body of the Juma Musjid Primary School v Essay* NO 2011 (8) BCLR 761 (CC) [37].

[176] ibid [42].

[177] ibid [45].

[178] See, eg, *Section 27 v Minister of Education* [2012] 3 All SA 579 (GNP) (textbooks a component of the right to basic education).

[179] See in general Jan Glazewski, *Environmental Law in South Africa* (London, LexisNexis Butterworths, 2005) and Michael Kidd, *Environmental Law* (Cape Town, Juta and Co, 2011).

[180] The World Bank describes the Gini-coefficient of inequality as 'the most commonly used measure of inequality. The coefficient varies between 0, which reflects complete equality and 1, which indicates complete inequality (one person has all the income or consumption, all others have none)'. See http://web.worldbank.org. South Africa's Gini coefficient rose from 0.64 in 1995 to 0.72 in 2005 (Haroon Bhorat, Carlene Van der Westhuizen and Toughedah Jacobs, 'Income and Non-Income Inequality in Post-Apartheid South Africa: Drivers and Possible Policy Interventions', Unpublished presentation, 29 September 2008, Development Policy Research Unit, University of Cape Town). According to government statistics, the Gini co-efficient hovered at around 0.68 for the period 2000–2008. Presidency of the RSA, *Development Indicators 2009* (2009).

partly mitigated by the government's social programmes.[181] If improvements in the provision of services have meant that non-income inequality has reduced, overall levels of poverty remain high, especially for black women.[182] High levels of gender-based violence,[183] recurrent xenophobia[184] and significant levels, of violent crime[185] suggest a society that is at war with itself. The majority of South Africans favour the death penalty.[186] Recent years have seen major political figures, including the immediate past and present presidents, use state institutions to serve sectional interests.[187] Reports of corruption suggest that tender abuse is widespread amongst public servants,[188] and evidence persists of arms deal corruption,[189] at the time of writing subject to a national commission of enquiry.[190] It is not difficult to illustrate the gap between the idea of a caring and compassionate society based on dignity, equality and freedom and daily life in South Africa, nor between an accountable, open and transparent government and problems of abuse of power, corruption and undermining the rule of law.

However, that would not also tell the whole story. Equally important is the plethora of laws that have been introduced to extend rights to previously excluded groups and set new norms of behaviour,[191] thus bridging the gap, at least in a formal sense, between constitutional values and reality. There is

[181] Bhorat, Van der Westhuizen and Jacobs, ibid.

[182] ibid. Statistics reveal that intra-group inequality has increased, although racial inequality between groups remains a dominant feature of South African society.

[183] It is estimated about one in nine women is raped in her lifetime. A recent study reveals that one in four men interviewed in two provinces (Kwazulu-Natal and the Eastern Cape) admit to having raped a woman. See generally: Rachel Jewkes, Y Sweyiya, Robert Morrell and Kristin Dunkle, 'Why, When and How Men Rape' (2010) 34 *SA Crime Quarterly* 23.

[184] See, eg, Loren Landau, Kaajal Ramjathan-Keogh and Gayatri Singh, 'Xenophobia in South Africa and Problems Related to it', Background Paper prepared for: Open hearings on 'Xenophobia and Problems Related to it' hosted by the South African Human Rights Commission with the Portfolio Committee of the Departments of Foreign Affairs and Home Affairs (January 2005).

[185] Statistics South Africa, *Victims of Crime Survey 2011* (2011).

[186] See Stephen Rule and Bongiwe Mncwango, 'Rights or Wrongs? An Exploration of Moral Values' in Udesh Pillay, Benjamin Roberts and Stephen Rule, *South African Social Attitudes. Changing Times, Diverse Voices.* (Pretoria, HSRC Press, 2006) ch 12, 257–62.

[187] While President Mbeki is alleged to have used the National Prosecuting Authority to influence charges in relation to his successor, Jacob Zuma, and police commissioner Jackie Selebi; President Zuma is alleged to have used the NPA to prevent charges being brought against him.

[188] Auditor-General of South Africa, *General Report on National Audit Putcome 2010–2011* (2012).

[189] Andew Feinstein, *The Shadow World: Inside the Global Arms Trade* (New York, Farrar, Straus and Giroux, 2011).

[190] The Commission of Inquiry into Allegations of Fraud, Corruption, Impropriety or Irregularity In The Strategic Defence Procurement Package was established by Proclamation of the President of the Republic of South Africa No R 4, 2012, *Government Gazette* No 350238, February 2012.

[191] A substantial number of laws have been passed to address a broad range of issues, including discrimination, gender-based violence, corruption, reproductive choice, same sex marriage etc.

also evidence of the state being held to account under the Constitution,[192] of participatory democracy asserting its power[193] and of poor people successfully claiming their rights in court;[194] in short, evidence of constitutional democracy working. Far more difficult to document, because of its location in the private, is evidence of communities assisting victims of xenophobia, breaking down racial barriers and reaching across old divides.

There are many reasons for the persistence of inequality, violence and authoritarian practices, as well as for accountability, participation, compassion and solidarity. At least some of these relate to the values that drive public and private behaviour, and by which we hold ourselves, and others, to account. Given the trajectory of South Africa's political transition, the Constitution is a foundational repository of the values of the new order. Giving meaning and life to these values plays an important role in constituting our democracy—giving it traction and substance. As interpreters of the Constitution, the courts, and especially the Constitutional Court, must 'through thoroughly reasoned engagement with the constitutional text, produce a normative framework of sufficient density to guide other political actors, organs of state and social agents'.[195] In doing so, courts and judges should also promote a 'dialogue' with others in the state and civil society, as they too act by advancing and debating policies, laws and practices that give substance to the Constitution.

In their role as arbiters, and thus as guardians of the Constitution, judges carry a heavy responsibility to provide a basis for democratic debate and to ensure that other state actors are held to account and remain within the boundaries of the Constitution. Judicial independence is critical for this, so too is the need for judges to be accountable in providing well-reasoned decisions, based on a clear exposition of the values of the Constitution.

[192] In particular cases on gender equality, sexual orientation and same-sex marriage. For a critical discussion, see Catherine Albertyn, 'Substantive Equality and Transformation in South Africa' (2007) 23 *South African Journal on Human Rights* 253.

[193] See, eg, *Doctors for Life International v Speaker of the National Assembly* 2006 (12) BCLR 1399 (CC), 2006 (6) SA 416 (CC); *Matatiele Municipality v President of the RSA* (2) (2007) 1 BCLR (CC) 47.

[194] See, in particular, cases of socio-economic rights: *Minister of Health v Treatment Action Campaign (No 2)* 2002 (5) SA 721 (CC)—rights of HIV-positive pregnant women in public sector hospitals to antiretroviral treatment to reduce transmission of HIV to their babies; *Khosa v Minister of Social Development* 2004 (6) 505 (CC), 2004 (6) BCLR 569 (CC)—rights of destitute permanent residents to social grants; *Port Elizabeth Municipality v Various Occupiers* 2005 (1) SA 217 (CC), 2004 (12) BCLR 1268 (CC)—rights of poor, unlawful occupiers not to rendered homeless through eviction by municipality in the absence of compelling evidence; *Occupiers of 51 Olivia Road, Berea v City of Johannesburg* 2008 (5) BCLR 475 (CC)—rights to temporary accommodation when evicted by local authority; *Residents of Joe Slovo Community v Thubelisha Homes* 2009 (9) BCLR 847 (CC)—rights to alternative accommodation where eviction would render poor community homeless.

[195] Stu Woolman and Henk Botha, 'Limitations. Shared Constitutional Intrepretation, An Appropriate Normative Framework and Hard Choices' in Stu Woolman and Michael Bishop (eds), *Constitutional Conversations* (Pretoria, Pretoria University Law Press, 2008) 149, 150.

The record of the Constitutional Court suggests that it has not fully stepped up to this role. Even the relatively brief survey of values in this chapter suggests that the foundational values of dignity, equality and freedom have not been fully explicated, either individually or in relation to each other. Within these 'conjoined, reciprocal and covalent values',[196] it is dignity that has been given the most substance and which has been elevated above the other two values—both of which remain undeveloped. In failing to develop these values, the Court has also failed to address the tensions between them.[197] The relationship between freedom and equality, for example, remains uncertain, yet it is critical to understanding the nature of our democracy. In the main, dignity has provided a way of negotiating the potential tensions between freedom and equality, and avoiding substantive choices about their meaning. Other values also remain undeveloped—*ubuntu* is an example of a value that is deployed to bolster a point about community or solidarity or nation, but its actual role within the constitutional value system remains unclear. Values of democracy (accountability, participation etc) have seen some development, but without a clear consensus on the deeper meaning of democracy itself.[198]

Early in the Constitutional Court's life, Alfred Cockrell wrote that the inclusion of values in the Constitution required a particular form of adjudication, one that relied on substantive rather than formal reasoning. Judicial decisions needed to be justified with reference to moral, ethical and political reasons, embedded in a deeper theoretical articulation of the values of the Constitution.[199] In Cockrell's analysis, and in many of those that followed, the Court was found to have engaged in a shallower form of reasoning, relying on formalism and legalism in which values were part of a fuzzy 'rainbow jurisprudence'.[200] Du Plessis has argued that values tend to be used for 'rhetorical rather than analytic purposes, and most often in order to lend force to what a judicial interpreter has already concluded, with reference to an issue at hand, an ideal state of affairs in democratic South Africa should be'.[201]

[196] *S v Mamabolo (E TV Intervening)* 2001 (3) SA 409 (CC), 2001 (5) BCLR 449 (CC) [41] (Kriegler J).

[197] Halton Cheadle and Dennis Davis, 'Structure of the Bill of Rights' in Halton Cheadle, Dennis Davis and Nicholas Haysom, *South African Constitutional Law: The Bill of Rights* (Durban, Butterworths, 2002) ch 1, p 7; Lourens du Plessis, 'Interpretation' in Woolman et al (eds), *Constitutional Law of South Africa*, 2nd edn (Cape Town, Juta and Co, 2008).

[198] See, eg, Theunis Roux, 'Democracy' in Woolman et al (eds), *Constitutional Law of South Africa*, 2nd edn (Cape Town, Juta and Co, 2006) ch 10.

[199] Alfred Cockrell, 'Rainbow Jurisprudence' (1996) 12 *South African Journal on Human Rights* 1.

[200] Dennis Davis, 'Transformation: The Constitutional Promise And Reality' (2010) 26 *South African Journal on Human Rights* 85.

[201] Lourens du Plessis, speaking particularly about the use of values in the limitations analysis (n 197) ch 32, p 129.

There are many reasons for this gap between the idea of the Court articulating a constitutional vision of a 'democratic future', a basic normative framework for democracy, and the more limited reality. Iain Currie, drawing on the work of Cass Sunstein, has suggested such judicious avoidance was a strategic act, deciding only what is necessary for their case.[202] Several authors have also pointed to the benefits of maintaining a level of indeterminacy in the content of values, granting the Court flexibility in defining the boundaries of rights and negotiating separation of powers issues.[203] It is important, too, to consider the fact that the Constitutional Court is a new institution in a new democracy, thus constructing legitimacy and building institutional security would have been important concerns.

As guardians of the Constitution, courts may occupy a precarious position within a democracy 'based on the will of the people'. Negotiating the 'majoritarian dilemma', and successfully holding other state institutions to account for their constitutional failures, requires much of a court. Theunis Roux has argued that constitutional courts in emerging democracies such as South Africa have negotiated a jurisprudential path between principled and strategically pragmatic decisions as a means of securing and defending institutional security. Roux suggests that the South African Constitutional Court has been particularly concerned to develop legitimacy with the ruling ANC elite, rather than to develop popular support amongst the public, and that it has been relatively successful in doing this. In so doing, the Court is able to conserve space to interpret the Bill of Rights and defend the rule of law.[204]

The fact that courts act strategically is unsurprising to critical scholars. It remains a moot question, however, as to whether the Court has acted strategically in *not* sufficiently developing the constitutional value system further, and in *not* achieving more popular support through accessible and reasoned judgments. This has become an important question in contemporary South Africa as the courts have increasingly been a site of struggle for competing political interests, a bruising political battle that has seen the judiciary and individual judges attacked for political bias and even 'counter-revolutionary' activities.[205] While, the ruling party has mostly reasserted its commitment to the Constitution, an independent judiciary and the rule of law; deep uncertainties remain about the possibilities of the government reining in an independent judiciary that, despite the criticisms articulated in this chapter, has

[202] Iain Currie, 'Judicious Avoidance' (1999) 15 *South African Journal on Human Rights* 138.

[203] Catherine Albertyn and Beth Goldblatt, 'Equality' in Woolman et al (eds), *Constitutional Law of South Africa*, 2nd edn (Cape Town, Juta and Co, 2007) ch 35, 14.

[204] Theunis Roux, 'Principle and Pragmatism in the South African Constitutional Court' (2008) *International Journal of Constitutional Law* 106.

[205] See, eg, Catherine O'Regan, 'A Forum for Reason: Reflections on the Role and Work of the Constitutional Court' (2012) 28 *South African Journal on Human Rights* 116, 117–18.

made powerful judgments that constrain state power and affirm the claims of the poor and marginalised.

Perhaps the lesson of this chapter is that courts need to work with what they have in creating legitimacy and security vis-à-vis the state *and* the public as a whole. The South African courts have a powerful Constitution, underpinned by strong democratic values that enable judges to speak to the aspirations of the majority who live in conditions of grinding inequality. The judiciary is authorised to engage, even to lead, a debate about the nature of our democracy, the meaning of the rule of law and the values of our society. It has undoubtedly done so in many of its judgments, and the importance of continuing to do so is undiminished.

14

Values in the UK Constitution

JEFFREY JOWELL AND COLM O'CINNEIDE

I. INTRODUCTION AND CONTEXT

IT IS OFTEN said that the United Kingdom has no constitution.[1] That is wrong. Its constitutional foundations are deeply rooted and well-established, although it is right to say that they are not set out in any single document. It is also not accurate to say that the British constitution is unwritten. A great deal of its content is based on written sources, including many statutes and decided cases (the common law). However, its content is also based upon unwritten sources, including settled expectations arising from conventional patterns of political behaviour and accepted democratic principles (such as the primacy of representative government, the rule of law and equality). These different strands of content, although not contained in any single overriding text, interweave to form a sturdy fabric of democratic constitutionalism.[2]

This constitutional fabric has acquired its current shape and texture through a process of open-ended, incremental and often turbulent development. The principal agents of this development have been Parliament (seeking to reflect public opinion) and the courts (seeking to reflect principles of justice). The two interact and together shape and define the values that we consider in this chapter.

The modern British constitutional system first emerged in embryonic form out of the struggles between King and Parliament in the seventeenth century. In the wake of the 'Glorious Revolution' of 1688, the provisions

[1] A note on terminology—the phrase 'British constitution' is used as shorthand throughout this chapter to refer to the constitutional system of the United Kingdom. This reflects common usage, although it should be borne in mind that the UK is composed of the union of Great Britain and Northern Ireland, and the geographical term 'Britain' only applies to the island of that name.

[2] Murkens has criticised the use of the term 'constitutionalism' in public law discourse in the UK, arguing that it often lacks precise definition: here, it is used as a shorthand to indicate the system of normative values that structures and controls the use of public power in the UK. See J Murkens, 'The Quest for Constitutionalism in UK Public Law Discourse' (2009) 29(3) *Oxford Journal of Legal Studies* 427–55.

of the Bill of Rights of 1689 established that Parliament had the sole right to levy taxes and enact legislation, thereby affirming the principle of parliamentary supremacy in the legislative sphere. The text of the Bill of Rights also recognised the existence of certain basic liberties, including the right to jury trial and entitlement to freedom from 'cruel and unusual punishment'. Many of these civil liberties had been described as the immemorial entitlement of all Englishmen in the Magna Carta of 1215: the Bill of Rights now presented liberty and representative governance as marching hand in hand, and these two values became established by the political settlement of 1688 as the twin pillars of the new emerging constitutional order.

Subsequently, the eighteenth and early nineteenth centuries saw the gradual decay of monarchical power, the extension of parliamentary control over the exercise of the royal prerogative (ie, the executive powers of the Crown), and the long struggle by radicals, trade unionists and others to expand the scope of civil liberties. The British constitution finally took its modern form with the extension of the franchise to working-class men and finally to women in the late nineteenth and the first half of the twentieth centuries respectively and the confirmation of the supremacy of the elected House of Commons over the unelected House of Lords in the Parliament Act 1911. This led in turn to the emergence of mass participatory democracy and modern political parties, the creation of the welfare state in the wake of the two world wars, and the ensuing expansion of the power and responsibilities of the executive branch of government.

The British constitution continues to evolve. The entry of the UK into what is now the European Union via the enactment of the European Communities Act 1972, the introduction of sweeping privatisation measures in the 1980s, the incorporation of the European Convention on Human Rights ('the ECHR') into UK law via the Human Rights Act 1998 ('the HRA') and the devolution of powers to legislative assemblies in Scotland, Wales and Northern Ireland are all fresh constitutional milestones laid down over the last few decades.[3] They raise profound questions about whether the UK's legal and political culture is indeed homogenous, and whether it fits with values of the wider Europe in which it is embedded.

Furthermore, the contours of the current constitutional settlement remain contested. At the time of writing, the UK's continuing membership of the EU remains a matter of serious public debate. Furthermore, the HRA and the influence exerted by the European Court of Human Rights ('the ECtHR') over domestic UK law have attracted a considerable degree of media and political hostility. Leading politicians within the centre-right Conservative Party have proposed replacing the HRA with a home-grown 'British

[3] Simpson has also noted the importance of the end of the British Empire to the shaping of constitutional culture post-1945: B Simpson, *Human Rights and the End of Empire: Britain and the Genesis of the European Convention on Human Rights* (Oxford, OUP, 2001).

Bill of Rights', with a view to minimising the impact of European human rights law on the development of national law and policy.[4] A referendum on Scottish independence took place in September 2014: it resulted in a clear vote against Scotland leaving the UK, but support for Scottish independence increased considerably during the referendum campaign, and in the aftermath of the vote significant new powers have been transferred to the Scottish Parliament in Edinburgh. In general, Scotland, Wales and Northern Ireland are becoming increasingly self-governing, while debate continues in Westminster as to how existing constitutional arrangements should be adjusted to reflect the reality that the UK is becoming a quasi-federal state. In general, the British constitution remains a work in progress, and it is difficult to predict its future development.

This state of permanent flux has led some prominent scholars to describe the UK constitutional system as lacking any definite content. For example, John Griffith once famously described the British constitution as simply 'what happens' when actors within the system exercise state power at any given time.[5] Other scholars have viewed the UK constitutional system as consisting of a set of rules which govern how power should be exercised in a democratic manner, and suggest that it lacks any substantive normative dimension beyond a basic commitment to democratic governance.[6]

However, both these different perspectives overlook how the historical evolution of the British constitutional system has given rise to a set of relatively 'thick' and deeply embedded normative expectations as to how state power should be exercised. Adherence to democratic constitutionalism in the UK is assumed to involve respect for a range of values that go beyond a minimalist commitment to representative democracy. While the UK lacks a definite legal mechanism for determining when something is or is not 'constitutional', these values generate normative standards against which the legitimacy of the acts of public bodies is judged. These values also dictate the content of the uncodified conventions, behavioural expectations and written legal rules that together shape the UK's dense democratic constitutionalist fabric. In other words, as with any other constitutional system, the UK has embedded constitutional values.

Three core values in particular underlie the British constitutional system. The first is the presumption of liberty. 'Liberty' in this context connotes an understanding that people have a right to do what is not explicitly and

[4] For an analysis of these proposals, see C O'Cinneide, *Human Rights and the UK Constitution* (London, British Academy, 2012), available at www.britac.ac.uk/policy/Human-rights.cfm.

[5] JAG Griffith, 'The Political Constitution' (1979) 42 *Modern Law Review* 1, 19.

[6] See the analysis of the existing state of the UK constitutional system in ch 1 of V Bogdanor, *The New British Constitution* (Oxford, Hart, 2009). For a normative defence of a purely 'political' constitutional order, see R Bellamy, *Political Constitutionalism: A Republican Defence of the Constitutionality of Democracy* (Cambridge, CUP, 2007).

lawfully forbidden. The second is the imperative of representative government, which endorses the notion of parliamentary sovereignty and requires decisions as to where the public interest lies to be made by the elected government of the day. The third value, the rule of law, mediates between the first two, seeking a balance between unrestrained freedom and unrestrained governmental authority and which itself contains a number of explicit secondary values.

Other values also exist which are accorded considerable weight in the functioning of the UK's constitutional system, such as respect for individual autonomy and human dignity, a commitment to equality and tolerance, and adherence to the principle of transparent, accountable and effective governance. However, these 'secondary' values have not yet been embedded into the bedrock of the British constitution: they influence the design and functioning of the UK's constitutional system, as distinct from the three core values which serve as its normative foundations.

II. THE PRESUMPTION OF LIBERTY

For many years it has been argued that the UK does not need a constitutional bill of rights—an entrenched framework of positive rights—because such rights and freedoms are in any event legally protected under the common law. Professor Dicey, in a work written in 1885[7] which attained huge authority, believed that liberties were better protected in England through the common law than in countries with written constitutions and a separate system of public law, such as in France at that time. Individuals were free to do anything not prohibited by law, and the UK's political culture of respect for personal freedom ensured that Parliament would not pass laws which unduly infringed individual autonomy.

It must be doubtful now (whatever may have been the case in the past) whether Dicey's argument that freedoms are better protected under the English common law system than under other European legal systems is necessarily correct, given the continental European embrace of strong constitutional democracy since 1945. However, he rightly observed that many of the fundamental freedoms generally enjoyed by citizens of democratic states across the world have in the UK been recognised by the courts to be inherent in law, and do not need to be explicitly granted or affirmed by statute. This creates a default presumption of personal liberty, which in turn has the effect of ensuring that public authorities must have a clear legal basis for any action that they may take which infringes upon individual freedom.

[7] AV Dicey, *Introduction to the Study of the Law of the Constitution* (London, Macmillan, 1885; 10th edn, 1959).

In the absence of legislative or common law authorisation, the state cannot interfere with how an individual lives their life.[8]

Historically, this presumption of liberty was of great importance. It gave rise to the canon of statutory interpretation that legislation creating criminal offences should be interpreted and applied narrowly by the courts, which continues to be of prime importance in limiting the potential over-reach of the criminal law.[9] The presumption also lead to the restrictive interpretation of police and public order powers, which was of immense historical significance in the eighteenth century when cases such as *Entick v Carrington*[10] established that interference with an individual's property or person would constitute trespass unless the existence of lawful justification could be established.

The presumption of liberty also remains central to the protection of liberties to this day, as illustrated by the decision of the House of Lords in *R (on the application of Laporte) v Chief Constable of Gloucestershire*, where police intervention in the interest of maintaining public order to prevent anti-war protesters picketing an air force base was held to be unlawful on the basis that the relevant public order legislation could not be interpreted widely so as to authorise the action taken against the protestors.[11]

The presumption of liberty thus continues to limit the reach of executive power. For example, there exists no general freestanding basis for executive action in the UK constitutional system that impacts upon individual freedom: there is no equivalent of the civil law concept of the *L'ordre publique*. The presumption of liberty also operates to protect individuals from paternalistic intrusion by the state or other private individuals which lacks a clear legal basis.[12] Its deeply embedded status in the UK's constitutional culture is also reflected in political debates in Parliament and elsewhere, where an emphasis on individual autonomy is a recurring theme.

However, in a society dependant on collective provision to ensure the achievement of key social objectives, individual liberty can inevitably come in tension with other important values, or with the liberty claims of others. As a consequence, liberty alone cannot serve as the dominant core value of a constitutional system: the tensions generated by a strong emphasis on individual freedom need to be mediated by a collective decision-making process.

[8] See eg, *R v Secretary of State for the Home Department, ex p Simms* [1999] 3 All ER 400, HL, [1999] 3 WLR 328.

[9] For a recent example of this see *R v Zafar* [2008] EWCA Crim 184, where the Court of Appeal adopted a restrictive interpretation of the provisions of s 57 of the Terrorism Act 2000, which prohibited the possession of material for a 'purpose connected with the commission, preparation or instigation of an act of terrorism'.

[10] *Entick v Carrington* (1765) 19 St Tr 1029.

[11] *R (on the application of Laporte) v Chief Constable of Gloucestershire* [2006] UKHL 55.

[12] See eg *Re F, F v West Berkshire Health Authority* [1989] 2 All ER 545.

Hobbes recognised this need to mediate individual liberty with collective rule in his seminal text, the *Leviathan*, when he posited the need for society to submit to governance by a sovereign ruler to prevent chaos. Locke subsequently went a step further and recognised that self-governance via representative democracy best mediated the tension between the collective and the individual, involving as it does the collective exercise of liberty (expressed through democratic choice in the selection of representatives) to determine questions of the common good.[13] Locke's 'social contract' analysis both influenced and was influenced by the new British constitutional order that emerged after 1688. Therefore, from the beginning of the modern UK constitutional system, the core value of personal liberty has been regarded as intimately intertwined with a second core value, the primacy of representative government.[14]

The status of liberty as a core constitutional value now also needs to be understood in the context of the massive expansion of the role of the state since the Victorian era, in particular with the establishment of the modern welfare state in the wake of the two world wars. This expanded role of the state has often been achieved through the use of broadly framed enabling legislation, which has given public authorities wide legal authority to intervene in areas of an individual's life that would have been seen as off limits in previous eras. This has limited the scope of personal liberty, at least if understood in the sense of untrammelled individual freedom from state interference: it has also reduced the impact of the presumption of liberty, as much wider legal bases now exist for state action than was the case in previous eras.

However, this new and more active role of the state can also be said to have enhanced substantive freedom, through measures such as the introduction of anti-discrimination law, protection against abuse in the home and the provision of social security. This illustrates Berlin's argument that liberty can be understood as having a 'negative' and a 'positive' face.[15] The presumption of liberty is based upon a negative understanding of the value of freedom, but the positive dimension is also often invoked to justify the extension of state regulation. Once again, this brings us back to the role of representative governance, which in the UK system is given the authority to determine where the balance should be struck between these different concepts of liberty.

[13] See in general J Locke, *Two Treatises of Government* [1690], P Laslett (ed), (Cambridge, CUP, 1988).

[14] The text of the Bill of Rights 1689, which established the principle of parliamentary supremacy in the legislative sphere, explicitly treats representative government as a manifestation of 'ancient rights and liberties'.

[15] I Berlin, 'Two Concepts of Liberty' in I Berlin, *Four Essays on Liberty* (Oxford, OUP, 1969) 118–72.

The presumption of liberty thus remains a value of considerable importance in the UK constitutional system: it frames and limits the exercise of state power in requiring that interference with individual freedom must rest upon a firm legal basis. However, it is another core value, the primacy of representative government, which tends to dictate who can confer such a legal basis and thereby authorise inference with personal liberty in the name of the common good or the promotion of the freedom of others.

III. THE PRIMACY OF REPRESENTATIVE GOVERNMENT (OR SOVEREIGNTY OF PARLIAMENT)

The principle of popular self-governance lies at the heart of the value system of all democratic societies. The UK is no exception. However, in the British constitutional system, particular emphasis is placed on representative government as the potentially unrestrained mechanism through which the democratic will of the British people is expressed. The UK Parliament is conventionally considered to be 'sovereign', meaning that legislation passed in Westminster cannot be challenged, nullified or overruled by any other organ of the state.[16] Under the doctrine of parliamentary sovereignty, Parliament can make and remake all law, a power which extends to reshaping the contours of the British constitutional system.[17] This sovereign status of Parliament is justified on the basis that it represents the people and serves as the vehicle through which popular self-governance is exercised. Therefore, the primacy of representative government in the form of the doctrine of the sovereignty of Parliament is established as a core value of the UK system: supreme power is understood to be exercised by the will of the people as expressed through their elected representatives in Parliament.[18]

The origins of this assumption lie in the particular historical development of the British constitutional system. As already discussed, the transition from rule by the monarch to rule by Parliament was, in the UK, relatively free from disruptive revolutions, insurrections or sustained civil war, after the Glorious Revolution of 1688. As the authority of the monarch contracted, the Parliament of the people effectively inherited the 'sovereignty' formerly residing in the Crown. As a result, Parliament became the mechanism through which the British people collectively came to exercise their

[16] This doctrine does not command universal assent: alternative understandings exist as to the status of the Westminster Parliament: see D Feldman, 'None, One or Several? Perspectives on the UK's Constitution(s)' (2005) 64(2) *Cambridge Law Journal* 329–51.

[17] See Dicey, n 7 above.

[18] In systems with written constitutions, popular sovereignty is considered to be expressed through the constitutional text from which all organs of the state derive their powers: in contrast, in the UK, popular sovereignty is viewed as expressed through the decisions of the sovereign Parliament, which functions in a way like a constituent assembly in permanent session.

democratic rights. In this way, the principle of parliamentary sovereignty became accepted as the appropriate constitutional embodiment of the democratic principle of popular self-government: the conferral of supreme power upon Parliament was seen as a full and adequate proxy for the conferral of power upon the people.

In general, Parliament has proved to be an effective vehicle for the expression of the popular will. It also has served as an engine for the definition and renewal of social values. Compared to the USA, it is the legislature, rather than the courts, which has played the primary role in imposing legal prohibitions on racial, gender and other forms of discrimination. The legislature has also introduced universal benefits such as health care, ensured that women have general access to abortion services, abolished capital punishment and made provision for same-sex marriage.

However, over the years, the automatic identification of the doctrine of parliamentary sovereignty with the principle of democratic self-governance has come under strain. Giving unlimited power to the sovereign Parliament has meant the adoption of a majoritarian view of democracy: a political party which controls a majority of seats in the House of Commons can wield its sovereign power, subject only to the constraints imposed by the prevailing political climate. The growth of unified and disciplined political parties has also meant that the day-to-day workings of Parliament tend to be controlled by the party leaderships. Furthermore, there is no legal constraint on the sovereign Parliament conferring extensive delegated powers upon the executive, police or other public authorities: as a result, more and more discretionary power in areas such as land use and planning, social security, immigration and policing functions has been conferred upon ministers and other public officials, who often operate relatively free of any effective parliamentary supervision.

Taken together, these trends have called into question the normative basis for the doctrine of parliamentary sovereignty, as they highlight how representative governance can struggle to give substantive effect to the principle of democratic self-governance, permit the erosion of liberties and give scant regard to the interests of unpopular minorities. The need to develop transnational forms of democratic governance in response to globalisation and the process of European integration, taken together with the partial transfer of legislative authority from Westminster to the devolved legislatures in Scotland, Wales and Northern Ireland, has also generated debate about the conceptual basis of parliamentary sovereignty: some critics have questioned the suitability of the doctrine in an era of multi-layered constitutional governance.[19]

[19] M Elliott, 'Parliamentary Sovereignty and the New Constitutional Order: Legislative Freedom, Political Reality and Convention' (2002) 22 *Legal Studies* 340.

The sovereign authority of the Westminster Parliament is now in any case subject to certain de facto constraints. For example, the establishment of devolved assemblies in Scotland, Northern Ireland and Wales with law-making powers has involved a delegation of authority by the Westminster Parliament to these new representative institutions. While in theory the sovereign Westminster Parliament could retract this delegation of power, in reality any substantial adjustment of the existing devolution settlement would require popular approval via referendum vote at least in the areas concerned.[20]

In addition, UK membership of the European Union (EU) as established by the European Communities Act 1972 means that EU law becomes part of UK law and must be treated by British courts as superior to any conflicting domestic laws: the House of Lords confirmed in the case of *Factortame* that even acts of the sovereign Parliament should not be applied by domestic courts if they are not in conformity with EU law.[21] As with the devolution settlement, the supremacy of EU law does not in itself contradict the doctrine of parliamentary sovereignty, as it takes effect in UK law by virtue of the European Communities Act 1972, a legislative enactment which the sovereign UK Parliament could presumably repeal.[22] However, repeal of the 1972 Act would be essentially incompatible with continuing UK membership of the EU: there is a general political consensus that any such fundamental shift in the UK's relationship with the EU will require popular approval via a referendum process, given that entry into what was then the EEC was approved via a popular referendum in 1975. As a result, UK membership of the EU means that parliamentary sovereignty is in practice limited by the requirement to conform to EU law, and any departure from this situation will require a direct appeal to the people, rather than being based solely upon the principle of the primacy of representative governance.[23]

Another contrast between the existence of de facto limits on the day-to-day exercise of parliamentary sovereignty and the persistence of the ultimate de jure sovereign power of Parliament can be seen through the European Convention on Human Rights (ECHR) which has been incorporated into UK law through the Human Rights Act 1998 (HRA). The ECHR does not have the status of EU law within domestic law: the courts lack the power under the HRA to strike down or suspend parliamentary legislation and must give effect to such legislation even if they consider it to

[20] G Little, 'Scotland and Parliamentary Sovereignty' (2006) 24(2) *Legal Studies* 540–67.

[21] *R v Secretary of State for Transport ex p Factortame Ltd (No 2)* [1991] 1 AC 603. See also the more recent judgment of *R (HS2 Action Alliance Ltd) v Secretary of State for Transport* [2014] UKSC 3.

[22] See in this respect s 18 of the European Union Act 2011.

[23] The European Union Act 2011 requires that a popular referendum must be held to approve any UK ratification of amendments to the existing core EU treaty framework.

be incompatible with the Convention.[24] However, the courts may issue a declaration of incompatibility which states their opinion that the legislation in question is incompatible with the Convention and a special fast-track mechanism allows for legislation to be amended rapidly in response to such a declaration.[25] Successive UK governments have in practice given effect to judgments of the European Court of Human Rights which have found the UK to be in breach of the ECHR, by ensuring that offending legislation was amended to reflect the conclusions of the Strasbourg court. In other words, the UK generally considers itself bound to adhere to the Convention and acts accordingly to maintain conformity with its provisions: this means that in practice domestic law is often made subservient to the requirements of the ECHR.

The sovereign Parliament still retains the power to disregard a declaration of incompatibility made by a UK court under the HRA, or refuse to give effect to a judgment of the European Court of Human Rights. The erosion of the day-to-day significance of Parliamentary sovereignty in the field of human rights nevertheless remains significant. For example, at the time of writing, there is strong parliamentary opposition to amending UK legislation relating to the voting rights of prisoners to bring it into conformity with the judgment of the Strasbourg Court of Human Rights in *Hirst v UK (No 2)*.[26] However, a Joint Committee of parliamentarians established to consider the issue concluded in December 2013 that a refusal to give effect to the Court's judgment would constitute a breach of the principle of the rule of law as long as the UK remained within the ECHR system.[27] The Committee's views do not bind Parliament, and the issue remains unresolved: however, its conclusions illustrate how the UK's human rights commitments form part of the framework of rule of law that Parliament is expected to respect (see below). Furthermore, EU member states since 2009 must act in conformity with the requirements of the EU Charter of Fundamental Rights when giving effect to EU law, which again imposes certain limits on the sovereign authority of the Westminster Parliament.

The existence of these constraints is controversial. Many parliamentarians have argued that they are incompatible with the principle of democratic

[24] See ss 3, 4 and 6 of the Human Rights Act 1998. For commentary on the relationship between these statutory provisions and the distinction by the HRA between parliamentary legislation and acts of public authorities, see A Kavanagh, *Constitutional Review under the Human Rights Act* (Cambridge, CUP, 2009); T Hickman, *Public Law after the Human Rights Act* (Oxford, Hart, 2010).

[25] Since the HRA came into force in 2000, Parliament has decided to amend legislation in response to every declaration of incompatibility issued by the courts bar the specific situation of prisoner voting rights. See O'Cinneide, *Human Rights and the UK Constitution*, n 4 above, p 38.

[26] *Hirst v UK (No 2)* 42 EHRR 41.

[27] *Report of the Joint Committee on the Draft Voting Eligibility (Prisoners) Bill*, Session 2013–14, HL Paper 103 HC 924, 18 December 2013.

self-governance.[28] In general, the values that animate both the ECHR system of rights protection and EU law—in particular the idea (uncontroversial in most European states) that the authority of national legislatures must be subordinated to overarching human rights principles and the goal of deeper European integration—can be difficult to reconcile with the primacy accorded to representative government in the UK constitutional scheme of values.[29] Furthermore, even though sound constitutional justifications exist as to why EU law and the ECHR should enjoy primacy, there exists a widespread cultural hostility to supranational European regulation: Lord Neuberger, the President of the UK Supreme Court, has recently outlined a number of reasons why 'when compared with people in other European countries, the British are peculiarly averse to, and particularly suspicious of, being told what they can and can't do by pan-European bodies'.[30] However, unless and until political calls for repeal of the HRA/renunciation of the ECHR/withdrawal from the EU become a reality, parliamentary sovereignty is subject to de facto limits arising from the requirements of national and European human rights norms, which in turn both reinforce and derive support from the UK's commitment to the rule of law (as discussed further below).

In general, the primacy of representative governance as expressed through the doctrine of parliamentary sovereignty remains a constitutional keystone. In the final analysis, it constitutes the default mechanism for determining the shape and content of the UK's unwritten constitutional system. However, the nominally unlimited power of Parliament is increasingly circumscribed in practice.[31] Furthermore, as discussed in the following section, question marks have even begun to appear over the de jure status of parliamentary sovereignty: the widening scope of the third core value, commitment to the rule of law, is beginning to call into question the presumptive priority historically accorded to the principle of representative government within the UK's constitutional system.

[28] See the criticisms directed against the Strasbourg Court by MPs during the House of Commons debate on prisoner voting rights, HC Deb 10 February 2011, cols 493–586.

[29] For the contrary view, see O'Cinneide, *Human Rights and the UK Constitution*, n 4 above.

[30] (Lord) David Neuberger, *The British and Europe*, Cambridge Freshfields Annual Law Lecture 2014, 12 February 2014, text available at https://www.supremecourt.uk/docs/speech-140212.pdf.

[31] For further analysis, see V Bogdanor, 'Imprisoned by a Doctrine: The Modern Defence of Parliamentary Sovereignty' (2012) 32(1) *Oxford Journal of Legal Studies* 179–95; J Goldsworthy, *Parliamentary Sovereignty: Contemporary Debates* (Cambridge, CUP, 2010); AL Young, 'Sovereignty: Demise, Afterlife or Partial Resurrection?' (2011) 9(1) *International Journal of Constitutional Law* 163–71; NW Barber, 'The Afterlife of Parliamentary Sovereignty' (2011) 9(1) *International Journal of Constitutional Law* 144–54. And see J Jowell, 'Parliamentary Sovereignty under the New Constitutional Hypothesis' [2006] PL 562.

IV. COMMITMENT TO THE RULE OF LAW

Superficially, the two values already discussed, the presumption of liberty and the primacy of representative governance as manifested through the doctrine of the sovereignty of Parliament, appear to be contradictory: if Parliament has the legal authority to extinguish any liberties, either by passing a law or by conferring discretionary power to an official who then may disregard any so-called inherent freedoms, then the presumption of liberty appears to lack all force. It is here, however, that the rule of law comes into play, seeking to place some restraint upon the unfettered use or exercise of Parliament's powers and in so doing to preserve some space for the presumption of liberty to apply. Even Dicey, who was in no doubt that the rule of law could be overridden by Parliament, considered the rule of law to be a significant constitutional principle guiding the exercise of all public decisions and regarded respect for this principle as a core value of the UK's uncodified constitutional order.

The pressure to conform to the rule of law emanates from the deeply rooted set of expectations relating to the nature of law and the exercise of power in a constitutional democracy. Law should be accessible, stable, relatively certain and predictable. Official decisions should not be arbitrary. The law must be enforced equally. Individuals must be able to challenge official action by way of fair trial before an independent judge. State action that fails to conform to the rule of law will lack legitimacy: it will be subject to the various forms of legal sanction developed in UK public law to ensure compliance with rule of law norms and, even if cloaked in the sovereign garb of an Act of Parliament, will also be exposed to political sanction generated by the embedded expectations that have accumulated in the UK public sphere as to how state power should be exercised.[32]

The content of the rule of law is not defined in any overriding constitutional or statutory document. The rule of law is a principle rather than a fixed rule. When in conflict with other constitutional principles or standards, a decision may have to be made as to which gives way: commitment to the rule of law as understood within the UK constitutional system is based upon the expectation that the principle of rule of law should be given due weight and is presumed to apply; not that it constitutes a trump card in all cases.

Also, the content of the rule of law is open-textured and often context-dependent. In the UK context, it is not understood as extending to all conventional civil and political rights: the substantive content of human rights treaty instruments such as the ECHR may often echo the concerns of the

[32] See T Bingham, *The Rule of Law* (London, Penguin, 2010); J Jowell, 'The Rule of Law' in J Jowell and D Oliver (eds), *The Changing Constitution* 8th edn (Oxford, OUP, 2015).

rule of law, but the two sets of norms are by and large regarded as separate and distinct, if often mutually reinforcing as discussed further below.[33] However, the content of the rule of law is regarded as encompassing a number of important values of a mixed procedural and substantive nature. These include:

Legality

At its most fundamental, the rule of law requires legality in the sense of obedience to law. The requirement that the law must be followed is reflected in the popular demand that 'law and order' must be maintained, both by the public and also by officials such as the police who are expected to enforce the law. However, legality goes further than that, as it also addresses the actions of public officials, requiring that their acts be legally authorised.

It is often unclear whether a statute, say, which confers very broad discretion on an official (perhaps to act 'as he may see fit') imposes any limits on his exercise of that discretion. During the first half of the twentieth century, the courts gave considerable leeway to public officials on whom broad discretionary powers had been conferred. Insofar as the rule of law was accepted, it was transmuted into an obligation, on the part of the courts and all officials, to secure the smooth implementation of Parliament's designs.

Perhaps the best known example of this tendency is the decision of the House of Lords in *Liversidge v Anderson*,[34] where the broad powers conferred by Parliament upon the Home Secretary during the Second World War to detain individuals whom he considered to be a threat to national security were interpreted as not requiring a justification to be offered for a decision to intern numbers of people, many of whom had fled persecution in Nazi Germany. Notwithstanding a powerful and subsequently acclaimed dissent by Lord Atkin, the majority of the House of Lords considered that the will of Parliament would best be fulfilled by giving the Home Secretary a free hand to exercise his powers as he saw fit.

This obligation that the judges imposed upon themselves to facilitate the perceived intent of Parliament was reinforced by a trusting faith in ministers, the career civil service, the police and other servants of the state to get things as right as they could be. This was coupled with a longstanding and

[33] Compliance with the principle of rule of law can nevertheless be viewed as requiring compliance with judgments of the European Court of Human Rights and other judicial determinations in the field of human rights law, as discussed above in the context of the *Hirst v UK (No 2)* judgment of the Strasbourg Court in respect of prisoner voting rights.

[34] *Liversidge v Anderson* [1942] AC 206.

deeply rooted mistrust of the use of legal techniques of dispute-resolution to regulate the activities of public bodies, which was shared by judges, administrators, academics and politicians alike. During the first half of the twentieth century the rule of law was viewed suspiciously, as a device that could inhibit the free exercise of official discretion.[35] The Labour government of 1945 explicitly sought to avoid 'judicial sabotage of socialist legislation' and even the highest judges regarded themselves as 'handmaidens of the administration'.[36]

However, this approach has been radically revised in recent years. In interpreting the scope of powers conferred upon ministers and other public bodies by legislation, the courts now look not merely at the letter of the relevant law but also at the broader purpose of discretionary power, treating the exercise of such power as bound and shaped by the background requirements of the rule of law. As a result, it has become clear that no discretion can be regarded any longer as wholly unfettered.[37]

Certainty

For Dicey, the essence of the rule of law was that the law should be certain and predictable. Dicey mistrusted the grant of virtually any discretionary power on the ground that it inherently permitted arbitrary decisions. He and his followers, such as Hewart and Hayek, preferred officials to act on the basis of known rules which formed the basis on which people could plan their lives. They were less concerned that laws were harsh than that they should be known in advance.

Certainty in this sense is an instrumental value in that it allows people to know clearly where they stand. However, it can also achieve substantive fairness—for example, when it prohibits the punishment of someone on the basis of an action which was lawful when it was carried out, or when it forbids penalising someone for breach of a law which they were unable to discover.

The notion of legal certainty was opposed for a long time by those who, as we have said, considered Dicey's preference for rules over discretion as a device to impede welfare provisions which required for their

[35] This suspicion was linked to distrust among socialist politicians and intellectuals of judicial elites, generated in particular by the use of the rhetoric of constitutionalism to attack the actions of the trade unions in the General Strike of 1926, as well as by the emphasis on *laissez-faire* individualism in the trans-Atlantic economic rights jurisprudence of the US Supreme Court in cases such as *Lochner v New York* 198 US 45 (1905).

[36] See generally, H Woolf, J Jowell, A Le Sueur, C Donnelly and I Hare, *de Smith's Judicial Review*, 7th edn (London, Sweet & Maxwell, 2013), chs 1 and 5.

[37] This was stated in the seminal case of *Padfield v Minister of Agriculture, Fisheries and Food* [1968] AC 997.

implementation the exercise of discretionary powers. For example, in the 1970s a lively debate took place on the question of whether recipients of discretionary welfare payments (known as Supplementary Benefit) should have definite and legally recognised entitlements to receive certain forms of benefit (described as 'welfare rights'). At that time, decisions were given on the basis of a secret code, the 'A Code', which did not allow welfare recipients to know the rules by which they were judged, and gave few opportunities for appeal or review of the decision about the extent of their benefits. Many leading thinkers who were themselves the architects of the 'welfare state' introduced by the Labour government of 1945, were strongly of the opinion that the administration of welfare benefits should be carried out under the benevolent and expert discretion of civil servants, and warned of a 'pathology of legalism' that would occur if the advocates of 'welfare rights' had their way.[38]

Today, the tide of intellectual and judicial opinion has been virtually reversed. With unexpected suddenness, from about 1960, the courts through judicial review of administrative powers (administrative law) increasingly required discretionary power to be exercised in conformity with the rule of law. In so doing, they were slowly subverting an essentially 'political constitution' based upon the exercise of wide-ranging and often untrammelled discretion by public officials subject only to often dilute forms of political accountability, and replacing it with a 'legal constitution', where the exercise of discretionary powers became subject to judicially imposed controls designed to ensure greater certainty, predictability and equality in their application.[39] Parliament also played a role in this shift, by setting standards for the control of administrative discretion and the possibility of its appeal or review.[40]

Judicial review has thus expanded exponentially, and the courts endorsed the notion of certainty by requiring that 'legitimate expectations' ought to be fulfilled and that decisions in like cases be treated consistently. The critics of Dicey's call for legal certainty had a point that a modern interventionist state requires broad discretionary powers. However, the law has shown itself able to balance the need for certainty with that of flexibility, by for example protecting legitimate expectations while also giving effect to the competing principle that no decision-maker should 'fetter their discretion'.[41]

[38] See *de Smith*, n 36 above, ch 5, para 5-006ff.

[39] T Hickman, 'In Defence of the Legal Constitution' (2005) 55(4) *University of Toronto Law Journal* 981–1022.

[40] See eg the 'positive equality duty' imposed upon public authorities by s 149 of the Equality Act 2010.

[41] See eg *British Oxygen v Minister for Technology* [1971] AC 610.

Participation

Another central normative requirement of the rule of law as understood in the UK and elsewhere is that no person should be condemned unheard—that there should be no punishment or imposition of a civil penalty without a trial where the defendant has been given the opportunity to participate and present their case. This requirement of 'due process', or 'natural justice' or 'procedural fairness' is associated with that of legality, as it assumes that the person will be able to challenge the implementation of any announced rule, or indeed the rule itself.

To do this, the claimant will need access to a court, so another feature of the rule of law is access to justice (which must include sufficient legal aid). For participation to be fair and access to justice to be meaningful, another aspect of the rule of law is engaged, namely, that the decision-maker be unbiased, which is to say both independent (in the sense of free from improper external pressure) and impartial (not apparently interested in the outcome of the case in favour of any one of the participants). Judicial independence is a key facet of this aspect of the rule of law, but it extends to all public officials exercising quasi-judicial functions.

The notion of participation is not only a procedural value. It also endorses the notion that every person is entitled to be treated with due regard to the proper merits of their cause. Failure to provide that treatment diminishes a person's sense of individual worth and impairs their dignity. When a decision is challenged, it has to be justified so that a concept of justification also emerges as a further value. Nor is the scope of participation limited to challenges to existing decisions. It also entitles individuals to engage in the formulation of decisions yet to be made, by means of making meaningful representations to the relevant decision-maker.

The value of participation as expressed in its different aspects has become embedded in the constitutional system of the UK over an extended period, commencing with the emergence of common law due process requirements in criminal trials in the eighteenth century.[42] The creation of the modern welfare state opened up new opportunities: the founding charter of the UK welfare state, the Beveridge Report, emphasised the central importance of legal aid as a crucial tool for opening up access to justice. Now, with the greater willingness of the UK judiciary since 1960 to apply judicial review controls to regulate and constrain the power of public authorities, the values associated with participation have acquired a new vibrancy. The right of access to the courts has been recognised, in cases such as *Ex p Witham,*[43] as an inherent aspect of the rule of law

[42] For a celebrated analysis of these developments, see EP Thompson, *Whigs and Hunters: The Origins of the Black Act* (London, Allen Lane, 1975).

[43] *R v Lord Chancellor ex p Witham* [1998] QB 575.

and thus presumed to apply unless Parliament indicates clearly to the contrary. In addition, the obligation on public authorities to give reasons for decisions which affect important elements of an individual's life and therefore make possible challenges to that decision has been strengthened, extended and reinforced by both Parliament and the courts (although not quite yet evolved into a constitutional requirement).[44]

Accountability

Linked to the notion of participation is the concept of accountability of decision-makers to those they serve, another key element of the rule of law as understood in the UK constitutional system. Political accountability is achieved in different ways, primarily through the requirement of regular elections. But there is also a notion of legal accountability, under which all officials may be sanctioned for departing from accepted standards. Where the official is guided by a rule, rather than acting under broad discretion, those rules provide a published standard against which to measure the legality of the official's decisions. An announced level of welfare assistance thus allows a person who qualifies but who is refused assistance to mount a legal challenge to the decision.

Once again, the expansion of judicial review controls in recent decades has strengthened legal methods of accountability, in particular, the development of case law on the obligations to respect legitimate expectations and to give reasons for administrative decisions (although there is still not a general duty to give reasons for all decisions). Parliament has also taken steps to expand the scope of political accountability mechanisms, including enacting freedom of information legislation, establishing an ombudsman system and strengthening the powers, role and functions of parliamentary select committees.

A developed concept of the rule of law, combining procedural and substantive elements, is thus now firmly embedded in the UK constitutional system. It forms the backbone of administrative law, and provides a well-established set of normative values that regulate the conduct and behaviour of public authorities through both political and legal forms of accountability.

With its focus on these notions of legality, certainty, participation and accountability, the UK constitutional system has been described as adhering to a 'formal' concept of the rule of law. However, under the influence of international human rights law, in particular the ECHR, and comparative jurisprudence, British courts began in the 1990s to adopt a more 'substantive' conception of the rule of law, whereby public authorities were expected

[44] See *de Smith*, n 36 above, para 7-085 ff.

not only to adhere to the 'formal' virtues of legality, certainty and so on but also to respect certain basic rights and entitlements such as freedom of expression, equality of treatment and freedom from destitution.[45] Building on existing case law, the common law was interpreted as containing built-in presumptions that state action which infringed upon one of these 'common law rights' would be unlawful unless it could be shown to rest upon a clear legal basis.

Thus in *Simms*, restrictions placed by a prison governor upon a prisoner's correspondence with a journalist were held to be unlawful, as the House of Lords considered that the general provisions of the Prisoner's Rules which enabled the governor to maintain good order in the prison could not be read as conferring a specific power to interfere with the prisoner's common law entitlements to free speech and to seek access to justice by contesting his sentence.[46] In *Ex p Witham*, a case already mentioned, ministerial regulations restricting access to legal aid were held to be incompatible with the common law right to access justice, with the courts interpreting the relevant power-conferring legislation as not contemplating the exercise of these powers to deny access to this basic right.[47]

However, the 'substantive' interpretation of the rule of law, as adopted in cases like *Simms* and *JCWI,* remains a work in progress.[48] The extent to which the common law can be seen as containing an embedded and comprehensive set of fundamental rights is uncertain, as the scope and extent of the 'common law rights' recognised by the courts remains unclear. Uncertainty also exists about how commitment to the rule of law should be reconciled with the other core values of the UK constitutional system, and in particular with the nominally untrammelled power of the sovereign Parliament. This links to a broader issue, namely the question of how the three core values of the UK's constitutional system should be reconciled when they come into tension with each other.

V. THE RESOLUTION OF CONFLICT BETWEEN THE PRESUMPTION OF LIBERTY, THE RULE OF LAW AND THE SOVEREIGNTY OF PARLIAMENT

The relationship between the core value of commitment to the rule of law and the other two core values of the presumption of liberty and the commitment to the primacy of representative governance is ever-shifting. As already

45 P Craig, 'Formal and Substantive Concepts of the Rule of Law' [1997] *Public Law* 467.
46 [1999] 3 All ER 400.
47 [1997] 2 All ER 779.
48 See *Osborn v Parole Board* [2013] UKSC 61 and *Kennedy v Charity Commission* [2014] UKSC 20 for a recent development of rule of law principles.

noted, the various facets of the rule of law, whether 'formal' or 'substantive' in nature, may be challenged by other considerations, such as the need for effective governance and broad flexibility in administrative decision-making. When this occurs, the UK constitutional system is generally understood as giving Parliament the final say as to how this tension should be resolved, in accordance with the primacy given to representative governance. In other words, where there is a clear conflict between the will of the sovereign Parliament and the rule of law, the former prevails. The same is true when the presumption of liberty runs up against competing considerations: Parliament has been regarded as having the final word.

Parliament could thus in theory interfere with the rule of law or abrogate any fundamental human right. In practice, however, the presumption of liberty and the rule of law have tended to exercise a profound restraining influence upon how Parliament uses its powers. In addition, the incorporation of the ECHR via the HRA and the superior status of EU law have considerably strengthened, extended and reinforced the restraints imposed by the principle of the rule of law on the exercise of legislative and executive power.[49]

The expanding reach of the rule of law principle has even begun to call the primacy of representative governance into question. Lord Woolf (then Lord Chief Justice of England and Wales) raised the possibility that the UK judiciary might treat parliamentary sovereignty as limited in scope during the 'ouster clause' controversy in 2004, when the UK government attempted to pass legislation through Parliament that would have removed the possibility of seeking judicial review of decisions in asylum claims. This proposal met substantial resistance in the House of Lords and was eventually withdrawn.[50] However, before this retreat, Lord Woolf in a speech at the Cambridge Law Faculty suggested that the courts might refuse to give effect to legislation of this sort which aimed to deny individuals the right to access the courts, even if the ouster of judicial review was stated in express terms on the face of the Act.[51]

In so doing, Lord Woolf appeared to be drawing upon the theory of 'common law constitutionalism'. This alternative constitutional theory has been advanced by Lord Justice Laws, Trevor Allen and other commentators since

[49] The ECHR rights reinforce rule of law entitlements in the area of procedural justice, in particular through the content of the right to fair trial protected by art 6 of the Convention, while also deepening, widening and extending the uncertain scope of protection offered by the substantive common law rights. EU law contains its own distinct set of rule of law norms, described as the 'general principles' of European law, while the provisions of the EU Charter of Fundamental Rights are applied by the Court of Justice of the EU and domestic courts in interpreting European legislation and national laws designed to implement EU directives.

[50] R Rawlings, 'Review, Revenge and Retreat' (2005) 68(3) *Modern Law Review* 378–410.

[51] Lord Woolf, 'The Rule of Law and a Change in the Constitution' (2004) 63 *Cambridge Law Journal* 317–30.

the early 1990s.[52] These echo the approach of Coke CJ in his 1610 judgment in *Bonham's Case*, where he pronounced that 'in many cases the common law will control acts of Parliament and sometime adjudge them to be utterly void: for when an act of Parliament is against common right or reason, or repugnant, or impossible to be performed, the common law will control it and adjudge such an Act to be void'.[53] This theory suggests that the doctrine of parliamentary sovereignty is a common law norm which may in certain circumstances be capable of being overridden by more fundamental common law norms—and in particular the core elements of the principle of the rule of law, such as access to justice.[54]

Subsequently, Lord Steyn in *Jackson v Attorney General*, speaking obiter, adopted a similar approach in asserting that the doctrine of parliamentary sovereignty was limited: in his view, Parliament lacked the power to pass legislation which would deny fundamental rights or erode the democratic basis of the state.[55] Baroness Hale in *Jackson* suggested that the question of whether parliamentary sovereignty was absolute remains unsettled, Lord Hope's judgment in the same case appeared to affirm that Parliament retained its sovereign status as a matter of law.

However, Lord Hope also highlighted the existence of substantial constraints on the ability of Parliament to legislate contrary to fundamental principles of the rule of law. In so doing, he made it clear that while the primacy of representative governance constituted a core value of the UK constitutional system, the exercise of this power was conditioned by the expectation that the rule of law would be observed and fundamental rights respected. Subsequently, Lord Hope returned to this theme in his judgment in *AXA General Insurance v Lord Advocate*, where he stated that 'the question of whether the principle of the sovereignty of the United Kingdom Parliament is absolute or may be subject to limitation in exceptional circumstances is still under discussion', while also affirming that the rule of law was the 'ultimate controlling principle on which our constitution is based'.[56]

Taken together, these dicta affirm that the UK constitutional system is based on a complex interaction of the three core values of the presumption

[52] Sir John Laws, 'Is the High Court the Guardian of Fundamental Constitutional Rights?' [1993] *Public Law* 59; Sir John Laws, 'Law and Democracy' [1995] *Public Law* 72; J Jowell, 'Beyond the Rule of Law: Towards Constitutional Judicial Review' [2000] *Public Law* 671–83; T Allan, 'The Rule of Law as the Rule of Reason: Consent and Constitutionalism' (1999) 115 *Law Quarterly Review* 221.

[53] *Bonham's Case* (1610) 8 Coke's Reports 114, 118. See also *Thomas v Sorrell* (1674) Vaughan 330: 'A law which a man cannot obey, nor act according to it, is void and no law; and it is impossible to obey contradictions, or act according to them.'

[54] S Lakin, 'Debunking the Idea of Parliamentary Sovereignty: the Controlling Factor of Legality in the British Constitution' (2008) 28 *Oxford Journal of Legal Studies* 709.

[55] *Jackson v Attorney General* [2005] UKHL 56.

[56] *AXA General Insurance v Lord Advocate* [2011] UKSC 46 [50]–[51].

of liberty, the primacy of representative governance and commitment to the rule of law. Furthermore, the shift in how courts have interpreted the rule of law principle since 1960, combined with the impact of parliamentary legislation and in particular the HRA and the European Communities Act, has greatly altered the balance struck between all three core values. Previously, the UK tended to place overwhelming emphasis upon the primacy of representative governance and adopted a 'political' conception of the constitution: now, the British constitutional system is based upon a more 'legal' conception, with legislative and executive power increasingly hemmed in by the requirements of rule of law and associated fundamental rights norms.

Majoritarian democracy and the exercise of wide discretionary powers by public bodies have thus conceded ground to a rights-based conception of democracy and a greater commitment to an expanded concept of the rule of law, even if the primacy of representative governance still retains central importance in the UK constitutional order. However, the extent of this shift remains disputed. Different judges have expressed different views as to the extent to which the principle of rule of law imposes substantive constraints on executive action.[57] The controversy surrounding the HRA and the place of ECHR rights in the UK legal system has already been mentioned. It remains to be seen how the balance is struck in the years ahead between the three core values of the British constitution, and whether Lord Hope's suggestion that the rule of law is the 'ultimate controlling principle' of the system will be vindicated in practice.[58]

VI. THE 'SECONDARY' CONSTITUTIONAL VALUES AND THEIR IMPACT ON PUBLIC AND PRIVATE LAW

Over the course of the evolution of the British constitution, state power has been exercised through the institutional and normative framework established by the interaction of the three core values already discussed to give effect to other important norms. These values can be described as 'secondary' constitutional values in the sense that they a) concern key elements of the relationship between the state and the individual which may be of profound significance to the lives of citizens, or to the nature of the UK as a democratic state; b) are considered to be basic norms to which it is desirable to give effect; yet c) are not treated as fundamental norms affecting the basic structure of the constitutional system.

[57] See eg the narrow approach advocated by Jonathan Sumption QC in his FA Mann lecture entitled 'Judicial and Political Decision-making: The Uncertain Boundary', 8 November 2011, text available at www.legalweek.com/digital_assets/3704/MANNLECTURE_final.pdf.

[58] In this context, the sweeping cuts to legal aid that have been implemented by successive UK governments over the period 2000–14 should be mentioned: these have the potential to limit access to justice in a manner that is arguably inconsistent with a serious commitment to rule of law.

These values can be of major importance to individuals, such as the value of respect for human life or the value of human dignity. However, they are not (yet) core norms: their expression is instead shaped by the three established and deeply embedded core values, whose interaction affects how the secondary values are given effect and manifested through the functioning of the UK's constitutional system.

For example, prior to the expansion of judicial review from 1960 on, the tendency for much of the twentieth century had been to use parliamentary legislation, ministerial regulation and the exercise of discretionary powers to give effect to secondary values, in particular through the creation of the post-war welfare state. In the new era of enhanced emphasis on the rule of law, an increased emphasis is now also placed on protecting such values through the use of administrative law remedies and the application of fundamental rights norms.

In other words, the shift in the underlying value framework of the UK constitutional system from a 'political' to a more 'legal' concept of the constitutional order is mirrored in how the secondary constitutional values are expressed and protected. In this regard, the importance of the ECHR rights and EU law deserves a mention: both have become important mechanisms for expressing and protecting secondary values. This is particularly the case in respect of the ECHR rights as incorporated by the HRA: in the absence of a national Bill of Rights set out in a written constitution or a fully developed framework of common law rights, the HRA steps in and partially fills this gap.[59]

It is also worth noting that UK law lacks a clear distinction between public and private law. The ECHR rights as incorporated by the HRA apply only to bodies performing public functions as defined by section 6 HRA.[60] Judicial review remedies may similarly only be obtained against bodies performing functions of a public nature, even if this test is defined in wider terms than the HRA definition of public authorities.[61] However, the ECHR rights as incorporated by the HRA bind the courts as 'public authorities', which has been interpreted as requiring the courts to interpret and apply private law in a manner compatible with the UK's obligations under the Convention, ie to give indirect horizontal effect to the ECHR rights.[62] The case law of the European Court of Human Rights has also recognised the existence of positive obligations on states to take positive steps to protect individual

[59] See in general A Kavanagh, *Constitutional Review under the Human Rights Act* (Cambridge, CUP, 2009).

[60] *YL v Birmingham* CC [2007] UKHL 27—but note the provisions of s 145 of the Health and Social Care Act 2008.

[61] J Miles, 'Standing under the Human Rights Act: Theories of Rights Enforcement and the Nature of Public Law Adjudication' (2000) 59(1) *Cambridge Law Journal* 133–67.

[62] *X v Y* [2004] EWCA Civ (28 May 2004).

rights against third parties or official neglect.[63] Furthermore, remedies in tort, contract and other areas of 'private law' regulation may be sought against public authorities. This means that core values are often manifested not alone through public law remedies but also through other areas of legal regulation. For example, the presumption of liberty is given effect through public law remedies against unlawful state action, but also through the tort of interference with the person: an unlawful arrest by the police will be a public law 'wrong', but also will constitute false imprisonment and thereby take the form of a tortious act.[64]

Therefore, the porous distinction between public and private law in the UK constitutional order readily allows the influence of the secondary constitutional values to seep from the vertical state-individual axis into horizontal relationships between private legal entities and individuals. As a result, secondary values are both protected and expressed through both public and private law: Dawn Oliver has argued that similar values animate both legal spheres,[65] even if the core values of the UK constitutional order are themselves not readily transplantable into private law. Therefore, a secondary value such as respect for individual autonomy or for equality and non-discrimination will thus often receive parallel expression in both public and private law.

Different accounts exist of what values could be said to qualify as having some sort of 'constitutional' status. Oliver has identified autonomy, respect, status, security, and dignity as key values immanent in both public and private law. Gearty has identified the importance of the value of 'civil liberties', namely the basic civil rights that make democratic participation possible, and of human dignity in addition to a core value that he describes as 'legality'.[66] Feldman in contrast has suggested that 'the constitutional significance of dignity seems less fundamental in practice than, for example, effectiveness of government, accountability and representativeness', and suggests that it ranks well below values such as autonomy and security.[67] Cane has provided a list of values linked to good governance, political accountability and transparent public decision-making in addition to those associated with the core value of commitment to the rule of law,[68] while Harlow and

[63] *X and Y v The Netherlands* (1985) 8 EHRR 235.

[64] *R (on the application of Laporte) v Chief Constable of Gloucestershire Constabulary* [2007] 2 All ER 529.

[65] D Oliver, *Common Values and the Public-Private Divide* (London, Butterworths, 1999).

[66] C Gearty, *Principles of Human Rights Adjudication* (Oxford, OUP, 2004).

[67] D Feldman, 'Human Dignity as a Legal Value—Part I' [1999] *Public Law* 682–702; 'Human Dignity as a Legal Value—Part II' [2000] *Public Law* 61–76.

[68] P Cane, 'Theory and Values in Public Law' in P Craig and R Rawlings (eds), *Law and Administration in Europe: Essays in Honour of Carol Harlow* (Oxford, OUP, 2003) 3–21: for criticism of his approach, see P Craig, 'Theory and Values in Public Law: A Response' in the same volume, 23–46; M Loughlin, 'Theory and Values in Public Law: An Interpretation' (2005) *Public Law* 48–66.

Rawlings have suggested that there is no 'finite set of values' in the common law beyond the 'administrative law values' such as participation and accountability linked with the rule of law.[69] Tomkins has suggested that a 'republican' interpretation of the UK system is possible, with three values at its core: 'popular sovereignty; freedom as non-domination; and political accountability'.[70]

Some of these lists mix up core and secondary values as distinguished here: others reflect the original thinking of their authors. However, if we are careful to separate out core and secondary values, recognising the dependent nature of the latter upon the former it is possible to identify a brief list of well-established 'second tier' values which are protected and expressed in tangible form in the British constitutional system. Most are linked to and grow out of one or more of the core values of the system, often deriving their status in part from their relationship to their deeply embedded and foundational 'core' cousins. In general, these second tier values have put down firm roots in the UK's constitutional system—however, their status is nevertheless often uncertain and contested, and substantial differences of view often exist as to how they should be given effect in law and policy.[71]

A. Respect for Individual Autonomy

Respect for individual autonomy can be considered to be a secondary constitutional value. It is closely linked to the core value of the presumption of liberty, but has more substantive content: respect for this value involves both protecting the 'negative' liberty of individuals from interference by the state and also securing their 'positive' liberty through the provision of social support, security and an adequate living environment.

The ECHR rights as incorporated by the HRA give effect to the value of autonomy by protecting essential facets of human freedom such as freedom of expression (article 10 ECHR), freedom of religion and thought (article 9 ECHR), freedom of association (article 11 ECHR), the right to life (article 2 ECHR), the right to private life, home life and family life (article 8 ECHR), and freedom from inhuman and degrading treatment (article 3 ECHR). The common law rights recognised as key elements of the rule of law have a similar impact, protecting freedom of expression, freedom to protest and other

[69] C Harlow and R Rawlings, *Law and Administration*, 3rd edn (Cambridge, Cambridge University Press, 2009), 46–48.

[70] A Tomkins, *Our Republican Constitution* (Oxford, Hart, 2005).

[71] Giving effect to these secondary values will often involve the allocation of scarce resources and the expenditure of taxpayer funds: this amplifies the extent to which they are the subject of political contestation and the vicissitudes of changing public opinion.

core liberties. The key elements of the rule of law, in particular the notions of participation, accountability and certainty, also help create the necessary conditions for autonomy and individual freedom of action.

Tort law also protects individual freedom and self-determination through the existence of causes of action such as trespass to the person, negligence and nuisance, which apply to both state and private actors: for example, any interference with bodily integrity will require lawful justification or else constitute an unlawful trespass to the person. The value of autonomy also underlies the law of contract and manifests itself in the protection offered by UK employment, discrimination and consumer protection laws, as well as through once-off legislative enactments such as the Protection from Harassment Act 1997.

Personal privacy is a concept often linked to the value of individual autonomy. However, this aspect of autonomy has struggled to find full expression in the UK context. Data protection legislation, the 1997 Act referred to above, aspects of tort law and other regulatory provisions have conferred some substantive legal protection to reinforce the embedded cultural expectation that individuals should enjoy protection for their privacy. However, these scattered provisions have failed to generate a comprehensive set of privacy norms, and the extent to which privacy should be treated as an important value remains contested: the use of CCTV and other forms of state and private surveillance is common in the UK and backed by government, while the press campaign vigorously for press freedom to be accorded a much higher status than privacy.

However, the ECHR has begun to infuse privacy values into UK law. The European Court of Human Rights has found the UK government to be in violation of article 8 ECHR on account of the amount of DNA samples retained at the national DNA database,[72] while confirming in *Peck v UK*[73] that the UK was under a positive obligation to protect individuals against publication of private information. The UK courts have responded to this by developing a common law tort of privacy, but it remains to be seen whether this dimension to individual autonomy makes the jump to qualifying as a substantive norm in the UK constitutional order: it is arguably still a long way from that point at present.

Respecting autonomy is not all about the operation of legal controls focused on individual rights. The social welfare safety net established in the wake of the two world wars, the universal health care (including access to abortion) available through the National Health Service (NHS), the security provided by the regulated police service, the independent office of the Director of Public Prosecutions and the court system, and the regulatory framework that protects the living environment all contribute to protecting

[72] *S and Marper v UK* (2009) 48 EHRR 50.
[73] *Peck v UK* (2003) 36 EHRR 41.

individual autonomy. These systems provide the positive support necessary to make the freedom of the individual a meaningful reality.

B. Respect for Human Dignity

As Feldman has argued, human dignity is less developed as a value in the UK constitutional system than in other jurisdictions.[74] It remains a somewhat ill-defined concept, which has nevertheless been described by judges and commentators as underpinning the ECHR rights and key elements of the common law, including important elements of criminal, tort and anti-discrimination law.[75] It also finds expression in legislation, as for example when the final statutory provisions providing for the possibility of the death penalty to be applied were repealed in 1998, which permitted the UK to ratify Protocol 13 to the ECHR in 2004 that prohibits the death penalty under all circumstances.[76]

The positive obligations imposed on states under the ECHR are important in this context, as they oblige public authorities to protect individuals against state neglect or acts of third parties which attack their essential dignity as human beings. In *Z v UK*, neglect by public authorities which exposed children to abuse was held to violate the UK's obligation under article 3 of the Convention to protect individuals against inhuman and degrading treatment:[77] this judgment has been reflected in the subsequent development of the common law of tort, with a broadening of the circumstances in which a duty of care will be imposed upon public authorities.[78]

The Law Lords in *R (Adam) v Secretary of State for the Home Department* also interpreted the protection given against inhuman and degrading treatment by article 3 ECHR as extending to protect individuals against state denial of welfare support which could drive them into destitution, on the basis that this constituted an assault on human dignity.[79] This echoes the acknowledgement of the Court of Appeal in *JCWI* of the existence of a common law entitlement not to be subject to destitution: in this case, the Court of Appeal held that ministerial regulations depriving asylum seekers of the right to welfare support were ultra vires, on the basis that Parliament could

[74] Feldman, 'Human Dignity', n 67 above. See also Ronald Dworkin, *Judges in Robes* (Cambridge MA, Harvard University Press, 2006) for his view of the importance of human dignity arising out the requirement of equal respect; A Barak, *Human Dignity* (Cambridge, CUP, 2015); R Dworkin, *Justice for Hedgehogs* (Boston, MA, Harvard UP, 2011) at 191ff.

[75] Feldman, ibid.

[76] The last execution was carried out in 1964.

[77] *Z v UK* [2001] 2 FCR 246.

[78] See eg *Phelps v Hillingdon London Borough Council* [2001] 2 AC 619.

[79] *R (Adam) v Secretary of State for the Home Department* [2005] UKHL 66.

be presumed not have intended the relevant immigration powers would be used to drive individuals into a state of destitution.[80]

The UK's social welfare, social protection and health care systems reinforce legal expressions of the value of dignity by providing positive support for individuals who could otherwise be reduced to a state of degradation and extreme poverty. The Beveridge Report of 1942 laid the foundation for the emergence of the post-war welfare state, in recommending state intervention to combat five 'giant evils': want, disease, ignorance, squalor and idleness. The recommendations of the Report, acclaimed by the then Archbishop of Canterbury as the 'first time anyone had set out to embody the whole spirit of the Christian ethic in an Act of Parliament',[81] were based on the belief that the British state should actively intervene to provide social protection for those in need. Its conclusions inspired the establishment of the post-war welfare state, which was founded on five central pillars: universal free access to medical care, universal free access to education, guarantees of social welfare support, the provision of adequate public housing and the provision of access to free legal aid for the needy.

The emergence of the welfare state thus represented the emergence of a new understanding of the role of the state, which was no longer conceptualised as a 'night watchman': instead, state action was expected to reflect an ethic of compassion and care, expressed through the administrative architecture and positive social provision of the welfare state. The free to all, taxpayer-funded NHS was a particular example of how this ethic was manifested through positive state provision and underpinned by deeply engrained public expectations as to the appropriate role of the state. However, in recent years, social provision has been allowed to deteriorate in the UK, calling into doubt the extent to which the commitment to protecting human dignity is actually being tangibly manifested in socio-economic policy.

C. Equality

Giving effect to the core value of commitment to the rule of law requires respect for the principle of formal equality, understood in the Aristotelian sense of treating like cases alike: if public authorities are to comply with the notions of legality, certainty, transparency, participation and accountability,

[80] *R v Secretary of State for Social Security ex p Joint Council for the Welfare of Immigrants* [1997] 1 WLR 275. Parliament subsequently introduced primary legislation expressly designed to subject certain categories of asylum seekers to the regime of enforced destitution which had been condemned by the Court of Appeal: see A Sweeney, 'The Human Rights of Failed Asylum Seekers in the United Kingdom' [2008] *Public Law* 277.

[81] See C Barnett, *The Audit of War* (London, Pan, 2001) 29.

then they are obliged to treat similarly-situated individuals and groups in a similar manner. Laws which are addressed to all persons must be applied equally to all: this requirement of consistency provides clarity and certainty, while also enabling participation and accountability by providing a common standard by which the actions of state officials and private individuals can be judged.

Case law has also recognised the general contours of a more substantive common law right to equal treatment without discrimination, on the basis that the use of distinctions based on 'suspect' characteristics such as race, ethnicity or sexual orientation will lack a rational basis and thereby fall foul of the requirements of the rule of law, unless a reasonable justification exists for their use.[82] This common law right is again bound up with the core value of commitment to the rule of law: it is a facet of the limits imposed upon discretionary decision-making by the demand to conform to the notions of legality, certainty and the equal application of the law.

A more developed substantive understanding of equality, whereby individuals and groups are protected against invidious discrimination or social disadvantage, constitutes another important secondary value of the UK constitutional system. This value is given effect through the mechanisms of the welfare state, in particular through the universal health care system. It is also expressed via legislation, case law and other forms of legal regulation. For example, the formal equality of all citizens in the political process is protected through the legislation governing entitlement to vote, the secret ballot and the right to stand for public office, while election expenditure rules and media regulation attempt to ensure a level playing-field.

The UK's comprehensive system of anti-discrimination law also gives effect to the value of substantive equality. At present, discrimination on the grounds of race, ethnicity, religion or belief, gender, disability, sexual orientation, gender reassignment, marital status and age is prohibited in Britain, while the Equality Act 2010 has clarifed and harmonised the levels of protection offered against discrimination on these grounds across the different spheres of human activity such as employment, access to goods and services and the performance of public functions. (Discrimination on the grounds of political opinion is also prohibited in Northern Ireland.) In addition, positive duties to eliminate discrimination and promote equality of opportunity are imposed on public authorities throughout the UK, which must give 'due regard' to these duties in carrying out their functions.[83]

[82] J Jowell, 'Is Equality a Constitutional Principle?' (1994) 7 *Current Legal Problems* 1; C McCrudden, 'Equality and Non-Discrimination' in D Feldman, *English Public Law* (Oxford, OUP, 2009) ch 11, 499–572; R Singh, 'Equality: The Neglected Virtue' [2004] *European Human Rights Law Review* 141–57; Baroness Hale, 'The Quest for Equal Treatment' [2005] *Public Law* 571–85.

[83] Eg s 49 of the Equality Act 2010. Duties to promote equality of opportunity are also imposed upon certain categories of private sector employers in Northern Ireland under the Fair Employment and Treatment (Northern Ireland) Order 1998.

The Equality Act 2006 established the Equality and Human Rights Commission, which is given powers to enforce anti-discrimination law and to promote respect for human rights: the Commission, which was formed out of a merger of the existing gender, race and disability equality commissions, plays an important institutional role in promoting respect for substantive equality. While the ECHR contains no general right to equal treatment, and the UK has refused to sign or ratify Protocol 12 to the Convention, which would insert such a general equality right into its text, article 14 ECHR provides a guarantee of non-discrimination in the enjoyment of other Convention rights. This has been given a reasonably wide interpretation by the European Court of Human Rights and by the UK courts through the Human Rights Act, with the result that reasonably strong protection against discrimination is available through human rights law.[84]

This substantive concept of equality is also reflected in government policy on widening access to the labour market, in particular for ethnic minorities, older persons and disabled persons, and an assortment of other initiatives taken to address group under-representation in a variety of activities across British society, including political life.[85] A concern to address inequalities based on ethnicity, gender, disability and religion in particular is embedded in public policy, and again reflects expectations that state action should be directed to addressing the consequences of structural discrimination. The Constitutional Reform Act 2005 requires the Judicial Appointments Commission, set up under that statute, to take into account the issue of diversity in the appointment of judges.

The value of substantive equality has thus been given wide effect in UK law and policy, in particular over the last 10 years. Controversy is often triggered by the question as to how effect should be given to this value in complex situations where non-discrimination rights come into conflict, or competing public goals clash. Nevertheless, the status of substantive equality as a secondary constitutional value now appears to be established: this complements the recognition given to formal equality as an aspect of the core value of commitment to the rule of law.[86]

D. Tolerance

The emergence of substantive equality as a constitutional value is linked to the emphasis placed on the value of tolerance in UK law and policy.

[84] See in general C O'Cinneide, 'Fumbling Towards Coherence: The Slow Evolution of Equality Law in England and Wales' (2006) *Northern Ireland Legal Quarterly* 57–102.

[85] The Sex Discrimination (Election Candidates) Act 2002 permits political parties to women in selecting candidates for elected office.

[86] Bamforth has described anti-discrimination law as taking a 'constitutional turn': see N Bamforth, 'Conceptions of Anti-discrimination Law' (2004) 24(4) *Oxford Journal of Legal Studies* 693.

In the wake of the religious and political turmoil of the seventeenth century, religious tolerance became established as an important value, expressed through state practice, legislation and social expectations. The Church of England remains as an established church, with the Queen as head of state also serving as head of the Church. However, culturally the UK has become a highly secular society. This has generated strong expectations that state action should respect and adopt as neutral a stance as possible between different forms of religious and philosophical belief. A position of de facto secularism has become the norm: however, there is no fixed and well-defined constitutional value of secularism as such. Instead, a more ad hoc value of tolerance, linked to the concept of substantive equality, is expressed through UK law and policy.

Common law offences such as blasphemy which conferred greater protection Christianity than on other religions have recently been abolished, while prohibitions on inciting religious hatred have been inserted into law, albeit with reinforced protection for freedom of speech. Church of England bishops have reserved seats in the House of Lords, but representatives of other faiths are now also allocated seats. The public schooling system consists of a majority of non-denominational comprehensive schools combined with a substantial minority of state-supported schools with a distinct religious ethos, including Church of England, Catholic, Muslim and Jewish state schools. There are in general no restrictions on the wearing of clothing or symbols associated with particular religious faiths: while schools may set their own uniform policy, the imposition of any restrictions on the wearing of religiously mandated clothing or symbols will need to be shown to be objectively justified, or else will violate anti-discrimination law.[87]

This ad hoc approach is reflected in legal and policy approaches to the ever-diversifying multicultural nature of UK society. Since the late 1960s, the UK as a state has tended to adopt an approach which places emphasis on equal opportunity and managing diversity, rather than insisting on assimilation within the dominant British culture.[88] Roy Jenkins MP, then the UK Home Secretary, expressed this particular manifestation of the value of tolerance in a speech in 1967:

> Integration is perhaps a rather loose word. I do not regard it as meaning the loss, by immigrants, of their own national characteristics and culture. I do not think we need in this country a melting pot, which will turn everybody out in a common mould, as one of a series of someone's misplaced vision of the stereotyped Englishman … I define integration, therefore, not as a flattening process of assimilation

[87] See eg *Eweida and Others v UK* App nos 48420/10, 59842/10, 51671/10 and 36516/10 (ECtHR, Judgment of 15 January 2013),

[88] See UK Performance and Innovation Unit, *Ethnic Minorities and the Labour Market: Interim Report* (London, Cabinet Office, 2002) 4.49.2, p 112.

> but as equal opportunity, coupled with cultural diversity, in an atmosphere of mutual tolerance.[89]

This relatively *laissez-faire* approach was however also complemented by strong immigration controls, and has since 9/11 given way at times to a new emphasis on integration.[90] However, UK law and policy remains in general wedded to the relatively ad hoc value of tolerance, rather than to any more clearly defined set of values such as Canadian-style multiculturalism or French-style republican secularism.

E. Transparency, Openness and Political Accountability

Tolerance also plays an important role in creating and maintaining the space for the expression of conflicting views within a democracy. Other secondary constitutional values also exist which relate closely to political life within the collective democratic order of the UK. A key such value is the emphasis that exists on the maintenance of transparency and openness in public life. This value is intimately linked to the core value of the primacy of representative governance: transparency permits the electorate and the press to monitor what their elected representatives get up to.

This value is also linked to the notions of accountability and participation that are integral elements of the rule of law: the rule of law requirements ensure public bodies exercise state power in an accountable manner which also opens the door to participation by those affected, while the value of transparency and openness is expressed through state action that conform to these norms. Together, these linked values give substance to another value which could be seen as both a key element of the core value of the primacy of representative governance and a free-standing secondary value in its own right, namely political accountability.

This secondary value is given effect in a variety of ways. Legal regulation in the form of the Freedom of Information Act 2000 now makes provision for access to official information, remedying a long-standing gap in British law. Press freedom is embedded within UK political culture and is even reinforced by a special provision of the HRA (section 12), which requires the courts to place particular emphasis on the importance of freedom of expression when applying Convention rights.

The value of transparency and openness and their central importance to political accountability also underpin the conventions that have grown up in the UK constitutional system as to where responsibility lies for the failure of public officials. Ministers take responsibility for the performance of

[89] R Jenkins, *Essays and Speeches* (London, 1967) 267.

[90] S Poulter, *Ethnicity, Law and Human Rights: The English Experience* (Oxford, Clarendon Press, 1998).

civil servants, while the Cabinet as a whole adopts collective responsibility for government policy at large. These specific lines of accountability ensure transparency as to where responsibility lies, which in turn reinforces political accountability.

Linked to the value of respect for transparency and openness is a corresponding emphasis placed on the value of adherence to honesty and integrity in political life. Expectations exist, which have emerged since Victorian rectitude replaced the corruption of the eighteenth century, that those who wield state power will do so without dishonesty. This has generated a political culture where systematic corruption is rare and rule-bending tends to take minor forms.

However, periodic infractions have tended to expose complacency as to the extent of dishonesty in UK public life. Therefore, reliance on the well-established political culture of honesty and integrity in public life has been bolstered by a series of legal mechanisms. The common law tort of misfeance in public office permits civil liability to be imposed upon dishonest public officials, while an assortment of criminal offences also exist which are designed to rein in corruption. Local authority auditors may surcharge councillors for wrongfully wasting public money.

At parliamentary level, a Parliamentary Commissioner for Standards and the Committee on Standards and Privileges enforces the codes of conduct to which Members of Parliament are expected to adhere, including the requirement to register relevant private interests. Similar bodies exist at the devolved level. Nevertheless, the expenses scandal of 2009, when numerous Members of Parliament were exposed as having abused their expense claim system, has given rise to a new institutional framework for giving expression to the value of honesty and integrity, with the establishment of the Independent Parliamentary Standards Authority (IPSA) to oversee adherence to this value on the part of elected representatives.

F. Effective Governance

A final 'political' value which is often overlooked in accounts of the UK's constitutional order, but which is nevertheless integral to its functioning, is the emphasis placed on the value of effective governance, understood as involving the exercise of state power by a government which can claim a clear popular mandate and has considerable freedom of action to implement its policies.

It may seem strange to characterise this as a constitutional value: it would appear to bear little resemblance to values such as respect for dignity or life. However, within the UK constitutional order, considerable importance is attached to this value. It is often seen as a necessary corollary to the core value of the primacy of representative governance, and also as linked to the secondary values of electoral participation, transparency and political accountability. A deeply rooted assumption exists that the elected representatives of the people should be duty-bound to exercise the power conferred upon them in an effective, efficient, and timely manner.

This value is given expression through the UK constitutional system in a variety of ways. The 'first past the post' election system used in UK parliamentary elections (but not used for elections to the devolved bodies and the European Parliament) makes it possible for a political party to gain a clear majority in the House of Commons while only gaining a plurality of votes over its competitors, and also ensures that it is difficult for smaller parties to enter Parliament. The unfairness inherent in this system is generally deemed to be a price worth paying for a decisive electoral outcome: however, declining support for the historically dominant Conservative and Labour parties means that coalition or minority governments may increasingly become the norm in the UK, which in turn may undermine the argument that the 'first past the post' system is better able to deliver stable parliamentary majorities than other electoral systems.

The emphasis on effective governance is also manifested in the discipline exercised by the major political parties over MPs in Parliament, reinforced by a strong whipping system. This ensures that parliamentary business, the member of select committees and the legislative timetable are largely controlled or heavily influenced by the party leadership. It also ensures that the UK has adopted a separation of powers system based upon a fused legislative-executive, with the leadership of the majority party in the Commons both controlling the executive branch and dominating the day-to-day work of Parliament.

A concern to maintain the effectiveness of governmental machinery is also periodically manifested in judicial decisions applying rule of law or human rights norms, in particular when interpreting the scope of discretionary powers. These cases tend to highlight the potential for the value of effective governance to come into serious tension with other secondary values, and even at times to cut across rule of law principles.

G. Latent Values

Other secondary values could be recognised, relating to the environment, community, education and other important collective goods. However, it is difficult to identify the existence of agreement as to the basic contours of these collective goods: they remain subjects of contestation, debate and ever-shifting regulation. In contrast with the secondary values set out above, there exists sufficient clarity about their basic scope and content to recognise them as embedded constitutional values, even if how they are interpreted and expressed in law and policy may generate considerable disagreement. The

UK constitutional system is in a state of permanent evolution, but change and adjustment takes time: while certain secondary values such as substantive equality have become expressed in a more or less cohesive form in UK law and policy over the last few decades, other latent values remain largely inchoate.

VII. CONCLUSION—THE GAP BETWEEN VALUES AND REALITY

Despite a state of permanent flux, the UK constitution has managed to maintain institutional continuity and stable governance while placing democratic choice and rule of law principles at the heart of its underlying system of values. This ensures that political and legal change takes place within the well-established framework of democratic constitutionalism.

This framework is built around the three core values of the presumption of liberty, the primacy of representative governance and commitment to the rule of law. The content of these core values changes and evolves, as demonstrated by the development of a more substantive concept of the rule of law in recent decades, accompanied by the recognition by the courts of the existence of common law rights. This in turn generates adjustments in how these three values interact, which in turn causes incremental shifts in the foundations of the UK constitutional system.

These core values are supplemented by the secondary constitutional values, which are given effect and expressed through the constitutional framework formed by the interaction of the three core values. These secondary values include respect for individual autonomy, respect for human dignity, respect for the right to life, a commitment to an ethic of compassion and care, a commitment to equality in both a formal and a substantive sense, a commitment to tolerance, and a set of commitments to respect values that relate to democratic governance, namely transparency, openness and political accountability, honesty and integrity, electoral participation and effective governance. There also exist latent values which may over time find coherent and sustained expression in UK law and policy, but remain for now indefinite and inchoate.

The flexibility of the UK's unwritten constitutional system has allowed it to adjust over time to close the gaps that have periodically opened up between the values to which the system formally adheres and the actual reality of how state power is exercised. However, the gap between values and reality can at times loom large. At present, the expanding substantive concept of the rule of law, combined with the greater expression given to secondary values such as respect for autonomy, dignity and equality, rub up against other values, including in particular the majoritarian orientation built into the primacy given to representative governance and the secondary value of effective governance (as it has been understood in the UK context, ie meaning the enabling of an elected government to implement its political agenda).

This tension is manifested in different ways. To begin with, the executive in the UK still wields wide-ranging discretionary powers, subject at times to minimal oversight. This barely limited discretion can dilute the commitment to the rule of law. It also can in certain circumstances cut across the commitment to certain secondary values such as individual autonomy and dignity, in particular where national security or public interest concerns are invoked. In addition, considerable power is concentrated in the executive due to the modern party political system. The representatives of the people in parliament have immense power in constitutional theory, but in practice the role of Parliament is limited and mechanisms for holding those who wield state power accountable to parliament are often underdeveloped. The formal primacy given to representative governance conceals a more complex reality, where the executive wields great power and effectively controls the day-to-day business of Parliament. Representative governance in the UK at present does not reflect the idealised picture of how it should work.

The majoritarian orientation of representative governance in the UK, combined with the lingering persistence of the doctrine of parliamentary sovereignty, also results at times in the dilution of the commitment to values such as equality, autonomy and dignity. This is particularly true where non-citizens, and in particular immigrants and asylum-seekers, are concerned: their lack of a political voice has at times made it easy to deny their fundamental rights. The emphasis placed on effective governance can also conflict with other values: too often, maintaining the efficiency of the government machine trumps other considerations.

Resolving these tensions may prove challenging, even for the flexible UK constitutional system. A key issue is the extent to which the UK can be said to be shifting from a 'political' to a 'legal' conception of its unwritten constitution, and to what degree substantive rule of law and fundamental rights principles should be acknowledged as core values rather than secondary norms. Substantive rule of law principles, including common law rights, are now partially embedded in the British constitutional system. The HRA, the ECHR and EU law, taken together with the operation of 'domestic' administrative law, confer substantial protection to values such as autonomy, dignity and equality, even if human rights law remains embroiled in political controversy. In light of these developments, it remains to be seen whether the primacy of representative governance, as expressed through the concept of parliamentary sovereignty, will continue to dominate the UK's system of constitutional values. Furthermore, it also remains to be seen whether values such as autonomy and equality will graduate from their secondary status and become de facto core values of the system. Much remains to be decided in the years ahead: may be that only a written constitution, if that ever comes about, will adequately crystallise the values that presently underlie, to differing degrees, the United Kingdom's flexible constitutional order and define in clear terms their complex inter-relationship.

15

Global Constitutional Values in the United States

RUTI TEITEL

I. INTRODUCTION

THIS CHAPTER ARGUES that the central US constitutional values are freedom and equality. While there is no stated hierarchy in the US Constitution, nor in its founding documents, still, since its founding, it is clear that the value of freedom has importance, reaching its apogee following the Civil War and up until the New Deal period.[1] With the growth of the modern state, there is greater tolerance of limits on this value by the protection of other values, such as equality; nevertheless, constitutional doctrine regarding freedom of expression continues to reflect this primary commitment. Rather than a substantive normative turn, what change there is has evolved out of the transformation of the public sphere and the related change in the understanding of the role and meaning of constitutionalism. Particularly, vis-à-vis the role of the state in its guarantees, one can see that judicial interpretation plays a role in an expanding view of the relevant constitutional subject, with consequences for the meaning of constitutional values.

II. FOUNDING VALUES

This section addresses the question of what values are explicitly articulated in the United States Founding documents, such as the Declaration of Independence, the Bill of Rights and the United States Constitution, as well as the writings of the founding fathers. We can see the commitment to freedom very clearly in their writings, such as in the Federalist Papers, the writings of Thomas Jefferson and Thomas Paine. Indeed, the very revolution and

[1] See Gordon Wood, *The Creation of the American Republic* (Chapel Hill, NC, University of North Carolina Press, 1969).

split from Britain was justified on freedom-liberation grounds; a grounding experience which colours much of later developments. Of course, the historical postcolonial experience continues to inform a constitution, which is now being applied by some way beyond its original circumstances—both at home, and beyond US borders.

A. Freedom/Independence

'Secur[ing] the blessings of liberty' are among the purposes of the Constitution, as set out in its Preamble.

The overarching value articulated in the United States Bill of Rights of the 1789 Constitution is freedom. Even before the constitutional founding, the Declaration of Independence stated that 'Life, Liberty and the Pursuit of Happiness' were unalienable rights such that 'whenever any Form of Government becomes destructive of these ends, it is the Right of the People to alter or to abolish it ... and to institute new Government, laying its foundation on such principles and organizing its powers in such form, as to them shall seem most likely to affect their Safety and Happiness.'

In the constitutional text, the Bill of Rights, the freedom and independence of the individual is protected in composite in each of the first 10 Amendments, some of which are discussed below. Most of the discussion that ensues concerns only some of these, those most illustrative of the American focus on individual freedoms.

The First Amendment protects the rights of the people, and specifically of the individual, to be free from government interference in religion, in both the Establishment Clause and the Free Exercise Clause, as well as the freedom of speech, petition and assembly. Subsumed within the First Amendment is the freedom of association.[2] Therefore, as we can see, there are constitutional declarations which appear to be absolute as to protections of liberty—at both the individual and the collective levels.

After decades of controversy over its meaning, in a recent term, an opinion by Justice Scalia held, despite ambiguity regarding the original meaning of the Second Amendment, that the right to bear arms constitutes an *individual* right.[3] Justice Breyer, in his own dissent, stated that the entire Court subscribes to the proposition that 'the amendment protects an "individual" right—i.e., one that is separately possessed, and may be enforced, by each person on whom it is conferred.' Hence, *Heller* can be understood to underscore the significance of what makes for a living constitution—access to

[2] *Healy v James*, 408 US 169, 181 (1972).
[3] *DC v Heller*, 554 US 570 (2008).

review and remedy—ie, and with respect to rights, the importance of the reality of individual rights enforcement. This informs ongoing interpretation.

Relatedly, the Third Amendment, prohibiting the quartering of troops, also protects the rights of an individual within the home. Though seldom invoked today, it is best understood from a transitional perspective as indicative of the strong interests in privacy following the Revolution.[4]

The Fourth Amendment protects the liberty/privacy interest of the individual at his home and person. 'The right of the people to be secure in their persons, houses, papers, and effects, against unreasonable searches and seizures, shall not be violated.'

The Fifth Amendment similarly recognises the liberty right in requiring due process of law before an individual may be deprived of 'life, liberty, or property'.[5]

The concept of liberty protected those personal rights that are fundamental, and is not confined to the specific terms of the Bill of Rights. Thus, the Ninth Amendment recognises the potential for other liberties not specifically enumerated in the Bill of Rights by providing '[t]he enumeration in the Constitution, of certain rights, shall not be construed to deny or disparage others retained by the people.'[6] The Ninth Amendment asserts that freedoms other than those enumerated exist—a reminder of the Founders' shared natural law rights sensibility, going back to the writing of John Locke, etc, as has been documented by Suzanna Sherry and others.

In sum, the US Constitution's Bill of Rights' enumeration of rights conceives of rights in individual terms, and justifies these rights in terms of the individual's freedom and independence, and delimits the ways the state ought not encroach on the individual's essential freedoms.

i. Constitutional Incongruence

Despite the early Founding Documents and the constitutional commitments discussed above, a wrenching inconsistency in the country's actualisation of the liberty value is its range of application, and that in US history, not 'all persons' could claim freedom until much later—after the Civil War. Indeed, it was just the reverse, where the protected 'liberties' in the infamous *Dred Scott* case included the freedom to have slaves.[7] It would not be until 1865 and the constitutional amendments, when Congress passed the Thirteenth Amendment, that all persons in the United States were finally free from slavery and other involuntary servitude. The Thirteenth Amendment

[4] See Ruti G Teitel, *Transitional Justice* (Oxford, Oxford University Press, 2000) 195 for a discussion of transitional constitutionalism.

[5] See *Paul v Davis*, 424 US 693 (1976).

[6] See *Griswold v Connecticut*, 381 US 479, 85 (Goldberg J).

[7] *Dred Scott v Sandford*, 60 US 393, 416 (1856), superseded (1868).

provides: 'Neither slavery nor involuntary servitude, except as a punishment for crime where of the party shall have been duly convicted, shall exist within the United States, or any place subject to their jurisdiction.'

B. Equality

Equality is the other core American constitutional value, which as we will see has often been in tension with liberty rights. While equality is set out as a fundamental right in a number of documents associated with the founding, since its origins, the country has been deeply divided over its scope.

Paragraph 2 of the Virginia Declaration of Rights, drafted in 1776, and which influenced both the Declaration of Independence and the Bill of Rights, opens: 'all men are by nature equally free and independent … [and] cannot, by any compact, deprive or divest their posterity; namely, the enjoyment of life and liberty.'

The Declaration of Independence echoes this sentiment in proclaiming as 'self-evident truth' that 'all men are created equal'.

i. Constitutional Incongruence

The value of equality was not deemed applicable to all Americans until the post-Civil War constitutional amendments, and, even later, insofar as women and other minorities were concerned. However, as early as the pre-constitutional Declaration of Independence, the Framers expressed the idea of all men being created equal in unequivocal terms, even if the norm was not applied as broadly as the words would suggest.

Nevertheless, the value is clearly reaffirmed following the Civil War. The concept of equality is most pronounced in the Fourteenth Amendment's equal protection clause, which proclaims that no state shall 'deny to any person within its jurisdiction the equal protection of the laws.'

The Fifteenth Amendment also contributes to the equality value by requiring that the right of US citizens to vote 'shall not be denied or abridged by the United States or by any State on account of race, color, or previous condition of servitude.' This mandate itself did not amount to actual equality until the Nineteenth Amendment was ratified in 1920, finally guaranteeing that '[t]he right of citizens of the United States to vote shall not be denied or abridged by the United States or by any State on account of sex.'

Despite the formal language set out in the post-war Reconstruction Amendments, it would not be until later case law that this had any real meaning, as slavery gave way to a system of 'Jim Crow' laws, essentially, legal apartheid as exemplified in *Plessy v Ferguson*.[8] America's brand of

[8] *Plessy v Ferguson* 163 US 537 (1896).

apartheid would not be overturned, until the 1950s, with the landmark case *Brown v Board of Education*,[9] involving segregation in the context of primary school education, which overturned the notion that separate could be equal in education, which was considered the building block to equal citizenship, as protected in the post-Civil War Reconstruction Amendments.

ii. Prioritisation

The constitutional documents, whether of the Constitution or the Bill of Rights, lack any explicit hierarchy regarding the ranking or balancing of the above constitutional values. Yet, one might say the hierarchy emerges via constitutional interpretation in the case law.

For some time, following *Lochner v New York*,[10] involving labour conditions in a bakery, there was a constitutional priority of liberty of contract, which prevailed over other social interests. But after the Depression, the challenge of social-economic welfare and the development of the modern state, and years of struggle in the courts, this notion was finally abandoned, as discussed later on in the chapter.

In other case law involving constitutional values conflict, there is a balancing where the meaningful assurance of individual freedoms regarding religion for example have been sacrificed to assure purported formal equality under the law generally, eg, *Employment Division v Smith*.[11] This issue has introduced the question of what level of state involvement is expected to assure meaningful protection of constitutional norms.

III. FREE SPEECH/EXPRESSION

In the United States, the essence of its constitutional system is justified in terms of the protections of liberty through the institution of judicial review. It is through this process that the rights set out in the founding documents and post-Civil War constitutional amendments are made real. Through constitutional adjudication, countervailing laws are struck down and constitutional rights and liberties protected—despite countervailing majoritarian interests.

> The very essence of civil liberty certainly consists in the right of every individual to claim the protection of the laws, whenever he receives an injury. One of the first duties of government is to afford that protection. In Great Britain the king himself is sued in the respectful form of a petition, and he never fails to comply with the judgment of his court.

[9] *Brown v Board of Education*, 349 US 254 (1955).

[10] *Lochner v New York*, 198 US 45 (1905).

[11] See *Employment Division, Department of Human Resources of Oregon v Smith*, 494 US 872, 889 (1990).

> ... Certainly all those who have framed written constitutions contemplate them as forming the fundamental and paramount law of the nation, and consequently the theory of every such government must be, that an act of the legislature, repugnant to the constitution, is void.[12]

In this foundational case, the Court would hold that constitutional protections trump ordinary legislation. In so doing, the Court insured a mechanism and process for protection of political and other rights, as well as affirming the place of constitutional values in the American system.

The first part of the twentieth century involved many challenges to regulation of government policy regarding expression, and particularly regarding political speech. There was growing litigation involving political expression, whether regarding Socialist revolution, the growing labour movement in the US, or the rise of the Communist Party, including landmark cases, where the court was very deferential to the government.[13] It was not until the 1930s and 40s that evolution of case law openly protected space for political dissent and organisation, establishing the notion of a public forum.[14]

The leading case establishing the high status of freedom of speech is *Brandenburg v Ohio*.[15] This case supports the liberty value by affirming the freedom of individuals to express thoughts and ideas, even where those views might well be deemed offensive to the majority of society. This commitment to freedom of thought and belief is especially evident in Justice Douglas's concurrence (in which he was joined by Justice Black). Although via a concurrence, Justice Douglas articulates the strictest and most literal meaning of the First Amendment, where he declares that 'Congress shall make *no law* restricting the freedom of speech.'

At once, *Brandenburg* reflects the tension between the abstract purpose behind the First Amendment to protect *all* opinions, thoughts, and ideas, and the facts of the case, the protection of a Ku Klux Klan rally. Here, the court chose a case to annunciate its more long-lasting doctrine in the area of freedom of expression—notwithstanding the fact that the appellant was a Klan member arrested for his ideas of *intolerance*—taking the opportunity to mandate tolerance of all opinions, thoughts and ideas, provided they do not result in imminent lawless action. 'Constitutional guarantees of free speech and free press do not permit a State to forbid or proscribe advocacy of the use of force or of law violation except where such advocacy is directed to inciting or producing imminent lawless action and is likely to incite or produce such action.'[16] This landmark decision has come to exemplify the

[12] *Marbury v Madison*, 5 US 137, 163, 178 (1803).
[13] *Schenk v US*, 249 US 47 (1919).
[14] See *Schneider v State of New Jersey*, 308 US (1939).
[15] *Brandenburg v Ohio*, 395 US 444 (1969).
[16] ibid, 447.

breadth of the US protection of freedom of expression. By illustrating the toleration of the intolerant, it displays the values of tolerance. Insofar as the Court considers the countervailing danger, it addresses the problem of the danger to the broader society and constitutional system, through the rule of law, that is via the promise of an effective judiciary capable of reviewing the facts and context to see if 'there is a likelihood of imminent harm.' This highly deferential standard became a landmark precedent in the area of speech protection, defining a characteristically American approach to racist 'hate' speech.

i. Prioritisation and Congruence

The US Constitution does not have an explicit system of prioritisation, in that it does not provide for a hierarchical principle providing that one constitutional right or value prevails over another. All that we can deduce about priorities derives from interpretation in the context of constitutional adjudication, particularly where there are rights in conflict.

In a number of cases, in particular during wartime, the primacy of the free speech right has been tested. During the Cold War, the Court deferred to the legislature and its regulation of expression with a very weak iteration of the meaning of clear and present danger.[17] In *Brandenburg*, however, Justice Douglas seems to imply that the war power ('the greatest leveler of them all') might trump freedom of speech and for that matter any other value.[18] Yet, the *Brandenberg* majority opinion does not address this, and it is not clear from any other cases exactly when the war power might trump other constitutional guarantees. History has seen many rights and protections erode during wartime (eg, habeas corpus), as well as rights to equal protection of the laws.[19] Indeed, one might rationalise the prior case law by interpreting *Brandenburg* through this lens.

Moreover, there are times when this value has come into conflict with the morals of the community. Popular American values include tolerance, inclusiveness, diversity, etc.; the idea of a melting pot. Nevertheless, as much as the US may value diversity and racial tolerance in its communities, even those who do not share those values are given the right to express those beliefs, however offensive they may be to the majority of the population (which is to some extent at odds with democracy itself). So, while a majority may disagree with any given opinion, nonetheless that opinion is

[17] *Dennis v United States*, 341 US 494 (1951).
[18] 395 US, 451 (1969).
[19] *Korematsu v US*, 323 US 214 (1944).

protected—here, tolerance requires that intolerance must also be protected. To cite from Justice Douglas's opinion in *Brandenburg*:

> One's beliefs have long been thought to be sanctuaries which government could not invade … I think that all matters of belief are beyond the reach of subpoenas or the probing of investigators … The line between what is permissible and not subject to control and what may be made impermissible and subject to regulation is the line between ideas and overt acts.[20]

Nevertheless, as far as the lived values of the community go, free speech has often been at odds with typical community mores, as exemplified in the opinion of Justice Scalia in *RAV v City of St Paul*.[21]

In the 1950s, there was a lessened commitment to freedom of speech where it came into conflict with language that was considered offensive. However, the modern period has made very clear that this is no longer the relevant approach. In a number of cases concerning offensive language, such as *Cohen v California* ('F—k the Draft'), involving displays of profanity at a courthouse, the Supreme Court explored the parameters of the outer limits of freedom of expression.[22] In Justice Harlan's opinion for the majority in *Cohen*, the dangers associated with government efforts to control or limit speech outweigh the dangers of allowing unpunished outrageous speech.

In *RAV*, a case involving cross-burning regulation, the Court found that it implicated the freedom of expression, raising some of the same tensions as in *Brandenburg* but, even more explicitly, at issue was a cross-burning statute which specifically prohibited bias-motivated conduct if it was based on race, colour, creed, religion or gender. As in *Brandenburg*, the protection of individual freedom of expression had to be reconciled with other values, such as equal respect and dignity. Once again, the extent of protection of this freedom is best seen in this judicial context. St Paul's law at stake in *RAV* sought to 'to communicate to minority groups that it does not condone the "group hatred" of bias-motivated speech does not justify selectively silencing speech on the basis of its content.'[23] Nevertheless, the Court struck down the restriction, holding that the Constitution protects beliefs and expression, so that laws cannot be based on heightened disapproval of some ideas and not others.

In finding the statute unconstitutional, the decision declared that any sense of the protections traditionally afforded to those groups (regarding equality of status) yields where freedom of expression is at stake. In *RAV*, Justice Antonin Scalia's majority opinion reaffirmed the Court's commitment to protect even offensive and unpopular speech (expression) because while 'burning a cross in someone's front yard is reprehensible … [the

[20] 395 US 444, 456 (1969).
[21] *RAV v City of St Paul*, 505 US 377 (1992).
[22] *Cohen v California* 403 US 15 (1971).
[23] *RAV v City of St Paul*, 505 US 377, 392 (1992).

government] has sufficient means at its disposal to prevent such behavior without adding the First Amendment to the fire.'[24]

Here, one might contrast the American approach with that of countries in Europe, such as Germany, where constitutional protection of freedom of expression is not so absolute that government cannot restrict it in favour of promoting other goals, such as outlawing of Holocaust denial and protection against hate speech levelled against vulnerable groups. Throughout much of Europe one can see that constitutions have incorporated a militant democracy approach, a vigilance of speech used to protect against racism, given the pre-war history particularly of ethnicist political propaganda.[25] One might categorise the US approach as neo-liberal, particularly in the light of the following: '[t]he point of the First Amendment is that majority preferences must be expressed in some fashion other than silencing speech based on the basis of its content.'[26]

IV. FREEDOM OF RELIGIOUS EXERCISE

In the discussion of the parameters of freedom of expression, one sees echoes of references to another of the core freedoms set out in the US Constitution—that of freedom of religion. This constitutionally protected freedom extends to both individual religious exercise, as well as separation of church and state: 'Congress shall make no law respecting an establishment of religion, or prohibiting the free exercise thereof.'

It would not be till the mid-twentieth century and waves of immigration that there was litigation surrounding the meaning of these textual protections, in particular, the extent to which these rights belonged to individuals, without regard to the nature of the state action, extending beyond Congress, from federal regulation to state laws, ie, raising the question of whether these were rights so fundamental that they ought to be incorporated through the Fourteenth Amendment.

This the Court had no trouble doing; for example, in *Pierce v Society of Sisters*,[27] involving protection of the parental right to shape the education of their children. The Court saw that the protection of speech, which was high on the constitutional agenda, often dovetailed with religion-related rights, such as the freedom of religious exercise. Indeed, where churches depend for their adherents upon proselytising, one can see these coincide:'The free exercise of religion means, first and foremost, the right to believe and profess whatever religious doctrine one desires. Thus, the First Amendment

[24] ibid, 396.

[25] See R Teitel, 'Militating Democracy: Comparative Constitutional Perspectives' 2008 (29) *Michigan International Law Journal* 49.

[26] 505 US 377, 392 (1992).

[27] *Pierce v Society of Sisters*, 268 US 510 (1925).

obviously excludes all governmental regulation of religious *beliefs* as such.'[28] '[T]he First Amendment was enacted precisely to protect the rights of those whose religious practices are not shared by the majority and may be viewed with hostility. The history of our free exercise doctrine amply demonstrates the harsh impact of majoritarian rule on unpopular or emerging religious groups such as the Jehovah's Witnesses and the Amish.'[29]

In early case law, reaching its peak in the 1960s and 70s, the Court seemed to regard meaningful constitutional protection as going beyond formal equality to substantive accommodations for those with particular religious obligations, such as Sabbatarians, in *Sherbert v Verner*,[30] or the Amish, in *Wisconsin v Yoder*,[31] allowing an exemption to compulsory education in light of the conflict of values, in particular, their religiously-inspired need of separation from modern society.

While historically, the Court had interpreted this constitutional value as requiring accommodation: namely, that the freedom couldn't be limited without a compelling justification, the Court expounded on a narrowing of protection of freedom of religious exercise in *Smith*, all in the name of equality under the law, as rule of law. Nevertheless, subsequently in more recent case law, the Court has held that the constitutional guarantee to free exercise of religion could be circumscribed by neutral laws of general applicability: '[g]enerally applicable, religion-neutral laws that have the effect of burdening a particular religious practice need not be justified by a compelling governmental interest'.[32] In so doing, the Court was reversing decades since the mid-twentieth century of constitutional protection of religious freedom, over less than compelling government interests. Moreover, in some regards, one can see that this direction runs counter to the rationale of the free speech cases, where the Court will look even at the incidental effect of a law on speech in deciding the law's constitutionality.

i. Prioritisation and Congruence

Although the First Amendment states that Congress and, by extension, the states, shall make no law 'prohibiting the free exercise' of religion, which had been interpreted for the last part of the twentieth century as prevailing over other values not of constitutional value, *Smith* appears to rewrite the doctrine essentially holding that where the law inhibiting the free exercise

[28] *Smith*, 494 US 872, 877 (1990).

[29] *Employment Division, Department of Human Resources of Oregon v Smith*, 494 US 872, 902 (1990).

[30] *Sherbert v Verner*, 374 US 398 (1963).

[31] *Wisconsin v Yoder*, 406 US 205 (1972).

[32] 494 US 872, 886 (1990).

rights is of general applicability, it is constitutional. One might conclude, therefore, that after *Smith*, the religious liberty value is diminished in favour of other regulatory interests such as drug prohibition laws (and safety, etc, for the public good).

This apparent diminishment of protection is seemingly incongruent with both the text of the First Amendment, as well as the Court's precedents in regarding both free exercise of religion and the Court's freedom of speech case law. The Scalia majority opinion in *Smith* reframes the free exercise right at issue as merely a matter of freedom of thought, rather than action, the right to 'believe and profess whatever religious doctrine one desires' and not necessarily the right to act according to one's religious desires.[33] Arguably, framing the issue this way brings *Smith* into line with the *Brandenburg* line of cases because the relevant distinction being drawn is between belief (or speech/advocacy) and action.

To refer further to the majority opinion, 'We have never held that an individual's religious beliefs excuse him from compliance with an otherwise valid law prohibiting conduct that the state is free to regulate.'[34] 'The only decisions in which we have held that the First Amendment bars application of a neutral, generally applicable law to religiously motivated action have involved not the Free Exercise Clause alone, but the Free Exercise Clause in conjunction with other constitutional protections, such as freedom of speech and of the press.'[35]

Here, the Court points to a new interpretive approach to the problem of hierarchy where the freedom of religious exercise becomes more weighty, demanding strict scrutiny so long as it is accompanied by another right, ie, becoming so-called 'hybrid rights'.

> Values that are protected against government interference through enshrinement in the Bill of Rights are not thereby banished from the political process. Just as a society that believes in the negative protection accorded to the press by the First Amendment is likely to enact laws that affirmatively foster the dissemination of the printed word, so also a society that believes in the negative protection accorded to religious belief can be expected to be solicitous of that value in its legislation as well ... It may fairly be said that leaving accommodation to the political process will place at a relative disadvantage those religious practices that are not widely engaged in; but that unavoidable consequence of democratic government must be preferred to a system in which each conscience is a law unto itself, or in which judges weigh the social importance of all laws against the centrality of all religious beliefs.[36]

In so doing, the Court seemed to deconstitutionalise religious freedoms, as stand alone rights.

[33] ibid, 877.
[34] ibid, 878–79.
[35] ibid, 881.
[36] ibid, 890.

While the majority opinion limited the religion rights protection, in her concurrence, Justice O'Conner would have applied the higher review standard of 'strict scrutiny', asserting: 'Because the First Amendment does not distinguish between religious belief and religious conduct, conduct motivated by sincere religious belief, like the belief itself, must be at least presumptively protected by the Free Exercise Clause.'[37]

In his dissent, Justice Blackmun, together with Justices Brennan and Marshall said: 'I do not believe the Founders thought their dearly bought freedom from religious persecution a "luxury", but an essential element of liberty-and they could not have thought religious intolerance "unavoidable", for they drafted the Religion Clauses precisely in order to avoid that intolerance.'[38] Reviewing the asserted state interests, Justice Blackmun declared: '[T]he values and interests of those seeking a religious exemption in this case are congruent, to a great degree, with those the State seeks to promote through its drug laws.'[39]

While in its later jurisprudence articulating a balanced rights approach, the Supreme Court has departed from its precedents; nevertheless, this approach appears to be harmonising with that of the European constitutional courts, where individual religion-related rights are often reconciled with the community interest.

Burwell v Hobby Lobby[40] involved Hobby Lobby, an arts and crafts company which dropped coverage for contraceptives in 2012 because the shareholders of the company considered that life began at conception, which they equated to fertilisation. Hence, they objected to their corporations providing health insurance coverage to their female employees for certain FDA approved contraceptives. The majority of the Court found for Hobby Lobby by way of a reliance on the Religious Freedom Restoration Act (RFRA), which required strict scrutiny when a law of general applicability substantially burdened the person's exercise of religious freedom. The majority of the Court held that the RFRA did apply to corporations, in that a for profit corporation could be considered a person under the RFRA; and that a statutory mandate to provide contraceptives substantially burdened the "exercise" of the right in religious freedom of the corporation. By contrast, Justice Ruth Bader Ginsburg delivered a powerful dissent, which included the following observations:

> [I]n a decision of startling breadth the court holds that commercial enterprises including corporations, along with partnerships and sole proprietorships, can opt out of any law (saving only tax laws) they judge incompatible with their sincerely

[37] ibid, 893.
[38] ibid, 909.
[39] ibid, 914.
[40] *Burwell v Hobby Lobby Stores*, 134 S Ct 2751 (2014).

> held religious beliefs ... Compelling governmental interests in uniform compliance with the law, and disadvantages that religion-based opt outs impose on others, hold no sway, the court decides, at least when there is a 'less restrictive alternative'. And such an alternative the Court suggests there will always be whenever, in lieu of tolling an enterprise claiming a religious-based exemption, the government i.e. the general public have to pick up the tab.[41]

She noted rightly that, until this decision, the Court had never recognised a profits corporations qualification for religious exemption from a generally applicable law, whether under the free exercise clause or under the RFRA.

Although the specific result in *Hobby Lobby* can be construed narrowly, in that it requires that the government extends to corporations with genuine religious objections, an accommodation with regard to who may pay the costs of free contraception, it does open the possibility to a broader set of religious exemptions from other forms of regulation.

V. OF LIBERTY AND DUE PROCESS

Historically, tensions in protecting liberty in due process have been sorely tested by the issues of race and equality; while, in more contemporary periods, it is being tested by concerns with security. Here, the rights implicated in protecting liberty and equality are often frequently in tension. Controversies concerning criminal justice processes, and particularly, the jury, go back to the very beginning of equal protection jurisprudence. In advocating the adoption of the Constitution, Alexander Hamilton argued: 'The friends and adversaries of the plan of the convention, if they agree in nothing else, concur at least in the value they set upon the trial by jury; or if there is any difference between them, it consists in this: the former regard it as a valuable safeguard to liberty, the latter represent it as the very palladium of free government.'[42]

In more contemporary case law, '[I]t is the jury that is a criminal defendant's fundamental 'protection of life and liberty against race or color prejudice.'[43] A contemporary case, *Batson v Kentucky*,[44] invokes the possibility of a 'liberty' analysis perspective, because the consequences of a criminal conviction involve deprivation of the convicted person's liberty in the most literal sense (and in some scenarios, of life), as well as fairness/justice, equality and due process.

[41] ibid, 2787.

[42] *The Federalist* No 83, p 519 (J Gideon ed, 1818); *McCleskey v Kemp*, 481 US 279, 310 (1987).

[43] 481 US 279, 309–10 (quoting *Strauder v West Virginia*, 100 US 303, 309 (1880)).

[44] *Batson v Kentucky*, 476 US 79 (1986).

i. Prioritisation and Congruence

There is a clear congruence here between liberty as a preeminent constitutional value, and due process as an additional value—supporting the right to due process also supports liberty, eg, in this context, serves the arms of justice and fairness by providing for jury of peers.

Where a black defendant is entitled to a jury of equals, does that mean that race becomes a valid denominator of equality? Where if race is a consideration for jury service, does that qualification also deprive the white juror of the right to participate in the justice process? 'Racial discrimination in selection of jurors harms not only the accused whose life or liberty they are summoned to try ... by denying a person participation in jury service on account of his race, the State unconstitutionally discriminated against the excluded juror.'[45] Although striking statistical evidence showed a profound racial disparity in the use of the death penalty, this evidence was deemed insufficient to invalidate the defendant's death sentence. Here, we can see that longstanding racial prejudice interferes with the country's theoretical commitment to due process rights.

VI. PRIVACY

From the turn of the twentieth century, and later in cases like *Palko v Connecticut*, the Court sought to provide a basic overview, where it defined the scope of fundamental right analysis: how do we know a right is fundamental? In particular, the case law addresses at what level constitutional rights are protected, and to what extent the question of the protection involves the federal government only, or statewide? Early cases concerned due process in criminal cases, leading to later interpretation of substantive due process.

> The right to trial by jury and the immunity from prosecution except as the result of an indictment may have value and importance. Even so, *they are not of the very essence of a scheme of ordered liberty*. To abolish them is not to violate a principle of justice so rooted in the traditions and conscience of our people as to be ranked as fundamental.[46]

i. Prioritisation and Congruence

In a more contemporary case, *Romer v Evans*,[47] involving a conflict between the freedom of association (of landlords) and equality rights, Justice Kennedy

[45] 476 US 79, 87. See *McCleskey v Kemp*, 481 US 279 (1987).
[46] *Palko v Connecticut* 302 US 319, 325 (1937).
[47] *Romer v Evans* 517 US 620 (1996).

for the Court, held that moral justification was not sufficient to support a legitimate governmental purpose argument. In apparently applying a rationality requirement, under the Fourteenth Amendment, this case reflects a limit to the notion of a liberty to contract; for the state will not protect private moralising that interferes with other equality in arbitrary ways. Concern for the equal protection of a targeted classification prevails over the freedom of association and liberty interest of landlords and employers. The case reflects unwillingness to allow the state to dictate morals, especially if a particular group will be judicial disadvantaged or harmed by the state's moral stance.

The following extract from Justice Kennedy's opinion captures this approach:

> The primary rationale the State offers for Amendment 2 is respect for other citizens' freedom of association, and in particular the liberties of landlords or employers who have personal or religious objections to homosexuality ... We cannot say that Amendment 2 is directed to any identifiable legitimate purpose or discrete objective. It is a status-based enactment divorced from any factual context from which we could discern a relationship to legitimate state interests; it is a classification of persons undertaken for its own sake, something the Equal Protection Clause does not permit. Class legislation ... [is] obnoxious to the prohibitions of the Fourteenth Amendment ... We must conclude that Amendment 2 classifies homosexuals not to further a proper legislative end but to make them unequal to everyone else. This Colorado cannot do. *A State cannot so deem a class of persons a stranger to its laws*. Amendment 2 violates the Equal Protection Clause.'[48]

In other areas, too, the Court has clearly limited the states' interests in legislating to preserve a broad private sphere. In a landmark case, the United States Supreme Court expanded its view of the liberty interest under the Fourteenth Amendment, to include within its ambit private consensual gay sex. In *Lawrence v Texas*,[49] the Court upheld a liberty interest in private, consensual sexual intimacy. liberty prevails over the state's regulatory authority to interfere in certain intimate spheres of its citizens' existence. Moral disapproval is not a legitimate government interest for the purpose of equal protection analysis.[50]

> Liberty protects the person from unwarranted government intrusions into a dwelling or other private places. In our tradition the State is not omnipresent in the home. And there are other spheres of our lives and existence, outside the home, where the State should not be a dominant presence. *Freedom extends beyond spatial bounds*. Liberty presumes an autonomy of self that includes freedom of thought, belief, expression, and certain intimate conduct. The instant case involves liberty of the person both in its spatial and in its more transcendent dimensions.[51]

[48] ibid, 635.
[49] *Lawrence v Texas*, 539 US 558 (2003) (Kennedy J).
[50] ibid.
[51] ibid, 562.

Here, Justice Kennedy looks to history and tradition in the United States and other Western democracies to determine whether the right to sexual privacy is a fundamental right, invoking the protection of human dignity, overruling *Bowers*. As he writes, 'The petitioners are entitled to respect for their private lives. The State cannot demean their existence or control their destiny by making their private sexual conduct a crime. Their right to liberty under the Due Process Clause gives them the full right to engage in their conduct without intervention of the government.'[52] The statute at issue, and the one presented in *Bowers*, was characterised as 'seek[ing] to control a personal relationship that, whether or not entitled to formal recognition in the law, is within the liberty of persons to choose without being punished as criminals.'[53] Invoking Justice Kennedy again: 'As the Constitution endures, persons in every generation can invoke its principles in their own search for greater freedom.'[54]

Other rights that pertain to the sphere of intimacy are abortion rights, where the Court has emphasised, the right derives from liberty. In the landmark case of *Roe v Wade*,[55] the United States Supreme Court extended constitutional protection to the right to abortion choice through the right of privacy. A right to a zone of personal privacy can be implied in the Constitution from 'penumbras of the Bill of Rights'. Nevertheless, even in this landmark case, the Court emphasised that the right to privacy was not absolute, and needed to be reconciled with the state's interests:

> The Constitution does not explicitly mention any right of privacy … [T]he Court has recognized that a right of personal privacy, or a guarantee of certain areas or zones of privacy, does exist under the Constitution. In varying contexts, the Court or individual Justices have, indeed, found at least the roots of that right in the First Amendment; in the Fourth and Fifth Amendments; in the penumbras of the Bill of Rights; in the Ninth Amendment (Goldberg, J, concurring); or in the concept of liberty guaranteed by the first section of the Fourteenth Amendment. These decisions make it clear that only personal rights that can be deemed 'fundamental' or 'implicit in the concept of ordered liberty,' are included in this guarantee of personal privacy. They also make it clear that the right has some extension to activities relating to marriage; procreation; contraception; family relationships; and child rearing and education.[56]

As Justice Stewart elucidated in his concurrence

> [T]he full scope of the liberty guaranteed by the Due Process Clause cannot be found in or limited by the precise terms of the specific guarantees elsewhere provided in the Constitution. This 'liberty' is not a series of isolated points pieced out in terms of the taking of property; the freedom of speech, press, and religion;

[52] ibid, 578.
[53] ibid, 567.
[54] ibid, 578–79.
[55] *Roe v Wade*, 410 US 113 (1973).
[56] ibid, 152–53.

> the right to keep and bear arms; the freedom from unreasonable searches and seizures; and so on. It is a rational continuum which, broadly speaking, includes a freedom from all substantial arbitrary impositions and purposeless restraints … and which also recognizes, what a reasonable and sensitive judgment must, that certain interests require particularly careful scrutiny of the state needs asserted to justify their abridgment. *Poe v Ullman*, 367 US 497, 543 … (opinion dissenting from dismissal of appeal).[57]

Both within and outside of the Court, the interpretative approach deployed in *Roe* has not been without controversy. To its detractors, 'to reach its result, the Court necessarily has had to find within the scope of the Fourteenth Amendment a right that was apparently completely unknown to the drafters of the Amendment.'[58]

For decades after it came down, the decision would spawn litigation, most recently *Planned Parenthood v Casey*,[59] where in a joint opinion by Justices O'Conner, Kennedy, Souter, the basic premise of *Roe* was reaffirmed:

> Liberty finds no refuge in a jurisprudence of doubt … The controlling word in the cases before us is 'liberty.' Although a literal reading of the [Due Process] Clause might suggest that it governs only the procedures by which a State may deprive persons of liberty, for at least 105 years, since *Mugler v Kansas*, 123 US 623, 660-661 … (1887), the Clause has been understood to contain a substantive component as well, one 'barring certain government actions regardless of the fairness of the procedures used to implement them.' *Daniels v Williams*, 474 US 327, 331 … (1986).[60]

As the majority said in *Planned Parenthood*,

> It is a promise of the Constitution that there is a realm of personal liberty which the government may not enter … Marriage is mentioned nowhere in the Bill of Rights and interracial marriage was illegal in most States in the 19th century, but the Court was no doubt correct in finding it to be an aspect of liberty protected against state interference by the substantive component of the Due Process Clause in *Loving v Virginia*, 388 US 1, 12, (1967) (relying, in an opinion for eight Justices, on the Due Process Clause).[61]

ii. Congruence

The limits to the abortion right as applied would become clear in *Harris v McRae*,[62] where the Court was confronted with a challenge to rights

57 ibid, 169.
58 ibid, 174.
59 *Planned Parenthood v Casey*, 505 US 833 (1992).
60 ibid, 846.
61 ibid, 847–48.
62 *Harris v McRae*, 448 US 297 (1980).

equality insofar as the exercise of a fundamental right (here, the ability to obtain an abortion) is frequently dependent on financial status. Although *Roe* declared that the right to seek an abortion was part of the fundamental right to privacy, *Harris v McRae* held that the state was not required to subsidise the exercise of the right.[63] The Court held that states participating in Medicaid programmes were not required to fund medically necessary abortions:

> [I]t simply does not follow that a woman's freedom of choice carries with it a constitutional entitlement to the financial resources to avail herself of the full range of protected choices ... Although the liberty protected by the Due Process Clause affords protection against unwarranted government interference with freedom of choice in the context of certain personal decisions, it does not confer an entitlement to such funds as may be necessary to realize all the advantages of that freedom. To hold otherwise would mark a drastic change in our understanding of the Constitution.[64]

While nowhere in the Constitution is there a requirement that the state fund the exercise of one's fundamental rights, such a requirement might have been seen as implicit in the equality principles espoused by the Constitution and the Fourteenth Amendment. Here, one can see the way controversies over the substance and extent of constitutional rights ultimately turn on the conception of the public sphere and, relatedly, the parameters of the state's regulation. In the words of the *Harris* dissent, Justice Brennan (with Justices Marshall and Blackmun) said: '[D]iscriminatory distribution of the benefits of governmental largesse can discourage the exercise of fundamental liberties just as effectively as can an outright denial of those rights through criminal and regulatory sanctions.'[65]

VII. THE EVOLUTION OF FREEDOM IN THE MODERN STATE

How far must the state go to protect a liberty interest framed in terms of constitutional values? Following on from the meaning of freedom beyond a negative rights view, ie, 'the right to be left alone', the modern state raises the question of to what extent might it require funding, or, other government support? To what extent might it require added political support beyond the protection of a negative freedom? This question involves juxtaposing positive versus negative freedoms, yet this discourse of rights seems increasingly obsolete. After all, rights protection, even when not socio-economic, implies

[63] ibid, 316.
[64] ibid, 317–18.
[65] ibid, 334.

costs relating to meaningful enforcement, occasioning expenses of a judicial nature as well as police protection.[66]

The other remaining challenge in the US system involves the increasing role of private actors, and the question of the extent to which constitutional rights protection should be limited to state actors. In an age of globalisation, to what extent do such restrictions make sense for the meaningful realisation of constitutional values?

Here, one can see the full elaboration and risks, which displays the danger of a liberal state that implicitly privileges freedom over other values. In a modern example, in the context of child abuse, the Court held in *DeShaney* that there was no affirmative duty for the state to protect its citizens against a private actor. This is a profoundly troubling opinion, particularly where children's lives are at stake, which one might regard as illustrating the real limits to freedom as the country's paramount constitutional value.[67]

The Roberts Court has begun to provide significant constitutional protection to corporations, a protection framed in terms of rights which previously would have been thought to have been held only by individual rights bearers. In 2010, in *Citizens United v FEC*,[68] the Court held that corporations could not be restricted with regard to their political expenditures, and the majority opinion of the Court equated corporations and human beings when it came to First Amendment rights of free speech.

In a fairly contemporary illustration, in *McCutcheon v FEC*,[69] the majority of the Court rejected Congress's efforts to limit the distorting influence of campaign funding. The issue turned on 'aggregate' limits on the total amount individuals can donate to political candidates. While in the 1976 decision of *Buckley v Valeo* the Court had reasoned that contributions to candidates and independent political expenditure were protected by the First Amendment, but found that these contributions could be regulated because they could permit a wealthy party to directly influence a candidate and therefore subvert the idea of free and fair elections.[70]

The Court has now overruled its finding in *Buckley*. In keeping with its decision in *Citizens United*, the Court has now prevented Congress from

[66] See *Shapiro v Thompson*, 394 US 618 (1969) and *Saenz v Roe*, 526 US 489 (1999) (upholding aid where it violated the 'right to travel'). The modern Court has later stepped back from meaningful enforcement where it is seen to be imposing costs, See *Dandridge v Williams*, 397 US 471 (1970).

[67] See *DeShaney v Winnebago County Dep't of Social Services*, 489 US 189 (1989) (Justice Rehnquist holding): 'It is the State's affirmative act of restraining the individual's freedom to act on his own behalf—through incarceration, institutionalization, or other similar restraint of personal liberty—which is the "deprivation of liberty" triggering the protections of the Due Process Clause, not its failure to act to protect his liberty interests against harms inflicted by other means.' 489 US 189, 200.

[68] *Citizens United v FEC* 558 US 310 (2010).

[69] *McCutcheon v FEC*, 572 US (2014).

[70] *Buckley v Valeo*, 424 US 1, 288 (1976).

limiting the privileged access and ability to excessively influence elected representatives of wealthy donors. At least Chief Justice Roberts acknowledged the problem which the majority in *Citizen United* created when, in opening his opinion in *McCutcheon*, he wrote: 'Money and politics may at time seem repugnant to some but so to does much of what the First Amendment vigorously protects. If the First Amendment protects flag burning, funeral protest and Nazi parades—despite the profound offence such spectacles cause—it surely protects political campaigns speech despite popular opposition.'

While the court has employed the conception of liberty to weaken a whole range of regulatory frameworks designed to promote a more participative democracy, it has continued, in significant areas, to protect the liberty of individuals. Recently, for example, the Court declined to hear appeals from decisions in five states striking down bans on same-sex marriage.[71] In *Windsor v United States*, the Court struck down section 3 of the so-called Defense of Marriage Act of 1996 which denied legally married same-sex couples legal protection. By striking down this section the Court confirmed the majority opinion of Justice Kennedy: 'DOMA rejects a long established precept that the incidents, benefits and obligations of marriage are uniform for all married couples in each State, though they may vary, subject to constitutional guarantees from one state to the next.' The Court rejected the idea that federal government could override a community's considered perspective with regard to the evolution of the institution of marriage. It further upheld the idea that the Act constituted an interference with the equal dignity of same-sex marriages which had been conferred by certain states.

i. Prioritisation and Congruence

The welfare of the individual citizen is subordinated to due process formalities: '[O]ur cases have recognized that the *Due Process Clauses generally confer no affirmative right* to governmental aid, even where such aid may be necessary to secure life, liberty, or property interests of which the government itself may not deprive the individual.'[72]

A case like *DeShaney* illuminates the line between private and public impediments to the realisation of constitutional rights. Accordingly:

> [a] State's failure to protect an individual against private violence simply does not constitute a violation of the Due Process Clause.[73] The county had no duty under the due process clause to protect the boy against his father's violence, and therefore the county's failure to provide such protection did not deprive the child

[71] *New York Times*, 10 August 2014.

[72] *DeShaney v Winnebago County Dep't of Social Services*, 489 US 189, 196 (1989).

[73] ibid, 197.

> of liberty in violation of the due process clause'[74] ... the affirmative duty to protect arises not from the State's knowledge of the individual's predicament or from its expressions of intent to help him, but from the limitations which it has imposed on his freedom to act on his own behalf, through imprisonment, institutionalization, or other similar restraint of personal liberty.[75]
>
> But nothing in the language of the Due Process Clause itself requires the State to protect the life, liberty, and property of its citizens against invasion by private actors. The Clause is phrased as a limitation on the State's power to act, not as a guarantee of certain minimal levels of safety and security. It forbids the State itself to deprive individuals of life, liberty, or property without "due process of law", but its language cannot fairly be extended to impose an affirmative obligation on the State to ensure that those interests do not come to harm through other means. Nor does history support such an expansive reading of the constitutional text. *196 Like its counterpart in the Fifth Amendment, the Due Process Clause of the Fourteenth Amendment was intended to prevent government "from abusing [its] power, or employing it as an instrument of oppression"... Consistent with these principles, our cases have recognized that the Due Process Clauses generally confer no affirmative right to governmental aid, even where such aid may be necessary to secure life, liberty, or property interests of which the government itself may not deprive the individual.[76]

In this approach, there is a narrow view taken of the public sphere, aimed at drawing narrow distinctions between private and public rights.[77]

> In the substantive due process analysis, it is the State's *affirmative act of restraining the individual's freedom to act on his own behalf*—through incarceration, institutionalization, or other similar restraint of personal liberty—which is the 'deprivation of liberty' triggering the protections of the Due Process Clause, not its failure to act to protect his liberty interests against harms inflicted by other means.[78]

For as the *DeShaney* dissenters Justices Brennan, Marshall and Blackmun, asserted: '[I]naction can be every bit as abusive of power as action, that oppression can result when a State undertakes a vital duty and then ignores it.'[79]

A. The Debate Over Freedom of Contract

A countertrend, fortunately, relating to the evolution of the modern state is the rise and fall of the notion that constitutional rights protecting contract

[74] ibid, 197.
[75] ibid, 197.
[76] ibid, 195–96.
[77] Of course, there is a competing strand in US constitutional law as well, which appears in the approach taken to rights to minimal social welfare; for example, *Saenz v Roe*.
[78] 489 US 189, 200.
[79] ibid, 212.

as an enforceable freedom. At the beginning of the twentieth century, in *Lochner v New York*, there was a strong commitment to freedom of contract, seen even in the light of other regulatory concerns such as labour and other rights. The Court recognised freedom of contract and individual 'liberty of choice' as fundamental.[80]

At that time, the Court held the freedom of the individual to contract to be virtually absolute. The Fourteenth Amendment is put to the service of the right of property, here in the form of the right to contract for labour. Freedom of contract trumps police power of the state to enact protective legislation for the good of the worker. To quote from the majority opinion of Justice Peckham:

> The general right to make a contract in relation to his business is part of the liberty of the individual protected by the Fourteenth Amendment of the Federal Constitution ... Under that provision no State can deprive any person of life, liberty or property without due process of law. The right to purchase or to sell labor is part of the liberty protected by this amendment, unless there are circumstances which exclude the right.[81]

Yet with time and after a few decades of litigation, the *Lochner* decision protecting an untrammeled free market became more famous for Justice Holmes's dissent, asserting:

> The liberty of the citizen to do as he likes so long as he does not interfere with the liberty of others to do the same, which has been a shibboleth for some well-known writers, is interfered with by school laws, by the Post Office, by every state or municipal institution which takes his money for purposes thought desirable, whether he likes it or not. The Fourteenth Amendment does not enact Mr. Herbert Spencer's Social Statics.[82]

The unbridled approach to freedom of contract came to an end in *West Coast Hotel Co v Parrish*,[83] where the Supreme Court finally subordinated the ostensible freedom of contract to the broader social interest, upholding a statute requiring a ceiling on employee work hours.

i. Prioritisation and Congruence

With the growth of the modern state, there has been recognition in both the political and judicial branches of the state interest in protecting the community interest in ways that may well override an individual's freedom of contract.

[80] *Lochner v New York*, 198 US 45 (1905) (Peckham J).
[81] ibid, 54.
[82] ibid, 76.
[83] *West Coast Hotel Co v Parrish*, 300 US 379 (1937).

> The Constitution does not speak of freedom of contract. It speaks of liberty and prohibits the deprivation of liberty without due process of law. In prohibiting that deprivation *the Constitution does not recognize an absolute and uncontrollable liberty*. Liberty in each of its phases has its history and connotation. But the liberty safeguarded is liberty in a social organization which requires the protection of law against the evils which menace the health, safety, morals and welfare of the people. Liberty under the Constitution is thus necessarily subject to the restraints of due process, and regulation which is reasonable in relation to its subject and is adopted in the interests of the community is due process.[84]

VIII. CONCLUSION

Animated by its colonial and postcolonial experiences, US constitutional doctrine privileges individual freedom as its overarching constitutional value. Over the years, this freedom has developed in various directions, particularly regarding the elaboration of constitutional values of freedom of expression, religious exercise, and privacy. Recently, as noted, the Court has afforded equal rights to corporations and has paid less attention to the power of wealthy corporations and individuals to influence the political process.

The evolution of this jurisprudence reflects the nuancing of the notion of absolute rights protection, harmonising with other constitutional values, such as equality. These developments can be understood in the context of the evolution of the subject of the right, where there was until recently an evident expansion of the constitutional community. We have also seen, in some instances, the substance of constitutional values as more nuanced by way of the interpretation of the implicated liberties, in light of the broader value of judicial protection of individual rights review, the best example being the opinion in *Roe v Wade*.

The impact of the values contained in the Constitution and the consequence of the Court's jurisprudence for the nature of American society has certainly been significantly affected by the Roberts Court.

The record of the contemporary Roberts Court is difficult to define with precision. The Court has affirmed the rights of married gays and lesbians who receive federal benefits. It has upheld healthcare and struck down anti-immigrant laws that would have imposed onerous penalties on foreign nationals who exceeded the limits of their visas. On the other hand, in its treatment of detainees, particularly those who hold to Islam as a religion, the Court has shifted away from decades of jurisprudence in which the Court envisaged its role as the protector of human dignity of those who lacked the political power to vindicate their own rights.[85] It has also

[84] ibid, 391.
[85] See Eric L Lewis, *New York Times*, 4 October 2014.

invalidated campaign finance regulations. Here, the Court has turned in a clear direction, reflecting a general scepticism about government regulation shoring up a laissez-faire view of the role of the Court in protecting the freedom of the market.[86]

[86] See for a comprehensive analysis of this point, David Cole, 'The Anti-Court Court' *New York Review of Books* 14 August 2014.

16

Global Values in the Venezuelan Constitution: Some Prioritisations and Several Incongruences

ALLAN R BREWER-CARÍAS

I. INTRODUCTION AND CONSTITUTIONAL BACKGROUND

VENEZUELA WAS THE first Latin American country to gain independence from the Spanish Crown, in 1810. A general congress of representatives of the former colonial provinces of the *Capitanía General de Venezuela* enacted on 21 December 1811 the Federal Constitution for the States of Venezuela, the first constitution on the South American continent, and only the third in modern constitutional history.[1] This Constitution followed the general principles of modern constitutionalism derived from the North American and French Revolutions, organising the state according to the principles of constitutional supremacy; sovereignty of the people, republicanism and political representation, separation of power, presidential system, checks and balances and superiority of the law as expression of the general will; territorial distribution of power with a federal system of government and municipal organisation; an extended declaration of fundamental rights of Man and Society; and a judiciary integrated by judges imparting justice in the name of the nation with judicial review powers.

[1] See on the constitutional texts of Venezuelan independence: Allan R Brewer-Carías, *Documentos Constitucionales de la Independencia/Constitucional Documents of the Independence 1811*, Colección Textos Legislativos No 52 (Caracas, Editorial Jurídica Venezolana, 2012). This book contains a facsimile text of the book: *Interesting Documents relating to Caracas/ Documentos Interesantes relativos a Caracas; Interesting Official Documents relating to the United Provinces of Caracas, viz Preliminary Remarks, The Act of Independence. Proclamation, Manifesto to the World of the Causes which have impelled the said provinces to separate from the Mother Country; together with the Constitution framed for the Administration of their Government. In Spanish and English*, published in a bilingual format in London, 1812 (pp 301–637).

The constitutional history of the two hundred years of republicanism shows the persistent attempts to consolidate such principles, concluding for instance with the adoption of a comprehensive system of judicial review, now common in almost all the Latin American countries, that combines the concentrated method (European model) attributed to the Constitutional Chamber of the Supreme Tribunal, with powers to annul statutes on the grounds of unconstitutionality when reached by means of popular actions, with the diffuse method (American model) empowering all courts to declare the inapplicability of statutes in cases or controversies when considered unconstitutional.[2] In addition, as in all the Latin American countries, in Venezuela there also exists the amparo action as a specific judicial mean that can be exercised before any court for the protection of constitutional rights.[3]

Since 1811 the Constitution has been modified (reformed or amended) on 26 occasions, having been substantially reformed in 1830, 1864, 1901, 1947, and 1999.[4] The twentieth-century democratic system of government effectively began in 1958 after the main political parties signed a political pact known as 'Pacto de Punto Fijo', which conditioned the drafting of the 1961 Constitution which governed the democratic system for the four last decades of the twentieth century. At the end of that period, the political parties entered into a profound political crisis that affected their leadership, leaving a political vacuum that was filled by an authoritarian, centralised and militaristic government led by Hugo Chávez Frias, who was elected in 1998 and re-elected in 2006. In 1999, a new Constitution[5] was sanctioned by a Constituent Assembly,[6] and subsequently approved by referendum in

[2] See Allan R Brewer-Carías, 'Judicial Review in Venezuela' (2007) 45(3) *Duquesne Law Review* 439–65.

[3] See Allan R Brewer-Carías, 'The Amparo Proceeding in Venezuela: Constitutional Litigation and Procedural Protection of Constitutional Rights and Guarantees' (2011) 49 *Duquesne Law Review* 161–241.

[4] For a detailed study of the historical constitutional periods in Venezuelan constitutionalism, see Allan R Brewer-Carías, *Instituciones Políticas y Constitucionales*, vol I Evolución Histórica del Estado (Caracas, San Cristóbal, 1996) 257–389; Allan R Brewer-Carías, 'Estudio Preliminar', *Las Constituciones de Venezuela*, vol I (Caracas, Academia de Ciencias Políticas y Sociales, 2008) 25–526; and Allan R Brewer-Carías, *Historia Constitucional de Venezuela* (Caracas, Editorial Alfa, 2008) 2 vols.

[5] See Allan R Brewer-Carías, *La Constitución de 1999. Derecho Constitucional Venezolano* (Caracas, Editorial Jurídica Venezolana, 2004), 2 vols; Hildegard Rondón de Sansó, *Análisis de la Constitución Venezolana de 1999* (Caracas, Editorial Ex Libris, 2001); Ricardo Combellas, *Derecho Constitucional: una introducción al estudio de la Constitución de la República Bolivariana de Venezuela* (Caracas, McGraw Hill, 2001); and Alfonso Rivas Quintero, *Derecho Constitucional* (Valencia, Paredes Editores, 2002).

[6] This author was elected a member of the Constituent Assembly, being one of the four members (of 131 members) that opposed the project proposed by President Hugo Chávez. See Allan R Brewer-Carías, *Debate Constituyente (Aportes a la Asamblea Nacional Constituyente)*, Tomo I (8 agosto-8 septiembre 1999); Tomo II (9 septiembre-17 octubre 1999), Tomo III (18 octubre-30 noviembre 1999) (Caracas, Fundación de Derecho Público-Editorial Jurídica Venezolana, 1999). On the 1999 constitution-making process see: Allan R Brewer-Carías,

the midst of the most severe political crisis of the country affecting the democratic parties and democracy itself.

The Constitution defines Venezuela as a democratic and social rule of law and justice state (*Estado democratico y social de derecho y de justicia*), declaring that the rule of law (*Estado de Derecho*) guarantees that the state submits to legality. It establishes a complete judicial review system in order to ensure control of constitutionality (articles 334 and 336) and legality of all state acts and actions (article 259).

The 1999 Venezuelan Constitution contains not only an extensive amount of articles devoted to enumerating human rights (120), but also a rich text full of values, principles and global declarations. The Constitutional Chamber of the Supreme Tribunal of Justice has said that the Constitution is 'an instrument with legal spirit that connects, according to the nature of the applicable precept, both the bodies of the State and the individuals'; and that imposes constitutional juridical situations 'with reference to indispensable values for the assurance of human freedom, equality and dignity' guaranteed by the judiciary.[7]

Constitutional values in the Venezuelan Constitution are expressed not only in its Preamble but in many of its articles, as goals intending to guide the state, society and general conduct of individuals.[8] Consequently, in Venezuela, global values and principles do not derive from the sole interpretation and application of the Constitution by the courts, but from provisions in the Constitution itself.[9] Nonetheless, by means of constitutional judicial decisions, the sense, the scope and the priority character of many of these constitutional principles and values have been defined and enriched; and also, unfortunately, in many cases, some constitutional incongruences have been established between the constitutional text and the political practice of government.

II. CONSTITUTIONAL VALUES AND THEIR PRIORITISATION

The Preamble to the Constitution began by declaring that it was adopted by the representatives of the Venezuelan people, having in mind the achievement

'The 1999 Venezuelan Constitution-Making Process as an Instrument for Framing the development of an Authoritarian Political Regime' in Laura E Miller (ed), *Framing the State in Times of Transition. Case Studies in Constitution Making* (Washington DC, United States Institute of Peace Press, 2010) 505–31.

7 See Decision N° 963 dated June 5, 2001. *José A Guía y otros v Ministerio de Infraestructura*, *Revista de Derecho Público*, N° 85–88 (Caracas, Editorial Jurídica Venezolana, 2001) 447.

8 See Allan R Brewer-Carías, 'La constitucionalización del derecho administrativo', *Derecho Administrativo*, Vol I (Bogotá, Universidad Externado de Colombia, 2005) 215 ff.

9 See Allan R Brewer-Carías, *Principios fundamentales del derecho público* (Caracas, Editorial Jurídica Venezolana, 2005).

of a series of goals 'guided by social, economic, political and judicial values',[10] in order to inspire the action of the state, 'which must respond to equalitarian, international, democratic, moral and historical principles'.

In this context, the state is defined as a 'state of justice, federal and decentralised', that must develop its action to enforce the values of 'freedom, independence, peace, solidarity, common good, territorial integrity, cohabitation and the empire of the law for these and all future generations', in a society that is qualified as 'democratic, participatory, multi-ethnic and pluricultural', which is confirmed, for instance, by the express recognition in the Constitution of the indigenous populations' status (articles 119 et seq).

These goals represent the fundamental principles and constitutional values that inspire the constitutional text as a whole. They have the same binding quality as constitutional provisions, and consequently are enforceable. As affirmed by the Constitutional Chamber of the Supreme Tribunal, 'the statutes must have those values as their guide, so those that do not follow them or that are contrary to those objectives become unconstitutional'.[11]

Besides the values guiding the configuration of the state declared in the Preamble, the Constitution also enumerates as superior values of the legal system and of the whole state activity: 'life, freedom, justice, equality, solidarity, democracy, social responsibility and, in general, the pre-eminence of human rights, ethics and political pluralism' (article 2).

Additionally, the Constitution identifies 'the defence and the development of the individual and the respect of his/her dignity, the democratic exercise of the popular will, the construction of a fair and peace loving society, the promotion of the prosperity and wellbeing of the people and the guarantee of the fulfilment of all principles, rights and duties recognised and enshrined in the Constitution' as essential goals of the state, considering 'education and work' as fundamental processes to achieve those ends (article 3).

The constitutional text also gave form to a series of social ends specified in the Preamble with the object of ensuring 'the right to a life, work, culture, education, social justice and equality without discrimination nor subordination of any kind'. Reference is also made in the Constitution regarding the social goals of society and of the state in order to achieve 'social justice'. The assurance of 'equality without discrimination nor subordination of any kind' is also specified as a fundamental social goal.

Referring to the Republic, particular further fundamental values are expressly emphasised in the Constitution: the principle that the nation's rights ('independence, freedom, sovereignty, immunity, territorial integrity

[10] Regarding the nature of the Preamble and its constitutional value, see the decision of the former Supreme Court of Justice in its Political-Administrative Chamber, dated August 8, 1989, *Revista de Derecho Público* Nº 39 (Caracas, Editorial Jurídica Venezolana, 1989) 102.

[11] See *Deudores hipotecarios v Superintendencia de Bancos*, *Revista de Derecho Público*, Nº 89–92 (Caracas, Editorial Jurídica Venezolana, 2002) 94 ff.

and the national self-determination') cannot be renounced or abandoned (article 1).

The Preamble sets out as one of the goals of the state, the 'peaceful cooperation between nations', which implies the commitment to look for the peaceful solution of controversies, and the rejection of war. This peaceful cooperation must be executed in accordance with the 'principle of the non-intervention' in the affairs of other countries, and the principle of 'self-determination of the people'. Also, it specifies that international cooperation must be carried out 'according to the universal and indivisible guarantee of human rights and the democratisation of the international society'.

References are also made in the Constitution to other values that must guide the international relations of the Republic, including 'nuclear disarmament, the ecological balance and the environment considered as a common and non-renouncable patrimony of humanity'. In particular, according to the Preamble, another fundamental goal that must serve as guidance of the state's actions is 'the impulse and consolidation of Latin-American integration' (article 153).

Some of the values declared in the Constitution have been prioritised in political practice and through judicial decisions, in the sense that they have been considered as having some kind of superior hierarchy regarding other principles that are governed by the former. This is the case for

— human dignity
— fairness/justice/rule of law/state of justice
— equality/respect/tolerance/diversity/multiculturalism
— democracy/participation/decentralisation/inclusion
— compassion/caring/solidarity/social justice/social state
— community/civil society
— family
— life
— honesty/integrity
— learning/education
— freedom/liberty/independence
— security
— responsibility/accountability/transparency
— environment.

It is to these that I now turn.

A. Human Dignity

The value of 'human dignity' is considered by the courts 'as inherent to the human condition' that exists 'before the state' and imposes on all branches of government the need to be 'at the service of the human being.'[12] This implies not only the existence of constitutional rights considered 'inherent to human beings' but the emergence of the 'principle of progressiveness' in their interpretation and enforcement. According to the criteria set out by the Constitutional Chamber of the Supreme Tribunal, the courts have an obligation 'to interpret the entire legal system in the light of the Right of the Constitution ... which also means, that they have to interpret the system congruently with the fundamental rights or human rights, that must be respected above all, making a progressive and complete interpretation'.[13]

The Constitution refers to this value in many articles, when guaranteeing to anybody deprived of liberty the right to be 'treated with respect due to the inherent dignity of the human being' (article 46); when guaranteeing that the judicial seizure of a person's home must be made 'always respecting human dignity' (article 47); when imposing the obligation on the state's security offices to always 'respect the human dignity and rights of all persons' (article 55); when establishing the duty of the state to protect senior citizens and disabled persons, always respecting their 'human dignity' (articles 80, 81); and when guaranteeing that the salary of every worker must be 'sufficient to enable him or her to live with dignity' (article 91).

The Constitutional Chamber of the Supreme Tribunal has considered human dignity as 'one of the values on which the Social rule of law and Justice State is based, and around which all the legal system and all the actions of the branches of government (public powers) must turn.' Based on this approach, the Chamber defined human dignity as 'the supremacy that persons have as an inherent attribute of their rational being, which imposes on public authorities the duty to watch for the protection and safe-conduct of the life, freedom and autonomy of men and women for the sole fact of their existence, independently of any other consideration.' Thus, 'the sole existence of man grants him the right to exist and to obtain all the guarantees needed to assure him a dignified life, that is, his own existence, proportional and rational to the recognition of his essence as a rational being.' This concept of human dignity implies the imposition 'upon the State of the duty to adopt the necessary protective measures to safeguard the legal assets that define man as a person, that is, life, integrity, freedom, autonomy.'[14]

[12] See Decision of the First Court of the Administrative Jurisdiction dated June 1, 2000, *Julio Rocco A*, *Revista de Derecho Público*, Nº 82 (Caracas, Editorial Jurídica Venezolana, 2000) 287 ff.

[13] ibid.

[14] With this purpose, the Constitution, in its art 3, 'establishes that the recognition of the human dignity constitutes a structural principle of the Social rule of law State and for that, it forbids, in its Title III, Chapter III, the forced disappearances, the degrading treatments, the tortures or cruel treatments that could harm the life as an inviolable right, the degrading punishments and all other inherent rights of the human person (articles 43 ff)' See Decision N° 2442, dated September 1, 2003, *Alejandro Serrano López*, *Revista de Derecho Público*, No 83–96 (Caracas, Editorial Jurídica Venezolana, 2003) 183 ff.

The Political-Administrative Chamber of the Supreme Tribunal of Justice has also emphasised the pre-eminent character of dignity, considering it the 'axiological' element representing 'the ideological base that supports the dogmatic order of the current Constitution', limiting the exercise of public power and establishing an effective judicial guarantee system.' Hence this 'prevalent position of human dignity' is considered as a 'superior value of the legal system'. It implies 'the obligation of the State and of all its bodies to protect and guarantee human rights as the main purpose and objective of its public action'. Consequently, the development of human dignity is considered by the Supreme Tribunal as 'one of the superior values of the legal system', seeing its 'defence and development' as 'one of the essential objectives of the State' (articles 2 and 3).[15]

Human dignity also promotes the idea of the 'pre-eminence of human rights' (Preamble); which according to the 'principle of progressiveness' (article 19) imposes the need for the interpretation of statutes in the most favourable way for their enjoyment. In this regard, article 19 of the 1999 Constitution begins the Title on 'Duties, Rights and Constitutional Guarantees' by setting forth that the state must guarantee every person, 'according to the progressiveness principle and without discrimination whatsoever, the enjoyment and non-renounceable, indivisible and interdependent exercise of human rights'. The provision adds that 'the respect and the guarantee of the rights are mandatory to all State bodies in accordance with the Constitution, the treaties on human rights signed and ratified by the Republic and the statutes.'[16] As affirmed by the courts, 'the interpretation of the corresponding constitutional provisions and any future constitutional revision must be performed in the most favourable way for the exercise and enjoyment of the rights', adding that 'this principle is so important that its application obliges the State to update legislation in favour of the defence of the human rights and in view to dignify the human condition, adapting the interpretation of the norms "to the sensibility, thought and needs of the new times in order to adapt them to the new established order and to reject any anachronistic precept that opposes their effective force"'.[17]

[15] See Decision N° 224 dated February 24, 2000, *Revista de Derecho Público*, N° 81 (2000, Editorial Jurídica Venezolana, Caracas) 131 ff. See also, decision of the Constitutional Chamber of the Supreme Tribunal N° 3215 dated June 15, 2004, *Revista de Derecho Público*, N° 97–98 (Caracas, Editorial Jurídica Venezolana, 2004) 428.

[16] About this principle, the Constitutional Chamber of the Supreme Tribunal of Justice, quoting art 2 of the American Convention on Human Rights, in Decision N° 1154, dated June 29, 2001, based on the same principle, has ruled that it is necessary 'to adapt the legal system in order to ensure the efficiency of said rights, being unacceptable the excuse of the inexistence or unsuitability of the means provided in the internal order for their protection and application.' *Revista de Derecho Público*, N° 85–88 (Caracas, Editorial Jurídica Venezolana, 2001) 111 ff.

[17] In this sense the First Court of the Administrative Jurisdiction has considered as its obligation 'to interpret the entire legal system in the light of the Right of the Constitution, even more, when acting in exercise of the constitutional power for protection, which also means, that we have to interpret the system congruently with the fundamental rights or human rights, that

In order to give human dignity its complete application, article 23 of the 1999 Constitution ensured that international treaties on human rights signed and ratified by Venezuela, 'prevail in the internal order when containing more favourable provisions regarding their enjoyment than those contained in the Constitution and the laws of the Republic.' The same article provides for the immediate and direct application of these treaties by state bodies, particularly the courts.[18]

On the other hand, in order to reinforce the constitutional value of human dignity, the human rights that are guaranteed and protected are not only the ones enumerated in the Constitution, but also those considered 'inherent to the human person' (article 22).[19] The last phrase of article 22 of the Constitution established that 'the lack of regulatory statutes regarding human rights do not diminish their exercise'; that is, their application 'cannot be conditioned by the existence of a statute developing it; and on the contrary, the lack of legal instruments regulating them does not diminish their exercise, being such rights 'of immediate and direct application by the courts and all other bodies of the State' (articles 22 and 23 of the Constitution).[20]

B. Fairness/Justice/Rule of Law/State of Justice

'Justice' has also been considered as a global and 'fundamental value' that must contribute to 'the construction of a just and peace-loving society

must be respected above all, making a progressive and complete interpretation.' See Decision dated June 1, 2000, Julio Rocco A, *Revista de Derecho Público*, N° 82 (Caracas, Editorial Jurídica Venezolana, 2000) 287 ff.

[18] The Constitutional Court of the Supreme Tribunal has for instance applied this provision regarding due process rights, preferentially applying art 8 of the American Convention on Human Rights. See Decision dated March 14, 2000 *CA Electricidad del Centro and CA Electricidad de los Andes*, *Revista de Derecho Público*, N° 81 (Caracas, Editorial Jurídica Venezolana, 2000) 157–58; quoted also in Decision N° 328 dated March 9, 2001, of the same Chamber, *Revista de Derecho Público*, N° 85–88 (Caracas, Editorial Jurídica Venezolana, 2001) 108. The Political-Administrative Chamber of the Supreme Tribunal interpreted and developed the criteria established by the Constitutional Chamber regarding the lack of application of art 185 of the Organic Law of the Supreme Court of Justice in Decision N° 802 dated April 13, 2000, *Elecentro v Superintendencia Procompetencia*, *Revista de Derecho Público*, N° 82 (Caracas, Editorial Jurídica Venezolana, 2000) 270. On a similar matter, see also, Decision N° 449 dated March 27, 2001, *Dayco de Construcciones v INOS*, *Revista de Derecho Público*, N° 85–88 (Caracas, Editorial Jurídica Venezolana, 2001). Nonetheless, the Political-Administrative Chamber has denied giving prevalence to art 8 of the American Convention regarding the requests made by corporate persons, understanding that the Convention only refers to the 'human' rights of individuals. See Decision N° 278 dated March 1, 2001, *Revista de Derecho Público*, N° 85–88 (Caracas, Editorial Jurídica Venezolana, 2001) 104.

[19] This open clause is more extensive in comparison with the original wording of the North American Constitution (Ninth Amendment), in the sense that it refers not only to the rights and guarantees not enumerated in the Constitution but also in the international instruments on human rights, which conforms a truly unlimited cast of unstated, but protected rights that are inherent to the human person.

[20] See Decision N° 723, dated May 15, 2001, *Revista de Derecho Público*, N° 85–88 (Caracas, Editorial Jurídica Venezolana, 2001) 111.

resulting from the democratic exercise of popular will' (article 3). The Constitutional Chamber has considered that 'the power to administer justice must be exercised in the name of the Republic and come from the citizens (article 253)', and 'must be executed with independence and impartiality' by judges 'free from subordinations and inadequate pressures' (articles 254 and 256 of the Constitution). This has been considered as 'a new paradigm about values and constitutional principles connected to the justice', which has led to the conception of the 'State of Justice', considering the judiciary not just one more branch of government but 'the integrating and stabilising State power with authority to control and even dissolve the rest of the branches of government' (Judicialist State).[21]

This conception of the 'State of Justice' (*Estado de Justicia*) not only flows from the provisions of the Preamble and of article 1 that declares justice as a constitutional value, but from the constitutional provisions establishing 'the prevalence of the notion of material justice over formalities and technicalities';[22] and providing for the 'effective judicial protection' of human rights by means of a system of justice that must be 'free, available, impartial, idoneous, transparent, autonomous, independent, responsible, fair and expeditious, without improper delays, formalisms or useless repositions' (article 26).[23] To that effect, the procedural laws must establish the 'simplification, uniformity and efficiency of the proceedings and adopt a brief, oral and public procedure, without sacrificing justice because of omission of non-essential formalities' (article 257).

C. Equality/Respect/Tolerance/Diversity/Multiculturalism

The Preamble to the Constitution also declares as a fundamental social value, 'equality without discrimination or subordination of any kind', which results from the traditional and historical egalitarian character of Venezuelan society, which rejects any kind of discrimination or servility (articles 19 and 21). This has also been considered 'as a fundamental principle of democracy'.[24]

[21] See Decision N° 659 of the Political-Administrative Chamber dated March 24, 2000, *Rosario Nouel v Consejo de la Judicatura y Comisión de Emergencia Judicial*, *Revista de Derecho Público* N° 81 (Caracas, Editorial Jurídica Venezolana, 2000) 103–04.

[22] See Supreme Tribunal of Justice, Decision N° 949 of the Political-Administrative Chamber dated April 26, 2000, *Revista de Derecho Público*, N° 82 (Caracas, Editorial Jurídica Venezolana, 2000) 163 ff.

[23] This conception of the 'State of Justice' has also been analysed by the Constitutional Chamber of the Supreme Tribunal of Justice, particularly in Decision N° 389 dated March 7, 2002, in which the principle of the informality of the process was repeated, also asserting the principle of *pro actione* as another principle of the State of Justice. See *Revista de Derecho Público*, N° 89–92 (Caracas, Editorial Jurídica Venezolana, 2002) 175 ff.

[24] See Decision N° 439 of the Political-Administrative Chamber dated October 6, 1992, *Revista de Derecho Público*, N° 52 (Caracas, Editorial Jurídica Venezolana, 1992) 91–92.

The principle of equality has been defined in a very explicit way in article 21 of the Constitution, stating that all persons are equal before the law, and consequently, no discrimination can be allowed based on race, sex, religion, social condition, or any other cause having the purpose or consequence of annulling or harming the recognition, enjoyment and exercise of rights and liberties in conditions of equality. For such purpose, the Constitution provides for the juridical and administrative conditions in order to effectively guarantee equality before the law; for instance providing for positive measures in favour of persons or groups that could be discriminated, marginalised or vulnerable; protecting persons located in circumstance of manifest weakness and punishing abuses and harms inflicted against them.

On matters of religion and belief, the Constitution expressly declares that the state must guarantee the freedom of 'cult and religion' (article 50); everybody having the right to profess religious faith and cults, and to express their beliefs in private or in public by teaching and other practices, provided that such beliefs are not contrary to moral, good customs or public order. No one shall invoke religious beliefs or discipline as a means for evading the compliance with the laws or preventing another person from the exercising of his rights. The autonomy and independence of religious confessions and churches is likewise guaranteed in the Constitution, subject only to such limitations as may derive from the Constitution and the law. The Constitution also entitles parents to determine the religious education to be given to their children in accordance with their convictions.

The Constitution guarantees freedom of conscience, although conscientious objections cannot be invoked in order to evade compliance with laws or prevent others from complying with it or exercising their rights (article 60).

Finally, the Preamble of the Constitution expressly declares the Venezuelan Society to be multi-ethnic and pluri-cultural.

D. Democracy/Participation/Decentralisation/Inclusion

The Constitution guarantees 'democracy' (Preamble), not only as a political regime and as a condition of government, but also as a way of life, founded in the ideas of political pluralism and equal 'participation' of everyone in the political processes. In this sense, the concept of the 'democratic state' (*Estado democrático*) is also identified as a constitutional principle that gives roots to the political organisation of the nation, as it derives from the Preamble ('democratic society') and from articles 2, 3, 5 and 6 of the Constitution. Democracy is also established in article 6 of the Constitution as an immutable regime of the government of the Republic and of its political entities (states and municipalities), by declaring that it is and always will be 'democratic, participative, elective, decentralised, alternative, responsible, pluralist, and of revocable mandates'.

The Constitutional Chamber of the Supreme Tribunal of Justice, in a decision N° 23 dated January 22, 2003 held that the intention of the 1999 Constitution was to 'establish a democratic, participative and protagonist society, which implies that it is not just the State who has to adopt and submit its institutions to the ways and principles of democracy, but it is also the society (formed by Venezuelan citizens) who must play a decisive and responsible role in the conduct of the Nation'.[25]

By establishing the concept of participation as a fundamental principle of democracy, the Constitution regulates it as a political constitutional right 'considering individuals as member of a determined political community, in order to take part in the formation of public decisions or of the will of the public institutions'; a right that is related to other political rights established in the Constitution, like the right to vote (article 63), to petition (article 51), to have access to public offices (article 62), to political association (article 67), to demonstration (article 68), and to be informed in due time and truthfully by public administration (article 143). It is also related to the social rights, like the right to health (article 84), educational rights (article 102) and environmental rights (article 127).[26]

'Participative democracy', in addition to 'representative' and 'direct' democracy, is promoted in other constitutional instruments established for the direct intervention of citizens in the decision making process of public affairs, and in particular, 'in political matter: the election of public office, the referendum, the revocation of the term of office, the initiative for legislation, for constitutional reforms and for the constituent process, the open municipal council and the citizens' assembly whose decisions will be of binding force' (article 70).

The Constitution directly regulates some mechanisms in order to guarantee direct participation of the representatives of the different sectors of the society in the adoption of some public decisions, particularly through the integration of 'Nominating Committees' for the appointment by the National Assembly of high public officials not popularly elected, namely, the Prosecutor General, the General Comptroller, the judges of the Supreme Court, and the members of the Electoral National Council, seeking to avoid the traditional agreements between political parties.[27] This was considered by the Constitutional Chamber of the Supreme Tribunal of Justice, in a decision N° 23 dated January 23, 2003, as a result of the 'struggles to change the negative political culture generated by decades of a centralized State of political parties (Cfr. Allan R. Brewer-Carías, *Problemas del Estado de*

[25] See *Interpretación del articulo 71 de la Constitución* in *Revista de Derecho Público*, N° 93–96 (Caracas, Editorial Jurídica Venezolana, 2003) 530 ff.

[26] ibid.

[27] See, eg, Allan R Brewer-Carías, *Los problemas del Estado de Partidos* (Caracas, Editorial Jurídica Venezolana, 1988).

Partidos, Caracas, 1988, pp. 39 ff.) that interfered with the development of democratic values, through the participation of the people which is no longer limited to electoral processes,' recognising their 'intervention in the formation, formulation and execution of public politics as a means to overcome the deficits of governability that have affected our political system due to the lack of harmony between the State and the society'; and radically changing 'from the root, the relations between State and society in which the latter receives back its legitimate and undeniable protagonist role by means of the exercise of its fundamental political rights.'[28]

In order to ensure the enforcement of citizens' right to political participation, the principle of federalism is promoted so that public power is territorially distributed among various levels of government, each of them with autonomous, democratic political institutions.

Article 4 of the 1999 Constitution formally defines the Republic of Venezuela 'as a decentralised Federal State under the terms set out in the Constitution' governed by the principles of 'territorial integrity, solidarity, concurrence and co-responsibility'. In practice, Venezuela continues to be a contradictory 'centralised federation'.[29]

Article 136 of the 1999 Constitution states that 'public power is distributed among the municipal, state and national entities', establishing a federation with three levels of political governments and autonomy: a national level exercised by the Republic (federal level); the states level, exercised by the 23 states and a Capital District; and the municipal level, exercised by the 338 existing municipalities. At each of these levels, the Constitution requires government that is 'democratic, participatory, elected, decentralised, alternative, responsible, plural and with revocable mandates' (article 6). Regarding the Capital District, this has substituted the former Federal District which was established in 1863, with the elimination of traditional federal interventions that existed regarding the authorities of the latter.

E. Compassion/Caring/Solidarity/Social Justice/Social State

Article 2 of the 1999 Constitution defines the Venezuelan state as a social and democratic rule of law state, in which the principle of 'social responsibility' (Preamble) prevails in guiding public policies, configuring the state as a 'Social State', with specific social duties regarding society. In particular, the Constitution refers to the social goal of society and of the state in order

[28] See *Interpretación del articulo 71 de la Constitución* in *Revista de Derecho Público*, N° 93–96 (Caracas, Editorial Jurídica Venezolana, 2003) 530 ff.

[29] See Allan R Brewer-Carías, *Federalismo y Municipalismo en la Constitución de 1999* (Caracas, Universidad Católica del Táchira-Editorial Jurídica Venezolana, 2001); 'Centralized Federalism in Venezuela' (2005) 43(4) *Duquesne Law Review* 629–43.

to ensure 'social justice', guaranteeing the equitable participation of all in the enjoyment of wealth, preventing its concentration in a few hands, avoiding unfair income differences, and seeking the guarantee of a dignified and prosperous existence for the collectivity (articles 112, 299).

This idea of a 'Social State' (*Estado Social*) refers to a State with social obligations that strives for social justice, which allows its intervention in social and economic activities, as a welfare state. Such social character mainly derives from the fundamental constitutional value of 'equality and non-discrimination' that comes from the Preamble, and from article 1 of the Constitution which, besides declaring it as a fundamental right (article 21), is the criterion of the performance of the state (article 2), and of the principle of 'social justice' as the base of the economic system (article 299).

This concept of a 'Social State' has been defined by the Constitutional Chamber of the Supreme Tribunal in a decision No 85 dated January, 24, 2002, thus:

> The Social State must protect people or groups that regarding others are in a situation of legal weakness, regardless of the principle of equality before the law, which in practice does not resolve anything, because unequal situations cannot be treated with similar solutions. In order to achieve the balance, the Social State not only intervenes in the labour and social security factor, protecting the salaried workers not related to the economic or political power, but it also protects their health, housing, education and economic relations. That is why the Economic Constitution must be seen from an essentially social perspective.
>
> ... The State is obligated to protect the weak, defend their interests protected by the Constitution, particularly through the courts; and regarding the strong, its duty is to watch that their freedom is not a load for everybody. As a juridical value, there cannot be constitutional protection at the expense of the fundamental rights of others...
>
> The Social State tries to harmonise the antagonistic interests of society, without allowing unlimited actions from social forces based on the silence of the statutes or their ambiguities, because otherwise that would lead to the establishment of an hegemony over the weak by those economically and socially stronger, in which the private power positions become an excessive diminution of the real freedom of the weak, in a subjugation that constantly encourages the social crisis.[30]

F. Community/Civil Society

The Constitution contains specific provisions that refer to the community, the family and civil society, implying the existence, in addition to personal and individual rights, of collective rights. These have been analysed by

[30] *Deudores hipotecarios v Superintendencia de Bancos*, *Revista de Derecho Público*, N° 89–92 (Caracas, Editorial Jurídica Venezolana, 2002) 94 ff.

the Constitutional Chamber of the Supreme Tribunal in decision N° 1395 dated November 21, 2000, as corresponding to the organised community (article 84), like the right to participate in the decision-making process of the public health institutions; to the Venezuelan people (articles 99 and 347), like the right to cultural values; to the community (article 118), like the right to develop associations of social and participative character; to the indigenous people (articles 121, 123 and 125), like the right to maintain their ethnic and cultural identity, and to maintain their own economic practices and to political participation. These are, according to the Chamber's doctrine, differentiated entities that are considered as holders of collective rights by express order of the Constitution.[31]

G. Family

The Constitution has established several personal rights to be protected by the state, beginning with the protection of the family and of families. Article 75 imposes on the state the obligation to protect families as a natural association in society, and as the fundamental space for the overall development of human beings. According to the same constitutional provision, family relationships must be based on equality of rights and duties, solidarity, common effort, mutual understanding and reciprocal respect among family members. In order to protect families, the state must guarantee protection to the mother, father or other person acting as head of a household.

Children and adolescents have the right to live, be raised and develop in their original family. When this proves to be impossible or contrary to their best interests, they shall have the right to have a substitute family, in accordance with law. Article 76 of the Constitution provides for the full protection of motherhood and fatherhood, whatever the marital status of the mother or father. Couples have the right to decide freely and responsibly how many children they wish to conceive, and are entitled to access to information and means necessary to guarantee the exercise of this right. The state guarantees overall assistance and protection for motherhood, in general, from the moment of conception, throughout pregnancy, delivery and the puerperal period, and guarantees full family planning services based on ethical and scientific values. The implication of this provision, particularly when protecting maternity from the moment of conception limits abortion as a right.

Article 77 of the Constitution also expressly 'protects marriage between a man and a woman, based on free consent and absolute equality of rights and obligations of the spouses'; consequently, same-sex 'marriages' are not protected in the Constitution, and only a stable de facto union between a

[31] *Revista de Derecho Público*, N° 84 (Caracas, Editorial Jurídica Venezolana, 2000) 331 ff.

man and a woman that meets the requirements established by law shall have the same effects as marriage.

Children and adolescents are considered as full legal persons whose rights are shall be protected by specialised courts, organs and legislation. The rights flow from the Constitution, the Convention on Children's Rights and other international treaty that may have been executed and ratified by the Republic in this field. The state, families and society shall guarantee their full protection as an absolute priority, taking into account their best interest in actions and decisions concerning them. The state shall promote their progressive incorporation into active citizenship, and shall create a national guidance system for the overall protection of children and adolescents (article 78).

Regarding senior citizens, article 80 of the Constitution imposes on the state the duty to guarantee the full exercise of their rights and guarantees; providing that the state, with the participation of families and society, is obliged to respect their human dignity, autonomy and to guarantee them full care and social security benefits to improve and guarantee their quality of life. Pension and retirement benefits granted through the social security system shall not be less than the urban minimum salary. Senior citizens shall be guaranteed the right to proper work if they indicate a desire to work and are capable of work.

H. Life

The most important civil right according to the Constitution is the right to life, article 43, as 'inviolable'. The Constitution thus prohibits the death penalty, providing that 'no law shall provide for the death penalty and no authority shall apply the same.' In addition, the article obliges the state to 'protect the life of persons who are deprived of liberty, are in military or civil services, or are subject to its authority in any other manner.' The right to life, therefore, is an absolute right that cannot be 'suspended' nor restricted in cases of states of exception decreed by the President of the Republic.

I. Learning/Education

A chapter in the Constitution is devoted to educational rights. In this respect, article 102 establishes that 'education is a human right and a fundamental social duty that is democratic, cost-free, and mandatory.' The consequence of this provision is an obligation imposed on the state to provide education as a function of greatest interest, at all levels and in all modes, as an instrument of scientific, humanistic and technical knowledge at the service of society. Every person has the right to a full, high-quality, ongoing education under conditions and circumstances of equality, subject only to personal aptitude, vocation or aspiration limitations. According to the Constitution, education is obligatory at all levels from day-care to the diversified secondary level.

Education is constitutionally declared to be a public service (article 102), although it states that, 'the State will stimulate and protect private education imparted which accords with the principles established in this Constitution and the Laws.' The Constitution establishes that education offered in state institutions is free of charge up to the undergraduate university level. The state shall create and maintain institutions and services sufficiently equipped to ensure the admission process, ongoing education and programme completion in the education system (article 103). The communications media, public and private, shall contribute to civil education. The state guarantees public radio and television services and library and computer networks, with a view to allowing universal access to information (article 108).

J. Honesty/Integrity

The Preamble to the Constitution refers to the values of 'ethics'. Ethical values are expressly mentioned in the provisions regarding education. Consequently, beyond the legal provisions referred to public ethics in public administration, there is a set of ethical norms that must guide society and state officials in the task of transforming the state and creating a new legal system. As for public administration, which must be 'at the service of the people', the Constitution also enumerates the principles and values on which it must be based: 'honesty, participation, celerity, efficiency, effectiveness, transparency, the accounting and responsibility in the execution of the public function, with complete subjection to the statutes and to the Law' (article 141).

As for elections, the Constitution enumerates the following principles that must be guaranteed regarding the electoral processes: 'equality, reliability, impartiality, transparency and efficiency', besides the 'personalisation of the vote and proportional representation' (article 293).

Regarding public services, the Constitution enumerates a series of governing principles in this respect: regarding the national public health system, it states that it must be 'inter-sectorial, decentralised and participative, and managed by the principles of gratuitousness, universality, integrality, impartiality, social integration and solidarity' (article 84); in respect of the social security system, it indicates that the system must be 'universal, integral, unified [*solidario*], unitary, efficient and participative financing, from direct or indirect contributions' (article 86); and as for the education, the Constitution expresses that it must be

> democratic, free and mandatory, based on the respect to all thought tendencies, in order to develop the creative potential of every human being and the complete exercise of his/her personality inside a democratic society based on the ethical valuation of labour and the active, conscientious and unified [*solidario*] participation in the processes of social transformation related with the values of the national identity and with a Latin-American and universal vision. (Article 102)

Regarding the socioeconomic regime of the Republic, the Constitution enumerates the following principles on which the system must be based:

> social justice, democracy, efficiency, free competition, environmental protection, productivity and solidarity, in order to guarantee the integral human development, a dignified and prosperous existence for the collectivity, the generation of labour sources, high national added value, elevation of the standard of living of the people and to strengthen the economical supremacy of the country, guaranteeing juridical security, stability, dynamism, supportability, permanence and equity of the economic growth, in order to achieve a fair distribution of the wealth by means of a democratic, participative and of open consultation strategic planning. (Article 299)

K. Freedom/Liberty/Independence

The Constitution establishes certain rights that cannot be renounced or waived, being 'independence, freedom, sovereignty, immunity, territorial integrity and national self-determination' (article 1).

Regarding independence, in the provisions referred to the territorial organisation of the state, particularly regarding the 'decentralised federal state' (article 4), it is established that it must be configured following the principles of 'territorial integrity, cooperation, solidarity, concurrence and co-responsibility' (article 4). As for the national statutes that can be sanctioned by the National Assembly regarding concurrent competences between the national, the states and the municipal levels, the Constitution prescribes that they must be oriented by 'the principles of independence, coordination, cooperation, co-responsibility and subsidiary' (article 165).

'Independence' is also affirmed in the Preamble, in the sense of reaffirming the existence of the Republic itself, which attained its independence from the Spanish monarchy in 1810, not subjected to any nature of foreign domination. Consequently, the 'territorial integrity' of the nation is also conceived as another fundamental value of the country, which impedes the modification of its borders in any way. Regarding the aims of 'peace', as a fundamental value, it implies the existential rejection of war.

On the other hand, 'freedom', according to the Preamble, is also one of the most fundamental values, understood in its most classical expression as the right of every individual to do anything that does not harm others; to not be obliged to do what the law does not order nor to be impeded from doing what it does not forbid; that is, the right to the 'free development of the personality', which is also expressly regulated (article 20) without any other limitation than those derived from the rights of others and the public and social order.

L. Security

According to article 55 of the Constitution, every person has the right to be protected by the state, through the entities established by law for the protection of citizens from situations that constitute a threat, vulnerability or risk to the physical integrity of individuals, their properties, and the enjoyment of their rights or the fulfilment of their duties. The citizens' participation in programmes for purposes of prevention, citizen safety and emergency management shall be regulated by a special law.

The Constitution guarantees that the state's security entities shall respect the human dignity and rights of all persons, and sets forth expressly that the use of weapons or toxic substances by police and security officers shall be limited by the principles of necessity, convenience, opportunity and proportionality in accordance with law.

The Constitution enumerates the following principles regarding the Nation's security: 'independence, democracy, equality, peace, freedom, justice, solidarity, promotion and conservation of the environment, the affirmation of the human rights and the progressive satisfaction of all individual and collective needs of the Venezuelan people' (article 326).

M. Responsibility/Accountability/Transparency

The Constitution establishes the general principle providing for state liability, incorporated in an express way in article 140, that 'The State is liable for the damages suffered by individuals in their goods and rights, provided that the injury be imputable to the functioning of Public Administration', being possible to comprise in the expression 'functioning of Public Administration' its normal or abnormal functioning. The Constitution provides for elected public officials to be subject to accountability (*rendición de cuentas*), establishing the possibility for them being subjected to repeal referendums for the revocation of mandates (article 6), which according to article 72 can only take place at the mid-point of a term in office. The corresponding petition for a repeal referendum can only be one of popular initiative that must be signed by at least 20 per cent of the registered voters in the corresponding jurisdiction. In order for a mandate to be repealed or revoked, the concurrence of a number of voters equal to or greater than the number that originally elected the official is needed, and the voters must total at least

25 per cent of the registered voters in the corresponding jurisdiction. If the repeal petition is approved, the substitute officer must be elected immediately according to the electoral procedures established in the Constitution and laws. This repeal referendum was distorted in 2004 regarding its application to the President of the Republic, and was transformed against the constitutional provision into a 'ratifying' referendum.[32]

Article 143 of the Constitution guarantees the rights of citizens to be informed and to have access to administrative information. In the first place, it provides for the right of citizens to be promptly and truly informed by public administration regarding the situation of the procedures in which they have a direct interest, and to know about the definitive resolutions therein adopted, to be notified of administrative acts and to be informed on the courses of the administrative procedure.

The constitutional article also establishes for the individual right everybody has to have access to administrative archives and registries, without prejudice of the acceptable limits imposed in a democratic society related to the national or foreign security, to criminal investigation, to the intimacy of private life, all according to the statutes regulating the matter of secret or confidential documents classification. The same article provides for the principle of prohibition of any previous censorship referring to public officials regarding the information they could give referring to matters under their responsibility.

N. Environment

The Constitution regulates the environment, declaring that each generation has the right and duty to protect and maintain the environment for its own benefit and that of the world of the future; and that everyone has the right, individually and collectively, to enjoy a safe, healthful and ecologically balanced life and environment.

The state shall protect the environment, biological and genetic diversity, ecological processes, national parks and natural monuments, and other areas of particular ecological importance. The genome of a living being shall not be patentable, and the field shall be regulated by the law relating to the principles of bioethics.

It is a fundamental duty of the state, with the active participation of society, to ensure to people their development in a pollution-free environment in which air, water, soil, coasts, climate, the ozone layer and living species receive special protection, in accordance with law (article 127).

[32] See Allan R Brewer-Carías, 'El secuestro del Poder Electoral y la confiscación del derecho a la participación política mediante el referendo revocatorio presidencial: Venezuela 2000–2004' (2005) 112 *Boletín Mexicano de Derecho Comparado*, Instituto de Investigaciones Jurídicas, Universidad Nacional Autónoma de México 11–73.

In order to guarantee the protection of the environment, article 129 of the Constitution prescribes that any activities capable of generating damage to ecosystems must be preceded by environmental and socio-cultural impact studies. The state shall prevent toxic and hazardous waste from entering the country, as well as preventing the manufacture and use of nuclear, chemical and biological weapons. A special law shall regulate the use, handling, transportation and storage of toxic and hazardous substances.

As a matter of public policy, article 128 of the Constitution imposes on the state the duty to develop a land-use policy taking into account ecological, geographic, demographic, social, cultural, economic and political realities, in accordance with the premises of sustainable development, including information, consultation and male/female participation by citizens. An organic law shall develop the principles and criteria for this zoning.

Article 106 of the Constitution ensures that environmental education is obligatory in the various levels and modes of the education system, as well as in informal civil education.

III. THE INCONGRUENCES BETWEEN DECLARED VALUES AND POLITICAL AND JUDICIAL PRACTICE

A. Subjection of the Superior Values of the Constitution to its 'Political Project' and the Rejection of the Supra-Constitutional Rank of International Instruments on Human Rights

The superior character of the values enshrined in the Constitution has been transformed by the Constitutional Chamber of the Supreme Tribunal of Justice, in its decision N° 23 of January 22, 2003. Thus, the universal meaning of the values has been eschewed by the Tribunal which has said that 'to interpret the legal system according to the Constitution, means to protect the Constitution itself from every diversion of principles and from every separation from the political project that it embodies by will of the people'. It added:

> [A] system of principles, assumed to be absolute and supra historical, cannot be placed above the Constitution, nor that its interpretation could eventually contradict the political theory that supports it. From this perspective, any theory that proposes absolute rights or goals must be rejected and … the interpretation or integration [of the Constitution] must be done according to the living cultural tradition whose sense and scope depends on the specific and historical analysis of the values shared by the Venezuelan people. Part of the protection and guarantee of the Constitution is established then, in an *in fieri* politic perspective, reluctant to the ideological connection with theories that can limit, under pretext of universal validities, the supremacy and the national self-determination, as demanded in article 1° *eiusdem*.[33]

[33] *Interpretación del article 71 de la Constitución*, *Revista de Derecho Público*, N° 93–96 (Caracas, Editorial Jurídica Venezolana, 2003) 530 ff.

This doctrine of subjection of the global constitutional values to a political project was ratified in Decision No 1.939 of December 18, 2009 (*Gustavo Álvarez Arias y otros*) in which the Constitutional Chamber declared a decision of the Inter American Court of Human Rights as non-enforceable in Venezuela, rejecting the existence of superior values which may trump government policy. The Chamber argued that the legal order 'is a normative theory at the service of politic defined in the axiological project of the Constitution'; that the standard in order to resolve conflicts between principles and provisions must be 'compatible with the political project of the Constitution', and such provisions 'cannot be affected with interpretations that could give prevalence to individual rights or that could give prevalence to the international order regarding the national one affecting the State sovereignty'; that no system of principles 'supposedly absolute and suprahistoric can be placed above the Constitution', and that 'theories based on universal values that pretend to limit the sovereignty and national autodetermination are unacceptable.'[34]

This rejection of superior and universal values has been followed by the rejection of the constitutional rank that the Constitution has given to international instruments of human rights and to their direct and immediate application by all courts.

In effect, article 23 of the 1999 Constitution, one of the most important provisions for the protection of human rights, provides for constitutional ranking of international treaties on human rights and their prevalence when containing provisions more favourable to their enjoyment than those established in the internal legal order. Its inclusion in the new Constitution was a significant advance in the completion of the protective framework of human rights.

Nonetheless, in the judicial practice and particularly regarding the provisions of the American Convention of Human Rights, the doctrine of the Supreme Tribunal in this case has been progressively restrictive, eventually rejecting the constitutional ranking of the international instruments of human rights. This restrictive approach by the Constitutional Chamber, that has affected the role of the Inter American institutions for the protection of human rights, began with a decision dated May 5, 2000, in which the Constitutional Chamber objected to the 'quasi-jurisdictional' powers of the Inter American Commission when issuing provisional protective measures regarding a state, qualifying it as 'unacceptable', stating that they 'imply a gross intrusion in the country's judiciary, like the suspension of the judicial proceeding against the plaintiff, measures that can only be adopted by the judges exercising their judicial attributions and independence, according to what is stated in the Constitution and the statutes of the Republic'.[35]

[34] See at www.tsj.gov.ve/decisiones/scon/Diciembre/1939-181208-2008-08-1572.html.

[35] See *Faitha M Nahmens L and Ben Ami Fihman Z* (*Revista Exceso*), Exp nº 00–0216, Decisión nº 386 dated May 17, 2000. See the reference in Carlos Ayala Corao, 'Recepción de la jurisprudencia internacional sobre derechos humanos por la jurisprudencia constitucional' (2004) 6 *Revista del Tribunal Constitucional* 275 ff.

The restrictive approach regarding the role and value of international institutions for the protection of human rights was also applied in Decision No 1.942 of July 15, 2003 (*Impugnación de artículos del Código Penal, Leyes de desacato*),[36] in which the Constitutional Chamber, when referring to International courts, stated that 'in Venezuela, in general, in relation to article 7 of the Constitution, no jurisdictional organ could exist above the Supreme Tribunal of Justice, and even in such case, its decisions when contradicting constitutional provisions are inapplicable in the country.'

This approach was extended in the decision of the Constitutional Chamber No 1.939 of December 18, 2008 (*Abogados Gustavo Álvarez Arias y otros*), in which it declared a decision of the Inter American Court on Human Rights as non enforceable in Venezuela. The decision of the former of August 5, 2008 (*Apitz Barbera y otros ('Corte Primera de lo Contencioso Administrativo') v Venezuela*)[37] condemned the Venezuelan state for the violation of the judicial guarantees of three former judges of a First Contentious Administrative Court that were dismissed by a Special Commission of the Supreme Tribunal. The Constitutional Chamber in its decision rejected the supra-constitutional character of the provisions of the American Convention, considering that in the event of contradiction of a provision of the Constitution and a provision of an international treaty, the judiciary should have the attribution to determine the applicable provisions.[38] The non-enforceability in Venezuela of the decisions of the Inter American Court of Human Rights was ratified by the Supreme Tribunal of Venezuela in decision No 1547 of October 17, 2011 (*Estado Venezolano vs. Corte Interamericana de Derechos Humanos*),[39] in which the Constitutional Chamber decided on the 'unconstitutionality' of the decision of the Inter American Court on Human Rights of September 1, 2011 (*Leopoldo López v Estado de Venezuela).*[40]

The problem with the interpretative role of the Court is that the Constitutional Chamber, unfortunately is overly controlled by the Executive.[41] This

[36] See en *Revista de Derecho Público*, No 93–96 (Caracas, Editorial Jurídica Venezolana, 2003) 136 ff.

[37] See in www.corteidh.or.cr. Excepción Preliminar, Fondo, Reparaciones y Costas, Serie C No 182.

[38] Available at www.tsj.gov.ve/decisiones/scon/Diciembre/1939-181208-2008-08-1572.html.

[39] Available at www.tsj.gov.ve/decisiones/scon/Octubre/1547-171011-2011-11-1130.html.

[40] Available at www.corteidh.or.cr/docs/casos/articulos/resumen_233_esp.pdf. See the comments in Allan R Brewer-Carías, 'El ilegítimo "control de constitucionalidad" de las sentencias de la Corte Interamericana de Derechos Humanos por parte la Sala Constitucional del Tribunal Supremo de Justicia de Venezuela: el caso *Leopoldo López vs Venezuela, septiembre 2011*' (2011) 128 *Revista de Derecho Público* 227–50.

[41] See Allan R Brewer-Carías, 'El juez constitucional al servicio del autoritarismo y la ilegítima mutación de la constitución: el caso de la Sala Constitucional del Tribunal Supremo de Justicia de Venezuela (1999–2009)' (2009) 180 *Revista de Administración Pública* 383–418.

has resulted in the rejection of the power of all courts to apply in a direct and immediate way, international instruments on human rights for the resolution of judicial cases.

B. The Erosion of Public Participation in Political Decision Making

The goal of participation requires some form of decentralisation, the inclusion of instruments of direct democracy in a representative democratic framework, and the possibility for the people to express their opinion on political decisions.

Referendums can be useful instruments in order to perfect democracy, but by themselves cannot satisfy the aim of participation. This is illustrated in the 2002–04 process concerning the Venezuelan presidential recall referendum, which was converted into a presidential 'ratification' referendum of a plebiscitary nature.[42] A recall referendum is a vote asking the people if the mandate of an elected official must be revoked or not; it is not a vote asking if the elected official must remain or not in office. In the first case, if the vote of the people for 'Yes' reaches the percentage established in the Constitution, the mandate of the elected official is considered automatically revoked or repealed, independently of the number of people that could have voted for 'No.' In the second case, it would be a 'plebiscite', based only on the majority of votes for 'Yes' or 'No,' which is not established in the Constitution. But in the 2004 recall referendum, the National Electoral Council, when giving the voting results, converted in an unconstitutional way the repeal referendum into a plebiscite, ratifying the President.

The result of the implementation of the 1999 Constitution is that Venezuelan democracy has been transformed, from being a representative democracy with more or less competitive and pluralist parties which alternated in government (1958–98), into a centralised plebiscite democracy, in which effectively all power lies with the President, supported by politically partisan votes of the National Assembly and the military, and more appropriate to a one-party system.

This plebiscite democracy system has created an illusion of popular participation, particularly by means of the uncontrolled distribution of state oil income among the poor through governmental social programmes that are not tailored to the promotion of investment and the creation of meaningful employment. This plebiscite democracy is less representative and less

[42] See Allan R Brewer-Carías, 'El secuestro del Poder Electoral y de la Sala Electoral del Tribunal Supremo y la confiscación del derecho a la participación política mediante el referendo revocatorio presidencial: Venezuela: 2000–2004' *Revista Costarricense de Derecho Constitucional*, Tomo V (San José, Costa Rica, Instituto Costarricense de Derecho Constitucional, Editorial Investigaciones Jurídicas SA, 2004) 167–312; and in (2004) 54 (55) *Revista Jurídica del Perú* 353–96.

participatory than the traditional representative party democracy, which, notwithstanding all the warnings[43] that were raised, the traditional parties have failed to preserve.

On the other hand, the only two constitutional provisions establishing means for direct participation of the people in political decisions process, in practice have been neutralised. This applies to the appointment of high officials of the Branches of Government (Prosecutor General, Comptroller General, People's Defender, National Electoral Council and Justices of the Supreme Court), that according to the Constitution must be nominated by specific Committees comprising of 'representatives of the various sectors of society' (articles 270, 279 and 295). Nonetheless the different statutes regulating their composition have organised such Committees as 'parliamentary commissions' subjected to the political party that control the majority of the National Assembly.[44]

The other provision established in the 1999 Constitution for the direct participation of the people in decision-making processes is the obligatory public consultation that has to be organised before sanctioning of statutes (article 211). This provision, in practice, has generally being ignored, because since 2001 almost all statutes have been issued by means of decree-laws, or delegate legislation, and the Executive Branch has never organised any sort of popular participation in order hear the opinion of the people. Additionally, the Constitutional Chamber of the Supreme Tribunal has expressly ruled in decision No 203 of March 25, 2014 (*Impugnación del Decreto de la Ley Orgánica de la Administración Pública*) that popular participation is not guaranteed in the Constitution when statutes are issued by the President of the Republic, only when sanctioned by the National Assembly.[45]

[43] See regarding this author's writings, Allan R Brewer-Carías, *El Estado. Crisis y reforma* (Caracas, Academia de Ciencias Políticas y Sociales, 1982); and *Problemas del Estado de partidos* (Caracas, Editorial Jurídica Venezolana, 1988); Allan R Brewer-Carías, 'La crisis de las instituciones: responsables y salidas' (1985) 11 *Revista del Centro de Estudios Superiores de las Fuerzas Armadas de Cooperación* 57–83; (1985) 64 *Revista de la Facultad de Ciencias Jurídicas y Políticas* 129–55. Also see Allan R Brewer-Carías, *Instituciones Políticas y Constitucionales*, Vol I, Evolución histórica del Estado (San Cristóbal-Caracas, Universidad Católica del Táchira, Editorial Jurídica Venezolana, 1996) 523–41.

[44] See Allan R Brewer-Carías, 'La participación ciudadana en la designación de los titulares de los órganos no electos de los Poderes Públicos en Venezuela y sus vicisitudes políticas', en *Revista Iberoamericana de Derecho Público y Administrativo* (San José, Costa Rica, Asociación Latinoamericana de Derecho Administrativo, 2005) 76–95.

[45] Available in *Revista de Derecho Público, Revista de Derecho Público*, No 137 (Caracas, Editorial Jurídica Venezolana, 2014) 100–03. See the comments on the decision in Allan R Brewer-Carías, 'El fin de la llamada "democracia participativa y protagónica" dispuesto por la Sala Constitucional en fraude a la Constitución, al justificar la emisión de legislación inconsulta en violación al derecho a la participación política', ibid, 157–64. See also Allan R Brewer-Carías, 'El derecho ciudadano a la participación popular y la inconstitucionalidad generalizada de los decretos leyes 2010–2012, por su carácter inconsulto', *Revista de Derecho Público*, No 130 (Caracas, Editorial Jurídica Venezolana, 2012) 85–88.

C. The Erosion of the Democratic Principle

The democratic principle embedded in the Constitution is one of its most important values, implying that all high officials of the state must be elected by direct or indirect popular vote, and that the will of the people manifested through an election must be respected. That also mean that only the people can directly or indirectly revoke the election made.

This implies that according to the Constitution, the representatives (*diputados*) of the National Assembly and the President of the Republic must always be elected by direct, secret and universal popular vote (articles 186, 228), and that only the vote of the people cast in a referendum organised by popular initiative can revoke the democratic mandate of the said representatives (*diputados*) of the National Assembly and the President of the Republic (articles 72, 198 and 233).

The same democratic principle applies regarding the election of the high official of the other three Branches of Government (Judicial, Citizens and Electoral Branches), in the sense that they can only be elected by indirect popular vote made by a qualified majority (two-thirds) of the representatives to the National Assembly acting as an electoral body. In this case, also their mandates can only be revoked by the representatives to the same Assembly, with the same qualified majority of votes (two–thirds) of the representatives (articles 265, 279 and 296).

Nonetheless, the incongruence in this case between the constitutional provisions and the practice of government has been notorious, basically resulting from decisions of the Constitutional Chamber of the Supreme Tribunal.[46] In January 2013, the Constitutional Chamber imposed a non-elected official (the then acting Executive Vice-President) to act as President of the Republic.[47] In 2014, the Constitutional Chamber revoked the popular electoral mandate of an elected representative to the National Assembly,[48] and of two

[46] See in general on the Supreme Tribunal decisions: Allan R Brewer-Carías, *El golpe a la democracia dado por la Sala Constitucional* (Caracas, Editorial Jurídica Venezolana, 2014).

[47] Decisions No 2 of January 9, 2013, available at http://www.tsj.gov.ve/decisio-nes/scon/Enero/02-9113-2013-12-1358.html, and No 141 of March 8, 2013, available at http://www.tsj.gov.ve.decisio-nes/scon/Marzo/141-9313-2013-13-0196.html. See the comments in Asdrúbal Aguiar (Compilator), *El Golpe de Enero en Venezuela (Documentos y testimonios para la historia)* (Caracas, Editorial Jurídica Venezolana, 2013) 85–90, 97–106, 133–48 and 297–314.

[48] Decision No 207 de 31 de marzo de 2014, available at en http://www.tsj.gov.ve/decisiones/scon/marzo/162546-207-31314-2014-14-0286.HTML, also published in *Official Gazette* No 40385 of April 2, 2014. See the comments in Allan R Brewer-Carías, 'La revocación del mandato popular de una diputada a la Asamblea Nacional por la Sala Constitucional del Tribunal Supremo de oficio, sin juicio ni proceso alguno (El caso de la Diputada María Corina Machado)', *Revista de Derecho Público*, 137 (Caracas, Editorial Jurídica Venezolana, 2014) 165–89.

elected municipal mayors.[49] In 2015, the Constitutional Chamber allowed the 'indirect election' of the Justices of the Supreme Tribunal, the Prosecutor General, the General Comptroller and the People's Defender by only a small majority of votes (51 per cent) of the representatives present in the session of the Assembly. And finally, also in 2015, the same Constitutional Chamber designated the members of the National Electoral Council, usurping the role of the National Assembly.[50]

D. The Contradictory State Intervention in the Internal Life of Civil Society Entities

In some cases, the incongruence between constitutional provisions is not the product of judicial rulings or of political application of the Constitution, but of norms contained in the Constitution. In this context, the Constitution, contrary to its participative phraseology, creates scope for intervention in the organisations of civil society by establishing the jurisdiction of the National Electoral Council for 'the organisation of the elections of trade unions, professional associations and organisations with political objectives' (article 293, 6).

According to this provision, the Constitution provides that the internal elections that can take place within political parties, trade unions and professionals associations of any kind, must be organised by the state through one of the branches of government. This represents a contradiction with the participatory feature attributed to the Constitution and with its declared goal of promoting citizens' participation.

Consequently, all the internal electoral processes within the political parties in Venezuela from 2000 are to be organised by the National Electoral Council, although this has not always been the case in practice.

[49] Decision No 138 of March 17, available at http://www.tsj.gov.ve/decisiones/scon/marzo/162025-138-17314-2014-14-0205.HTML 2014; and Decision No 245 of April, 9, 2014, available at: http://www.tsj.gov.ve/decisiones/scon/abril/162860-245-9414-2014-14-0205.HTML, Véase también en *Gaceta Oficial* No 40.391 de 10 de abril de 2014. See the comments in Allan R Brewer-Carías, 'La ilegítima e inconstitucional revocación del mandato popular de alcaldes por la Sala Constitucional del Tribunal Supremo, usurpando competencias de la jurisdicción penal, mediante un procedimiento "sumario" de condena y encarcelamiento (El caso de los Alcaldes Vicencio Scarano Spisso y Daniel Ceballo)', *Revista de Derecho Público,* 138 (Caracas, Editorial Jurídica Venezolana, 2014) 176–210.

[50] Decision No 1864 of December 22, 2014, available at: http://historico.tsj.gov.ve/decisiones/scon/diciembre/173494-1864-221214-2014-14-1341.HTML; and decision No 1865 of December 26, 2014, available at: http://historico.tsj.gov.ve/decisiones/scon/diciembre/173497-1865-261214-2014-14-1343.HTML. See the comments in Allan R Brewer-Carías, 'El golpe de Estado dado en diciembre de 2014, con la inconstitucional designación de las altas autoridades del Poder Público', *Revista de Derecho Público* 40 (Caracas, Editorial Jurídica Venezolana, 2014).

State intervention has been active regarding civil society organisations. For example, even though the trade unions are considered as not being 'inside the structure of the Venezuelan public organisation',[51] the Electoral Chamber of the Supreme Court, in Decision N° 46 dated March 11, 2002, justified state intervention and supervision regarding social organisations, arguing that it tends:

> To guarantee [internal] democracy in said organisations through the transparency and celerity of their electoral processes and the selection of the legitimate authorities that are called to represent the interests and rights of those affiliated in the negotiations and collective conflicts of labour; in the procedures of conciliation and arbitrage; in the promotion, negotiation, celebration, revision and modification of collective labour conventions, and in everything necessary for the guarantee of the patrimony and the interests of the trade union organisation.[52]

The Electoral Chamber of the Supreme Tribunal of Justice has decided in many cases to participate in the internal functioning of other forms of civic associations, as happened within neighbourhood associations. In a Decision N° 61 dated May 29, 2001, the Constitutional Chamber considered that the matter was about organisations 'that the constitutional text, itself, refers to as "civil society", being able to request, from the National Electoral Council, its intervention in order to organise their internal elections.'[53] In a decision dated November 1, 2000, in which the Electoral Chamber ruled against the electoral regulations issued by the Electoral Commission of a social club, considering that, even though the club was an association, 'the constitutional text itself refers to as forming part of "civil society", with authority to be freely constituted by its members, providing for their own organisation, being nonetheless able to request the intervention of the National Electoral Council for the organisation of their internal elections.'[54]

As for other civil associations, such as businesses and industrial or commercial chambers, the Electoral Chamber of the Supreme Tribunal, in Decision N° 18, dated February 15, 2001, considered that a civil association called 'Cámara de Comercios e Industrias del Estado Aragua' by virtue of its objectives to 'encourage for the economic development and the social progress of the region, providing the collective effort of the sectors that form it', as well as 'the defence and the strengthening of the free initiative and the freedom of the enterprise', constituted an indirect participative

[51] *Revista de Derecho Público*, N° 84 (Caracas, Editorial Jurídica Venezolana, 2000) 132 ff.

[52] *Revista de Derecho Público*, N° 89–92 (Caracas, Editorial Jurídica Venezolana, 2000) 148–49.

[53] See Exp 000064, *Asociación de Residentes de la Urbanización La Trinidad*. See the reference in Allan R Brewer-Carías, *Derecho Administrativo*, vol I (Bogotá, Universidad Externado de Colombia, 2005) 413 ff.

[54] See Exp 0115, *Asociación Civil Club Campestre Paracotos*. See the reference in Allan R Brewer-Carías, *Derecho Administrativo*, vol I (Bogotá, Universidad Externado de Colombia, 2005) 413 ff.

mechanism—both economically and socially—of a sector of the people in national society life; thus 'even if the referred civil association is of a private character, its objectives transcend the core particular interest'. For this reason, the Chamber considered that it was 'justified to include it as one of the organisations of the "civil society" implicitly stated in article 293, 6 of the Constitution', a reason for which it declared its jurisdiction to resolve a dispute challenging the election held in the association 'independently of the nature of the entity from which these proceed'.[55]

But in other cases, the Electoral Chamber has recognised the obligatory intervention of the National Electoral Council in the electoral processes of civil associations like those of university professors, as occurred regarding internal elections in the professors' association of the Universidad Central de Venezuela. Regarding these associations, the Electoral Chamber ruled in a Decision No 51 dated May 19, 2000, that article 293.6 refers to those 'groups of people that in their condition of professionals, unite to defend their common interests and to achieve improvements also of common character, independently from the fact that their conformation is not done by expressed disposition of a statute, but by common agreement from its members, under a form of private right'. The Electoral Chamber thus included associations established inside the Universities, formed by the professionals of diverse disciplines or knowledge areas that are part of the institution in their condition of professors, teachers or instructors, imposing on them the intervention of the state to organise their internal electoral processes.[56]

E. The Dangerous Expansion of Security and Defence Values

The Constitution made substantial departures from the provisions of the earlier 1961 Constitution regarding national security and defence and the military. The earlier Constitution contained only three provisions on the subject: article 133, establishing restrictions regarding the possession of arms; article 131, prohibiting the simultaneous exercise of civilian and military authority by any public official other than the President of the Republic as Commander in Chief of the Armed Forces; and article 132, referring to the general regulation of the Armed Forces.

[55] See Exp 000017, *Cámara de Comercios e Industrias del Estado Aragua*. This jurisprudence was ratified by the same Chamber according to verdict N° 162, Exp 2002–000077 dated 10–17–02 (Cámara de Comercio e Industrias del Estado Bolívar). See the reference in Allan R Brewer-Carías, *Derecho Administrativo*, Vol I (Bogotá, Universidad Externado de Colombia, 2005) 413 ff.

[56] See *Asociación de Profesores de la Universidad Central de Venezuela*, in *Revista de Derecho Público*, N° 82 (Caracas, Editorial Jurídica Venezolana, 2000) 92 ff.

By contrast, the Constitution promotes a markedly militarist shape to the state, with particular provisions regarding not only the military but the security and defence establishment.

Article 322 of the Constitution begins by stating that the security of the nation falls within the essential competence and responsibility of the state, founded upon the state's 'integral development;' the defence of the state being the responsibility of Venezuelans, and of all natural and legal persons, whether of public or private law, within the geographic territory of the state.

In addition, article 326 provides for general principles of national security, declaring that its preservation in 'economic, social, political, cultural, geographic, environmental and military areas' mutually corresponds ('co-responsibility') to the state and to civil society, in order to fulfil the principles of 'independence, democracy, equality, peace, liberty, justice, solidarity, promotion and conservation of the environment, the affirmation of human rights, and, the progressive satisfaction of the individual and collective needs of Venezuelans on the basis of sustainable and productive development fully covering the national community.' All of these principles are enumerated in the opening articles 1, 2 and 3 of the Constitution of 1999.

For this purpose, the Constitution created a new council, the National Council of Defence (article 323), as the nation's highest authority for defence planning, advice, and consultation to the state (public powers) on all matters related to the defence and security of the nation's sovereignty, territorial integrity, and strategic thinking. This Council is presided over by the President of the Republic, and integrated by the Executive Vice-President, the President of the National Assembly, the President of Supreme Tribunal of Justice, the President of the Moral Republican Council (Citizen Branch of government, article 237), the Ministers of the defence sectors: interior security, foreign relations, and planning, and others whose participation is considered pertinent.

Under the Constitution, the traditional national armed forces (comprised of the Army, the Navy, the Air Force, and the National Guard) have become integrated into a single institution, named the 'National Armed Force', which nonetheless, according to article 328, is comprised of the Army, the Navy, the Air Force, and the National Guard, each working within its area of competence to fulfil its mission, and with its own system of social security, as established by its respective organic legislation.

All these constitutional provisions reinforce a normative framework with clear marks of a militarist structure, which when combined with the centralisation of state power and the concentration of state power in the President by his control over the National Assembly. The result is a system that has shown authoritarian tendencies. In particular, the Constitution's provisions on military matters, the idea of the subjection or subordination of military authority to civilian authority has disappeared. Instead what has been created is a greater autonomy of the National Armed Forces, whose four branches (since 2008, five branches) have been unified into one institution with the possibility of intervention in civilian functions.

This militaristic tendency is evidenced by the following constitutional rules: first, the elimination of the traditional prohibition that military and civilian authority be exercised simultaneously, as was established by article 131 of the 1961 Constitution; second, the elimination of control by the National Assembly of senior military promotions, as provided in article 331 of the 1961 Constitution and throughout the country's traditional constitutionalism; third, the elimination of the constitutionally 'non-deliberative and apolitical' character of the military institution, as established in article 132 of the 1961 Constitution, which has opened the way for the Armed Force, as a military institution, to deliberate politically, intervene, and give its opinion on matters under resolution within the civil organs of the state; fourth, the elimination of the obligation of the Armed Force to ensure the stability of democratic institutions required by article 132 of the 1961 Constitution; fifth, the elimination of the obligation of the Armed Force to respect the Constitution and laws 'the adherence to which will always be above any other obligation' as was set forth in article 132 of the 1961 Constitution; sixth, the express right of suffrage granted to members of the military in article 330 of the 1999 Constitution, which in many cases has been politically incompatible with the principle of obedience; seventh, the submission of authority over the use of all weapons, for war or otherwise, to the Armed Force, while removing this authority from the civil administration of the state (article 324); eighth, the general attribution of police administrative functions to the Armed Force (article 329); ninth, the establishment of procedural privilege for generals and admirals in the sense that in order for them to be tried, the Supreme Tribunal of Justice must declare in advance of trial whether or not the proceeding has merit (article 266,3); and tenth, the adoption in the Constitution of the concept of the 'doctrine of national security,' as a global, totalistic, and omni-comprehensive doctrine in the sense that everything that happens in the state and in the nation concerns the security of the state, including economic and social development (article 326); with the duty for the Armed Force to have an 'active participation in national development' (article 328). All these provisions create a picture of militarism, unique in Venezuelan constitutional history, not found even in former military regimes.

IV. CONCLUSION

The Venezuelan Constitution incorporated in its text an express and extensive list of constitutional values and principles defined as goals intended to guide the conduct and activities of the state, society and individuals.

Thus, those global values and principles do not derive from the process of interpretation and application of the Constitution, particularly by the courts, but are expressly established in the text of the Constitution.

By means of constitutional interpretation, mainly through the Constitutional Chamber of the Supreme Tribunal of Justice, the sense, the scope and the priority character of many of the constitutional principles and values have been defined and enriched, even giving some of them a priority vis-à-vis others. Unfortunately, in practice these have been distorted by legislative practice and by the same Supreme Tribunal decisions[57] originating some constitutional incongruence between what is provided for in the Constitution and what has been decided in the political practice of government.

[57] See Allan R Brewer-Carías, *La patología de la justicia constitucional* (San José, Costa Rica, Investigaciones Jurídicas, 2012); Allan R Brewer-Carías, *Golpe a la democracia dado por la Sala Constitucional* (Caracas, Editorial Jurídica Venezolana, 2014).

17

Conclusion

DENNIS DAVIS, ALAN RICHTER AND CHERYL SAUNDERS

IN 1993, THE Secretary General of the United Nations, Boutros Boutros-Ghali, observed in his inaugural remarks to the 1993 Vienna Conference on Human Rights that human rights constituted 'a common language of humanity'.[1] In this way, he linked his argument to a view that the human rights discourse represents the only universal ideology, at the very least in the making, which simultaneously legitimates the exercise of power and holds out the possibility of an emancipatory politics.[2]

This line of argument enjoys a distinguished historical pedigree. More than 200 years ago Immanuel Kant wrote of the universality of the rights of 'men', conceiving of four elements which made up a cosmopolitan point of view, being: (1) the generalisation of republicanism as a way of government within all societies; (2) the establishment of a legal authority at the international level; (3) the extension of rights to foreigners; and (4) putting an end to the barbarities associated with colonialism.[3]

More recently, in the face of dramatic regionalisation and globalisation, others have argued to similar effect. To take only one prominent example: Peter Singer has observed that the globalisation of the later part of the twentieth century has taken the world in a direction of a global community and thus diminished the extent to which any national state can claim independently to determine its own future.[4] In Singer's view, not only is there a need to strengthen institutions for global decision-making and make them more accountable to affected communities, but there is now a basis for an agreement on a framework for international human rights law which would represent a common language of humanity.

[1] Upendra Baxi, *Human Rights in a Post Human World* (Oxford, Oxford University Press, 2007) 1.

[2] Mary Ann Glendon, *Rights Talk: The impoverishment of political discourse* (New York, Free Press, 1991).

[3] Robert Fine, 'Cosmopolitanism and Human Rights: Radicalism in a global age' (2009) 40 *Metaphilosophy* 8–23.

[4] Peter Singer, *One World. The ethics of globalisation* (New Haven CT, Yale University Press, 2004) 199.

Resisting the criticism of cultural imperialism, Singer contends for a view of ethics that admits to the possibility of a moral argument which transcends the limitations of a particular culture. Thus,

> [W]e can recognise that Western culture has no monopoly on wisdom, has often learned from other cultures, and still has much to learn. We can urge sensitivity to the values of other people and understanding for what gives them self-respect and a sense of identity. On that basis we can criticise the nineteenth century missionaries for their insensitivity to cultural differences, and for their further obsession with sexual behaviour, an area in which human relations take a wide variety of forms without any one pattern being clearly superior to others ... But once we accept that there is scope for rational argument and ethics, independent of any particular culture, we can also ask whether the values we are upholding are sound, defensible and justifiable.'[5]

Singer's argument is based upon, at the very least, the existence of a global ethic which is reflected in the development of international law and, in turn, is powered by the global recognition of human rights. Representing another tradition, which is sourced in religion, Hans Kung also makes a case for a basic consensus relating to binding values, irrevocable standards and moral attributes, which can be affirmed by all religions despite their undeniable divergences and theological differences and which, in his view, can also be supported by non-believers.[6] Much of the confidence in these lines of argument can be traced to the Declaration of the Rights of Man approved by the French National Assembly in August 1789, and the more contemporary proclamation in the form of the Universal Declaration of Human Rights by the General Assembly of the United Nations in December 1948.

These documents have been converted from their aspirational character into substantive legal commitments by way of a range of national constitutions, most of which were passed after the Second World War. There are now almost 200 such instruments. Most contain express protections for the rights of individuals, in varying forms and with varying effect. In many cases the protected rights extend beyond traditional categories of civil and political rights to social, economic and environmental rights as well.[7] In some cases they have a degree of horizontal as well as vertical effect. Even where constitutions do not protect rights, or particular rights, and even in the relatively few instances where there are no codified constitutions at all, the operation of the political and legal systems may provide mechanisms through which rights nevertheless are protected.

A vast number of these national constitutions were passed during the third wave of democracy, beginning in the 1970s with the emergence of

[5] ibid, 140.

[6] Hans Kung, *Justification* (Westminster, John Knox Press, 2014).

[7] David Law and Miles Versteeg, 'The evolution and ideology of global constitutionalism' (2011) 99 *California Law Review* 1165–1243.

numerous new states, and the process accelerated further following the end of the Cold War from 1989.[8] A rich field of national constitutional law has now provided the ideal terrain on which to test the suggestion in the arguments of, for example, Boutros-Ghali and Singer, that the human rights now incorporated through so many national constitutions promote a set of values which are the building blocks of a common language for humanity. If this perception is right, progress has commenced towards the form of cosmopolitanism of which Kant wrote in the eighteenth century and which is assumed by so much of the more recent literature on the internationalisation and globalisation of constitutional law.[9]

This volume was designed to test these claims, albeit tentatively, by way of an examination of a range of disparate national constitutions which promote certain basic human rights, and which are drawn from countries with different histories, cultures, legal and political systems. Even this objective requires careful description. Congruence of rights and the values which underpin them can prove to be an elusive concept. It can mean compatibility of values which are given express mention in the text. It can also mean the values that emerge from a group of rights or all the rights contained in the text. Authors were also asked to consider congruence between the values proclaimed in the text or by way of judicial work and the manner in which these values play out in society.

It is important to emphasise that this book does not concern international law and arguments concerning the possible establishment of a world constitution which may serve to represent an overarching constitutional order that sets the legal standard to which all national legal institutions should conform. In short, this book is not concerned with the controversial debate about the existence of an international legal order possessed of certain superior constitutional norms.[10] Neither is the primary focus of the work to explore the reasons why so many countries have moved towards the formal adoption of human rights standards—although this issue is canvassed within the context of the overall objective of exploring the claim of a shared constitutional language.

It has been suggested that the constitutions of the nation states which have adopted these instruments can be measured along a single ideological dimension: from the libertarian, in which a common law tradition of negative liberty and especially judicial protection from detention and bodily harm by officials purporting to represent the state constitutes the core of the enterprise, to those statist constitutions that provide for a far-reaching set of obligations

[8] Sujit Choudhry, *Constitutional Design for Divided Societies* (Oxford, Oxford University Press, 2008).

[9] Anne Marie Slaughter, *A New World Order* (Princeton NJ, Princeton University Press, 2004).

[10] Christine Schwobel, *Global Constitutionalism in International Legal Perspective* (Dordrecht, Martinus Nijhoff, 2011).

to be fulfilled by the state.[11] Our concern is that this determination cannot be derived from an examination of the texts alone. Indeed, absent an examination of the jurisprudence which clothes these texts with content, the exercise of comparison provides little guidance about the possible reflection of global values in the increasingly wide acceptance of introducing a constitution as a cornerstone of municipal law.

For this reason, the authors of the various chapters were specifically asked to analyse the jurisprudence of particular national constitutions and then develop an analysis which could begin to determine the possible existence of a set of 'global' values in these national constitutions, together with a description of any variations in the way that these values might be defined or implemented. This project proceeds from the perspective of national constitutions in general and the enumeration of rights entrenched in these constitutions in particular. In their study of the evolution of global constitutionalism, Law and Versteeg observe that, prior to the Second World War, most constitutions enumerated only a few specific civil and political rights.[12] By 1946, the average constitution contained 19 of the 56 substantive rights set out in their index. By 2006 the figure had increased to 33.[13] The rapid increase in rights which are entrenched in national constitutions provides a promising foundation to explore claims concerning the possible convergence of rights and the understanding of the values which underpin them as well as the differences in constitutional content and the reasons therefore. But as is apparent from the various chapters in this volume, the text without an interrogation of its interpretation by the courts and its application tells little of significance concerning congruence and difference.

Hence, the national studies interrogate the values which underpinned the various rights contained in the particular constitution in order to explore:

(a) Which values were or were not, shared, cosmopolitan or universal, on the basis of both constitutional form and content and national understanding of it.
(b) The prioritisation of the values, as an aid to assessing similarities and differences.
(c) The congruence between the Constitution, as interpreted and understood and the real, existing conditions in that country.

In discussion with the authors, it became apparent that the distinction between values and principles was not an easy one to draw with much confidence. Clearly, a right to which an obligation attaches is easily distinguishable from either a value or a principle. Even a constitutionally entrenched right which

[11] David Law and Miles Versteeg, 'The evolution and ideology of global constitutionalism' (2011) 99 *California Law Review* 1165, 1170.

[12] ibid, 1195.

[13] Law and Versteeg's index appears in an annexure to this chapter.

is subjected to the vagaries of interpretation owing to the open textured nature of many constitutional rights is different from a principle which, as Dworkin pointed out a long time ago, does not apply in an all or nothing way and is derived from the animating purpose of the rights contained in the text.[14] Values also form the basis of a normative framework but may be sourced independently from the text. In many of the texts which form the basis of this study, there is an express reference to standards that undoubtedly constitute 'values'—dignity, equality, fraternity, accountability, for example. Principles which are derived from an inferential reading of the text may well operate in similar fashion in the process of adjudication. We have chosen value as a term to be employed as, for our purposes, it can encompass principles and is distinct from the meaning of rights; that is, this book has been concerned with values which emerge from or are expressly or by implication to be derived from the relevant text. In the context of this book, the rights which are guaranteed in the text are both a means of achieving the underlying value (for example, freedom of expression promotes values of liberty and autonomy) and are interpreted through the animating value. In turn these values are shaped by context, with historical and political factors being of particular influence.

Indeed, from a reading of the chapters many of the contributors to this volume raised a major concern about the influence of vastly differing political and historical traditions upon the various constitutional texts, no matter how similar the wording thereof.

This concern is reflective of the criticism of a considerable literature dealing with international human rights of the kind reflected in the work of Singer to the effect of having produced a paradox, in that it seeks to foster a diversity but only under the guise of western political democracy.[15] Thus, any recognition of diversity is conflated into a liberal paradigm through which all difference is mediated. Mutua argues by contrast that

> this inelasticity and cultural parochialism of the human rights corpus needs urgent revision so that the ideals of the difference and diversity can be realised. The long term interests of the human rights movement are not likely to be served by the pious and righteous advocacy of human rights norms as frozen and fixed principles whose content and cultural relevance is unquestionable.[16]

At the same time, the engagement with issues of congruence and incompatibility allows for a discussion of the manner in which courts, whose task it is to interpret the Bill of Rights, are influenced not only by some abstract conception of justice or by a dominant perspective of the values underlining

[14] Ronald Dworkin, *Taking Rights Seriously* (Cambridge MA, Harvard University Press, 1978).

[15] Makau Mutua, 'The complexity of conversation in human rights' in Andreas Sajo (ed), *Human Rights with Modesty. The problem of universalism* (Dordrecht, Springer, 2004) 51–64.

[16] ibid, 55.

human rights instruments but also by the traditions of the legal culture in which the particular court is located, different styles of adjudication, which flow from different legal traditions, and broader political, historical and cultural influences which shape the society, whose constitution is the focus of the study. In this way the impact of the national studies, read together, cautions against any monist conception of this constitutional project. Even those writers renowned for arguing in favour of objectivity of values and some universal normative validity of rights are constrained to argue that at best political elites must try in good faith to respect the underlying principles of a text promoting human rights.[17]

Cognisant of this controversy and complexity about indeterminacy, this project adopted as a tentative working hypothesis a measure of convergence between the values underlying the various constitutional texts analysed in the book with specific emphasis on those contained in any Bills of Rights which formed part of the chosen constitutions. Authors were asked specifically to examine the manner in which the jurisprudence developed through the courts, the form in which the constitution operated and was given practical effect in the countries under review as well as the particular meanings which had been developed in respect of the various fundamental rights contained in the Constitution, whether expressly or by implication.

I. THE AMBIGUITIES: A CRITICAL ASSESSMENT

As noted, the idea that there is a development of human rights which represents an operative principle of global justice and/or governance draws its intellectual pedigree initially from the cosmopolitism of the Enlightenment, particularly as it was developed by Kant. But this study reveals that, whatever the similarity of a textual provision, the existence of significant differences or ambiguities dictate the adoption of great caution towards the existence of an operational cosmopolitanism within the twenty-first century, as is illustrated below.

A. Freedom/Independence

There is a major disjunction between the way in which most of the chapters have approached freedom (as individual freedom or autonomy) and independence (usually understood as national independence). In some cases (Iran for example), national independence may act as a limit on the exercise of individual freedoms. This reflects the well-known cultural dimension of Individualism versus collectivism.

[17] Eg, Ronald Dworkin, *Justice for Hedgehogs* (Cambridge MA, Harvard University Press, 2011).

B. Family/Community

There is a similar conceptual tension between family and community. In most systems, possible manifestations of community bear no relationship to the idea of the family. Perhaps 'family' and 'community' should be considered as separate values. On community, some chapters have also mentioned such matters as the general will, popular sovereignty, national sovereignty, the state and the (French) Republic as distinct values. These all go to the existence of some kind of collective identity.[18]

C. Respect/Tolerance

It is not clear what is encompassed by this value within the jurisprudence of the countries under review. Japan has a constitutional provision concerning 'respect' that is probably most analogous to 'dignity' in other systems, and has little in common with what other contributors have proposed as a guarantee of respect/tolerance in their countries. In general, this value seems to be directed towards respect for, and tolerance of, minority groups of a different race/religion/political belief, etc, rather than 'respect' at large. Even on a narrow understanding of this value, it is not clear what is required in order for a state to be said to exhibit adherence or commitment to respect/tolerance. Iran, for example, is clearly an Islamic state, and this perspective dominates much of its jurisprudence. There are certain rights accorded to specifically enumerated religious minorities, but it is doubtful whether this is sufficient to conclude that the state is tolerant of these minorities. A similar question arises in respect of fundamental principles as justice, when defined in accordance with Islamic teachings.

D. Democracy

Many chapters have alluded to the democratic nature of their polity as being of fundamental importance. To the extent that it is seen as a value, democracy is attributed to freedom, to responsibility/accountability, or even to community.

II. PRIORITISATION OF ASCRIBED MEANINGS

The challenge of assessing the prioritisation of these values is to develop a plausible measure for assessment. To this question we shall return after an initial examination of the various studies.

[18] The question however, is whether community is an appropriate rubric under which to discuss these values?

Human dignity is prioritised in six countries that expressly refer to it, as a foundational/core/fundamental/overarching/informing value from which rights are derived; widely considered an 'inherent' quality of every human being and thus inviolable and absolute following the Kantian philosophical tradition (see Germany and Venezuela); generally associated with protection of civil rights and freedoms, although the extent to which the right encompasses socio-economic rights (with concomitant positive duties imposed on the state) is contested.[19] In the case of Finland, socio-economic rights are given wider constitutional protection than is the case with equivalent rights which appear in international human rights conventions. In the United Kingdom a commitment to dignity and individual autonomy are secondary values that are not embedded into the bedrock of the British Constitution.

Life is recognised as a fundamental right in nine countries. The presence of a limitation clause means that strictly speaking the right enjoys no absolute recognition in Germany, Canada, Japan or Israel. The same holds true for China and Iran. Only Venezuela regards it as absolute and inviolable, and 'as the first and most important civil right'. In Germany, Canada, India and Japan, the right to life is connected to the value of individual autonomy or a meaningful life. Contrary to most countries, life and dignity are non-derogable in the South African constitutional jurisprudence. For this reason, they enjoy complete protection even in a state of emergency.

Equality is expressly protected in 10 constitutions, each however with a different scope accorded to the right. For example, there is a reluctance to extend the notion of equality to the economic sphere in Israel and Canada; in Iran, religion is not listed as a ground to be protected against discrimination with differential treatment under Islamic law permissible; affirmative action (ie, provision for positive state action to address existing inequality) is expressly permitted in Canada, India, Venezuela, Finland and Germany (the latter, specifically in regard to gender equality).

Freedom/liberty/independence is given a narrow, formal interpretation as individual freedom in Israel (as an absence of state interference; restricted to due process guarantees) but enjoys an expansive understanding as individual freedom (including the substantive/material preconditions necessary for the exercise of the right) in Germany and Venezuela. Similarly, a broader constitutional freedom is read into the 'right to the pursuit of happiness' in Japan. In Iran, the proclaimed guarantee of freedom (understood to cover 'all human, political, economic, social freedoms') is subject to restriction based on Islamic law and the rights of others, public rights and interests, interests of the country, national unity, independence and territorial integrity. Liberty, construed as a right of a person to do what is not explicitly and lawfully forbidden, is a core value in the United Kingdom.

[19] See eg, Venezuela and Israel in this regard.

With regard to fairness/justice/rule of law; the latter enjoys institutional protection in Germany, which is based on the post-war commitment of 'Never Again', and in turn is associated with human dignity. In Canada it is described as one of two 'foundational principles' under the constitution, Israel provides for the doctrine of separation of powers, the rule of law and an independent judiciary identified as a 'core component' of Israel's democracy. In Venezuela the Constitution provides for the designation as a 'state of justice' and proclaims the judiciary as the ultimate controlling branch of government, with Justice described as a 'fundamental value' in the Preamble and article 1 of the Constitution. The rule of law is central to the United Kingdom and mediates between unrestrained freedom and unrestrained governmental authority. In turn it promotes a number of secondary values, including transparency, accountability and participation.

Guarantees of justice are understood to include both *procedural and substantive* protections both in Finland and Germany (associated with human dignity as a precondition of justice), Canada, Japan, Israel, Iran (as Islamic/Qur'anic justice) and Venezuela (with an express provision for the prevalence of material justice over 'formalities and technicalities'). Justice and fairness expressly associated with equality are to be found in Japan, Venezuela and Iran (under Islamic law).

As regards security of the person, due process rights are widely recognised, as well as social protections. In certain jurisdictions, positive duties are imposed on the state, particularly in Germany and Canada (where these duties are associated with human dignity and personal integrity) and Japan, Venezuela (where they are associated closely with the right of human dignity) and Iran.[20]

Responsibility/accountability: government responsibility and accountability are recognised in most countries, as can be inferred from the annexure to this chapter. For example, in Japan, the principle is closely associated with the transition from traditional imperial sovereignty to popular sovereignty, while similar emphasis is placed on the principle of popular sovereignty; in Israel, government accountability is associated primarily with the notion of 'public trust' or 'faith' in government. Mutual responsibility of citizens is emphasised in Iran (in accordance with Islamic law) and Japan. Of the countries in this study, Finland has the most developed system of an Ombudsman, as the second country after Sweden to have established the institution.

Canada, Finland, Venezuela, Japan, Iran, Israel and South Africa recognise participation/democracy as a fundamental value, but there is a considerable variance in its conception: in Canada, democratic participation is viewed as a normative commitment underlying federalism, and implying government by consent, rule of law and political accountability; in Venezuela, *participatory* democracy (as opposed to direct/representative) is emphasised, while

[20] See, as regards national security, given prominence in Israel and Iran.

Japan defines its democracy as representative. In Iran, democracy is shaped by the overriding principle of guardianship. In Israel, it is qualified with the designation of Israel as a 'Jewish state'. In South Africa, the Bill of Rights chapter is proclaimed to be 'a cornerstone of democracy'. In the United Kingdom, liberty promotes the idea of representative government.

An emphasis on respect/tolerance is most broadly to be found in Canada and Venezuela, which states are recognised to be multicultural. In Canada, multicultural policies extend to immigration law, the recognition of aboriginal rights, protection of sexual minorities and their language rights and religious education. Freedom of religion is associated with respect for diversity, privacy of the family, integrity of faith-based communities and individual freedom. In Germany and Finland religious freedom for faiths is recognised, although the protection is subject to a standard limitation clause. Interpretations of the scope of the right to reputation vary greatly. The Finns have engaged in strict and narrow interpretations of honour/reputation, and this approach has been tested many times by the European Court of Human Rights, where Finland has been found to be in breach of the European Convention of Human Rights. In Israel, tolerance has mostly informed the right of free speech, especially with regard to sexual minorities. The right to free speech has been limited, however, on the basis of 'injury to public feelings'. In Iran, constitutional recognition extends only to specified Islamic and non-Islamic groups (protecting religious education and practices).

Honesty/integrity enjoys a variety of interpretations. In Canada and Germany, this is associated with physical integrity; and with government accountability in Israel, Iran, Venezuela and Japan (implicit only). Canada also associates integrity (of the individual and faith-based communities) with religious freedom. South Africa protects both bodily and psychological integrity.

Compassion/caring/socio-economic guarantees are entrenched in Venezuela, based on its designation as a 'social state': extensive socio-economic guarantees with the government constitutionally obliged to promote social justice, and an emphasis on 'solidarity' and social/community duties of citizens, with collective needs taking precedence over individual needs. In China, there are also detailed constitutional provisions on social and economic rights and social welfare. In Iran, there is provision for compassion and caring which are viewed as religious duties, giving rise to extensive government duties, and requiring that the government and all Muslims treat all others kindly and gently in conformity with the ethical norms of Islam. In Japan, no express mention is made of compassion/caring, but there are constitutional guarantees of 'the right to maintain a minimum standard of a wholesome and cultured life', with government obliged to extend social welfare. In Germany, the principle of the social state includes certain social protections and, in turn, has been employed by the courts to extend a range of rights. In Finland, the Nordic welfare state social policy model has strongly influenced the drafting of the national constitution. As already noted, Finland has extended socio-economic rights beyond those provided for example in the International Covenant for Social, Economic and Cultural Rights, including the right to free education up to university level and a range of subsidies which have had significant distributional consequences.[21]

The Indian courts employ directive principles of state policy contained in the Indian Constitution to give some socio-economic content to what might otherwise be considered to be civil and political rights. In Canada, there are no enumerated socio-economic rights, but the political tradition has appeared to support equitable social welfare distribution. South Africa guarantees a range of social and economic rights, but with the qualification that government's obligation are determined by what can reasonably be achieved with available resources. By contrast, in Israel, there is a clear reluctance to recognise socio-economic rights or impose concomitant duties on the state.

The value of family is given constitutional protection in most countries. It is narrowly defined in Japan, Israel, Venezuela and Iran to exclude same-sex marriages. Furthermore, in Iran, family relations must be based on Islamic rights and ethics, which are patriarchal. In both Japan and Venezuela, the Constitution expressly requires that family relations be based on equality. In Canada, the privacy of the family is expressly protected, and associated with the rights to liberty, security and freedom of religion.

With respect to community, collective rights and community integrity are expressly protected in Canada and Venezuela. In China, the value of community enjoys priority in the Constitution. Iran's Constitution refers to community at several levels: the Islamic community, that of the nation-state, that of the official religious group, the Twelve Shi'ite Islam. In contrast, the concept of community is not mentioned in Japan's Constitution, and scholars are sceptical of a proposed amendment to include respect for communal values. In Germany, concern with 'community' interests is implied only in the limitation of fundamental rights based on general/public interest. Similarly in Israel, there is no express protection of collective rights, but the identification of Israel as a 'Jewish state' defines the political community as an ethnic/religious community.

The right to education is expressly protected in Finland and Japan ('equal education' expressly guaranteed, with free compulsory education—interpreted as nine years of basic education—), as well as mainland China (PRC) and Taiwan (both constitutions provide for the right and duty to

[21] Significantly Richard Wilkinson and Kate Pickett observe that these measures have an effect: the ratio between the average take-home pay and the worst-off and the 20% best-off is just under 4 in the Nordic countries, 7 in the UK, and nearly 9 in the USA (Richard Wilkinson and Kate Pickett, *The Spirit Level. Why equality is better for everyone* (London, Penguin, 2009)).

receive education), Iran (Constitution guarantees 12 years of free education as well as free higher education to the extent required for the country's self-sufficiency), and Venezuela (also informed by the principle of equality, and free up to undergraduate university level). It also is guaranteed in South Africa, both in respect of basic education for children and adults and for further education, which the state, through reasonable measures, must make progressively available. It is not mentioned in Israel's Basic Law, but recognised by the Supreme Court as a basic right (including the need for equality in education), although the Court has yet to confirm it as a constitutional right. It is not constitutionally guaranteed in Germany (education is a state, not federal government responsibility) or in Canada.

The environment is expressly protected in Germany, Iran and Venezuela (the latter's Constitution having extensive provisions) and South Africa.

Peace/pacifism is specified as one of the three pillars of Japan's constitution (along with the guarantee of fundamental rights and the principle of popular sovereignty), and reflective of the peculiar post-war drafting history of Japan's Constitution. There remains a 'glaring gap' between the constitutional provisions mandating pacifism and the government's interpretation of its obligations in respect of them. The aim of peace is also mentioned as a fundamental value in Venezuela and Germany.

Spirituality fundamentally informs the Iranian Constitution, which is to be developed in terms of and is made subject to, Islamic law. To return to the question of prioritisation, this has proved to be extremely different, partly because of the significant range of rights contained in the texts and the differences of interpretation of these rights as they are proclaimed in the text. However dignity, life, equality and freedom appear to be a significant font for unremunerated rights which are then developed by the courts.

III. CONGRUENCE

A. The Relationship Between Theory and Practice

The various chapters also show that congruence, in the sense of a finding based upon the outcome of an examination and comparison between the text, its jurisprudence and the practical effect thereof, was incomplete in most, if not all, of the countries surveyed. Below is a summation of the findings in each of the countries whose constitutional jurisprudence was surveyed.

i. Australia

In the Australian system, it is difficult to measure congruence. The lived reality in Australia seems to be in consonance with the few clauses enshrined in the

Constitution and the legal order more generally. This is not surprising: one would expect the enactment of Acts of Parliament that are more reflective of the contemporary living *mores*. An example in point is the enactment of a law against racial discrimination. On the other hand, Australian practice is not entirely congruent with Australian international obligations, as decisions of the Human Rights Council suggest, pointing to some shortfall between aspirations and reality, in Australia as elsewhere. Notably also, some of the standards that in Australia are given effect through legislation or case law are the subject of dissention in the community; judicial decisions in relation to native title are a case in point.

ii. Brazil

Although courts have invoked constitutional values to adopt an activist role (on the bench at least), the social reality on the ground in Brazil is far removed from what these values require. For example, Brazil is still marred by vast inequality, crime, violence and precarious living standards.

iii. Canada

Generally, there is a strong correlation between the social (or lived) reality on the ground, and the values as enshrined in the Charter. But there is dissatisfaction in some sectors of society—those who support the Charter maintain that the court could do more to protect and to give effect to socio-economic rights.

iv. China

In China, whether or not the reality on the ground reflects constitutional values depends on three factors: (a) the degree to which the values are not abstracted from the lived social reality on the ground, (b) the effectiveness of the legal system to ensure that the law in the books is in fact the living law, and (c) the nature and features of the day's political order/system. China is an authoritarian state, possibly in transition, at least in economic terms. Therefore, it follows that the adherence to a plethora of the values appears to be at the mercy of the state. To compound the problem, the Constitution is not justiciable, and this poses serious challenges about enforcement. Where courts have ruled for the enforcement of rights such as those dealing with equality, such decisions were more theoretical than practical.

v. Finland

The congruence between constitutional values and reality is fairly strong. Perhaps the most significant exception are the breaches of provisions regarding timely judicial proceedings, the failure of the state to respond adequately to violence against women, human trafficking, societal discrimination against minorities, and foreign-born residents. Equality has been implemented to improve the equality in respect of gender. However xenophobia and intolerance of immigrants has revealed a significant gap between the values of equality and real-life experience of their communities. The Nordic Welfare State model has ensured that dignity encompasses not only personal freedom, but the kind of social and financial protection for the dignified life. In general the pressures of globalisation have posed great challenges for the implementation of social inclusivity.

vi. France

The issue of congruence in France is not entirely clear. However, it can be discerned from the discussion of France that certain of the values operate at an institutional level (for example between Council and Parliament), in particular freedom, equality and a sense of French community which shape the content of their relationship.

vii. Germany

There seems to be a high correlation between constitutional values and the social reality in Germany, to the extent that the values of the social state, and the importance of dignity are reflected in the socio-economic structure of the country. Further the importance of the core value of dignity, in particular, has meant that the fabric of society has been significantly influenced by the implementation of constitutional rights as developed by the Constitutional Court.

viii. India

The jurisprudence of the Supreme Court has ensured that social, economic, cultural and environmental rights have become justiciable issues. In turn this has affected the nature of government policy, in particular with regard to social and economic provisioning. The insistence by the courts that there is a basic structure to the Constitution has meant that it has become an impermeable wall against belligerent parliaments and executives who have commanded large enough majorities to amend the Constitution. The creation of a basic structure has protected the Constitution and hence Indian society from the eradication, or at least, a fundamental erosion of constitutional democracy.

ix. Iran

There is a glaring gap between values and practice in Iran. The text is not significantly different in important part from the other texts under investigation but the hegemony of the religious framework produces a far different, less open and tolerant society than the text would superficially appear to promise.

x. Israel

There seems to be a mismatch between values as they are institutionally understood and interpreted on the one hand, and social concerns on the ground on the other hand. The undemocratic occupation of Palestine detracts from Israel's purported commitment to a number of the values.

xi. Japan

Bearing in mind that Japan is a constitutional monarchy, it appears that there is appreciable congruence between the jurisprudence and the socio-economic reality—albeit that the Constitution was, in significant part, an imposed constitution which was introduced after the Second World War.

xii. South Africa

South Africa, like other transitional societies, remains a country under construction and it is difficult conclusively to answer the question of congruence. The values do appear regularly in public discourse, but they are not always put into effect. For example the country remains a very male-centred society. Although the value of equality is highly ranked, South Africa has one of the highest Gini-coefficients in the world. Tolerance is constantly challenged by both xenophobia and homophobia.

xiii. United Kingdom

The flexibility of the UK's unwritten constitutional system has allowed it to adjust over time to close the gaps that have periodically opened up between the values to which the system formally adheres and actual reality of how state power is exercised. However, the gap between values and reality can at times loom large. At present, the expanding substantive concept of the rule of law, combined with the greater expression given to secondary values such as respect for autonomy, dignity and equality, rub into the primacy given to representative governance and the secondary value of effective governance (as it has been understood in the UK context, ie, meaning the enabling of an elected government to implement its political agenda).

xiv. United States

The Supreme Court in the United States has preserved a concept of liberty which it has used trump the states' regulatory authority and hence intervene in a range of social and economic activity. Some protection in the sphere of intimacy, such as abortion rights, has proved to be extraordinarily controversial, but to date the landmark case in which these rights were proclaimed, *Roe v Wade*,[22] has not been overruled. Over time the court has also used the value of liberty to encroach upon the role of the federal government to regulate a range of issues which in other countries would be considered to be inextricably linked to government's role to promote a vibrant public sphere.

xv. Venezuela

It is generally difficult to give effect to the various constitutional values in Venezuela, owing to a rather illusory separation of powers. More directly, there seems to be much more control exerted on all other branches of government by the legislature; where certain members of the judiciary have sought to function independently, they have often been dismissed from office.

IV. WHERE DOES THIS LEAVE THIS PROJECT?

With these findings of the project in mind, the question to which we must return is whether these disparities clearly refute a claim that there is a move towards a cosmopolitanism in constitutional values; in particular as they inform human rights. Expressed differently, to what extent do the constitutions under this study support the argument of a movement towards a new common framework for humanity?

As noted earlier in this chapter, there is a danger that a cosmopolitan imagination can produce an uncritical positivism; that is an unquestioning endorsement of an existing conception of human rights which is to be found in certain Western societies. In turn, this can give rise to a problem of a constitutional framework for the existing global order which eschews the realisation of the cosmopolitan vision and becomes an argument for the subordination of power to the rule of a particular conception of international human rights law. This forces a focus upon the possible existence of any common understanding of values, a return to the idea of cosmopolitism which, in summation is: 'A way of thinking that declares its opposition to all forms of nationalism and religious fundamentalism, as well as to the economic imperatives of global capitalism.'[23] Thus, a cosmopolitan way of thinking emphasises the point of view of humanity as a whole.

[22] *Roe v Wade*, 410 US 113 (1973).

[23] Robert Fine, 'Cosmopolitanism and Human Rights: Radicalism in a global age' (2009) 40 *Metaphilosophy* 8–23.

Once this idea is taken seriously it must ultimately lead on to the possible transcendence of a nation state. As Sen argues, the position that every person in the world, irrespective of citizenship, residence, race, class, caste or community, has some basic rights, which others should respect, must hold great appeal.[24]

In its modern form, cosmopolitanism sets out to construct an enlightened vision of peaceful relations between nation states and human rights which are shared by all world citizens, as well as a global legal order supported by a global civil society.[25] For this particular project, which has been based upon an examination of national constitutions, there is a difficulty in rejecting the importance of the nation-state. Indeed the dominant approach to cosmopolitanism is one that centralises the nation-state. That the nation-state is central is evident by the selection of various jurisdictions examined in this volume. The question still remains as to whether, even within the framework of the nation-state, some common set of values is emerging to be recognised by humanity, no matter the differences.

The importance placed upon the nation-state requires further amplification. Within the legal context, it may be argued that cosmopolitanism has its roots in international law, but with a logic that goes beyond and at times contradicts the very origins thereof. While international law might be seen as the stage for a migration toward cosmopolitanism, various considerations set cosmopolitanism apart from international law; although there has been significant movement in this connection to extend the scope of international law.

However, the tentative steps taken by international institutions notwithstanding, it is more often than not the nation-state which serves as the entity against which such rights are claimed or enforced. It is through the nation-state that rights are enforced, and where appropriate, sanctions for non-compliance with human rights are located. For this reason, this study has focused attention upon the nation-state and the possibility of shared global values which inform national guarantees of human rights.

By contrast, in amplifying his argument in favour of the international law origins of cosmopolitanism, Singer notes that the commencement of a global trend towards one law must find root in the formation of an agency that would regulate and impose sanctions on those who are found of the commission of crimes against humanity. For Singer, the International Criminal Law (ICL) serves as a model of such an agency. Singer writes that the ICL was created as a practical consolidation of various responses to a range of wars or violations of the humanity of millions of victims of crimes against humanity. In the example he provides, the ICL culminated in the creation of

[24] Amartya Sen, *The Idea of Justice* (London, Allen Lane, 2009).

[25] Robert Fine, 'Cosmopolitanism and Human Rights: Radicalism in a global age' (2009) 40 *Metaphilosophy* 8–23.

the International Criminal Court (ICC), which exerts jurisdiction over states that are signatory to its statute.[26]

Both the ICL and its corollary the ICC, however, find application after a crime has been committed and punishment for the perpetrators needs to be determined. Something needs to be said about intervention to prevent a crime or to stop a crime that is being committed and punishment for the perpetrators needs to be determined. This would, in some instances, necessitate an intervention into the affairs of another state. The question for Singer in this regard is how far are we willing, or should we be willing, to erode the doctrine of state sovereignty? Singer seems to be sympathetic to the view that intervention in the affairs of another state is justified when it is in response to acts 'that shock the moral conscience of mankind'.[27] Theodor Meron argues that the purpose of international criminal law is to enforce international human rights which thus provide the basis for the enforcement by the ICL.[28]

The problem with this approach is that varying acts may trigger markedly differing responses. For example, homosexuality in some communities is regarded as offensive to the moral conscience, as are interracial relationships or being an atheist.

As noted, Singer is cognisant of the different understandings of 'moral consciousness' which have been confronted in this chapter and therefore by implication the debate among contributors to this volume. He therefore engages in a discussion of cultural relativism, and the question how one can avoid cultural relativism in determining what values ought to be discarded and which values ought to be retained. He commences a response to this question from the premise that an argument against cultural relativism can be founded on ethics that allows for the possibility of moral arguments that extend beyond the limits of a particular culture. Rooted in this conception of ethics, the argument against cultural relativism acknowledges that 'distinctive cultures embody ways of living that have been developed over countless generations, that when they are destroyed, the accumulated wisdom that they represent is lost, and that we are all enriched by being able to observe and appreciate the diversity of cultures'. This requires that we be sensitive to the cultural values of others, and have an 'understanding for what gives them self-respect and identity'.[29]

Singer then argues that, only after we have taken note of and accepted the 'scope for rational argument' that lies in an ethics which is 'independent of any particular culture', can we begin to question the soundness, defensibility or justifiability of the values to which we claim to adhere.[30]

[26] Singer, *One World* (n 4).
[27] ibid, 141.
[28] Theodore Meron, *The Making Of International Law: A View From The Bench* (Oxford, Oxford University Press, 2011).
[29] Singer, *One World* (n 4) 140.
[30] ibid.

Enter this book, which has sought through the prism of national constitutions which protect and promote human rights to examine this question: how does the impact of culture and politics influence the possibility of a common language of rights based upon certain agreed values and the meaning thereof? Is there sufficient justification to contend for any form of overlapping consensus. In turn, can cosmopolitanism accommodate inherent traditions and customs?

Tagore asserts that 'tradition without reason is blind, and reason without tradition is empty'. He rejects a cosmopolitan enterprise that is devoid of cultural or traditional content. For him, cosmopolitanism, as detached from reason, 'impoverishes the multi-hued richness of the human condition';[31] cosmopolitanism does not derive from abstractions but it is 'grounded in existential orientation'. It is grounded in 'a way of being in the world'.[32] Similarly, reason grounded in tradition is philosophically uncomfortable. Something very important is lost when tradition is devalued in the course of trying to attain cosmopolitanism. Martha Nussbaum contends, in similar fashion, that the source of our foundational moral obligations is the human community; that is, 'we should regard all human beings as our fellow citizens and neighbours', although this does not imply a relinquishment of local affinity, belief or identity.[33]

Amartya Sen has developed an argument which essentially follows that of Nussbaum, namely that cosmopolitism does not need to eschew considerations of tradition, belief, identity or local affinity. He acknowledges that

> no one should expect that there would be complete unanimity in what everyone in the world actually wants or that there is any hope that a dedicated racist or sexist would be inexorably reformed by the force of public argument. What sustainability of a judgment in favour of a form of common rights discourse demands is a general appreciation of the reach of reasoning in the favour of those rights, if and when others try to scrutinise claims on an impartial basis.[34]

V. THE IMPARTIAL SPECTATOR

A conceptual framework to do this work is therefore required to examine questions of possible convergence. Sen's impartial spectator may prove to be a promising starting point to engage with this question. In addition to its appeal to open impartiality, the impartial spectator insists on a constant engagement between the institutions and the reality of the people that they govern. This idea is tentatively employed as a basis for further examination.

[31] Sarandronath Tagore, 'Tagore Conception of Cosmopolitanism: A reconstruction' (2008) 77 *University of Toronto Quarterly* 1070, 1073.

[32] ibid, 1078.

[33] Martha Nussbaum, *Hiding from Humanity. Disgust, shame and the law* (Princeton, Princeton University Press, 2004) 84.

[34] Sen, *The Idea of Justice* (n 24) 386.

Sen uses a concept of open and closed impartiality to develop an idea of an objective basis with which to communicate and debate beliefs and values so that the engagement is not confined to an impermeable subjectivity of the communicator; that is, one should be able to communicate in a manner that enables the person to fully express her values and beliefs. Open impartiality involves making assessments which invoke judgments from outside the focal groups and thereby avoid parochial bias.

This enables people to engage in debates 'about the correctness of the claims made by different people'.[35]

In support, he cites Adam Smith:

> We can never survey our own sentiments and motives, we can never form any judgment concerning them; unless we remove ourselves, as it were, from our own natural station, and endeavour to view them as at a certain distance from us. But we can do this in no other way than by endeavouring to view them with the eyes of other people, or as other people are likely to view them.[36]

In examining the correctness of ethical propositions, what is important is the reasoning on which that proposition is based. It is here that objectivity plays a role. Sen explains that 'demands of ethical objectivity … relate closely to the ability to stand up to open public reasoning, and this, in turn, has close connection with the impartial nature of the proposed propositions and the arguments in their support'.[37] Impartiality is important to an understanding of justice so that we can arrive at an understanding of justice through a deliberative 'evaluation of social justice and the concomitant societal arrangements'.[38]

Thus the core idea behind the 'impartial spectator' is that we should 'examine our own conduct as we imagine any other fair and impartial spectator would examine it'[39]; meaning that we should evaluate our own actions with utmost objectivity. This supports the contention that the 'impartial spectator' is more concerned with 'open impartiality'. The difference between the idea of an impartial spectator as conceived by Smith, and Rawls' concept of social contract (based upon the original position) is that the former permits judgments by 'any other fair and impartial spectator'. It includes judgments by people who are close to, or who are part of the particular community, as well as judgments from those who are exterior to, and removed from that community.[40] By including judgments from 'outsiders' and 'insiders', the impartial spectator enables us to broaden the scope of our ethical enquiry. Again Adam Smith is employed to provide an explanation of the importance of the impartial spectator:

35 Sen, *The Idea of Justice* (n 24) 118.
36 ibid, 125.
37 ibid, 122.
38 ibid, 123.
39 ibid, 124.
40 ibid, 125.

> In solitude, we are apt to feel too strongly whatever relates to ourselves ... The conversation of a friend brings us to a better, that of a stranger to a still better temper. The man within the breast, the abstract and ideal spectator of our sentiments and conduct, requires often to be awakened and put in mind of his duty, by the presence of the real spectator: and it is always from that spectator, from whom we can expect the least sympathy and indulgence, that we are likely to learn the most complete lesson of self-command.[41]

In invoking the concept of the impartial spectator therefore, the point is to listen to other voices, as these 'may help us gain a full—fairer—understanding' of justice.[42]

Within the context of the enterprise undertaken in this study, the idea of the impartial spectator represents a protest against transcendental institutionalism and maintains that there is a multiplicity of values, even among reasonable people. To this extent, it goes beyond finding 'just institutions' and seeks social realisations regarding key issues.[43] Therefore, even if we cannot agree upon a comprehensive definition of the just without such a conception, we can still develop a common resolve to fight for the abolition of famine, genocide, terrorism, slavery, epidemics or illiteracy. It follows that the model of the impartial spectator rejects the argument that justice can only be institutionalised with the context of a sovereign state. Instead, the impartial spectator accepts that there are trans-border entities whose decisions have a bearing on people's lives globally. It acknowledges further that what may happen within the borders of one nation-state may have ramifications within the borders of another country which in turn cautions against the rejection of some basis of a common discourse.

VI. THE IMPLICATIONS WHICH FLOW FROM THIS STUDY

Unsurprisingly, there is a considerable overlap in values as they appear in the various texts under scrutiny. Freedom for example, receives almost unanimous mention in the various constitutions which are canvassed. The same holds true of the values of community/family and reverence for life. But that, alas tells us too little. As is apparent from the individual chapters, there are great variations in the emphasis placed on these rights and the meaning given thereto by the various constitutional courts which interpret these constitutions. As has been indicated in the discussion relating to the scope and limitations of the cosmopolitan approach, it is not entirely unsurprising that the achievement of a truly, universal agreement in respect of the content of human rights is unlikely to be achieved in the foreseeable future.

[41] Adam Smith, *The Theory of Moral Sentiment*, III.3.38 at 153–54 as quoted in Sen, ibid 125.
[42] Sen *The Idea of Justice* (n 24) 131.
[43] ibid, 143.

Notwithstanding the exponential growth in national constitutions which seek at least textually to promote similar forms of human rights, this study has shown that there is no consistent application of any of the rights which set laws which consistently transcend natural boundaries. Even amongst nation-states that may be described as democracies and would lay claim to sharing similar basic values, the historical, cultural and, in some cases, religious influences materially affect the jurisprudence of these countries and hence limit the achievement of shared and equal application of the textually guaranteed provisions. Furthermore, the legal cultures of these societies and, in particular the procedural traditions within the various legal systems which, examined in turn, reflect certain historical and cultural influences, continue to constitute an obstacle to a universal agreement on an agreed content of human rights norms and other constitutional values.

This study has however shown that as more constitutional texts are passed in countries with vastly different historical, cultural and legal traditions, an impartial spectator, reading the various chapters of this book, would be able to conclude that a framework of normative reasoning with regard to the values cannot entirely be discounted; that is, at the very least, practices which contravene a range of these values now require either rationalisation or justification from 'right abusers' rather than the claim that they can be justified on any coherent normative basis. As Sen observes:

> I would argue that taking rights seriously requires us to recognise that it would be bad—sometimes terrible—if they were violated. This does not imply that the recognition of a claim as a right requires us to assume that it must always overwhelm every other argument in the contrary direction (based, for example, on well-being, or a freedom not included in that right). It is perhaps not surprising that the opponents of the idea of human rights often thrusts on them remarkably all-conquering pretensions and then dismiss these rights on the grounds that these pretentions are highly implausible. Mary Wollstonecraft and Thomas Paine did not attribute unconditional all-conquering pretentions to the rights of human beings; nor do most of the people today who can be seen as human rights activists. They do, however, insist that human rights be taken seriously and be included among the powerful determinants of action, rather than being ignored or easily overwhelmed.[44]

This passage suggests that, while Singer's claim for a universal law may be overly optimistic, the contrary proposition, namely that no progress towards a set of common values has taken place, should enjoy even less plausibility.

In summary, demands for global justice make best sense when they are based on a shared humanity and some sense of common or shared discourse.[45] By adopting the model of the impartial spectator and its requirement of

[44] Sen, *The Idea of Justice* (n 24) 360–61.
[45] ibid, 143.

open impartiality, it may be possible to recognise that considerations of basic human rights and global values, including the importance of safeguarding elementary civil and political liberties, need not be contingent on citizenship and nationality, and may not be institutionally dependent on a nationally derived social contract. Further, there is no need to presume a world government, or even to invoke a hypothetical global social contract. The 'imperfect obligations' associated with the recognition of these human rights can be seen as falling broadly on anyone who is in a position to help.

The manifestation of global dialogue today, through the formal organisations such as the United Nations, the World Trade Organisation (WTO) and the International Criminal Court (ICC), through the 'media, political agitation' and the works of citizens across borders in their varied forms, all bear testament to some form of open impartiality. As Sen puts it, these factors provide evidence for the contention that 'the cause of open impartiality is not entirely neglected in the contemporary world'.[46] There is a case to be made in favour of an idea of interwoven global interests. In this sense, it is possible to see how a multitude of economic, climatic and terrorist induced crises support open impartiality that is demanded by the impartial spectator which speaks to that interconnectedness, as well as the promotion of debate and dialogue about global values. A focus on global institutions alone (which Sen rejects) understates the importance of conflicting interest to which the local identity and culture directs our attention. Therefore, instead of an idea of justice that is based on the concept of perfect institutions, what is needed is an 'agreement, based on public reasoning, on the rankings of alternatives that can be realised'.[47]

The key question raised in this book concerns the extent to which the exponential growth in national constitutions of which the texts studied in this book are but illustrative, may provide some evidence of the possibility of a common constitutional discourse which, in turn, is predicated on some measure of reasoned agreement about shared values.

The analysis of the country chapters reveals significant differences in interpretation and application of a variety of values which are all represented in the texts of the countries so studied. However, an impartial spectator, when examining the annexure shown on p 473, would have noticed significant overlaps in understanding to the extent that even the critical differences can be understood and debated within a framework of reasoned argument. Broad agreement on an idea of a rule of law, equality, and life, for example, and even a narrow agreement on freedom, in particular, reveals some significant transcendence of national boundaries as the expansion of the constitutional enterprise begins to prod countries towards some form of tentative, but developing common, global framework of values.

[46] ibid, 151.
[47] ibid, 17.

This work does not prove that the values which underpin the individual rights contained in the texts examined by the authors are free of moral ambiguity. But that acknowledgement is a long way from concluding that there is no basis for any finding of congruence. Of course, even a finding of congruence is subject to the exigencies of the political context. For example, since 9/11 torture as a means of dealing with security threats both real and perceived has threatened to trump the value of fairness and openness which underlies the right of due process. Thus, in public opinion polling, a bare majority of Americans oppose torturing prisoners in the struggle against terrorism, and support for torture has risen significantly in recent years.[48]

However, the very global constitutional enterprise which is the subject of this book has still given rise to a social practice in which political action is both justified and evaluated. Indeed very often governments lie about claims that they torture prisoners as a result of the social sanction which is sourced in the values so examined in this book. Further, while the chapter on China luminously illustrates many of the problems which have been discussed in this conclusion regarding a confident assertion of growing congruence, subsequent to the writing of the Chinese chapter the Chinese Communist Party's new General Secretary, Mr Xi Jinping, spoke of the need to enforce the Constitution and said 'the Constitution should be the legal weapon for people to defend their own rights'.[49] Whatever the justifiable doubts about whether this speech will be translated into practice, it does reveal that even a call for the Constitution to be implemented so that it can have 'life and authority' is illustrative of the shape of a discourse that is a product of some common understanding (dare we say congruence) in the scope and meaning of the rights and the values that underpin them.

Marti Koskenniemi has mounted a sustained and powerful critique of the rise of human rights centred discourse, particularly in international law.[50] He contends, in sharp contrast to those who advocate a cosmopolitan set of ideas, that the latter promote the myth that a set of contestable values possess historical inevitability and an uncontested global reach. However, he concedes that these constitutional and hence human rights vocabularies do not merely frame the internal world of politicians' consciousness of the contingency of their choices. They directly inform political struggles. In addition these values form the basis of a legal vocabulary which is mastered by technical and administrative bodies and which then is employed to articulate concerns which are considered to be important. It follows that, even Koskenniemi, arguably the most distinguished international lawyer who is opposed

[48] *New York Review of Books*, 7 February 2013, p 6.

[49] *New York Times*, 4 February 2013.

[50] See eg, Marti Koskenniemi, 'The fate of international law: Between technique and politics' (2007) 70 *Modern Law Review* 1–32; see also Koskenniemi, 'Vocabularies of Sovereignty: the powers of paradox' in H Kalmo and A Skinner (eds), *Sovereignty in Fragments* (Cambridge, Cambridge University Press, 2014) 222–42.

to any form of universal legal vocabulary, is compelled to concede that the 'myth', as he describes it, has profound practical consequences.

That these vocabularies are contested and conflicted is unsurprising, given the multitude of contexts in which they are located. But these rights and the values that inform them are not so different that they do not speak across national boundaries. There is, at the very least, some measure of an overlapping vocabulary. Hence, while this book cannot claim to have justified the conclusion that the basis of a coherent international language of values and system of recognised rights exists, there lies in the praxis of constitutionalism, the outline of a discernible framework which holds the possibility for a future cosmopolitan claim as outlined earlier in this chapter. And this conclusion in turn holds significant normative and legal possibilities for a form of shared political and legal discourse which may, at some point, transcend national boundaries, history and culture.

VII. ANNEXURE: LAW AND VERSTEEG (2011)*

Rank	Rights-related provisions	1946	1956	1966	1976	1986	1996	2006
1	Freedom of religion	81%	88%	87%	88%	92%	95%	97%
2	Freedom of the press and/or expression	87%	88%	84%	86%	87%	95%	97%
3	Equality guarantees	71%	77%	85%	88%	92%	95%	97%
4	Right to private property	81%	85%	81%	83%	87%	95%	97%
5	Right to privacy	83%	83%	78%	81%	83%	94%	95%
6	Prohibition of arbitrary arrest and detention	76%	81%	81%	79%	81%	92%	94%
7	Right of detention	73%	77%	73%	75%	81%	90%	94%
8	Right of association	72%	74%	78%	77%	80%	91%	93%
9	Women's rights	35%	51%	62%	70%	77%	90%	91%
10	Freedom of movement	50%	55%	58%	58%	64%	84%	88%

(continued)

* The Evolution and ideology of Global Constitutionalism by David Law and Mila Versteeg, Washington University Legal Studies Research Paper Series, June 2011.

Rank	Rights-related provisions	1946	1956	1966	1976	1986	1996	2006
11	Right of access to court	68%	68%	64%	62%	64%	85%	86%
12	Prohibition of torture	37%	37%	41%	45%	56%	80%	84%
13	Right to vote	63%	74%	73%	69%	74%	82%	84%
14	Right to work	55%	65%	59%	67%	65%	80%	82%
15	Positive rights to education at state expense	65%	72%	59%	65%	65%	78%	82%
16	Judicial review	25%	32%	53%	51%	58%	80%	82%
17	Prohibition of ex post facto laws	41%	51%	57%	60%	67%	77%	80%
18	Physical needs rights	44%	60%	52%	57%	61%	75%	79%
19	Right to life	33%	33%	38%	41%	51%	71%	78%
20	Presumption of innocence	8%	12%	31%	37%	49%	69%	74%
21	Right not to be expelled from home territory	30%	33%	38%	44%	48%	70%	73%
22	Limits on property rights	51%	63%	58%	68%	70%	69%	73%
23	Rights to present a defence	30%	37%	52%	57%	64%	69%	72%
24	Right to unionise and/or strike	25%	35%	49%	50%	50%	69%	72%
25	Right to counsel	10%	17%	31%	38%	47%	66%	70%
26	Right to public trial	43%	47%	46%	48%	53%	65%	69%
27	Rights for the family	28%	28%	38%	43%	46%	62%	67%
28	Right to form political parties	9%	16%	28%	26%	31%	63%	65%
29	Children's rights	25%	35%	30%	35%	40%	59%	65%

(continued)

30	Citizen duties	53%	62%	52%	59%	56%	63%	65%
31	Rights to a healthy environment	0%	0%	1%	8%	20%	52%	63%
32	Other workers' rights (freedom of education	32%	45%	38%	42%	46%	57%	59%
33	Negative education rights (freedom of education)	57%	56%	44%	38%	35%	52%	55%
34	Minority rights	16%	24%	20%	20%	26%	43%	51%
35	Prohibition of double jeopardy	16%	19%	26%	31%	37%	46%	50%
36	Right to remain silent	29%	29%	32%	31%	38%	47%	49%
37	Right to a timely trial	8%	11%	18%	22%	31%	40%	47%
38	Artistic freedom	10%	16%	13%	17%	23%	42%	45%
39	Rights for handicapped	0%	1%	3%	5%	13%	30%	43%
40	Ombudsman or human rights commission	5%	5%	4%	9%	15%	27%	37%
41	Right to marry	18%	31%	30%	28%	26%	32%	35%
42	Right to asylum	11%	21%	18%	21%	21%	32%	35%
43	Reference to international human rights treaties	0%	1%	18%	17%	15%	30%	35%
44	Rights for elderly	3%	3%	3%	7%	12%	26%	34%
45	Rights to information about government	2%	4%	3%	5%	8%	25%	34%
46	Separation of church and state	20%	25%	28%	25%	25%	36%	34%

(continued)

Rank	Rights-related provisions	1946	1956	1966	1976	1986	1996	2006
47	Right to protection of reputation	13%	11%	8%	10%	17%	29%	32%
48	Affirmative action	3%	9%	17%	20%	26%	27%	30%
49	Natural resources for benefit of all	8%	7%	8%	15%	19%	27%	29%
50	Right to appeal to higher court	8%	8%	7%	7%	8%	20%	25%
51	Prohibition of death penalty	10%	9%	8%	9%	12%	20%	24%
52	Official state religion	39%	39%	32%	27%	26%	24%	22%
53	Prisoner rights	10%	12%	9%	12%	10%	15%	18%
54	Consumer rights	0%	0%	0%	1%	6%	12%	16%
55	Rights to resist when rights are violated	8%	7%	4%	4%	4%	15%	16%
56	Substantive principle for education	11%	16%	10%	15%	15%	14%	14%
57	Prohibition of genocide/crimes against humanity	0%	0%	0%	1%	2%	6%	12%
58	Rights for victims of crimes	0%	0%	0%	0%	1%	7%	10%
59	Protection of foetuses	0%	0%	1%	1%	6%	7%	8%
60	Rights to bear arms	10%	8%	5%	4%	3%	3%	2%

Index

www.ingramcontent.com/pod-product-compliance
Ingram Content Group UK Ltd.
Pitfield, Milton Keynes, MK11 3LW, UK
UKHW020130290926
15471UKWH00003B/392

9 781509 917709